PRAISE FOR THE SIXTH EDITION OF *SECURITY ANALYSIS*

"The sixth edition of the iconic *Security Analysis* disproves the adage ''tis best to leave well enough alone.' An extraordinary team of commentators, led by Seth Klarman and James Grant, bridge the gap between the simpler financial world of the 1930s and the more complex investment arena of the new millennium. Readers benefit from the experience and wisdom of some of the financial world's finest practitioners and best informed market observers. The new edition of *Security Analysis* belongs in the library of every serious student of finance."

David F. Swensen
Chief Investment Officer
Yale University
author of *Pioneering Portfolio Management*
and *Unconventional Success*

"The best of the past made current by the best of the present. Tiger Woods updates Ben Hogan. It has to be good for your game."

Jack Meyer
Managing Partner and CEO
Convexity Capital

"*Security Analysis*, a 1940 classic updated by some of the greatest financial minds of our generation, is more essential than ever as a learning tool and reference book for disciplined investors today."

Jamie Dimon
Chairman and CEO
JPMorgan Chase

"While Coca-Cola found it couldn't improve on a time-tested classic, Seth Klarman, Jim Grant, Bruce Greenwald, et al., prove that a great book can be made even better. Seth Klarman's preface should be required reading for all investors, and collectively, the contributing editors' updates make for a classic in their own right. The enduring lesson is that an understanding of human behavior is a critical part of the process of security analysis."

Brian C. Rogers
Chairman
T. Rowe Price Group

"A classic has now been updated by some of the greatest and most thoughtful investors of our time. The book was a must read and has now been elevated to a new level."

Daniel S. Och
Senior Managing Member
Och-Ziff Capital Management Group

"Readers will find the updated version of Graham and Dodd's *Security Analysis* to be much improved from earlier editions. While the timeless advice from two of the greatest value investors continues to resonate, the essays that are contributed by some of the world's top value investors add immeasurably to the read. These investors practice what they preach in their essays and combine to make this edition the best ever! I highly recommend this volume to all investors—old and young—who will benefit from the tried and true principles of the past and the updated applications to today's turbulent markets!"

Morris Smith
Private Investor
Former Manager
Fidelity Magellan Fund

"No book empowers you with better tools for intelligent investing than *Security Analysis*. Seth Klarman and his fabulous team have produced a nonpareil edition of Ben Graham's classic for the new millennium."

Mason Hawkins
Chairman, Longleaf Partners
Southeastern Asset Management

"The ideas of Graham and Dodd have withstood all kinds of market conditions and 75 years of scrutiny—making them ever more relevant for modern-day investing. The essays by Klarman and other storied value investors lucidly illustrate that while the capital markets landscape may be vastly changed from years past, basic investor traits are not, and disciplined application of the principles of *Security Analysis* continues to provide an important edge in investing."

André F. Perold
George Gund Professor of Finance and Banking
Harvard Business School

SECURITY ANALYSIS

SECURITY ANALYSIS PRIOR EDITIONS

Graham and Dodd: *Security Analysis*, First Edition (1934)

Graham and Dodd: *Security Analysis*, Second Edition (1940)

Graham and Dodd: *Security Analysis*, Third Edition (1951)

Graham, Dodd, Cottle, and Tatham: *Security Analysis*, Fourth Edition (1962)

Graham, Dodd, Cottle, Murray, Block, & Leibowitz: *Security Analysis*, Fifth Edition (1988)

SECURITY ANALYSIS

Principles and Technique

BENJAMIN GRAHAM
Investment Fund Manager;
Lecturer in Finance
Columbia University

AND

DAVID L. DODD
Associate Professor of Finance
Columbia University

Sixth Edition

New York   Chicago   San Francisco   Lisbon   London   Madrid
Mexico City   Milan   New Delhi   San Juan   Seoul
Singapore   Sydney   Toronto

23   LCR   21 20

ISBN   P/N 978-0-07-160312-6 of set
       978-0-07-159253-6
MHID P/N 0-07-160312-3 of set
       0-07-159253-9

This publication is designed to provide accurate and authoritative information in regard to the subject matter covered. It is sold with the understanding that neither the author nor the publisher is engaged in rendering legal, accounting, futures/securities trading, or other professional service. If legal advice or other expert assistance is required, the services of a competent professional person should be sought.
—*From a Declaration of Principles jointly adopted by a Committee of the American Bar Association and a Committee of Publishers*

McGraw-Hill books are available at special quantity discounts to use as premiums and sales promotions, or for use in corporate training programs. To contact a representative, please visit the Contact Us pages at www.mhprofessional.com.

Library of Congress Cataloging-in-Publication Data
Graham, Benjamin.
    Security analysis / by Benjamin Graham and David L. Dodd.—6th ed.
       p. cm.
    Includes index.
    ISBN-13: 978-0-07-159253-6 (set)
    ISBN-10: 0-07-159253-9 (set)
    ISBN-13: 978-0-07-160312-6 (book)
    ISBN-10: 0-07-160312-3 (book)
    [etc.]
    1. Securities—United States. 2. Investment analysis. 3. Speculation. I. Dodd, David L. (David Le Fevre). II. Title.
    HG4910.G729 2008
    332.63'2042—dc22
                                                2008023115

BENJAMIN GRAHAM AND DAVID DODD forever changed the theory and practice of investing with the 1934 publication of *Security Analysis*. The nation, and indeed the rest of the world, was in the grips of the Great Depression, a period that brought unprecedented upheaval to the financial world. In 1940, the authors responded with a comprehensive revision. The second edition of *Security Analysis* is considered by many investors to be the definitive word from the most influential investment philosophers of our time.

Around the world, *Security Analysis* is still regarded as the fundamental text for the analysis of stocks and bonds. It is also considered to be the bible of value investing. To commemorate the 75th Anniversary of *Security Analysis*, McGraw-Hill is proud to publish this sixth edition.

Using the text of the 1940 edition, this new edition features lively and practical essays written by a stellar team that includes today's leading value investors, a prominent academic, and leading financial writers. The result is a contemporary bible of value investing.

The sixth edition, with a new design that pays homage to the original 1940 design, includes a CD that contains chapters from the original 1940 second edition. This book was printed and bound by R.R. Donnelley in Crawfordsville, Indiana.

*"Many shall be restored that now are fallen,
and many shall fall that now are in honor."*

HORACE—ARS POETICA.

CONTENTS

PART I

SURVEY AND APPROACH

PART II

FIXED-VALUE INVESTMENTS

PART III

SENIOR SECURITIES WITH SPECULATIVE FEATURES

Part IV

Theory of Common-stock Investment. The Dividend Factor

Part V

Analysis of the Income Account. The Earnings Factor in Common-stock Valuation

Part VI

Balance-sheet Analysis. Implications of Asset Values

PART VII

ADDITIONAL ASPECTS OF SECURITY ANALYSIS. DISCREPANCIES BETWEEN PRICE AND VALUE

Introduction to Part VII | The Great Illusion of the Stock Market and the Future of Value Investing • *by David Abrams*   617

PART VIII

GLOBAL VALUE INVESTING

Globetrotting with Graham and Dodd • *by Thomas A. Russo*   713

FOREWORD

BY WARREN E. BUFFETT

There are four books in my overflowing library that I particularly treasure, each of them written more than 50 years ago. All, though, would still be of enormous value to me if I were to read them today for the first time; their wisdom endures though their pages fade.

Two of those books are first editions of *The Wealth of Nations* (1776), by Adam Smith, and *The Intelligent Investor* (1949), by Benjamin Graham. A third is an original copy of the book you hold in your hands, Graham and Dodd's *Security Analysis*. I studied from *Security Analysis* while I was at Columbia University in 1950 and 1951, when I had the extraordinary good luck to have Ben Graham and Dave Dodd as teachers. Together, the book and the men changed my life.

On the utilitarian side, what I learned then became the bedrock upon which all of my investment and business decisions have been built. Prior to meeting Ben and Dave, I had long been fascinated by the stock market. Before I bought my first stock at age 11—it took me until then to accumulate the $115 required for the purchase—I had read every book in the Omaha Public Library having to do with the stock market. I found many of them fascinating and all interesting. But none were really useful.

My intellectual odyssey ended, however, when I met Ben and Dave, first through their writings and then in person. They laid out a roadmap for investing that I have now been following for 57 years. There's been no reason to look for another.

Beyond the ideas Ben and Dave gave me, they showered me with friendship, encouragement, and trust. They cared not a whit for reciprocation—toward a young student, they simply wanted to extend a one-way street of helpfulness. In the end, that's probably what I admire most about the two men. It was ordained at birth that they would be brilliant; they elected to be generous and kind.

Misanthropes would have been puzzled by their behavior. Ben and Dave instructed literally thousands of potential competitors, young fellows like me who would buy bargain stocks or engage in arbitrage transactions, directly competing with the Graham-Newman Corporation, which was Ben's investment company. Moreover, Ben and Dave would use current investing examples in the classroom and in their writings, in effect doing our work for us. The way they behaved made as deep an impression on me—and many of my classmates—as did their ideas. We were being taught not only how to invest wisely; we were also being taught how to live wisely.

The copy of *Security Analysis* that I keep in my library and that I used at Columbia is the 1940 edition. I've read it, I'm sure, at least four times, and obviously it is special.

But let's get to the fourth book I mentioned, which is even more precious. In 2000, Barbara Dodd Anderson, Dave's only child, gave me her father's copy of the 1934 edition of *Security Analysis*, inscribed with hundreds of marginal notes. These were inked in by Dave as he prepared for publication of the 1940 revised edition. No gift has meant more to me.

THE TIMELESS WISDOM OF GRAHAM AND DODD

BY SETH A. KLARMAN

Seventy-five years after Benjamin Graham and David Dodd wrote *Security Analysis*, a growing coterie of modern-day value investors remain deeply indebted to them. Graham and David were two assiduous and unusually insightful thinkers seeking to give order to the mostly uncharted financial wilderness of their era. They kindled a flame that has illuminated the way for value investors ever since. Today, *Security Analysis* remains an invaluable roadmap for investors as they navigate through unpredictable, often volatile, and sometimes treacherous financial markets. Frequently referred to as the "bible of value investing," *Security Analysis* is extremely thorough and detailed, teeming with wisdom for the ages. Although many of the examples are obviously dated, their lessons are timeless. And while the prose may sometimes seem dry, readers can yet discover valuable ideas on nearly every page. The financial markets have morphed since 1934 in almost unimaginable ways, but Graham and Dodd's approach to investing remains remarkably applicable today.

Value investing, today as in the era of Graham and Dodd, is the practice of purchasing securities or assets for less than they are worth—the proverbial dollar for 50 cents. Investing in bargain-priced securities provides a "margin of safety"—room for error, imprecision, bad luck, or the vicissitudes of the economy and stock market. While some might mistakenly consider value investing a mechanical tool for identifying bargains, it is actually a comprehensive investment philosophy that emphasizes the need to perform in-depth fundamental analysis, pursue long-term investment results, limit risk, and resist crowd psychology.

Far too many people approach the stock market with a focus on making money quickly. Such an orientation involves speculation rather than investment and is based on the hope that share prices will rise irrespective of valuation. Speculators generally regard stocks as pieces of paper to be quickly traded back and forth, foolishly decoupling them from business reality and valuation criteria. Speculative approaches—which pay little or no attention to downside risk—are especially popular in rising markets. In heady times, few are sufficiently disciplined to maintain strict standards of valuation and risk aversion, especially when most of those abandoning such standards are quickly getting rich. After all, it is easy to confuse genius with a bull market.

In recent years, some people have attempted to expand the definition of an investment to include any asset that has recently—or might soon—appreciate in price: art, rare stamps, or a wine collection. Because these items have no ascertainable fundamental value, generate no present or future cash flow, and depend for their value entirely on buyer whim, they clearly constitute speculations rather than investments.

In contrast to the speculator's preoccupation with rapid gain, value investors demonstrate their risk aversion by striving to avoid loss. A risk-averse investor is one for whom the perceived benefit of any gain is outweighed by the perceived cost of an equivalent loss. Once any of us has accumulated a modicum of capital, the incremental benefit of gaining more is typically eclipsed by the pain of having less.[1] Imagine how you

---

[1] Losing money, as Graham noted, can also be psychologically unsettling. Anxiety from the financial damage caused by recently experienced loss or the fear of further loss can significantly impede our ability to take advantage of the next opportunity that comes along. If an undervalued stock falls by half while the fundamentals—after checking and rechecking—are confirmed to be unchanged, we should relish the opportunity to buy significantly more "on sale." But if our net worth has tumbled along with the share price, it may be psychologically difficult to add to the position.

would respond to the proposition of a coin flip that would either double your net worth or extinguish it. Being risk averse, nearly all people would respectfully decline such a gamble. Such risk aversion is deeply ingrained in human nature. Yet many unwittingly set aside their risk aversion when the sirens of market speculation call.

Value investors regard securities not as speculative instruments but as fractional ownership in, or debt claims on, the underlying businesses. This orientation is key to value investing. When a small slice of a business is offered at a bargain price, it is helpful to evaluate it as if the whole business were offered for sale there. This analytical anchor helps value investors remain focused on the pursuit of long-term results rather than the profitability of their daily trading ledger.

At the root of Graham and Dodd's philosophy is the principle that the financial markets are the ultimate creators of opportunity. Sometimes the markets price securities correctly, other times not. Indeed, in the short run, the market can be quite inefficient, with great deviations between price and underlying value. Unexpected developments, increased uncertainty, and capital flows can boost short-term market volatility, with prices overshooting in either direction.[2] In the words of Graham and Dodd, "The price [of a security] is frequently an essential element, so that a stock . . . may have investment merit at one price level but not at another." (p. 106) As Graham has instructed, those who view the market as a weighing machine—a precise and efficient assessor of value—are part of the emotionally driven herd. Those who regard the market as a voting machine—

---

[2] Over the long run, however, as investors perform fundamental analysis, and corporate managements explain their strategies and manage their capital structures, share prices often migrate toward underlying business value. In particular, shares priced significantly below underlying value will attract bargain hunters and, ultimately, corporate acquirers, reinforcing the tendency toward longer-term share price efficiency. This tendency, however, is always subject to interruption by the short-term forces of greed and fear.

a sentiment-driven popularity contest—will be well positioned to take proper advantage of the extremes of market sentiment.

While it might seem that anyone can be a value investor, the essential characteristics of this type of investor—patience, discipline, and risk aversion—may well be genetically determined. When you first learn of the value approach, it either resonates with you or it doesn't. Either you are able to remain disciplined and patient, or you aren't. As Warren Buffett said in his famous article, "The Superinvestors of Graham-and-Doddsville," "It is extraordinary to me that the idea of buying dollar bills for 40 cents takes immediately with people or it doesn't take at all. It's like an inoculation. If it doesn't grab a person right away, I find you can talk to him for years and show him records, and it doesn't make any difference." [3,4] If *Security Analysis* resonates with you—if you can resist speculating and sometimes sit on your hands—perhaps you have a predisposition toward value investing. If not, at least the book will help you understand where you fit into the investing landscape and give you an appreciation for what the value-investing community may be thinking.

Just as Relevant Now

Perhaps the most exceptional achievement of *Security Analysis*, first published in 1934 and revised in the acclaimed 1940 edition, is that its lessons are timeless. Generations of value investors have adopted the teachings of Graham and Dodd and successfully implemented them across highly varied market environments, countries, and asset classes.

---

[3] "The Superinvestors of Graham-and-Doddsville," *Hermes*, the Columbia Business School magazine, 1984.

[4] My own experience has been exactly the one that Buffett describes. My 1978 summer job at Mutual Shares, a no-load value-based mutual fund, set the course for my professional career. The planned liquidation of Telecor and spin-off of its Electro Rent subsidiary in 1980 forever imprinted in my mind the merit of fundamental investment analysis. A buyer of Telecor stock was effectively creating an investment in the shares of Electro Rent, a fast-growing equipment rental company, at the giveaway valuation of approximately 1 times the cash flow. You always remember your first value investment.

This would delight the authors, who hoped to set forth principles that would "stand the test of the ever enigmatic future." (p. xliv)

In 1992, Tweedy, Browne Company LLC, a well-known value investment firm, published a compilation of 44 research studies entitled, "What Has Worked in Investing." The study found that what has worked is fairly simple: cheap stocks (measured by price-to-book values, price-to-earnings ratios, or dividend yields) reliably outperform expensive ones, and stocks that have underperformed (over three- and five-year periods) subsequently beat those that have lately performed well. In other words, value investing works! I know of no long-time practitioner who regrets adhering to a value philosophy; few investors who embrace the fundamental principles ever abandon this investment approach for another.

Today, when you read Graham and Dodd's description of how they navigated through the financial markets of the 1930s, it seems as if they were detailing a strange, foreign, and antiquated era of economic depression, extreme risk aversion, and obscure and obsolete businesses. But such an exploration is considerably more valuable than it superficially appears. After all, each new day has the potential to bring with it a strange and foreign environment. Investors tend to assume that tomorrow's markets will look very much like today's, and, most of the time, they will. But every once in a while,[5] conventional wisdom is turned on its head, circular reasoning is unraveled, prices revert to the mean, and speculative behavior is exposed as such. At those times, when today fails to resemble yesterday, most investors will be paralyzed. In the words of Graham and Dodd, "We have striven throughout to guard the student against overemphasis upon the superficial and the temporary," which is "at once the delusion and the nemesis of the world of finance." (p. xliv) It

---

[5] The credit crunch triggered by subprime mortgage losses that began in July 2007 is a recent and dramatic example.

is during periods of tumult that a value-investing philosophy is particularly beneficial.

In 1934, Graham and Dodd had witnessed over a five-year span the best and the worst of times in the markets—the run-up to the 1929 peak, the October 1929 crash, and the relentless grind of the Great Depression. They laid out a plan for how investors in any environment might sort through hundreds or even thousands of common stocks, preferred shares, and bonds to identify those worthy of investment. Remarkably, their approach is essentially the same one that value investors employ today. The same principles they applied to the U.S. stock and bond markets of the 1920s and 1930s apply to the global capital markets of the early twenty-first century, to less liquid asset classes like real estate and private equity, and even to derivative instruments that hardly existed when *Security Analysis* was written.

While formulas such as the classic "net working capital" test are necessary to support an investment analysis, value investing is not a paint-by-numbers exercise.[6] Skepticism and judgment are always required. For one thing, not all elements affecting value are captured in a company's financial statements—inventories can grow obsolete and receivables uncollectible; liabilities are sometimes unrecorded and property values over- or understated. Second, valuation is an art, not a science. Because the value of a business depends on numerous variables, it can typically be assessed only within a range. Third, the outcomes of all investments depend to some extent on the future, which cannot be predicted with certainty; for this reason, even some carefully analyzed investments fail to achieve profitable outcomes. Sometimes a stock becomes cheap for good reason: a broken business model, hidden liabilities, protracted liti-

---

[6] Graham and Dodd recommended that investors purchase stocks trading for less than two-thirds of "net working capital," defined as working capital less all other liabilities. Many stocks fit this criterion during the Depression years, far fewer today.

gation, or incompetent or corrupt management. Investors must always act with caution and humility, relentlessly searching for additional information while realizing that they will never know everything about a company. In the end, the most successful value investors combine detailed business research and valuation work with endless discipline and patience, a well-considered sensitivity analysis, intellectual honesty, and years of analytical and investment experience.

Interestingly, Graham and Dodd's value-investing principles apply beyond the financial markets—including, for example, to the market for baseball talent, as eloquently captured in *Moneyball*, Michael Lewis's 2003 bestseller. The market for baseball players, like the market for stocks and bonds, is inefficient—and for many of the same reasons. In both investing and baseball, there is no single way to ascertain value, no one metric that tells the whole story. In both, there are mountains of information and no broad consensus on how to assess it. Decision makers in both arenas misinterpret available data, misdirect their analyses, and reach inaccurate conclusions. In baseball, as in securities, many overpay because they fear standing apart from the crowd and being criticized. They often make decisions for emotional, not rational, reasons. They become exuberant; they panic. Their orientation sometimes becomes overly short term. They fail to understand what is mean reverting and what isn't. Baseball's value investors, like financial market value investors, have achieved significant outperformance over time. While Graham and Dodd didn't apply value principles to baseball, the applicability of their insights to the market for athletic talent attests to the universality and timelessness of this approach.

Value Investing Today

Amidst the Great Depression, the stock market and the national economy were exceedingly risky. Downward movements in share prices and business activity came suddenly and could be severe and protracted. Optimists were regularly rebuffed by circumstances. Winning, in a sense, was accomplished by not losing. Investors could achieve a margin of safety by buying shares in businesses at a large discount to their underlying value, and they needed a margin of safety because of all the things that could—and often did—go wrong.

Even in the worst of markets, Graham and Dodd remained faithful to their principles, including their view that the economy and markets sometimes go through painful cycles, which must simply be endured. They expressed confidence, in those dark days, that the economy and stock market would eventually rebound: "While we were writing, we had to combat a widespread conviction that financial debacle was to be the permanent order." (p. xliv)

Of course, just as investors must deal with down cycles when business results deteriorate and cheap stocks become cheaper, they must also endure up cycles when bargains are scarce and investment capital is plentiful. In recent years, the financial markets have performed exceedingly well by historic standards, attracting substantial fresh capital in need of managers. Today, a meaningful portion of that capital—likely totaling in the trillions of dollars globally—invests with a value approach. This includes numerous value-based asset management firms and mutual funds, a number of today's roughly 9,000 hedge funds, and some of the largest and most successful university endowments and family investment offices.

It is important to note that not all value investors are alike. In the aforementioned "Superinvestors of Graham-and-Doddsville," Buffett describes numerous successful value investors who have little portfolio overlap. Some value investors hold obscure, "pink-sheet shares" while others focus on the large-cap universe. Some have gone global, while others focus on a single market sector such as real estate or energy.

Some run computer screens to identify statistically inexpensive companies, while others assess "private market value"—the value an industry
buyer would pay for the entire company. Some are activists who aggressively fight for corporate change, while others seek out undervalued
securities with a catalyst already in place—such as a spin-off, asset sale,
major share repurchase plan, or new management team—for the partial
or full realization of the underlying value. And, of course, as in any profession, some value investors are simply more talented than others.

In the aggregate, the value-investing community is no longer the very
small group of adherents that it was several decades ago. Competition
can have a powerful corrective effect on market inefficiencies and mispricings. With today's many amply capitalized and skilled investors, what
are the prospects for a value practitioner? Better than you might expect,
for several reasons. First, even with a growing value community, there are
far more market participants with little or no value orientation. Most managers, including growth and momentum investors and market indexers,
pay little or no attention to value criteria. Instead, they concentrate
almost single-mindedly on the growth rate of a company's earnings, the
momentum of its share price, or simply its inclusion in a market index.

Second, nearly all money managers today, including some hapless
value managers, are forced by the (real or imagined) performance pressures of the investment business to have an absurdly short investment
horizon, sometimes as brief as a calendar quarter, month, or less. A value
strategy is of little use to the impatient investor since it usually takes
time to pay off.

Finally, human nature never changes. Capital market manias regularly
occur on a grand scale: Japanese stocks in the late 1980s, Internet and
technology stocks in 1999 and 2000, subprime mortgage lending in
2006 and 2007, and alternative investments currently. It is always difficult
to take a contrarian approach. Even highly capable investors can wither

under the relentless message from the market that they are wrong. The pressures to succumb are enormous; many investment managers fear they'll lose business if they stand too far apart from the crowd. Some also fail to pursue value because they've handcuffed themselves (or been saddled by clients) with constraints preventing them from buying stocks selling at low dollar prices, small-cap stocks, stocks of companies that don't pay dividends or are losing money, or debt instruments with below investment-grade ratings.[7] Many also engage in career management techniques like "window dressing" their portfolios at the end of calendar quarters or selling off losers (even if they are undervalued) while buying more of the winners (even if overvalued). Of course, for those value investors who are truly long term oriented, it is a wonderful thing that many potential competitors are thrown off course by constraints that render them unable or unwilling to effectively compete.

Another reason that greater competition may not hinder today's value investors is the broader and more diverse investment landscape in which they operate. Graham faced a limited lineup of publicly traded U.S. equity and debt securities. Today, there are many thousands of publicly traded stocks in the United States alone, and many tens of thousands worldwide, plus thousands of corporate bonds and asset-backed debt securities. Previously illiquid assets, such as bank loans, now trade regularly. Investors may also choose from an almost limitless number of derivative instruments, including customized contracts designed to meet any need or hunch.

Nevertheless, 25 years of historically strong stock market performance have left the market far from bargain-priced. High valuations and

---

[7] Another sort of constraint involves the "prudent man rule," which is a legal concept that divides permissible from impermissible investments. In the mid- to late 1970s, many interpreted this rule to preclude meaningful exposure to equities. Since then, prudence has become a moving target as investors, gaining comfort over time from the actions of their peers, have come to invest in more exotic and increasingly illiquid asset classes.

intensified competition raise the specter of lower returns for value investors generally. Also, some value investment firms have become extremely large, and size can be the enemy of investment performance because decision making is slowed by bureaucracy and smaller opportunities cease to move the needle.

In addition, because growing numbers of competent buy-side and sell-side analysts are plying their trade with the assistance of sophisticated information technology, far fewer securities seem likely to fall through the cracks to become extremely undervalued.[8] Today's value investors are unlikely to find opportunity armed only with a Value Line guide or by thumbing through stock tables. While bargains still occasionally hide in plain sight, securities today are most likely to become mispriced when they are either accidentally overlooked or deliberately avoided. Consequently, value investors have had to become thoughtful about where to focus their analysis. In the early 2000s, for example, investors became so disillusioned with the capital allocation procedures of many South Korean companies that few considered them candidates for worthwhile investment. As a result, the shares of numerous South Korean companies traded at great discounts from prevailing international valuations: at two or three times the cash flow, less than half the underlying business value, and, in several cases, less than the cash (net of debt) held on their balance sheets. Bargain issues, such as Posco and SK Telecom, ultimately attracted many value seekers; Warren Buffett reportedly profited handsomely from a number of South Korean holdings.

Today's value investors also find opportunity in the stocks and bonds of companies stigmatized on Wall Street because of involvement in pro-

---

[8] Great innovations in technology have made vastly more information and analytical capability available to all investors. This democratization has not, however, made value investors any better off. With information more widely and inexpensively available, some of the greatest market inefficiencies have been corrected. Developing innovative sources of ideas and information, such as those available from business consultants and industry experts, has become increasingly important.

tracted litigation, scandal, accounting fraud, or financial distress. The securities of such companies sometimes trade down to bargain levels, where they become good investments for those who are able to remain stalwart in the face of bad news. For example, the debt of Enron, perhaps the world's most stigmatized company after an accounting scandal forced it into bankruptcy in 2001, traded as low as 10 cents on the dollar of claim; ultimate recoveries are expected to be six times that amount. Similarly, companies with tobacco or asbestos exposure have in recent years periodically come under severe selling pressure due to the uncertainties surrounding litigation and the resultant risk of corporate financial distress. More generally, companies that disappoint or surprise investors with lower-than-expected results, sudden management changes, accounting problems, or ratings downgrades are more likely than consistently strong performers to be sources of opportunity.

When bargains are scarce, value investors must be patient; compromising standards is a slippery slope to disaster. New opportunities will emerge, even if we don't know when or where. In the absence of compelling opportunity, holding at least a portion of one's portfolio in cash equivalents (for example, U.S. Treasury bills) awaiting future deployment will sometimes be the most sensible option. Recently, Warren Buffett stated that he has more cash to invest than he has good investments. As all value investors must do from time to time, Buffett is waiting patiently.

Still, value investors are bottom-up analysts, good at assessing securities one at a time based on the fundamentals. They don't need the entire market to be bargain priced, just 20 or 25 unrelated securities—a number sufficient for diversification of risk. Even in an expensive market, value investors must keep analyzing securities and assessing businesses, gaining knowledge and experience that will be useful in the future. Value investors, therefore, should not try to time the market or guess whether it will rise or fall in the near term. Rather, they should rely on a bottom-up approach, sifting the financial markets for bargains and then buying them, regardless of the level or recent direction of the market or economy. Only when they cannot find bargains should they default to holding cash.

A Flexible Approach

Because our nation's founders could not foresee—and knew they could not foresee—technological, social, cultural, and economic changes that the future would bring, they wrote a flexible constitution that still guides us over two centuries later. Similarly, Benjamin Graham and David Dodd acknowledged that they could not anticipate the business, economic, technological, and competitive changes that would sweep through the investment world over the ensuing years. But they, too, wrote a flexible treatise that provides us with the tools to function in an investment landscape that was destined—and remains destined—to undergo profound and unpredictable change.

For example, companies today sell products that Graham and Dodd could not have imagined. Indeed, there are companies and entire industries that they could not have envisioned. *Security Analysis* offers no examples of how to value cellular phone carriers, software companies, satellite television providers, or Internet search engines. But the book provides the analytical tools to evaluate almost any company, to assess the value of its marketable securities, and to determine the existence of a margin of safety. Questions of solvency, liquidity, predictability, business strategy, and risk cut across businesses, nations, and time.

Graham and Dodd did not specifically address how to value private businesses or how to determine the value of an entire company rather than the value of a fractional interest through ownership of its shares.[9]

---

[9] They did consider the relative merits of corporate control enjoyed by a private business owner versus the value of marketability for a listed stock (p. 372).

But their analytical principles apply equally well to these different issues. Investors still need to ask, how stable is the enterprise, and what are its future prospects? What are its earnings and cash flow? What is the downside risk of owning it? What is its liquidation value? How capable and honest is its management? What would you pay for the stock of this company if it were public? What factors might cause the owner of this business to sell control at a bargain price?

Similarly, the pair never addressed how to analyze the purchase of an office building or apartment complex. Real estate bargains come about for the same reasons as securities bargains—an urgent need for cash, inability to perform proper analysis, a bearish macro view, or investor disfavor or neglect. In a bad real estate climate, tighter lending standards can cause even healthy properties to sell at distressed prices. Graham and Dodd's principles—such as the stability of cash flow, sufficiency of return, and analysis of downside risk—allow us to identify real estate investments with a margin of safety in any market environment.

Even complex derivatives not imagined in an earlier era can be scrutinized with the value investor's eye. While traders today typically price put and call options via the Black-Scholes model, one can instead use value-investing precepts—upside potential, downside risk, and the likelihood that each of various possible scenarios will occur—to analyze these instruments. An inexpensive option may, in effect, have the favorable risk-return characteristics of a value investment—regardless of what the Black-Scholes model dictates.

Institutional Investing

Perhaps the most important change in the investment landscape over the past 75 years is the ascendancy of institutional investing. In the 1930s, individual investors dominated the stock market. Today, by con-

trast, most market activity is driven by institutional investors—large
pools of pension, endowment, and aggregated individual capital. While
the advent of these large, quasi-permanent capital pools might have
resulted in the wide-scale adoption of a long-term value-oriented
approach, in fact this has not occurred. Instead, institutional investing
has evolved into a short-term performance derby, which makes it difficult for institutional managers to take contrarian or long-term positions.
Indeed, rather than standing apart from the crowd and possibly suffering
disappointing short-term results that could cause clients to withdraw
capital, institutional investors often prefer the safe haven of assured
mediocre performance that can be achieved only by closely following
the herd.

Alternative investments—a catch-all category that includes venture
capital, leveraged buyouts, private equity, and hedge funds—are the current institutional rage. No investment treatise written today could fail to
comment on this development.

Fueled by performance pressures and a growing expectation of low
(and inadequate) returns from traditional equity and debt investments,
institutional investors have sought high returns and diversification by
allocating a growing portion of their endowments and pension funds to
alternatives. *Pioneering Portfolio Management*, written in 2000 by David
Swensen, the groundbreaking head of Yale's Investment Office, makes a
strong case for alternative investments. In it, Swensen points to the
historically inefficient pricing of many asset classes,[10] the historically high
risk-adjusted returns of many alternative managers, and the limited

---

[10] Many investors make the mistake of thinking about returns to asset classes as if they were permanent. Returns are not inherent to an asset class; they result from the fundamentals of the underlying
businesses *and* the price paid by investors for the related securities. Capital flowing into an asset
class can, reflexively, impair the ability of those investing in that asset class to continue to generate
the anticipated, historically attractive returns.

performance correlation between alternatives and other asset classes. He highlights the importance of alternative manager selection by noting the large dispersion of returns achieved between top-quartile and third-quartile performers. A great many endowment managers have emulated Swensen, following him into a large commitment to alternative investments, almost certainly on worse terms and amidst a more competitive environment than when he entered the area.

Graham and Dodd would be greatly concerned by the commitment of virtually all major university endowments to one type of alternative investment: venture capital. The authors of the margin-of-safety approach to investing would not find one in the entire venture capital universe.[11] While there is often the prospect of substantial upside in venture capital, there is also very high risk of failure. Even with the diversification provided by a venture fund, it is not clear how to analyze the underlying investments to determine whether the potential return justifies the risk. Venture capital investment would, therefore, have to be characterized as pure speculation, with no margin of safety whatsoever.

Hedge funds—a burgeoning area of institutional interest with nearly $2 trillion of assets under management—are pools of capital that vary widely in their tactics but have a common fee structure that typically pays the manager 1% to 2% annually of assets under management and 20% (and sometimes more) of any profits generated. They had their start in the 1920s, when Ben Graham himself ran one of the first hedge funds.

What would Graham and Dodd say about the hedge funds operating in today's markets? They would likely disapprove of hedge funds that make investments based on macroeconomic assessments or that pursue

---

[11] Nor would they find one in leveraged buyouts, through which businesses are purchased at lofty prices using mostly debt financing and a thin layer of equity capital. The only value-investing rationale for venture capital or leveraged buyouts might be if they were regarded as mispriced call options. Even so, it is not clear that these areas constitute good value.

speculative, short-term strategies. Such funds, by avoiding or even selling undervalued securities to participate in one or another folly, inadvertently create opportunities for value investors. The illiquidity, lack of transparency, gargantuan size, embedded leverage, and hefty fees of some hedge funds would no doubt raise red flags. But Graham and Dodd would probably approve of hedge funds that practice value-oriented investment selection.

Importantly, while Graham and Dodd emphasized limiting risk on an investment-by-investment basis, they also believed that diversification and hedging could protect the downside for an entire portfolio. (p. 106) This is what most hedge funds attempt to do. While they hold individual securities that, considered alone, may involve an uncomfortable degree of risk, they attempt to offset the risks for the entire portfolio through the short sale of similar but more highly valued securities, through the purchase of put options on individual securities or market indexes, and through adequate diversification (although many are guilty of overdiversification, holding too little of their truly good ideas and too much of their mediocre ones). In this way, a hedge fund portfolio could (in theory, anyway) have characteristics of good potential return with limited risk that its individual components may not have.

Modern-day Developments

As mentioned, the analysis of businesses and securities has become increasingly sophisticated over the years. Spreadsheet technology, for example, allows for vastly more sophisticated modeling than was possible even one generation ago. Benjamin Graham's pencil, clearly one of the sharpest of his era, might not be sharp enough today. On the other hand, technology can easily be misused; computer modeling requires making a series of assumptions about the future that can lead to a spurious precision of which Graham would have been quite dubious. While Graham was interested in companies that produced consistent earnings, analysis in his day was less sophisticated regarding why some company's earnings might be more consistent than others. Analysts today examine businesses but also business models; the bottom-line impact of changes in revenues, profit margins, product mix, and other variables is carefully studied by managements and financial analysts alike. Investors know that businesses do not exist in a vacuum; the actions of competitors, suppliers, and customers can greatly impact corporate profitability and must be considered.[12]

Another important change in focus over time is that while Graham looked at corporate earnings and dividend payments as barometers of a company's health, most value investors today analyze free cash flow. This is the cash generated annually from the operations of a business after all capital expenditures are made and changes in working capital are considered. Investors have increasingly turned to this metric because reported earnings can be an accounting fiction, masking the cash generated by a business or implying positive cash generation when there is none. Today's investors have rightly concluded that following the cash— as the manager of a business must do—is the most reliable and revealing means of assessing a company.

In addition, many value investors today consider balance sheet analysis less important than was generally thought a few generations ago. With returns on capital much higher at present than in the past, most stocks trade far above book value; balance sheet analysis is less helpful in understanding upside potential or downside risk of stocks priced at

---

[12] Professor Michael Porter of Harvard Business School, in his seminal book *Competitive Strategy* (Free Press, 1980), lays out the groundwork for a more intensive, thorough, and dynamic analysis of businesses and industries in the modern economy. A broad industry analysis has become particularly necessary as a result of the passage in 2000 of Regulation FD (Fair Disclosure), which regulates and restricts the communications between a company and its actual or potential shareholders. Wall Street analysts, facing a dearth of information from the companies they cover, have been forced to expand their areas of inquiry.

such levels. The effects of sustained inflation over time have also wreaked havoc with the accuracy of assets accounted for using historic cost; this means that two companies owning identical assets could report very different book values. Of course, balance sheets must still be carefully scrutinized. Astute observers of corporate balance sheets are often the first to see business deterioration or vulnerability as inventories and receivables build, debt grows, and cash evaporates. And for investors in the equity and debt of underperforming companies, balance sheet analysis remains one generally reliable way of assessing downside protection.

Globalization has increasingly affected the investment landscape, with most investors looking beyond their home countries for opportunity and diversification. Graham and Dodd's principles fully apply to international markets, which are, if anything, even more subject to the vicissitudes of investor sentiment—and thus more inefficiently priced—than the U.S. market is today. Investors must be cognizant of the risks of international investing, including exposure to foreign currencies and the need to consider hedging them. Among the other risks are political instability, different (or absent) securities laws and investor protections, varying accounting standards, and limited availability of information.

Oddly enough, despite 75 years of success achieved by value investors, one group of observers largely ignores or dismisses this discipline: academics. Academics tend to create elegant theories that purport to explain the real world but in fact oversimplify it. One such theory, the Efficient Market Hypothesis (EMH), holds that security prices always and immediately reflect all available information, an idea deeply at odds with Graham and Dodd's notion that there is great value to fundamental security analysis. The Capital Asset Pricing Model (CAPM) relates risk to return but always mistakes volatility, or beta, for risk. Modern Portfolio Theory (MPT) applauds the benefits of diversification in constructing an

optimal portfolio. But by insisting that higher expected return comes
only with greater risk, MPT effectively repudiates the entire value-investing philosophy and its long-term record of risk-adjusted investment outperformance. Value investors have no time for these theories and
generally ignore them.

The assumptions made by these theories—including continuous
markets, perfect information, and low or no transaction costs—are unrealistic. Academics, broadly speaking, are so entrenched in their theories
that they cannot accept that value investing works. Instead of launching
a series of studies to understand the remarkable 50-year investment
record of Warren Buffett, academics instead explain him away as an aber-
ration. Greater attention has been paid recently to behavioral economics,
a field recognizing that individuals do not always act rationally and have
systematic cognitive biases that contribute to market inefficiencies and
security mispricings. These teachings—which would not seem alien to
Graham—have not yet entered the academic mainstream, but they are
building some momentum.

Academics have espoused nuanced permutations of their flawed theories for several decades. Countless thousands of their students have
been taught that security analysis is worthless, that risk is the same as
volatility, and that investors must avoid overconcentration in good ideas
(because in efficient markets there can be no good ideas) and thus diversify into mediocre or bad ones. Of course, for value investors, the propa-
gation of these academic theories has been deeply gratifying: the
brainwashing of generations of young investors produces the very inefficiencies that savvy stock pickers can exploit.

Another important factor for value investors to take into account is
the growing propensity of the Federal Reserve to intervene in financial
markets at the first sign of trouble. Amidst severe turbulence, the Fed
frequently lowers interest rates to prop up securities prices and restore

investor confidence. While the intention of Fed officials is to maintain orderly capital markets, some money managers view Fed intervention as a virtual license to speculate. Aggressive Fed tactics, sometimes referred to as the "Greenspan put" (now the "Bernanke put"), create a moral hazard that encourages speculation while prolonging overvaluation. So long as value investors aren't lured into a false sense of security, so long as they can maintain a long-term horizon and ensure their staying power, market dislocations caused by Fed action (or investor anticipation of it) may ultimately be a source of opportunity.

Another modern development of relevance is the ubiquitous cable television coverage of the stock market. This frenetic lunacy exacerbates the already short-term orientation of most investors. It foments the view that it is possible—or even necessary—to have an opinion on everything pertinent to the financial markets, as opposed to the patient and highly selective approach endorsed by Graham and Dodd. This sound-bite culture reinforces the popular impression that investing is easy, not rigorous and painstaking. The daily cheerleading pundits exult at rallies and record highs and commiserate over market reversals; viewers get the impression that up is the only rational market direction and that selling or sitting on the sidelines is almost unpatriotic. The hysterical tenor is exacerbated at every turn. For example, CNBC frequently uses a formatted screen that constantly updates the level of the major market indexes against a digital clock. Not only is the time displayed in hours, minutes, and seconds but in completely useless hundredths of seconds, the numbers flashing by so rapidly (like tenths of a cent on the gas pump) as to be completely unreadable. The only conceivable purpose is to grab the viewers' attention and ratchet their adrenaline to full throttle.

Cable business channels bring the herdlike mentality of the crowd into everyone's living room, thus making it much harder for viewers to stand apart from the masses. Only on financial cable TV would a commentator with a crazed persona become a celebrity whose pronouncements regularly move markets. In a world in which the differences between investing and speculating are frequently blurred, the nonsense on financial cable channels only compounds the problem. Graham would have been appalled. The only saving grace is that value investors prosper at the expense of those who fall under the spell of the cable pundits. Meanwhile, human nature virtually ensures that there will never be a Graham and Dodd channel.

Unanswered Questions

Today's investors still wrestle, as Graham and Dodd did in their day, with a number of important investment questions. One is whether to focus on relative or absolute value. Relative value involves the assessment that one security is cheaper than another, that Microsoft is a better bargain than IBM. Relative value is easier to determine than absolute value, the two-dimensional assessment of whether a security is cheaper than other securities *and* cheap enough to be worth purchasing. The most intrepid investors in relative value manage hedge funds where they purchase the relatively less expensive securities and sell short the relatively more expensive ones. This enables them potentially to profit on both sides of the ledger, long and short. Of course, it also exposes them to double-barreled losses if they are wrong.[13]

It is harder to think about absolute value than relative value. When is a stock cheap enough to buy and hold without a short sale as a hedge? One standard is to buy when a security trades at an appreciable—say, 30%, 40%, or greater—discount from its underlying value, calculated either as its liquidation value, going-concern value, or private-market

---

[13] Many hedge funds also use significant leverage to goose their returns further, which backfires when analysis is faulty or judgment is flawed.

value (the value a knowledgeable third party would reasonably pay for the business). Another standard is to invest when a security offers an acceptably attractive return to a long-term holder, such as a low-risk bond priced to yield 10% or more, or a stock with an 8% to 10% or higher free cash flow yield at a time when "risk-free" U.S. government bonds deliver 4% to 5% nominal and 2% to 3% real returns. Such demanding standards virtually ensure that absolute value will be quite scarce.

Another area where investors struggle is trying to define what constitutes a good business. Someone once defined the best possible business as a post office box to which people send money. That idea has certainly been eclipsed by the creation of subscription Web sites that accept credit cards. Today's most profitable businesses are those in which you sell a fixed amount of work product—say, a piece of software or a hit recording—millions and millions of times at very low marginal cost. Good businesses are generally considered those with strong barriers to entry, limited capital requirements, reliable customers, low risk of technological obsolescence, abundant growth possibilities, and thus significant and growing free cash flow.

Businesses are also subject to changes in the technological and competitive landscape. Because of the Internet, the competitive moat surrounding the newspaper business—which was considered a very good business only a decade ago—has eroded faster than almost anyone anticipated. In an era of rapid technological change, investors must be ever vigilant, even with regard to companies that are not involved in technology but are simply affected by it. In short, today's good businesses may not be tomorrow's.

Investors also expend considerable effort attempting to assess the quality of a company's management. Some managers are more capable or scrupulous than others, and some may be able to manage certain businesses and environments better than others. Yet, as Graham and

Dodd noted, "Objective tests of managerial ability are few and far from scientific." (p. 84) Make no mistake about it: a management's acumen, foresight, integrity, and motivation all make a huge difference in shareholder returns. In the present era of aggressive corporate financial engineering, managers have many levers at their disposal to positively impact returns, including share repurchases, prudent use of leverage, and a valuation-based approach to acquisitions. Managers who are unwilling to make shareholder-friendly decisions risk their companies becoming perceived as "value traps": inexpensively valued, but ultimately poor investments, because the assets are underutilized. Such companies often attract activist investors seeking to unlock this trapped value. Even more difficult, investors must decide whether to take the risk of investing—at any price—with management teams that have not always done right by shareholders. Shares of such companies may sell at steeply discounted levels, but perhaps the discount is warranted; value that today belongs to the equity holders may tomorrow have been spirited away or squandered.

An age-old difficulty for investors is ascertaining the value of future growth. In the preface to the first edition of *Security Analysis*, the authors said as much: "Some matters of vital significance, e.g., the determination of the future prospects of an enterprise, have received little space, because little of definite value can be said on the subject." (p. xliii)

Clearly, a company that will earn (or have free cash flow of) $1 per share today and $2 per share in five years is worth considerably more than a company with identical current per share earnings and no growth. This is especially true if the growth of the first company is likely to continue and is not subject to great variability. Another complication is that companies can grow in many different ways—for example, selling the same number of units at higher prices; selling more units at the same (or even lower) prices; changing the product mix (selling proportionately more of the higher-profit-margin products); or developing an entirely new product line. Obviously, some forms of growth are worth more than others.

There is a significant downside to paying up for growth or, worse, to obsessing over it. Graham and Dodd astutely observed that "analysis is concerned primarily with values which are supported by the facts and not with those which depend largely upon expectations." (p. 86) Strongly preferring the actual to the possible, they regarded the "future as a hazard which his [the analyst's] conclusions must encounter rather than as the source of his vindication." (p. 86) Investors should be especially vigilant against focusing on growth to the exclusion of all else, including the risk of overpaying. Again, Graham and Dodd were spot on, warning that "carried to its logical extreme, . . . [there is no price] too high for a good stock, and that such an issue was equally 'safe' after it had advanced to 200 as it had been at 25." (p. 105) Precisely this mistake was made when stock prices surged skyward during the Nifty Fifty era of the early 1970s and the dot-com bubble of 1999 to 2000.

The flaw in such a growth-at-any-price approach becomes obvious when the anticipated growth fails to materialize. When the future disappoints, what should investors do? Hope growth resumes? Or give up and sell? Indeed, failed growth stocks are often so aggressively dumped by disappointed holders that their price falls to levels at which value investors, who stubbornly pay little or nothing for growth characteristics, become major holders. This was the case with many technology stocks that suffered huge declines after the dot-com bubble burst in the spring of 2000. By 2002, hundreds of fallen tech stocks traded for less than the cash on their balance sheets, a value investor's dream. One such company was Radvision, an Israeli provider of voice, video, and data products whose stock subsequently rose from under $5 to the mid-$20s after the urgent selling abated and investors refocused on fundamentals.

Another conundrum for value investors is knowing when to sell. Buying bargains is the sweet spot of value investors, although how small a discount one might accept can be subject to debate. Selling is more difficult because it involves securities that are closer to fully priced. As with buying, investors need a discipline for selling. First, sell targets, once set, should be regularly adjusted to reflect all currently available information. Second, individual investors must consider tax consequences. Third, whether or not an investor is fully invested may influence the urgency of raising cash from a stockholding as it approaches full valuation. The availability of better bargains might also make one a more eager seller. Finally, value investors should completely exit a security by the time it reaches full value; owning overvalued securities is the realm of speculators. Value investors typically begin selling at a 10% to 20% discount to their assessment of underlying value—based on the liquidity of the security, the possible presence of a catalyst for value realization, the quality of management, the riskiness and leverage of the underlying business, and the investors' confidence level regarding the assumptions underlying the investment.

Finally, investors need to deal with the complex subject of risk. As mentioned earlier, academics and many professional investors have come to define risk in terms of the Greek letter beta, which they use as a measure of past share price volatility: a historically more volatile stock is seen as riskier. But value investors, who are inclined to think about risk as the probability and amount of potential loss, find such reasoning absurd. In fact, a volatile stock may become deeply undervalued, rendering it a very low risk investment.

One of the most difficult questions for value investors is how much risk to incur. One facet of this question involves position size and its impact on portfolio diversification. How much can you comfortably own of even the most attractive opportunities? Naturally, investors desire to profit fully from their good ideas. Yet this tendency is tempered by the fear of being unlucky or wrong. Nonetheless, value investors should concentrate their holdings in their best ideas; if you can tell a good investment from a bad one, you can also distinguish a great one from a good one.

Investors must also ponder the risks of investing in politically unstable countries, as well as the uncertainties involving currency, interest rate, and economic fluctuations. How much of your capital do you want tied up in Argentina or Thailand, or even France or Australia, no matter how undervalued the stocks may be in those markets?

Another risk consideration for value investors, as with all investors, is whether or not to use leverage. While some value-oriented hedge funds and even endowments use leverage to enhance their returns, I side with those who are unwilling to incur the added risks that come with margin debt. Just as leverage enhances the return of successful investments, it magnifies the losses from unsuccessful ones. More importantly, nonrecourse (margin) debt raises risk to unacceptable levels because it places one's staying power in jeopardy. One risk-related consideration should be paramount above all others: the ability to sleep well at night, confident that your financial position is secure whatever the future may bring.

Final Thoughts

In a rising market, everyone makes money and a value philosophy is unnecessary. But because there is no certain way to predict what the market will do, one must follow a value philosophy at all times. By controlling risk and limiting loss through extensive fundamental analysis, strict discipline, and endless patience, value investors can expect good results with limited downside. You may not get rich quick, but you will keep what you have, and if the future of value investing resembles its past, you are likely to get rich slowly. As investment strategies go, this is the most that any reasonable investor can hope for.

The real secret to investing is that there is no secret to investing. Every important aspect of value investing has been made available to the public many times over, beginning in 1934 with the first edition of *Security Analysis*. That so many people fail to follow this timeless and almost foolproof approach enables those who adopt it to remain successful. The foibles of human nature that result in the mass pursuit of instant wealth and effortless gain seem certain to be with us forever. So long as people succumb to this aspect of their natures, value investing will remain, as it has been for 75 years, a sound and low-risk approach to successful long-term investing.

SETH A. KLARMAN

Boston, Massachusetts, *May, 2008*

PREFACE TO THE SECOND EDITION

THE LAPSE OF six years since first publication of this work supplies the excuse, if not the necessity, for the present comprehensive revision. Things happen too fast in the economic world to permit authors to rest comfortably for long. The impact of a major war adds special point to our problem. To the extent that we deal with investment policy we can at best merely hint at the war's significance for the future. As for security analysis proper, the new uncertainties may complicate its subject matter, but they should not alter its foundations or its methods.

We have revised our text with a number of objectives in view. There are weaknesses to be corrected and some new judgments to be substituted. Recent developments in the financial sphere are to be taken into account, particularly the effects of regulation by the Securities and Exchange Commission. The persistence of low interest rates justifies a fresh approach to that subject; on the other hand the reaffirmance of Wall Street's primary reliance on *trend* impels us to a wider, though not essentially different, critique of this modern philosophy of investment.

Although too great insistence on up-to-date examples may prove something of a boomerang, as the years pass swiftly, we have used such new illustrations as would occur to authors writing in 1939–1940. But we have felt also that many of the old examples, which challenged the future when first suggested, may now possess some utility as verifiers of the proposed techniques. Thus we have borrowed one of our own ideas and have ventured to view the sequel to all our germane 1934 examples as a "laboratory test" of practical security analysis. Reference to each such case, in the text or in notes, may enable the reader to apply certain tests of his own to the pretensions of the securities analyst.

The increased size of the book results partly from a larger number of examples, partly from the addition of clarifying material at many points, and perhaps mainly from an expanded treatment of railroad analysis and the addition of much new statistical material bearing on the exhibits of all the industrial companies listed on the New York Stock Exchange. The general arrangement of the work has been retained, although a few who use it as a text have suggested otherwise. We trust, however, that the order of the chapters can be revised in the reading, without too much difficulty, to convenience those who prefer to start, say, with the theory and practice of common-stock analysis.

BENJAMIN GRAHAM AND DAVID L. DODD
New York, New York, *May, 1940*

PREFACE TO THE FIRST EDITION

THIS BOOK IS intended for all those who have a serious interest in security values. It is not addressed to the complete novice, however, for it presupposes some acquaintance with the terminology and the simpler concepts of finance. The scope of the work is wider than its title may suggest. It deals not only with methods of analyzing individual issues, but also with the establishment of general principles of selection and protection of security holdings. Hence much emphasis has been laid upon distinguishing the investment from the speculative approach, upon setting up sound and workable tests of safety, and upon an understanding of the rights and true interests of investors in senior securities and owners of common stocks.

In dividing our space between various topics the primary but not the exclusive criterion has been that of relative importance. Some matters of vital significance, *e.g.*, the determination of the future prospects of an enterprise, have received little space, because little of definite value can be said on the subject. Others are glossed over because they are so well understood. Conversely we have stressed the technique of discovering *bargain issues* beyond its relative importance in the entire field of investment, because in this activity the talents peculiar to the securities analyst find perhaps their most fruitful expression. In similar fashion we have accorded quite detailed treatment to the characteristics of privileged senior issues (convertibles, etc.), because the attention given to these instruments in standard textbooks is now quite inadequate in view of their extensive development in recent years.

Our governing aim, however, has been to make this a critical rather than a descriptive work. We are concerned chiefly with concepts, methods, standards, principles, and, above all, with logical reasoning. We have stressed theory not for itself alone but for its value in practice. We have tried to avoid prescribing standards which are too stringent to follow, or technical methods which are more trouble than they are worth.

The chief problem of this work has been one of perspective—to blend the divergent experiences of the recent and the remoter past into a synthesis which will stand the test of the ever enigmatic future. While we were writing, we had to combat a widespread conviction that financial debacle was to be the permanent order; as we publish, we already see resurgent the age-old frailty of the investor—that his money burns a hole in his pocket. But it is the conservative investor who will need most of all to be reminded constantly of the lessons of 1931–1933 and of previous collapses. For what we shall call *fixed-value investments* can be soundly chosen only if they are approached—in the Spinozan phrase—"from the viewpoint of calamity." In dealing with other types of security commitments, we have striven throughout to guard the student against overemphasis upon the superficial and the temporary. Twenty years of varied experience in Wall Street have taught the senior author that this overemphasis is at once the delusion and the nemesis of the world of finance.

Our sincere thanks are due to the many friends who have encouraged and aided us in the preparation of this work.

BENJAMIN GRAHAM AND DAVID L. DODD
New York, New York, *May, 1934*

SECURITY ANALYSIS

BENJAMIN GRAHAM AND *SECURITY ANALYSIS*: THE HISTORICAL BACKDROP

BY JAMES GRANT

I t was a distracted world before which McGraw-Hill set, with a thud, the first edition of *Security Analysis* in July 1934. From Berlin dribbled reports of a shake-up at the top of the German government. "It will simplify the Führer's whole work immensely if he need not first ask some-body if he may do this or that," the Associated Press quoted an informant on August 1 as saying of Hitler's ascension from chancellor to dictator. Set against such epochal proceedings, a 727-page textbook on the fine points of value investing must have seemed an unlikely candidate for bestsellerdom, then or later.

In his posthumously published autobiography, *The Memoirs of the Dean of Wall Street*, Graham (1894–1976) thanked his lucky stars that he had entered the investment business when he did. The timing seemed not so propitious in the year of the first edition of *Security Analysis*, or, indeed, that of the second edition—expanded and revised—six years later. From its 1929 peak to its 1932 trough, the Dow Jones Industrial Average had lost 87% of its value. At cyclical low ebb, in 1933, the national unemployment rate topped 25%. That the Great Depression ended in 1933 was the considered judgment of the timekeepers of the National Bureau of Economic Research. Millions of Americans, however—not least, the relatively few who tried to squeeze a living out of a profit-less Wall Street—had reason to doubt it.

The bear market and credit liquidation of the early 1930s gave the institutions of American finance a top-to-bottom scouring. What was left of them presently came in for a rough handling by the first Roosevelt administration. Graham had learned his trade in the Wall Street of the mid–nineteen teens, an era of lightly regulated markets. He began work on *Security Analysis* as the administration of Herbert Hoover was giving the country its first taste of thoroughgoing federal intervention in a peacetime economy. He was correcting page proofs as the Roosevelt administration was implementing its first radical forays into macroeconomic management. By 1934, there were laws to institute federal regulation of the securities markets, federal insurance of bank deposits, and federal price controls (not to put a cap on prices, as in later, inflationary times, but rather to put a floor under them). To try to prop up prices, the administration devalued the dollar. It is a testament to the enduring quality of Graham's thought, not to mention the resiliency of America's financial markets, that *Security Analysis* lost none of its relevance even as the economy was being turned upside down and inside out.

Five full months elapsed following publication of the first edition before Louis Rich got around to reviewing it in the *New York Times*. Who knows? Maybe the conscientious critic read every page. In any case, Rich gave the book a rave, albeit a slightly rueful one. "On the assumption," he wrote, on December 2, 1934, "that despite the debacle of recent history there are still people left whose money burns a hole in their pockets, it is hoped that they will read this book. It is a full-bodied, mature, meticulous and wholly meritorious outgrowth of scholarly probing and practical sagacity. Although cast in the form and spirit of a textbook, the presentation is endowed with all the qualities likely to engage the liveliest interest of the layman."[1]

How few laymen seemed to care about investing was brought home to Wall Street more forcefully with every passing year of the unprosper-

---

[1] Louis Rich, "Sagacity and Securities," *New York Times,* December 2, 1934, p. BR13.

ous postcrash era. Just when it seemed that trading volume could get no smaller, or New York Stock Exchange seat prices no lower, or equity valuations more absurdly cheap, a new, dispiriting record was set. It required every effort of the editors of the Big Board's house organ, the *Exchange* magazine, to keep up a brave face. "*Must There Be* an End to Progress?" was the inquiring headline over an essay by the Swedish economist Gustav Cassel published around the time of the release of Graham and Dodd's second edition (the professor thought not).[2] "Why Do Securities Brokers Stay in Business?" the editors posed and helpfully answered, "Despite wearying lethargy over long periods, confidence abounds that when the public recognizes fully the value of protective measures which lately have been ranged about market procedure, investment interest in securities will increase." It did not amuse the *Exchange* that a New York City magistrate, sarcastically addressing in his court a collection of defendants hauled in by the police for shooting craps on the sidewalk, had derided the financial profession. "The first thing you know," the judge had upbraided the suspects, "you'll wind up as stock brokers in Wall Street with yachts and country homes on Long Island."[3]

In ways now difficult to imagine, Murphy's Law was the order of the day; what could go wrong, did. "Depression" was more than a long-lingering state of economic affairs. It had become a worldview. The academic exponents of "secular stagnation," notably Alvin Hansen and Joseph Schumpeter, each a Harvard economics professor, predicted a long decline in American population growth. This deceleration, Hansen contended in his 1939 essay, "together with the failure of any really important innovations of a magnitude to absorb large capital outlays, weighs very heavily as an explanation for the failure of the recent recovery to reach full employment."[4]

---

[2] Gustav Cassel, "Must There Be an End to Progress?" *Exchange,* January 1940.

[3] *Exchange,* "Why Do Securities Brokers Stay in Business?" September 1940.

[4] James Grant, *The Trouble with Prosperity* (New York: Random House, 1996), p. 84.

Neither Hansen nor his readers had any way of knowing that a baby boom was around the corner. Nothing could have seemed more unlikely to a world preoccupied with a new war in Europe and the evident decline and fall of capitalism. Certainly, Hansen's ideas must have struck a chord with the chronically underemployed brokers and traders in lower Manhattan. As a business, the New York Stock Exchange was running at a steady loss. From 1933, the year in which it began to report its financial results, through 1940, the Big Board recorded a profit in only one year, 1935 (and a nominal one, at that). And when, in 1937, Chelcie C. Bosland, an assistant professor of economics at Brown University, brought forth a book entitled *The Common Stock Theory of Investment,* he remarked as if he were repeating a commonplace that the American economy had peaked two decades earlier at about the time of what was not yet called World War I. The professor added, quoting unnamed authorities, that American population growth could be expected to stop in its tracks by 1975.[5] Small wonder that Graham was to write that the acid test of a bond issuer was its capacity to meet its obligations not in a time of middling prosperity (which modest test today's residential mortgage–backed securities struggle to meet) but in a depression. Altogether, an investor in those days was well advised to keep up his guard. "The combination of a record high level for bonds," writes Graham in the 1940 edition, "with a history of two catastrophic price collapses in the preceding 20 years and a major war in progress is not one to justify airy confidence in the future." (p. 142)

Wall Street, not such a big place even during the 1920s' boom, got considerably smaller in the subsequent bust. Ben Graham, in conjunction with his partner Jerry Newman, made a very small cog of this low-horse-power machine. The two of them conducted a specialty investment business at 52 Wall Street. Their strong suits were arbitrage, reorganizations,

---

[5] Chelcie C. Bosland, *The Common Stock Theory of Investment* (New York: Ronald Press, 1937), p. 74.

bankruptcies, and other complex matters. A schematic drawing of the financial district published by *Fortune* in 1937 made no reference to the Graham-Newman offices. Then again, the partnerships and corporate headquarters that did rate a spot on the Wall Street map were themselves—by the standards of twenty-first-century finance—remarkably compact. One floor at 40 Wall Street was enough to contain the entire office of Merrill Lynch & Co. And a single floor at 2 Wall Street was all the space required to house Morgan Stanley, the hands-down leader in 1936 corporate securities underwriting, with originations of all of $195 million. Compensation was in keeping with the slow pace of business, especially at the bottom of the corporate ladder.[6] After a 20% rise in the new federal minimum wage, effective October 1939, brokerage employees could earn no less than 30 cents an hour.[7]

In March 1940, the *Exchange* documented in all the detail its readers could want (and possibly then some) the collapse of public participation in the stock market. In the first three decades of the twentieth century, the annual volume of trading had almost invariably exceeded the quantity of listed shares outstanding, sometimes by a wide margin. And in only one year between 1900 and 1930 had annual volume amounted to less than 50% of listed shares—the exception being 1914, the year in which the exchange was closed for $4^1/_2$ months to allow for the shock of the outbreak of World War I to sink in. Then came the 1930s, and the annual turnover as a percentage of listed shares struggled to reach as high as 50%. In 1939, despite a short-lived surge of trading on the outbreak of World War II in Europe, the turnover ratio had fallen to a shockingly low 18.4%. (For comparison, in 2007, the ratio of trading volume to listed shares amounted to 123%.) "Perhaps," sighed the author of the study, "it is a fair statement that if the farming industry showed a similar record, gov-

---

[6] *Fortune,* "Wall Street, Itself," June 1937.

[7] *New York Times,* October 3, 1939, p. 38.

ernment subsidies would have been voted long ago. Unfortunately for Wall Street, it seems to have too little sponsorship in officialdom."[8]

If a reader took hope from the idea that things were so bad that they could hardly get worse, he or she was in for yet another disappointment. The second edition of *Security Analysis* had been published only months earlier when, on August 19, 1940, the stock exchange volume totaled just 129,650 shares. It was one of the sleepiest sessions since the 49,000-share mark set on August 5, 1916. For the entire 1940 calendar year, volume totaled 207,599,749 shares—a not very busy two hours' turnover at this writing and 18.5% of the turnover of 1929, that year of seemingly irrecoverable prosperity. The cost of a membership, or seat, on the stock exchange sank along with turnover and with the major price indexes. At the nadir in 1942, a seat fetched just $17,000. It was the lowest price since 1897 and 97% below the record high price of $625,000, set—naturally—in 1929.

"'The Cleaners,'" quipped Fred Schwed, Jr., in his funny and wise book *Where Are the Customers' Yachts?* (which, like Graham's second edition, appeared in 1940), "was not one of those exclusive clubs; by 1932, everybody who had ever tried speculation had been admitted to membership."[9] And if an investor did, somehow, manage to avoid the cleaner's during the formally designated Great Depression, he or she was by no means home free. In August 1937, the market began a violent sell-off that would carry the averages down by 50% by March 1938. The nonfinancial portion of the economy fared little better than the financial side. In just nine months, industrial production fell by 34.5%, a sharper contraction even than that in the depression of 1920 to 1921, a slump that, for Graham's generation, had seemed to set the standard for the most economic damage in the shortest elapsed time.[10] The Roosevelt administration insisted that the

---

[8] *Exchange,* March 1940.

[9] Fred Schwed, Jr., *Where Are the Customers' Yachts?* (New York: Simon and Schuster, 1940), p. 28.

[10] Benjamin M. Anderson, *Economics and the Public Welfare* (New York: Van Nostrand, 1949), p. 431.

slump of 1937 to 1938 was no depression but rather a "recession." The national unemployment rate in 1938 was, on average, 18.8%.

In April 1937, four months before the bottom fell out of the stock market for the second time in 10 years, Robert Lovett, a partner at the investment firm of Brown Brothers Harriman & Co., served warning to the American public in the pages of the weekly *Saturday Evening Post*. Lovett, a member of the innermost circle of the Wall Street establishment, set out to demonstrate that there is no such thing as financial security—none, at least, to be had in stocks and bonds. The gist of Lovett's argument was that, in capitalism, capital is consumed and that businesses are just as fragile, and mortal, as the people who own them. He invited his millions of readers to examine the record, as he had done: "If an investor had purchased 100 shares of the 20 most popular dividend-paying stocks on December 31, 1901, and held them through 1936, adding, in the meantime, all the melons in the form of stock dividends, and all the plums in the form of stock split-ups, and had exercised all the valuable rights to subscribe to additional stock, the aggregate market value of his total holdings on December 31, 1936, would have shown a shrinkage of 39% as compared with the cost of his original investment. In plain English, the average investor paid $294,911.90 for things worth $180,072.06 on December 31, 1936. That's a big disappearance of dollar value in any language." In the innocent days before the crash, people had blithely spoken of "permanent investments." "For our part," wrote this partner of an eminent Wall Street private bank, "we are convinced that the only permanent investment is one which has become a total and irretrievable loss."[11]

Lovett turned out to be a prophet. At the nadir of the 1937 to 1938 bear market, one in five NYSE-listed industrial companies was valued in the market for less than its net current assets. Subtract from cash and quick assets all liabilities and the remainder was greater than the com-

---

[11] Robert A. Lovett, "Gilt-Edged Insecurity," *Saturday Evening Post*, April 3, 1937.

pany's market value. That is, business value was negative. The Great Atlantic & Pacific Tea Company (A&P), the Wal-Mart of its day, was one of these corporate castoffs. At the 1938 lows, the market value of the common and preferred shares of A&P at $126 million was less than the value of its cash, inventories, and receivables, conservatively valued at $134 million. In the words of Graham and Dodd, the still-profitable company was selling for "scrap." (p. 673)

A Different Wall Street

Few institutional traces of that Wall Street remain. Nowadays, the big broker-dealers keep as much as $1 trillion in securities in inventory; in Graham's day, they customarily held none. Nowadays, the big broker-dealers are in a perpetual competitive lather to see which can bring the greatest number of initial public offerings (IPOs) to the public market. In Graham's day, no frontline member firm would stoop to placing an IPO in public hands, the risks and rewards for this kind of offering being reserved for professionals. Federal securities regulation was a new thing in the 1930s. What had preceded the Securities and Exchange Commission (SEC) was a regime of tribal sanction. Some things were simply beyond the pale. Both during and immediately after World War I, no self-respecting NYSE member firm facilitated a client's switch from Liberty bonds into potentially more lucrative, if less patriotic, alternatives. There was no law against such a business development overture. Rather, according to Graham, it just wasn't done.

A great many things weren't done in the Wall Street of the 1930s. Newly empowered regulators were resistant to financial innovation, transaction costs were high, technology was (at least by today's digital standards) primitive, and investors were demoralized. After the vicious bear market of 1937 to 1938, not a few decided they'd had enough. What was the point of it all? "In June 1939," writes Graham in a note to a discussion about corporate finance in the second edition, "the S.E.C. set a salutary precedent by refusing to authorize the issuance of 'Capital Income Debentures' in the reorganization of the Griess-Pfleger Tanning Company, on the ground that the devising of new types of hybrid issues had gone far enough." (p. 115, fn. 4) In the same conservative vein, he expresses his approval of the institution of the "legal list," a document compiled by state banking departments to stipulate which bonds the regulated savings banks could safely own. The very idea of such a list flies in the face of nearly every millennial notion about good regulatory practice. But Graham defends it thus: "Since the selection of high-grade bonds has been shown to be in good part a process of exclusion, it lends itself reasonably well to the application of definite rules and standards designed to disqualify unsuitable issues." (p. 169) No collateralized debt obligations stocked with subprime mortgages for the father of value investing!

The 1930s ushered in a revolution in financial disclosure. The new federal securities acts directed investor-owned companies to brief their stockholders once a quarter as well as at year-end. But the new standards were not immediately applicable to all public companies, and more than a few continued doing business the old-fashioned way, with their cards to their chests. One of these informational holdouts was none other than Dun & Bradstreet (D&B), the financial information company. Graham seemed to relish the irony of D&B not revealing "its own earnings to its own stockholders." (p. 92, fn. 4) On the whole, by twenty-first-century standards, information in Graham's time was as slow moving as it was sparse. There were no conference calls, no automated spreadsheets, and no nonstop news from distant markets—indeed, not much truck with the world outside the 48 states. *Security Analysis* barely acknowledges the existence of foreign markets.

Such an institutional setting was hardly conducive to the development of "efficient markets," as the economists today call them—markets in which information is disseminated rapidly, human beings process it flawlessly, and prices incorporate it instantaneously. Graham would have scoffed at such an idea. Equally, he would have smiled at the discovery—so late in the evolution of the human species—that there was a place in economics for a subdiscipline called "behavioral finance." Reading *Security Analysis*, one is led to wonder what facet of investing is not behavioral. The stock market, Graham saw, is a source of entertainment value as well as investment value: "Even when the underlying motive of purchase is mere speculative greed, human nature desires to conceal this unlovely impulse behind a screen of apparent logic and good sense. To adapt the aphorism of Voltaire, it may be said that if there were no such thing as common-stock analysis, it would be necessary to counterfeit it." (p. 348)

Anomalies of undervaluation and overvaluation—of underdoing it and overdoing it—fill these pages. It bemused Graham, but did not shock him, that so many businesses could be valued in the stock market for less than their net current assets, even during the late 1920s' boom, or that, in the dislocations to the bond market immediately following World War I, investors became disoriented enough to assign a higher price and a lower yield to the Union Pacific First Mortgage 4s than they did to the U.S. Treasury's own Fourth Liberty $4^{1}/_{4}$s. Graham writes of the "inveterate tendency of the stock market to exaggerate." (p. 679) He would not have exaggerated much if he had written, instead, "all markets."

Though he did not dwell long on the cycles in finance, Graham was certainly aware of them. He could see that ideas, no less than prices and categories of investment assets, had their seasons. The discussion in *Security Analysis* of the flame-out of the mortgage guarantee business in the early 1930s is a perfect miniature of the often-ruinous competition in which financial institutions periodically engage. "The rise of the newer and more aggressive real estate bond organizations had a most unfortunate effect upon the policies of the older concerns," Graham writes of his time and also of ours. "By force of competition they were led to relax their standards of making loans. New mortgages were granted on an increasingly liberal basis, and when old mortgages matured, they were frequently renewed in a larger sum. Furthermore, the face amount of the mortgages guaranteed rose to so high a multiple of the capital of the guarantor companies that it should have been obvious that the guaranty would afford only the flimsiest of protection in the event of a general decline in values." (p. 217)

Security analysis itself is a cyclical phenomenon; it, too, goes in and out of fashion, Graham observed. It holds a strong, intuitive appeal for the kind of businessperson who thinks about stocks the way he or she thinks about his or her own family business. What would such a fount of common sense care about earnings momentum or Wall Street's pseudo-scientific guesses about the economic future? Such an investor, appraising a common stock, would much rather know what the company behind it is worth. That is, he or she would want to study its balance sheet. Well, Graham relates here, that kind of analysis went out of style when stocks started levitating without reference to anything except hope and prophecy. So, by about 1927, fortune-telling and chart-reading had displaced the value discipline by which he and his partner were earning a very good living. It is characteristic of Graham that his critique of the "new era" method of investing is measured and not derisory. The old, conservative approach—his own—had been rather backward looking, Graham admits. It had laid more emphasis on the past than on the future, on stable earning power rather than tomorrow's earnings prospects. But new technologies, new methods, and new forms of corporate organization had introduced new risks into the post–World War I economy. This fact—"the increasing instability of the typical business"—had blown a small hole in the older analytical approach that emphasized stable earnings power over forecast earnings growth. Beyond that mitigating consideration, however, Graham does not go. The new era approach, "which turned upon the earnings trend as the sole criterion of value, . . . was certain to end in an appalling debacle." (p. 366) Which, of course, it did, and—in the CNBC-driven markets of the twenty-first century—continues to do at intervals today.

A Man of Many Talents

Benjamin Graham was born Benjamin Grossbaum on May 9, 1894, in London, and sailed to New York with his family before he was two. Young Benjamin was a prodigy in mathematics, classical languages, modern languages, expository writing (as readers of this volume will see for themselves), and anything else that the public schools had to offer. He had a tenacious memory and a love of reading—a certain ticket to academic success, then or later. His father's death at the age of 35 left him, his two brothers, and their mother in the social and financial lurch. Benjamin early learned to work and to do without.

No need here for a biographical profile of the principal author of *Security Analysis*: Graham's own memoir delightfully covers that ground. Suffice it to say that the high school brainiac entered Columbia College as an Alumni Scholar in September 1911 at the age of 17. So much material had he already absorbed that he began with a semester's head start, "the highest possible advanced standing."[12] He mixed his academic studies with a grab bag of jobs, part-time and full-time alike. Upon his graduation in 1914, he started work as a runner and board-boy at the New York Stock Exchange member firm of Newberger, Henderson & Loeb. Within a year, the board-boy was playing the liquidation of the

---

[12] Benjamin Graham, *The Memoirs of the Dean of Wall Street,* edited by Seymour Chatman (New York: McGraw-Hill, 1996), p. 106.

Guggenheim Exploration Company by astutely going long the shares of Guggenheim and short the stocks of the companies in which Guggenheim had made a minority investment, as his no-doubt bemused elders looked on: "The profit was realized exactly as calculated; and everyone was happy, not least myself."[13]

Security Analysis did not come out of the blue. Graham had supplemented his modest salary by contributing articles to the *Magazine of Wall Street*. His productions are unmistakably those of a self-assured and superbly educated Wall Street moneymaker. There was no need to quote expert opinion. He and the documents he interpreted were all the authority he needed. His favorite topics were the ones that he subsequently developed in the book you hold in your hands. He was partial to the special situations in which Graham-Newman was to become so successful. Thus, when a high-flying, and highly complex, American International Corp. fell from the sky in 1920, Graham was able to show that the stock was cheap in relation to the evident value of its portfolio of miscellaneous (and not especially well disclosed) investment assets.[14] The shocking insolvency of Goodyear Tire and Rubber attracted his attention in 1921. "The downfall of Goodyear is a remarkable incident even in the present plenitude of business disasters," he wrote, in a characteristic Graham sentence (how many financial journalists, then or later, had "plenitude" on the tips of their tongues?). He shrewdly judged that Goodyear would be a survivor.[15] In the summer of 1924, he hit on a theme that would echo through *Security Analysis:* it was the evident non sequitor of stocks valued in the market at less than the liquidating value of the companies that issued them. "Eight Stock Bargains Off the Beaten Track," said

---

[13] Ibid., p. 145.

[14] Benjamin Graham, "The 'Collapse' of American International," *Magazine of Wall Street,* December, 11, 1920, pp. 175–176, 217.

[15] Benjamin Graham, "The Goodyear Reorganization," *Magazine of Wall Street,* March 19, 1921, pp. 683–685.

the headline over the Benjamin Graham byline: "Stocks that Are Covered Chiefly by Cash or the Equivalent—No Bonds or Preferred Stock Ahead of These Issues—An Unusually Interesting Group of Securities." In one case, that of Tonopah Mining, liquid assets of $4.31 per share towered over a market price of just $1.38 a share.[16]

For Graham, an era of sweet reasonableness in investment thinking seemed to end around 1914. Before that time, the typical investor was a businessman who analyzed a stock or a bond much as he might a claim on a private business. He—it was usually a he—would naturally try to determine what the security-issuing company owned, free and clear of any encumbrances. If the prospective investment was a bond—and it usually was—the businessman-investor would seek assurances that the borrowing company had the financial strength to weather a depression.

"It's not undue modesty," Graham wrote in his memoir, "to say that I had become something of a smart cookie in my particular field." His specialty was the carefully analyzed out-of-the-way investment: castaway stocks or bonds, liquidations, bankruptcies, arbitrage. Since at least the early 1920s, Graham had preached the sermon of the "margin of safety." As the future is a closed book, he urged in his writings, an investor, as a matter of self-defense against the unknown, should contrive to pay less than "intrinsic" value. Intrinsic value, as defined in *Security Analysis*, is "that value which is justified by the facts, e.g., the assets, earnings, dividends, definite prospects, as distinct, let us say, from market quotations established by artificial manipulation or distorted by psychological excesses." (p. 64)

He himself had gone from the ridiculous to the sublime (and sometimes back again) in the conduct of his own investment career. His quick and easy grasp of mathematics made him a natural arbitrageur. He would sell one stock and simultaneously buy another. Or he would buy

---

[16] Benjamin Graham, "Eight Stock Bargains Off the Beaten Track," *Magazine of Wall Street*, July 19,1924, pp. 450–453.

or sell shares of stock against the convertible bonds of the identical issuing company. So doing, he would lock in a profit that, if not certain, was
as close to guaranteed as the vicissitudes of finance allowed. In one
instance, in the early 1920s, he exploited an inefficiency in the relationship between DuPont and the then red-hot General Motors (GM).
DuPont held a sizable stake in GM. And it was for that interest alone
which the market valued the big chemical company. By implication, the
rest of the business was worth nothing. To exploit this anomaly, Graham
bought shares in DuPont and sold short the hedge-appropriate number
of shares in GM. And when the market came to its senses, and the price
gap between DuPont and GM widened in the expected direction, Graham took his profit.[17]

However, Graham, like many another value investor after him, sometimes veered from the austere precepts of safe-and-cheap investing. A
Graham only slightly younger than the master who sold GM and bought
DuPont allowed himself to be hoodwinked by a crooked promoter of a
company that seems not actually to have existed—at least, in anything
like the state of glowing prosperity described by the manager of the
pool to which Graham entrusted his money. An electric sign in Colum-
bus Circle, on the upper West Side of Manhattan, did bear the name of
the object of Graham's misplaced confidence, Savold Tire. But, as the
author of *Security Analysis* confessed in his memoir, that could have been
the only tangible marker of the company's existence. "Also, as far as I
knew," Graham added, "nobody complained to the district attorney's
office about the promoter's bare-faced theft of the public's money." Certainly, by his own telling, Graham didn't.[18]

By 1929, when he was 35, Graham was well on his way to fame and
fortune. His wife and he kept a squadron of servants, including—for the
first and only time in his life—a manservant for himself. With Jerry

---

[17] Graham, *Memoirs*, p. 188.

[18] Ibid., pp. 181–184.

Newman, Graham had compiled an investment record so enviable that the great Bernard M. Baruch sought him out. Would Graham wind up his business to manage Baruch's money? "I replied," Graham writes, "that I was highly flattered—flabbergasted, in fact—by his proposal, but I could not end so abruptly the close and highly satisfactory relations I had with my friends and clients."[19] Those relations soon became much less satisfactory.

Graham relates that, though he was worried at the top of the market, he failed to act on his bearish hunch. The Graham-Newman partnership went into the 1929 break with $2.5 million of capital. And they controlled about $2.5 million in hedged positions—stocks owned long offset by stocks sold short. They had, besides, about $4.5 million in outright long positions. It was bad enough that they were leveraged, as Graham later came to realize. Compounding that tactical error was a deeply rooted conviction that the stocks they owned were cheap enough to withstand any imaginable blow.

They came through the crash creditably: down by only 20% was, for the final quarter of 1929, almost heroic. But they gave up 50% in 1930, 16% in 1931, and 3% in 1932 (another relatively excellent showing), for a cumulative loss of 70%.[20] "I blamed myself not so much for my failure to protect myself against the disaster I had been predicting," Graham writes, "as for having slipped into an extravagant way of life which I hadn't the temperament or capacity to enjoy. I quickly convinced myself that the true key to material happiness lay in a modest standard of living which could be achieved with little difficulty under almost all economic conditions"—the margin-of-safety idea applied to personal finance.[21]

It can't be said that the academic world immediately clasped *Security Analysis* to its breast as the definitive elucidation of value investing, or of anything else. The aforementioned survey of the field in which Graham

[19] Ibid., p. 253.

[20] Ibid., p. 259.

[21] Ibid., p. 263.

and Dodd made their signal contribution, *The Common Stock Theory of Investment*, by Chelcie C. Bosland, published three years after the appearance of the first edition of *Security Analysis*, cited 53 different sources and 43 different authors. Not one of them was named Graham or Dodd.

Edgar Lawrence Smith, however, did receive Bosland's full and respectful attention. Smith's *Common Stocks as Long Term Investments*, published in 1924, had challenged the long-held view that bonds were innately superior to equities. For one thing, Smith argued, the dollar (even the gold-backed 1924 edition) was inflation-prone, which meant that creditors were inherently disadvantaged. Not so the owners of common stock. If the companies in which they invested earned a profit, and if the managements of those companies retained a portion of that profit in the business, and if those retained earnings, in turn, produced future earnings, the principal value of an investor's portfolio would tend "to increase in accordance with the operation of compound interest."[22]

Smith's timing was impeccable. Not a year after he published, the great Coolidge bull market erupted. *Common Stocks as Long Term Investments*, only 129 pages long, provided a handy rationale for chasing the market higher. That stocks do, in fact, tend to excel in the long run has entered the canon of American investment thought as a revealed truth (it looked anything but obvious in the 1930s). For his part, Graham entered a strong dissent to Smith's thesis, or, more exactly, its uncritical bullish application. It was one thing to pay 10 times earnings for an equity investment, he notes, quite another to pay 20 to 40 times earnings. Besides, the Smith analysis skirted the important question of what asset values lay behind the stock certificates that people so feverishly and uncritically traded back and forth. Finally, embedded in Smith's argument was the assumption that common stocks could be counted on to deliver in the future what they had done in the past. Graham was not a believer. (pp. 362–363)

---

[22] Grant, *The Trouble with Prosperity*, p. 43.

If Graham was a hard critic, however, he was also a generous one. In 1939 he was given John Burr Williams's *The Theory of Investment Value* to review for the *Journal of Political Economy* (no small honor for a Wall Street author-practitioner). Williams's thesis was as important as it was concise. The investment value of a common stock is the present value of all future dividends, he proposed. Williams did not underestimate the significance of these loaded words. Armed with that critical knowledge, the author ventured to hope, investors might restrain themselves from bidding stocks back up to the moon again. Graham, in whose capacious brain dwelled the talents both of the quant and behavioral financier, voiced his doubts about that forecast. The rub, as he pointed out, was that, in order to apply Williams's method, one needed to make some very large assumptions about the future course of interest rates, the growth of profit, and the terminal value of the shares when growth stops. "One wonders," Graham mused, "whether there may not be too great a discrepancy between the necessarily hit-or-miss character of these assumptions and the highly refined mathematical treatment to which they are subjected." Graham closed his essay on a characteristi- cally generous and witty note, commending Williams for the refreshing level-headedness of his approach and adding: "This conservatism is not really implicit in the author's formulas; but if the investor can be per- suaded by higher algebra to take a sane attitude toward common-stock prices, the reviewer will cast a loud vote for higher algebra."[23]

   Graham's technical accomplishments in securities analysis, by them- selves, could hardly have carried *Security Analysis* through its five edi- tions. It's the book's humanity and good humor that, to me, explain its long life and the adoring loyalty of a certain remnant of Graham readers, myself included. Was there ever a Wall Street moneymaker better

---

[23] Benjamin Graham, "Review of John Burr Williams's *The Theory of Investment Value* [Cambridge, Mass.: Harvard University Press, 1938]," *Journal of Political Economy*, vol. 47, no. 2 (April 1939), pp. 276–278.

steeped than Graham in classical languages and literature *and* in the financial history of his own time? I would bet "no" with all the confidence of a value investor laying down money to buy an especially cheap stock.

Yet this great investment philosopher was, to a degree, a prisoner of his own times. He could see that the experiences through which he lived were unique, that the Great Depression was, in fact, a great anomaly. If anyone understood the folly of projecting current experience into the unpredictable future, it was Graham. Yet this investment-philosopher king, having spent 727 pages (not including the gold mine of an appendix) describing how a careful and risk-averse investor could prosper in every kind of macroeconomic conditions, arrives at a remarkable conclusion.

What of the institutional investor, he asks. How should he invest? At first, Graham diffidently ducks the question—who is he to prescribe for the experienced financiers at the head of America's philanthropic and educational institutions? But then he takes the astonishing plunge. "An institution," he writes, "that can manage to get along on the low income provided by high-grade fixed-value issues should, in our opinion, confine its holdings to this field. We doubt if the better performance of common-stock indexes over past periods will, in itself, warrant the heavy responsibilities and the recurring uncertainties that are inseparable from a common-stock investment program." (pp. 709–710)

Could the greatest value investor have meant that? Did the man who stuck it out through ruinous losses in the Depression years and went on to compile a remarkable long-term investment record really mean that common stocks were not worth the bother? In 1940, with a new world war fanning the Roosevelt administration's fiscal and monetary policies, high-grade corporate bonds yielded just 2.75%, while blue-chip equities yielded 5.1%. Did Graham mean to say that bonds were a safer proposition than stocks? Well, he did say it. If Homer could nod, so could Graham—and so can the rest of us, whoever we are. Let it be a lesson.

Introduction to the Second Edition

PROBLEMS OF
INVESTMENT POLICY

ALTHOUGH, STRICTLY speaking, security analysis may be carried on without reference to any definite program or standards of investment, such a specialization of functions would be quite unrealistic. Critical examination of balance sheets and income accounts, comparisons of related or similar issues, studies of the terms and protective covenants behind bonds and preferred stocks—these typical activities of the securities analyst are invariably carried on with some practical idea of purchase or sale in mind, and they must be viewed against a broader background of investment principles, or perhaps of speculative precepts. In this work we shall not strive for a precise demarcation between investment theory and analytical technique but at times shall combine the two elements in the close relationship that they possess in the world of finance.

It seems best, therefore, to preface our exposition with a concise review of the problems of policy that confront the security buyer. Such a discussion must be colored, in part at least, by the conditions prevailing when this chapter was written. But it is hoped that enough allowance will be made for the possibility of change to give our conclusions more than passing interest and value. Indeed, we consider this element of change as a central fact in the financial universe. For a better understanding of this point we are presenting some data, in conspectus form, designed to illustrate the reversals and upheavals in values and standards that have developed in the past quarter century.

The three reference periods 1911–1913, 1923–1925, and 1936–1938 were selected to represent the nearest approximations to "normal," or relative stability, that could be found at intervals during the past quarter century. Between the first and second triennium we had the war collapse and hectic prosperity, followed by the postwar hesitation, inflation, and deep depression. Between 1925 and 1936 we had the "new-era boom," the great

FINANCIAL AND ECONOMIC DATA FOR THREE REFERENCE PERIODS

Period	1911–1913			1923–1925			1936–1938		
	High	Low	Average	High	Low	Average	High	Low	Average
Business index*	118.8	94.6	107.9	174.9	136.0	157.9	164.9	106.0	137.0
Bond yields*	4.22%	4.02%	4.09%	4.82%	4.55%	4.68%	3.99%	3.36%	3.65%
Index of industrial stock prices*	121.6	92.2	107.6	198.6	128.6	153.4	293.4	124.8	211.1
Dow-Jones Industrial Average (per unit):									
Price range	94	72	82	159	86	112	194	97	149
Earnings	$8.69	$7.81	$8.12	$13.54	$10.52	$11.81	$11.41	$6.02	$9.14
Dividends	5.69	4.50	5.13	7.09	5.51	6.13	8.15	4.84	6.66
Price-earnings ratio†	11.6x	8.9x	10.1x	13.5x	7.3x	9.5x	21.2x	10.6x	16.3x
Dividend yield†	5.5%	7.1%	6.3%	3.9%	7.1%	5.5%	3.4%	6.9%	4.5%
U. S. Steel:‡									
Price range	82	50	65	139	86	111	178	53	96
Earnings per share	$11.00	$5.70	$7.53	$16.40	$11.80	$13.70	$11.22	(d)$5.30	$3.33
Dividends per share	5.00	5.00	5.00	7.00	5.25	6.42	1.40	Nil	0.42
Price-earnings ratio†	10.9x	6.6x	8.6x	10.1x	6.3x	8.1x	53.4x	15.9x	28.8x
Dividend yield†	6.1%	10.0%	7.7%	4.6%	7.5%	5.8%	0.2%	0.8%	0.4%
General Electric:§									
Price range	196	142	172	524	262	368	1,580	664	1,070
Earnings per share	$16.72	$12.43	$14.27	$32.10	$27.75	$30.35	$53.50	$23.40	$38.00
Dividends per share‖	10.40	8.00	8.80	19.80	19.80	19.80	53.50	21.85	38.90
Price-earnings ratio†	13.7x	10.0x	12.1x	17.2x	8.6x	13.8x	41.5x	17.5x	28.2x
Dividend yield†	4.5%	6.2%	5.1%	3.8%	7.6%	5.4%	2.5%	5.9%	3.6%

American Can:§									
Price range	47	9	25	297	74	150	828	414	612
Earnings per share	$8.86	$0.07	$4.71	$32.75	$19.64	$24.30	$36.48	$26.10	$32.46
Dividends per share	Nil	Nil	Nil	7.00	5.00	6.00	30.00	24.00	26.00
Price-earnings ratio†	10.0x	1.9x	5.3x	12.2x	3.0x	6.2x	25.5x	12.7	18.8x
Dividend yield†	Nil	Nil	Nil	2.0%	8.1%	4.0%	3.1%	6.3%	4.2%
Pennsylvania R.R.:									
Price range	65	53	60	55	41	46	50	14	30
Earnings per share	$4.64	$4.14	$4.33	$6.23	$3.82	$5.07	$2.94	$0.84	$1.95
Dividends per share	3.00	3.00	3.00	3.00	3.00	3.00	2.00	0.50	1.25
Price-earnings ratio†	15.0x	12.2x	13.8x	10.9x	8.1x	9.2x	25.6x	7.2x	15.5x
Dividend yield†	4.6%	5.7%	5.0%	5.5%	7.3%	6.5%	2.5%	8.9%	4.1%
American Tel. & Tel.:									
Price range	153	110	137	145	119	130	190	111	155
Earnings per share	$9.58	$8.64	$9.26	$11.79	$11.31	$11.48	$9.62	$8.16	$9.05
Dividends per share	8.00	8.00	8.00	9.00	9.00	9.00	9.00	9.00	9.00
Price-earnings ratio†	16.5x	11.9x	14.8x	12.6x	10.4x	11.3x	21.0x	12.3x	17.1x
Dividend yield†	5.2%	7.3%	5.8%	6.2%	7.6%	6.9%	4.7%	8.1%	5.8%

* Axe-Houghton indexes of business activity and of industrial stock prices, both unadjusted for trend; yields on 10 high-grade railroad bonds—all by courtesy of E. W. Axe & Co., Inc.
† High, low, and average prices are compared with *average* earnings and dividends in each period.
‡ 1936–1938 figures adjusted to reflect 40% stock dividend.
§ Figures adjusted to reflect various stock dividends and split-ups between 1913 and 1930, equivalent ultimately to about 25 shares in 1936 for 1 share in 1912.
‖ Exclusive of one share of Electric Bond and Share Securities Corporation distributed as a dividend in 1925.
¶ 1936–1938 figures adjusted to reflect six-for-one exchange of shares in 1926.

collapse and depression, and a somewhat irregular recovery towards normal. But if we examine the three-year periods themselves, we cannot fail to be struck by the increasing tendency toward instability even in relatively normal times. This is shown vividly in the progressive widening of the graphs in Chart A, page 26, which trace the fluctuations in general business and industrial stock prices during the years in question.

It would be foolhardy to deduce from these developments that we must expect still greater instability in the future. But it would be equally imprudent to minimize the significance of what has happened and to return overreadily to the comfortable conviction of 1925 that we were moving steadily towards both greater stability and greater prosperity. The times would seem to call for caution in embracing any theory as to the future and for flexible and open-minded investment policies. With these caveats to guide us, let us proceed to consider briefly certain types of investment problems.

A. INVESTMENT IN HIGH-GRADE BONDS AND PREFERRED STOCKS

Bond investment presents many more perplexing problems today than seemed to be true in 1913. The chief question then was how to get the highest yield commensurate with safety; and if the investor was satisfied with the lower yielding standard issues (nearly all consisting of railroad mortgage bonds), he could supposedly "buy them with his eyes shut and put them away and forget them." Now the investor must wrestle with a threefold problem: safety of interest and principal, the future of bond yields and prices, and the future value of the dollar. To describe the dilemma is easy; to resolve it satisfactorily seems next to impossible.

1. Safety of Interest and Principal. Two serious depressions in the past twenty years, and the collapse of an enormous volume of railroad issues once thought safe beyond question, suggest that the future may have further rude shocks for the complacent bond investor. The old idea of "permanent investments," exempt from change and free from care, is no doubt permanently gone. Our studies lead us to conclude, however, that by sufficiently stringent standards of selection and reasonably frequent scrutiny thereafter the investor should be able to escape most of the serious losses that have distracted him in the past, so that his collection of interest and principal should work out at a satisfactory percentage even in times of depression. Careful selection must include a due regard to future prospects, but we do not consider that the investor need be clairvoyant or that he must confine himself to companies that hold forth exceptional promise of expanding profits. These remarks relate to (really) high-grade preferred stocks as well as to bonds.

2. Future of Interest Rates and Bond Prices. The unprecedentedly low yields offered by both short- and long-term bond issues may well cause concern to the investor for other reasons than a natural dissatisfaction with the small return that his money brings him. If these low rates should prove temporary and are followed by a rise to previous levels, long-term bond prices could lose some 25%, or more, of their market value. Such a price decline would be equivalent to the loss of perhaps ten years' interest. In 1934 we felt that this possibility must be taken seriously into account, because the low interest rates then current might well have been a phenomenon of subnormal business, subject to a radical advance with returning trade activity. But the persistence of these low rates for many years, and in the face of the considerable business expansion of 1936–1937, would argue strongly for the acceptance of this condition as a well-established result of a plethora of capital or of governmental fiscal policy or of both.

A new uncertainty has been injected into this question by the outbreak of a European war in 1939. The first World War brought about a sharp increase in interest rates and a corresponding severe fall in high-grade bond prices. There are sufficient similarities and differences, both, between the 1914 and the 1939 situations to make prediction too risky for comfort. Obviously the danger of a substantial fall in bond prices (from the level of early 1940) is still a real one; yet a policy of noninvestment awaiting such a contingency is open to many practical objections. Perhaps a partiality to maturities no longer than, say, fifteen years from purchase date may be the most logical reaction to this uncertain situation.

For the small investor, United States Savings Bonds present a perfect solution of this problem (as well as the one preceding), since the right of redemption at the *option of the holder* guarantees them against a lower price. As we shall point out in a more detailed discussion, the advent of these baby bonds has truly revolutionized the position of most security buyers.

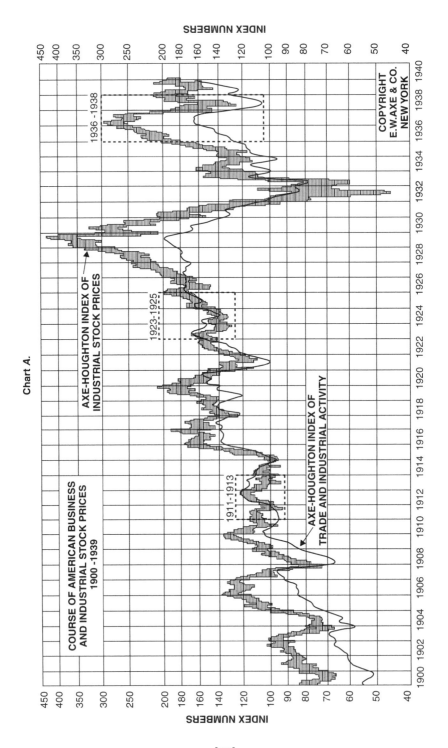

Chart A.

COURSE OF AMERICAN BUSINESS
AND INDUSTRIAL STOCK PRICES
1900 -1939

AXE-HOUGHTON INDEX OF
INDUSTRIAL STOCK PRICES

AXE-HOUGHTON INDEX OF
TRADE AND INDUSTRIAL ACTIVITY

COPYRIGHT
E.W.AXE & CO.
NEW YORK

[26]

Chart *B*.

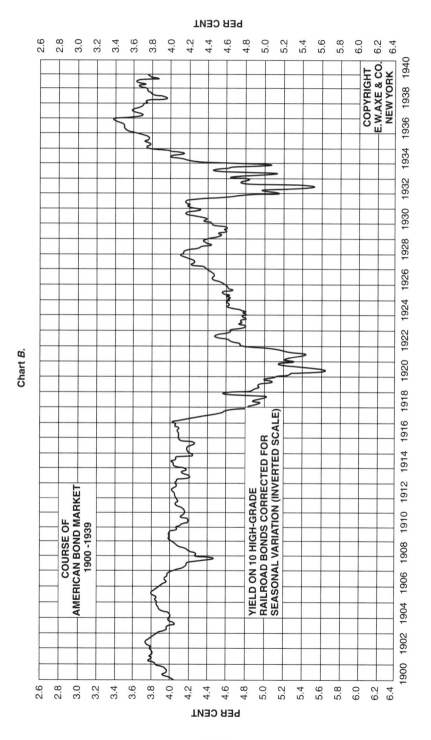

COURSE OF
AMERICAN BOND MARKET
1900 -1939

YIELD ON 10 HIGH-GRADE
RAILROAD BONDS CORRECTED FOR
SEASONAL VARIATION (INVERTED SCALE)

PER CENT

[27]

3. The Value of the Dollar. If the investor were certain that the purchasing power of the dollar is going to decline substantially, he undoubtedly should prefer common stocks or commodities to bonds. To the extent that inflation, in the sense commonly employed, remains a possibility, the investment policy of the typical bond buyer is made more perplexing. The arguments for and against ultimate inflation are both unusually weighty, and we must decline to choose between them. The course of the price level since 1933 would seem to belie inflation fears, but the past is not necessarily conclusive as to the future. Prudence may suggest some compromise in investment policy, to include a component of common stocks or tangible assets, designed to afford some protection against a serious fall in the dollar's value. Such a hybrid policy would involve difficult problems of its own; and in the last analysis each investor must decide for himself which of the alternative risks he would prefer to run.

B. SPECULATIVE BONDS AND PREFERRED STOCKS

The problems related to this large class of securities are not inherent in the class itself, but are rather derived from those of investment bonds and of common stocks, between which they lie. The broad principles underlying the purchase of speculative senior issues remain, in our opinion, the same as they always were: (1) A risk of principal loss may not be offset by a higher yield alone but must be accompanied by a commensurate chance of principal profit; (2) it is generally sounder to approach these issues as if they were common stocks, but recognizing their limited claims, than it is to consider them as an inferior type of senior security.

C. THE PROBLEM OF COMMON-STOCK INVESTMENT

Common-stock speculation, as the term has always been generally understood, is not so difficult to understand as it is to practice successfully. The speculator admittedly risks his money upon his guess or judgment as to the general market or the action of a particular stock or possibly on some future development in the company's affairs. No doubt the speculator's problems have changed somewhat with the years, but we incline to the view that the qualities and training necessary for success, as well as the mathematical odds against him, are not vitally different now from what they were before. But stock speculation, as such, does not come within the scope of this volume.

Current Practice. We are concerned, however, with common-stock *investment*, which we shall define provisionally as purchases based upon analysis of value and controlled by definite standards of safety of principal. If we look to current practice to discern what these standards are, we find little beyond the rather indefinite concept that "a good stock is a good investment." "Good" stocks are those of either (1) leading companies with satisfactory records, a combination relied on to produce favorable results in the future; or (2) any well-financed enterprise believed to have especially attractive prospects of increased future earnings. (As of early 1940, we may cite Coca-Cola as an example of (1), Abbott Laboratories as an example of (2), and General Electric as an example of both.)

But although the stock market has very definite and apparently logical ideas as to the *quality* of the common stocks that it buys for investment, its *quantitative* standards—governing the relation of price to determinable value—are so indefinite as to be almost nonexistent. Balance-sheet values are considered to be entirely out of the picture. Average earnings have little significance when there is a marked trend. The so-called "price-earnings ratio" is applied variously, sometimes to the past, sometimes to the present, and sometimes to the near future. But the ratio itself can scarcely be called a standard, since it is controlled by investment practice instead of controlling it. In other words the "right" price-earnings ratio for any stock is what the market says it is. We can find no evidence that at any time from 1926 to date common-stock investors as a class have sold their holdings because the price-earnings ratios were too high.

How the present practice of common-stock investors, including the investment trusts almost without exception, can properly be termed *investment*, in view of this virtual absence of controlling standards, is more than we can fathom. It would be far more logical and helpful to call it "speculation in stocks of strong companies." Certainly the results in the stock market of such "investment" have been indistinguishable from those of old-time speculation, except perhaps for the margin element. A striking confirmation of this statement, as applied to the years after the 1929 crash, is found by comparing the price range of General Electric since 1930 with that of common stocks generally. The following figures show that General Electric common, which is perhaps the premier and undoubtedly the longest entrenched investment issue in the industrial field today, has fluctuated more widely in market price than have the rank and file of common stocks.

PRICE RANGES OF GENERAL ELECTRIC COMMON, DOW-JONES INDUSTRIALS, AND STANDARD
STATISTICS' INDUSTRIAL STOCK INDEX, 1930–1939

	General Electric		Dow-Jones Industrials		Standard Statistics Industrials[1]	
Year	High	Low	High	Low	High	Low
1930	$95^3/_8$	$41^1/_2$	294.1	157.5	174.1	98.2
1931	$54^3/_4$	$22^7/_8$	194.4	73.8	119.1	48.5
1932	$26^1/_8$	$8^1/_2$	88.8	41.2	63.5	30.7
1933	$30^1/_4$	$10^1/_2$	108.7	50.2	92.2	36.5
1934	$25^1/_4$	$16^7/_8$	110.7	85.5	93.3	69.3
1935	$40^7/_8$	$20^1/_2$	148.4	96.7	113.2	72.8
1936	55	$34^1/_2$	184.9	143.1	148.5	109.1
1937	$64^7/_8$	34	194.4	113.6	158.7	84.2
1938	48	$27^1/_4$	158.4	99.0	119.3	73.5
1939	$44^5/_8$	31	155.9	121.4	118.3	86.7

[1] Weekly indexes of prices (1926 = 100) of 350 industrial issues in 1939 and 347 issues in earlier years.

It was little short of nonsense for the stock market to say in 1937 that General Electric Company was worth $1,870,000,000 and almost precisely a year later that it was worth only $784,000,000. Certainly nothing had happened within twelve months' time to destroy more than half the value of this powerful enterprise, nor did investors even pretend to claim that the falling off in earnings from 1937 to 1938 had any permanent significance for the future of the company. General Electric sold at $64^7/_8$ because the public was in an optimistic frame of mind and at $27^1/_4$ because the same people were pessimistic. To speak of these prices as representing "investment values" or the "appraisal of investors" is to do violence either to the English language or to common sense, or both.

Four Problems. Assuming that a common-stock buyer were to seek definite investment standards by which to guide his operations, he might well direct his attention to four questions: (1) the general future of corporation profits, (2) the differential in quality between one type of company and another, (3) the influence of interest rates on the dividends or earnings return that he should demand, and finally (4) the extent to which his purchases and sales should be governed by the factor of timing as distinct from price.

The General Future of Corporate Profits. If we study these questions in the light of past experience, our most pronounced reaction is likely to be a wholesome scepticism as to the soundness of the stock market's judgment on all broad matters relating to the future. The data in our first table show quite clearly that the market underestimated the attractiveness of industrial common stocks as a whole in the years prior to 1926. Their prices generally represented a rather cautious appraisal of past and current earnings, with no signs of any premium being paid for the possibilities of growth inherent in the leading enterprises of a rapidly expanding commonwealth. In 1913 railroad and traction issues made up the bulk of investment bonds and stocks. By 1925 a large part of the investment in street railways had been endangered by the development of the automobile, but even then there was no disposition to apprehend a similar threat to the steam railroads.

The widespread recognition of the factor of future growth in common stocks first asserted itself as a stock-market influence at a time when in fact the most dynamic factors in our national expansion (territorial development and rapid accretions of population) were no longer operative, and our economy was about to face grave problems of instability arising from these very checks to the factor of growth. The overvaluations of the new-era years extended to nearly every issue that had even a short period of increasing earnings to recommend it, but especial favor was accorded the public-utility and chain-store groups. Even as late as 1931 the high prices paid for these issues showed no realization of their inherent limitations, just as five years later the market still failed to appreciate the critical changes taking place in the position of railroad bonds as well as stocks.

Quality Differentials. The stock market of 1940 has its well-defined characteristics, founded chiefly on the experience of the recent past and on the rather obvious prospects of the future. The tendency to favor the larger and stronger companies is perhaps more pronounced than ever. This is supported by the record since 1929, which indicates, we believe, both better resistance to depression and a more complete recovery of earning power in the case of the leading than of the secondary companies. There is also the usual predilection for certain industrial groups, including companies of smaller size therein. Most prominent are the chemical and aviation shares—the former because of their really remarkable record of growth through research, the latter because of the great influx of armament orders.

But these preferences of the current stock market, although easily understood, may raise some questions in the minds of the sceptical. First to be considered is the extraordinary disparity between the prices of prominent and less popular issues. If average earnings of 1934–1939 are taken as a criterion, the "good stocks" would appear to be selling about two to three times as high as other issues. In terms of asset values the divergence is far greater, since obviously the popular issues have earned a much larger return on their invested capital. The ignoring of asset values has reached a stage where even current assets receive very little attention, so that even a moderately successful enterprise is likely to be selling at considerably less than its liquidating value if it happens to be rich in working capital.

The relationship between "good stocks" and other stocks must be considered in the light of what is to be expected of American business generally. Any prediction on the latter point would be highly imprudent; but it is in order to point out that the record of the last fifteen years does not in itself supply the basis for an expectation of a long-term upward movement in volume and profits. In so far as we judge the future by the past we must recognize a rather complete transformation in the *apparent* outlook of 1940 against that in 1924. In the earlier year a secular rise in production and a steady advance in the figure taken as "normal" were accepted as a matter of course. But so far as we can see now, the 1923–1925 average of industrial production, formerly taken as 100 on the Federal Reserve Board's index,[1] must still be considered as high a normal as we have any right to prognosticate. Needless to say, the investor will not deny the *possibility* of a renewed secular rise, but the important point for him is that he cannot count upon it.

---

[1] In 1940 the Board revised this index. New components were added, and the average of 1935–1939 was adopted as the base.

If this is the working hypothesis of the present stock market, it follows that stock buyers are expecting in general a further growth in the earnings of large companies *at the expense* of smaller ones and of favorably situated industries at the expense of all others. Such an expectation appears to be the theoretical basis for the high price of the one group and the low prices found elsewhere. That stocks with good past trends and favorable prospects are worth more than others goes without saying. But is it not possible that Wall Street has carried its partiality too far—in this as in so many other cases? May not the typical large and prosperous company be subject to a twofold limitation: first, that its very size precludes spectacular further growth; second, that its high rate of earnings on invested capital makes it vulnerable to attack if not by competition then perhaps by regulation?

Perhaps, also, the smaller companies and the less popular industries as a class may be definitely undervalued, both absolutely and in relation to the favored issues. Surely this can be true in theory, since at *some* price level the good stocks must turn out to have been selling too high and the others too low. There are strong, if not conclusive, reasons for arguing that this point may have already been reached in 1940. The two possible points of weakness in the "good stocks" are paralleled by corresponding favorable possibilities in the others. The numerous issues selling below net current asset value, even in normal markets, are a powerful indication that Wall Street's favoritism has been overdone. Finally, if we carry the analysis further, we must realize that the smaller listed companies are representative of the hundreds of thousands of private enterprises, of all sizes, throughout the country. Wall Street is apparently predicting the continued decline of *all* business except the very largest, which is to flourish mightily. In our own opinion such a development appears neither economically probable nor politically possible.

Similar doubts may be voiced as to the stock market's emphasis on certain favored industries. This is something that, by the nature of the case, must always be overdone—since there are no quantitative checks on the public's enthusiasm for what it likes. Not only has the market invariably carried its optimism too far, but it has shown a surprising aptitude for favoring industries that soon turned out to be facing adverse developments. (Witness the baking stocks in 1925, the radio and refrigeration issues in 1927, the public utility and chain stores in 1928–1929, the liquor issues in 1933.) It is interesting to compare the "investor's" eagerness to buy Abbott Laboratories in 1939 and his comparative indifference to American Home Products—the one kind of pharmaceutical company being thought to have brilliant, and the other to have only mediocre, prospects in store. This distinction may prove to have been soundly and shrewdly drawn; but the student who remembers the market's not so remote enthusiasm for American Home Products itself and its companions (particularly Lambert) in 1927 can hardly be too confident of the outcome.[2]

Interest Rates. Coming now to the third point of importance, *viz.*, the relation between interest rates and common-stock prices, it is clear that if current low bond yields are permanent, they must produce a corresponding decline in average stock yields and an advance in the value of a dollar of expected earning power, as compared with the situation, say, in 1923–1925. The more liberal valuation of earnings in 1936–1938, as shown by the data relating to the Dow-Jones Industrial Average on page 22, would thus appear to have been justified by the change in the long-term interest rate. The disconcerting question presents itself, however, whether or not the fall in interest rates is not closely bound up with the cessation of the secular expansion of business and with a decline in the average profitability of invested capital. If this is so, the debit factors in stock values generally may outweigh the credit influence of low interest rates, and a typical dollar of earning power in 1936–1938 may not really have been worth more than it should have been worth a decade and a half previously.

The Factor of Timing. Increasing importance has been ascribed in recent years to the desirability of buying and selling at the right time, as distinguished from the right price. In earlier periods, when the prices of investment issues did not usually fluctuate over a wide range, the time of purchase was not considered of particular importance. Between 1924 and 1929, a comfortable but quite misleading confidence developed in the unlimited future growth of sound stocks, so that any mistake in timing was sure to be rectified by the market's recovery to ever higher levels. The past decade has witnessed very wide fluctuations without a long-term upward trend, except in a relatively small number of issues. Under these

---

[2] Data relating to these three companies are given in Appendix Note 1, p. 733 on accompanying CD.

conditions it is not surprising that successful investment seems, like successful speculation, to be bound up inescapably with the choice of the right moment to buy and to sell. We thus find that forecasting of the major market swings appears now to be an integral part of the art of investment in common stocks.

The validity of stock-market forecasting methods is a subject for extensive inquiry and perhaps vigorous controversy. At this point we must content ourselves with a summary judgment, which may reflect our own prejudices along with our investigations. It is our view that stock-market timing cannot be done, with general success, unless the time to buy is related to an attractive price level, as measured by analytical standards. Similarly, the investor must take his cue to sell primarily not from so-called technical market signals but from an advance in the price level beyond a point justified by objective standards of value. It may be that within these paramount limits there are refinements of stock-market technique that can make for better timing and more satisfactory over-all results. Yet we cannot avoid the conclusion that the most generally accepted principle of timing—*viz.*, that purchases should be made only *after* an upswing has definitely announced itself—is basically opposed to the essential nature of investment. Traditionally the investor has been the man with patience and the courage of his convictions who would buy when the harried or disheartened speculator was selling. If the investor is now to hold back until the market itself encourages him, how will he distinguish himself from the speculator, and wherein will he deserve any better than the ordinary speculator's fate?

Conclusion. Our search for definite investment standards for the common-stock buyer has been more productive of warnings than of concrete suggestions. We have been led to the old principle that the investor should wait for periods of depressed business and market levels to buy representative common stocks, since he is unlikely to be able to acquire them at other times except at prices that the future may cause him to regret. On the other hand, the thousands of so-called "secondary companies" should offer at least a moderate number of true investment opportunities under all conditions, except perhaps in the heydey of a bull market. This wide but quite unpopular field may present the more logical challenge to the interest of the bona fide investor and to the talents of the securities analyst.

PART I
SURVEY AND
APPROACH

THE ESSENTIAL LESSONS

BY ROGER LOWENSTEIN

I f the modern reader were asked, what did the junk bonds of the 1980s, the dot-com stocks of the late 1990s, and, more recently, the various subprime mortgage portfolios of the 2000s all have in common, the first correct answer is that each of them took a nosedive from a highly inflated price to one rather closer to zero. You can throw in, for good measure, the net asset value and reputation of the world's most intelligent hedge fund, Long-Term Capital Management (LTCM). The second right answer is that each was an investment disaster whose perils could have been avoided by a patient reading of *Security Analysis*. Graham and Dodd wrote the first edition in 1934 and first revised it in 1940—some four decades before Michael Milken became a household name and three score years in advance of the frenzy for no-documentation, adjustable-rate mortgages. The authors advocated more than a merely generalized skepticism. They prescribed (as we will see) a series of specific injunctions, each of which would have served as a prophylactic against one or more of the above-named fiascos and their associated investment fads.

While the book was received by serious investors as an instant classic, I cannot say it elevated Wall Street or the public above their tendency to speculate. If I can venture a guess as to why, it is that even the experienced investor is too often like the teenage driver first taking over the wheel. He hears the advice about being careful, avoiding icy patches and so forth, and consigns it to the remote part of his brain reserved for archived parental instructions. He surely does not want to wreck the family car, but avoiding an accident is a low priority because he does not think it will happen to him. Thus with our investor: he is focused on making money, not with averting the myriad potential wrecks in the investment landscape. And I suspect that Graham and Dodd have been ignored by those who suffer from the misconception that trying to make serious money requires that one take serious risks. In fact, the converse is true. Avoiding serious loss is a *precondition* for sustaining a high compound rate of growth.

In 25 years as a financial journalist, virtually all of the investors of this writer's acquaintance who have consistently earned superior profits have been Graham-and-Dodders. The most famous, of course, is Warren Buffett, and he is also the most illustrative. Buffett became Graham's pupil and disciple in 1950, when as a scrawny 20-year-old, he confided to a friend that he would be studying under a pair of "hotshots" (meaning Benjamin Graham and his assistant David Dodd) at the Columbia Business School.[1] And he was also, years later, the first to admit that he had moved beyond the stocks that lay within his master's ken. Buffett was an adapter; he did not imitate his mentor stroke for stroke. He began with Ben Graham types of stocks such as Berkshire Hathaway, which was then a struggling textile maker, and he moved on to Walt Disney and American Express, which possessed less in the way of tangible assets but more in economic value. Yet his *approach* remained consistent (even if the choice of securities it yielded did not).

It is this approach, successfully applied by a devoted minority of other professional and individual investors, that makes *Security Analysis* an enduring roadmap. It is still the bible for avoiding those icy patches— perhaps that much seems obvious—but it is also an instruction manual for identifying investments that are superior as well as safe.

---

[1] Roger Lowenstein, *Buffett: The Making of an American Capitalist* (New York: Random House, 1995), p. 35.

This was known without a doubt to the working investors who enrolled in Graham's classes, some of whom would bolt from the lecture hall to call their brokers with the names of the stocks that Professor Graham had used as examples. One later successful broker maintained that Graham's tips had been so valuable that the class actually paid for his degree. Whatever the literal truth, Graham was the rare academic who was both theoretician and working practitioner. Some brief knowledge of the man will elucidate his approach.[2] At a personal level, Graham was a caricature of the absent-minded professor, a devotee of the classics, a student of Latin and Greek, and a translator of Spanish poetry who could dress for work in mismatched shoes and who evidenced little interest in money. But intellectually, his curiosity was unrivaled. When he graduated from Columbia in 1914, he was offered positions in English, mathematics, and philosophy. Taking the advice of a college dean, he went to Wall Street, which he treated rather like another branch of academia—that is, as a discipline that was subject to logical and testable principles (albeit ones that had yet to be discovered). He gravitated to money management, in which he excelled, eventually combining it with writing and teaching. It took Graham 20 years—which is to say, a complete cycle from the bull market of the Roaring Twenties through the dark, nearly ruinous days of the early 1930s—to refine his investment philosophy into a discipline that was as rigorous as the Euclidean theorems he had studied in college.

An Analytical Discipline

This analytical approach is evident from the first chapter; indeed, it is the cornerstone of Part I, in which Graham and Dodd set forth the fundamentals. They promise to use "established principles and sound logic," or what the authors term "the scientific method," and yet they recognize

---

[2] Lowenstein, *Buffett,* p. 37.

that, as with law or medicine, investing is not hard science but a discipline in which both skill and chance play a role. *Security Analysis* is their prescription for maximizing the influence of the former and minimizing that of the latter. If you want to trust your portfolio to luck, this is not the book for you. It is addressed primarily to the *investor,* as opposed to the speculator, and the distinction that Graham and Dodd drew between them remains the heart of the work.

The investors in Graham's day, of course, operated in a vastly different landscape than today's. They suffered periodic and often severe economic depressions, as distinct from the occasional and generally mild recessions that have been the rule of late. They had less faith that the future would deliver prosperity, and they had less reliable information about specific securities. For such reasons, they were more inclined to invest in bonds than in stocks, most often in the bonds of well-known industrial companies. And the names of the leading companies didn't change much from year to year or even from decade to decade. American industry was increasingly regulated, and it was not as dynamic as it has been in recent times. Wall Street was an exclusive club, and investing was a rich person's game, not the popular sport it has become. The range of investment possibilities was also narrower. As for "alternative investments"—suffice to say that investing in a start-up that had yet to earn any profits would have been considered positively daft.

The changes in the marketplace have been so profound that it might seem astonishing that an investment manual written in the 1930s would have any relevance today. But human nature doesn't change. People still oscillate between manic highs and depressive lows, and in their hunger for instant profits, their distaste for the hard labor of serious study and for independent thought, modern investors look very much like their grandfathers and even their great-grandfathers. Then as now, it takes discipline to overcome the demons (largely emotional) that impede most investors. And the essentials of security analysis have not much changed.

In the 1930s, there was a common notion that bonds were safe—suitable for "investment"—while stocks were unsafe. Graham and Dodd rejected this mechanical rule, as they did, more generally, the notion of relying on the *form* of any security. They recognized that the various issues in the corporate food chain (senior bonds, junior debt, preferred stock, and common) were not so much dissimilar but rather part of a continuum. And though a bondholder, it is true, has an economic, and also a legal, priority over a stockholder, it is not the contractual obligation that provides safety to the bondholder, the authors pointed out, but "the ability of the debtor corporation to meet its obligations." And it follows that (leaving aside the tax shield provided from interest expense) the bondholder's claim cannot be worth more than the company's net worth would be to an owner who held it free and clear of debt.

This might seem obvious, but it was in no way apparent to the creditors of Federated Department Stores (which operated Bloomingdale's and other high-end retailers) during the junk bond mania of the late 1980s. Investment banks had discovered, without any sense of shame, that they could sell junk bonds to a credulous public irrespective of the issuers' ability to repay them. In 1988, Federated agreed to a leveraged acquisition by the Canadian developer and corporate raider Robert Campeau, which committed the company to annual interest charges thereafter of $600 million. This was rather an interesting figure because Federated was earning only $400 million.[3] The Federated bonds thus violated the rule that creditors can never extract more from a company than it actually has. (They also violated common sense.) Not two years

---

[3] Louis Lowenstein, University Lecture, Columbia University, Spring 1989.

later, Federated filed for bankruptcy and its bonds crashed. Needless to say, the investors hadn't read Graham and Dodd.

In accordance with the customs of its era, *Security Analysis* spends more time on bonds than it would were it written today (another sign of its Great Depression vintage is that there is scant mention of the risk that inflation poses to bondholders). But the general argument against evaluating securities on the basis of their type or formal classification is as trenchant as ever. Investors may have overcome (to a fault) their fear of stocks, but they fall into equally simplistic traps, such as supposing that investing in a stock market index is always and ever prudent—or even, until recently, that real estate "never goes down." Graham and Dodd's rejoinder was timeless: *at a price*, any security can be a suitable investment, but, to repeat, none is safe merely by virtue of its form. Nor does the fact that a stock is "blue chip" (that is, generally respected and widely owned) protect investors from loss. Graham and Dodd cited AT&T, which tumbled from a price of $494 a share in 1929 to a Depression low of $36. Modern readers will think of Ma Bell's notorious offspring, Lucent Technologies, which in the late 1990s was the bluest of blue chips—the darling of institutional investors—until it tumbled from $80 to less than a dollar.

Graham and Dodd went from AT&T and from the general madness of the late 1920s to argue that the standard for an investment could not be based on "psychological" factors such as popularity or renown—for it would allow the market to invent new standards as it went along. The parallel to the Internet bubble of the late 1990s is eerie, for making up standards is exactly what so-called investors did. Promoters claimed that stocks no longer needed earnings, and the cream of Wall Street—firms such as Morgan Stanley, Goldman Sachs, and Merrill Lynch—thought nothing of touting issues of companies that did not have a prayer of realizing profits.

Beware of Capitalizing Hope

When Graham and Dodd warned against "the capitalization of entirely conjectural future prospects," they could have been referring to the *fin-de-siècle* saga of Internet Capital Group (ICG), which provided seed money to Web-based start-ups, most of which were trying to start online businesses. It put money in some 47 of these prospects, and its total investment was about $350 million. Then, in August 1999, ICG itself went public at a price of $6 a share. By year-end, amidst the frenzy for Internet stocks, it was trading at $170. At that price, it was valued at precisely $46 billion. Since the company had little of value besides its investments in the start-ups, the market was assuming that, on average, its 47 seedlings would provide an average return of better than 100 to 1. Talk about capitalizing hope! Most investors do not realize a 100-for-1 return even once in their lifetimes. Alas, within a couple of years ICG's shares had been reappraised by the market at 25 cents.

Such vignettes, though useful as well as entertaining, are merely proscriptive; they tell us what *not* to do. It is only when, after considerable discussion, Graham and Dodd delineate the boundary line between investment and speculation that we get our first insight of what *to* do. "An investment," we are told in a carefully chosen phrase, is an operation "that promises safety of principal and a satisfactory return."

The operative word here is "promises." It does not assume an ironclad guarantee (some promises after all are broken, and some investments do lose money). But it assumes a high degree of certainty. No one would have said of an Internet Capital Group that it "promised" safety. But that is perhaps too easy a case. Let us look at a more established and, indeed, a more reasonably priced stock, that of Washington Mutual. Most of its shareholders at the end of 2006 presumably would have classified themselves as "investors." The bank was large and geographically diverse; it had increased earnings nine straight years before falling off, only slightly, in 2006. Its stock over those 10 years had well more than doubled.

True, "WaMu," as it is known, had a large portfolio of mortgages, including subprime mortgages. Across the United States, such mortgages had been extended on an increasingly flimsy basis (that is, to borrowers of dubious credit), and defaults had started to tick up. But WaMu was held in high regard. It was said to have the most sophisticated tools for risk assessment, and its public statements were reassuring. The chairman's year-end letter applauded his company for being "positioned . . . to deliver stronger operating performance in 2007." The casual stock picker, even the professional, would have had no trouble describing WaMu as an "investment."

Graham and Dodd, however, insisted that "safety must be based on study and on standards," in particular, study of the published financials. For 2006, WaMu's annual report indicated a balance of $20 billion of subprime loans, which (though WaMu didn't make the connection) was equal to 80% of its total stockholder equity. What's more, the subprime portfolio had doubled in four years. WaMu had made it a practice of getting such loans off its balance sheet by securitizing them and selling them to investors, but, as it noted, if delinquency rates were to rise, investors might have less appetite for subprime loans and WaMu could wind up stuck with them. And delinquency rates *were* rising. Subprime loans classified as "nonperforming" had jumped by 50% in the past year and had tripled in four years. The risk of nonpayment was especially acute because WaMu had issued many loans above the traditional limit of 80% of home value—meaning that if the real estate market were to weaken, some customers would owe more than their homes were worth.

WaMu had a much larger portfolio, about $100 billion, of traditional mortgages (those rated higher than subprime). But even many of these loans were not truly "traditional." On 60% of the mortgages in its total portfolio, the interest rate was due to adjust within one year, meaning that its customers could face sharply higher—and potentially unafford-able—rates. WaMu disclosed that such folks had been spared the possi-bility of foreclosure by the steady rise in home prices. This was a rather powerful admission, especially as, the bank observed, "appreciation lev-els experienced during the past five years may not continue." In fact, the real estate slump was becoming national news. WaMu had bet the ranch on a rising market and now the market was tanking.

Parsing such disclosures may seem like a lot of effort (WaMu's report is 194 pages), and indeed it does entail work. But no one who took the trouble to read WaMu's annual report would have concluded that WaMu promised safety. The Graham and Dodd investor therefore would have been spared the pain when home prices fell and subprime losses sharply escalated. Such losses would soon prove catastrophic. Late in 2007 WaMu abandoned the subprime business and laid off thousands of employees. For the fourth quarter, it reported a loss of nearly $2 billion, and over the full year its shares suffered a 70% decline.

Since (as WaMu discovered) market trends can quickly reverse, Graham and Dodd counseled readers to invest on a sounder foundation, that is, on the basis of a security's intrinsic value. They never—surprise to say— define the term, but we readily grasp its meaning. "Intrinsic value" is the worth of an enterprise to one who owns it "for keeps." Logically, it must be based on the cash flow that would go to a continuing owner over the long run, as distinct from a speculative assessment of its resale value.

The underlying premise requires a tiny leap of faith. Occasionally, stocks and bonds trade for less than intrinsic value, thus the opportunity. But sooner or later—here is where faith comes into the picture—such securities should revert to intrinsic value (else why invest in them?). To summarize the core of Part I in plain English, Graham and Dodd told investors to look for securities at a hefty discount to what they are worth.

A Range of Values

The rub, then and now, is how to calculate that worth. I suspect the authors deliberately refrained from defining intrinsic value, lest they convey the misleading impression that the value of a security can be precisely determined. Given the practical limits of people's ability to forecast (an earnings report, a romance, the weather, or anything), the authors urge that investors think in terms of a range of values. Happily, this is quite satisfactory for the purposes of investors. To quote Graham and Dodd: "It is quite possible to decide by inspection that a woman is old enough to vote without knowing her age or that a man is heavier than he should be without knowing his weight." (p. 66)

Precision is in any case unnecessary because the aim is to pay a good deal *less* than intrinsic value, so as to provide a margin of safety. Just as it would be tempting fate to cross a bridge while carrying the maximum allowable tonnage, buying a stock at full value would involve "a speculative component" (since one's calculation of value could be off).

A somewhat similar cautionary note is that favorable odds will *not* endow the gambler with the element of safety required for investing. Graham and Dodd used the example of a mythical roulette wheel in which the odds had been reversed to 19 to 18 in favor of the customer. "If the player wagers all his money on a single number, the small odds in his favor are of slight importance," the authors note. In fact, the investor would be ill advised to risk his all on a single spin even if the odds were *strongly* in his favor.

The Long-Term Capital Management hedge fund made just such a bet, or a series of bets, in 1998. Each of its trades had been mathematically calculated (the fund had a pair of Nobel Prize winners in residence), and its previous experience suggested that on each of its trades the odds were in its favor. However, LTCM, which was highly leveraged, risked far more than it could afford to lose. And its various bets, though superficially unrelated, were linked thematically (each was a bet that the risk premiums on bonds would narrow). When one trade fell, they all did, and the legendary fund was wiped out.

So we are back to the question of what *will* qualify as an investment. There is a well-traveled myth that Graham and Dodd exclusively relied on a company's book value to determine a safe threshold. While intrinsic value measures the economic potential—what an owner might hope to get *out* of an asset—book value is an arithmetic computation of what has been invested *into* it.[4] But book value alone cannot be determinative. If you invested an equal sum in, say, two auto companies, one run by Toyota and the other by General Motors, the book values would be equal, but their intrinsic or economic values would be very different. Graham and Dodd did *not* fall into this error; they stated plainly that, in terms of forecasting the course of stock prices, book value was "almost worthless as a practical matter."

But Graham frequently found securities that, solely on the basis of their assets and after putting them to hard study, met the safety-of-principal test. In the 1930s, markets were so depressed that it was not uncommon for stocks to sell at less than the value of their cash on hand, even after subtracting their debt. (This was akin to buying a home for less than the amount of money in the bedroom safe and getting to keep the safe as well!) Such hypercheap investments are scarcer today due to the broader-based interest in the stock market and to the armies of investors, often armed with computer screens, perpetually looking for bargains.

---

[4] Technically, book value equals the sum of what has been invested in a company, plus accumulated profits less the dividends it has paid. An alternate but mathematically equivalent definition is that book value is equal to the total assets minus the total liabilities.

Bargain Hunting

Nonetheless, they do exist. Individual stocks are often cheap when a whole industry or group of securities has been sold down indiscriminately. In the early 1980s, for instance, the savings and loan industry was depressed, and for good reason. Following the elimination of regulatory ceilings on interest rates, thrifts had been forced to pay higher rates for short-term deposits than they were receiving on long-term loans. Mutual savings banks (owned by their depositors) began to go public to attract more capital, and as they did so, their stocks fetched very low values. United Savings Bank of Tacoma, for one, traded at only 35% of book value. Though many thrifts of the day were weak, Tacoma was profitable and well capitalized. "People didn't understand them," says one investor who did. "They had just converted [from mutual ownership], they were small, they were off people's radar." Within a year, the investor had quintupled his money.

Another opportunity beckoned in 1997, after the contagious melt-down of Asian stock and currency markets. Once again, the selling was indiscriminate—it tarred good companies and bad alike. Graham and Dodd investors responded opportunistically, booking flights to Hong Kong, Singapore, and Kuala Lumpur. Greg Alexander, who manages money for Ruane Cunniff & Goldfarb, read the annual report of every Asian company he had heard of and determined that South Korea, which previously had discouraged foreign investment and was thus especially short on capital, offered the best bargains. He flew to Seoul and, though still in a jet-lagged stupor, realized he was in a Graham-and-Dodders' heaven. Cheap stocks were hanging on the market like overripe fruit. Shinyoung Securities, a local brokerage firm that had stocked up on high-yielding South Korean government bonds when interest rates were at a peak, was trading at less than half of book value. Surprisingly, even as late as 2004, Daekyo Corp., an after-school tutoring company, was trading at only $20 a share, even though each share represented $22.66

in cash in addition to a slice of the ongoing business. In Graham and Dodd terms, such stocks promised safety because they were selling for less than their tangible worth. Alexander bought a dozen South Korean stocks; each would rise manyfold within a relatively short time.

The competition for such values is fiercer in the United States, but they can be found, especially, again, when some broader trend punishes an entire sector of the market. In 2001, for instance, energy stocks were cheap (as was the price of oil). Graham and Dodd would not have advised speculating on the price of oil—which is dependent on myriad uncertain factors from OPEC to the growth rate of China's economy to the weather. But because the industry was depressed, drilling companies were selling for less than the value of their equipment. Ensco International was trading at less than $15 per share, while the replacement value of its rigs was estimated at $35. Patterson-UTI Energy owned some 350 rigs worth about $2.8 billion. Yet its stock was trading for only $1 billion. Investors were getting the assets at a huge discount. Though the subsequent oil price rise made these stocks home runs, the key point is that the investments weren't dependent on the oil price. Graham and Dodd investors bought into these stocks with a substantial margin of safety.

A more common sort of asset play involves peering through the corporate shell to the various subsidiaries: sometimes, the pieces add up to more than the whole. An interesting case was Xcel Energy in 2002. Xcel owned five subsidiaries, so analyzing the stock required some mathematical deconstruction (Graham had a natural affinity for such calculations). Four of the subsidiaries were profitable utilities; the other was an alternative energy supplier that was overloaded with debt and apparently headed for bankruptcy. The parent was not responsible for the subsidiary's debt. However, in the aftermath of the Enron collapse, utility holding companies were shunned by investors. "It was a strange time," recalled a hedge fund manager. "People were selling first and examining second. The market was irrational."

Xcel's bonds were trading at 56 cents on the dollar (thus, you could buy a $1,000 obligation of the parent for only $560). And the bonds paid an attractive coupon of 7%. The question was whether Xcel could *pay* the interest. The hedge fund investor discovered that Xcel had $1 billion of these bonds outstanding and that the book value of its healthy subsidiaries was $4 billion (these are the sort of endlessly useful figures that can be dug out of corporate disclosures). On paper, then, its assets were enough to redeem the bonds with plenty to spare. The hedge fund investor bought every bond he could find.

When no more of the bonds were available, the investor began to look at Xcel's stock, which was depressed for the same reason as its bonds. The stock wasn't quite as safe (in a bankruptcy, bondholders get paid off first). Still, the investor's calculations had convinced him that the parent company would not file for bankruptcy. And the profitable subsidiaries were earning $500 million, more than $1 a share. The stock was trading at $7, or less than seven times earnings. So the investor bought the stock too.

The weak subsidiary did file for bankruptcy, but as expected this did not detract from the value of the parent. Within a year, the panic over such utilities subsided, and Wall Street reevaluated Xcel. The bonds went from $56 to $105. The stock also soared. The investor doubled his money on each of his Xcel trades. Neither had been a roll of the dice; rather, each was quantifiably demonstrable as a Graham and Dodd investment. "It was a safe, steady industry," the investor agreed. "Not a lot of business-cycle risks. I think Ben Graham would have approved."

As intriguing as Xcel types of puzzles may be, most stocks will simply be valued on their earnings. In reality, the process isn't "simple." Valuing equities involves a calculation of what a company should be able to earn each year, going forward, as distinct from taking a snapshot of the assets it has at the moment. Graham and Dodd reluctantly endorsed this exercise—"reluctantly" because the future is never as certain as the present.

Forecasting Flows

To forecast earnings with any degree of confidence is extremely difficult. The best guide can only be what a company has earned in the past. But capitalism is dynamic. Graham and Dodd frowned on trying to estimate earnings for businesses of "inherently unstable character." Due to the rapidity with which technology evolves, many high-tech companies are innately unstable or at least unpredictable. In the late 1990s, Yahoo! was vulnerable to the risk that somebody would invent a better search engine (somebody did: Google). McDonald's doesn't face that risk. Its business depends largely on its brand, whose strength is unlikely to change much from one year to the next. And no one is going to reinvent the hamburger. It should be noted, though, that even McDonald's cannot stand still; it has recently introduced espresso on its menu, in part to fend off competitors such as Starbucks.

Some present-day Graham-and-Dodders (perhaps because Buffett has had a well-publicized aversion to high tech) have a mistaken notion that all technology is impossible to analyze and is therefore off-limits. Such a wooden rule violates the Graham and Dodd precept that analysts make a fact-determinant, company-specific analysis. One example of a high-tech company that submits to a Graham type of analysis is Amazon.com. Though it does business exclusively on the Web, Amazon is essentially a retailer, and it may be evaluated in the same way as Wal-Mart, Sears, and so forth. The question, as always, is, does the business provide an adequate margin of safety at a given market price. For much of Amazon's short life, the stock was wildly overpriced. But when the dot-com bubble burst, its securities collapsed. Buffett himself bought Amazon's deeply discounted bonds after the crash, when there was much fearful talk that Amazon was headed for bankruptcy. The bonds subsequently rose to par, and Buffett made a killing. Another example is Intel, now a relatively mature manufacturer whose chip volume varies with the performance of the economy much as General Motors' did in earlier eras. Indeed, Intel has been around for far longer than GM had been when Graham and Dodd were writing this book.

In estimating future earnings (for any sort of business), *Security Analysis* provides two vital rules. One, as noted, is that companies with stable earnings are easier to forecast and hence preferable. The world having become more changeable, this precept might be modestly updated, to wit: the more volatile a firm's earnings, the more cautious one should be in estimating its future and the further back into its past one should look. Graham and Dodd suggested 10 years.

The second point relates to the tendency of earnings to fluctuate, at least somewhat, in a cyclical pattern. Therefore, Graham and Dodd made a vital (and oft-overlooked) distinction. A firm's *average* earnings can provide a rough guide to the future; the earnings *trend* is far less reliable. Any baseball fan knows that just because a .250 hitter hits .300 for a week, it cannot be assumed that he will necessarily hit that well for the rest of the season. And even if he does, the odds are he will revert to form the next year. But investors get seduced by the trend; perhaps they want to be seduced, for as Graham and Dodd observed, "Trends carried far enough into the future will yield any desired result."

To understand the distinction between the average and the trend, let's look at the earnings per share of Microsoft over the last half of the 1990s. (Each year is for the 12-month period ended in June.)

1995	$0.16
1996	$0.23
1997	$0.36
1998	$0.46
1999	$0.77
2000	$0.91

Although the average for the period is 48 cents, the more recent numbers are higher, and the upward trend is unmistakable. Projecting the trend into the future, a casual analyst at the turn of the century might have penciled in numbers like this:

$1.10
$1.30
$1.55

Give or take a few pennies, this is exactly what so-called analysts were doing. Early in 2000, the stock was trading above $50, based on the expectation that earnings would continue to soar. But 2000 was the peak of the cycle for ordering new computers. As new orders fell, Microsoft's earnings plummeted. In 2001, it earned 72 cents. The next year, it earned only 50 cents, virtually equal to its average for the mid-1990s. The stock plunged into the low $20s.

Microsoft, however, was not some Internet fly-by-night. Over 20 years, it has always been profitable, and aside from the 2001–2002 cyclical slump, its earnings have steadily increased. Investors arguably overreacted to the slump much as, in the past, they overreacted to favorable news. They became fearful that Google might invade Microsoft's turf, though this concern was highly speculative. Microsoft continued to dominate operating software (indeed, it has had a virtual monopoly in that business) and to generate a prodigious cash flow. Also, since it has little need for reinvestment, it is free to employ its cash as it chooses. (By contrast, an airline must continually reinvest in new planes.) In that sense, Microsoft is an inherently good business. By fiscal 2007, it was trading at a multiple of only 15 times earnings, well less than its intrinsic characteristics justified given the strength of the franchise. Once Wall Street reawakened to the fact, the stock quickly rose 50% from its low. This demonstrates the continuing *pas de deux* of price and value. At a high price, Microsoft was a sheer speculation; at a low one, a sound investment.

The mention of cash flow points to an area in which *Security Analysis* is truly dated. In the 1930s, companies did not have to publish cash flow reports, and virtually none of them did. Today, detailed cash flow statements are required, and for serious investors they are indispensable. The income statement gives the company's accounting profit; the cash flow statement reports what happened to its money.

Companies that try to cook the books such as Enron or Waste Management can always dress up the earnings statement, at least for a while. But they can't manufacture cash. Thus, when the income statement and the cash flow statement start to diverge, it's a signal that something is amiss. At Sunbeam, the high-flying appliance company run by "Chainsaw" Al Dunlap, sales of blenders were reportedly (reported by the company, that is) going through the roof, but the cash flow wasn't. It turned out that Dunlap was engaged in a massive fraud. Though he sold the company, it collapsed soon after, and "Chainsaw" was sawed off by the SEC from ever again serving as an officer or director in a public company.

Similarly, when Lucent's stock was sky-high, it was not actually collecting cash for many of the phone systems it was delivering, in particular to customers in developing countries. It was, in effect, loaning them out pending payment. Though these "sales" were booked into earnings, once again, the cash flow statement didn't lie.

This is a mischief that Graham would have discovered because an uncollected item goes on the balance sheet as a receivable, and Graham was a fiend for reading balance sheets. Graham and Dodd paid more attention to the balance sheet, which records a moment in financial time, than to earnings and cash flow statements, which depict the change over a previous quarter or year, because such information was either not available or not very detailed. Even the requirement for quarterly earnings was new in 1940, and earnings statements did not come freighted, as they do today, with detailed footnotes and discussions of significant risks.

Graham supplemented the published financials (though they were his primary source) with a highly eclectic mix of trade and government publications. When researching a coal stock, he consulted reports of the U.S. Coal Commission; on autos, *Cram's Auto Service*. For contemporary investors, *in most cases*, published financials are both exhaustive and reliable. Also, today, industry data are more widely available.

An investor in U.S. securities thus faces a challenge unimaginable to Graham and Dodd. Where the latter suffered a paucity of information, investors today confront a surfeit. Company financials are denser, and the information on the Internet is, of course, unlimited—a worrisome fact given its uneven quality. The challenge is to weed out what is irrelevant, insignificant, or just plain wrong, or rather, to identify what in particular *is* important. This would have meant identifying cash flow issues at Lucent or subprime exposure in the case of WaMu before the stocks ran into trouble.

As a rule of thumb, investors should spend the bulk of their time on the disclosures of the security under study, and they should spend significant time on the reports of competitors. The point is not just to memorize the numbers but to understand them; as we have seen, both the balance sheet and the statement of cash flow will throw significant light on the number that Wall Street pays the most attention to, the reported earnings.

There cannot be an absolute recommendation regarding investors' sources because people learn in different ways. Walter Schloss, a Graham employee and later a famed investor in his own right, and his son and associate Edwin shared a single telephone so that neither would spend too much time talking on it. (The Schlosses worked in an office that has been compared to a closet.) Like the Schlosses, many investors work best in teams. On the other hand, Buffett, who works in an unpretentious office in Omaha, is famously solitary. His partner, Charlie Munger, resides in Los Angeles, 1,500 miles west, and in a day-to-day sense, Buffett operates largely on his own. And while some investors rely strictly on the published financials, others do substantial legwork. Eddie Lampert, the hedge fund manager, visited dozens of outlets of auto-parts retailer AutoZone before he bought a controlling stake in it. This was Lampert's way of getting into his comfort zone.

Information at a Premium

In general, the greater dispersion of public information today puts a premium on information that is exclusive. The most likely source of exclusive information (apologies to Schloss) is the telephone. Some mutual funds employ former journalists to ferret out investing "scoops." They call former employees for a candid appraisal of management; they talk to suppliers and competitors. One mutual fund discovered that a just-named CEO of a prominent financial company had confessed to an associate that he was nervous about taking the job because he couldn't read financial statements. The fund, which had been looking at the stock, immediately lost interest. Though not everyone has the resources to hire a private sleuth, some research is eminently affordable. An enterprising stockbroker kept tabs on one of his stocks, Jones Soda, by chatting up baristas at Starbucks, one of the outlets where Jones was sold. When they told him that Starbucks was dropping the brand, he sold the stock pronto. Also, there is a certain kind of conviction that can be gleaned only from hearing management answer unscripted questions. Be forewarned, though; some executives will lie.

Graham was particularly mistrustful of executives (he did not like to visit managements for this reason). He and Dodd warned that "objective tests of managerial ability are few." Just as it is difficult to apportion proper credit to a winning coach, it is hard to say how much of a company's success is attributable to the executives. Investors often ascribe to managerial prowess what could be the residue of favorable conditions (or simply of good luck). Coca-Cola's earnings were rising sharply in the early and mid-1990s, and the company's aggressively promotional CEO, Roberto Goizueta, was feted on the cover of *Fortune*. Goizueta was talented, but his talent was fully reflected in Coca-Cola's earnings, and the earnings were reflected in the price of the stock. Investors, however, went a further step, pushing the stock to a lofty 45 times earnings due to their faith in management to increase earnings. Graham and Dodd referred to this as "double-counting"—that is, investors buy the stock on the basis of their faith in management and then, seeing that the stock has risen, take it as additional proof of management's powers and bid the stock up further. In 1997, an analyst at Oppenheimer was so smitten by Goizueta, who died later that year, that he wrote that Coca-Cola had "absolute control over near-term results."[5]

Such faith was misplaced on three accounts. First, Goizueta's talent was already factored into the stock. Second, the notion that management had "absolute control" was a myth, as was demonstrated when growth tapered off. Third, to the extent it did have control, it was by "managing" Coca-Cola's earnings, with the aid of dubious accounting contrivances. For instance, Coca-Cola made a practice of selling stakes in bottling plants and booking the gains into operating earnings to make its numbers. The suggestion that Goizueta was a magically talented guru was a warning signal. Rather than prove that Goizueta had the power to levitate earnings in the future, it raised questions about the quality of

---

[5] Roger Lowenstein, *Origins of the Crash: The Great Bubble and Its Undoing* (New York: Penguin Press, 2004), p. 70.

the earnings he had achieved in the past. As reality caught up with Coca-Cola, the stock went into a decadelong funk.

Such examples should demonstrate that investing is hardly less risky today than in Graham and Dodd's era, nor is the human spirit less vulnerable to temptation and error. The complexity of our markets has further enhanced the need for an investing guide that is straightforward, logical, detailed, and, most especially, prudent. This and no more was the authors' brief. Herewith Part I—a primer on intrinsic value, an exploration of investment as distinct from speculation, and an introduction to Graham and Dodd's approach, their philosophy, their stratagems and guidance, and their tools.

Chapter 1

THE SCOPE AND LIMITATIONS OF SECURITY ANALYSIS. THE CONCEPT ·OF INTRINSIC VALUE

ANALYSIS CONNOTES the careful study of available facts with the attempt to draw conclusions therefrom based on established principles and sound logic. It is part of the scientific method. But in applying analysis to the field of securities we encounter the serious obstacle that investment is by nature not an exact science. The same is true, however, of law and medicine, for here also both individual skill (art) and chance are important factors in determining success or failure. Nevertheless, in these professions analysis is not only useful but indispensable, so that the same should probably be true in the field of investment and possibly in that of speculation.

In the last three decades the prestige of security analysis in Wall Street has experienced both a brilliant rise and an ignominious fall—a history related but by no means parallel to the course of stock prices. The advance of security analysis proceeded uninterruptedly until about 1927, covering a long period in which increasing attention was paid on all sides to financial reports and statistical data. But the "new era" commencing in 1927 involved at bottom the abandonment of the analytical approach; and while emphasis was still seemingly placed on facts and figures, these were manipulated by a sort of pseudo-analysis to support the delusions of the period. The market collapse in October 1929 was no surprise to such analysts as had kept their heads, but the extent of the business collapse which later developed, with its devastating effects on established earning power, again threw their calculations out of gear. Hence the ultimate result was that serious analysis suffered a double discrediting: the first—prior to the crash—due to the persistence of imaginary values, and the second—after the crash—due to the disappearance of real values.

The experiences of 1927–1933 were of so extraordinary a character that they scarcely provide a valid criterion for judging the usefulness of security analysis. As to the years since 1933, there is perhaps room for a difference of opinion. In the field of bonds and preferred stocks, we believe that sound principles of selection and rejection have justified themselves quite well. In the common-stock arena the partialities of the market have tended to confound the conservative viewpoint, and conversely many issues appearing cheap under analysis have given a disappointing performance. On the other hand, the analytical approach would have given strong grounds for believing representative stock prices to be too high in early 1937 and too low a year later.

THREE FUNCTIONS OF ANALYSIS:
1. DESCRIPTIVE FUNCTION

The functions of security analysis may be described under three headings: descriptive, selective, and critical. In its more obvious form, descriptive analysis consists of marshalling the important facts relating to an issue and presenting them in a coherent, readily intelligible manner. This function is adequately performed for the entire range of marketable corporate securities by the various manuals, the Standard Statistics and Fitch services, and others. A more penetrating type of description seeks to reveal the strong and weak points in the position of an issue, compare its exhibit with that of others of similar character, and appraise the factors which are likely to influence its future performance. Analysis of this kind is applicable to almost every corporate issue, and it may be regarded as an adjunct not only to investment but also to intelligent speculation in that it provides an organized factual basis for the application of judgment.

2. THE SELECTIVE FUNCTION OF
SECURITY ANALYSIS

In its selective function, security analysis goes further and expresses specific judgments of its own. It seeks to determine whether a given issue should be bought, sold, retained, or exchanged for some other. What types of securities or situations lend themselves best to this more positive activity of the analyst, and to what handicaps or limitations is it subject? It may be well to start with a group of examples of analytical judgments, which could later serve as a basis for a more general inquiry.

Examples of Analytical Judgments. In 1928 the public was offered a large issue of 6% noncumulative preferred stock of St. Louis-San Francisco Railway Company priced at 100. The record showed that in no year in the company's history had earnings been equivalent to as much as 1¹/₂ times the fixed charges and preferred dividends combined. The application of well-established standards of selection to the facts in this case would have led to the rejection of the issue as insufficiently protected.

A contrasting example: In June 1932 it was possible to purchase 5% bonds of Owens-Illinois Glass Company, due 1939, at 70, yielding 11% to maturity. The company's earnings were many times the interest requirements—not only on the average but even at that time of severe depression. The bond issue was amply covered by current assets alone, and it was followed by common and preferred stock with a very large aggregate market value, taking their lowest quotations. Here, analysis would have led to the recommendation of this issue as a strongly entrenched and attractively priced investment.

Let us take an example from the field of common stocks. In 1922, prior to the boom in aviation securities, Wright Aeronautical Corporation stock was selling on the New York Stock Exchange at only $8, although it was paying a $1 dividend, had for some time been earning over $2 a share, and showed more than $8 per share in cash assets in the treasury. In this case analysis would readily have established that the intrinsic value of the issue was substantially above the market price.

Again, consider the same issue in 1928 when it had advanced to $280 per share. It was then earning at the rate of $8 per share, as against $3.77 in 1927. The dividend rate was $2; the net-asset value was less than $50 per share. A study of this picture must have shown conclusively that the market price represented for the most part the capitalization of entirely conjectural future prospects—in other words, that the intrinsic value was far less than the market quotation.

A third kind of analytical conclusion may be illustrated by a comparison of Interborough Rapid Transit Company First and Refunding 5s with the same company's Collateral 7% Notes, when both issues were selling at the same price (say 62) in 1933. The 7% notes were clearly worth considerably more than the 5s. Each $1,000 note was secured by deposit of $1,736 face amount of 5s; the principal of the notes had matured; they were entitled either to be paid off in full or to a sale of the collateral for their benefit. The annual interest received on the collateral was equal to about $87 on each 7% note (which amount was actually being distributed to the note holders), so that the current income on the 7s was considerably greater than that on the 5s. Whatever technicalities might be invoked to prevent the note holders from asserting their contractual rights promptly and completely, it was difficult to imagine conditions under which the 7s would not be intrinsically worth considerably more than the 5s.

A more recent comparison of the same general type could have been drawn between Paramount Pictures First Convertible Preferred selling at 113 in October 1936 and the common stock concurrently selling at 15 7/8. The preferred stock was convertible at the holders' option into seven times as many shares of common, and it carried accumulated dividends of about $11 per share. Obviously the preferred was cheaper than the common, since it would have to receive very substantial dividends before the common received anything, and it could also share fully in any rise of the common by reason of the conversion privilege. If a common stockholder had accepted this analysis and exchanged his shares for one-seventh as many preferred, he would soon have realized a large gain both in dividends received and in principal value.[1]

Intrinsic Value vs. Price. From the foregoing examples it will be seen that the work of the securities analyst is not without concrete results of considerable practical value, and that it is applicable to a wide variety of situations. In all of these instances he appears to be concerned with the intrinsic value of the security and more particularly with the discovery of discrepancies between the intrinsic value and the market price. We must recognize, however, that intrinsic value is an elusive concept. In general terms it is understood to be that value which is justified by the facts, *e.g.*, the assets, earnings, dividends, definite prospects, as distinct, let us say, from market quotations established by artificial manipulation or distorted by psychological excesses. But it is a great mistake to imagine that intrinsic value is as definite and as determinable as is the market price. Some time ago intrinsic value (in the case of a common stock) was thought to be about the same thing as "book value," *i.e.*, it was equal to the net assets of the business, fairly priced. This

---

[1] For the sequels to the six examples just given, see Appendix Note 2, p. 734 on accompanying CD.

view of intrinsic value was quite definite, but it proved almost worthless as a practical matter because neither the average earnings nor the average market price evinced any tendency to be governed by the book value.

Intrinsic Value and "Earning Power." Hence this idea was superseded by a newer view, *viz.*, that the intrinsic value of a business was determined by its earning power. But the phrase "earning power" must imply a fairly confident expectation of certain future results. It is not sufficient to know what the past earnings have averaged, or even that they disclose a definite line of growth or decline. There must be plausible grounds for believing that this average or this trend is a dependable guide to the future. Experience has shown only too forcibly that in many instances this is far from true. This means that the concept of "earning power," expressed as a definite figure, and the derived concept of intrinsic value, as something equally definite and ascertainable, cannot be safely accepted as a *general premise* of security analysis.

Example: To make this reasoning clearer, let us consider a concrete and typical example. What would we mean by the intrinsic value of J. I. Case Company common, as analyzed, say, early in 1933? The market price was $30; the asset value per share was $176; no dividend was being paid; the average earnings for ten years had been $9.50 per share; the results for 1932 had shown a *deficit* of $17 per share. If we followed a customary method of appraisal, we might take the average earnings per share of common for ten years, multiply this average by ten, and arrive at an intrinsic value of $95. But let us examine the individual figures which make up this ten-year average. They are as shown in the table on page 66. The average of $9.50 is obviously nothing more than an arithmetical resultant from ten unrelated figures. It can hardly be urged that this average is in any way representative of *typical* conditions in the past or representative of what may be expected in the future. Hence any figure of "real" or intrinsic value derived from this average must be characterized as equally accidental or artificial.[2]

---

[2] Between 1933 and 1939 the earnings on Case common varied between a deficit of $14.66 and profits of $19.20 per share, averaging $3.18. The price ranged between 30$\frac{1}{2}$ and 191$\frac{3}{4}$, closing in 1939 at 73$\frac{3}{4}$.

EARNINGS PER SHARE OF J.I. CASE COMMON

1932	$17.40(d)
1931	2.90(d)
1930	11.00
1929	20.40
1928	26.90
1927	26.00
1926	23.30
1925	15.30
1924	5.90(d)
1923	2.10(d)
Average	$9.50

(d) Deficit.

The Role of Intrinsic Value in the Work of the Analyst. Let us
try to formulate a statement of the role of intrinsic value in the work of
the analyst which will reconcile the rather conflicting implications of our
various examples. The essential point is that security analysis does not
seek to determine exactly what is the intrinsic value of a given security.
It needs only to establish either that the value is *adequate*—e.g., to protect a bond or to justify a stock purchase—or else that the value is considerably higher or considerably lower than the market price. For such
purposes an indefinite and approximate measure of the intrinsic value
may be sufficient. To use a homely simile, it is quite possible to decide
by inspection that a woman is old enough to vote without knowing
her age or that a man is heavier than he should be without knowing his
exact weight.

This statement of the case may be made clearer by a brief return to
our examples. The rejection of St. Louis-San Francisco Preferred did not
require an exact calculation of the intrinsic value of this railroad system.
It was enough to show, very simply from the earnings record, that the
margin of value above the bondholders' and preferred stockholders'
claims was too small to assure safety. Exactly the opposite was true for
the Owens-Illinois Glass 5s. In this instance, also, it would undoubtedly
have been difficult to arrive at a fair valuation of the business; but it was
quite easy to decide that this value in any event was far in excess of the
company's debt.

In the Wright Aeronautical example, the earlier situation presented a set of facts which demonstrated that the business was worth substantially more than $8 per share, or $1,800,000. In the later year, the facts were equally conclusive that the business did not have a reasonable value of $280 per share, or $70,000,000 in all. It would have been difficult for the analyst to determine whether Wright Aeronautical was actually worth $20 or $40 a share in 1922—or actually worth $50 or $80 in 1929. But fortunately it was not necessary to decide these points in order to conclude that the shares were attractive at $8 and unattractive, intrinsically, at $280.

The J. I. Case example illustrates the far more typical common-stock situation, in which the analyst cannot reach a dependable conclusion as to the relation of intrinsic value to market price. But even here, *if the price had been low or high enough*, a conclusion might have been warranted. To express the uncertainty of the picture, we might say that it was difficult to determine in early 1933 whether the intrinsic value of Case common was nearer $30 or $130. Yet if the stock had been selling at as low as $10, the analyst would undoubtedly have been justified in declaring that it was worth more than the market price.

Flexibility of the Concept of Intrinsic Value. This should indicate how flexible is the concept of intrinsic value as applied to security analysis. Our notion of the intrinsic value may be more or less distinct, depending on the particular case. The degree of indistinctness may be expressed by a very hypothetical "range of approximate value," which would grow wider as the uncertainty of the picture increased, e.g., $20 to $40 for Wright Aeronautical in 1922 as against $30 to $130 for Case in 1933. It would follow that even a very indefinite idea of the intrinsic value may still justify a conclusion if the current price falls far outside either the maximum or minimum appraisal.

More Definite Concept in Special Cases. The Interborough Rapid Transit example permits a more precise line of reasoning than any of the others. Here a given market price for the 5% bonds results in a very definite valuation for the 7% notes. If it were certain that the collateral securing the notes would be acquired for and distributed to the note holders, then the mathematical relationship—*viz.*, $1,736 of value for the 7s against $1,000 of value for the 5s—would eventually be established at this ratio in the market. But because of quasi-political complications in the picture, this normal procedure could not be expected with certainty. As a practical matter, therefore, it is not possible to say that the 7s are actually worth 74% more than the 5s, but it may be said with assurance that the 7s are worth *substantially more*—which is a very useful conclusion to arrive at when both issues are selling at the same price.

The Interborough issues are an example of a rather special group of situations in which analysis may reach more definite conclusions respecting intrinsic value than in the ordinary case. These situations may involve a liquidation or give rise to technical operations known as "arbitrage" or "hedging." While, viewed in the abstract, they are probably the most satisfactory field for the analyst's work, the fact that they are specialized in character and of infrequent occurrence makes them relatively unimportant from the broader standpoint of investment theory and practice.

Principal Obstacles to Success of the Analyst. *a. Inadequate or Incorrect Data.* Needless to say, the analyst cannot be right all the time. Furthermore, a conclusion may be logically right but work out badly in practice. The main obstacles to the success of the analyst's work are threefold, *viz.*, (1) the inadequacy or incorrectness of the data, (2) the uncertainties of the future, and (3) the irrational behavior of the market. The first of these drawbacks, although serious, is the least important of the three. Deliberate falsification of the data is rare; most of the misrepresentation flows from the use of accounting artifices which it is the function of the capable analyst to detect. Concealment is more common than misstatement. But the extent of such concealment has been greatly reduced as the result of regulations, first of the New York Stock Exchange and later of the S.E.C., requiring more complete disclosure and fuller explanation of accounting practices. Where information on an important point is still withheld, the analyst's experience and skill should lead him to note this defect and make allowance therefor—if, indeed, he may not elicit the facts by proper inquiry and pressure. In some cases, no doubt, the concealment will elude detection and give rise to an incorrect conclusion.

b. Uncertainties of the Future. Of much greater moment is the element of future change. A conclusion warranted by the facts and by the apparent prospects may be vitiated by new developments. This raises the question of how far it is the function of security analysis to anticipate changed conditions. We shall defer consideration of this point until our discussion of various factors entering into the processes of analysis. It is manifest, however, that future changes are largely unpredictable, and that security analysis must ordinarily proceed on the assumption that the past record affords at least a rough guide to the future. The more questionable this assumption, the less valuable is the analysis. Hence this technique is more useful when applied to senior securities (which are protected against change) than to common stocks; more useful when applied to a business of inherently stable character than to one subject to wide variations; and, finally, more useful when carried on under fairly normal general conditions than in times of great uncertainty and radical change.

c. The Irrational Behavior of the Market. The third handicap to security analysis is found in the market itself. In a sense the market and the future present the same kind of difficulties. Neither can be predicted or controlled by the analyst, yet his success is largely dependent upon them both. The major activities of the investment analyst may be thought to have little or no concern with market prices. His typical function is the selection of high-grade, fixed-income-bearing bonds, which upon investigation he judges to be secure as to interest and principal. The purchaser is supposed to pay no attention to their subsequent market fluctuations, but to be interested solely in the question whether the bonds will continue to be sound investments. In our opinion this traditional view of the investor's attitude is inaccurate and somewhat hypocritical. Owners of securities, whatever their character, are interested in their market quotations. This fact is recognized by the emphasis always laid in investment practice upon *marketability*. If it is important that an issue be readily salable, it is still more important that it command a satisfactory price. While for obvious reasons the investor in high-grade bonds has a lesser concern with market fluctuations than has the speculator, they still have a strong psychological, if not financial, effect upon him. Even in this field, therefore, the analyst must take into account whatever influences may adversely govern the market price, as well as those which bear upon the basic safety of the issue.

In that portion of the analyst's activities which relates to the discovery of undervalued, and possibly of overvalued securities, he is more directly concerned with market prices. For here the vindication of his judgment must be found largely in the ultimate market action of the issue. This field of analytical work may be said to rest upon a twofold assumption: first, that the market price is frequently out of line with the true value; and, second, that there is an inherent tendency for these disparities to correct themselves. As to the truth of the former statement, there can be very little doubt—even though Wall Street often speaks glibly of the "infallible judgment of the market" and asserts that "a stock is worth what you can sell it for—neither more nor less."

The Hazard of Tardy Adjustment of Price Value. The second assumption is equally true in theory, but its working out in practice is often most unsatisfactory. Undervaluations caused by neglect or prejudice may persist for an inconveniently long time, and the same applies to inflated prices caused by overenthusiasm or artificial stimulants. The particular danger to the analyst is that, because of such delay, new determining factors may supervene before the market price adjusts itself to the value as he found it. In other words, by the time the price finally does reflect the value, this value may have changed considerably and the facts and reasoning on which his decision was based may no longer be applicable.

The analyst must seek to guard himself against this danger as best he can: in part, by dealing with those situations preferably which are not subject to sudden change; in part, by favoring securities in which the popular interest is keen enough to promise a fairly swift response to value elements which he is the first to recognize; in part, by tempering his activities to the general financial situation—laying more emphasis on the discovery of undervalued securities when business and market conditions are on a fairly even keel, and proceeding with greater caution in times of abnormal stress and uncertainty.

The Relationship of Intrinsic Value to Market Price. The general question of the relation of intrinsic value to the market quotation may be made clearer by the following chart, which traces the various steps culminating in the market price. It will be evident from the chart that the influence of what we call analytical factors over the market price is both *partial* and *indirect*—partial, because it frequently competes with purely speculative factors which influence the price in the opposite direction; and indirect, because it acts through the intermediary of people's sentiments and decisions. In other words, the market is not a *weighing machine*, on which the value of each issue is recorded by an exact and impersonal mechanism, in accordance with its specific qualities. Rather should we say that the market is a *voting machine*, whereon countless individuals register choices which are the product partly of reason and partly of emotion.

RELATIONSHIP OF INTRINSIC VALUE FACTORS TO MARKET PRICE

I. *General market factors.*

II. *Individual factors.*

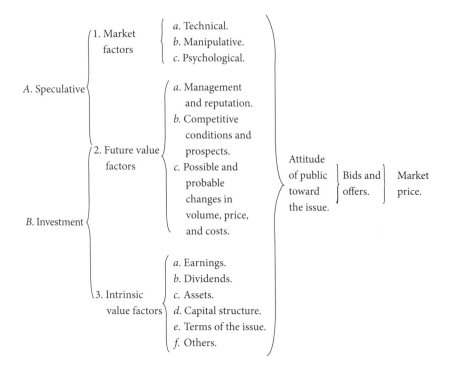

ANALYSIS AND SPECULATION

It may be thought that sound analysis should produce successful results in any type of situation, including the confessedly speculative, *i.e.*, those subject to substantial uncertainty and risk. If the selection of speculative issues is based on expert study of the companies' position, should not this approach give the purchaser a considerable advantage? Admitting future events to be uncertain, could not the favorable and unfavorable developments be counted on to cancel out against each other, more or less, so that the initial advantage afforded by sound analysis will carry through into an eventual average profit? This is a plausible argument but a deceptive one; and its over-ready acceptance has done much to lead analysts astray. It is worth while, therefore, to detail several valid arguments against placing chief reliance upon analysis in speculative situations.

In the first place, what may be called the mechanics of speculation involves serious handicaps to the speculator, which may outweigh the benefits conferred by analytical study. These disadvantages include the payment of commissions and interest charges, the so-called "turn of the market" (meaning the spread between the bid and asked price), and, most important of all, an inherent tendency for the average loss to exceed the average profit, unless a certain technique of trading is followed, which is opposed to the analytical approach.

The second objection is that the underlying analytical factors in speculative situations are subject to swift and sudden revision. The danger, already referred to, that the intrinsic value may change before the market price reflects that value, is therefore much more serious in speculative than in investment situations. A third difficulty arises from circumstances surrounding the unknown factors, which are necessarily left out of security analysis. Theoretically these unknown factors should have an equal chance of being favorable or unfavorable, and thus they should neutralize each other in the long run. For example, it is often easy to determine by comparative analysis that one company is selling much lower than another in the same field, in relation to earnings, although both apparently have similar prospects. But it may well be that the low price for the apparently attractive issue is due to certain important unfavorable factors which, though not disclosed, are known to those identified with the company—and *vice versa* for the issue seemingly selling above its relative value. In speculative situations, those "on the inside" often have an advantage of this kind which nullifies the premise that good and bad changes in the picture should offset each other, and which loads the dice against the analyst working with some of the facts concealed from him.[3]

The Value of Analysis Diminishes as the Element of Chance Increases.
The final objection is based on more abstract grounds, but, nevertheless, its practical importance is very great. Even if we grant that analysis can give the speculator a mathematical advantage, it does not assure him a profit. His ventures remain hazardous; in any individual case a loss may be taken; and after the operation is concluded, it is difficult to determine whether the analyst's contribution has been a benefit or a

---

[3] See Appendix Note 3, p. 735 on accompanying CD, for the result of a study of the market behavior of "high price-earnings ratio stocks" as compared with "low price-earnings ratio stocks."

detriment. Hence the latter's position in the speculative field is at best uncertain and somewhat lacking in professional dignity. It is as though the analyst and Dame Fortune were playing a duet on the speculative piano, with the fickle goddess calling all the tunes.

By another and less imaginative simile, we might more convincingly show why analysis is inherently better suited to investment than to speculative situation. (In anticipation of a more detailed inquiry in a later chapter, we have assumed throughout this chapter that investment implies expected safety and speculation connotes acknowledged risk.) In Monte Carlo the odds are weighted 19 to 18 in favor of the proprietor of the roulette wheel, so that on the average he wins one dollar out of each 37 wagered by the public. This may suggest the odds against the untrained investor or speculator. Let us assume that, through some equivalent of analysis, a roulette player is able to reverse the odds for a limited number of wagers, so that they are now 18 to 19 in his favor. If he distributes his wagers evenly over all the numbers, then whichever one turns up he is certain to win a moderate amount. This operation may be likened to an investment program based upon sound analysis and carried on under propitious general conditions.

But if the player wagers all his money on a single number, the small odds in his favor are of slight importance compared with the crucial question whether chance will elect the number he has chosen. His "analysis" will enable him to win a little more if he is lucky; it will be of no value when luck is against him. This, in slightly exaggerated form perhaps, describes the position of the analyst dealing with essentially speculative operations. Exactly the same mathematical advantage which practically assures good results in the investment field may prove entirely ineffective where luck is the overshadowing influence.

It would seem prudent, therefore, to consider analysis as an *adjunct* or *auxiliary* rather than as a *guide* in speculation. It is only where chance plays a subordinate role that the analyst can properly speak in an authoritative voice and accept responsibility for the results of his judgments.

3. THE CRITICAL FUNCTION OF SECURITY ANALYSIS

The principles of investment finance and the methods of corporation finance fall necessarily within the province of security analysis. Analytical judgments are reached by applying standards to facts. The analyst is concerned, therefore, with the soundness and practicability of the standards of selection. He is also interested to see that securities, especially bonds and preferred stocks, be issued with adequate protective provisions, and—more important still—that proper methods of enforcement of these covenants be part of accepted financial practice.

It is a matter of great moment to the analyst that the facts be fairly presented, and this means that he must be highly critical of accounting methods. Finally, he must concern himself with all corporate policies affecting the security owner, for the value of the issue which he analyzes may be largely dependent upon the acts of the management. In this category are included questions of capitalization set-up, of dividend and expansion policies, of managerial compensation, and even of continuing or liquidating an unprofitable business.

On these matters of varied import, security analysis may be competent to express critical judgments, looking to the avoidance of mistakes, to the correction of abuses, and to the better protection of those owning bonds or stocks.

Chapter 2

FUNDAMENTAL ELEMENTS IN THE PROBLEM OF ANALYSIS. QUANTITATIVE AND QUALITATIVE FACTORS

IN THE PREVIOUS chapter we referred to some of the concepts and materials of analysis from the standpoint of their bearing on what the analyst may hope to accomplish. Let us now imagine the analyst at work and ask what are the broad considerations which govern his approach to a particular problem, and also what should be his general attitude toward the various kinds of information with which he has to deal.

FOUR FUNDAMENTAL ELEMENTS

The object of security analysis is to answer, or assist in answering, certain questions of a very practical nature. Of these, perhaps the most customary are the following: What securities should be bought for a given purpose? Should issue S be bought, or sold, or retained?

In all such questions, four major factors may be said to enter, either expressly or by implication. These are:

1. The security.
2. The price.
3. The time.
4. The person.

More completely stated, the second typical question would run, Should security S be bought (or sold, or retained) at price P, at this time T, by individual I? Some discussion of the relative significance of these four factors is therefore pertinent, and we shall find it convenient to consider them in inverse order.

The Personal Element. The personal element enters to a greater or lesser extent into every security purchase. The aspect of chief importance is usually the financial position of the intending buyer. What might be an attractive speculation for a business man should under no circumstances be attempted by a trustee or a widow with limited income. Again, United States Liberty $3^{1}/_{2}$s should not have been purchased by those to whom their complete tax-exemption feature was of no benefit, when a considerably higher yield could be obtained from partially taxable governmental issues.[1]

Other personal characteristics that on occasion might properly influence the individual's choice of securities are his financial training and competence, his temperament, and his preferences. But however vital these considerations may prove at times, they are not ordinarily determining factors in analysis. Most of the conclusions derived from analysis can be stated in impersonal terms, as applicable to investors or speculators as a class.

The Time. The time at which an issue is analyzed may affect the conclusion in various ways. The company's showing may be better, or its outlook may seem better, at one time than another, and these changing circumstances are bound to exert a varying influence on the analyst's viewpoint toward the issue. Furthermore, securities are selected by the application of standards of quality and yield, and both of these—particularly the latter—will vary with financial conditions in general. A railroad bond of highest grade yielding 5% seemed attractive in June 1931 because the average return on this type of bond was 4.32%. But the same offering made six months later would have been quite unattractive, for in the meantime bond prices had fallen severely and the yield on this group had increased to 5.86%. Finally, nearly all security commitments are influenced to some extent by the current view of the financial and business outlook. In speculative operations these considerations are of controlling importance; and while conservative investment is ordinarily supposed to disregard these elements, in times of stress and uncertainty they may not be ignored.

Security analysis, as a study, must necessarily concern itself as much as possible with principles and methods which are valid at all times—or, at least, under all ordinary conditions. It should be kept in mind,

---

[1] In 1927 the yield on these $3^{1}/_{2}$s was 3.39%, while U. S. Liberty $4^{1}/_{4}$s, due about the same time, were yielding 4.08%.

however, that the practical applications of analysis are made against a background largely colored by the changing times.

The Price. The price is an integral part of every complete judgment relating to securities. In the selection of prime investment bonds, the price is usually a subordinate factor, not because it is a matter of indifference but because in actual practice the price is rarely unreasonably high. Hence almost entire emphasis is placed on the question whether the issue is adequately secured. But in a special case, such as the purchase of high-grade *convertible* bonds, the price may be a factor fully as important as the degree of security. This point is illustrated by the American Telephone and Telegraph Company Convertible $4^1/2$s, due 1939, which sold above 200 in 1929. The fact that principal (at par) and interest were safe beyond question did not prevent the issue from being an extremely risky purchase *at that price*—one which in fact was followed by the loss of over half its market value.[2]

In the field of common stocks, the necessity of taking price into account is more compelling, because the danger of paying the wrong price is almost as great as that of buying the wrong issue. We shall point out later that the new-era theory of investment left price out of the reckoning, and that this omission was productive of most disastrous consequences.

The Security: Character of the Enterprise and the Terms of the Commitment. The roles played by the security and its price in an investment decision may be set forth more clearly if we restate the problem in somewhat different form. Instead of asking, (1) In what security? and (2) At what price? let us ask, (1) In what enterprise? and (2) On what terms is the commitment proposed? This gives us a more comprehensive and evenly balanced contrast between two basic elements in analysis. By the *terms* of the investment or speculation, we mean not only the price but also the provisions of the issue and its status or showing at the time.

---

[2] Annual price ranges for American Telephone and Telegraph Company Convertible $4^1/2$s, due in 1939, were as follows:

Year	High	Low
1929	227	118
1930	$193^3/8$	116
1931	135	95

Example of Commitment on Unattractive Terms. An investment in the soundest type of enterprise may be made on unsound and unfavorable terms. Prior to 1929 the value of urban real estate had tended to grow steadily over a long period of years; hence it came to be regarded by many as the "safest" medium of investment. But the purchase of a preferred stock in a New York City real estate development in 1929 might have involved *terms* of investment so thoroughly disadvantageous as to banish all elements of soundness from the proposition. One such stock offering could be summarized as follows[3]:

1. *Provisions of the Issue.* A preferred stock, ranking junior to a large first mortgage and without unqualified rights to dividend or principal payments. It ranked ahead of a common stock which represented no cash investment so that the common stockholders had nothing to lose and a great deal to gain, while the preferred stockholders had everything to lose and only a small share in the possible gain.

2. *Status of the Issue.* A commitment in a new building, constructed at an exceedingly high level of costs, with no reserves or junior capital to fall back upon in case of trouble.

3. *Price of the Issue.* At par the dividend return was 6%, which was much less than the yield obtainable on real-estate second mortgages having many other advantages over this preferred stock.[4]

Example of a Commitment on Attractive Terms. We have only to examine electric power and light financing in recent years to find countless examples of unsound securities in a fundamentally attractive industry. By way of contrast let us cite the case of Brooklyn Union

---

[3] The financing method described is that used by the separate owning corporations organized and sponsored by the Fred F. French Company and affiliated enterprises, with the exception of some of the later Tudor City units in the financing of which interest-bearing notes, convertible par for par into preferred stock at the option of the company, were substituted for the preferred stock in the financial plan. See *The French Plan* (10th ed., December 1928) published and distributed by the Fred F. French Investing Company, Inc. See also *Moody's Manual;* "Banks and Finance," 1933, pp. 1703–1707.

[4] The real-estate enterprise from which this example is taken gave a bonus of common stock with the preferred shares. The common stock had no immediate value, but it did have a potential value which, *under favorable conditions*, might have made the purchase profitable. From the investment standpoint, however, the preferred stock of this enterprise was subject to all of the objections which we have detailed. Needless to say, purchasers of these issues fared very badly in nearly every case.

Elevated Railroad First 5s, due 1950, which sold in 1932 at 60 to yield 9.85% to maturity. They are an obligation of the Brooklyn-Manhattan Transit System. The traction, or electric railway, industry has long been unfavorably regarded, chiefly because of automobile competition but also on account of regulation and fare-contract difficulties. Hence this security represents a comparatively unattractive *type* of enterprise. Yet the *terms* of the investment here might well make it a satisfactory commitment, as shown by the following:

1. *Provisions of the Issue.* By contract between the operating company and the City of New York, this was a first charge on the earnings of the combined subway and elevated lines of the system, both company and city owned, representing an investment enormously greater than the size of this issue.

2. *Status of the Issue.* Apart from the very exceptional specific protection just described, the bonds were obligations of a company with stable and apparently fully adequate earning power.

3. *Price of Issue.* It could be purchased to yield somewhat more than the Brooklyn-Manhattan Transit Corporation 6s, due 1968, which occupied a subordinate position. (At the low price of 68 for the latter issue in 1932, its yield was 9% against 9.85% for the Brooklyn Union Elevated 5s.[5])

Relative Importance of the Terms of the Commitment and the Character of the Enterprise.
Our distinction between the character of the enterprise and the terms of the commitment suggests a question as to which element is the more important. Is it better to invest in an attractive enterprise on unattractive terms or in an unattractive enterprise on attractive terms? The popular view unhesitatingly prefers the former alternative, and in so doing it is instinctively, rather than logically, right. Over a long period, experience will undoubtedly show that less money has been lost by the great body of investors through paying too high a price for securities of the best regarded enterprises than by trying to secure a larger income or profit from commitments in enterprises of lower grade.

---

[5] By 1936 the price of the Brooklyn Union Elevated 5s had advanced to 115$^{1}/_{2}$. After 1937 the earnings of the B.M.T. declined, and the price of this issue fell to 59. In the purchase of the system by New York City in 1940, however, the strong position of this issue was recognized, and its price recovered again to 92.

From the standpoint of analysis, however, this empirical result does not dispose of the matter. It merely exemplifies a rule that is applicable to all kinds of merchandise, *viz.*, that the *untrained buyer* fares best by purchasing goods of the highest reputation, even though he may pay a comparatively high price. But, needless to say, this is not a rule to guide the expert merchandise buyer, for he is expected to judge quality by examination and not solely by reputation, and at times he may even sacrifice certain definite degrees of quality if that which he obtains is adequate for his purpose and attractive in price. This distinction applies as well to the purchase of securities as to buying paints or watches. It results in two principles of quite opposite character, the one suitable for the untrained investor, the other useful only to the analyst.

1. Principle for the untrained security buyer: *Do not put money in a low-grade enterprise on any terms.*
2. Principle for the securities analyst: *Nearly every issue might conceivably be cheap in one price range and dear in another.*

We have criticized the placing of exclusive emphasis on the choice of the enterprise on the ground that it often leads to paying too high a price for a good security. A second objection is that the enterprise itself may prove to be unwisely chosen. It is natural and proper to prefer a business which is large and well managed, has a good record, and is expected to show increasing earnings in the future. But these expectations, though seemingly well-founded, often fail to be realized. Many of the leading enterprises of yesterday are today far back in the ranks. Tomorrow is likely to tell a similar story. The most impressive illustration is afforded by the persistent decline in the relative investment position of the railroads as a class during the past two decades. The standing of an enterprise is in part a matter of fact and in part a matter of opinion. During recent years investment opinion has proved extraordinarily volatile and undependable. In 1929 Westinghouse Electric and Manufacturing Company was quite universally considered as enjoying an unusually favorable industrial position. Two years later the stock sold for much less than the net current assets alone, presumably indicating widespread doubt as to its ability to earn *any* profit in the future. Great Atlantic and Pacific Tea Company, viewed as little short of a miraculous enterprise in 1929, declined from 494 in that year to 36 in 1938. At the latter date the common sold for less than its cash assets, the preferred being amply covered by other current assets.

These considerations do not gainsay the principle that untrained investors should confine themselves to the best regarded enterprises. It should be realized, however, that this preference is enjoined upon them because of the greater risk for them in other directions, and not because the most popular issues are necessarily the safest. The analyst must pay respectful attention to the judgment of the market place and to the enterprises which it strongly favors, but he must retain an independent and critical viewpoint. Nor should he hesitate to condemn the popular and espouse the unpopular when reasons sufficiently weighty and convincing are at hand.

QUALITATIVE AND QUANTITATIVE FACTORS IN ANALYSIS

Analyzing a security involves an analysis of the business. Such a study could be carried to an unlimited degree of detail; hence practical judgment must be exercised to determine how far the process should go. The circumstances will naturally have a bearing on this point. A buyer of a $1,000 bond would not deem it worth his while to make as thorough an analysis of an issue as would a large insurance company considering the purchase of a $500,000 block. The latter's study would still be less detailed than that made by the originating bankers. Or, from another angle, a less intensive analysis should be needed in selecting a high-grade bond yielding 3% than in trying to find a well-secured issue yielding 6% or an *unquestioned bargain* in the field of common stocks.

Technique and Extent of Analysis Should Be Limited by Character and Purposes of the Commitment. The equipment of the analyst must include a sense of proportion in the use of his technique. In choosing and dealing with the materials of analysis he must consider not only inherent importance and dependability but also the question of accessibility and convenience. He must not be misled by the availability of a mass of data—*e.g.*, in the reports of the railroads to the Interstate Commerce Commission—into making elaborate studies of nonessentials. On the other hand, he must frequently resign himself to the lack of significant information because it can be secured only by expenditure of more effort than he can spare or the problem will justify. This would be true frequently of some of the elements involved in a complete "business analysis"—as, for example, the extent to which an enterprise is dependent upon patent protection or geographical advantages or favorable labor conditions which may not endure.

Value of Data Varies with Type of Enterprise. Most important of all, the analyst must recognize that the value of a particular kind of data varies greatly with the type of enterprise which is being studied. The five-year record of gross or net earnings of a railroad or a large chain-store enterprise may afford, if not a conclusive, at least a reasonably sound basis for measuring the safety of the senior issues and the attractiveness of the common shares. But the same statistics supplied by one of the smaller oil-producing companies may well prove more deceptive than useful, since they are chiefly the resultant of two factors, *viz.*, price received and production, both of which are likely to be radically different in the future than in the past.

Quantitative vs. Qualitative Elements in Analysis. It is convenient at times to classify the elements entering into an analysis under two headings: the quantitative and the qualitative. The former might be called the company's statistical exhibit. Included in it would be all the useful items in the income account and balance sheet, together with such additional specific data as may be provided with respect to production and unit prices, costs, capacity, unfilled orders, etc. These various items may be subclassified under the headings: (1) capitalization, (2) earnings and dividends, (3) assets and liabilities, and (4) operating statistics.

The qualitative factors, on the other hand, deal with such matters as the nature of the business; the relative position of the individual company in the industry; its physical, geographical, and operating characteristics; the character of the management; and, finally, the outlook for the unit, for the industry, and for business in general. Questions of this sort are not dealt with ordinarily in the company's reports. The analyst must look for their answers to miscellaneous sources of information of greatly varying dependability—including a large admixture of mere opinion.

Broadly speaking, the quantitative factors lend themselves far better to thoroughgoing analysis than do the qualitative factors. The former are fewer in number, more easily obtainable, and much better suited to the forming of definite and dependable conclusions. Furthermore the financial results will themselves epitomize many of the qualitative elements, so that a detailed study of the latter may not add much of importance to the picture. The typical analysis of a security—as made, say, in a brokerage-house circular or in a report issued by a statistical service—will treat the qualitative factors in a superficial or summary fashion and devote most of its space to the figures.

Qualitative Factors: Nature of the Business and Its Future Prospects. The qualitative factors upon which most stress is laid are the nature of the business and the character of the management. These elements are exceedingly important, but they are also exceedingly difficult to deal with intelligently. Let us consider, first, the nature of the business, in which concept is included the general idea of its future prospects. Most people have fairly definite notions as to what is "a good business" and what is not. These views are based partly on the financial results, partly on knowledge of specific conditions in the industry, and partly also on surmise or bias.

During most of the period of general prosperity between 1923 and 1929, quite a number of major industries were backward. These included cigars, coal, cotton goods, fertilizers, leather, lumber, meat packing, paper, shipping, street railways, sugar, woolen goods. The underlying cause was usually either the development of competitive products or services (*e.g.,* coal, cotton goods, tractions) or excessive production and demoralizing trade practices (*e.g.,* paper, lumber, sugar). During the same period other industries were far more prosperous than the average. Among these were can manufacturers, chain stores, cigarette producers, motion pictures, public utilities. The chief cause of these superior showings might be found in unusual growth of demand (cigarettes, motion pictures) or in absence or control of competition (public utilities, can makers) or in the ability to win business from other agencies (chain stores).

It is natural to assume that industries which have fared worse than the average are "unfavorably situated" and therefore to be avoided. The converse would be assumed, of course, for those with superior records. But this conclusion may often prove quite erroneous. Abnormally good or abnormally bad conditions do not last forever. This is true not only of general business but of particular industries as well. Corrective forces are often set in motion which tend to restore profits where they have disappeared, or to reduce them where they are excessive in relation to capital.

Industries especially favored by a developing demand may become demoralized through a still more rapid growth of supply. This has been true of radio, aviation, electric refrigeration, bus transportation, and silk hosiery. In 1922 department stores were very favorably regarded because of their excellent showing in the 1920–1921 depression; but they did not maintain this advantage in subsequent years. The public utilities were unpopular in the 1919 boom, because of high costs; they became speculative and investment favorites in 1927–1929; in 1933–1938 fear of inflation, rate regulation, and direct governmental competition again undermined the public's confidence in them. In 1933, on the other hand, the cotton-goods industry—long depressed—forged ahead faster than most others.

The Factor of Management. Our appreciation of the importance of selecting a "good industry" must be tempered by a realization that this is by no means so easy as it sounds. Somewhat the same difficulty is met with in endeavoring to select an unusually capable management. Objective tests of managerial ability are few and far from scientific. In most cases the investor must rely upon a reputation which may or may not be deserved. The most convincing proof of capable management lies in a superior comparative record over a period of time. But this brings us back to the quantitative data.

There is a strong tendency in the stock market to value the management factor twice in its calculations. Stock prices reflect the large earnings which the good management has produced, *plus* a substantial increment for "good management" considered separately. This amounts to "counting the same trick twice," and it proves a frequent cause of overvaluation.

The Trend of Future Earnings. In recent years increasing importance has been laid upon the *trend of earnings*. Needless to say, a record of increasing profits is a favorable sign. Financial theory has gone further, however, and has sought to estimate future earnings by projecting the past trend into the future and then used this projection as a basis for valuing the business. Because figures are used in this process, people mistakenly believe that it is "mathematically sound." But while a trend shown in the past is a fact, a "future trend" is only an assumption. The factors that we mentioned previously as militating against the maintenance of abnormal prosperity or depression are equally opposed to the indefinite continuance of an upward or downward trend. By the time the trend has become clearly noticeable, conditions may well be ripe for a change.

It may be objected that as far as the future is concerned it is just as logical to expect a past trend to be maintained as to expect a past average to be repeated. This is probably true, but it does not follow that the trend is more useful to analysis than the individual or average figures of the past. For security analysis does not assume that a past average will be repeated, but only that it supplies a *rough index* to what may be expected of the future. A trend, however, cannot be used as a rough index; it represents a definite prediction of either better or poorer results, and it must be either right or wrong.

This distinction, important in its bearing on the attitude of the analyst, may be made clearer by the use of examples. Let us assume that in 1929 a railroad showed its interest charges earned three times on the average during the preceding seven years. The analyst would have ascribed great weight to this point as an indication that its bonds were sound. This is a judgment based on quantitative data and standards. But it does not imply a prediction that the earnings in the next seven years will average three times interest charges; it suggests only that earnings are not likely to fall so much under three times interest charges as to endanger the bonds. In nearly every actual case such a conclusion would have proved correct, despite the economic collapse that ensued.

Now let us consider a similar judgment based primarily upon the trend. In 1929 nearly all public-utility systems showed a continued growth of earnings, but the fixed charges of many were so heavy—by reason of pyramidal capital structures—that they consumed nearly all the net income. Investors bought bonds of these systems freely on the theory that the small margin of safety was no drawback, since earnings were certain to continue to increase. They were thus making a clear-cut prediction as to the future, upon the correctness of which depended the justification of their investment. If their prediction were wrong—as proved to be the case—they were bound to suffer serious loss.

Trend Essentially a Qualitative Factor. In our discussion of the valuation of common stocks, later in this book, we shall point out that the placing of preponderant emphasis on the trend is likely to result in errors of overvaluation or undervaluation. This is true because no limit may be fixed on how far ahead the trend should be projected; and therefore the process of valuation, while seemingly mathematical, is in reality psychological and quite arbitrary. For this reason we consider the trend as a *qualitative* factor in its practical implications, even though it may be stated in quantitative terms.

Qualitative Factors Resist Even Reasonably Accurate Appraisal.

The trend is, in fact, a statement of future prospects in the form of an exact prediction. In similar fashion, conclusions as to the nature of the business and the abilities of the management have their chief significance in their bearing on the outlook. These qualitative factors are therefore all of the same general character. They all involve the same basic difficulty for the analyst, *viz.*, that it is impossible to judge how far they may properly reflect themselves in the price of a given security. In most cases, if they are recognized at all, they tend to be overemphasized. We see the same influence constantly at work in the general market. The recurrent excesses of its advances and declines are due at bottom to the fact that, when values are determined chiefly by the outlook, the resultant judgments are not subject to any mathematical controls and are almost inevitably carried to extremes.

Analysis is concerned primarily with values which are supported by the facts and not with those which depend largely upon expectations. In this respect the analyst's approach is diametrically opposed to that of the speculator, meaning thereby one whose success turns upon his ability to forecast or to guess future developments. Needless to say, the analyst must take possible future changes into account, but his primary aim is not so much to *profit* from them as to *guard against* them. Broadly speaking, he views the business future as a hazard which his conclusions must encounter rather than as the source of his vindication.

Inherent Stability a Major Qualitative Factor.

It follows that the qualitative factor in which the analyst should properly be most interested is that of *inherent stability*. For stability means resistance to change and hence greater dependability for the results shown in the past. Stability, like the trend, may be expressed in quantitative terms—as, for example, by stating that the earnings of General Baking Company during 1923–1932 were never less than ten times 1932 interest charges or that the operating profits of Woolworth between 1924 and 1933 varied only between $2.12 and $3.66 per share of common. But in our opinion stability is really a qualitative trait, because it derives in the first instance from the character of the business and not from its statistical record. A stable record suggests that the business is inherently stable, but this suggestion may be rebutted by other considerations.

Examples: This point may be brought out by a comparison of two preferred-stock issues as of early 1932, *viz.,* those of Studebaker (motors) and of First National (grocery) Stores, both of which were selling above par. The two exhibits were similar, in that both disclosed a continuously satisfactory margin above preferred-dividend requirements. The Studebaker figures were more impressive, however, as the following table will indicate:

NUMBER OF TIMES PREFERRED DIVIDEND WAS COVERED

First National Stores		Studebaker	
Period	Times covered	Calendar year	Times covered
Calendar year, 1922	4.0	1922	27.3
Calendar year, 1923	5.1	1923	30.5
Calendar year, 1924	4.9	1924	23.4
Calendar year, 1925	5.7	1925	29.7
15 mos. ended Mar. 31, 1927	4.6	1926	24.8
Year ended Mar. 31, 1928	4.4	1927	23.0
Year ended Mar. 31, 1929	8.4	1928	27.3
Year ended Mar. 31, 1930	13.4	1929	23.3
Annual average	6.3		26.2

But the analyst must penetrate beyond the mere figures and consider the inherent character of the two businesses. The chain-store grocery trade contained within itself many elements of relative stability, such as stable demand, diversified locations, and rapid inventory turnover. A typical large unit in this field, provided only it abstained from reckless expansion policies, was not likely to suffer tremendous fluctuations in its earnings. But the situation of the typical automobile manufacturer was quite different. Despite fair stability in the industry as a whole, the individual units were subject to extraordinary variations, due chiefly to the vagaries of popular preference. The stability of Studebaker's earnings could not be held by any convincing logic to demonstrate that this company enjoyed a special and permanent immunity from the vicissitudes to which most of its competitors had shown themselves subject. The soundness of Studebaker Preferred rested, therefore, largely upon a stable statistical showing which was at variance with the general character of the industry, so far as its individual units were concerned. On the other hand, the satisfactory exhibit of First National Stores Preferred was in thorough accord with what was generally thought to be the inherent character of the business. The later consideration should have carried great weight with the analyst and should have made First National Stores Preferred appear intrinsically sounder as a fixed-value investment than Studebaker Preferred, despite the more impressive *statistical* showing of the automobile company.[6]

Summary. To sum up this discussion of qualitative and quantitative factors, we may express the dictum that the analyst's conclusions must always rest upon the figures and upon established tests and standards. These figures alone are not *sufficient;* they may be completely vitiated by qualitative considerations of an opposite import. A security may make a satisfactory statistical showing, but doubt as to the future or distrust of the management may properly impel its rejection. Again, the analyst is likely to attach prime importance to the qualitative element of *stability,* because its presence means that conclusions based on past results are not so likely to be upset by unexpected developments. It is also true that he will be far more confident in his selection of an issue if he can buttress an adequate quantitative exhibit with unusually favorable qualitative factors.

But whenever the commitment depends to a substantial degree upon these qualitative factors—whenever, that is, the price is considerably higher than the figures alone would justify—then the analytical basis of approval is lacking. In the mathematical phrase, a satisfactory statistical exhibit is a *necessary* though by no means a *sufficient condition* for a favorable decision by the analyst.

---

[6] First National Stores has since maintained its earning power with little change; the preferred stock was redeemed in 1934 and subsequently. Studebaker's earnings fell off sharply after 1930; a receiver was appointed in 1933; and the preferred stock lost nearly all its value.

Chapter 3

SOURCES OF INFORMATION

IT IS IMPOSSIBLE to discuss or even to list all the sources of information which the analyst may find it profitable to consult at one time or another in his work. In this chapter we shall present a concise outline of the more important sources, together with some critical observations thereon; and we shall also endeavor to convey, by means of examples, an idea of the character and utility of the large variety of special avenues of information.

DATA ON THE TERMS OF THE ISSUE

Let us assume that in the typical case the analyst seeks data regarding: (1) the terms of the specific issue, (2) the company, and (3) the industry. The provisions of the issue itself are summarized in the security manuals or statistical services. For more detailed information regarding a bond contract the analyst should consult the indenture (or deed of trust), a copy of which may be obtained or inspected at the office of the trustee. The terms of the respective stock issues of a company are set forth fully in the charter (or articles of incorporation), together with the by-laws. If the stock is listed, these documents are on file with the S.E.C. and also with the proper stock exchange. In the case of both bonds and stocks, the listing applications—which are readily obtainable—contain nearly all the significant provisions. Prospectuses of new issues also contain these provisions.

DATA ON THE COMPANY

Reports to Stockholders (Including Interim News Releases). Coming now to the *company*, the chief source of statistical data is, of course, the reports issued to the stockholders. These reports vary widely with respect to both frequency and completeness, as the following summary will show:

All important railroads supply *monthly* figures down to net after rentals (net railway operating income). Most carry the results down to the balance for dividends (net income). Many publish carloading figures *weekly*, and a few have published gross earnings weekly. The pamphlet annual reports publish financial and operating figures in considerable detail.[1]

The ruling policy of public-utility companies varies between *quarterly* and *monthly* statements. Figures regularly include gross, net after taxes, and balance for dividends. Some companies publish only a moving twelve-month total—*e.g.*, American Water Works and Electric Company (monthly), North American Company (quarterly). Many supply *weekly* or *monthly* figures of kilowatt-hours sold.

Industrials. The practices followed by industrial companies are usually a matter of individual policy. In some industrial groups there is a tendency for most of the companies therein to follow the same course.

1. *Monthly Statements.* Most chain stores announce their monthly sales in dollars. Prior to 1931, copper producers regularly published their monthly output. General Motors publishes monthly sales in units.

Between 1902 and 1933, United States Steel Corporation published its unfilled orders each month, but in 1933 it replaced this figure by monthly deliveries in tons. Baldwin Locomotive Works has published monthly figures of shipments, new orders, and unfilled orders in dollars. The "Standard Oil Group" of pipeline companies publish monthly statistics of operations in barrels.

Monthly figures of net earnings are published by individual companies from time to time, but such practices have tended to be sporadic or temporary (*e.g.*, Otis Steel, Mullins Manufacturing, Alaska Juneau).[2] There is a tendency to inaugurate monthly statements during periods of improvement and to discontinue them with earnings decline. Sometimes figures by months are included in the quarterly statements—*e.g.*, United States Steel Corporation prior to 1932.

---

[1] Some railroads now send all stockholders a condensed annual statement but offer to send a more comprehensive report on request.

[2] The Alaska Juneau figures—somewhat abbreviated—have continued from about 1925 to the end of 1939. In 1938 Caterpillar Tractor began to publish monthly a complete income account and a balance sheet. This is not really so extraordinary, for most companies supply these data to their directors.

2. *Quarterly Statements.* Publication of results quarterly is considered as the standard procedure in nearly all lines of industry. The New York Stock Exchange has been urging quarterly reports with increasing vigor and has usually been able to make its demands effective in connection with the listing of new or additional securities. Certain types of businesses are considered—or consider themselves—exempt from this requirement, because of the seasonal nature of their results. These lines include sugar production, fertilizers, and agricultural implements. Seasonal fluctuations may be concealed by publishing quarterly a moving twelve-months' figure of earnings. This is done by Continental Can Company.[3]

It is not easy to understand why all the large cigarette manufacturers and the majority of department stores should withhold their results for a full year. It is inconsistent also for a company such as Woolworth to publish sales monthly but no interim statements of net profits. Many individual companies, belonging to practically every division of industry, still fail to publish quarterly reports. In nearly every case such interim figures are available to the management but are denied to the stockholders without adequate reason.

The data given in the quarterly statements vary from a single figure of net earnings (sometimes without allowance for depreciation or federal taxes) to a fully detailed presentation of the income account and the balance sheet, with president's remarks appended. General Motors Corporation is an outstanding example of the latter practice.

3. *Semiannual Reports.* These do not appear to be standard practice for any industrial group, except possibly the rubber companies. A number of individual enterprises report semiannually—*e.g.*, American Locomotive and American Woolen.

4. *Annual Reports.* Every listed company publishes an annual report of some kind. The annual statement is generally more detailed than those covering interim periods. It frequently contains remarks—not always illuminating—by the president or the chairman of the board, relating to the past year's results and to the future outlook. The distinguishing feature of the annual report, however, is that it invariably presents the balance-sheet position.

---

[3] In March 1936 the New York Stock Exchange suggested that all listed companies follow this procedure instead of publishing the usual quarterly earnings. This suggestion aroused great opposition and was withdrawn the next month.

The information given in the income account varies considerably in extent. Some reports give no more than the earnings available for dividends and the amount of dividends paid, *e.g.*, United States Leather Company.[4]

The Income Account. In our opinion an annual income account is not reasonably complete unless it contains the following items: (1) sales, (2) net earnings (before the items following), (3) depreciation (and depletion), (4) interest charges, (5) nonoperating income (in detail), (6) income taxes, (7) dividends paid, (8) surplus adjustments (in detail).

Prior to the passage of the Securities and Exchange Act it was unfortunately true that less than half of our industrial corporations supplied this very moderate quota of information. (By contrast, data relative to railroads and public utilities have long been uniformly adequate.) The S.E.C. regulations now require virtually all this information to be published in the original registration statement (Form 10) and the succeeding annual reports (Form 10-K). Quite a number of companies have requested the S.E.C. to keep their sales figures confidential, on the ground that publication would be detrimental to the enterprise. Most of these requests have been either withdrawn or denied.[5]

---

[4] Pocohantas Fuel Company appears to have been the only enterprise that, although listed on the New York Stock Exchange, published an annual balance sheet only and provided no income statement of any kind. Its bonds were removed from listing in October 1934.

The New York Curb dealings include a number of so called "unlisted issues"—dating from pre-S.E.C. days—which are not subject to requirements of the S.E.C. Among these are companies like American Book, which does not publish an income account, and New Jersey Zinc, which publishes an income account but no balance sheet.

Companies whose issues are dealt in "over-the-counter," and are thus not subject to S.E.C. regulation, generally publish annual reports only. They tend to be less detailed than the statements of listed companies, being especially prone to omit sales and depreciation figures. The great majority supply both a balance sheet and income account, but exceptions are fairly numerous. An amusing example is Dun & Bradstreet Corporation. This purveyor of financial information does not reveal its own earnings to its stockholders. Other companies omitting income accounts are Bemis Brothers' Bag, Joseph Dixon Crucible (since 1935), Glenwood Range, Goodman Manufacturing, Perfection Stove, Regal Shoe, etc.

[5] A few companies, *e.g.*, Celanese Corporation of America, succeeded in obtaining a confidential status for their sales figures in certain years prior to 1938. In some, possibly most, of the cases later requests were denied, and sales figures were subsequently published.

Our study of the 1938 reports of practically all the industrial companies listed on the New York Stock Exchange (648 enterprises) disclosed that only eight had failed to reveal their sales figures by the end of the following year. The S.E.C. advised that confidential treatment of the sales figure had been granted to one company (United Fruit) and that no

The standard of *reasonable completeness* for annual reports, suggested above, by no means includes all the information which might be vouchsafed to shareholders. The reports of United States Steel Corporation may be taken as a model of comprehensiveness. The data there supplied embrace, in addition to our standard requirements, the following items:

1. Production and sales in units. Rate of capacity operated.
2. Division of sales as between:
   Domestic and foreign.
   Intercompany and outsiders.
3. Details of operating expenses:
   Wages, wage rates, and number of employees.
   State and local taxes paid.
   Selling and general expense.
   Maintenance expenditures, amount and details.
4. Details of capital expenditures during the year.
5. Details of inventories.
6. Details of properties owned.
7. Number of stockholders.

The Balance Sheet. The form of the balance sheet is better standardized than the income account, and it does not offer such frequent grounds for criticism. Formerly a widespread defect of balance sheets was the failure to separate intangible from tangible fixed assets, but this is now quite rare in the case of listed issues. (Among the companies that since 1935 have disclosed the amount of good-will formerly included in their property accounts are American Steel Foundries, American Can, Harbison

---

decision had been reached with respect to the other seven (American Sumatra Tobacco, Bon Ami, Collins & Aikman, Mathieson Alkali, Mesta Machine, Sheaffer Pen, United Engineering and Foundry), as late as December 1939.

Various issues, *e.g.*, Trico Products Corporation, failed to register and were dropped from listing, presumably because of their unwillingness to supply sales figures. The withdrawal of Marlin Rockwell Corporation from listing in 1938 may be ascribed to the same reason. The stock exchanges have favored an amendment to the law requiring full disclosure in the case of over-the-counter issues, to remove what they regard as an unfair advantage.

Many companies still provide their stockholders in their annual reports with much less information than they file with the S.E.C. The Standard Statistics *Corporation Records Service*, however, regularly publishes the S.E.C. figures as supplementary data.

Walker Refractories, Loose-Wiles Biscuit, and United States Steel. In nearly all these cases the good-will was written off against surplus.)

Criticism may properly be voiced against the practice of a great many companies in stating only the *net* figure for their property account without showing the deduction for depreciation. Other shortcomings sometimes met are the failure to state the market value of securities owned—*e.g.*, Oppenheim Collins and Company in 1932; to identify "investments" as marketable or nonliquid—*e.g.*, Pittsburgh Plate Glass Company; to value the inventory at lower of cost or market—*e.g.*, Celanese Corporation of America in 1931; to state the nature of miscellaneous reserves—*e.g.*, Hazel-Atlas Glass Company; and to state the amount of the company's own securities held in the treasury—*e.g.*, American Arch Company.[6]

Periodic Reports to Public Agencies. Railroads and most public utilities are required to supply information to various federal and state commissions. Since these data are generally more detailed than the statements to shareholders, they afford a useful supplementary source of material. A few practical illustrations of the value of these reports to commissions may be of interest.

For many years prior to 1927 Consolidated Gas Company of New York (now Consolidated Edison Company of New York) was a "mystery stock" in Wall Street because it supplied very little information to its stockholders. Great emphasis was laid by speculators upon the undisclosed value of its interest in its numerous subsidiary companies. However, complete operating and financial data relating to both the company and its subsidiaries were at all times available in the annual reports of the Public Service Commission of New York. The same situation pertained over a long period with respect to the Mackay Companies, controlling Postal Telegraph and Cable Corporation, which reported no details to its stockholders but considerable information to the Interstate Commerce Commission. A similar contrast exists between the unilluminating reports of Fifth Avenue Bus Securities Company to its shareholders and the complete

---

[6] Several of these points were involved in a protracted dispute between the New York Stock Exchange and Allied Chemical and Dye Corporation, which was terminated to the satisfaction of the Stock Exchange in 1933. But the annual reports of the company to shareholders are still inadequate in that they fail to furnish figures for sales, operating expenses, or depreciation.

information filed by its operating subsidiary with the New York Transit Commission.

Finally, we may mention the "Standard Oil Group" of pipeline companies, which have been extremely chary of information to their stockholders. But these companies come under the jurisdiction of the Interstate Commerce Commission and are required to file circumstantial annual reports at Washington. Examination of these reports several years ago would have disclosed striking facts about these companies' holdings of cash and marketable securities.

The voluminous data contained in the *Survey of Current Business*, published monthly by the United States Department of Commerce, have included sales figures for individual chain-store companies which were not given general publicity—*e.g.*, Waldorf System, J. R. Thompson, United Cigar Stores, Hartman Corporation, etc. Current statistical information regarding particular companies is often available in trade publications or services.

Examples: Cram's Auto Service gives weekly figures of production for each motor-car company. Willett and Gray publish several estimates of sugar production by companies during the crop year. The *Oil and Gas Journal* often carries data regarding the production of important fields by companies. The *Railway Age* supplies detailed information regarding equipment orders placed. Dow, Jones and Company estimate weekly the rate of production of United States Steel.

Listing Applications. In pre-S.E.C. days these were the most important nonperiodic sources of information. The reports required by the New York Stock Exchange, as a condition to admitting securities to its list, are much more detailed than those usually submitted to the stockholders. The additional data may include sales in dollars, output in units, amount of federal taxes, details of subsidiaries' operations, basis and amount of depreciation and depletion charges. Valuable information may also be supplied regarding the properties owned, the terms of contracts, and the accounting methods followed.

The analyst will find these listing applications exceedingly helpful. It is unfortunate that they appear at irregular intervals, and therefore cannot be counted upon as a steady source of information.

Registration Statements and Prospectuses. As a result of the S.E.C. legislation and regulations, the information available regarding all listed securities and all *new* securities (whether listed or not) is much more comprehensive than heretofore. These data are contained in registration statements filed with the Commission in Washington and available for inspection or obtainable in copy upon payment of a fee. The more important information in the registration statement must be included in the prospectus supplied by the underwriters to intending purchasers of new issues. Similar registration statements must be filed with the S.E.C. under the terms of the Public Utility Act of 1935, which applies to holding companies, some of which might not come under the other legislation. Although it is true that the registration statements are undoubtedly too bulky to be read by the typical investor, and although it is doubtful if he is even careful to digest the material in the abbreviated prospectus (which still may cover more than 100 pages), there is no doubt that this material is proving of the greatest value to the analyst and through him to the investing public.

Miscellaneous Official Reports. Information on individual companies may be unearthed in various kinds of official documents. A few examples will give an idea of their miscellaneous character. The report of the United States Coal Commission in 1923 (finally printed as a Senate Document in 1925) gave financial and operating data on the anthracite companies which had not previously been published. Reports of the Federal Trade Commission have recently supplied a wealth of information heretofore not available concerning utility operating and holding companies, and natural-gas and pipe-line companies, unearthed in an elaborate investigation extending over a period of about nine years. In 1938 and 1939 the Commission published detailed reports on the farm implement and automobile manufacturers. In 1933 a comprehensive study of the pipe-line companies was published under the direction of the House Committee on Interstate and Foreign Commerce. Voluminous studies of the American Telephone and Telegraph System have emanated from the investigation carried on by the Federal Communications Commission pursuant to a Congressional resolution adopted in 1935.[7] Some

[7] These reports have been published respectively as Sen. Doc. 92, pts. 1–84D, 70th Congress, 1st Session (1928–1937); House Doc. 702, pts. 1 and 2, 75th Congress, 3d Session (1938); House Doc. 468, 76th Congress, 1st Session (1939); House Report No. 2192, pts. 1 and 2, 72d Congress, 2d Session (1933); House Doc. 340, 76th Congress, 1st Session (1939), together with supplementary reports mentioned on pp. 609–611 thereof; and Proposed Report, Telephone Investigation Pursuant to Public Resolution No. 8, 74th Congress (1938).

of the opinions of the Interstate Commerce Commission have contained material of great value to the analyst. Trustees under mortgages may have information required to be supplied by the terms of the indenture. These figures may be significant. For example, unpublished reports with the trustee of Mason City and Fort Dodge Railroad Company 4s, revealed that the interest on the bonds was not being earned, that payment thereof was being continued by Chicago Great Western Railroad Company as a matter of policy only, and hence that the bonds were in a far more vulnerable position than was generally suspected.

Statistical and Financial Publications. Most of the information required by the securities analyst in his daily work may be found conveniently and adequately presented by the various statistical services. These include comprehensive manuals published annually with periodic supplements (Poor's, Moody's); descriptive stock and bond cards, and manuals frequently revised (Standard & Poor's, Fitch); daily digests of news relating to individual companies (Standard Corporation Records, Fitch).[8] These services have made great progress during the past 20 years in the completeness and accuracy with which they present the facts. Nevertheless they cannot be relied upon to give all the data available in the various original sources above described. Some of these sources escape them completely, and in other cases they may neglect to reproduce items of importance. It follows therefore that in any thoroughgoing study of an individual company, the analyst should consult the original reports and other documents wherever possible, and not rely upon summaries or transcriptions.

In the field of financial periodicals, special mention must be made of *The Commercial and Financial Chronicle*, a weekly publication with numerous statistical supplements. Its treatment of the financial and industrial field is unusually comprehensive; and its most noteworthy feature is perhaps its detailed reproduction of corporate reports and other documents.

Requests for Direct Information from the Company. Published information may often be supplemented to an important extent by private inquiry of or by interview with the management. There is no reason why stockholders should not ask for information on specific points, and

---

[8] During 1941 Poor's Publishing Company and Standard Statistics Company merged into Standard & Poor's Corp. The separate Poor's services have been discontinued.

in many cases part at least of the data asked for will be furnished. It must never be forgotten that a stockholder is an *owner* of the business and an *employer* of its officers. He is entitled not only to ask legitimate questions but also to have them answered, unless there is some persuasive reason to the contrary.

Insufficient attention has been paid to this all-important point. The courts have generally held that a bona fide stockholder has the same right to full information as a partner in a private business. This right may not be exercised to the detriment of the corporation, but the burden of proof rests upon the management to show an improper motive behind the request or that disclosure of the information would work an injury to the business.

Compelling a company to supply information involves expensive legal proceedings and hence few shareholders are in a position to assert their rights to the limit. Experience shows, however, that vigorous demands for legitimate information are frequently acceded to even by the most recalcitrant managements. This is particularly true when the information asked for is no more than that which is regularly published by other companies in the same field.

INFORMATION REGARDING THE INDUSTRY

Statistical data respecting industries as a whole are available in abundance. The *Survey of Current Business*, published by the United States Department of Commerce, gives monthly figures on output, consumption, stocks, unfilled orders, etc., for many different lines. Annual data are contained in the Statistical Abstract, the World Almanac, and other compendiums. More detailed figures are available in the Biennial Census of Manufactures.

Many important summary figures are published at frequent intervals in the various trade journals. In these publications will be found also a continuous and detailed picture of the current and prospective state of the industry. Thus it is usually possible for the analyst to acquire without undue difficulty a background of fairly complete knowledge of the history and problems of the industry with which he is dealing.

In recent years the leading statistical agencies have developed additional services containing basic surveys of the principal industrial groups, supplemented frequently by current data designed to keep the basic surveys up to date.[9]

---

[9] For description of these services see *Handbook of Commercial and Financial Services*, Special Libraries Association, New York, 1939.

Chapter 4

DISTINCTIONS BETWEEN INVESTMENT AND SPECULATION

General Connotations of the Term "Investment." Investment or investing, like "value" in the famous dictum of Justice Brandeis, is "a word of many meanings." Of these, three will concern us here. The first meaning, or set of meanings, relates to putting or having money in a business. A man "invests" $1,000 in opening a grocery store; the "return on investment" in the steel industry (including bonded debt and retained profits) averaged 2.40% during 1929–1938.[1] The sense here is purely descriptive; it makes no distinctions and pronounces no judgments. Note, however, that it accepts rather than rejects the element of risk—the ordinary business investment is said to be made "at the risk of the business."

The second set of uses applies the term in a similar manner to the field of finance. In this sense all securities are "investments." We have investment dealers or brokers, investment companies[2] or trusts, investment lists. Here, again, no real distinction is made between investment and other types of financial operations such as speculation. It is a convenient omnibus word, with perhaps an admixture of euphemism—*i.e.*, a desire to lend a certain respectability to financial dealings of miscellaneous character.

Alongside of these two indiscriminate uses of the term "investment" has always been a third and more limited connotation—that of investment as opposed to speculation. That such a distinction is a useful one

---

[1] *Dollars behind Steel*, pamphlet of American Iron and Steel Institute, New York, 1939.

[2] Note that in October 1939 the S.E.C. listed under the title of "Investment Company" the offering of stock of "The Adventure Company, Ltd.," a new enterprise promoted by "The Discovery Company, Ltd." The fact that 1¢ par value stock was offered at $10 per share, although not really significant, has a certain appropriateness.

is generally taken for granted. It is commonly thought that investment, in this special sense, is good for everybody and at all times. Speculation, on the other hand, may be good or bad, depending on the conditions and the person who speculates. It should be essential, therefore, for anyone engaging in financial operations to know whether he is investing or speculating and, if the latter, to make sure that his speculation is a justifiable one.

The difference between investment and speculation, when the two are thus opposed, is understood in a general way by nearly everyone; but when we try to formulate it precisely, we run into perplexing difficulties. In fact something can be said for the cynic's definition that an investment is a successful speculation and a speculation is an unsuccessful investment. It might be taken for granted that United States government securities are an investment medium, while the common stock, say, of Radio Corporation of America—which between 1931 and 1935 had neither dividends, earnings, nor tangible assets behind it—must certainly be a speculation. Yet operations of a definitely speculative nature may be carried on in United States government bonds (*e.g.*, by specialists who buy large blocks in anticipation of a quick rise); and on the other hand, in 1929 Radio Corporation of America common was widely regarded as an investment, to the extent in fact of being included in the portfolios of leading "Investment Trusts."

It is certainly desirable that some exact and acceptable definition of the two terms be arrived at, if only because we ought as far as possible to know what we are talking about. A more forceful reason, perhaps, might be the statement that the failure properly to distinguish between investment and speculation was in large measure responsible for the market excesses of 1928–1929 and the calamities that ensued—as well as, we think, for much continuing confusion in the ideas and policies of would-be investors. On this account we shall give the question a more thorough-going study than it usually receives. The best procedure might be first to examine critically the various meanings commonly intended in using the two expressions, and then to endeavor to crystallize therefrom a single sound and definite conception of investment.

Distinctions Commonly Drawn between the Two Terms. The chief distinctions in common use may be listed in the following table:

Investment	Speculation
1. In bonds.	In stocks.
2. Outright purchases.	Purchases on margin.
3. For permanent holding.	For a "quick turn."
4. For income.	For profit.
5. In safe securities.	In risky issues.

The first four distinctions have the advantage of being entirely definite, and each of them also sets forth a characteristic which is applicable to the *general run* of investment or speculation. They are all open to the objection that in numerous individual cases the criterion suggested would not properly apply.

1. Bonds vs. Stocks. Taking up the first distinction, we find it corresponds to a common idea of investing as opposed to speculating, and that it also has the weight of at least one authority on investment who insists that only bonds belong in that category.[3] The latter contention, however, runs counter to the well-nigh universal acceptance of high-grade preferred stocks as media of investment. Furthermore, it is most dangerous to regard the bond form as possessing inherently the credentials of an investment, for a poorly secured bond may not only be thoroughly speculative but the most unattractive form of speculation as well. It is logically unsound, furthermore, to deny investment rating to a strongly entrenched common stock merely because it possesses profit possibilities. Even the popular view recognizes this fact, since at all times certain especially sound common stocks have been rated as investment issues and their purchasers regarded as investors and not as speculators.

2 and 3. Outright vs. Marginal Purchases; Permanent vs. Temporary Holding. The second and third distinctions relate to the customary *method* and *intention*, rather than to the innate character of investment and speculative operations. It should be obvious that buying a stock outright does not *ipso facto* make the transaction an investment.

---

[3] Lawrence Chamberlain at p. 8 of *Investment and Speculation* by Chamberlain and William W. Hay, New York, 1931.

In truth the most speculative issues, *e.g.*, "penny mining stocks," *must* be purchased outright, since no one will lend money against them. Conversely, when the American public was urged during the war to buy Liberty Bonds with borrowed money, such purchases were nonetheless universally classed as investments. If strict logic were followed in financial operations—a very improbable hypothesis!—the common practice would be reversed: the safer (investment) issues would be considered more suitable for marginal purchase, and the riskier (speculative) commitments would be paid for in full.

Similarly the contrast between permanent and temporary holding is applicable only in a broad and inexact fashion. An authority on common stocks has defined an investment as any purchase made with the intention of holding it for a year or longer; but this definition is admittedly suggested by its convenience rather than its penetration.[4] The inexactness of this suggested rule is shown by the circumstance that *short-term investment* is a well-established practice. *Long-term speculation* is equally well established as a rueful fact (when the purchaser holds on hoping to make up a loss), and it is also carried on to some extent as an intentional undertaking.

4 and 5. Income vs. Profit; Safety vs. Risk. The fourth and fifth distinctions also belong together, and so joined they undoubtedly come closer than the others to both a rational and a popular understanding of the subject. Certainly, through many years prior to 1928, the typical investor had been interested above all in safety of principal and continuance of an adequate income. However, the doctrine that common stocks are the best long-term investments has resulted in a transfer of emphasis from current income to future income and hence inevitably to future enhancement of principal value. In its complete subordination of the income element to the desire for profit, and also in the prime reliance it places upon favorable developments expected in the future, the new-era style of investment—as exemplified in the general policy of the investment trusts—is practically indistinguishable from speculation. In fact this so-called "investment" can be accurately defined as speculation in the common stocks of strongly situated companies.

---

[4] Sloan, Laurence H., *Everyman and His Common Stocks*, pp. 8–9, 279 *ff.*, New York, 1931.

It would undoubtedly be a wholesome step to go back to the accepted idea of income as the central motive in investment, leaving the aim toward profit, or capital appreciation, as the typical characteristic of speculation. But it is doubtful whether the true inwardness of investment rests even in this distinction. Examining standard practices of the past, we find some instances in which current income was not the leading interest of a bona fide investment operation. This was regularly true, for example, of bank stocks, which until recent years were regarded as the exclusive province of the wealthy investor. These issues returned a smaller dividend yield than did high-grade bonds, but they were purchased on the expectation that the steady growth in earnings and surplus would result in special distributions and increased principal value. In other words, it was the earnings accruing to the stockholder's credit, rather than those distributed in dividends, which motivated his purchase. Yet it would not appear to be sound to call this attitude speculative, for we should then have to contend that only the bank stocks which paid out most of their earnings in dividends (and thus gave an adequate current return) could be regarded as investments, while those following the conservative policy of building up their surplus would therefore have to be considered speculative. Such a conclusion is obviously paradoxical; and because of this fact it must be admitted that an investment in a common stock might conceivably be founded on its earning power, without reference to current dividend payments.

Does this bring us back to the new-era theory of investment? Must we say that the purchase of low-yielding industrial shares in 1929 had the same right to be called investment as the purchase of low-yielding bank stocks in prewar days? The answer to this question should bring us to the end of our quest, but to deal with it properly we must turn our attention to the fifth and last distinction in our list—that between safety and risk.

This distinction expresses the broadest concept of all those underlying the term *investment*, but its practical utility is handicapped by various shortcomings. If safety is to be judged by the result, we are virtually begging the question, and come perilously close to the cynic's definition of an investment as a successful speculation.[5] Naturally the safety must be posited in advance, but here again there is room for much that is indefinite and

---

[5] For a *serious* suggestion along these lines see Felix I. Shaffner, *The Problem of Investment*, pp. 18–19, New York, 1936.

purely subjective. The race-track gambler, betting on a "sure thing," is convinced that his commitment is safe. The 1929 "investor" in high-priced common stocks also considered himself safe in his reliance upon future growth to justify the figure he paid and more.

Standards of Safety. The concept of safety can be really useful only if it is based on something more tangible than the psychology of the purchaser. The safety must be assured, or at least strongly indicated, by the application of definite and well-established standards. It was this point which distinguished the bank-stock buyer of 1912 from the common-stock investor of 1929. The former purchased at price levels which he considered conservative in the light of experience; he was satisfied, from his knowledge of the institution's resources and earning power, that he was getting his money's worth in full. If a strong speculative market resulted in advancing the price to a level out of line with these standards of value, he sold his shares and waited for a reasonable price to return before reacquiring them.

Had the same attitude been taken by the purchaser of common stocks in 1928–1929, the term *investment* would not have been the tragic misnomer that it was. But in proudly applying the designation "blue chips" to the high-priced issues chiefly favored, the public unconsciously revealed the gambling motive at the heart of its supposed investment selections. These differed from the old-time bank-stock purchases in the one vital respect that the buyer did not determine that they were worth the price paid by the application of firmly established standards of value. The market made up new standards as it went along, by accepting the current price—however high—as the sole measure of value. Any idea of safety based on this uncritical approach was clearly illusory and replete with danger. Carried to its logical extreme, it meant that no price could possibly be too high for a good stock, and that such an issue was equally "safe" after it had advanced to 200 as it had been at 25.

A Proposed Definition of Investment. This comparison suggests that it is not enough to identify investment with expected safety; the expectation must be based on study and standards. At the same time, the investor need not necessarily be interested in current income; he may at times legitimately base his purchase on a return which is accumulating to his credit and realized by him after a longer or shorter wait. With these observations in mind, we suggest the following definition of investment as one in harmony with both the popular understanding of the term and the requirements of reasonable precision:

> *An investment operation is one which, upon thorough analysis, promises safety of principal and a satisfactory return. Operations not meeting these requirements are speculative.*

Certain implications of this definition are worthy of further discussion. We speak of an *investment operation* rather than an issue or a purchase, for several reasons. It is unsound to think always of investment character as inhering in an issue *per se*. The price is frequently an essential element, so that a stock (and even a bond) may have investment merit at one price level but not at another. Furthermore, an investment might be justified in a group of issues, which would not be sufficiently safe if made in any one of them singly. In other words, diversification might be necessary to reduce the risk involved in the separate issues to the minimum consonant with the requirements of investment. (This would be true, in general, of purchases of common stocks for investment.)

In our view it is also proper to consider as investment operations certain types of arbitrage and hedging commitments which involve the sale of one security against the purchase of another. In these operations the element of safety is provided by the combination of purchase and sale. This is an extension of the ordinary concept of investment, but one which appears to the writers to be entirely logical.

The phrases *thorough analysis, promises safety*, and *satisfactory return* are all chargeable with indefiniteness, but the important point is that their meaning is clear enough to prevent serious misunderstanding. By *thorough analysis* we mean, of course, the study of the facts in the light of established standards of safety and value. An "analysis" that recommended investment in General Electric common at a price forty times its highest recorded earnings merely because of its excellent prospects would be clearly ruled out, as devoid of all quality of thoroughness.

The *safety* sought in investment is not absolute or complete; the word means, rather, protection against loss under all normal or reasonably likely conditions or variations. A safe bond, for example, is one which could suffer default only under exceptional and highly improbable circumstances. Similarly, a safe stock is one which holds every prospect of being worth the price paid except under quite unlikely contingencies.

Where study and experience indicate that an appreciable chance of loss must be recognized and allowed for, we have a speculative situation.

A *satisfactory return* is a wider expression than *adequate income*, since it allows for capital appreciation or profit as well as current interest or dividend yield. "Satisfactory" is a subjective term; it covers any rate or amount of return, however low, which the investor is willing to accept, provided he acts with reasonable intelligence.

It may be helpful to elaborate our definition from a somewhat different angle, which will stress the fact that investment must always consider the *price* as well as the *quality* of the security. Strictly speaking, there can be no such thing as an "investment issue" in the absolute sense, *i.e.*, implying that it remains an investment regardless of price. In the case of high-grade bonds, this point may not be important, for it is rare that their prices are so inflated as to introduce serious risk of loss of principal. But in the common-stock field this risk may frequently be created by an undue advance in price—so much so, indeed, that in our opinion the great majority of common stocks of strong companies must be considered speculative during most of the time, simply because their price is too high to warrant safety of principal in any intelligible sense of the phrase. We must warn the reader that prevailing Wall Street opinion does not agree with us on this point; and he must make up his own mind which of us is wrong.

Nevertheless, we shall embody our principle in the following additional criterion of investment:

> *An investment operation is one that can be justified on* both *qualitative and quantitative grounds.*

The extent to which the distinction between investment and speculation may depend upon the underlying facts, including the element of price, rather than on any easy generalization, may be brought home in somewhat extreme fashion by two contrasting examples based upon General Electric Special (*i.e.*, Preferred) stock, which occurred in successive months.

Example 1: In December 1934 this issue sold at 12³/₄. It paid 6% on $10 par and was callable on any dividend date at 11. In spite of the pre-eminent quality of this issue, as far as safety of dividends was concerned, the buyer at 12³/₄ was *speculating* to the extent of more than 10% of his principal. He was virtually wagering that the issue would not be called for some years to come.[6] As it happened, the issue was called that very month for redemption at $11 per share on April 15, 1935.

Example 2: After the issue was called, the price promptly declined to 11. At that time the issue offered an unusual opportunity for profitable *short-term investment on margin.* Brokers buying the shares at 11 (without paying commission), say on January 15, 1935, could have borrowed $10 per share thereon at not more than 2% per annum. This operation would have netted a sure return at the rate of 40% per annum on the capital invested—as shown by the following calculation:

Cost of 1,000 shares at 11 net..$11,000
Redeemed Apr. 15, 1935, at 11 plus dividend.....................................11,150
  Gross profit 150
Less 3 months' interest at 2% on $10,000...50
  Net profit...100

Net profit of $100 on $1,000 in 3 months is equivalent to annual return of 40%.

Needless to say, the safety, and the resultant *investment* character, of this unusual operation derived solely from the fact that the holder could count absolutely on the redemption of the shares in April 1935.

The conception of investment advanced above is broader than most of those in common use. Under it investment may conceivably—though not usually—be made in stocks, carried on margin, and purchased with the chief interest in a quick profit. In these respects it would run counter to the first four distinctions which we listed at the outset. But to offset this seeming laxity, we insist on a satisfactory assurance of safety based on adequate analysis. We are thus led to the conclusion that the viewpoint of analysis and the viewpoint of investment are largely identical in their scope.

---

[6] In recent years many United States Government short-term securities have been purchased at prices yielding less than nothing to maturity in the expectation that the holders would be given valuable exchange privileges into new issues. According to our definition all such purchases must be called speculative to the extent of the premium paid above par and interest to maturity.

OTHER ASPECTS OF INVESTMENT
AND SPECULATION

Relation of the Future to Investment and Speculation. It may be said, with some approximation to the truth, that investment is grounded on the past whereas speculation looks primarily to the future. But this statement is far from complete. Both investment and speculation must meet the test of the future; they are subject to its vicissitudes and are judged by its verdict. But what we have said about the analyst and the future applies equally well to the concept of investment. For investment, the future is essentially something to be guarded against rather than to be profited from. If the future brings improvement, so much the better; but investment as such cannot be founded in any important degree upon the expectation of improvement. Speculation, on the other hand, may always properly—and often soundly—derive its basis and its justification from prospective developments that differ from past performance.

Types of "Investment." Assuming that the student has acquired a fairly clear concept of investment in the distinctive sense that we have just developed, there remains the confusing effect of the prevalent use of the term in the broader meanings referred to at the beginning of this chapter. It might be useful if some descriptive adjective were regularly employed, when care is needed, to designate the particular meaning intended. Let us tentatively suggest the following:

1. Business investment	Referring to money put or held in a business.
2. Financial investment or investment generally	Referring to securities generally.
3. Sheltered investment	Referring to securities regarded as subject to small risk by reason of their prior claim on earnings or because they rest upon an adequate taxing power.
4. Analyst's investment	Referring to operations that, upon thorough study, promise safety of principal and an adequate return.

Evidently these different types of investment are not mutually exclusive. A good bond, for example, would fall under all four headings. Unless we specify otherwise, we shall employ the word "investment," and its relatives, in the sense of "analyst's investment," as developed in this chapter.

Types of Speculation. The distinction between speculation and gambling assumes significance when the activities of Wall Street are subjected to critical scrutiny. It is more or less the official position of the New York Stock Exchange that "gambling" represents the creation of risks not previously existing—*e.g.*, race-track betting—whereas "speculation" applies to the taking of risks that are implicit in a situation and so must be taken by someone. A formal distinction between "intelligent speculation" and "unintelligent speculation" is no doubt open to strong theoretical objections, but we do think that it has practical utility. Thus we suggest the following:

1. Intelligent speculation	The taking of a risk that appears justified after careful weighing of the pros and cons.
2. Unintelligent speculation	Risk taking without adequate study of the situation.

In the field of general business most well-considered enterprises would belong in the class of intelligent speculations as well as representing "business investments" in the popular sense. If the risk of loss is very small—an exceptional occurrence—a particular business venture may qualify as an analyst's investment in our special sense. On the other hand, many ill-conceived businesses must be called unintelligent speculations. Similarly, in the field of finance, a great deal of common-stock buying is done with reasonable care and may be called intelligent speculation; a great deal, also, is done upon inadequate consideration and for unsound reasons and thus must be called unintelligent; in the exceptional case a common stock may be bought on such attractive terms, qualitative and quantitative, as to set the inherent risk at a minimum and justify the title of analyst's investment.

Investment and Speculative Components. A proposed purchase that cannot qualify as an "analyst's investment" automatically falls into the speculative category. But at times it may be useful to view such a purchase somewhat differently and to divide the price paid into an investment and a speculative component. Thus the analyst, considering General Electric common at its average price of $38 in 1939, might conclude that up to, say, $25 per share is justified from the strict standpoint of investment value. The remaining $13 per share will represent the stock market's average appraisal of the company's excellent long-term prospects, including therein, perhaps, a rather strong psychological bias in favor of this outstanding enterprise. On the basis of such a study, the analyst would declare that the price of $38 for General Electric includes an investment component of some $25 per share and a speculative component of about $13 per share. If this is sound, it would follow that at a price of 25 or less, General Electric common would constitute an "analyst's investment" completely; but above that price the buyer should recognize that he is paying something for the company's very real speculative possibilities.[7]

Investment Value, Speculative Value, and Intrinsic Value. The foregoing discussion suggests an amplification of what was said in Chap. 1 on the concept of "intrinsic value," which was there defined as "value justified by the facts." It is important to recognize that such value is by no means limited to "value for investment"—*i.e.*, to the investment component of total value—but may properly include a substantial component of speculative value, provided that such speculative value is intelligently arrived at. Hence the market price may be said to exceed intrinsic value only when the market price is clearly the reflection of unintelligent speculation.

Generally speaking, it is the function of the stock market, and not of the analyst, to appraise the speculative factors in a given common-stock picture. To this important extent the market, not the analyst, determines intrinsic value. The range of such an appraisal may be very wide, as illustrated by our former suggestion that the intrinsic value of J. I. Case common in 1933 might conceivably have been as high as 130 or as low as 30. At any point between these broad limits it would have been necessary to accept the market's verdict—changeable as it was from day to day—as representing the best available determination of the intrinsic value of this volatile issue.

---

[7] We have intentionally, and at the risk of future regret, used an example here of a highly controversial character. Nearly everyone in Wall Street would regard General Electric stock as an "investment issue" irrespective of its market price and, more specifically, would consider the average price of $38 as amply justified from the investment standpoint. But we are convinced that to regard investment quality as something independent of price is a fundamental and dangerous error. As to the point at which the investment value of General Electric ceases and its speculative value begins, there is naturally room for a fairly wide difference of opinion. Our figure is only illustrative.

Chapter 5

CLASSIFICATION OF SECURITIES

SECURITIES ARE CUSTOMARILY divided into the two main groups of bonds and stocks, with the latter subdivided into preferred stocks and common stocks. The first and basic division recognizes and conforms to the fundamental legal distinction between the creditors' position and the partners' position. The bondholder has a fixed and prior claim for principal and interest; the stockholder assumes the major risks and shares in the profits of ownership. It follows that a higher degree of safety should inhere in bonds as a class, while greater opportunity of speculative gain—to offset the greater hazard—is to be found in the field of stocks. It is this contrast, of both legal status and investment character, as between the two kinds of issues, which provides the point of departure for the usual textbook treatment of securities.

Objections to the Conventional Grouping: 1. Preferred Stock Grouped with Common. While this approach is hallowed by tradition, it is open to several serious objections. Of these the most obvious is that it places preferred stocks with common stocks, whereas, so far as investment practice is concerned, the former undoubtedly belong with bonds. The typical or standard preferred stock is bought for fixed income and safety of principal. Its owner considers himself not as a partner in the business but as the holder of a claim ranking ahead of the interest of the partners, *i.e.*, the common stockholders. Preferred stockholders are partners or owners of the business only in a technical, legalistic sense; but they resemble bondholders in the purpose and expected results of their investment.

2. Bond Form Identified with Safety. A weightier though less patent objection to the radical separation of bonds from stocks is that it tends to identify the *bond form* with the idea of safety. Hence investors are led to believe that the very name "bond" must carry some especial assurance against loss. This attitude is basically unsound, and on frequent occasions is responsible for serious mistakes and loss. The investor has been spared even greater penalties for this error by the rather accidental fact that fraudulent security promoters have rarely taken advantage of the investment prestige attaching to the bond form.[1] It is true beyond dispute that bonds as a whole enjoy a degree of safety distinctly superior to that of the average stock. But this advantage is not the result of any essential virtue of the bond form; it follows from the circumstance that the typical American enterprise is financed with some honesty and intelligence and does not assume fixed obligations without a reasonable expectation of being able to meet them. But it is not the obligation that creates the safety, nor is it the legal remedies of the bondholder in the event of default. *Safety depends upon and is measured entirely by the ability of the debtor corporation to meet its obligations.*

The bond of a business without assets or earning power would be every whit as valueless as the stock of such an enterprise. Bonds representing all the capital placed in a new venture are no safer than common stock would be, and are considerably less attractive. For the bondholder could not possibly get more out of the company by virtue of his fixed claim than he could realize if he owned the business in full, free and clear.[2] This simple principle seems too obvious to merit statement; yet because of the traditional association of the bond form with superior safety, the investor has often been persuaded that by the mere act of limiting his return he obtained an assurance against loss.

3. Failure of Titles to Describe Issues with Accuracy. The basic classification of securities into bonds and stocks—or even into three main classes of bonds, preferred stocks, and common stocks—is open to the third objection that in many cases these titles fail to supply an accurate description of the issue. This is the consequence of the steadily mounting

---

[1] For an example of fraudulent sales of bonds see Securities Act of 1933: Release No. 2112, dated Dec. 4, 1939, relating to conviction of various parties in connection with the sale of American Terminals and Transit Company bonds and Green River Valley Terminal Company notes.

[2] See Appendix Note 4, p. 736 on accompanying CD, for a phase of the liquidation of the United States Express Company illustrating this point and for the more recent example of Court-Livingston Corporation.

percentage of securities which do not conform to the standard patterns, but instead modify or mingle the customary provisions.

Briefly stated, these standard patterns are as follows:

I. The bond pattern comprises:
   A. The unqualified right to a fixed interest payment on fixed dates.
   B. The unqualified right to repayment of a fixed principal amount on a fixed date.
   C. No further interest in assets or profits, and no voice in the management.
II. The preferred-stock pattern comprises:
   A. A stated rate of dividend in priority to any payment on the common. (Hence full preferred dividends are mandatory if the common receives any dividend; but if nothing is paid on the common, the preferred dividend is subject to the discretion of the directors).
   B. The right to a stated principal amount in the event of dissolution, in priority to any payments to the common stock.
   C. Either no voting rights, or voting power shared with the common.
III. The common-stock pattern comprises:
   A. A pro rata ownership of the company's assets in excess of its debts and preferred stock issues.
   B. A pro rata interest in all profits in excess of prior deductions.
   C. A pro rata vote for the election of directors and for other purposes.

Bonds and preferred stocks conforming to the above standard patterns will sometimes be referred to as *straight bonds* or *straight preferred stocks*.

Numerous Deviations from the Standard Patterns. However, almost every conceivable departure from the standard pattern can be found in greater or less profusion in the security markets of today. Of these the most frequent and important are identified by the following designations: *income* bonds; *convertible* bonds and preferred stocks; bonds and preferred stocks with *stock-purchase warrants* attached; *participating* preferred stocks; common stocks with *preferential features; nonvoting* common stock. Of recent origin is the device of making bond interest or preferred dividends payable either in cash or in common stock at the holder's *option.* The *callable feature* now found in most bonds may also be termed a lesser departure from the standard provision of fixed maturity of principal.

Of less frequent and perhaps unique deviations from the standard patterns, the variety is almost endless.[3] We shall mention here only the glaring instance of Great Northern Railway Preferred Stock which for many years has been in all respects a plain common issue; and also the resort by Associated Gas and Electric Company to the insidious and highly objectionable device of bonds convertible into preferred stock *at the option of the company* which are, therefore, not true bonds at all.

More striking still is the emergence of completely distinctive types of securities so unrelated to the standard bond or stock pattern as to require an entirely different set of names. Of these, the most significant is the option warrant—a device which during the years prior to 1929 developed into a financial instrument of major importance and tremendous mischief-making powers. The option warrants issued by a single company—American and Foreign Power Company—attained in 1929 an aggregate market value of more than a *billion dollars*, a figure exceeding our national debt in 1914. A number of other newfangled security forms, bearing titles such as allotment certificates and dividend participations, could be mentioned.[4]

The peculiarities and complexities to be found in the present day security list are added arguments against the traditional practice of pigeonholing and generalizing about securities in accordance with their *titles*. While this procedure has the merit of convenience and a certain rough validity, we think it should be replaced by a more flexible and accurate basis of classification. In our opinion, the criterion most useful for purposes of study would be the *normal behavior* of the issue after purchase—in other words its risk-and-profit characteristics as the buyer or owner would reasonably view them.

New Classification Suggested. With this standpoint in mind, we suggest that securities be classified under the following three headings:

---

[3] The reader is referred to Appendix Note 3 of the first edition of this work for a comprehensive list of these deviations, with examples of each. To save space that material is omitted from this edition.

[4] In June 1939 the S.E.C. set a salutary precedent by refusing to authorize the issuance of "Capital Income Debentures" in the reorganization of the Griess-Pfleger Tanning Company, on the ground that the devising of new types of hybrid issues had gone far enough. See S.E.C. Corporate Reorganization Release No. 13, dated June 16, 1939. Unfortunately, the court failed to see the matter in the same light and approved the issuance of the new security.

Class	Representative Issue
I. Securities of the fixed-value type.	A high-grade bond or preferred stock.
II. Senior securities of the variable-value type.	
A. Well-protected issues with profit possibilities.	A high-grade convertible bond.
B. Inadequately protected issues.	A lower-grade bond or preferred stock.
III. Common-stock type.	A common stock.

An approximation to the above grouping could be reached by the use of more familiar terms, as follows:

I.   Investment bonds and preferred stocks.
II.   Speculative bonds and preferred stocks.
   A. Convertibles, etc.
   B. Low-grade senior issues.
III.   Common stocks.

The somewhat novel designations that we employ are needed to make our classification more comprehensive. This necessity will be clearer, perhaps, from the following description and discussion of each group.

Leading Characteristics of the Three Types. The first class includes issues, of whatever title, in which prospective change of value may fairly be said to hold minor importance.[5] The owner's dominant interest lies in the safety of his principal and his sole purpose in making the commitment is to obtain a steady income. In the second class, prospective changes in the value of the principal assume real significance. In Type *A*, the investor hopes to obtain the safety of a straight investment, with an added possibility of profit by reason of a conversion right or some similar privilege. In Type *B*, a definite risk of loss is recognized, which is presumably offset

---

[5] The actual fluctuations in the price of long-term investment bonds since 1914 have been so wide (see chart on p. 27) as to suggest that these price changes must surely be of more than minor importance. It is true, nonetheless, that the investor habitually acts as *if* they were of minor importance to him, so that, subjectively at least, our criterion and title are justified. To the objection that this is conniving at self-delusion by the investor, we may answer that on the whole he is likely to fare better by overlooking the price variations of high-grade bonds than by trying to take advantage of them and thus transforming himself into a trader.

by a corresponding chance of profit. Securities included in Group II*B* will differ from the common-stock type (Group III) in two respects: (1) They enjoy an effective priority over some junior issue, thus giving them a certain degree of protection. (2) Their profit possibilities, however substantial, have a fairly definite limit, in contrast with the unlimited percentage of possible gain theoretically or optimistically associated with a fortunate common-stock commitment.

Issues of the fixed-value type include all *straight* bonds and preferred stocks of high quality selling at a normal price. Besides these, there belong in this class:

1. Sound convertible issues where the conversion level is too remote to enter as a factor in the purchase. (Similarly for participating or warrant-bearing senior issues.)
2. Guaranteed common stocks of investment grade.
3. "Class *A*" or prior-common stocks occupying the status of a high-grade, straight preferred stock.

On the other hand, a bond of investment grade which happens to sell at any unduly low price would belong in the second group, since the purchaser might have reason to expect and be interested in an appreciation of its market value.

Exactly at what point the question of price fluctuation becomes material rather than minor is naturally impossible to prescribe. The price level itself is not the sole determining factor. A long-term 3% bond selling at 60 may have belonged in the fixed-value class (*e.g.*, Northern Pacific Railway 3s, due 2047 between 1922 and 1930), whereas a one-year maturity of any coupon rate selling at 80 would *not* because in a comparatively short time it must either be paid off at a 20-point advance or else default and probably suffer a severe decline in market value. We must be prepared, therefore, to find marginal cases where the classification (as between Group I and Group II) will depend on the personal viewpoint of the analyst or investor.

Any issue which displays the main characteristics of a common stock belongs in Group III, whether it is entitled "common stock," "preferred stock" or even "bond." The case, already cited, of American Telephone and Telegraph Company Convertible $4^1/2$s, when selling about 200, provides an apposite example. The buyer or holder of the bond at so high a level was to all practical purposes making a commitment in the common stock, for the bond and stock would not only advance together but also decline together over an exceedingly wide price range. Still more definite illustration of this point was supplied by the Kreuger and Toll Participating Debentures at the time of their sale to the public. The offering price was so far above the amount of their prior claim that their title had no significance at all, and could only have been misleading. *These "bonds" were definitely of the common-stock type.*[6]

The opposite situation is met when issues, senior in name, sell at such low prices that the junior securities can obviously have no real equity, *i.e.,* ownership interest, in the company. In such cases, the low-priced bond or preferred stock stands virtually in the position of a common stock and should be regarded as such for purposes of analysis. A preferred stock selling at 10 cents on the dollar, for example, should be viewed not as a preferred stock at all, but as a common stock. On the one hand it lacks the prime requisite of a senior security, *viz.,* that it should be followed by a junior investment of substantial value. On the other hand, it carries all the profit features of a common stock, since the amount of possible gain from the current level is for all practical purposes unlimited.

The dividing line between Groups II and III is as indefinite as that between Groups I and II. Borderline cases can be handled without undue difficulty however, by considering them from the standpoint of either category or of both. For example, should a 7% preferred stock selling at 30 be considered a low-priced senior issue or as the equivalent of a common stock? The answer to this question will depend partly on the exhibit of the company and partly on the attitude of the prospective buyer. If real value may conceivably exist in excess of the par amount of the preferred stock, the issue may be granted some of the favored status of a senior security. On the other hand, whether or not the buyer should consider it in the same light as a common stock may also depend on whether he would be amply satisfied with a possible 250% appreciation, or is looking for even greater speculative gain.[7]

---

[6] See Appendix Note 5, p. 737 on accompanying CD, for the terms of this issue.

[7] There were many preferred stocks of this kind in 1932—*e.g.,* Interstate Department Stores Preferred which sold at an average price of about 30 in 1932 and 1933 and then advanced to 107 in 1936 and 1937. A similar remark applies to low-priced bonds, such as those mentioned in the table on p. 330.

From the foregoing discussion the real character and purpose of our classification should now be more evident. Its basis is not the title of the issue, but the practical significance of its specific terms and status to the owner. Nor is the primary emphasis placed upon what the owner is legally entitled to demand, but upon what he is likely to get, or is justified in expecting, under conditions which appear to be probable at the time of purchase or analysis.

PART II

FIXED-VALUE INVESTMENTS

UNSHACKLING BONDS

BY HOWARD S. MARKS

M y first exposure to *Security Analysis* came in 1965. As a Wharton undergraduate, I was assigned readings from the masterwork of Benjamin Graham and David Dodd (joined by that time by editor Sidney Cottle).

We're talking about the early days, when a career in investment management mostly meant working for a bank, a trust company, or an insurance company. The first institutional investment boutique that I remember—Jennison Associates—was still a few years away from its founding. Common stock investors referenced the Dow Jones Industrial Average, not the S&P 500, and there was no talk of quartiles or deciles. In fact, it was just a few years earlier, at the University of Chicago's Center for Research in Security Prices, that daily stock prices since 1926 had been digitized, permitting calculation of the 9.2% historic return on equities.

The term "growth stock investing" was relatively new (and in its absence, there was no need for the contrasting term "value investing"). The invention of the hedge fund had yet to be recognized, and I'm not sure the description even existed. No one had ever heard of a venture capital fund, a private equity fund, an index fund, a quant fund, or an emerging market fund. And, interestingly, "famous investor" was largely an oxymoron—the world hadn't yet heard of Warren Buffett, for example, and only a small circle recognized his teacher at Columbia, Ben Graham.

The world of fixed income bore little resemblance to that of today. There was no way to avoid uncertainty regarding the rate at which interest payments could be reinvested because zero-coupon bonds had not been invented. Bonds rated below investment grade couldn't be issued as such, and the fallen angels that were outstanding had yet to be labeled "junk" or "high yield" bonds. Of course, there were no leveraged loans, residential mortgage–backed securities (RMBSs), or collateralized bond, debt, and loan obligations. And today's bond professionals might give some thought to how their predecessors arrived at yields to maturity before the existence of computers, calculators, or Bloomberg terminals.

But I'm lucky to have begun my studies in the mid-1960s because the finance and investment theory I would go on to learn at the University of Chicago Graduate School of Business was new and hadn't yet spread broadly. Thus my college experience did not include exposure to the Efficient Market Hypothesis, which told the next few generations of students of finance that there was no use for *Security Analysis*: a guidebook to the impossible task of beating an inefficient market.

* * *

I learned a lot from this book, which was generally accepted in 1965 as the bible of security analysis. And yet I came away with a negative reaction as well, feeling that it contained too much dogma and too many formulas incorporating numerical constants like "multiply by x" or "count only y years."

My more recent reading of the chapters on fixed income securities in the 1940 edition of *Security Analysis* served to remind me of some of the rules I had found too rigid. But it also showed me the vast wealth of less quantitative and more flexible common sense contained in the book, as well as some of the forward-looking insights.

To my mind, some of the most interesting aspects of the book—and of developments in the investment world over the last several decades—are seen in Graham and Dodd's perspective on the evolution of investment standards.

- At least through 1940, there were well-accepted and very specific standards for what was proper and what was not, especially in fixed income. Rules and attitudes governed the actions of fiduciaries and the things they could and could not do. In this environment, a fiduciary who lost money for his beneficiaries in a nonqualifying investment could be "surcharged"—forced to make good the losses—without reference to how well he did his job overall or whether the whole portfolio made money.
- Then, there was the concept of the "prudent man," based on a nineteenth-century court case. Was this something that a prudent person would do, judged in the light of the circumstances under which the decision was made and in the context of the portfolio as a whole? Thus individual losing investments need not give rise to penalties if the fiduciary's decisions and results were acceptable *in toto*.
- As part of the development of the finance theory that is attributed to the "Chicago School," in the 1950s Harry Markowitz contributed the notion that, based on an understanding of correlation, the addition of a "risky asset" to a portfolio could reduce the portfolio's overall riskiness by increasing its diversification.
- Finally, the ultimate contribution of the Chicago School came through the assertion that the "goodness" of an investment—and of a performance record—had to be evaluated based on the relationship between its risk and its return. A safe investment is not a good investment, and a risky investment is not a bad investment. Good-enough performance prospects can compensate for the riskiness of a risky investment, rendering it attractive and prudent.

Thus, today we see few absolute rules of investing. In fact, it's hard to think of anything that's off-limits, and most investors will do almost anything to make a buck. The 1940 edition of *Security Analysis* marks an interesting turn toward what we would consider very modern thinking—it references some absolute standards but dismisses many others and reflects an advanced attitude toward sensible fixed income investing.

Investment Absolutes

The 1940 edition certainly contains statements that seem definite. Here are some examples:

> Deficient safety cannot be compensated for by an abnormally high coupon rate. The selection of all bonds for investment should be subject to rules of exclusion and to specific quantitative tests. (p. 144)

> If a company's junior bonds are not safe, its first-mortgage bonds are not a desirable fixed-value investment. For if the second mortgage is unsafe the company itself is weak, and generally speaking there can be no high-grade obligations of a weak enterprise. (p. 148)

> Bonds of smaller industrial companies are not well qualified for consideration as fixed-value investments. (p. 161)

When I began to manage high yield bonds in 1978, most institutional portfolios were governed by rules that limited bond holdings to either "investment grade" (triple B or better) or "A or better." Rules like these that put certain securities off-limits to most buyers had the effect of making bargains available to those of us who weren't so restricted. At first glance, Graham and Dodd's proscriptions would seem to be among those rules.

Investment versus Speculation

As I reread the chapters that are the subject of this updating, I came across a number of statements like these, to the effect that some bond is or is not appropriate for investment. No mention of price or yield; just yes or no . . . good or bad. To someone whose career in portfolio management has dealt almost exclusively with speculative-grade assets, this would seem to rule out whole sections of the investment universe. The ideas that potential return can compensate for risk and that the debt of a financially troubled company can get so cheap that it's a screaming buy appear to fight the authors' principles.

Then it dawned on me that Graham and Dodd were saying one thing and I was reading another. They didn't mean that something shouldn't be bought—but rather that it shouldn't be bought, to use their phrase, "on an investment basis." Today people attach the word "investment" to anything purchased for the purpose of financial gain—as opposed to something bought for use or consumption. People invest today in not just stocks and bonds but also in jewelry, vacation-home timeshares, collectibles, and art. But 75 years ago, investing meant the purchase of financial assets that by their intrinsic nature satisfied the requirements of conservatism, prudence, and, above all, safety.

Securities qualified for investment on the basis of quality, not prospective return. They either were eligible for investment or they were not. In the extreme, there were hard-and-fast rules, such as those promulgated by each of the states for its savings banks. In New York, for example, savings banks could buy railroad, gas, and electric bonds but not the bonds of street railway or water companies. Bonds secured by first mortgages on real estate qualified as investments, but—startlingly—industrial bonds did not.

Investments that hewed to the accepted standards were "safe" (and probably litigation-proof for the fiduciary who bought them), while speculating was chancy. It was this rigid, exclusionary, black-and-white attitude toward investment propriety that likely led John Maynard Keynes to his trenchant observation that "a speculator is one who runs risks of which he is aware and an investor is one who runs risks of which he is unaware."

Thus a more modern attitude—and, like Keynes's, well ahead of its time—would be based on the notion that virtually any asset can be a good investment if bought knowledgeably and at a low-enough price. The opposite is also something that I insist is true: there's no asset so good that it can't be a bad investment if bought at too high a price. Everyone now realizes that membership on a list of "acceptable investments" certainly doesn't provide protection against loss. If you don't agree with that statement, try looking for the bonds that were rated AAA a few decades ago or mortgage-backed securities that went from AAA to junk status in 2007.

In *Security Analysis*, the principle is developed and reiterated that "a high coupon rate is not adequate compensation for the assumption of substantial risk of principal." (p. 125 on accompanying CD) This statement would seem to rule out investing in high yield bonds, which has been successfully pursued over the last 30 years with absolute and risk-adjusted returns well above those on investment-grade bonds. A more thorough reading, however, shows that securities that the authors say should not be purchased "on an investment basis" can still be considered "for speculation." Nevertheless, today Graham and Dodd's blanket statement certainly seems doctrinaire—especially in that it implements a distinction that has almost entirely ceased to exist.

The statement that certain assets either are or aren't appropriate for purchase on an investment basis is probably one of the dicta to which I reacted negatively 43 years ago. But now, in this rereading, I was able to see further.

Investment Realism

Over the last four or five decades, the investment world has seen what could be described as the development of a much more pragmatic approach to making money: judging investment merit not on absolute notions of quality and safety but rather on the relationship between expected return and expected risk. Alternatively, of course, this could be described as a lowering of standards; what ever happened to concepts like fiduciary duty and preservation of capital?

Graham and Dodd seem to operate in something of a middle ground. They propound absolute requirements for purchases on an investment basis, but they also admit that apparent quality and safety alone shouldn't be expected to make some things successful investments or rule out others. Here are several examples:

> [Given that fixed income securities lack the upside potential of equities,] the essence of proper bond selection consists, therefore, in obtaining specific and convincing factors of safety in compensation for the surrender of participation in profits. (p. 143)

> The conception of a mortgage lien as a guaranty of protection independent of the success of the business itself is in most cases a complete fallacy. . . . The established practice of stating the original cost or appraised value of the pledged property as an inducement to purchase bonds is entirely misleading. (p. 145)

> The debentures of a strong enterprise are undoubtedly sounder investments than the mortgage issues of a weak company. (p. 148)

> It is clear . . . that the investor who favors the Cudahy first-lien 5s [yielding $5^{1}/_{2}$ versus the junior $5^{1}/_{2}$'s yielding over 20%] is paying a premium of about 15% per annum (the difference in yield) for only a *partial* insurance against loss. On this basis he is undoubtedly giving up too much for what he gets in return. (p. 149)

> [On the other hand,] where the first-mortgage bond yields only slightly less, it is undoubtedly wise to pay the small insurance premium for protection against unexpected trouble. (p. 149)

> [In reviewing bond collapses among railroads between 1931 and 1933,] the fault appears to be that the stability of the transportation industry

was overrated, so that investors were satisfied with a margin of protection which proved insufficient. *It was not a matter of imprudently disregarding old established standards of safety . . . but of being content with old standards when conditions called for more stringent requirements. . . . If [the investor] had required his railroad bonds to meet the same tests that he applied to industrial issues, he would have been compelled to confine his selection to a relatively few of the strongly situated lines. As it turned out, nearly all of these have been able to withstand the tremendous loss of traffic since 1929 without danger to their fixed charges.* (p. 158, emphasis added)

It is clear in these citations and many others that Graham and Dodd are insistent on substance over form, and on logic rather than rules. It's how likely a bond is to pay that matters, not what it is labeled. Credit standards must not be fixed but instead must evolve. Mortgages are not automatically better than unsecured debentures. Safer bonds are not necessarily better buys than their juniors. Superior yield can render riskier issues more attractive.

A thorough reading makes it clear that Graham and Dodd are true investment pragmatists. More echoing Keynes than diverging from him, they argue for thorough analysis followed by intelligent risk bearing (as opposed to knee-jerk risk avoidance).

Our Methodology for Bond Investing

To examine the relevance of *Security Analysis* to fixed income investments, I reviewed Graham and Dodd's process for bond investing, and I compared their approach to the one applied by my firm, Oaktree Capital Management, L.P.

The bottom line is that, while Graham and Dodd's thoughts may be expressed differently, most are highly applicable to today's investment world. In fact, they strongly parallel the approach and methodology developed and applied in the area of high yield bonds over the last 30 years by my partner, Sheldon Stone, and me.

1. *Our entire approach is based on recognition of the asymmetry that underlies all nondistressed bond investing.* Gains are limited to the promised yield plus perhaps a few points of appreciation, while credit losses can cause the disappearance of most or all of one's principal. Thus the key to success lies in avoiding losers, not in searching for winners. As Graham and Dodd note:

   > Instead of associating bonds primarily with the presumption of *safety*—as has long been the practice—it would be sounder to start with what is not presumption but fact, *viz.*, that a (straight) bond is an investment with *limited return.* . . .
   >
   > Our primary conception of the bond as a commitment with limited return leads us to another important viewpoint toward bond investment. Since the chief emphasis must be placed on avoidance of loss, bond selection is primarily a negative art. It is a process of exclusion and rejection, rather than of search and acceptance. (p. 143)

2. *Our high yield bond portfolios are focused.* We work mostly in that part of the curve where healthy yields on B-rated bonds can be earned and where the risk of default is limited. For us, higher-rated bonds don't have enough yield, and lower-rated bonds have too much uncertainty. This B zone is where our clients expect us to operate.

   > It would be sounder procedure to start with minimum standards of safety, which all bonds must be required to meet in order to be eligible for further consideration. Issues failing to meet these minimum requirements should be automatically disqualified as straight investments, regardless of high yield, attractive prospects, or other grounds for partiality. . . . Essentially, bond selection should consist of working upward from definite minimum standards rather than working downward in haphazard fashion from some ideal but unacceptable level of maximum security. (pp. 167–168)

3. *Credit risk stems primarily from the quantum of leverage and the firm's basic instability, the interaction of which in tough times can erode the margin by which interest coverage exceeds debt service requirements.* A company with very stable cash flows can support high leverage and a heavy debt service. By the same token, a company with limited leverage and modest debt service requirements can survive severe fluctuations in its cash flow. But the combination of high leverage and undependable cash flow can result in a failure to service debt, as investors are reminded painfully from time to time. Graham and Dodd cite the very same elements.

Studying the 1931–1933 record, we note that price collapses [among industrial bonds] were not due primarily to unsound financial structures, as in the case of utility bonds, nor to a miscalculation by investors as to the margin of safety needed, as in the case of railroad bonds. We are confronted in many cases by a sudden disappearance of earning power, and a disconcerting question as to whether the business can survive. (p. 157)

4. *Analysis of individual issues calls for a multifaceted approach.* Since 1985, my team of analysts has applied an eight-factor credit analysis process developed by Sheldon Stone. Most of the elements are reflected in—perhaps ultimately were inspired by—aspects of Graham and Dodd's thinking. Our concerns are with industry, company standing, management, interest coverage, capital structure, alternative sources of liquidity, liquidation value, and covenants. *Security Analysis* reflects many of these same concerns.

On company standing: "The experience of the past decade indicates that dominant or at least substantial size affords an element of protection against the hazards of instability." (p. 178)

On interest coverage: "The present-day investor is accustomed to regard the ratio of earnings to interest charges as the most important specific test of safety." (p. 128 on accompanying CD)

On capital structure: "The biggest company may be the weakest if its
bonded debt is disproportionately large." (p. 179)

5. *"Buy-and-hold" investing is inconsistent with the responsibilities of the
professional investor, and the creditworthiness of every issuer represented in the portfolio must be revisited no less than quarterly.*

Even before the market collapse of 1929, the danger ensuing from neglect
of investments previously made, and the need for periodic scrutiny or
supervision of all holdings, had been recognized as a new canon in Wall
Street. This principle, directly opposed to the former practice, is frequently
summed up in the dictum, "There are no permanent investments." (p. 253)

6. *Don't engage in market timing based on interest rate forecasts.* Instead,
we confine our efforts to "knowing the knowable," which can result
only from superior efforts to understand industries, companies, and
securities.

It is doubtful if trading in bonds, to catch the market swings, can be carried
on successfully by the investor. . . . We are sceptical of the ability of any
paid agency to provide reliable forecasts of the market action of either
bonds or stocks. Furthermore we are convinced that any combined effort
to advise upon the choice of individual high-grade investments and upon
the course of bond *prices* is fundamentally illogical and confusing. Much as
the investor would like to be able to buy at just the right time and to sell
out when prices are about to fall, experience shows that he is not likely to
be brilliantly successful in such efforts and that by injecting the trading
element into his investment operations he will . . . inevitably shift his interest into speculative directions. (p. 261)

7. *Despite our best efforts, defaults will creep into our portfolios, whether
due to failings in credit analysis or bad luck.* In order for the incremental
yield gained from taking risks to regularly exceed the losses incurred
as a result of defaults, individual holdings have to be small enough so
that a single default won't dissipate a large amount of the portfolio's

capital. We have always thought of our approach to risk as being akin to that of an insurance company. In order for the actuarial process to work, the risk has to be spread over many small holdings and the expected return given a chance to prove out. Thus, you should not invest in high yield bonds unless you can be thoroughly diversified.

> The investor cannot prudently turn himself into an insurance company and incur risks of losing his principal in exchange for annual premiums in the form of extra-large interest coupons. One objection to such a policy is that sound insurance practice requires a very wide distribution of risk, in order to minimize the influence of luck and to allow maximum play to the law of probability. The investor may endeavor to attain this end by diversifying his holdings, but as a practical matter, he cannot approach the division of risk attained by an insurance company. (pp. 165–166)

To wrap up on the subject of investment approach, we feel the successful assumption of credit risk in the fixed income universe depends on the successful assessment of the company's ability to service its debts. Extensive financial statement analysis is not nearly as important as a few skilled judgments regarding the company's prospects.

> The selection of a fixed-value security for limited-income return should be, relatively, at least, a simple operation. The investor must make certain by quantitative tests that the income has been amply above the interest charges and that the current value of the business is well in excess of its debts. In addition, he must be satisfied in his own judgment that the character of the enterprise is such as to promise continued success in the future, or more accurately speaking, to make failure a highly unlikely occurrence. (p. 160 on accompanying CD)

In the end, though, we diverge from Graham and Dodd in one important way. In selecting bonds for purchase, we make judgments about the issuers' prospects, and here's why: When I began to analyze and manage high yield bonds in 1978, the widely held view was that investing in bonds and assessing the future are fundamentally incompatible, and that prudent bond investing must be based on solid inferences from past data as opposed to speculation regarding future events. But credit risk is prospective, and thus substantial credit risk can be borne intelligently only on the basis of skilled judgments about the future.

In large part, the old position represented a prejudice: that buying stocks—an inherently riskier proposition—can be done intelligently on the basis of judgments regarding the future, but depending on those same judgments in the more conservative world of bond investing just isn't right. Some of the greatest—and most profitable—market inefficiencies I have encountered have been the result of prejudices that walled off certain opportunities from "proper investing" . . . and thus left them for flexible investors to pick off far below their fair value. This seems to be one of these prejudices.

One of the reasons I started First National City Bank's high yield bond portfolio in 1978 was my immediately prior experience as the bank's director of research for equities. All I had to do, then, was apply the future-oriented process for analyzing common stocks to the universe of bonds rated below triple B.

Few walls still stand in the investment world today, and it is widely understood that forward-looking analysis can be profitably applied to instruments of all sorts. That lesson remained to be learned in 1940.

Common Sense

Much of the value of *Security Analysis* lies not in its specific instructions but in its common sense. Several of their lessons have specific relevance to the present. More importantly, Graham and Dodd's insight and thought process show how investors should try to dig beneath customary, superficial answers to investment questions.

> Security prices and yields are not determined by any exact mathematical calculation of the expected risk, but they depend rather upon the popularity of the issue. (p. 164) [Markets are not clinically efficient.]

It may be pointed out further that the supposed actuarial computation of investment risks is out of the question theoretically as well as in practice. There are no experience tables available by which the expected "mortality" of various types of issues can be determined. Even if such tables were prepared, based on long and exhaustive studies of past records, it is doubtful whether they would have any real utility for the future. In life insurance, the relation between age and mortality rate is well defined and changes only gradually. The same is true, to a much lesser extent, of the relation between the various types of structures and the fire hazard attaching to them. But the relation between different types of investments and the risk of loss is entirely too indefinite, and too variable with changing conditions, to permit of sound mathematical formulation. This is particularly true because investment losses are not distributed fairly evenly in point of time, but tend to be concentrated at intervals, *i.e.*, during periods of general depression. Hence the typical investment hazard is roughly similar to the conflagration or epidemic hazard, which is the exceptional and incalculable factor in fire or life insurance. (pp. 164–165, emphasis added) [So much for reliable quantitative models.]

Among [the aspects of the earnings picture to which the investor would do well to pay attention] are the *trend*, the *minimum* figure, and the *current* figure. The importance of each of these cannot be gainsaid, but they do not lend themselves effectively to the application of hard and fast rules. (p. 133 on accompanying CD)

The investor . . . will be *attracted* by: (*a*) a rising trend in profits; (*b*) an especially good current showing; and (*c*) a satisfactory margin over interest charges in *every* year during the period studied. If a bond is deficient in any one of these three aspects, the result should not necessarily be to condemn the issue but rather to exact an average earnings coverage well in excess of the minimum and to require closer attention to the general or qualitative elements in the situation. (pp. 133–134 on accompanying CD)

If [a ratio of] $1 of stock to $1 of bonds is taken as the "normal" requirement for an industrial company, would it not be sound to demand, say, a $2-to-$1 ratio when stock prices are inflated, and conversely to be satisfied with a 50-cent-to-$1 ratio when quotations are far below intrinsic values? But this suggestion is impracticable for two reasons, the first being that it implies that the bond buyer can recognize an unduly high or low level of stock prices, which is far too complimentary an assumption. The second is that it would require bond investors to act with especial caution when things are booming and with greater confidence when times are hard. This is a counsel of perfection which it is not in human nature to follow. Bond buyers are people, and they cannot be expected to escape entirely either the enthusiasm of bull markets or the apprehensions of a severe depression. (pp. 157–158 on accompanying CD)

"In the purely speculative field the objection to paying for advice is that if the adviser *knew* whereof he spoke he would not need to bother with a consultant's duties." (p. 261) Not much different from Warren Buffett's observation that "Wall Street is the only place that people ride to in a Rolls-Royce to get advice from those who take the subway."[1]

There are many instances in which Graham and Dodd offer common-sense advice or, even more interestingly, in which they refute existing rules of investing, substituting common sense for "accepted wisdom," that great oxymoron. To me, this represents the greatest strength of the section on fixed income securities. In the end, Graham and Dodd remind us, "Investment theory should be chary of easy generalizations." (p. 171)

Security Analysis through the Years

Many of Graham and Dodd's specific ideas have withstood the test of time and, in fact, been picked up and carried forward by others.

- Their observation that "an investor may reject any number of good bonds with virtually no penalty at all" (p. 143) may have inspired Warren Buffett, who draws a very apt comparison to batters in baseball. Buffett reminds us that a baseball hitter will be called out if he fails to

[1] *Los Angeles Times Magazine*, April 7, 1991.

swing at three pitches in the strike zone, while an investor can let any
number of investment opportunities go by without being penalized.

- Likewise, Graham and Dodd submitted that "the best criterion that we
  are able to offer [for the purpose of assessing the margin of assets over
  indebtedness] is the ratio of the *market value* of the capital stock to the
  total funded debt." (p. 150 on accompanying CD) This was paralleled
  exactly by the market-adjusted debt (MAD) ratios popularized by
  Michael Milken when he pioneered the issuance of high yield bonds at
  Drexel Burnham Lambert in the 1970s and 1980s. Market values are far
  from perfect, but accounting data are purely historical and thus are
  often out-of-date at best and irrelevant at worst.

- Importantly, Graham and Dodd highlight the importance of cash flow
  stability in a company's ability to service its debts in an adverse environment. "Once it is admitted—as it always must be—that the industry can suffer *some* reduction in profits, then the investor is compelled
  to estimate the possible extent of the shrinkage and compare it with
  the surplus above the interest requirements. He thus finds himself . . .
  vitally concerned with the ability of the company to meet the vicissitudes of the future." (p. 155) This consideration contributed to the fact
  that, in its infancy in the mid-1970s, the leveraged buyout industry
  restricted its purchases to noncyclical companies. Of course, like all
  important investment principles, this one is often ignored in bullish
  periods; enthusiasm and optimism gain sway and the stable-cash-flow
  rule can be easily forgotten.

A Few More Thoughts

In considering the relevance 68 years later of the 1940 edition of *Security
Analysis*, a number of additional observations deserve to be made.

First, most of the timing that interested Graham and Dodd concerned
"depressions" and their impact on creditworthiness. They cite three

depressions—1920 to 1922, 1930 to 1933, and 1937 to 1938—whereas we talk today about there having been only one in this century: the Great Depression. Clearly, Graham and Dodd are talking about what we call "recessions."

Second, they were not concerned with predicting interest-rate fluctuations. The primary reason for this may be that interest rates didn't fluctuate much in those days. A table on page 157 shows, for example, that in the 13 years from 1926 to 1938—a period that sandwiched a famous boom between two "depressions"—the yield on 40 utility bonds moved only between 3.9% and 6.3%. At the time the 1940 edition was published, then, interest rates were low and fairly steady.

Third, it is important to note that several of Graham and Dodd's warnings against risk taking are directed not at professionals but at the individual investors who appear to have been the authors' target audience.

> As a practical matter it is not so easy to distinguish in advance between the underlying bonds that come through reorganization unscathed and those which suffer drastic treatment. Hence the ordinary investor may be well advised to leave such issues out of his calculations and stick to the rule that only strong companies have strong bonds. (p. 153)

> The individual is not qualified to be an insurance underwriter. It is not his function to be paid for incurring risks; on the contrary it is to his interest to pay others for insurance against loss. . . . Even assuming that the high coupon rates [on higher yielding securities] will, in the great aggregate, more than compensate on an *actuarial* basis for the risks accepted, such bonds are still undesirable investments from the *personal* standpoint of the average investor. (pp. 165–166)

Thus concern for the safety of nonprofessional investors appears to be the source of many of *Security Analysis*'s most rigid dicta. I would not differ with the proposition that direct investment in distressed debt and high yield bonds should be left to professionals.

Into the Future

Few books can be read nearly 70 years after their publication with the reasonable expectation that everything they say—and the way they say it—will be thoroughly up-to-date. General wisdom and occasional nuggets of insight are usually the most that can be hoped for. Anyone wondering how the 1940 edition of *Security Analysis* comes through in this regard needs only consider Graham and Dodd's discussion of mortgage investing in the light of the subprime and collateralized debt obligation (CDO) experience of 2007:

> During the great and disastrous development of the real estate mortgage-bond business between 1923 and 1929, the only datum customarily presented to support the usual bond offering—aside from an estimate of future earnings—was a statement of the *appraised value* of the property, which almost invariably amounted to some 66^2/$_3$% in excess of the mortgage issue. If these appraisals had corresponded to the market values which experienced buyers of or lenders on real estate would place upon the properties, they would have been of real utility in the selection of sound real estate bonds. But unfortunately they were purely artificial valuations, to which the appraisers were willing to attach their names for a fee, and whose only function was to deceive the investor as to the protection which he was receiving. . . .
>
> This whole scheme of real estate financing was honeycombed with the most glaring weaknesses, and it is sad commentary on the lack of principle, penetration, and ordinary common sense on the part of all parties concerned that it was permitted to reach such gigantic proportions before the inevitable collapse. (p. 185)

Paid-for home appraisals (and security ratings) that led to undeserved confidence—and thus uninformed risk bearing—on the part of unknowing investors: what could better describe recent events? And what better evidence could there be of the relevance of the 1940 edition of *Security Analysis* to the decades since its writing . . . and the decades to come?

Chapter 6

THE SELECTION OF FIXED-VALUE INVESTMENTS

HAVING SUGGESTED a classification of securities by character rather than by title, we now take up in order the principles and methods of selection applicable to each group. We have already stated that the fixed-value group includes:

1. High-grade straight bonds and preferred stocks.
2. High-grade privileged issues, where the value of the privilege is too remote to count as a factor in selection.
3. Common stocks which through guaranty or preferred status occupy the position of a high-grade senior issue.

Basic Attitude toward High-grade Preferred Stocks. By placing gilt-edged preferred stocks and high-grade bonds in a single group, we indicate that the same investment attitude and the same general method of analysis are applicable to both types. The very definite inferiority of the preferred stockholders' legal claim is here left out of account, for the logical reason that the soundness of the best investments must rest not upon legal rights or remedies but upon ample financial capacity of the enterprise. Confirmation of this viewpoint is found in the investor's attitude toward such an issue as National Biscuit Company Preferred, which for nearly 40 years has been considered as possessing the same *essential investment character* as a good bond.[1]

Preferred Stocks Not Generally Equivalent to Bonds in Investment Merit. But it should be pointed out immediately that issues with the history and standing of National Biscuit Preferred constitute a

---

[1] See Appendix Note 6, p. 737 on accompanying CD, for supporting data.

very small percentage of all preferred stocks. Hence, we are by no means asserting the investment equivalence of bonds and preferred stocks *in general.* On the contrary, we shall in a later chapter be at some pains to show that the *average* preferred issue deserves a lower rank than the average bond, and furthermore that preferred stocks have been much too readily accepted by the investing public. The majority of these issues have not been sufficiently well protected to assure continuance of dividends *beyond any reasonable doubt.* They belong properly, therefore, in the class of variable or speculative senior issues (Group II), and in this field the contractual differences between bonds and preferred shares are likely to assume great importance. A sharp distinction must, therefore, be made between the typical and the exceptional preferred stock. It is only the latter which deserves to rank as a fixed-value investment and to be viewed in the same light as a good bond. To avoid awkwardness of expression in this discussion we shall frequently use the terms "investment bonds" or merely "bonds" to represent all securities belonging to the fixed-value class.

Is Bond Investment Logical? In the 1934 edition of this work we considered with some seriousness the question whether or not the extreme financial and industrial fluctuations of the preceding years had not impaired the fundamental logic of bond investment. Was it worth while for the investor to limit his income return and to forego all prospect of speculative gain, if despite these sacrifices he must still subject himself to serious risk of loss? We suggested in reply that the phenomena of 1927–1933 were so completely abnormal as to afford no fair basis for investment theory and practice. Subsequent experience seems to have borne us out, but there are still enough uncertainties facing the bond buyer to banish, perhaps for a long time, his old sense of complete security. The combination of a record high level for bonds (in 1940) with a history of two catastrophic price collapses in the preceding twenty years and a major war in progress is not one to justify airy confidence in the future.

Bond Form Inherently Unattractive: Quantitative Assurance of Safety Essentials. This situation clearly calls for a more critical and exacting attitude towards bond selection than was formerly considered necessary by investors, issuing houses, or authors of textbooks on investment.

Allusion has already been made to the dangers inherent in the acceptance of the bond *form* as an assurance of safety, or even of smaller risk than is found in stocks. Instead of associating bonds primarily with the presumption of *safety* as has long been the practice—it would be sounder to start with what is not presumption but fact, *viz.*, that a (straight) bond is an investment with *limited return*. In exchange for limiting his participation in future profits, the bondholder obtains a prior claim and a definite promise of payment, while the preferred stockholder obtains only the priority, without the promise. But neither priority nor promise is itself an *assurance* of payment. This assurance rests in the ability of the enterprise to fulfill its promise, and must be looked for in its financial position, record, and prospects. The essence of proper bond selection consists, therefore, in obtaining specific and convincing factors of safety in compensation for the surrender of participation in profits.

Major Emphasis on Avoidance of Loss. Our primary conception of the bond as a commitment with limited return leads us to another important viewpoint toward bond investment. Since the chief emphasis must be placed on avoidance of loss, bond selection is primarily a negative art. It is a process of exclusion and rejection, rather than of search and acceptance. In this respect the contrast with common-stock selection is fundamental in character. The prospective buyer of a given common stock is influenced more or less equally by the desire to avoid loss and the desire to make a profit. The penalty for mistakenly rejecting the issue may conceivably be as great as that for mistakenly accepting it. But an investor may reject any number of good bonds with virtually no penalty at all, provided he does not eventually accept an unsound issue. Hence, broadly speaking, there is no such thing as being unduly captious or exacting in the purchase of fixed-value investments. The observation that Walter Bagehot addressed to commercial bankers is equally applicable to the selection of investment bonds. "If there is a difficulty or a doubt the security should be declined."[2]

Four Principles for the Selection of Issues of the Fixed-value Type. Having established this general approach to our problem, we may

---

[2] *Lombard Street*, p. 245, New York, 1892.

now state four additional principles of more specific character which are applicable to the selection of individual issues:

I. *Safety is measured not by specific lien or other contractual rights, but by the ability of the issuer to meet all of its obligations.*[3]

II. *This ability should be measured under conditions of depression rather than prosperity.*

III. *Deficient safety cannot be compensated for by an abnormally high coupon rate.*

IV. *The selection of all bonds for investment should be subject to rules of exclusion and to specific quantitative tests corresponding to those prescribed by statute to govern investments of savings banks.*

A technique of bond selection based on the above principles will differ in significant respects from the traditional attitude and methods. In departing from old concepts, however, this treatment represents not an innovation but the recognition and advocacy of viewpoints which have been steadily gaining ground among intelligent and experienced investors. The ensuing discussion is designed to make clear both the nature and the justification of the newer ideas.[4]

I. SAFETY NOT MEASURED BY LIEN BUT BY ABILITY TO PAY

The basic difference confronts us at the very beginning. In the past the primary emphasis was laid upon the specific security, *i.e.*, the character and supposed value of the property on which the bonds hold a lien. From our standpoint this consideration is quite secondary; the dominant element must be the strength and soundness of the obligor enterprise. There is here a clearcut distinction between two points of view. On the one hand the bond is regarded as a claim against *property*; on the other hand, as a claim against a *business*.

The older view was logical enough in its origin and purpose. It desired to make the bondholder independent of the risks of the business by

---

[3] This is a general rule applicable to the majority of bonds of the fixed-value type, but it is subject to a number of exceptions which are discussed later.

[4] These ideas are neither so new nor so uncommon in 1940 as they were in 1934, but we doubt whether they may be considered standard as yet.

giving him ample security on which to levy in the event that the enterprise proved a failure. If the business became unable to pay his claim, he could take over the mortgaged property and pay himself out of that. This arrangement would be excellent if it worked, but in practice it rarely proves to be feasible. For this there are three reasons:

1. The shrinkage of property values when the business fails.
2. The difficulty of asserting the bondholders' supposed legal rights.
3. The delays and other disadvantages incident to a receivership.

Lien Is No Guarantee against Shrinkage of Values. The conception of a mortgage lien as a guaranty of protection independent of the success of the business itself is in most cases a complete fallacy. In the typical situation, the value of the pledged property is vitally dependent on the earning power of the enterprise. The bondholder usually has a lien on a railroad line, or on factory buildings and equipment, or on power plants and other utility properties, or perhaps on a bridge or hotel structure. These properties are rarely adaptable to uses other than those for which they were constructed. Hence if the enterprise proves a failure its fixed assets ordinarily suffer an appalling shrinkage in realizable value. For this reason the established practice of stating the original cost or appraised value of the pledged property as an inducement to purchase bonds is entirely misleading. The value of pledged assets assumes practical importance only in the event of default, and in any such event the book figures are almost invariably found to be unreliable and irrelevant. This may be illustrated by Seaboard-All Florida Railway First Mortgage 6s, selling in 1931 at 1 cent on the dollar shortly after completion of the road.[5]

Impracticable to Enforce Basic Legal Rights of Lien Holder. In cases where the mortgaged property is actually worth as much as the debt, the bondholder is rarely allowed to take possession and realize upon it. It must be recognized that the procedure following default on a corporation bond has come to differ materially from that customary in the case of a mortgage on privately owned property. The basic legal rights of the lien holder are supposedly the same in both situations. But in practice we find a very definite disinclination on the part of the courts to permit

---

[5] See Appendix Note 7, p. 738 on accompanying CD, for supporting data.

corporate bondholders to take over properties by foreclosing on their liens, if there is any possibility that these assets may have a fair value in excess of their claim.[6] Apparently it is considered unfair to wipe out stockholders or junior bondholders who have a potential interest in the property but are not in a position to protect it. As a result of this practice, bondholders rarely, if ever, come into actual possession of the pledged property unless its value at the time is substantially less than their claim. In most cases they are required to take new securities in a reorganized company. Sometimes the default in interest is cured and the issue reinstated.[7] On exceedingly rare occasions a defaulted issue may be paid off in full, but only after a long and vexing delay.[8]

Delays Are Wearisome. This delay constitutes the third objection to relying upon the mortgaged property as protection for a bond investment. The more valuable the pledged assets in relation to the amount of the lien, the more difficult it is to take them over under foreclosure, and the longer the time required to work out an "equitable" division of interest among the various bond and stock issues. Let us consider the most favorable kind of situation for a bondholder in the event of receivership. He would hold a comparatively small first mortgage followed by a substantial junior lien, the requirements of which have made the company insolvent. It may well be that the strength of the first-mortgage bondholder's position is such that at no time is there any real chance of eventual loss to him. Yet the financial difficulties of the company usually have a depressing effect on the market price of all its securities, even those presumably unimpaired in real value. As the receivership drags on, the market decline becomes accentuated, since investors are constitutionally averse to buying into a troubled situation. Eventually the first-mortgage bonds may come through the reorganization undisturbed, but during a wearisome and protracted period the owners have faced a severe impairment in the quoted value of their holdings and at least some degree of doubt and worry as to the outcome. Typical examples of such an experience can be found in the case of Missouri, Kansas and Texas Railway Company First 4s and Brooklyn

---

[6] The failure to foreclose on Interborough Rapid Transit Secured 7s for seven years after default of principal (discussed on p. 734) well illustrates this point.

[7] See Appendix Note 8, p. 738 on accompanying CD, for supporting data.

[8] See Appendix Note 9, p. 739 on accompanying CD, for supporting data.

Union Elevated Railroad First 5s.[9] The subject of receivership and reorganization practice, particularly as they affect the bondholder, will receive more detailed consideration in a later chapter.

Basic Principle Is to Avoid Trouble. The foregoing discussion should support our emphatic stand that the primary aim of the bond buyer must be to avoid trouble and not to protect himself in the event of trouble. Even in the cases where the specific lien proves of real advantage, this benefit is realized under conditions which contravene the very meaning of *fixed-value* investment. In view of the severe decline in market price almost invariably associated with receivership, the mere fact that the investor must have recourse to his indenture indicates that his investment has been unwise or unfortunate. The protection that the mortgaged property offers him can constitute at best a mitigation of his mistake.

Corollaries from This First Principle. 1. *Absence of Lien of Minor Consequence.* From Principle I there follow a number of corollaries with important practical applications. Since specific lien is of subordinate importance in the choice of high-grade bonds, the absence of lien is also of minor consequence. The debenture,[10] *i.e.*, unsecured, obligations of a

---

[9] See Appendix Note 10, p. 739 on accompanying CD, for supporting data. On the subject of delays in enforcing bondholders' claims, it should be pointed out that, with up to one-third of the country's railroad mileage in bankruptcy, not a single road emerged from trusteeship in the six years following passage of the Sec. 77 amendment to the Bankruptcy Act in 1933—a step designed to *accelerate* reorganization.

[10] The term "debenture" in American financial practice has the accepted meaning of "unsecured bond or note." For no good reason, the name is sometimes given to other kinds of securities without apparently signifying anything in particular. There have been a number of "secured debentures," *e.g.*, Chicago Herald and Examiner Secured Debenture 6^{1}/2s, due 1950, and Lone Star Gas Debenture 3^{1}/2s, due 1953. Also, a number of preferred issues are called debenture preferred stock or merely debenture stock, *e.g.*, Du Pont Debenture Stock (called in 1939); General Cigar Company Debenture Preferred (called in 1927).

Sometimes debenture issues, properly so entitled because originally unsecured, later acquire specific security through the operation of a protective covenant, *e.g.*, New York, New Haven and Hartford Railroad Company Debentures, discussed in Chap. 19. Another example was the Debenture 6^{1}/2s of Fox New England Theaters, Inc., reorganized in 1933. These debentures acquired as security a block of first-mortgage bonds of the same company, which were surrendered by the vendor of the theaters because it failed to meet a guarantee of future earnings.

Observe that there is no clear-cut distinction between a "bond" and a "note" other than the fact that the latter generally means a relatively short-term obligation, *i.e.*, one maturing not more than, say, ten years after issuance.

strong corporation, amply capable of meeting its interest charges, may qualify for acceptance almost as readily as a bond secured by mortgage. Furthermore the debentures of a strong enterprise are undoubtedly sounder investments than the mortgage issues of a weak company. No first-lien bond, for example, enjoys a better investment rating than Standard Oil of New Jersey Debenture 3s, due 1961. An examination of the bond list will show that the debenture issues of companies having no secured debt ahead of them will rank in investment character at least on a par with the average mortgage bond, because an enterprise must enjoy a high credit rating to obtain funds on its unsecured long-term bond.[11]

2. *The Theory of Buying the Highest Yielding Obligation of a Sound Company.* It follows also that if any obligation of an enterprise deserves to qualify as a fixed-value investment, then all its obligations must do so. Stated conversely, if a company's junior bonds are not safe, its first-mortgage bonds are not a desirable fixed-value investment. For if the second mortgage is unsafe the company itself is weak, and generally speaking there can be no high-grade obligations of a weak enterprise. The theoretically correct procedure for bond investment, therefore, is first to select a company meeting every test of strength and soundness, and then to purchase its highest yielding obligation, which would usually mean its junior rather than its first-lien bonds. Assuming no error were ever made in our choice of enterprises, this procedure would work out perfectly well in practice. The greater the chance of mistake, however, the more reason to sacrifice yield in order to reduce the potential loss in capital value. But we must recognize that in favoring the lower yielding first-mortgage issue, the bond buyer is in fact expressing a lack of confidence in his own judgment as to the soundness of the business—which, if carried far enough, would call into question the advisability of his making an investment in *any* of the bonds of the particular enterprise.

Example: As an example of this point, let us consider the Cudahy Packing Company First Mortgage 5s, due 1946, and the Debenture 5¹/₂s of the same company, due 1937. In June 1932 the First 5s sold at 95 to yield about 5¹/₂%, whereas the junior 5¹/₂s sold at 59 to yield over 20% to

---

[11] This point is strikingly substantiated by the industrial bond financing between 1935 and 1939. During these years, when only high-grade issues could be sold, by far the greater part of the total was represented by *debentures.*

maturity. The purchase of the 5% bonds at close to par could only be justified by a confident belief that the company would remain solvent and reasonably prosperous, for otherwise the bonds would undoubtedly suffer a severe drop in market price. But if the investor has confidence in the future of Cudahy, why should he not buy the debenture issue and obtain an enormously greater return on his money? The only answer can be that the investor wants the superior protection of the first mortgage in the event his judgment proves incorrect and the company falls into difficulties. In that case he would probably lose less as the owner of the first-mortgage bonds than through holding the junior issue. Even on this score it should be pointed out that if by any chance Cudahy Packing Company were to suffer the reverses that befell Fisk Rubber Company, the loss in market value of the first-mortgage bonds would be fully as great as those suffered by the debentures; for in April 1932 Fisk Rubber Company First 8s were selling as low as 17 against a price of 12 for the unsecured 5¹/₂% Notes. It is clear, at any rate, that the investor who favors the Cudahy first-lien 5s is paying a premium of about 15% per annum (the difference in yield) for only a *partial* insurance against loss. On this basis he is undoubtedly giving up too much for what he gets in return. The conclusion appears inescapable either that he should make no investment in Cudahy bonds or that he should buy the junior issue at its enormously higher yield.[12] This rule may be laid down as applying to the general case where a first-mortgage bond sells at a fixed-value price (*e.g.*, close to par) and junior issues of the same company can be bought to yield a much higher return.[13]

3. *Senior Liens Are to Be Favored, Unless Junior Obligations Offer a Substantial Advantage.* Obviously a junior lien should be preferred only if the advantage in income return is substantial. Where the first-mortgage bond yields only slightly less, it is undoubtedly wise to pay the small insurance premium for protection against unexpected trouble.

Example: This point is illustrated by the relative market prices of Atchison Topeka and Santa Fe Railway Company General (first) 4s and Adjustment (second mortgage) 4s, both of which mature in 1995.

---

[12] Both of the Cudahy issues were retired at 102¹/₂ in 1935.

[13] Exceptions to this rule may be justified in rare cases where the senior security has an unusually preferred status—*e.g.*, a very strongly entrenched underlying railroad bond. But see *infra* pp. 152–153.

PRICE OF ATCHISON GENERAL 4S AND ADJUSTMENT 4S AT VARIOUS DATES

Date	Price of General 4s	Price of Adjustment 4s	Spread
Jan. 2, 1913	97$^1/_2$	88	9$^1/_2$
Jan. 5, 1917	95$^1/_2$	86$^3/_4$	8$^3/_4$
May 21, 1920	70$^1/_4$	62	8$^1/_4$
Aug. 4, 1922	93$^1/_2$	84$^1/_2$	9
Dec. 4, 1925	89$^1/_4$	85$^1/_4$	4
Jan. 3, 1930	93$^1/_4$	93	$^1/_4$
Jan. 7, 1931	98$^1/_2$	97	1$^1/_2$
June 2, 1932	81	66$^1/_2$	14$^1/_2$
June 19, 1933	93	88	5
Jan. 9, 1934	94$^1/_4$	83	11$^1/_4$
Mar. 6, 1936	114$^5/_8$	113$^1/_2$	1$^1/_8$
Apr. 26, 1937	103$^1/_2$	106$^3/_4$	3$^1/_4$
Apr. 14, 1938	99$^1/_4$	75$^1/_4$	24
Dec. 29, 1939	105$^3/_4$	85$^1/_4$	20$^1/_2$

Prior to 1924 the Atchison General 4s sold usually at about 7 to 10 points above the Adjustment 4s and yielded about $^1/_2$% less. Since both issues were considered safe without question, it would have been more logical to purchase the junior issue at its 10% lower cost. After 1923 this point of view asserted itself, and the price difference steadily narrowed. During 1930 and part of 1931 the junior issue sold on numerous occasions at practically the same price as the General 4s. This relationship was even more illogical than the unduly wide spread in 1922–1923, since the advantage of the Adjustment 4s in price and yield was too negligible to warrant accepting a junior position, even assuming unquestioned safety for both liens.

Within a very short time this rather obvious truth was brought home strikingly by the widening of the spread to over 14 points during the demoralized bond-market conditions of June 1932. As the record appeared in 1934, it could be inferred that a reasonable differential between the two issues would be about 5 points and that either a substantial widening or a virtual disappearance of the spread would present an opportunity for a desirable exchange of one issue for another. Two such opportunities did in fact appear in 1934 and 1936, as shown in our table.

But this example is of further utility in illustrating the all-pervasive factor of change and the necessity of taking it into account in bond analysis. By 1937 the failure of Atchison's earnings to recover within striking distance of its former normal, and the actual inadequacy of the margin above interest requirements as judged by conservative standards, should have warned the investor that the "adjustment" (*i.e.*, contingent) element in the junior issue could not safely be ignored. Thus a price relationship that was logical at a time when safety of interest was never in question could not be relied upon under the new conditions. In 1938 the poor earnings actually compelled the road to defer the May 1 interest payment on the adjustment bonds, as a result of which their price fell to $75\frac{1}{4}$ and the spread widened to 24 points. Although the interest was later paid in full and the price recovered to 96 in 1939, it would seem quite unwise for the investor to apply pre-1932 standards to this bond issue.

A junior lien of Company *X* may be selected in preference to a first-mortgage bond of Company *Y*, on one of two bases:

1. The protection for the total debt of Company *X* is adequate and the yield of the junior lien is substantially higher than that of the Company *Y* issue; or
2. If there is no substantial advantage in yield, then the indicated protection for the total debt of Company *X* must be considerably better than that of Company *Y*.

Example of 2:

Issue	Price in 1930	Fixed charges earned, 1929*
Pacific Power and Light Co. First 5s, due 1955	101	1.53 times
American Gas and Electric Co. Debenture 5s, due 2028	101	2.52 times

* Average results approximately the same.

The appreciably higher coverage of total charges by American Gas and Electric would have justified preferring its junior bonds to the first-mortgage issue of Pacific Power and Light, when both were selling at about the same price.[14]

---

[14] In 1937 the low price of Pacific Power and Light 5s was 51, against a low of 104 for the American Gas and Electric Debentures.

Special Status of "Underlying Bonds." In the railroad field an especial investment character is generally supposed to attach to what are known as "underlying bonds." These represent issues of relatively small size secured by a lien on especially important parts of the obligor system, and often followed by a series of "blanket mortgages." The underlying bond usually enjoys a first lien, but it may be a second- or even a third-mortgage issue, provided the senior issues are also of comparatively small magnitude.

Example: New York and Erie Railroad Third Mortgage Extended 4½s, due 1938, are junior to two small prior liens covering an important part of the Erie Railroad's main line. They are followed by four successive blanket mortgages on the system, and they have regularly enjoyed the favored status of an underlying bond.

Bonds of this description have been thought to be entirely safe, regardless of what happens to the system as a whole. They have almost always come through reorganization unscathed; and even during a receivership interest payments are usually continued as a matter of course, largely because the sum involved is proportionately so small. They are not exempt, however, from fairly sharp declines in market value if insolvency overtakes the system.

Examples: In the case of New York and Erie Third 4½s (which had been voluntarily extended on maturity in 1923 and again in 1933), principal and interest were defaulted in March 1938, following the bankruptcy of the Erie two months earlier. The bid price declined to as low as 61. However, the various reorganization plans filed to the end of 1939 all provided for the payment of principal and interest in full on this issue.

Chicago and Eastern Illinois Consolidated 6s, due 1934, were finally paid off in full in 1940, with further interest at 4%—but not until their price had fallen as low as 32 in 1933.

Pacific Railway of Missouri First 4s and Second 5s and Missouri Pacific Railway Third 4s, all extended from their original maturities to 1938, are underlying bonds of the Missouri Pacific system. They continued to receive interest and were left undisturbed in the receivership of 1915. Following the second bankruptcy in 1933, they continued to receive interest until their maturity date. At that time payment of principal was defaulted, but interest payments were continued through 1939. The various reorganization plans virtually provided for these bonds in full, by offering them prior-lien, fixed-interest obligations of the new company. But since 1931, the price of these three issues has been as low as 65, 60, and 53, respectively.

Other bonds, however, once regarded as underlying issues, have not fared so well following insolvency.

Example: Milwaukee, Sparta and Northwestern First 4s, due 1947, ranked as an underlying bond of the Chicago and North Western Railway, and for many years their price was not far below that of the premier Union Pacific First 4s, due the same year. Yet the receivership of the Chicago and North Western was followed by default of interest on this issue in 1935 and collapse of its price to the abysmal low of $8^{1}/_{8}$ as late as 1939.

From the foregoing it would appear that *in some cases* underlying bonds may be viewed as exceptions to our rule that a bond is not sound unless the company is sound. For the most part such bonds are owned by institutions or large investors. (The same observations may apply to certain first-mortgage bonds of operating subsidiaries of public-utility holding-company systems.)

In railroad bonds of this type, the location and strategic value of the mileage covered are of prime importance. First-mortgage bonds on nonessential and unprofitable parts of the system, referred to sometimes as "divisional liens," are not true underlying bonds in the sense that we have just used the term. Divisional first liens on poorly located mileage may receive much less favorable treatment in a reorganization than blanket mortgage bonds ostensibly junior to them.

Example: Central Branch Union Pacific Railway First 4s, due 1938, were said to "underly" the Missouri Pacific First and Refunding mortgage, which provided for their retirement. Yet the reorganization plans presented to the end of 1939 all offered better treatment for the Missouri Pacific First and Refunding 5s than for the ostensibly senior Central Branch bonds.

As a practical matter it is not so easy to distinguish in advance between the underlying bonds that come through reorganization unscathed and those which suffer drastic treatment. Hence the ordinary investor may be well advised to leave such issues out of his calculations and stick to the rule that only strong companies have strong bonds.

Chapter 7

THE SELECTION OF FIXED-VALUE INVESTMENTS: SECOND AND THIRD PRINCIPLES

II. BONDS SHOULD BE BOUGHT ON A DEPRESSION BASIS

The rule that a sound investment must be able to withstand adversity seems self-evident enough to be termed a truism. Any bond can do well when conditions are favorable; it is only under the acid test of depression that the advantages of strong over weak issues become manifest and vitally important. For this reason prudent investors have always favored the obligations of old-established enterprises which have demonstrated their ability to come through bad times as well as good.

Presumption of Safety Based upon Either the Character of the Industry or the Amount of Protection. Confidence in the ability of a bond issue to weather depression may be based on either of two different reasons. The investor may believe that the particular business will be immune from a drastic shrinkage in earning power, or else that the margin of safety is so large that it can undergo such a shrinkage without resultant danger. The bonds of light and power companies have been favored principally for the first reason, the bonds of United States Steel Corporation subsidiaries for the second. In the former case it is the *character* of the industry, in the latter it is the *amount* of protection, which justifies the purchase. Of the two viewpoints, the one which tries to avoid the perils of depression appeals most to the average bond buyer. It seems much simpler to invest in a depression-proof enterprise than to have to rely on the company's financial strength to pull its bonds through a period of poor results.

No Industry Entirely Depression-proof. The objection to this theory of investment is, of course, that there is no such thing as a depression-proof industry, meaning thereby one that is immune from the danger of *any* decline in earning power. It is true that the Edison companies have shown themselves subject to only minor shrinkage in profits, as compared, say, with the steel producers. But even a small decline may prove fatal if the business is bonded to the limit of prosperity earnings. Once it is admitted—as it always must be—that the industry can suffer *some* reduction in profits, then the investor is compelled to estimate the possible extent of the shrinkage and compare it with the surplus above the interest requirements. He thus finds himself in the same position as the holder of any other kind of bond, vitally concerned with the ability of the company to meet the vicissitudes of the future.[1]

The distinction to be made, therefore, is not between industries which are *exempt* from and those which are *affected* by depression, but rather between those which are more and those which are less subject to fluctuation. The more stable the type of enterprise, the better suited it is to bond financing and the larger the portion of the supposed normal earning power which may be consumed by interest charges. As the degree of instability increases, it must be offset by a greater margin of safety to make sure that interest charges will be met; in other words, a smaller portion of total capital may be represented by bonds. If there is such a lack of inherent stability as to make survival of the enterprise doubtful under continued unfavorable conditions (a question arising frequently in the case of industrial companies of secondary size), then the bond issue cannot meet the requirements of fixed-value investment, even though the margin of safety—measured by past performance—may be exceedingly large. Such a bond will meet the quantitative but not the qualitative test, but both are essential to our concept of investment.[2]

----

[1] Note that a large number of utility holding-company issues (and even some overbonded operating companies) defaulted in 1931–1932, whereas the subsidiary bonds of the United States Steel Corporation maintained a high investment rating despite the exceedingly bad operating results.

[2] For examples of this important point, see our discussion of Studebaker Preferred stock on p. 87 and of Willys-Overland Company First $6^1/_2$s on p. 767 of accompanying CD.

Investment Practice Recognizes Importance of Character of the Industry. This conception of diverse margins of safety has been solidly grounded in investment practice for many years. The threefold classification of enterprises—as railroads, public utilities, or industrials—was intended to reflect inherent differences in relative stability and consequently in the coverage to be required above bond interest requirements. Investors thought well, for example, of any railroad which earned its bond interest twice over, but the same margin in the case of an industrial bond was ordinarily regarded as inadequate. In the decade between 1920 and 1930, the status of the public-utility division underwent some radical changes. A sharp separation was introduced between light, heat, and power services on the one hand, and street-railway lines on the other, although previously the two had been closely allied. The trolley companies, because of their poor showing, were tacitly excluded from the purview of the term "public utility," as used in financial circles, and in the popular mind the name was restricted to electric, gas, water, and telephone companies. (Later on, promoters endeavored to exploit the popularity of the public utilities by applying this title to companies engaged in all sorts of businesses, including natural gas, ice, coal, and even storage.) The steady progress of the utility group, even in the face of the minor industrial setbacks of 1924 and 1927, led to an impressive advance in its standing among investors, so that by 1929 it enjoyed a credit rating fully on a par with the railroads. In the ensuing depression, it registered a much smaller shrinkage in gross and net earnings than did the transportation industry, and its seems logical to expect that bonds of soundly capitalized light and power companies will replace high-grade railroad bonds as the premier type of corporate investment. (This seems true to the authors despite the distinct recession in the popularity of utility bonds and stocks since 1933, due to a combination of rate reductions, governmental competition and threatened dangers from inflation.)

Depression Performance as a Test of Merit. Let us turn our attention now to the behavior of these three investment groups in the two recent depression tests—that of 1931–1933 and that of 1937–1938. Of these, the former was of such unexampled severity that it may seem unfair and impractical to ask that any investment now under consideration should be measured by its performance in those disastrous times. We have felt, however, that the experiences of 1931–1933 may be profitably

COMPARISON OF RAILROAD AND PUBLIC-UTILITY GROSS AND NET WITH THE AVERAGE
YIELD ON HIGH-GRADE RAILROAD AND UTILITY BONDS, 1926–1938 (UNIT $1,000,000)

Year	Railroads			Public utilities		
	Gross[1]	Net railway operating income[2]	Yield on railroad bonds, %[3]	Gross[4]	Net[5] (index %)	Yield on public-utility bonds, %[3]
1926	$6,383	$1,213	5.13	$1,520	100.0	5.11
1927	6,136	1,068	4.83	1,661	106.8	4.96
1928	6,112	1,173	4.85	1,784	124.0	4.87
1929	6,280	1,252	5.18	1,939	142.5	5.14
1930	5,281	869	4.96	1,991	127.7	5.05
1931	4,188	526	6.09	1,976	123.5	5.27
1932	3,127	326	7.61	1,814	96.6	6.30
1933	3,095	474	6.09	1,755	98.2	6.25
1934	3,272	463	4.96	1,832	88.1	5.40
1935	3,452	500	4.95	1,912	92.9	4.43
1936	4,053	667	4.24	2,045	120.7	3.88
1937	4,166	590	4.34	2,181	125.8	3.93
1938	3,565	373	5.21	2,195	106.0	3.87

[1] Railway operating revenues for all Class I railroads in the United States (I.C.C.).
[2] Net railway operating income for the same roads (I.C.C.).
[3] Average yields on 40 rail and 40 utility bonds, respectively, as compiled by Moody's.
[4] Revenues from the sale of electric power to ultimate consumers, compiled by Edison Electric Institute. Data from 90% of the industry are adjusted to cover 100% of the industry (*Survey of Current Business*).
[5] Index of corporate profits of 15 public utilities, compiled by Standard Statistics Company, Inc. Figures are annual averages of quarterly relatives in which 1926 is the base year.

viewed as a "laboratory test" of investment standards, involving degrees of stress not to be expected in the ordinary vicissitudes of the future. Even though the conditions prevalent in those years may not be duplicated, the behavior of various types of securities at the time should throw a useful light on investment problems.

Various Causes of Bond Collapses. 1. *Excessive Funded Debt of Utilities.* If we study the bond issues which suffered collapse in the post-bubble period, we shall observe that different causes underlay the troubles of each group. The public-utility defaults were caused not by a disappearance of earnings but by the inability of overextended debt structures to withstand a relatively moderate setback. Enterprises capitalized on a reasonably sound basis, as judged by former standards, had little difficulty in meeting bond interest. This did not hold true in the case of many holding companies with pyramided capital structures which had absorbed nearly every dollar of peak-year earnings for fixed charges and so had scarcely any margin available to meet a shrinkage in profits. The widespread difficulties of the utilities were due not to any weakness in the light and power *business*, but to the reckless extravagance of its financing methods. The losses of investors in public-utility bonds could for the most part have been avoided by the exercise of ordinary prudence in bond selection. Conversely, the unsound financing methods employed must eventually have resulted in individual collapses, even in the ordinary course of the business cycle. In consequence, the theory of investment in sound public-utility bonds appears in no sense to have been undermined by 1931–1933 experience.

2. *Stability of Railroad Earnings Overrated.* Turning to the railroads, we find a somewhat different situation. Here the fault appears to be that the stability of the transportation industry was overrated, so that investors were satisfied with a margin of protection which proved insufficient. It was not a matter of imprudently disregarding old established standards of safety, as in the case of the weaker utilities, but rather of being content with old standards when conditions called for more stringent requirements. Looking back, we can see that the failure of the carriers generally to increase their earnings with the great growth of the country since pre-war days was a sign of a weakened relative position, which called for a more cautious and exacting attitude by the investor. If he had required his railroad bonds to meet the same tests that he applied to industrial issues, he would have been compelled to confine his selection to a relatively few of the strongly situated lines.[3] As it turned out, nearly all of these have been able to withstand the tremendous loss of traffic since 1929 without danger to their fixed charges. Whether or not this is a case

---

[3] If, for example, the investor had restricted his attention to bonds of roads which in the prosperous year 1928 covered their fixed charges $2^1/_2$ times or better, he would have confined his selections to bonds of: Atchison; Canadian Pacific; Chesapeake and Ohio; Chicago, Burlington and Quincy; Norfolk and Western; Pere Marquette; Reading; and Union Pacific. (With the exception of Pere Marquette, the bonds of these roads fared comparatively well in the depression. Note, however, that the foregoing test may be more stringent than the one we propose later on: *average* earnings = twice fixed charges.)

of wisdom after the event is irrelevant to our discussion. Viewing past experience as a lesson for the future, we can see that *selecting railroad bonds on a depression basis* would mean requiring a larger margin of safety in normal times than was heretofore considered necessary.

The 1937–1938 Experience. These conclusions with respect to railroad and utility bonds are supported by the behavior of the two groups in the 1937–1938 recession. Nearly all issues which met reasonably stringent quantitative tests at the beginning of 1937 came through the ensuing slump with a relatively small market decline and no impairment of inherent position. On the other hand, bonds of both groups showing a substandard earnings coverage for 1936 suffered in most cases a really serious loss of quoted value, which in some instances proved the precursor of financial difficulties for the issuer.[4]

3. *Depression Performance of Industrial Bonds.* In the case of industrial obligations, the 1937–1938 pattern and the 1931–1933 pattern are appreciably different, so that the investor's attitude toward this type of security may depend somewhat on whether he feels it necessary to guard against the more or the less serious degree of depression. Studying the 1931–1933 record, we note that price collapses were not due primarily to unsound financial structures, as in the case of utility bonds, nor to a miscalculation by investors as to the margin of safety needed, as in the case of railroad bonds. We are confronted in many cases by a sudden disappearance of earning power, and a disconcerting question as to whether the business can survive. A company such as Gulf States Steel, for example, earned its 1929 interest charges at least $3^1/_2$ times in every year from 1922 to 1929. Yet in 1930 and 1931 operating losses were so large as to threaten its solvency.[5] Many basic industries, such as the Cuban sugar producers and our own coal mines, were depressed prior to the 1929 debacle. In the past, such eclipses had always proven to be temporary, and investors felt justified in holding the bonds of these companies in the expectation of a speedy recovery. But in this instance the continuance of adverse conditions beyond all previous experience defeated their calculations and destroyed the values behind their investment.

---

[4] See Appendix Note 11, p. 740 on accompanying CD, for a summary of the performance of representative railroad and utility bonds in 1937–1938, as related to earnings coverage for 1936.

[5] See Appendix Note 12, p. 741 on accompanying CD, for supporting data and other examples.

From these cases we must conclude that even a high margin of safety in good times may prove ineffective against a succession of operating losses caused by prolonged adversity. The difficulties that befell industrial bonds, therefore, cannot be avoided in the future merely by more stringent requirements as to bond-interest coverage in normal years.

If we examine more closely the behavior of the industrial bond list in 1932–1933 (taking all issues listed on the New York Stock Exchange), we shall note that the fraction that maintained a price reflecting reasonable confidence in the safety of the issue was limited to only 18 out of some 200 companies.[6]

The majority of these companies were of outstanding importance in their respective industries. This point suggests that *large size* is a trait of considerable advantage in dealing with exceptionally unfavorable developments in the industrial world, which may mean in turn that industrial investments should be restricted to major companies. The evidence, however, may be objected to on the ground of having been founded on an admittedly abnormal experience. The less drastic test of 1937–1938 points rather towards the conventional conclusion that issues strongly buttressed by past earnings can be relied on to withstand depressions.[7] If, however, we go back over a longer period—say, since 1915—we shall find perennial evidence of the instability of industrial earning power. Even in the supposedly prosperous period between 1922 and 1929, the bonds of smaller industrial enterprises did not prove a dependable medium of investment. There were many instances wherein an apparently well-established earning power suffered a sudden disappearance.[8] In fact these unpredictable variations were sufficiently numerous to suggest the conclusion that there is an inherent lack of stability in the small

---

[6] These companies were: American Machine and Foundry, American Sugar Refining Company, Associated Oil Company, Corn Products Refining Company, General Baking Company, General Electric Company, General Motors Acceptance Corporation, Humble Oil and Refining Company, International Business Machine Corporation, Liggett and Myers Tobacco Company, P. Lorillard Company, National Sugar Refining Company, Pillsbury Flour Mills Company, Smith (A.O.) Corporation, Socony-Vacuum Corporation, Standard Oil Company of Indiana, Standard Oil Company of New Jersey and United States Steel Corporation.

[7] Appendix Note 13, p. 742 on accompanying CD, summarizes the performance of industrial bonds in 1937–1938, as related to earnings for a period ended in 1936.

[8] See Appendix Note 14, p. 743 on accompanying CD, for examples.

or medium-sized industrial enterprise, which makes them ill-suited to bond financing. A tacit recognition of this weakness has been responsible in part for the growing adoption of conversion and subscription-warrant privileges in connection with industrial-bond financing.[9] To what extent such embellishments can compensate for insufficient safety will be discussed in our chapters on Senior Securities with Speculative Features. But in any event the widespread resort to these profit-sharing artifices seems to confirm our view that bonds of smaller industrial companies are not well qualified for consideration as fixed-value investments.

Unavailability of Sound Bonds No Excuse for Buying Poor Ones.

However, if we recommend that straight bond investment in the industrial field be confined to companies of dominant size, we face the difficulty that such companies are few in number and many of them have no bonds outstanding. It may be objected further that such an attitude would severely handicap the financing of legitimate businesses of secondary size and would have a blighting effect on investment-banking activities. The answer to these remonstrances must be that no consideration can justify the purchase of unsound bonds at an investment price. The fact that no good bonds are available is hardly an excuse for either issuing or accepting poor ones. Needless to say, the investor is never forced to buy a security of inferior grade. At some sacrifice in yield he can always find issues that meet his requirements, however stringent; and, as we shall point out later, attempts to increase yield at the expense of safety are likely to prove unprofitable. From the standpoint of the corporations and their investment bankers, the conclusion must follow that if their securities cannot properly qualify as straight investments, they must be given profit-making possibilities sufficient to compensate the purchaser for the risk he runs.

Conflicting Views on Bond Financing.

In this connection, observations are in order regarding two generally accepted ideas on the subject of bond financing. The first is that bond issues are an element of weakness in a company's financial position, so that the elimination of funded debt is always a desirable object. The second is that when companies are unable to finance through the sale of stock it is proper to raise

---

[9] See footnote 3, p. 290.

money by means of bond issues. In the writers' view both of these wide-spread notions are quite incorrect. Otherwise there would be no really sound basis for any bond financing. For they imply that only weak companies should be willing to sell bonds—which, if true, would mean that investors should not be willing to buy them.

Proper Theory of Bond Financing. The proper theory of bond financing, however, is of quite different import. A reasonable amount of funded debt is of advantage to a prosperous business, because the stockholders can earn a profit above interest charges through the use of the bondholders' capital. It is desirable for both the corporation and the investor that the borrowing be limited to an amount which can safely be taken care of under all conditions. Hence, from the standpoint of sound finance, there is no basic conflict of interest between the strong corporation which floats bonds and the public which buys them. On the other hand, whenever an element of unwillingness or compulsion enters into the creation of a bond issue by an enterprise, these bonds are *ipso facto* of secondary quality and it is unwise to purchase them on a straight investment basis.

Unsound Policies Followed in Practice. Financial policies followed by corporations and accepted by the public have for many years run counter to these logical principles. The railroads, for example, have financed the bulk of their needs through bond sales, resulting in an over-balancing of funded debt as against stock capital. This tendency has been repeatedly deplored by all authorities, but accepted as inevitable because poor earnings made stock sales impracticable. But if the latter were true, they also made bond purchases inadvisable. It is now quite clear that investors were imprudent in lending money to carriers which themselves complained of the necessity of having to borrow it.

While investors were thus illogically lending money to weak borrowers, many strong enterprises were paying off their debts through the sale of additional stock. But if there is any thoroughly sound basis for corporate borrowing, then this procedure must also be regarded as unwise. If a reasonable amount of borrowed capital, obtained at low interest rates, is advantageous to the stockholder, then the replacement of this debt by added stock capital means the surrender of such advantage. The elimination of debt will naturally simplify the problems of the management, but surely there must be some point at which the return to the stockholders must also be considered. Were this not so, corporations would be constantly raising money from their owners and they would never pay any part of it back in dividends. It should be pointed out that the mania for debt retirement in 1927–1929 has had a disturbing effect upon our banking situation, since it eliminated most of the good commercial borrowers and replaced them by second-grade business risks and by loans on stock collateral, which were replete with possibilities of harm.

Significance of the Foregoing to the Investor. The above analysis of the course of industrial bond borrowing in the last 15 years is not irrelevant to the theme of this chapter, *viz.*, the application of depression standards to the selection of fixed-value investments. Recognizing the necessity of ultra-stringent criteria of choice in the industrial field, the bond buyer is faced by a further narrowing of eligible issues due to the elimination of funded debt by many of the strongest companies. Clearly his reaction must not be to accept the issues of less desirable enterprises, in the absence of better ones, but rather to refrain from any purchases on an investment basis if the suitable ones are not available. It appears to be a financial axiom that whenever there is money to invest, it is invested; and if the owner cannot find a good security yielding a fair return, he will invariably buy a poor one. But a prudent and intelligent investor should be able to avoid this temptation, and reconcile himself to accepting an unattractive yield from the best bonds, in preference to risking his principal in second-grade issues for the sake of a large coupon return.

Summary. The rule that bonds should be bought on the basis of their ability to withstand depression has been part of an old investment tradition. It was nearly lost sight of in the prosperous period culminating in 1929, but its importance was made painfully manifest during the following collapse and demonstrated again in the 1937–1938 recession. The bonds of reasonably capitalized electric and gas companies have given a satisfactory account of themselves during this decade and the same is true—to a lesser degree—of the relatively few railroads which showed a large margin above interest charges prior to 1930. In the industrial list, however, even an excellent past record has in many cases proved undependable, especially where the company is of small or moderate size. For this reason, the investor would seem to gain better protection against adverse developments by confining his industrial selections to companies which meet the two requirements of (1) dominant size and (2) substantial margin of earnings over bond interest.

III. THIRD PRINCIPLE: UNSOUND TO SACRIFICE SAFETY FOR YIELD

In the traditional theory of bond investment a mathematical relationship is supposed to exist between the interest rate and the degree of risk incurred. The interest return is divided into two components, the first constituting "pure interest"—*i.e.*, the rate obtainable with *no* risk of loss—and the second representing the premium obtained to compensate for the risk assumed. If, for example, the "pure interest rate" is assumed to be 2%, then a 3% investment is supposed to involve one chance in a hundred of loss, while the risk incurred in an 7% investment would be five times as great, or 1 in 20. (Presumably the risk should be somewhat less than that indicated, to allow for an "insurance profit.")

This theory implies that bond-interest rates are closely similar to insurance rates, and that they measure the degree of risk on some reasonably precise actuarial basis. It would follow that, by and large, the return from high-and low-yielding investments should tend to equalize, since what the former gain in income would be offset by their greater percentage of principal losses, and *vice versa*.

No Mathematical Relationship between Yield and Risk. This view, however, seems to us to bear little relation to the realities of bond investment. Security prices and yields are not determined by any exact mathematical calculation of the expected risk, but they depend rather upon the *popularity* of the issue. This popularity reflects in a general way the investors' view as to the risk involved, but it is also influenced largely by other factors, such as the degree of familiarity of the public with the company and the issue (seasoning) and the ease with which the bond can be sold (marketability).

It may be pointed out further that the supposed actuarial computation of investment risks is out of the question theoretically as well as in practice. There are no experience tables available by which the expected "mortality" of various types of issues can be determined. Even if such tables were prepared, based on long and exhaustive studies of past records, it is doubtful whether they would have any real utility for the future. In life insurance the relation between age and mortality rate is well defined and changes only gradually. The same is true, to a much lesser extent, of the relation between the various types of structures and the fire hazard attaching to them. But the relation between different kinds of investments and the risk of loss is entirely too indefinite, and too variable with changing conditions, to permit of sound mathematical formulation. This is particularly true because investment losses are not distributed fairly evenly in point of time, but tend to be concentrated at intervals, *i.e.*, during periods of general depression. Hence the typical investment hazard is roughly similar to the conflagration or epidemic hazard, which is the exceptional and incalculable factor in fire or life insurance.

Self-insurance Generally Not Possible in Investment. If we were to assume that a precise mathematical relationship does exist between yield and risk, then the result of this premise should be inevitably to recommend the lowest yielding—and therefore the safest—bonds to all investors. For the individual is not qualified to be an insurance underwriter. It is not his function to be paid for incurring risks; on the contrary it is to his interest to pay others for insurance against loss. Let us assume a bond buyer has his choice of investing $1,000 for $20 per annum without risk, or for $70 per annum with 1 chance out of 20 each year that his principal would be lost. The $50 additional income on the second investment is mathematically equivalent to the risk involved. But in terms of *personal requirements*, an investor cannot afford to take even a small chance of losing $1,000 of principal in return for an extra $50 of income. Such a procedure would be the direct opposite of the standard procedure of *paying* small annual sums to protect property values against loss by fire and theft.

The Factor of Cyclical Risks. The investor cannot prudently turn himself into an insurance company and incur risks of losing his principal in exchange for annual premiums in the form of extra-large interest coupons. One objection to such a policy is that sound insurance practice requires a very wide distribution of risk, in order to minimize the influence of luck and to allow maximum play to the law of probability. The investor may endeavor to attain this end by diversifying his holdings, but as a practical matter he cannot approach the division of risk attained by an insurance company. More important still is the danger that many risky investments may collapse together in a depression period, so that the investor in high-yielding issues will find a period of large income (which he will probably spend) followed suddenly by a deluge of losses of principal.

It may be contended that the higher yielding securities on the whole return a larger premium above "pure interest" than the degree of risk requires; in other words, that in return for taking the risk, investors will in the long run obtain a *profit* over and above the losses in principal suffered. It is difficult to say definitely whether or not this is true. But even assuming that the high coupon rates will, in the great aggregate, more than compensate on an *actuarial* basis for the risks accepted, such bonds are still undesirable investments from the *personal* standpoint of the average investor. Our arguments against the investor turning himself into an insurance company remain valid even if the insurance operations all told may prove profitable. The bond buyer is neither financially nor psychologically equipped to carry on extensive transactions involving the setting up of reserves out of regular income to absorb losses in substantial amounts suffered at irregular intervals.

Risk and Yield Are Incommensurable. The foregoing discussion leads us to suggest the principle that income return and risk of principal should be regarded as *incommensurable*. Practically speaking, this means that acknowledged risks of losing principal should not be offset merely by a high coupon rate, but can be accepted only in return for a corresponding opportunity for enhancement of principal, *e.g.*, through the purchase of bonds at a substantial discount from par, or possibly by obtaining an unusually attractive conversion privilege. While there may be no real *mathematical* difference between offsetting risks of loss by a higher income or by a chance for profit, the *psychological* difference is very important. The purchaser of low-priced bonds is fully aware of the risk he is running; he is more likely to make a thorough investigation of the issue and to appraise carefully the chances of loss and of profit; finally—most important of all—he is prepared for whatever losses he may sustain, and his profits are in a form available to meet his losses. Actual investment experience, therefore, will not favor the purchase of the typical high-coupon bond offered at about par, wherein, for example, a

7% interest return is imagined to compensate for a distinctly inferior grade of security.[10]

Fallacy of the "Business Man's Investment." An issue of this type is commonly referred to in the financial world as a "business man's investment" and is supposedly suited to those who can afford to take some degree of risk. Most of the foreign bonds floated between 1923 and 1929 belonged in that category. The same is true of the great bulk of straight preferred stock issues. According to our view, such "business man's investments" are an illogical type of commitment. The security buyer who can afford to take some risk should seek a commensurate opportunity of enhancement in price and pay only secondary attention to the income obtained.

Reversal of Customary Procedure Recommended. Viewing the matter more broadly, it would be well if investors reversed their customary attitude toward income return. In selecting the grade of bonds suitable to their situation, they are prone to start at the top of the list, where maximum safety is combined with lowest yield, and then to calculate how great a concession from ideal security they are willing to make for the sake of a more attractive income rate. From this point of view, the ordinary investor becomes accustomed to the idea that the type of issue suited to his needs must rank somewhere below the very best, a frame of mind which is likely to lead to the acceptance of definitely unsound bonds, either because of their high income return or by surrender to the blandishments of the bond salesman.

It would be sounder procedure to start with minimum standards of safety, which all bonds must be required to meet in order to be eligible for further consideration. Issues failing to meet these minimum requirements should be automatically disqualified as straight investments, regardless of high yield, attractive prospects, or other grounds for partiality. Having thus delimited the field of eligible investments, the buyer may then apply such further selective processes as he deems appropriate. He may desire elements of safety far beyond the accepted minima, in which case he must ordinarily make some sacrifice of yield. He may also indulge

---

[10] In an exceptional year such as 1921 strongly entrenched bonds were offered bearing a 7% coupon, due to the prevailing high money rates.

his preferences as to the nature of the business and the character of the management. But, essentially, bond selection should consist of working upward from definite minimum standards rather than working downward in haphazard fashion from some ideal but unacceptable level of maximum security.

Chapter 8

SPECIFIC STANDARDS FOR
BOND INVESTMENT

IV. FOURTH PRINCIPLE: DEFINITE STANDARDS OF SAFETY MUST BE APPLIED

Since the selection of high-grade bonds has been shown to be in good part a process of exclusion, it lends itself reasonably well to the application of definite rules and standards designed to disqualify unsuitable issues. Such regulations have in fact been set up in many states by legislative enactment to govern the investments made by savings banks and by trust funds. In most such states, the banking department prepares each year a list of securities which appear to conform to these regulations and are therefore considered "legal," *i.e.*, eligible for purchase under the statute.

It is our view that the underlying idea of fixed standards and minima should be extended to the entire field of straight investment, *i.e.*, investment for income only. These legislative restrictions are intended to promote a high average level of investment quality and to protect depositors and beneficiaries against losses from unsafe securities. If such regulations are desirable in the case of institutions, it should be logical for individuals to follow them also. We have previously challenged the prevalent idea that the ordinary investor can afford to take greater investment risks than a savings bank, and need not therefore be as exacting with respect to the soundness of his fixed-value securities. The experience since 1928 undoubtedly emphasizes the need for a general tightening of investment standards, and a simple method of attaining this end might be to confine all straight-bond selections to those which meet the legal tests of eligibility for savings banks or trust funds. Such a procedure would appear directly consonant with our fundamental principle that straight investments should be made only in issues of unimpeachable soundness, and that securities of inferior grade must be bought only on an admittedly speculative basis.

New York Savings-bank Law as a Point of Departure. As a matter of *practical policy*, an individual bond buyer is likely to obtain fairly satisfactory results by subjecting himself to the restrictions which govern the investment of savings banks' funds. But this procedure cannot be seriously suggested as a *general principle of investment*, because the legislative provisions are themselves far too imperfect to warrant their acceptance as the best available theoretical standards. The acts of the various states are widely divergent; most of them are antiquated in important respects; none is entirely logical or scientific. The legislators did not approach their task from the viewpoint of establishing criteria of sound investments for universal use; consequently they felt free to impose arbitrary restrictions on savings-bank and trust funds, which they would have hesitated to prescribe for investors generally. The New York statute, generally regarded as the best of its class, is nevertheless marred by a number of evident defects. In the formulation of comprehensive investment standards, the New York legislation may best be used, therefore, as a guide or point of departure, rather than as a final authority. The ensuing discussion will follow fairly closely the pattern set forth in the statutory provisions (as they existed in 1939); but these will be criticized, rejected, or amplified, whenever such emendation appears desirable.

GENERAL CRITERIA PRESCRIBED BY THE NEW YORK STATUTE

The specific requirements imposed by the statute upon bond investments may be classified under seven heads, which we shall proceed to enumerate and discuss:

1. The *nature* and *location* of the business or government.
2. The *size* of the enterprise, or the issue.
3. The *terms* of the issue.
4. The *record* of solvency and dividend payments.
5. The relation of *earnings* to interest requirements.
6. The relation of the *value* of the property to the funded debt.
7. The relation of *stock* capitalization to the funded debt.

NATURE AND LOCATION

The most striking features of the laws governing savings-bank investments is the complete exclusion of bonds in certain broad categories. The New York provisions relative to permitted and prohibited classes may be summarized as follows (subject to a 1938 amendment soon to be discussed):

Admitted	Excluded
United States government, state and municipal bonds.	Foreign government and foreign corporation bonds.
Railroad bonds and electric, gas and telephone mortgage bonds.	Street railway and water bonds. Debentures of public utilities.
Bonds secured by first mortgages on real estate.	All industrial bonds.
	Bonds of financial companies (investment trusts, credit concerns, etc.).

The Fallacy of Blanket Prohibitions. The legislature was evidently of the view that bonds belonging to the excluded categories are essentially too unstable to be suited to savings-bank investment. If this view is entirely sound, it would follow from our previous reasoning that all issues in these groups are unsuited to conservative investment generally. Such a conclusion would involve revolutionary changes in the field of finance, since a large part of the capital now regularly raised in the investment market would have to be sought on an admittedly speculative basis.

In our opinion, a considerable narrowing of the investment category is in fact demanded by the unsatisfactory experience of bond investors over a fairly long period. Nevertheless, there are strong objections to the application of blanket prohibitions of the kind now under discussion. Investment theory should be chary of easy generalizations. Even if full recognition is given, for example, to the unstable tendencies of industrial bonds, as discussed in Chap. 7, the elimination of this entire major group from investment consideration would seem neither practicable nor desirable. The existence of a fair number of industrial issues (even though a small percentage of the total) which have maintained an undoubted investment status through the severest tests, would preclude investors generally from adopting so drastic a policy. Moreover, the confining of investment demand to a few eligible types of enterprise is likely to make for scarcity, and hence for the acceptance of inferior issues merely because they fall within these groups. This has in fact been one of the unfortunate results of the present legislative restrictions.

Individual Strength May Compensate for Inherent Weakness of a Class. It would seem a sounder principle, therefore, to require a stronger exhibit by the *individual* bond to compensate for any weakness supposedly inherent in its *class*, rather than to seek to admit all bonds of certain favored groups and to exclude all bonds of others. An industrial bond may properly be required to show a larger margin of earnings over interest charges and a smaller proportion of debt to going-concern value than would be required of an obligation of a gas or electric enterprise. The same would apply in the case of traction bonds. In connection with the exclusion of *water-company bonds* by the New York statute, it should be noted that this group is considered by most other states to be on a par with gas, electric, and telephone obligations. There seems to be no good reason for subjecting them to more stringent requirements than in the case of other types of public-service issues.

The 1938 Amendment to the Banking Law. In 1938 the New York legislature, recognizing the validity of these objections to categorical exclusions, proceeded to relieve the situation in a rather peculiar manner. It decreed that the Banking Board could authorize savings banks to invest in interest-bearing obligations not otherwise eligible for investment, provided application for such authorization shall have been made by not less than 20 savings banks, or by a trust company, all of the capital stock of which is owned by not less than 20 savings banks. (This meant the Savings Bank Trust Company of New York.)

Clearly this amendment goes much farther than a mere widening of the categories of savings-bank investment. What it does, in fact, is to supersede—potentially, at least—all the specific requirements of the law (other than the primary insistence on interest-paying bonds) by the combined judgment of the savings banks themselves and the Banking Board. This means that, in theory, all seven of the criteria imposed by the law may be set aside by agreement of the parties. Obviously there is no practical danger that the legislative wisdom of the statute will be completely flouted. In fact, investments authorized by virtue of this new provision up to the end of 1939 are all unexceptionable in character. They include previously ineligible debenture issues of very strong telephone and industrial companies. (Curiously enough, no industrial mortgage bond has as yet been approved, but this may serve to confirm our previous statement that good industrial bonds are likely to be debentures.)

The action to date under the 1938 amendment has represented a praiseworthy departure from the unduly narrow restrictions of the statute itself, which we have criticized above. We are by no means convinced, however, that the legislation as it now stands is in really satisfactory form. There seems to be something puerile about enacting a long list of rules and then permitting an administrative body to waive as many of them as it sees fit. Would it not be better to prescribe a few really important criteria, which must be followed in every instance, and then give the Banking Board discretionary power to *exclude* issues that meet these minimum requirements but still are not sound enough in its conservative judgment?

Obligations of Foreign Governments. We have argued against any broad exclusions of entire categories of bonds. But in dealing with foreign-government debts, a different type of reasoning may conceivably be justified. Such issues respond in but small degree to financial analysis, and investment therein is ordinarily based on general considerations, such as confidence in the country's economic and political stability and the belief that it will faithfully endeavor to discharge its obligations. To a much greater extent, therefore, than in the case of other bonds, an opinion may be justified or even necessitated as to the *general desirability* of foreign-government bonds for fixed-value investment.

The Factor of Political Expediency. Viewing objectively the history of foreign-bond investment in this country since it first assumed importance during the World War, it is difficult to escape an unfavorable conclusion on this point. In the final analysis, a foreign-government debt is an unenforceable contract. If payment is withheld, the bondholder has no direct remedy. Even if specific revenues or assets are pledged as security, he is practically helpless in the event that these pledges are broken.[1]

---

[1] Among the numerous examples of this unhappy fact we may mention the pledge of specific revenues behind the Dawes Loan (German government) 7s, due 1949, and the Sao Paulo Secured 7s, due 1956. Following default of service of these two loans in 1934 and 1932, respectively, nothing whatever was done, or could have been done, to enforce the claim against the pledged revenues.

It follows that while a foreign-government obligation is in theory a claim against the entire resources of the nation, the extent to which these resources are actually drawn upon to meet the external debt burden is found to depend in good part on political expediency. The grave international dislocations of the postwar period made some defaults inevitable, and supplied the pretext for others. In any event, because nonpayment has become a familiar phenomenon, its very frequency has removed much of the resultant obloquy. Hence the investor has, seemingly less reason than of old to rely upon herculean efforts being made by a foreign government to live up to its obligations during difficult times.

The Foreign-trade Argument. It is generally argued that a renewal of large-scale international lending is necessary to restore world equilibrium. More concretely, such lending appears to be an indispensable adjunct to the restoration and development of our export trade. But the investor should not be expected to make unsound commitments for idealistic reasons or to benefit American exporters. As a *speculative operation*, the purchase of foreign obligations at low prices, such as prevailed in 1932, might prove well justified by the attendant possibilities of profit; but these tremendously depreciated quotations are in themselves a potent argument against later purchases of new foreign issues at a price close to 100% of face value, no matter how high the coupon rate may be set.

The Individual-record Argument. It may be contended, however, that investment in foreign obligations is essentially similar to any other form of investment in that it requires discrimination and judgment. Some nations deserve a high credit rating based on their past performance, and these are entitled to investment preference to the same degree as are domestic corporations with satisfactory records. The legislatures of several states have recognized the superior standing of Canada by authorizing savings banks to purchase its obligations, and Vermont has accepted also the dollar bonds of Belgium, Denmark, Great Britain, Holland, and Switzerland.

A strong argument in the contrary direction is supplied by the appended list of the various countries having debts payable in dollars, classified according to the credit rating indicated by the market action of their bonds during the severe test of 1932.

1. Countries whose bonds sold on an investment basis: Canada, France, Great Britain, Netherlands, Switzerland.

2. Countries whose bonds sold on a speculative basis: Argentina, Australia, Austria, Bolivia, Brazil, Bulgaria, Chile, China, Colombia, Costa Rica, Cuba, Czecho-Slovakia, Denmark, Dominican Republic, Esthonia, Finland, Germany, Guatemala, Greece, Haiti, Hungary, Japan, Jugoslavia, Mexico, Nicaragua, Panama, Peru, Poland, Rumania, Russia, Salvador, Uruguay.

3. Borderline countries: Belgium, Ireland, Italy, Norway, Sweden.

Of the five countries in the first or investment group, the credit of two, *viz.*, France and Great Britain, was considered speculative in the preceding depression of 1921–1922. Out of 42 countries represented, therefore, only three (Canada, Holland, and Switzerland) enjoyed an unquestioned investment rating during the twelve years ending in 1932.

Twofold Objection to Purchase of Foreign-government Bonds. This evidence suggests that the purchase of foreign-government bonds is subject to a twofold objection of *generic* character: theoretically, in that the basis for credit is fundamentally intangible; and practically, in that experience with the foreign group has been preponderantly unsatisfactory. Apparently it will require a considerable betterment of world conditions, demonstrated by a fairly long period of punctual discharge of international obligations, to warrant a revision of this unfavorable attitude toward foreign bonds as a class.

Canadian issues may undoubtedly be exempted from this blanket condemnation, both on their record and because of the closeness of the relationship between Canada and the United States. Individual investors, for either personal or statistical reasons, may be equally convinced of the high credit standing of various other countries, and will therefore be ready to purchase their obligations as high-grade investments. Such commitments may prove to be fully justified by the facts; but for some years, at least, it would be well if the investor approached them in the light of *exceptions* to a general rule of avoiding foreign bonds, and required them accordingly to present exceptionally strong evidence of stability and safety.[2]

---

[2] The foregoing section relating to foreign-government bonds is reproduced without change from the 1934 edition of this work. War conditions existing in 1940 add emphasis to our conclusions. Note that at the end of 1939 the dollar bonds of only Argentina, Canada, and Cuba were selling on better than a 6% basis in our markets. (Certain Cuban bonds were selling to yield over 6%. Note also that Great Britain, Netherlands, Sweden, and Switzerland had no dollar bonds outstanding.) For data concerning foreign-bond defaults see various news releases and reports of Foreign Bondholders' Protective Council, Inc.

Bonds of Foreign Corporations. In *theory*, bonds of a corporation, however prosperous, cannot enjoy better security than the obligations of the country in which the corporation is located. The government, through its taxing power, has an unlimited prior claim upon the assets and earnings of the business; in other words, it can take the property away from the private bondholder and utilize it to discharge the national debt. But in actuality, distinct limits are imposed by political expediency upon the exercise of the taxing power. Accordingly we find instances of corporations meeting their dollar obligations even when their government is in default.[3]

Foreign-corporation bonds have an advantage over governmental bonds in that the holder enjoys specific legal remedies in the event of nonpayment, such as the right of foreclosure. Consequently it is probably true that a foreign company is under greater *compulsion* to meet its debt than is a sovereign nation. But it must be recognized that the conditions resulting in the default of government obligations are certain to affect adversely the position of the corporate bondholder. Restrictions on the transfer of funds may prevent the payment of interest in dollars even though the company may remain amply solvent.[4] Furthermore, the distance separating the creditor from the property, and the obstacles interposed by governmental decree, are likely to destroy the practical value of his mortgage security. For these reasons the unfavorable conclusions reached with respect to foreign-government obligations as fixed-value investments must be considered as applicable also to foreign-corporation bonds.

SIZE

The bonds of very small enterprises are subject to objections which disqualify them as media for conservative investment. A company of relatively minor size is more vulnerable than others to unexpected happenings, and it is likely to be handicapped by the lack of strong banking connections or of technical resources. Very small businesses, therefore, have never been able to obtain public financing and have depended on private capital, those supplying the funds being given the double inducement

---

[3] See Appendix Note 15, p. 743 on accompanying CD, for examples.

[4] See Appendix Note 16, p. 744 on accompanying CD, for examples.

of a share in the profits and a direct voice in the management. The objections to bonds of undersized corporations apply also to tiny villages or microscopic townships, and the careful investor in municipal obligations will ordinarily avoid those below a certain population level.

The establishment of such minimum requirements as to size necessarily involves the drawing of arbitrary lines of demarcation. There is no mathematical means of determining exactly at what point a company or a municipality becomes large enough to warrant the investor's attention. The same difficulty will attach to setting up any other quantitative standards, as for example the margin of earnings above interest charges, or the relation of stock or property values to bonded debt. It must be borne in mind, therefore, that all these "critical points" are necessarily rule-of-thumb decisions, and the investor is free to use other amounts if they appeal to him more. But however arbitrary the standards selected may be, they are undoubtedly of great practical utility in safeguarding the bond buyer from inadequately protected issues.

Provisions of New York Statute. The New York statute has prescribed various standards as to minimum size in defining investments eligible for savings banks. As regards municipal bonds, a population of not less than 10,000 is required for states adjacent to New York, and of 30,000 for other states. Railroads must either own 500 miles of standard-gauge line or else have operating revenues of not less than $10,000,000 per annum. Unsecured and income bonds of railroad companies are admitted only if (among other special requirements) the *net income* available for dividends amounts to $10,000,000. For gas and electric companies, gross revenues must have averaged $1,000,000 per year during the preceding five years; but in the case of telephone bonds, this figure must be $5,000,000. There are further provisions to the effect that the size of the bond issue itself must be not less than $1,000,000 for gas and electric companies, and not less than $5,000,000 in the case of telephone obligations.

Some Criticisms of These Requirements. The figures of minimum gross receipts do not appear well chosen from the standpoint of bond investment in general. The distinctions as to population requirements would scarcely appeal to investors throughout the country. The alternative tests for railroads, based on either mileage or revenues, are confusing and unnecessary. The $10,000,000-gross requirement by itself is too high; it would have eliminated, for example, the Bangor and Aroostook Railroad, one of the few lines to make a satisfactory exhibit during the 1930–1933 depression as well as before. Equally unwarranted is the requirement of $5,000,000 gross for telephone concerns, as against only $1,000,000 for gas and electric utilities. This provision would have ruled out the bonds of Tri-State Telephone and Telegraph Company prior to 1927, although they were then (and since) obligations of unquestioned merit. We believe that the following proposed requirements for minimum size, although by necessity arbitrarily taken, are in reasonable accord with the realities of sound investment:

Minimum Requirement of Size

Municipalities	10,000 population
Public-utility enterprises	$2,000,000 gross
Railroad systems	$3,000,000 gross
Industrial companies	$5,000,000 gross

Industrial Bonds and the Factor of Size. Since industrial bonds are not eligible for savings banks under the New York law, no minimum size is therein prescribed. We have expressed the view that industrial obligations may be included among high-grade investments provided they meet stringent tests of safety. The experience of the past decade indicates that dominant or at least substantial size affords an element of protection against the hazards of instability to which industrial enterprises are more subject than are railroads or public utilities. A cautious investor, seeking to profit from recent lessons, would apparently be justified in deciding to confine his purchases of fixed-value bonds to perhaps the half dozen leading units in each industrial group, and also perhaps in adding the suggested minimum requirement of $5,000,000 annual sales.

Such minimum standards may be criticized as unduly stringent, in that if they were universally applied (which in any event is unlikely) they would make it impossible for sound and prosperous businesses of moderate size to finance themselves through straight bond issues. It is conceivable that a general stabilization of industrial conditions in the United States may invalidate the conclusions derived from the extreme variations of the past ten years. But until such a tendency in the direction of stability has actually demonstrated itself, we should favor a highly exacting attitude toward the purchase of industrial bonds *at investment levels.*

Large Size Alone No Guarantee of Safety. These recommendations on the subject of minimum size do not imply that enormous dimensions are in themselves a guarantee of prosperity and financial strength. The biggest company may be the weakest if its bonded debt is disproportionately large. Moreover, in the railroad, public-utility, and municipal groups, no practical advantage attaches to the very largest units as compared with those of medium magnitude. Whether the gross receipts of an electric company are twenty millions or a hundred millions has, in all probability, no material effect on the safety of its bonds; and similarly a town of 75,000 inhabitants may deserve better credit than would a city of several millions. It is only in the industrial field that we have suggested that the bonds of a very large enterprise may be inherently more desirable than those of middle-sized companies; but even here a thoroughly satisfactory statistical showing on the part of the large company is necessary to make this advantage a dependable one.

Other Provisions Rejected. The New York statute includes an additional requirement in respect to unsecured railroad bonds, *viz.*, that the *net* earnings after interest charge must equal $10,000,000. This does not appear to us to be justified, since we have previously argued against attaching particular significance to the possession or lack of mortgage security. There is a certain logical fallacy also in the further prescription of a minimum size for the bond issue itself in the case of public utilities. If the enterprise is large enough as measured by its gross business, then the smaller the bond issue the easier it would be to meet interest and principal requirements. The legislature probably desired to avoid the inferior marketability associated with very small issues. In our view, the element of marketability is generally given too much stress by investors; and in this case we do not favor following the statutory requirement with respect to the size of the issue as a general rule for bond investment.

See accompanying CD for Chapter 9, "Specific Standards for Bond Investment *(Continued)*."

Chapter 10

SPECIFIC STANDARDS FOR
BOND INVESTMENT (*Continued*)

THE RELATION OF THE VALUE OF THE PROPERTY TO THE FUNDED DEBT

In our earlier discussion (Chap. 6) we pointed out that the soundness of the typical bond investment depends upon the ability of the obligor corporation to take care of its debts, rather than upon the value of the property on which the bonds have a lien. This broad principle naturally leads directly away from the establishment of any *general* tests of bond safety based upon the value of the mortgaged assets, where this value is considered apart from the success or failure of the enterprise itself.

Stating the matter differently, we do not believe that in the case of the ordinary corporation bond—whether railroad, utility, or industrial—it would be advantageous to stipulate any minimum relationship between the value of the physical property pledged (taken at either original or reproduction cost) and the amount of the debt. In this respect we are in disagreement with statutory provisions in many states (including New York) which reflect the traditional emphasis upon property values. The New York law, for example, will not admit as eligible a gas, electric, or telephone bond, unless it is secured by property having a value $66^2/3\%$ in excess of the bond issue. This value is presumably book value, which either may be the original dollar cost less depreciation or may be some more or less artificial value set up as a result of transfer or reappraisal.

Special Types of Obligations: 1. Equipment Obligations. It is our view that the book value of public-utility properties—and of railroads and the typical industrial plant as well—is no guidance in determining the safety of the bond issues secured thereon. There are, however, various *special* types of obligations, the safety of which is in great measure

[180]

dependent upon the assets securing them, as distinguished from the going-concern value of the enterprise as a whole. The most characteristic of these, perhaps, is the railroad-equipment trust certificate, secured by title to locomotives, freight cars, or passenger cars, and by the pledge of the lease under which the railroad is using the equipment. The investment record of these equipment obligations is very satisfactory, particularly because until recently even the most serious financial difficulties of the issuing road have very rarely prevented the prompt payment of interest and principal.[1] The primary reason for these good results is that the specific property pledged is removable and usable by other carriers. Consequently it enjoys an independent salable value, similar to automobiles, jewelry, and other chattels on which personal loans are made. Even where there might be great difficulty in actually selling the rolling stock to some other railroad at a reasonable price, this mobility still gives the equipment obligation a great advantage over the mortgages on the railroad itself. Both kinds of property are essential to the operation of the line, but the railroad bondholder has no alternative save to permit the receiver to operate his property, while the holder of the equipment lien can at least threaten to take the rolling stock away. It is the possession of this *alternative* which in practice has proved of prime value to the owner of equipment trusts because it has virtually compelled the holders even of the first mortgages on the road itself to subordinate their claim to his.

It follows that the holder of equipment-trust certificates has two separate sources of protection, the one being the credit and success of the borrowing railway, the other being the value of the pledged rolling stock. If the latter value is sufficiently in excess of the money loaned against it, he may be able to ignore the first or credit factor entirely, in the same way as a pawn-broker ignores the financial status of the individual to whom he lends money and is content to rely exclusively on the pledged property.

The conditions under which equipment trusts are usually created supply a substantial degree of protection to the purchaser. The legal forms are designed to facilitate the enforcement of the lienholder's rights in the event of nonpayment. In practically all cases at least 20% of the cost of the equipment is provided by the railway, and consequently the amount of the equipment obligations is initially not more than 80% of the value

---

[1] See Appendix Note 17, p. 744 on accompanying CD, for information on the investment record of such issues.

of the property pledged behind them. The principal is usually repayable in 15 equal annual installments, beginning one year from issuance, so that the amount of the debt is reduced more rapidly than ordinary depreciation would require.

The protection accorded the equipment-trust holder by these arrangements has been somewhat diminished in recent years, due partly to the drop in commodity prices which has brought reproduction (and therefore, salable) values far below original cost, and also to the reduced demand for equipment, whether new or used, because of the smaller traffic handled. Since 1930 certain railroads in receivership (e.g., Seaboard Air Line and Wabash) have required holders of maturing equipment obligations to extend their maturities for a short period or to exchange them for trustee's or receiver's certificates carrying a lower coupon. In the unique case of one Florida East Coast Railway issue (Series "D") the receivers permitted the equipment-trust holders to take over and sell the pledged equipment, which seemed to have been less valuable than that securing other series. In this instance the holders realized only 43 cents on the dollar from the sale and have a deficiency judgment (of doubtful value) against the road for the balance. These maneuvers and losses suggest that the claim of "almost absolute safety" frequently made in behalf of equipment issues will have to be moderated; but it cannot be denied that this form of investment enjoys a positive and substantial advantage through the realizability of the pledged assets.[2] (This conclusion may be supported by a concrete reference to the sale in November 1939 of Chicago and North Western new Equipment Trust $2^{1}/_{2}$s, due 1940–1949, at prices to yield only from 0.45 to 2.35%, despite the fact that all the mortgage issues of that road were then in default.)

2. Collateral-trust Bonds. Collateral-trust bonds are obligations secured by the pledge of stocks or other bonds. In the typical case, the collateral consists of bonds of the obligor company itself, or of the bonds or stocks of subsidiary corporations. Consequently the realizable value of the collateral is usually dependent in great measure on the success of the enterprise as a whole. But in the case of the collateral-trust issues of investment companies, a development of recent years, the holder may be said to have a primary interest in the market value of the pledged

---

[2] See Appendix Note 18, p. 747 on accompanying CD, for comment and supporting data.

securities, so that it is quite possible that by virtue of the protective conditions in the indenture, he may be completely taken care of under conditions which mean virtual extinction for the stockholders. This type of collateral-trust bond may therefore be ranked with equipment-trust obligations as exceptions to our general rule that the bond buyer must place his chief reliance on the success of the enterprise and not on the property specifically pledged.

Going behind the form to the substance, we may point out that this characteristic is essentially true also of investment-trust *debenture* obligations. For it makes little practical difference whether the portfolio is physically pledged with a trustee, as under a collateral-trust indenture, or whether it is held by the corporation subject to the claim of the debenture bondholders. In the usual case the debentures are protected by adequate provisions against increasing the debt, and frequently also by a covenant requiring the market price of the company's assets to be maintained at a stated percentage above the face amount of the bonds.

Example: The Reliance Management Corporation Debenture 5s, due 1954, are an instance of the working of these protective provisions. The enterprise as a whole was highly unsuccessful, as is shown vividly by a decline in the price of the stock from 69 in 1929 to 1 in 1933. In the case of the ordinary bond issue, such a collapse in the stock value would have meant almost certain default and large loss of principal. But here the fact that the assets could be readily turned into cash gave significance to the protective covenants behind the debentures. It made possible and compelled the repurchase by the company of more than three-quarters of the issue, and it even forced the stockholders to contribute additional capital to make good a deficiency of assets below the indenture requirements. This resulted in the bonds selling as high as 88 in 1932 when the stock sold for only $2^{1}/_{2}$. The balance of the issue was called at $104^{1}/_{4}$ in February 1937.

In Chap. 18, devoted to protective covenants, we shall refer to the history of a collateral-trust bond issue of an investment company (Financial Investing Company), and we shall point out that the intrinsic strength of such obligations is often impaired—unnecessarily, in our opinion—by hesitation in asserting the bondholders' rights.

3. Real Estate Bonds. Of much greater importance than either of the two types of securities just discussed is the large field of real estate

mortgages and real estate mortgage bonds. The latter represent participations of convenient size in large individual mortgages. There is no
doubt that in the case of such obligations the value of the pledged land
and buildings is of paramount importance. The ordinary real estate loan
made by an experienced investor is based chiefly upon his conclusions as
to the fair value of the property offered as security. It seems to us, however, that in a broad sense the values behind real estate mortgages are
going-concern values; i.e., they are derived fundamentally from the earning power of the property, either actual or presumptive. In other words,
the value of the pledged asset is not something *distinct* from the success
of the enterprise (as is possibly the case with a railroad-equipment trust
certificate), but is rather *identical* therewith.

This point may be made clearer by a reference to the most typical form
of real estate loan, a first mortgage on a single-family dwelling house.
Under ordinary conditions a home costing $10,000 would have a rental
value (or an equivalent value to an owner-tenant) of some $1,200 per year,
and would yield a net income of about $800 after taxes and other
expenses. A 5% first-mortgage loan on the savings-bank basis, *i.e.,* 60%
of value, or $6,000, would therefore be protected by a normal *earning
power* of over twice the interest requirements. Stated differently, the rental
value could suffer a reduction of over one-third before the ability to meet
interest charges would be impaired. Hence the mortgagee reasons that
regardless of the ability of the then owner of the house to pay the carrying charges, he could always find a tenant or a new purchaser who would
rent or buy the property on a basis at least sufficient to cover his 60% loan.
(By way of contrast, it may be pointed out that a typical *industrial plant,*
costing $1,000,000 and bonded for $600,000, could not be expected to
sell or rent for enough to cover the 5% mortgage if the issuing company
went into bankruptcy.)

Property Values and Earning Power Closely Related. This illustration
shows that under normal conditions obtaining in the field of *dwellings,
offices,* and *stores,* the property values and the rental values go hand in
hand. In this sense it is largely immaterial whether the lender views mortgaged property of this kind as something with salable value or as something with an earning power, the equivalent of a going concern. To some
extent this is true also of vacant lots and unoccupied houses or stores,
since the market value of these is closely related to the *expected* rental

when improved or let. (It is emphatically not true, however, of buildings erected for a special purpose, such as factories, etc.)

Misleading Character of Appraisals. The foregoing discussion is important in its bearing on the correct attitude that the intending investor in real estate bonds should take towards the property values asserted to exist behind the issues submitted to him. During the great and disastrous development of the real estate mortgage-bond business between 1923 and 1929, the only datum customarily presented to support the usual bond offering—aside from an estimate of future earnings—was a statement of the *appraised value* of the property, which almost invariably amounted to some 66²/₃% in excess of the mortgage issue. If these appraisals had corresponded to the market values which experienced buyers of or lenders on real estate would place upon the properties, they would have been of real utility in the selection of sound real estate bonds. But unfortunately they were purely artificial valuations, to which the appraisers were willing to attach their names for a fee, and whose only function was to deceive the investor as to the protection which he was receiving.

The method followed by these appraisals was the capitalization on a liberal basis of the rental expected to be returned by the property. By this means, a typical building which cost $1,000,000, including liberal financing charges, would immediately be given an "appraised value" of $1,500,000. Hence a bond issue could be floated for almost the entire cost of the venture so that the builders or promoters retained the equity (*i.e.,* the ownership) of the building, without a cent's investment, and in many cases with a goodly cash profit to boot.[3] This whole scheme of real estate financing was honeycombed with the most glaring weaknesses, and it is sad commentary on the lack of principle, penetration, and ordinary common sense on the part of all parties concerned that it was permitted to reach such gigantic proportions before the inevitable collapse.[4]

---

[3] The 419–4th Avenue Corporation (Bowker Building) floated a $1,230,000 bond issue in 1927 with a paid-in capital stock of only $75,000. (By the familiar process, the land and building which cost about $1,300,000 were appraised at $1,897,788.) Default and receivership in 1931–1932 were inevitable.

[4] See Appendix Note 19, p. 748 on accompanying CD, for report of Real Estate Securities Committee of the Investment Bankers Association of America commenting on defaults in this field.

Abnormal Rentals Used as Basis of Valuation. It was indeed true that the scale of rentals prevalent in 1928–1929 would yield an abundantly high rate of income on the cost of a new real estate venture. But this condition could not properly be interpreted as making a new building immediately worth 50% in excess of its actual cost. For this high income return was certain to be only temporary, since it could not fail to stimulate more and more building, until an oversupply of space caused a collapse in the scale of rentals. This overbuilding was the more inevitable because it was possible to carry it on without risk on the part of the owner, who raised all the money needed from the public.

Debt Based on Excessive Construction Costs. A collateral result of this overbuilding was an increase in the cost of construction to abnormally high levels. Hence even an apparently conservative loan made in 1928 or 1929, in an amount not exceeding two-thirds of *actual cost*, did not enjoy a proper degree of protection, because there was the evident danger (subsequently realized) that a sharp drop in construction costs would reduce fundamental values to a figure below the amount of the loan.

Weakness of Specialized Buildings. A third general weakness of real estate-bond investment lay in the entire lack of discrimination as between various types of building projects. The typical or standard real estate loan was formerly made on a home, and its peculiar virtue lay in the fact that there was an indefinitely large number of prospective purchasers or tenants to draw upon, so that it could always be disposed of at some moderate concession from the current scale of values. A fairly similar situation is normally presented by the ordinary apartment house, or store, or office building. But when a structure is built for some *special* purpose, such as a hotel, garage, club, hospital, church, or factory, it loses this quality of rapid disposability, and *its value becomes bound up with the success of the particular enterprise for whose use it was originally intended.* Hence mortgage bonds on such structures are not actually real estate bonds in the accepted sense, but rather *loans extended to a business;* and consequently their safety must be judged by all the stringent tests surrounding the purchase of an industrial obligation.

This point was completely lost sight of in the rush of real estate financing preceding the collapse in real estate values. Bonds were floated to build hotels, garages, and even hospitals, on very much the same basis as loans made on apartment houses. In other words, an appraisal showing a "value" of one-half to two-thirds in excess of the bond issue was considered almost enough to establish the safety of the loan. It turned out, however, that when such new ventures proved commercially unsuccessful and were unable to pay their interest charges, the "real estate" bondholders were in little better position than the holders of a mortgage on an unprofitable railroad or mill property.[5]

Values Based on Initial Rentals Misleading. Another weakness should be pointed out in connection with apartment-house financing. The rental income used in determining the appraised value was based on the rentals to be charged at the outset. But apartment-house tenants are accustomed to pay a substantial premium for space in a new building, and they consider a structure old, or at least no longer especially modern and desirable, after it has been standing a very few years. Consequently, under normal conditions the rentals received in the first years are substantially larger than those which can conservatively be expected throughout the life of the bond issue.

Lack of Financial Information. A defect related to those discussed above, but of a different character, was the almost universal failure to supply the bond buyer with operating and financial data after his purchase. This drawback applies generally to companies that sell bonds to the public but whose stock is privately held—an arrangement characteristic of real estate financing. As a result, not only were most bondholders unaware of the poor showing of the venture until default had actually taken place, but—more serious still—at that time they frequently found that large unpaid taxes had accrued against the property while the owners were "milking" it by drawing down all available cash.

Suggested Rules of Procedure. From this detailed analysis of the defects of real estate bond financing in the past decade, a number of specific rules of procedure may be developed to guide the investor in the future.

In the case of single-family dwellings, loans are generally made directly by the mortgage holder to the owner of the home, *i.e.*, without the intermediary of a real estate mortgage *bond* sold by a house of issue. But an extensive business has also been transacted by mortgage companies (*e.g.*, Lawyers Mortgage Company, Title Guarantee and Trust Company) in

---

[5] See Appendix Note 20, p. 750 on accompanying CD, for example (Hudson Towers).

guaranteed mortgages and mortgage-participation certificates, secured on such dwellings.[6] Where investments of this kind are made, the lender should be certain: (a) that the amount of the loan is not over $66^2/3\%$ of the value of the property, as shown either by actual recent cost or by the amount which an experienced real estate man would consider a fair price *to pay* for the property; and (b) that this cost or fair price does not reflect recent speculative inflation and does not greatly exceed the price levels existing for a long period previously. If so, a proper reduction must be made in the maximum relation of the amount of mortgage debt to the current value.

The more usual real estate mortgage *bond* represents a participation in a first mortgage on a new apartment house or office building. In considering such offerings the investor should ignore the conventional "appraised values" submitted and demand that the actual cost, fairly presented, should exceed the amount of the bond issue by at least 50%. Secondly, he should require an estimated income account, conservatively calculated to reflect losses through vacancies and the decline in the rental scale as the building grows older. This income account should forecast a margin of at least 100% over interest charges, after deducting from earnings a depreciation allowance to be actually expended as a sinking fund for the gradual retirement of the bond issue. The borrower should agree to supply the bond-holders with regular operating and financial statements.

Issues termed "first-*leasehold* mortgage bonds" are in actuality second mortgages. They are issued against buildings erected on leased land and the ground rent operates in effect as a first lien or prior charge against the entire property. In analyzing such issues the ground rent should be added to the bond-interest requirements to arrive at the total interest charges of the property. Furthermore, it should be recognized that in the field of real estate obligations the advantage of a first mortgage over a junior lien is much more clean-cut than in an ordinary business enterprise.[7]

---

[6] Since 1933 real estate financing on single-family homes has been taken over so substantially by the Federal government, through the Federal Housing Administration (F.H.A.), that practically no real estate bonds of this type have been sold to investors. Financing on larger buildings has been greatly restricted. Practically all of it has been provided by financial institutions (insurance companies, etc.), and there have been virtually no sales of real estate securities to the general public (to the end of 1939).

[7] See Appendix Note 21, p. 750 on accompanying CD, for examples and comment.

In addition to the above quantitative tests, the investor should be satisfied in his own mind that the location and type of the building are such as to attract tenants and to minimize the possibility of a large loss of value through unfavorable changes in the character of the neighborhood.[8]

Real estate loans should not be made on buildings erected for a special or limited purpose, such as hotels, garages, etc. Commitments of this kind must be made in the venture itself, considered as an individual business. From our previous discussion of the standards applicable to a high-grade industrial-bond purchase, it is difficult to see how any bond issue on a new hotel, or the like, could logically be bought on a straight investment basis. All such enterprises should be financed at the outset by private capital, and only after they can show a number of years of successful operation should the public be offered either bonds or stock therein.[9]

---

[8] Footnote to 1934 edition: "One of the few examples of a conservatively financed real estate-bond issue extant in 1933 is afforded by the Trinity Buildings Corporation of New York First $5^1/2$s, due 1939, secured on two well-located office buildings in the financial district of New York City. This issue was outstanding in the amount of $4,300,000, and was secured by a first lien on land and buildings assessed for taxation at $13,000,000. In 1931, gross earnings were $2,230,000 and the net after depreciation was about six times the interest on the first-mortgage bonds. In 1932, rent income declined to $1,653,000, but the balance for first-mortgage interest was still about $3^1/2$ times the requirement. In September 1933 these bonds sold close to par."

This footnote and the sequel well illustrate the importance of the location factor referred to in the text. Despite the improvement in general business conditions since 1933, the lessened activity in the financial district resulted in a loss of tenants and a severe decline in rental rates. The net earnings of Trinity Building Corporation failed even to cover depreciation charges in 1938 and were less than interest charges, even ignoring depreciation; principal and interest were defaulted at maturity in 1939; the guarantee by United States Realty and Improvement Company, the parent enterprise, proved inadequate; and the holders were faced with the necessity of extending their principal and accepting a reduction in the fixed coupon rate. In this instance an undoubtedly conservative financial set-up (a *quantitative* factor) did not prove strong enough to offset a decline in the rental value of the neighborhood (a *qualitative* factor).

[9] The subject of guaranteed real estate mortgage issues is treated in Chap. 17.

See accompanying CD for Chapter 11, "Specific Standards for Bond Investment *(Continued)*"; Chapter 12, "Special Factors in the Analysis of Railroad and Public-utility Bonds"; Chapter 13, "Other Special Factors in Bond Analysis"; and Chapter 14, "The Theory of Preferred Stocks."

Chapter 15

TECHNIQUE OF SELECTING PREFERRED STOCKS FOR INVESTMENT

OUR DISCUSSION of the theory of preferred stocks led to the practical conclusion that an investment preferred issue must meet all the requirements of a good bond, with an extra margin of safety to offset its contractual disadvantages. In analyzing a senior stock issue, therefore, the same tests should be applied as we have previously suggested and described with respect to bonds.

More Stringent Requirements Suggested. In order to make the quantitative tests more stringent, some increase is needed in the minimum earnings coverage above that prescribed for the various bond groups. The criteria we propose are as follows:

MINIMUM AVERAGE-EARNINGS COVERAGE

Class of enterprise	For investment bonds	For investment preferred stocks
Public utilities	1³/₄ times fixed charges	2 times fixed charges plus preferred dividends
Railroads	2 times fixed charges	2¹/₂ times fixed charges plus preferred dividends
Industrials	3 times fixed charges	4 times fixed charges plus preferred dividends

These increases in the earnings coverage suggest that a corresponding advance should be made in the stock-value ratio. It may be argued that since this is a secondary test it is hardly necessary to change the figure. But consistency of treatment would require that the minimum stock-value coverage be raised in some such manner as shown in the table on page 191.

The margins of safety above suggested are materially higher than those hitherto accepted as adequate, and it may be objected that we are imposing requirements of unreasonable and prohibitive stringency. It is true that these requirements would have disqualified a large part of the preferred-stock financing done in the years prior to 1931, but such severity would have been of benefit to the investing public. A general stabilization of business and financial conditions may later justify a more lenient attitude towards the minimum earnings coverage, but until such stabilization has actually been discernible over a considerable period of time the attitude of investors towards preferred stocks must remain extremely critical and exacting.

	Minimum current stock-value ratio	
Class of enterprise	For investment bonds	For investment preferred stocks
Public utilities	$2 bonds to $1 stock	$1¹/₂ bonds and preferred to $1 junior stock
Railroads	$1¹/₂ bonds to $1 stock	$1 bonds and preferred to $1 junior stock
Industrials	$1 bonds to $1 stock	$1 bonds and preferred to $1¹/₂ junior stock

Referring to the list of preferred stocks given on page 192 of accompanying CD, it will be noted that in the case of all the *industrial* issues the stock-value ratio at its lowest exceeded 1.6 to 1, and also that the average earnings coverage exceeded 5.6 times.[1]

Mere Presence of Funded Debt Does Not Disqualify Preferred Stocks for Investment. It is proper to consider whether an investment rating should be confined to preferred stocks not preceded by bonds. That the absence of funded debt is a desirable feature for a preferred issue goes without saying; it is an advantage similar to that of having a first mortgage on a property instead of a second mortgage. It is not surprising, therefore, that preferred stocks without bonds ahead of them have *as a*

[1] We do not consider it necessary to suggest an increase in minimum *size* above the figures recommended for investment bonds.

class made a better showing than those of companies with funded debt. But from this rather obvious fact it does not follow that *all* preferred stocks with bonds preceding are unsound investments, any more than it can be said that *all* second-mortgage bonds are inferior in quality to *all* first-mortgage bonds. Such a principle would entail the rejection of all public-utility preferred stocks (since they invariably have bonds ahead of them) although these are better regarded as a group than are the "non-bonded" industrial preferreds. Furthermore, in the extreme test of 1932, a substantial percentage of the preferred issues which held up were preceded by funded debt.[2]

To condemn a powerfully entrenched security such as General Electric preferred in 1933 because it had an infinitesimal bond issue ahead of it, would have been the height of absurdity. This example should illustrate forcibly the inherent unwisdom of subjecting investment selection to hard and fast rules of a *qualitative* character. In our view, the presence of bonds senior to a preferred stock is a fact which the investor must take carefully into account, impelling him to greater caution than he might otherwise exercise; but if the company's exhibit is sufficiently impressive the preferred stock may still be accorded an investment rating.

Total-deductions Basis of Calculation Recommended. In calculating the earnings coverage for preferred stocks with bonds preceding, it is absolutely essential that the bond interest and preferred dividend be taken *together*. The almost universal practice of stating the earnings on the preferred stock separately (in dollars per share) is exactly similar to, and as fallacious as, the prior-deductions method of computing the margin above interest charges on a junior bond. If the preferred stock issue is much smaller than the funded debt, the earnings per share will indicate that the preferred dividend is earned more times than is the bond interest. Such a statement must either have no meaning at all, or else it will imply that the preferred dividend is safer than the bond interest of the same company—an utter absurdity.[3] (See the examples on page 194.)

---

[2] Out of the 21 such issues listed on p. 192 of accompanying CD eleven were preceded by bonds, *viz.*, five public utilities, one railroad, and five (out of 15) industrials.

[3] See Appendix Note 28, p. 760 on accompanying CD, for comment upon neglect of this point by writers of textbooks on investment.

The West Penn Electric Company Class *A* stock is in reality a second preferred issue. In this example the customary statement makes the preferred dividend appear safer than the bond interest; and because the Class *A* issue is small, it makes this second preferred issue appear much safer than either the bonds or the first preferred. The correct statement shows that the Class *A* requirements are covered 1.26 times instead of 7.43 times—a tremendous difference. The erroneous method of stating the earnings coverage was probably responsible in good part for the high price at which the Class *A* shares sold in 1937 (108). It is interesting to observe that although the Class *A* shares had declined to 25 in 1932, they later sold repeatedly at a higher price than the 7% preferred issue. Evidently some investors were still misled by the per-share earnings figures, and imagined the second preferred safer than the first preferred.

An Apparent Contradiction Explained. Our principles of preferred-dividend coverage lead to an apparent contradiction, *viz.*, that the preferred stockholders of a company must require a larger minimum coverage than the bondholders of the same company, yet by the nature of the case the actual coverage is bound to be smaller. For in any corporation the bond interest alone is obviously earned with a larger margin than the bond interest and preferred dividends combined. This fact has created the impression among investors (and some writers) that the tests of a sound preferred stock may properly be less stringent than those of a sound bond.[4] But this is not true at all. The real point is that where a company has both bonds and preferred stock the preferred stock can be safe

---

[4] See, for example, the following quotations from R. E. Badger and H. G. Guthmann, *Investment Principles and Practices*, New York, 1941:

"Similarly, it is a general rule that, on the average, the interest on industrial bonds should be covered at least three times, in order that the bond should be considered safe" (p. 316).

"From the authors' viewpoint, an industrial preferred stock should be regarded as speculative unless combined charges and dividend requirements are earned at least twice over a period of years" (p. 319).

"One is probably safe in stating that, where combined charges are twice earned, including interest charges on the bonds of the holding company, the presumption is in favor of the soundness of such holding company issue. Likewise, where combined prior charges and preferred dividend requirements are earned 1.5 times, the preferred stock of the holding company will be favorably regarded" (p. 421).

See also F. F. Burtchett, *Investments and Investment Policy*, New York, 1938, p. 325, where the author requires larger coverage of fixed charges on bonds than on preferred stocks of merchandising enterprises.

EXAMPLES OF CORRECT AND INCORRECT METHODS OF CALCULATING EARNINGS COVERAGE
FOR PREFERRED STOCKS

A. Colorado Fuel and Iron Company: 1929 figures
   Earned for bond interest $3,978,000
   Interest charges 1,628,000
   Preferred dividends 160,000
   Balance for common 2,190,000

Customary but incorrect statement	Correct statement
Int. charges earned. ....2.4 times	Int. charges earned ....2.4 times
Preferred dividend earned ....14.7 times	Interest and preferred
Earned per share of preferred $117.50	dividends earned ......2.2 times
Note: The preceding statement of	
earnings on the preferred stock	
alone is either worthless or	
dangerously misleading.	

B. Warner Bros. Pictures, Inc.:   Year ended Aug. 28, 1937
   Earned for interest $10,760,000
   Interest charges 4,574,000
   Preferred dividends 397,000
   Balance for common 5,789,000

Customary but incorrect statement	Correct statement
Int. charges earned ....2.35 times	Int. charges earned ......2.35 times
Preferred dividends earned ....14.8 times	Interest and preferred
Earned per share of preferred $56.99	dividends earned ....2.1 times

C. West Penn Electric Company: 1937 figures
   Gross $40,261,000
   Net before charges 13,604,000
   Fixed charges (include preferred dividends of subsidiaries) 8,113,000
   Dividends on 7% and 6% preferred issues 2,267,000
   Dividends on Class A stock (junior to 6% and 7% Pfd.). 412,000
   Balance for Class B and common 2,812,000

Customary but incorrect statement		Correct statement
Times interest or	Earned	Times earned
dividends earned	per share	
Fixed charges... 1.68 times		Fixed charges..............1.68 times
6% and 7%		Charges and
preferred		preferred
(combined)...2.42 times	$16.11	dividends ....1.31 times
Class A..........7.43 times	54.79	Fixed charges,
		preferred dividends,
		and Class A dividends .1.26 times

Year	Liggett & Myers Tobacco Co.		Commonwealth & Southern Corp.	
	Number of times interest earned	Number of times int. and pfd. dividend earned	Number of times fixed charges earned	Number of times fixed charges and pfd. dividend earned
1930	15.2	7.87	1.84	1.48
1929	13.9	7.23	1.84	1.55
1928	12.3	6.42	1.71	1.44
1927	11.9	6.20	1.62	1.37
1926	11.2	5.85	1.52	1.31
1925	9.8	5.14	1.42	1.28

enough *only if the bonds are much safer than necessary.* Conversely, if the bonds are only just safe enough, the preferred stock cannot be sound. This is illustrated by two examples, as follows:

The Liggett and Myers preferred-dividend coverage (including, of course, the bond interest as well) is substantially above our suggested minimum of four times. The bond-interest coverage alone is therefore far in excess of the smaller minimum required for it, *viz.*, three times. On the other hand, the Commonwealth and Southern fixed-charge coverage in 1930 was just about at the proposed minimum $1^3/_4$ times. This meant that while the various bonds *might* qualify for investment, the 6% preferred stock could not possibly do so, and the purchase of that issue at a price above par in 1930 was an obvious mistake.

"Dollars-per-share" Formula Misleading. When a preferred stock has no bonds ahead of it, the earnings may be presented either as so many dollars per share or as so many times dividend requirements. The second form is distinctly preferable, for two reasons. The more important one is that the use of the "dollars per share" formula in cases where there are no bonds is likely to encourage its use in cases where there are bonds. Security analysts and intelligent investors should make special efforts to avoid and decry this misleading method of stating preferred-dividend coverage, and this may best be accomplished by dropping the dollars-per-share form of calculation entirely. As a second point, it should be noted that the significance of the dollars earned per share is dependent upon the market price of the preferred stock. Earnings of $20 per share would be much more favorable for a preferred issue selling at 80 than for a preferred

selling at 125. In the one case the earnings are 25%, and in the other only 16%, on the market price. The dollars-per-share figure loses all comparative value when the par value is less than $100, or when there is no-par stock with a low dividend rate per share. Earnings of $18.60 per share in 1931 on S. H. Kress and Company 6% Preferred (par $10) are of course far more favorable than earnings of $20 per share on some 7% preferred stock, par $100.

Calculation of the Stock-value Ratio.

The technique of applying this test to preferred stocks is in all respects similar to that of the earnings-coverage test. The bonds, if any, and the preferred stock must be taken together and the total compared with the market price of the common stock only. When calculating the protection behind a bond, the preferred issue is part of the stock equity; but when calculating the protection behind the preferred shares, the common stock is now, of course, the only junior security. In cases where there are both a first and second preferred issue, the second preferred is added to the common stock in calculating the equity behind the first preferred.

EXAMPLE OF CALCULATION OF STOCK-VALUE RATIOS FOR PREFERRED STOCKS

PROCTER AND GAMBLE COMPANY

Capitalization	Face amount	Low price 1932	Value at low price in 1932
Bonds	$10,500,000		
8% pfd. (1st pfd.)	2,250,000	@ 140	$3,150,000
5% pfd. (2d pfd.)	17,156,000	@ 81	13,900,000
Common	6,140,000*	@ 20	128,200,000

* Number of shares.

A. Stock-value ratio for bonds

$$\frac{3,150,000 + 13,900,000 + 128,200,000}{10,500,000} = 13.8:1$$

B. Stock-value ratio for 1st pfd.

$$\frac{13,900,000 + 128,200,000}{10,500,000 + 3,150,000} = 10.4:1$$

C. Stock-value ratio for 2d pfd.

$$\frac{128,200,000}{10,500,000 + 3,150,000 + 13,900,000} = 4.6:1$$

Should the market value of the common stock be compared with the *par* value or the *market* value of the preferred? In the majority of cases it will not make any vital difference which figure is used. There are, however, an increasing number of no-par-value preferreds (and also a number like Island Creek Coal Company Preferred and Remington Rand, Inc., Second Preferred in which the real par is entirely different from the stated par).[5] In these cases an equivalent would have to be constructed from the dividend rate. Because of such instances and also those where the market price tends to differ materially from the par value (*e.g.*, Norfolk and Western Railway Company 4% Preferred in 1932 or Eastman Kodak 6% Preferred in 1939), it would seem the better rule to use the *market price* of preferred stocks regularly in computing stock-value ratios. On the other hand the regular use of the *face value* of bond issues, rather than the market price, is recommended, because it is much more convenient and does not involve the objections just discussed in relation to preferred shares.

Noncumulative Issues. The theoretical disadvantage of a noncumulative preferred stock as compared with a cumulative issue is very similar to the inferiority of preferred stocks in general as compared with bonds. The drawback of not being able to compel the payment of dividends on preferred stocks generally is almost matched by the handicap in the case of noncumulative issues of not being able to receive in the future the dividends withheld in the past. This latter arrangement is so patently inequitable that new security buyers (who will stand for almost anything) object to noncumulative issues, and for many years new offerings of straight preferred stocks have almost invariably had the cumulative feature.[6] Noncumulative issues have generally come into existence as the result of reorganization plans in which old security holders have been

---

[5] Island Creek Coal Preferred has a stated par of $1 and Remington Rand, Inc., Second Preferred has a stated par of $25, but both issues carry a $6 dividend and they are entitled to $120 per share and $100 per share respectively in the event of liquidation. Their true par is evidently $100. The same is true of American Zinc Lead and Smelting First $5 Prior Preferred and $6 (Second) Preferred; par of each is $25.

[6] The only important "straight," noncumulative preferred stock sold to stockholders or the public since the war was St. Louis-San Francisco Railway Company Preferred. In the case of Illinois Central Railroad Company Noncumulative Preferred, the conversion privilege was the overshadowing inducement at the time of issue.

virtually forced to accept whatever type of security was offered them. But in recent years the preferred issues created through reorganization have been preponderantly cumulative, though in some cases this provision becomes operative only after a certain interval. Austin Nichols and Company $5 Preferred, for example, was issued under a Readjustment Plan in 1930 and became cumulative in 1934. National Department Stores Preferred, created in 1935, became fully cumulative in 1938.

Chief Objection to Noncumulative Provision. One of the chief objections to the noncumulative provision is that it permits the directors to withhold dividends even in good years, when they are amply earned, the money thus saved inuring to the benefit of the common stockholders. Experience shows that noncumulative dividends are seldom paid unless they are necessitated by the desire to declare dividends on the common; and if the common dividend is later discontinued, the preferred dividend is almost invariably suspended soon afterwards.[7]

Example: St. Louis-San Francisco Railway Company affords a typical example. No dividends were paid on the (old) preferred issue between 1916 and 1924, although the dividend was fully earned in most of these years. Payments were not commenced until immediately before dividends were initiated on the common; and they were continued (on the new preferred) less than a year after the common dividend was suspended in 1931.

The manifest injustice of such an arrangement led the New Jersey courts (in the United States Cast Iron Pipe case)[8] to decide that if dividends are earned on a noncumulative preferred stock but not paid, then the holder is entitled to receive such amounts later before anything can be paid on the common. This meant that in New Jersey a noncumulative preferred stock was given a cumulative claim on dividends to the extent that they were earned. The United States Supreme Court however, handed

---

[7] Kansas City Southern Railway Company 4% Noncumulative Preferred, which paid dividends between 1907 and 1929 while the common received nothing, is an outstanding exception to this statement. St. Louis Southwestern Railway Company 5% Noncumulative Preferred received full dividends during 1923–1929 while no payments were made on the common; but for a still longer period preferred dividends, although earned, were wholly or partially withheld (and thus irrevocably lost).

[8] *Day v. United States Cast Iron Pipe and Foundry Company*, 94 N.J. Eq. 389, 124 Atl. 546 (1924), *aff'd.* 96 N.J. Eq. 738, 126 Atl. 302 (1925); *Moran v. United States Cast Iron Pipe and Foundry Company*, 95 N.J. Eq. 389, 123 Atl. 546 (1924), *aff'd*, 96 N.J. Eq. 698, 126 Atl. 329 (1925).

down a contrary decision (in the Wabash Railway case)[9] holding that while the noncumulative provision may work a great hardship on the holder, he has nevertheless agreed thereto when he accepted the issue. This is undoubtedly sound law, but the inherent objections to the non-cumulative provision are so great (chiefly because of the opportunity it affords for unfair policies by the directors) that it would seem to be advisable for the legislatures of the several states to put the New Jersey decision into statutory effect by prohibiting the creation of completely noncumulative preferred stocks, requiring them to be made cumulative at least to the extent that the dividend is earned. This result has been attained in a number of individual instances through insertion of appropriate charter provisions.[10]

Features of the List of 21 Preferred Issues of Investment Grade.

Out of some 440 preferred stocks listed on the New York Stock Exchange in 1932, only 40, or 9%, were noncumulative. Of these, 29 were railroad or street-railway issues and only 11 were industrial issues. The reader will be surprised to note, however, that out of only 21 preferred stocks selling continuously on an investment basis in 1932, no less than four were non-cumulative. Other peculiarities are to be found in this favored list, and they may be summarized as follows (see page 192 of accompanying CD):

1. Both the number of noncumulative issues and the number of preferred stocks preceded by bonds are proportionately higher among the 21 "good" companies than in the Stock Exchange list as a whole.
2. The industry best represented is the *snuff* business, with three companies.

---

[9] *Wabash Railway Company et al. v. Barclay et al.*, 280 U.S. 197 (1930), reversing *Barclay v. Wabash Railway*, 30 Fed. (2d) 260 (1929). See discussion in A. A. Berle, Jr., and G. C. Means, *The Modern Corporation and Private Property*, pp. 190–192.

[10] See, for example, the provisions of George A. Fuller Company $3 Convertible Stock; Aeolian Company 6% Class *A* Preferred; United States Lines Company Convertible Second Preferred. A trend in the direction of preferred stocks with this type of provision is observable in numerous recent reorganization plans of railroads. See various plans presented in 1936–1938 for Chicago and Eastern Illinois Railroad, Missouri Pacific Railroad, Erie Railroad, St. Louis-San Francisco Railroad. An early example of this type of preferred is that of Pittsburgh, Youngstown and Ashtabula Railway. But here the dividend becomes cumulative only if the full $7 rate is earned and less has been paid.

3. Miscellaneous peculiarities:
   a. Only one issue has a sinking fund provision.
   b. One issue is a second preferred (Procter and Gamble).
   c. One issue has a par value of only $1 (Island Creek Coal).
   d. One issue was callable at close to the lowest market price of 1932–1933 (General Electric).

Matters of Form, Title, or Legal Right Relatively Immaterial. We trust that no overzealous exponent of the inductive method will conclude from these figures either: (1) that noncumulative preferreds are superior to cumulative issues; or (2) that preferreds preceded by bonds are superior to those without bonds; or (3) that the snuff business presents the safest opportunity for investment. The real significance of these unexpected results is rather the striking confirmation they offer to our basic thesis that matters of form, title, or legal right are relatively immaterial, and that the showing made by the individual issue is of paramount importance. If a preferred stock could always be expected to pay its dividend without question, then whether it is cumulative or noncumulative would become an academic question solely, in the same way that the inferior contractual rights of a preferred stock as compared with a bond would cease to have practical significance. Since the dividend on United States Tobacco Company Preferred was earned more than sixteen times in the depression year 1931—and since, moreover, the company had been willing to buy in a large part of the preferred issue at prices ranging up to $125 per share—the lack of a cumulative provision caused the holders no concern at all. This example must of course, be considered as exceptional; and as a point of practical investment policy we should suggest that no matter how impressive may be the exhibit of a noncumulative preferred stock, it would be better to select a cumulative issue for purchase in order to enjoy better protection in the event of unexpected reverses.[11]

---

[11] See, for example, the record of American Car and Foundry Company 7% Noncumulative Preferred. For many years prior to 1928 this issue sold higher than United States Tobacco Company 7% Noncumulative Preferred. By 1929 it had completed 30 years of uninterrupted dividend payments, during the last 20 of which its market price had never fallen below 100. Yet in 1932 the dividend was passed and the quotation declined to 16. Similarly, Atchison, Topeka and Santa Fe Railway Company Preferred, a 5% noncumulative issue, paid full dividends between 1901 and 1932 and was long regarded as a gilt-edged investment. As late as

Amount Rather Than Mere Presence of Senior Obligations Important. The relatively large number of companies in our list having bonds outstanding is also of interest, as demonstrating that it is not the mere *presence* of bonds, but rather the *amount* of the prior debt which is of serious moment. In three cases the bonds were outstanding in merely a nominal sum, as the result of the fact that nearly all of these companies had a long history, so that some of them carried small residues of old bond financing.[12]

By a coincidence all three of the noncumulative industrial preferred stocks in our list belong to companies in the *snuff* business. This fact is interesting, not because it proves the investment primacy of snuff, but because of the strong reminder it offers that the investor cannot safely judge the merits or demerits of a security by his personal reaction to the kind of business in which it is engaged. An outstanding record for a long period in the past, plus strong evidence of inherent stability, plus the absence of any concrete reason to expect a substantial change for the worse in the future, afford probably the only sound basis available for the selection of a *fixed-value* investment. The miscellaneous peculiarities in our list (mentioned under 3, above) are also useful indications that matters of form or minor drawbacks have no essential bearing on the quality of an investment.

1931 the price reached 108¹/₄, *within a half-point of the highest level in its history*, and a yield of only 4.6%. The very next year the price fell to 35, and in the following year the dividend was reduced to a $3 basis. It was later restored to 5% but in 1938 the dividend was omitted entirely. This history might be pondered by investors willing to pay 112 for Norfolk and Western 4% Noncumulative Preferred in 1939.

[12] These companies were General Electric, American Tobacco, and Corn Products Refining. The University of Michigan study by Dr. Rodkey recognizes this point in part by ignoring certain bond issues amounting to less than 10% of capital and surplus.

Chapter 16

Income Bonds and
Guaranteed Securities

I. INCOME BONDS

The contractual position of an income bond (sometimes called an adjustment bond) stands midway between that of a straight bond and a preferred stock. Practically all income obligations have a definite maturity, so that the holder has an unqualified right to repayment of his principal on a fixed date. In this respect his position is entirely that of the ordinary bondholder. However, it should be pointed out that income bonds are almost always given a long maturity date, so that the right of repayment is not likely to be of practical importance in the typical case studied. In fact we have discovered only one instance of income bondholders actually having received repayment of their principal in full by reason of maturity.[1]

Interest Payment Sometimes Wholly Discretionary. In the matter of interest payments some income bonds are almost precisely in the position of a preferred stock, because the directors are given practically complete discretion over the amounts to be paid to the bondholders. The

---

[1] This was a $500,000 issue of Milwaukee Lake Shore and Western Income 6s, issued in 1881, assumed by the Chicago and Northwestern in 1891, and paid off at maturity in 1911. St. Louis-San Francisco Railway Company Income 6s and Adjustment 6s were both *called* for repayment at par in 1928, which was 32 and 27 years, respectively, prior to their maturity. This proved fortunate for the bondholders since the road went into receivership in 1932. The history of the 'Frisco between its emergence from receivership in 1916 and its subsequent relapse into receivership in 1932 is an extraordinary example of the heedlessness of both investors and speculators, who were induced by a moderate improvement, shown in a few years of general prosperity, to place a high rating on the securities of a railroad with a poor previous record and a top-heavy capital structure.

[202]

customary provisions require that interest be paid to the extent that income is available, but many indentures permit the directors to set aside whatever portion of the income they please for capital expenditures or other purposes, before arriving at the "available" balance. In the case of the Green Bay and Western Railroad Company Income Debentures "Series B," the amounts paid out between 1922 and 1931, inclusive, aggregated only 6% although the earnings were equal to only slightly less than 22%. The more recent indentures (*e.g.*, Colorado Fuel and Iron Company Income 5s, due 1970) tend to place definite limits on the percentage of earnings which may be withheld in this manner from the income bond-holders; but a considerable degree of latitude is usually reserved to the directors. It may be said that individual income-bond issues may be found illustrating almost every step in the range of variation between straight preferred stocks and ordinary bonds.

Low Investment Rating of Income Bonds as a Class. Since the contractual rights of income bonds are always more or less superior to those of preferred stocks, it might be thought that a greater proportion of income bonds than of preferred stocks would deserve an investment rating. Such is not the case, however. In fact we know of only one income obligation which has maintained an investment standing continuously over any length of time, *viz.*, Atchison, Topeka and Santa Fe Railway Company Adjustment 4s, due 1995.[2] We have here a contrast between

---

[2] After more than forty years of uninterrupted interest payments, this issue lapsed temporarily from grace in 1938. May 1 interest (on bonds entitled to semiannual interest) was deferred but paid six months later. The price dropped from $103^{1}/_{4}$ to $75^{1}/_{8}$ but recovered to $96^{1}/_{4}$—all in the year 1938. This recovery is a striking commentary on the eagerness of investors for so-called "prime bonds."

Some guaranteed income bonds of leased railroads have maintained a high investment standing, similar to that of guaranteed railroad stocks.

Example: Elmira and Williamsport Railroad Income 5s, due 2862, guaranteed by Pennsylvania Railroad and by an important subsidiary. (Note the 1,000-year maturity.) Also observe the superior position of Chicago, Terre Haute, and Southeastern Income 5s, guaranteed by the Chicago, Milwaukee, St. Paul and Pacific Railroad, in the reorganization of that system (*infra* p. 209).

Among the newer crop of income bonds, one has qualified as an investment issue almost from the start: Allied Owners Corporation 4s-5s, virtually guaranteed by Loews, Inc. In the authors' view, there was no excuse for making this an income bond in the reorganization of 1936.

theory and actuality, the reason being, of course, that income bonds have been issued almost exclusively in connection with corporate reorganizations and have therefore been associated with companies of secondary credit standing. The very fact that the interest payments are dependent on earnings implies the likelihood that the earnings may be insufficient. Preferred-stock dividends are equally dependent upon earnings, but the same implication is not associated with them. Hence the general investment status of income bonds as a class is seen to have been governed by the circumstances under which they are created rather than by the legal rights which attach to them. To use an analogy: If it had been the general practice here, as in England, to avoid mortgage-bond issues wherever possible, using them only where doubtful credit made this protection necessary, then we might find that mortgage bonds in general would occupy an investment position distinctly inferior to that of debenture bonds.[3]

Increased Volume of Income Bonds Probable. Looking forward, it may be true that in the future income obligations will show a larger proportion of investment issues than will be found among preferred stocks. The numerous reorganizations growing out of the 1930–1933 depression and the continued weakness of railway earnings have created a large new crop of income bonds, and some of these companies may later so improve their position as to place their income obligations in the investment class, as happened to the Atchison, Topeka and Santa Fe after its reorganization in 1895. There is also the point, so far almost overlooked, that income bonds effect a substantial saving in corporation taxes as compared with preferred stocks, without important offsetting disadvantages. Some strong companies may some day be led to replace their present preferred stocks—or to do their new financing—by income obligations, for the sake of this tax saving, in the same way as they are now creating artificially low par values for their shares to reduce the transfer taxes thereon. A development of this kind in the future might result in a

---

[3] This actually proved to be the case in the *industrial* financing of 1937–1939. Practically all the bond issues were debentures and were sold at unusually low interest rates. It may be said, we believe, that *industrial* debentures now connote a higher type of security than industrial mortgage bonds.

respectable number of income-bond issues deserving to rank as fixed-value investments.[4]

Calculations of Margins of Safety for Income Bonds.

The technique of analyzing an income-bond exhibit is identical with that for a preferred stock. Computations of earnings on the issue taken separately must, of course, be rigorously avoided, although such calculations are given by the statistical agencies.

We suggest that the minimum earnings coverage recommended in the preceding chapter for preferred stocks be required also for income bonds when selected as fixed-value investments.

Example: The following analysis of the Missouri-Kansas-Texas Railroad Company income account for 1930 will illustrate the proper method of dealing with all the senior securities of a company having adjustment bonds. It also shows how the two methods of figuring the fixed charges of a railroad system (discussed in Chap. 12 on accompanying CD) are to be applied to the analysis of income bonds and preferred stock.

Note that interest on income or adjustment bonds is not part of the total interest charges when calculating the coverage for the *fixed-interest* bonds. In this respect the position of an income bond is exactly that of a preferred stock. Note also that the statement made by the statistical services that 57.29% was earned on the M-K-T Adjustment 5s. (*i.e.*, that the "interest was covered" more than eleven times) is valueless or misleading.

Significance of These Figures for the Investor in Early 1931. The 1930 earnings were somewhat lower than the ten-year average and could then apparently be viewed as a fair indication of the normal earning power of M-K-T. The coverage for the preferred stock was clearly inadequate from any investment standpoint. The coverage for the adjustment-bond interest on the more conservative basis (the net-deductions method) was

---

[4] The Associated Gas and Electric Company used the device of "bonds" convertible into preferred stock *at the option of the company*, and obtained this tax saving without the burden of a fixed-bond obligation. The income-bond form would have been far less misleading to the ordinary investor than this extraordinary invention.

Income bonds have been favored over preferred stocks in railroad reorganizations because of legal restrictions on insurance companies which would prohibit them from holding preferred shares in place of their old bonds. Conceivably this consideration, as well as the tax saving, could induce corporations to do *new* financing through income bonds in lieu of preferred stocks.

Missouri-Kansas-Texas Railroad Company, Calendar Year 1930
(All dollar figures in thousands)

Gross revenue $45,949

Railway operating income (net after taxes) .13,353

Gross income (net after rents, plus other income) 12,009

Fixed charges (fixed interest and other deductions) 4,230

Balance for adjustment interest 7,779

Adjustment interest 696

Balance for dividends (net income) 7,083

Preferred dividends 4,645

Balance for common 2,438

Net after taxes exceeds gross income. Hence use net-deductions test.

Net deductions = difference between net after taxes and balance for
adjustment interest
= $13,353 − $7,779.

Times earned

Net deductions	= $ 5,574	$\frac{\$13,353}{\$5,574}$ = 2.40
Net deductions and adjustment interest = 6,270		$\frac{\$13,353}{\$6,270}$ = 2.14
Net deductions, adjustment interest, and preferred dividends	= $10,915	$\frac{\$13,353}{\$10,915}$ = 1.22

below our minimum requirement of $2^{1}/_{2}$ times, so that this issue would not have qualified for investment. The coverage for the fixed-bond interest was substantially above our minimum and indicated a satisfactory degree of protection.

Naturally the disastrous decline of earnings in 1931–1933 could not have been foreseen or fully guarded against. The market price of M-K-T fixed obligations suffered severely in 1932; but since the company's debt structure was relatively conservative, it did not come so close to insolvency as the majority of other carriers. In fact, the 1932–1934 interest was paid on the adjustment bonds, although such payment was not obligatory.

Subsequent developments are worth describing because of their practical bearing on bond investment. The following table should prove instructive:

Year	Balance for interest	Net deductions earned, times	Range for year 4¹/₂s, 1978	Range for year Adj. 5s
1930	11,999,000	2.40	92¹/₂–101	86– 108¹/₂
1931	5,579,000	1.22	43¹/₂– 98	34– 95
1932	4,268,000	1.01	36– 70³/₄	13– 60
1933	3,378,000	0.86	55– 77¹/₂	32³/₄–65
1934	2,093,000	0.65	63¹/₈– 83³/₄	29– 62¹/₂
1935	2,457,000	0.71	28¹/₂– 64	11¹/₄–36¹/₂
1936	4,773,000	1.09	52¹/₂– 83	30³/₄–74³/₄
1937	3,274,000	0.86	38– 79³/₄	18¹/₂–80
1938	1,120,000	0.49	25– 45³/₄	10– 24

It will be seen that the 1930 earnings did not in fact prove a guide to the future normal earning power of M-K-T. Yet this mistake need not have proved very costly to an individual investor who bought the fixed-interest bonds in 1931. Despite the decline in earnings and investment quality, he had several opportunities to sell out advantageously during the next six years. As we point out later (Chap. 21), proper investment technique would have compelled such a sale, in view of the changed exhibit.

After 1934, interest on the adjustment bonds was paid only in 1937. The price range of that issue is interesting chiefly as a reflection of the heedlessness of bond buyers. Note that at the 1937 highs they paid the same price for the adjustment 5s as for the 4¹/₂s, despite the totally inadequate earnings coverage, and despite the fact that in 1932, 1934 and 1935 the senior issue had sold more than twice as high as the adjustments.

Senior Income Bonds. There are a few instances of income bonds which are senior in their lien to other bonds bearing fixed interest. The Atchison Adjustment 4s are the best known example, being followed by 4% fixed-interest debenture issues which have regularly sold at a lower price except briefly in 1938. The situation holds true also with respect to St. Louis Southwestern Railway Company Second Income 4s.[5] While the

---

[5] The various reorganization plans for this road (1936–1939) all give the Second Income 4s much better treatment than is offered the junior fixed-interest issues. An unusual case is afforded by Wabash Railway Noncumulative Income Debenture 6s, due 1939, interest on which was payable "from net income." Although called debentures, they are secured by a direct lien and have priority over the Wabash *Railroad* Refunding and General Mortgage. Although entitled by their terms only to noncumulative interest dependent on earnings, this

theoretical status of such bonds is rather confusing, the practical procedure called for is, obviously, to treat the interest thereon as part of the
company's *fixed charges*, when dealing with the system as a whole.

II. GUARANTEED ISSUES

No special investment quality attaches to guaranteed issues as such. Inex-
perienced investors may imagine that the word "guaranteed" carries a
positive assurance of safety; but, needless to say, the value of any guaranty depends strictly upon the financial condition of the guarantor. If the
guarantor has nothing, the guaranty is worthless. In contrast with the attitude of the financial novice, Wall Street displays a tendency to *underestimate* the value of a guaranty, as shown by the lower prices often current
for guaranteed issues in comparison with the debentures or even the preferred stock of the guarantor. This sophisticated distrust of guarantees
dates back to the Kanawha and Hocking Coal and Coke Company case
in 1915, when the guarantor railroad endeavored to escape its liability by
claiming that the guaranty, made in 1901, was beyond its corporate powers and hence void. This attempt at evasion, encouraged by the outcome
of antitrust suits in the Ohio and federal courts, in the end proved completely unsuccessful; but it cast a shadow over the value of all guarantees,
from which they have not completely emerged even after 25 years.[6] We
know of no important case in which a solvent company has escaped the
consequences of its guaranty through legal technicalities.[7]

---

interest was paid regularly from 1916 through 1938, despite the fact that the company
entered receivership in 1931 and defaulted upon the junior-mortgage (fixed) interest in
1932. This issue was also given superior treatment in the various reorganization plans for the
Wabash filed to the end of 1939.

[6] See Appendix Note 29, p. 761, for a condensed history of this famous case.

[7] However, the shadowy form of "insolvency" provided for in Chap. XI of the Chandler
(Federal Bankruptcy) Act has been availed of to induce holders of guaranteed issues to modify their contract without sacrifice by the guarantor company and to force acceptance of the
modified terms by minority holders. *Example:* Modification of guaranty of Trinity Building
5^{1}/2s by United States Realty and Improvement proposed in March 1939.

Contrast this with the full payment in October 1932 of the unpurchased portion of Savoy
Plaza Corporation Debenture 5^{1}/2s, which had also been guaranteed by United States Realty
and Improvement. At that time unguaranteed *First Mortgage* bonds of Savoy Plaza had been
selling as low as 5. Note also the full payment in 1939 of Utica, Clinton and Binghamton
Railroad First 5s through funds supplied by Delaware and Hudson Railroad, the guarantor,
although Delaware and Hudson had not been operating the line for a great many years.

Status of Guaranteed Issues. If a company guarantees interest, dividend, or principal payments, its failure to meet this obligation will expose it to insolvency. The claim against the guarantor ranks equally with an unsecured debt of the company, so that guaranteed issues deserve the same rating as a debenture bond of the guarantor and a better rating than its preferred stock. A guaranteed issue may also be entitled to an investment rating because of its own position and earning power independent of the guaranty. In such cases the guaranty may add to its security, but it cannot detract therefrom even if the guarantor company itself is in bad straits.

Examples: The Brooklyn Union Elevated Railroad 5s (see pages 78–79) were guaranteed by the Brooklyn Heights Railroad Company, which went into receivership in 1919; but the bond came through the reorganization unscathed because of its own preferred position in the Brooklyn Rapid Transit System. Similarly U. S. Industrial Alcohol Company Preferred dividends were guaranteed by Distilling Company of America; the latter enterprise became bankrupt, but the Alcohol Company was easily able to continue the dividend out of its own earnings and later to retire the preferred issue at 125.

A common or preferred stock fully guaranteed by another company has the status of a bond issue as far as the guarantor is concerned. If the guaranty proves worthless, it would naturally return to the position of a stock—usually a weak issue, but possibly a strong one, as in the case of U. S. Industrial Alcohol Company Preferred just mentioned. A similar situation obtains with respect to income bonds of one company guaranteed by another (*e.g.*, Chicago, Terre Haute, and Southeastern Railway Company Income 5s,[8] *guaranteed* by the Chicago, Milwaukee, St. Paul and Pacific Railroad Company).

The value of a guarantee is sometimes very evident when part of an issue is guaranteed and part is not.

---

[8] Interest was continued on these income bonds (through 1939) despite receivership of the guarantor company in 1935 and default on all its own obligations. This was due not to the guarantee but to the strategic importance and substantial earnings of the Terre Haute division. Note that in this case a *divisional second-mortgage income bond* fared substantially better than the first mortgage on the main line of the system. *Not the terms but the facts determine investment performance.*

Example:

ANACOSTIA AND POTOMAC RIVER RAILROAD FIRST 5S, DUE 1949

$500,000 guaranteed by Washington Ry. & Elec. Co. .... price 110 in 1939
$2,100,000 unguaranteed .... price 80 in 1939

In this case the Anacostia company's earnings coverage was inadequate (1.36 times in 1938), but that of the guarantor company was high (over 4 times in 1938 on a consolidated basis and over 11 times in that year on a parent-only basis inclusive of interest for which it was contingently liable).

Exact Terms of Guaranty Are Important. The exact terms of a guaranty have obviously a vital influence upon its value. A guaranty of interest only is likely to be much less significant than a guaranty of principal as well.

Examples: Philippine Railway Company First 4s, due 1937, were guaranteed as to interest only by the Philippine government. The earnings of the road itself were poor. Interest was paid promptly up to maturity, but principal was defaulted. The price of the bond reflected this situation, having sold no higher than 39 since 1929.[9]

Minneapolis, St. Paul and Saulte Saint Marie Railroad First Consolidated 4s and 5s due 1938: All the 4% bonds and about half the 5% bonds were guaranteed as to interest only by Canadian Pacific Railway. Principal was defaulted on maturity, and the Canadian Pacific ceased to pay interest, the price of the bonds declining to 6.[10]

On the other hand, this company's First and Refunding 5 1/2s, Series *B*, due 1978,—a junior lien—are also guaranteed as to interest by Canadian Pacific and in accordance with the guaranty continued to receive interest after the senior lien was in default. These bonds sold at 64 in 1939, whereas

---

[9] Efforts made by a protective committee to induce the Philippine government to buy the bonds or assume liability for the principal resulted only in a scandal and a jail sentence for the chairman of the committee in 1939. The bonds sold at 7 in 1939.

[10] Bondholders brought legal action in 1939 to compel Canadian Pacific to continue to pay interest until the principal was discharged.

the senior issues sold at 6. Note that in 1931 they sold as low as 35, whereas the 1st Consolidated Guaranteed 5s, due 1938, sold at 45 and the Canadian Pacific (unsecured) Debenture stock sold at $56^7/8$. It is clear that the value of the *long-term* Canadian Pacific guaranty was not fully appreciated in 1931.

A similar disadvantage attaches to a guaranty of dividends running for a limited period.

Examples: The actual working out of such a situation was shown in the case of American Telegraph and Cable Company common stock, which was guaranteed as to 5% dividends (only) for 50 years from 1882 by the Western Union Telegraph Company under a lease terminating in 1932. Because of the long record of dividend payments, investors came finally to consider the dividend as a fixture, and as late as 1922 the stock sold at 70. But in the meantime the strategic or trade value of the leased cable properties was rapidly diminishing, so that the value of the stock at the expiration of the lease was likely to be very small. A settlement was made in 1930 with Western Union under which the American Telegraph and Cable stockholders received the equivalent of about $20 for the principal of their stock.[11]

A rather unusual example of the importance of the exact terms of a guaranty was supplied by Pratt and Whitney Preferred (retired in 1928). According to the security manuals, the dividend on this issue was "guaranteed" by its parent company, Niles-Bement-Pond. But in fact the Niles company agreed to make up unpaid dividends on Pratt and Whitney Preferred only to the extent that Niles had earnings available therefor after payment of its own preferred dividends. Hence no dividends were received by Pratt and Whitney Preferred stockholders from November 1924 to June 1926 without any claim being enforceable against Niles-Bement-Pond. In view of the possibility of such special provisions, particular care must be exercised to obtain complete information regarding the terms of a guaranty before purchasing any security on the strength thereof.

---

[11] An alert investor might have taken warning of this possibility from statements contained in the annual reports of Western Union, starting with 1913, wherein this company's own holdings of American Telegraph and Cable stock were written down annually towards an estimated value of $10 per share in 1932.

Joint and Several Guarantees. Such guarantees are given by more than one company to cover the same issue, and each company accepts responsibility not only for its pro rata share but also for the share of any other guarantor who may default. In other words, each guarantor concern is potentially liable for the entire amount of the issue. Since two or more sponsors are better than one, bonds bearing a joint and several guarantee are likely to have special advantages.

Example: The most familiar class of issues backed by such a guaranty are the bonds of union railroad stations. An outstanding example is supplied by Kansas City Terminal Railway Company First 4s, due 1960, which are guaranteed jointly and severally by no less than 12 railroads, all of which use the company's facilities. The 12 guarantors are as follows: Atchison, Alton, Burlington, St. Paul, Great Western, Rock Island, Kansas City Southern, M-K-T, Missouri Pacific, 'Frisco, Union Pacific and Wabash.

The value of each of these individual guarantees has varied greatly from road to road and from time to time, but at least three of the companies have consistently maintained sufficient financial strength to assure a Terminal bondholder that his obligation would be met without difficulty. Investors have not fully appreciated the superior protection accorded by the combined responsibility of the 12 carriers as compared with the liability of any one of them singly. The price record shows that the Kansas City Terminal Railway Company 4s frequently sold at no higher prices than representative issues of individual guarantor companies which later turned out to be of questionable soundness, whereas at no time was the safety of the Terminal bond ever a matter of doubt.[12]

It would seem good policy for investors, therefore, to favor bonds of this type, which carry the guaranty of a *number* of substantial enterprises, in preference to the obligations of a single company.

---

[12] See Appendix Note 30, p. 762 on accompanying CD, for supporting data.

Federal Land Bank Bonds. A somewhat different aspect of the joint and several guarantee appears in the important case of the Federal Land Bank bonds, which are secured by deposit of farm mortgages. The obligations of each of the 12 separate banks are guaranteed by the 11 others, so that each Federal Land Bank bond is in reality a liability of the entire system. When these banks were organized, there was created concurrently a group of Joint Stock Land Banks which also issued bonds, but the obligations of one Joint Stock Bank were not guaranteed by the others.[13] Both sets of land banks were under United States government supervision and the bonds of both were made exempt from federal taxation. Practically all of the stock of the Federal Land Banks was subscribed for originally by the United States government (which, however, did not assume liability for their bonds); the Joint Stock Land Bank shares were privately owned.

At the inception of this dual system, investors were disposed to consider the federal supervision and tax exemption as a virtual guarantee of the safety of the *Joint Stock* Land Bank bonds, and they were therefore willing to buy them at a yield only $1/2$% higher than that returned by the *Federal* Land Bank bonds. In comparing the nonguaranteed Joint Stock bonds with the mutually guaranteed federal bonds, the following observations might well have been made:

1. Assuming the complete success of the farm-loan system, the guarantee would be superfluous, since each bond issue separately would have enjoyed ample protection.

2. Assuming complete failure of the system, the guarantee would prove worthless, since all the banks would be equally insolvent.

3. For any intermediate stage between these two extremes, the joint and several guarantee might prove extremely valuable. This would be particularly true as to bonds of a farm-loan district subjected to extremely adverse conditions of a *local* character.

---

[13] The word "Joint" in the title referred to the ownership of the stock by various interests, but it may have created an unfortunate impression among investors that there was a joint responsibility by the group of banks for the liabilities of each. For a comprehensive account and criticism of these banks, see Carl H. Schwartz, "Financial Study of the Joint Stock Land Banks," Washington, D. C., 1938.

In view of the fact that the farm-loan system was a new and untried undertaking, investors therein should have assured themselves of the largest possible measure of protection. Those who in their eagerness for the extra $1/2\%$ of income return dispensed with the joint guarantee committed a patent mistake of judgment.[14]

---

[14] A number of the Joint Stock bond issues defaulted during 1930–1932, a large proportion sold at receivership prices, and all of them declined to a speculative price level. On the other hand, not only were there no defaults among the Federal Land Bank bonds, but their prices suffered a relatively moderate shrinkage, remaining consistently on an investment level. This much more satisfactory experience of the investor in the Federal Land Bank bonds was due in good part to the additional capital subscribed by the United States government to these Banks, and to the closer supervision to which they were subjected, but the joint and several guarantee undoubtedly proved of considerable benefit.

Note also that Joint Stock Land Bank bonds were made legal investments for trust funds in many states, and remained so after 1932 despite their undoubtedly inadequate security. Since May 1933 the Joint Stock Land Banks have been prohibited from taking on new business, and orderly liquidation has been in process.

Chapter 17

GUARANTEED SECURITIES (*Continued*)

GUARANTEED REAL ESTATE MORTGAGES
AND MORTGAGE BONDS

The practice of guaranteeing securities reached its widest development in the field of real estate mortgages. These guarantees are of two different types: the first being given by the corporation engaged in the sale of the mortgages or mortgage participations (or by an affiliate); the second and more recent form being the guaranty given by an independent surety company, which assumes the contingent liability in return for a fee.

The idea underlying real estate mortgage guarantees is evidently that of insurance. It is to the mortgage holder's advantage to protect himself, at some cost in income return, against the possibility of adverse developments affecting his particular property (such as a change in the character of the neighborhood). It is within the province of sound insurance practice to afford this protection in return for an adequate premium, provided of course, that all phases of the business are prudently handled. Such an arrangement will have the best chance of success if:

1. The mortgage loans are conservatively made in the first instance.
2. The guaranty or surety company is large, well managed, independent of the agency selling the mortgages, and has a diversification of business in fields other than real estate.
3. Economic conditions are not undergoing fluctuations of abnormal intensity.

The collapse in real estate values after 1929 was so extreme as to contravene the third of these conditions. Accordingly the behavior of real estate mortgage guarantees during this period may not afford a really fair guide to their future value. Nevertheless, some of the characteristics which they revealed are worthy of comment.

[215]

This Business Once Conservatively Managed. In the first place a striking contrast may be drawn between the way in which the business of guaranteeing mortgages had been conducted prior to about 1924 and the lax methods which developed thereafter, during the very time that this part of the financial field was attaining its greatest importance.

If we consider the policies of the leading New York City institutions which guaranteed real estate mortgages (*e.g.*, Bond and Mortgage Guarantee Company, Lawyers Mortgage Company), it is fair to say that for many years the business was conservatively managed. The amount of each mortgage was limited to not more than 60% of the value, carefully determined; large individual mortgages were avoided; and a fair diversification of risk, from the standpoint of location, was attained. It is true that the guarantor companies were not independent of the selling companies, nor did they have other types of surety business. It is true also that the general practice of guaranteeing mortgages due only three to five years after their issuance contained the possibility, later realized, of a flood of maturing obligations at a most inconvenient time. Nevertheless, the prudent conduct of their activities had enabled them successfully to weather severe real estate depressions such as occurred in 1908 and 1921.

New and Less Conservative Practices Developed. The building boom which developed during the "new era" was marked by an enormous growth of the real estate mortgage business and of the practice of guaranteeing obligations of this kind. New people, new capital, and new methods entered the field. Several small local concerns which had been in the field for a long period were transformed into highly aggressive organizations doing a gigantic and nation-wide business. Great emphasis was laid upon the long record of success in the past, and the public was duly impressed—not realizing that the size, the methods, and the personnel were so changed that they were in fact dealing with a different institution. In a previous chapter we pointed out how recklessly unsound were the methods of financing real estate ventures during this period. The weakness of the mortgages themselves applied equally to the guarantees which were frequently attached thereto for an extra consideration. The guarantor companies were mere subsidiaries of the sellers of the bonds. Hence, when the crash came, the value of the properties, the real estate bond company, and the affiliated guarantor company all collapsed together.

Evil Effects of Competition and Contagion. The rise of the newer and more aggressive real estate bond organizations had a most unfortunate effect upon the policies of the older concerns. By force of competition they were led to relax their standards of making loans. New mortgages were granted on an increasingly liberal basis, and when old mortgages matured, they were frequently renewed in a larger sum. Furthermore, the face amount of the mortgages guaranteed rose to so high a multiple of the capital of the guarantor companies that it should have been obvious that the guaranty would afford only the flimsiest of protection in the event of a general decline in values.

When the real estate market broke in 1931, the first consequence was the utter collapse of virtually every one of the newer real estate bond companies and their subsidiary guarantor concerns. As the depression continued, the older institutions gave way also. The holders of guaranteed mortgages or participations therein (aggregating about $3,000,000,000 guaranteed by New York title and mortgage companies alone) found that the guaranty was a mere name and that they were entirely dependent upon the value of the underlying properties. In most cases these had been mortgaged far more heavily than reasonable prudence would have permitted. Apparently only a very small fraction of the mortgages outstanding in 1932 were created under the conservative conditions and principles that had ruled up to, say, eight years previously.

Guarantees by Independent Surety Companies. During the 1924–1930 period several of the independent surety and fidelity companies extended their operations to include the guaranteeing of real-estate mortgages for a fee or premium. Theoretically, this should have represented the soundest method of conducting such operations. In addition to the strength and general experience of the surety company there was the important fact that such a guarantor, being entirely independent, would presumably be highly critical of the issues submitted for its guaranty. But this theoretical advantage was offset to a great extent by the fact that the surety companies began the practice of guaranteeing real estate mortgage bonds only a short time prior to their debacle, and they were led by the general overoptimism then current to commit serious errors in judgment. In most cases the resultant losses to the guarantor were greater than it could stand; several of the companies were forced into receivership (notably National Surety Company), and holders of bonds with such guarantees failed to obtain full protection.[1]

LEASEHOLD OBLIGATIONS EQUIVALENT TO GUARANTEES

The property of one company is often leased to another for a fixed annual rental sufficient to pay interest and dividends on the former's capital issues. Frequently the lease is accompanied by a specific guaranty of such interest and dividend payments, and in fact the majority of guaranteed corporate issues originate in this fashion.[2] But even if there is no explicit guaranty, a lease or other contract providing fixed annual payments will supply the equivalent of a guaranty on the securities of the lessee company.

Examples: An excellent instance of the value of such an arrangement is afforded by the Westvaco Chlorine Products Corporation 5^{1}/$_{2}$s, issued in 1927 and maturing in 1937. The Westvaco Company agreed to sell part of its output to a subsidiary of Union Carbide and Carbon Corporation, and the latter enterprise guaranteed that monthly payments would be made to the trustee sufficient to take care of the interest and retirement of the 5^{1}/$_{2}$% bonds. In effect this arrangement was a guaranty of interest and principal of the Westvaco issue by Union Carbide and Carbon, a very strong concern. By reason of this protection and the continuous purchases for redemption made thereunder, the price of the issue was maintained at 99 or higher throughout 1932–1933. This contrasts with a decline in the price of Westvaco common stock from 116^{1}/$_{2}$ in 1929 to 3 in 1932. (The entire bond issue was called at 100^{1}/$_{2}$ in September 1935.)

Another interesting example is supplied by the Tobacco Products Corporation of New Jersey 6^{1}/$_{2}$s, due 2022. The properties of this company were leased to American Tobacco Company under a 99-year contract,

---

[1] But in the case of the independent surety companies the guarantees proved of substantial, if only partial, value. The bankruptcy estate of National Surety Company yielded a large cash payment to holders of bonds bearing its guarantee. Some of the other companies managed to remain solvent by affecting a kind of composition with bondholders, involving the issuance of new bonds carrying a guarantee of interest at rather low rates, though not of principal. *Examples:* Metropolitan Casualty Company, Maryland Casualty Company, United States Fidelity and Guaranty Company.

[2] For example Pittsburgh, Fort Wayne and Chicago Railway Company Preferred and Common receive 7% dividends under a 999-year lease to the Pennsylvania Railroad Company. These dividends are also guaranteed by the Pennsylvania.

expiring also in 2022, providing for annual payments of $2,500,000 (with the privilege to the lessee to settle by a lump-sum payment equivalent to the then present value of the rental, discounted at 7% per annum). By means of a sinking-fund arrangement these rental payments were calculated to be sufficient to retire the bond issue in full prior to maturity, in addition to taking care of the interest. These Tobacco Products $6^{1}/_{2}$s were the equivalent of fixed obligations of American Tobacco Company. As such they ranked ahead of American Tobacco Preferred, dividends on which, of course, are not a fixed charge. When the bonds were created in 1931 the investing public was either sceptical of the validity of the lease or—more probably—was not familiar with this situation, for American Tobacco Preferred sold at a much higher relative price than the Tobacco Products bonds. At the low price of 73 in 1932 the bonds yielded 8.90%, while American Tobacco preferred was selling at 95, to yield 6.32%. In January 1935 the lease was commuted by a lump-sum payment resulting in the redemption of the Tobacco Products $6^{1}/_{2}$s at par.

Specific Terms of Lease Important. *Example:*

As in the case of guaranteed issues, the details of the lease arrangement may have a vital bearing on the status of the issue benefiting therefrom. Some of the elements here involved are illustrated by the following example:

Georgia Midland Railway First 3s, due 1946. Not guaranteed, but property leased to Southern Railway until 1995, at a rental equal to present bond interest. (Price in January 1939, 35.)

In this case the lease agreement is fully equivalent to a guarantee of *interest* up to and far beyond the maturity date. The value of the guaranty itself depends upon the solvency of the Southern Railway. The status of the bond issue at maturity in 1946 will depend, however, on a number of other factors as well, *e.g.:*

1. The market value of a long-term rental obligation of Southern Railway. If interest rates are low enough, and the credit of Southern Railway high enough, the issue could be refunded at the same 3% interest rate into a longer maturity. (This would seem far from probable in 1939.)

2. The value of the Georgia Midland mileage. If this mileage actually earns substantially more than the rental paid, then Southern Railway could be expected to make a special effort to pay the bonds at maturity, for fear of otherwise losing control of the property. This would involve

an agreement to pay such higher rental (*i.e.*, interest rate) as may be necessary to permit extension or refunding of the bond maturity. (However, traffic-density data in private hands in 1939 indicated that this mileage was not a valuable part of the Southern Railway System.)

3. Possible payment on grounds of convenience, etc. If the Southern Railway is prosperous in 1946, it may take care of this maturity merely to avoid insolvency for part of the system. There is also the technical possibility that by the terms of its own "blanket" Development and General Mortgage (under which sufficient bonds are reserved to refund the Georgia Midland 3s at maturity), it may be considered to have an obligation to provide for payment of these bonds in 1946. (Here also, as in the two previous paragraphs, the bondholder in 1939 could not be too confident of the strength of his position).

The foregoing discussion will perhaps adequately explain the low price of the Georgia Midland 3s at the beginning of 1939. It is interesting to note, as an element of security analysis, that the key fact in this situation—the unprofitable character of the mileage covered—was not a matter of public record but required a check into supplementary sources of information.

Guaranteed Issues Frequently Undervalued. The Tobacco Products example illustrates the fairly frequent undervaluation of guaranteed or quasi-guaranteed issues as compared with other securities of the guarantor enterprise. A well-known instance was that of San Antonio and Aransas Pass Railway Company First 4s, due 1943, guaranteed as to principal and interest by Southern Pacific Company. Although these enjoyed a mortgage security in addition to the guaranty they regularly sold at prices yielding higher returns than did the unsecured obligations of the Southern Pacific.[3]

---

[3] A. S. Dewing, in his *A Study of Corporation Securities*, pp. 293–297, New York, 1934, makes the following statements with respect to guaranteed bonds:

"There may be, however, instances in which a holding or controlling corporation will maintain the interest or rental on an unprofitable subsidiary's bonds for strategic reasons." (Here follow examples, including details concerning San Antonio and Aransas Pass First 4s, due 1943, showing failure of the issuer to earn its charges in most years.) "Yet its [San Antonio and Aransas Pass Railway's] importance to the Southern Pacific Company's lines is such that the guarantor company very wisely meets the bond interest deficit... In spite of such instances, the rule holds good almost always that the strength of a guaranteed bond is no greater than that of the corporation issuing it and the earning capacity of the property directly covered by it."

Examples: A more striking contrast was afforded by the price of Barnhart Bros. and Spindler Company First and Second Preferred (both guaranteed as to principal and dividends by American Type Founders Company) in relation to the price of the guarantor's own preferred stock which was not a fixed obligation. Additional examples of this point are afforded by the price of Huyler's of Delaware, Inc., Preferred, guaranteed by Schulte Retail Stores Corporation, as compared with the price of Schulte Preferred; and by the price of Armour and Company of Delaware guaranteed preferred, as compared with the preferred stock of the guarantor company, Armour and Company of Illinois. Some comparative quotations relating to these examples are given below.

COMPARATIVE PRICES AND YIELDS OF GUARANTEED SECURITIES AND
SECURITIES OF THE GUARANTOR*

Issue	Date	Price	Yield, %
San Antonio & Aransas Pass 1st 4s/1943 (GTD)	Jan. 2, 1920	56$^1/_4$	8.30
Southern Pacific Co. Debenture 4s/1929	Jan. 2, 1920	81	6.86
Barnhart Bros. & Spindler 7% 1st Pfd. (GTD)	1923 low price	90	7.78
Barnhart Bros. & Spindler 7% 2d Pfd. (GTD)	1923 low price	80	8.75
American Type Founders 7% Pfd	1923 low price	95	7.37
Huyler's of Delaware 7% Pfd. (GTD)	April 11, 1928	102$^1/_2$	6.83
Schulte Retail Stores 8% Pfd.	April 11, 1928	129	6.20
Armour of Delaware 7% Pfd. (GTD)	Feb. 13, 1925	95$^1/_8$	7.36
Armour of Illinois 7% Pfd.	Feb. 13, 1925	92$^7/_8$	7.54

* If the reader traces the subsequent history of the various issues in this table, he will find a great variety of developments, including assumption through merger (San Antonio and Aransas Pass Railroad), redemption (Barnhart Brothers and Spindler), and default (Huylers of Delaware, Inc.). But the fact that the guaranteed issues were *relatively* undervalued is demonstrated by the sequel in each case.

It is obvious that in cases of this sort advantageous exchanges can be made from the lower yielding into the higher yielding security with no

It seems clear to us that these statements misinterpret the essential character of the obligation under a guarantee. Southern Pacific met the San Antonio and Aransas Pass bond interest deficit, not out of "wisdom" but by compulsion. The strength of a guaranteed bond *may be very much greater than* that of the corporation issuing it, because that strength rests upon the dual claim of the holder against *both* the issuing corporation and the guarantor.

impairment of safety; or else into a much better secured issue with little sacrifice of yield, and sometimes with an actual gain.[4]

INCLUSION OF GUARANTEES AND RENTALS IN THE CALCULATION OF FIXED CHARGES

All obligations equivalent to bond interest should be included with a company's interest charges when calculating the coverage for its bond issues. This point has already been explained in some detail in connection with railroad fixed charges, and it was touched upon briefly in our discussion of public-utility bonds. The procedure in these groups offers no special difficulties. But in the case of certain types of industrial companies, the treatment of rentals and guarantees may offer confusing variations. This question is of particular moment in connection with retail enterprises, theater companies, etc., in which rent or other obligations related to buildings occupied may be an important element in the general picture. Such a building may be owned by the corporation and paid for by a bond issue, in which case the obligation will be fully disclosed in both the balance sheet and the income account. But if another company occupies a similar building under long-term lease, no separate measure of the rental obligation appears in the income account and no indication thereof can be found in the balance sheet. The second company may *appear* sounder than the first, but that is only because its obligations are undisclosed; essentially, both companies are carrying a similar burden. Conversely, the outright ownership of premises free and clear carries an important advantage (from the standpoint of preferred stock, particularly) over operation under long-term lease, although the capitalization set-up will not reveal this advantage.

Examples: If Interstate Department Stores Preferred had been compared with The Outlet Company Preferred in 1929 the two exhibits might have appeared closely similar; the earnings coverage averaged about the same, and neither company showed any bond or mortgage liability. But Outlet's position was in actuality by far the stronger, because it owned its land and buildings while those of Interstate (with a minor exception) were held under lease. The real effect of this situation was to place a substantial

---

[4] In Note 31 of the Appendix, p. 762 on accompanying CD, will be found a concise discussion of certain interesting phases of guarantees and rentals, as illustrated by the N. Y. and Harlem Railroad and the Mobile and Ohio Railroad situations.

fixed obligation ahead of Interstate Department Stores Preferred which did not exist in the case of Outlet. In the chain-store field a similar observation would apply to a comparison of J. C. Penney Preferred and S. H. Kress Preferred in 1932; for the latter company owned more than half of its store properties, while nearly all the Penney locations were leased.

Lease Liabilities Generally Overlooked. The question of liability under long-term leases received very little attention from the financial world until its significance was brought home rudely in 1931 and 1932, when the high level of rentals assumed in the preceding boom years proved intolerably burdensome to many merchandising companies.

Example: The influence of this factor upon a supposed investment security is shown with striking force in the case of United Cigar Stores Preferred. This issue, and its predecessor, had for many years shown every sign of stability and had sold accordingly at a consistently high level. For 1928 the company reported "no funded debt" and earnings equal to about seven times the preferred dividend. Yet so crushing were the liabilities under its long-term leases (and to carry properties acquired by subsidiaries), that in 1932 bankruptcy was resorted to and the preferred stock was menaced with extinction.

Such Liabilities Complicated Analysis. It must be admitted that in the case of companies where the rental factor is important, its obtrusion has badly complicated the whole question of bond or preferred stock analysis. Fortunately the investor now has some data as to the extent of such leasehold obligations, since they are now required to be summarized in registration statements filed with the S.E.C., and the actual rent payments must be stated each year (on Form 10-K).[5] But the problem remains whether or not these rentals should be treated, in whole or in part, as the equivalent of fixed charges. To some extent, certainly, they are identical rather with fixed "overhead"—*e.g.*, depreciation, taxes, general expense—which it has not been found feasible to add in with bond interest for the purpose of figuring a margin of safety. One type of solution is obvious: If the company meets the earnings test, even after adding rents paid to bond interest, the rent situation need not worry the investor.

---

[5] The S.E.C. forms group "rents and royalties" together, but in the typical case this entire item relates to rents and can be treated as such.

Example:

SWIFT AND COMPANY 3³/4S, DUE 1950

	1934–1938 Average Results
Balance for dividends	$8,630,000
Interest paid	2,107,000
Rentals paid	996,000
Interest earned	5.1 times
Interest and rentals earned	3.8 times

We feel, however, that it would be neither fair nor practicable to require every company to meet a test so severe. A compromise suggestion based on some study of actual exhibits may be hazarded, *viz.:* (1) that one-third the annual rentals (for building space) be included with fixed charges (and preferred dividends), to compute the earnings coverage; and (2) that in the case of retail establishments (chain stores, department stores) the minimum coverage required for interest plus one-third of rentals be reduced from 3 to 2. This reduction would recognize the relative stability of retail business, after allowance is made for the special burden attaching to the rental factor. The corresponding coverage required for a retail company's preferred stock would be reduced from 4 to 2$^1/_2$.

Examples:

(*A*) NONRETAIL BOND ISSUE LOEW'S, INC., 3¹/2S, DUE 1946

	August 1934–August 1938 Average Results
Balance for dividends	$10,097,000
Interest (and subsid. preferred dividends) paid.	2,614,000
One-third of rentals paid	1,107,000
Interest, etc., earned	4.86 times
Interest and one-third of rentals earned	3.71 times

(*B*) RETAIL ENTERPRISE PREFERRED STOCK

1934–1938 Average Results

	McCrory Stores Corp. 6% Preferred	McLellan Stores Co. 6% Preferred
Balance for common stock	$1,682,000	$1,148,000
Interest on bonds	abt. 200,000	
One-third of rentals	770,000*	434,000
Preferred dividends	300,000	180,000
Preferred dividend (and interest earned) ...	4.36 times	7.38 times
Preferred dividend, interest and ¹/3 of rentals earned	2.33 times	2.87 times

* 1935–1938 average.

Conclusions: Loew's 3^1/$_2$s pass our quantitative test for nonretail bond issues. McLellan Preferred does, but McCrory Preferred does not, pass our suggested test for retail-store preferred stocks.

The four preceding examples illustrate a simplified technique for earnings coverage. Instead of first computing the amount available for the charges, we divide the charges (and preferred dividends) into the balance *after* charges (and preferred dividends) and add 1 to the quotient.

The reader is warned that these suggested standards and the calculations illustrating them are submitted with considerable hesitation. They represent a new departure in analytical method; the data for rentals paid are available only at some effort; most serious of all, the arithmetical standards proposed are arbitrary and perhaps not the best that can be devised. We might point out, further, that the new test may yield some unexpected results. Note that McLellan Preferred has sold (in 1939) at a lower price than McCrory Preferred—a point that *may* be justified by other factors. Note, further, that if the same calculation as above is applied to W. T. Grant 5% Preferred—a high-priced issue, which earned its dividend nearly ten times over in 1934–1938—we should find that the preferred dividend plus one-third of rentals was covered not quite 2^1/$_2$ times.[6]

Status of Guaranteed Obligations. Some additional observations may properly be made as to the computation of earnings coverage in the case of guaranteed obligations. In the typical case the properties involved in the guarantee form part of the whole enterprise; hence both the earnings therefrom and the guaranteed payments are included in a single income statement.

Example: Neisner Realty Corporation 6s, due 1948, are guaranteed by Neisner Brothers, Inc. The corporation's operations and interest charges are included in the parent company's consolidated statement.

When the guaranteed security is outstanding against a separately operated property, its standing may depend either on its own results or on those of the guarantor. Hence the issue need be required to pass only one of three alternative tests, based on (1) earnings of issuing company, independent of the guarantee; or (2) combined earnings and charges of the issuing and guarantor companies; or (3) earnings of guarantor company applied to its own charges plus its guarantees.

---

[6] This stock, par 20, sold at 25 in 1939 although callable at 22.

Examples: a. Indiana Harbor Belt Railway General 4s and $4^1/_2$s, due
1957. Guaranteed as to principal and interest by New York Central Railroad and an important subsidiary. The Standard Statistics Bond Guide
gives as the interest coverage that of the guarantor, the New York Central
System. But the showing of the company itself is much better, *e.g.:*

	Charges earned	
	N. Y. Central System	Indiana Harbor Belt
1938	0.59 times	2.98 times
1937	1.12 times	3.81 times

b. This is the typical situation, in which coverage is calculated from a
consolidated income account, including operations of both the parent
(guarantor) company and its guaranteed subsidiaries.

c. Minneapolis, St. Paul and Sault Sainte Marie $5^1/_2$s, due 1978, guaranteed as to interest by Canadian Pacific Railway. The "Soo line" shows
earnings of only a small part of total interest charges. Coverage for this
issue might best be computed by applying earnings of Canadian Pacific
Railway to the total of its own interest charges plus the guaranteed interest on these and other bonds guaranteed by Canadian Pacific Railway.

SUBSIDIARY COMPANY BONDS

The bonds of a subsidiary of a strong company are generally regarded as
well protected, on the theory that the parent company will take care of all
its constituents' obligations. This viewpoint is encouraged by the common method of setting up consolidated income accounts, under which
all the subsidiary bond interest appears as a charge against all the combined earnings, ranking ahead of the parent company's preferred and
common stocks. If, however, the parent concern is not contractually
responsible for the subsidiary bonds, by guaranty or lease (or direct
assumption), this form of statement may prove to be misleading. For if a
particular subsidiary proves unprofitable, its bond interest may conceivably not be taken care of by the parent company, which may be willing to
lose its investment in this part of its business and turn it over to the subsidiary's bondholders. Such a development is unusual, but the possibility
thereof was forcibly demonstrated in 1932–1933 by the history of United
Drug Company 5s, due 1953.

Examples: United Drug was an important subsidiary of Drug, Inc., which had regularly earned and paid large dividends, gained chiefly from the manufacture of proprietary medicines and other drugs. In the first half of 1932, the consolidated income account showed earnings equal to ten times the interest on United Drug 5s, and the record of previous years was even better. While this issue was not assumed or guaranteed by Drug, Inc., investors considered the combined showing so favorable as to assure the safety of the United Drug 5s beyond question. But United Drug owned, as part of its assets and business, the stock of Louis K. Liggett Company, which operated a large number of drug stores and which was burdened by a high-rental problem similar to that of United Cigar Stores. In September 1932 Liggett's notified its landlords that unless rents were reduced it would be forced into bankruptcy.

This announcement brought rudely home to investors the fact that the still prosperous Drug, Inc., was not assuming responsibility for the liabilities of its (indirect) subsidiary, Liggett's, and they immediately became nervously conscious of the fact that Drug, Inc., was not responsible for interest payments on United Drug 5s either. Sales of these bonds resulting from this discovery depressed the price from 93 earlier in the year down to 42. At the latter figure, the $40,000,000 of United Drug 5s were quoted at only $17,000,000, although the parent company's stock was still selling for more than $100,000,000 (3,500,000 shares at about 30). In the following year the "Drug, Inc., System" was voluntarily dissolved into its component parts—an unusual development—and the United Drug Co. resumed its entirely separate existence. (It has since shown an inadequate coverage for the 5% bonds.)

Consolidated Traction Company of New Jersey First 5s were obligations of a large but unprofitable subsidiary of Public Service Corporation of New Jersey. The bonds were not guaranteed by the parent company. When they matured in 1933 many of the holders accepted an offer of 65 for their bonds made by the parent company.

Saltex Looms, Inc., 1st 6s, due 1954, were obligations of a subsidiary of Sidney Blumenthal & Co., Inc., but in no way guaranteed by the parent company. The consolidated earning statements of Blumenthal regularly deducted the Saltex bond interest before showing the amount available for its own preferred stock. Interest on the bonds was defaulted, however, in 1939; and in 1940 the bonds sold at 7 while Blumenthal preferred was quoted above 70.

Separate Analysis of Subsidiary Interest Coverage Essential.
These examples suggest that just as investors are prone to underestimate
the value of a guaranty by a strong company, they sometimes make the
opposite mistake and attach undue significance to the fact that a company is controlled by another. From the standpoint of fixed-value investment, nothing of importance may be taken for granted. Hence a
subsidiary bond should not be purchased on the basis of the showing of
its parent company, unless the latter has assumed direct responsibility for
the bond in question. In other cases the exhibit of the subsidiary itself can
afford the only basis for the acceptance of its bond issues.[7]

If the above discussion is compared with that on page 179 of accompanying CD, it will be seen that investors in bonds of a *holding company*
must insist upon a consolidated income account, in which the subsidiary
interest—whether guaranteed or not—is shown as a prior charge; but that
purchasers of unguaranteed *subsidiary* bonds cannot accept such consolidated reports as a measure of their safety, and must require a statement
covering the subsidiary alone. These statements may be obtainable only
with some difficulty, as was true in the case of United Drug 5s, but they
must nevertheless be insisted upon.

---

[7] As a practical matter, the financial interest of the parent company in its subsidiary, and
other business reasons, may result in its protecting the latter's bonds even though it is not
obligated to do so. This would be a valid consideration, however, only in deciding upon a
purchase on a *speculative* basis (*i.e.*, carrying a chance of principal profit), but would not justify buying the bond at a full investment price. Concretely stated, it might have made United
Drug 5s an excellent speculation at 45, but they were a poor investment at 93.

Chapter 18

PROTECTIVE COVENANTS AND REMEDIES OF SENIOR SECURITY HOLDERS

IN THIS AND the two succeeding chapters we shall consider the provisions usually made to protect the rights of bond owners and preferred stockholders against impairment, and the various lines of action which may be followed in the event of nonfulfillment of the company's obligations. Our object here, as throughout this book, is not to supply information of a kind readily available elsewhere, but rather to subject current practices to critical examination and to suggest feasible improvements therein for the benefit of security holders generally. In this connection a review of recent developments in the field of reorganization procedure may also be found of value.

Indenture or Charter Provisions Designed to Protect Holder of Senior Securities. The contract between a corporation and the owners of its bonds is contained in a document called the *indenture or deed of trust*. The corresponding agreements relating to the rights of preferred stockholders are set forth in the Articles, or Certificate, of Incorporation. These instruments usually contain provisions designed to prevent corporate acts injurious to senior security holders and to afford remedies in case of certain unfavorable developments. The more important occurrences for which such provision is almost always made may be listed under the following heads:

1. In the case of bonds:
   a. Nonpayment of interest, principal, or sinking fund.
   b. Default on other obligations, or receivership.
   c. Issuance of new secured debt.
   d. Dilution of a conversion (or subscription) privilege.

2. In the case of preferred stocks:

    a. Nonpayment of (cumulative) preferred dividends for a period of time.

    b. Creation of funded debt or a prior stock issue.

    c. Dilution of a conversion (or subscription) privilege.

A frequent, but less general, provision requires the maintenance of working capital at a certain percentage of the bonded debt of industrial companies. (In the case of investment-trust or holding-company bonds it is the *market value* of all the assets which is subject to this provision.)

The remedies provided for bondholders in cases falling under 1*a* and 1*b* above are fairly well standardized. Any one of these untoward developments is designated as an "event of default" and permits the trustee to declare the principal of the bond issue due and payable in advance of the specified maturity date. The provisions therefor in the indenture are known as "acceleration clauses." Their purpose in the main is to enable the bondholders to assert the full amount of their claim in competition with the other creditors.

Contradictory Aspects of Bondholders' Legal Rights. In considering these provisions from a critical standpoint, we must recognize that there are contradictory aspects to the question of the bondholders' legal rights. Receivership[1] is a dreaded word in Wall Street; its advent means ordinarily a drastic shrinkage in the price of all the company's securities, including the bonds for the "benefit" of which the receivership was instituted. As we pointed out in a former chapter, the market's appraisal of a bond in default is no higher on the whole, and perhaps lower, than that of a non-dividend-paying preferred stock of a solvent company.

The question arises, therefore, whether the bondholders might not be better off if they did not have any enforceable claim to principal or interest payments *when conditions are such as to make prompt payment impossible.* For at such times the bondholder's legal rights apparently succeed

---

[1] "Receivership" was formerly a convenient term, applying to all kinds of financial difficulties that involved court action. As a result of the Chandler Act (Bankruptcy Act of 1938), receivers have been largely replaced by trustees. No doubt the word "receivership" will continue to be used—for a while at least—because the terms "trusteeship" and "bankruptcy" are not quite satisfactory, the former being somewhat ambiguous, the latter having an overdrastic connotation. "Insolvency" is a suitable word but awkward to use at times.

So-called "equity receivers" will still be appointed in the future in connection with stockholder's suits, voluntary liquidations, and other special matters.

only in ruining the corporation without benefiting the bondholder. As long as the interest or principal is not going to be paid anyway, would it not be to the interest of the bondholders themselves to postpone the date of payment and keep the enterprise out of the courts?

Corporate Insolvency and Reorganization. This question leads into the broad field of corporate insolvency and reorganization. We must try, within as brief a space as possible, first, to describe the procedure followed prior to the amendatory legislation beginning in 1933; secondly, to summarize the changes brought about by the recent statutes; and, finally, to evaluate the bondholder's position as it now appears. (The latter will be especially difficult, since the new laws have not yet had time to prove their merits or deficiencies in actual practice.)

The old pattern for corporate reorganization went usually as follows: Inability to pay interest or principal of indebtedness led to an application by the corporation itself for a receiver.[2] It was customary to select a "friendly" court; the receiver was generally the company's president; the bondholders' interests were represented by protective committees ordinarily formed by the investment banking houses that had floated the issues. A reorganization plan was agreed upon by the committees and then approved by the court. The plan usually represented a compromise of the conflicting interests of the various ranks of security holders, under which, generally speaking, everyone retained *some* interest in the new company and everyone made some sacrifice. (In numerous cases, however, small and well-entrenched issues at the top were paid off or left undisturbed; and in hopeless situations stock issues were sometimes completely wiped out.) The actual mechanics of reorganization was through a foreclosure or bankruptcy sale. The properties were bought in in behalf of the assenting security holders; and creditors who refused to participate received in cash their pro rata share, if any, of the sale price. This price was usually set so low that everyone was better off to join in the plan and take new securities rather than to stay out and take cash.

Between 1933 and 1939 this procedure was completely transformed by a series of remedial laws, the most important of which was the Chandler

---

[2] Other "events of default"—*e.g.*, failure to meet sinking-fund or working-capital requirements—rarely resulted in receivership. Almost always bondholders preferred to overlook, or negotiate over, these matters rather than harm themselves by throwing the company in the courts.

Act. The defects for which a cure was desired were of two kinds: On the one hand the necessity for paying nonassenting bondholders had developed into a dilemma; because unduly low "upset," or minimum, foreclosure-sale prices were being frowned on by the courts, whereas payment of a fair price involved often an insuperable problem of finding the cash. More serious was the fact that the whole mechanics of reorganization tended to keep complete dominance of the situation in the hands of the old controlling group—who may have been inefficient or even dishonest, and who certainly had special interests to serve.

Beginning with the 1933 changes, a reorganization technique was set up under which a plan accepted by two-thirds of the creditors and a majority of the stockholders (if they had some "equity"), and approved by the court, was made binding on all the security holders. This has done away with the cumbersome and otherwise objectionable device of the foreclosure sale. As perfected by the Chandler Act and the Trust Indenture Act of 1939, the new procedure for other than railroad companies includes the following additional important points:[3]

1. The company must be turned over to at least one disinterested trustee. This trustee must decide whether any claims should be asserted against the old management and also whether or not the business is worth continuing.

2. Actual responsibility for devising a reorganization plan devolves on three disinterested agencies: (1) the trustee, who must present the plan in the first instance; (2) the S.E.C. (when the liabilities exceed $3,000,000), who may submit an advisory opinion thereon; (3) and the judge, who must officially approve it. Although the security holders and their protective committees may make suggestions, their acceptance is not asked for until the disinterested agencies have done their work. Furthermore, apparently wide powers are now given the court to force acceptance upon

---

[3] Provisions 1 to 4 appear in Chap. X of the Chandler Act, an outgrowth of the famous Sec. 77B, which was added to the old bankruptcy act in 1933. Railroad reorganizations are governed by Sec. 77, which was carried over into the Chandler Act intact, and by Chap. XV, added in 1939 (see footnote 12, p. 238). There is also a Chap. XI proceeding under the Chandler Act, relating to "arrangements" of unsecured indebtedness only. Note resort to such proceedings by Haytian Corporation in 1938 and by United States Realty and Improvement Company in 1939. In the latter case the only matter affected was its guarantee of Trinity Buildings Corporation $5^1/2$s, the company seeking to keep its own structure unchanged. Difficulties developed, and the proceedings were replaced by others.

classes of holders who have failed to approve in the requisite percentage; but the exact extent of these powers is still uncertain.

3. The reorganization plan must meet a number of standards of fairness prescribed in the statute, including provisions relating to voting power, publication of reports, etc. The court must specifically approve the new management.

4. The activities of protective committees are subject to close scrutiny and supervision. Reorganization costs of all kinds, including compensation to all and sundry, must receive court sanction.

5. As distinct from reorganization procedure proper, the Trust Indenture Act prescribes a number of requirements for trustees acting under bond indentures. These are designed both to obviate certain conflicts in interest that have caused considerable complaint and also to insure a more active attitude by the trustee in behalf of the bondholders.

There is no doubt at all in our minds that in the typical case the recent legislation[4] will prove highly beneficial. It should eliminate a number of the abuses formerly attaching to receiverships and reorganizations. It should also speed up materially the readjustment process. This should be true, especially, after more definite standards of fairness in reorganization plans have come to be established, so that there will not be so much room as heretofore for protracted disputes between the different ranks of security holders.[5]

---

[4] Legislation analogous to the mechanics of the 77B and Chandler Act provisions was applied to real estate readjustments in the Schackno and Burchill Acts passed by the New York State Legislature in 1933. In the same year The Companies' Creditors Arrangement Act, adopted in Canada, provided that insolvent Canadian Companies might escape proceedings under the Bankruptcy Act and work out compromises with creditors with the sanction of the court. When properly approved, such compromises are binding on minority groups. See W. S. Lighthall, *The Dominion Companies Act* 1934, *annotated*, pp. 289, 345 *ff.*, Montreal, 1935.

[5] The tendency of the S.E.C. advisory opinions, as well as the findings of the I.C.C. in railroad reorganizations, has been strongly in the direction of eliminating stockholders when there appears to be no chance that earnings will cover former interest charges. For a discussion of this point by one of the authors, see Benjamin Graham, "Fair Reorganization Plans under Chapter X of the Chandler Act," *Brooklyn Law Review*, December 1938.

Despite the improvements in the law, railroad reorganizations have been subject to extraordinary delays since 1933. In our opinion, however, this was due not so much to weaknesses remaining in the statute as it was to the extraordinary problem of devising fair plans for extremely complicated corporate structures when the question of future earning power was both highly controversial and of critical importance.

Alternative Remedy Suggested. Despite these undoubted reforms in reorganization technique, we shall be bold enough to venture the assertion that the ideal protective procedure for bondholders may often be found along other and simpler lines. In our opinion—given a sufficiently simple debt structure—the best remedy for all injuries suffered by bondholders is the immediate vesting in them of voting control over the corporation, together with an adequate mechanism to assure the intelligent exercise of such control. In many cases the creditors would then be able to marshal the company's resources and earnings for their own protection in such a way as to avoid recourse to expensive and protracted judicial proceedings.

Our suggestion falls into two parts: First, voting control by bondholders would, by the terms of the indenture, constitute the sole immediate remedy for any event of default, including nonpayment of interest or principal. During such control, unpaid interest or principal would be considered subject to a grace period. But the directors representing the bondholders should have the right to apply for a trusteeship under the Chandler Act, if they feel that comprehensive reorganization is preferable to an indefinite continuance of the moratorium plus control. Secondly, this voting control could best be implemented through the indenture trustee— a large and financially experienced institution, which is competent to represent the bondholders generally and to recommend to them suitable candidates for the controlling directorships. Stockholder's interests should continue to be represented on the board by minority directors.

What this arrangement would mean in effect is the turning of a fixed-interest bond into an income bond during the period of bondholders' control; and the postponement of maturing debt until voluntary extension or refinancing becomes feasible or else until liquidation or sale is found to be the desirable course. It should also be feasible to extend the basic technique and principle of voluntary recapitalization by statute (now applying only to the various stock issues) to include a bond issue as well, when the plan emanates from bondholders' representatives who have the alternative of keeping control and merely waiting.

Obviously, however, control cannot well be vested in creditors when they belong to several classes with conflicting interests. In such cases Chandler Act proceedings would seem necessary to cut the Gordian knot. But, theoretically at least, a voting-control arrangement is possible with a simple senior and a simple junior lien. If default should occur only with respect to the junior lien, voting control would pass to that issue. If the senior lien is defaulted, it would take control as a single class.

Although these suggestions may inspire doubt because of their novelty, it should be pointed out that the idea of voting by bondholders is both an old one and growing in vogue. Although in the past it was an exceptional arrangement, we now find that many reorganization plans, providing for issuance of income bonds, give voting powers to these securities, generally calling for control of the board of directors until all or most of the issue is retired or if interest is not paid in full.[6] Furthermore, many indentures covering fixed-interest bonds now provide for a vote by bondholders on amendments to the indenture.[7] It is also common for Canadian trust indentures to provide for meetings of bondholders in order to amend the terms of the indenture, including even the postponement or change of interest or principal payments.[8] Such meetings may be called by the trustee, by a stated proportion of the bondholders, or in certain instances by the company itself.

It may be objected that the suggested arrangement would really give a bondholder no better legal rights than a preferred stockholder and would thus relegate him to the unsatisfactory position of having both a limited

---

[6] *Examples:* The reorganization plan of New York State Railways (Syracuse System), dated February 1939, provides that the holders of the new income notes shall be entitled to elect two-thirds of the directors until at least 80% of the notes have been retired. Commercial Mackay Corporation Income Debentures, due 1967, elect one-third of the directors until all bonds are retired.

National Hotel of Cuba Income 6s, due 1959 (issued in 1929), were given voting control in the event of default of one year's interest. Older examples of voting rights given to bondholders include Erie Railroad Prior Lien 4s and General 4s, Mobile and Ohio Railroad General 4s, Third Avenue Railway Adjustment 5s.

The 1934 reorganization of Maple Leaf Milling Company, Ltd. (Canada), provided that the Indenture Trustee of the $5^{1}/_{2}$s due 1949 (later extended to 1958) would exercise effective control of the company by ownership (in trust) of 2 out of 3 management or voting shares.

[7] Generally excluded from this provision are changes in maturity dates of principal or interest, the rate of interest, the redemption price and the conversion rate. *Examples:* Richfield Oil Corporation Debenture 4s, due 1952. The Industrial Rayon First $4^{1}/_{2}$s, due 1948, are unusual in that the indenture permits a two-thirds vote of bondholders to postpone interest payments. However, the New York Stock Exchange required an undertaking not to invoke this clause, as a condition of listing the issue.

[8] See the S.E.C. *Report on the Study and Investigation of the Work, Activities, Personnel and Functions of Protective and Reorganization Committees*, Pt. VI, pp. 135–177, especially pp. 138–143, 164–177, Washington, 1936.

interest and an unenforceable claim. Our answer must be that, if the control device can be developed properly, it would provide an adequate remedy for both bondholders and preferred stockholders. In that case the basic contractual advantage of bonds over preferred shares would vanish, except to the extent of the right of bonds to repayment at a fixed date. We repeat, in conclusion, the point made in our discussion of the theory of preferred stocks (page 188 on accompanying CD) that the contractual disadvantage of preferred shares is, at bottom, not so much a matter of inherent legal rights as it is of practical corporate procedure and of the investor's own shortcomings.

Tendency of Securities of Insolvent Companies to Sell below Their Fair Value.

Some additional aspects of the corporate-reorganization question deserve attention. The first relates to the market action of securities of insolvent companies. Receiverships in the past have been productive generally of a vast and pervasive uncertainty, which threatens extinction to the stockholders but fails to promise anything specific to the bondholders. As a result there has been a tendency for the securities of companies in receivership to sell below their fair value in the aggregate; and also a tendency for illogical relationships to be established between the price of a bond issue in default and the price of the junior stock issues.

Examples: The Fisk Rubber Company case is an excellent example of the former point; the Studebaker Corporation situation in September 1933 illustrates the latter.

MARKET VALUE OF FISK RUBBER SECURITIES IN APRIL 1932

$7,600,000 First 8s @ 16	$ 1,200,000
8,200,000 Debenture 5$^1/_2$s @ 11	.900,000
Stock issues	Nominal
Total market value of the company	$ 2,100,000

BALANCE SHEET, JUNE 30, 1932

Cash	$ 7,687,000
Receivables (less reserve of $1,425,000)	4,838,000
Inventories (at lower of cost or market)	3,216,000
	$15,741,000
Accounts Payable	363,000
Net current assets	$15,378,000
Fixed assets (less $8,400,000 depreciation)	23,350,000

The company's securities were selling together for less than one-third of the cash alone, and for only one-seventh of the net current assets, allowing nothing for the fixed property.[9]

STUDEBAKER CORPORATION, SEPTEMBER 1933

Issue	Face amount	Market price	Market value
10-year 6% notes and other claims	$22,000,000	40	$8,800,000
Preferred stock	5,800,000	27	$1,500,000
Common stock (*2,464,000* shares)		6	14,700,000
Total value of stock issues			$16,200,000

The company's debt, selling at 40 cents on the dollar, was entitled to *prompt payment in full* before the stockholder received anything. Nevertheless, the market placed a much larger value upon the stock issues than upon the prior debt.

Voluntary Readjustment Plans. Realization of the manifest disadvantages of receivership has often led bondholders to accept suggestions emanating from the management for a voluntary reduction of their contractual claims. Arrangements of this kind have varied from the old-fashioned type of "composition" (in which creditors extended or even curtailed their claims, while the stockholders retained their interest intact) to cases where the bondholders received a substantial part of the stock equity.

Examples: At the end of 1931 Radio-Keith-Orpheum Corporation, needing funds to meet pressing obligations, found ordinary financing impossible. The stockholders ratified a plan under which in effect they surrendered 75% of their stock interest, which was given in turn as a bonus to those who supplied the $11,600,000 required by purchasing debenture notes. (Continued large losses, however, forced the company into receivership a year later.)

In 1933 Fox Film Corporation effected a recapitalization of the same general type. The stockholders gave up over 80% of their holdings, and this stock was in turn *exchanged* for nearly all of approximately $40,000,000 of 5-year notes and bank debt.

---

[9] As pointed out in Chap. 50, below, the Fisk Rubber 8s later proved to be worth close to 100 and the 5^1/2s more than 70.

The Kansas City Public Service Company readjustment plan, also consummated in 1933, was designed to meet the simpler problem of reducing interest charges during a supposedly temporary period of subnormal earnings. It provided that the coupon rate on the 6% first-mortgage bonds should be reduced to 3% during the four years 1933–1936, restored to 6% for 1937–1938, and advanced to 7% for 1939–1951, thus making up the 12% foregone in the earlier years. A substantial sinking fund, contingent upon earnings; was set up to retire the issue gradually and to improve its market position.

It was obvious that the Kansas City Public Service bondholders were better off to accept temporarily the 3% which could be paid rather than to insist on 6% which could not be paid and thereby precipitate a receivership. (The previous receivership of the enterprise, terminated in 1926, had lasted six years.) In this case the stockholders were not required to give up any part of their junior interest to the bondholders in return for the concessions made. While theoretically some such sacrifice and transfer would be equitable, it was not of much practical importance here because any stock bonus given to the bondholders would have had a very slight market value.[10] It should be recognized as a principle, however, that the waiving of any important right by the bondholders entitles them to some *quid pro quo* from the stockholders—in the form either of a contribution of cash to the enterprise or of a transfer of some part of their claim on future earnings to the bondholders.[11]

In 1939 additional legislation of a temporary nature was adopted, designed to facilitate so-called "voluntary reorganizations" of railroads by making them binding on all security holders.[12] This statute was

---

[10] In 1936 the company effected a second voluntary rearrangement, under which the interest rate was fixed at 4%, and the bondholders received a rather nugatory bonus of common stock. In 1939 still a third voluntary modification was accepted, in which bondholders took 30% in cash and 70% in preferred stock for their bonds—the money being advanced as a loan by the R.F.C.

[11] The reorganization of Industrial Office Building Company in 1932–1933 is a remarkable example of the conversion of fixed-interest bonds into income bonds without sacrifice of any kind by the stockholders. A detailed discussion of this instance is given in the Appendix Note 32, p. 763 on accompanying CD.

[12] This is the Chandler Railroad Readjustment Act of 1939, which actually adds a new Chap. XV to the Bankruptcy Act. Action thereunder must be begun before July 31, 1940, and must be substantially concluded within a year after its initiation. As far as the reorganization technique

intended specifically to aid the Baltimore and Ohio and Lehigh Valley roads, which had previously proposed voluntary reorganization plans. These were designed to reduce fixed-interest charges and to extend current and near maturities. The stockholders, in each case, were to retain their interests intact.

As we have previously stated, it is our opinion that voluntary readjustment plans are desirable in themselves, but they should be proposed *after* voting control over the corporation has passed to the bondholders, and they are in a position to choose between alternative courses of action.

Change in the Status of Bond Trustees. Not the least important of the remedial legislation enacted since 1933 is the "Trust Indenture Act of 1939." This undertakes to correct a number of inadequacies and abuses in the administration of their duties by bond trustees. The chief criticism of the behavior of indenture trustees in the past is that they did not act as trustees at all but merely as agents of the bondholders. This meant that as a general rule they took no action on their own initiative but only when directed to do so and were fully indemnified by a certain percentage of the bondholders.[13] Indentures have said practically nothing about the duties of a trustee but a great deal about his immunities and indemnification.

The 1939 statute aims directly at this unsatisfactory situation by including the following provision (in Section 315):

Duties of the Trustee in Case of Default

(c) The indenture to be qualified shall contain provisions requiring the indenture trustee to exercise in case of default (as such term is defined in the indenture) such of the rights and powers vested in it by such indenture, and to use the same degree of care and skill in their exercise, as a prudent man would exercise or use under the circumstances in the conduct of his own affairs.

There are further provisions limiting the use of so-called "exculpatory clauses," which in the past made it impossible to hold a trustee to account

---

is concerned, it is not significantly different from that provided in Section 77. In both cases approval of the I.C.C., of a court, and of a suitable percentage of security holders is required. The important difference is that under the new Chap. XV there is no bankruptcy in the involved legal sense. The company continues to administer its own affairs, and no contracts or other obligations are affected except those specifically included in the plan of readjustment.

[13] See Appendix Note 33, p. 766 on accompanying CD, for further discussion and an example on this point appearing in the first edition of this work.

for anything except provable fraud or else negligence so gross as to be equivalent thereto.

A further cause of complaint arose from the fact that the indenture trustee has frequently been a creditor of the obligor (*e.g.*, a trust company holding its promissory notes) or else has been controlled by the same interests. These situations have created conflicts of interest, or an unwillingness to act impartially and vigorously, which have militated strongly against the bondholders. The Trust Indenture Act of 1939 contains stringent provisions designed to terminate these abuses.[14]

The Problem of the Protective Committee. Reform in the status of indenture trustees may lead to a solution of the vexing problem of the protective committee. Since 1929 the general status of protective committees has become uncertain and most unsatisfactory. Formerly it was taken for granted that the investment bankers who floated the issue would organize a protective committee in the event of default. But in recent years there has been a growing tendency to question the propriety or desirability of such action. Bondholders may lack faith in the judgment of the issuing house, or they may question its ability to represent them impartially because of other interests in or connections with the enterprise; or they may even consider the underwriters as legally responsible for the losses incurred. The arguments in favor of *competent* representation by agencies *other* than the houses of issue are therefore quite convincing. The difficulty lies however, in securing such competent representation. With the original issuing houses out of the picture, anybody can announce himself as chairman of a protective committee and invite deposits. The whole procedure has become unstandardized and open to serious abuses. Duplicate committees often appear; an undignified scramble for deposits takes place; persons with undesirable reputations and motives can easily inject themselves into the situation.

The new bankruptcy legislation of 1938 introduced some improvement into this situation by subjecting the activities and compensation of

---

[14] The remedial legislation was an outgrowth of a trust indenture study made by the S.E.C. and was greatly stimulated by the opinion delivered by Judge Rosenman in 1936 denying the claims of holders of National Electric Power (secured) debentures to hold the trustee of the issue accountable for the huge losses suffered by them. The judge held that the exculpatory clauses saved the trustee in this case but that the whole system of indenture trusteeship was in need of radical reform.

protective committees to court scrutiny. (In the case of railroads a committee cannot take part in a proceeding without prior permission from the I.C.C.) Further legislation will probably be enacted regulating in more detail the formation as well as the subsequent conduct of protective committees.

A Recommended Reform. The whole procedure might readily be clarified and standardized now that the trustee under the indenture is expected to assume the duty of *actively* protecting the bond issue. The large institutions which hold these positions have the facilities, the experience, and the standing required for the successful discharge of such a function. There seems no good reason, in the ordinary case, why the trustee should not itself organize the protective committee, with one of its executive officers as chairman and with the other members selected from among the larger bondholders or their nominees. The possible conflict of interest between the trustee as representative of all the bondholders and the protective committee as representative of the depositing holders only will be found on analysis rarely to be of more than technical and minor consequence. Such a conflict, if it should arise, could be solved by submission of the question to the court. There is no difficulty about awarding sufficient compensation to the trustee and its counsel for their labors and accomplishment on behalf of the bondholders.

This arrangement envisages effective cooperation between the trustee and a group of bondholders who in the opinion of the trustee are qualified to represent the issue as a whole. The best arrangement might be to establish this bondholders' group at the time the issue is sold, *i.e.*, without waiting for an event of default to bring it into being, in order that there may be from the very start some responsible and interested agency to follow the affairs of the corporation from the bondholders' standpoint, and to make objections, if need be, to policies which may appear to threaten the safety of the issue. Reasonable compensation for this service should be paid by the corporation. This would be equivalent in part to representation of the bondholders on the board of directors. If the time were to arrive when the group would have to act as a protective committee on behalf of the bondholders, their familiarity with the company's affairs should prove of advantage.

Chapter 19

PROTECTIVE COVENANTS (*Continued*)

Prohibition of Prior Liens. A brief discussion is desirable regarding certain protective provisions other than those dealing with the ordinary events of default. (The matter of safeguarding conversion and other participating privileges against dilution will be covered in the chapters dealing with Senior Securities with Speculative Features.) Dealing first with mortgage bonds, we find that indentures almost always prohibit the placing of any new prior lien on the property. Exceptions are sometimes made in the case of bonds issued under a reorganization plan, when it is recognized that a prior mortgage may be necessary to permit raising new capital in the future.

Example: In 1926 Chicago, Milwaukee, St. Paul, and Pacific Railroad Company issued $107,000,000 of Series *A* Mortgage 5% bonds and, junior thereto, $185,000,000 of Convertible Adjustment Mortgage 5s, in exchange for securities of the bankrupt Chicago, Milwaukee, and St. Paul Railway Company. The indentures permitted the later issuance of an indefinite amount of First and Refunding Mortgage Bonds, which would rank ahead of the Series *A* Mortgage 5s.[1]

Equal-and-ratable Security Clause. When a bond issue is unsecured it is almost always provided that it will share equally in any mortgage lien later placed on the property.

Example: The New York, New Haven, and Hartford Railroad Company sold a number of debenture issues between 1897 and 1908. These bonds were originally unsecured, but the indentures provided that they should be equally secured with any mortgage subsequently placed upon the property. In 1920 a first and refunding mortgage was authorized by

---

[1] In 1933 the St. Paul was granted permission to issue some of the new first and refunding bonds, to be held as collateral for short-term loans made by the United States government.

the stockholders; consequently the earlier issues have since been equally secured with bonds issued under the new mortgage. They still carry the title of "debentures," but this is now a misnomer. There is, however, an issue of 4% debentures, due in 1957, which did not carry this provision and hence are unsecured. In 1939 the (unsecured) debenture 4s, due 1957, sold at one-third the price of the (secured) debenture 4s, due 1956, *e.g.,* 5 vs. 16.[2]

Purchase-money Mortgages. It is customary to permit without restriction the assumption of *purchase-money mortgages.* These are liens attaching only to new property subsequently acquired, and their assumption is not regarded as affecting the position of the other bondholders. The latter supposition is not necessarily valid, of course, since it is possible thereby to increase the ratio of total debt of the enterprise to the total shareholder's equity in a manner which might jeopardize the position of the existing bondholders.

Subordination of Bond Issues to Bank Debt in Reorganization. In the case of bonds or notes issued under a reorganization plan it is sometimes provided that their claim shall be junior to that of present or future bank loans. This is done to facilitate bank borrowings which otherwise could be effected only by the pledging of receivables or inventories as security. An example of this arrangement is afforded by Aeolian Company Five-year Secured 6% Notes, due in 1937, which were issued under a capital readjustment plan in partial exchange for the Guaranteed 7% Preferred Stock of the company. The notes were subordinated to $400,000 of bank loans, which were later paid.

Safeguards against Creation of Additional Amounts of the Same Issue. Nearly all bonds or preferred issues enjoy adequate safeguards in respect to the creation of additional amounts of the issue. The customary provisions require a substantial margin of earnings above the requirements of the issue as thus enlarged. For example, additional

---

[2] In exceptional cases, debenture obligations are entitled to a *prior lien* on the property in the event that a subsequent mortgage is placed thereon. *Example:* National Radiator Corporation Debenture 6^1/2s, due 1947, and the successor corporation's income debenture 5s, due 1946. In a second reorganization, effected in 1939, these debentures were replaced by stock. Here is an excellent example of the relative unimportance of protective provisions, as compared with profitable operations.

New York Edison Company First Lien and Refunding Mortgage Bonds may not be issued, except for refunding purposes, unless consolidated net earnings for a recent 12-month period have been at least $1^3/4$ times the annual interest charges on the aggregate bonded indebtedness of the company, including those to be issued. In the case of Wheeling Steel Corporation First Mortgage bonds the required ratio is 2 times.[3]

Provisions of this kind with reference to earnings-coverage are practically nonexistent in the railroad field, however. Railroad bonds of the blanket-mortgage type more commonly restrict the issuance of additional bonds through a provision that the total funded indebtedness shall not exceed a certain ratio to the capital stock outstanding, and by a limitation upon the emission of new bonds to a certain percentage of the *cost* or *fair value* of newly acquired property. (See, for example, the Baltimore and Ohio Railroad Company Refunding and General Mortgage Bonds and the Northern Pacific Railway Company Refunding and Improvement Bonds.) In the older bond issues it was customary to close the mortgage at a relatively small fixed amount, thus requiring that additional funds be raised by the sale of junior securities. This provision gave rise to the favorably situated "underlying bonds" to which reference was made in Chap. 6.

In the typical case additional issues of mortgage bonds may be made only against pledge of new property worth considerably more than the increase in debt. (See, for examples: Youngstown Sheet and Tube Company First Mortgage, under which further bonds may be issued to finance 75% of the cost of additions or improvements to the mortgaged properties; New York Edison Company, Inc., First Lien and Refunding Mortgage, under which bonds may be issued in further amounts to finance additions and betterments up to 75% of the actual and reasonable expenditure therefor; Pere Marquette Railway Company First-mortgage bonds, which may be issued up to 80% of the cost or fair value, whichever is the lower, of newly constructed or acquired property.)

These safeguards are logically conceived and almost always carefully observed. Their practical importance is less than might appear, however, because in the ordinary instance the showing stipulated would be needed anyway in order to attract buyers for the additional issue.

---

[3] For similar provisions in the case of preferred stocks see Consolidated Edison Company of New York $5 Preferred, General Foods Corporation $4.50 Preferred and Gotham Silk Hosiery Company 7% Preferred.

Working-capital Requirements. The provisions for maintaining working capital at a certain percentage of bonded debt, and for a certain ratio of current assets to current liabilities, are by no means standardized. They appear only in industrial bond indentures.[4]

The required percentages vary, and the penalties for nonobservance vary also. In most cases the result is merely the prohibition of dividends until the proper level or ratio of working capital is restored. In a few cases the principal of the bond issue may be declared due.

Examples: 1. *Sole penalty, prohibition of dividends.* B. F. Goodrich First 4^1/4s, due 1956, and Wilson and Company First 4s, due 1955, require current assets to equal total indebtedness, *i.e.,* net quick assets to equal funded debt. In the case of West Virginia Pulp and Paper First 4^1/2s, due 1952, subsidiary preferred stocks are included with funded debt.

The provisions of Fairbanks, Morse and Company Debenture 4s, due 1956, require that current assets equal (*a*) 110% of total liabilities and (*b*) 200% of current liabilities. In the case of Wheeling Steel First 4^1/2s, due 1966, and Republic Steel General 4^1/2s, due 1956, current assets must equal 300% of current liabilities, and net current assets must equal 50% of the funded debt.

2. *Failure to meet requirement is an event of default.* Skelly Oil Debenture 4s, due 1951, and Serial Notes, due 1937–1941. Here the company agrees to maintain current assets equal to at least 200% of current liabilities. In the case of Continental Steel 4^1/2s, due 1946, the required ratio is 115%.

Among former examples may be cited American Machine and Foundry 6s, due 1939, which had a twofold provision: the first prohibiting dividends unless net current assets equal 150% of the outstanding bond issue, and the second requiring unconditionally that the net current assets be maintained at 100% of the face value of outstanding bonds. In the case of United States Radiator Corporation 5s, due 1938, the company agreed at all times to maintain net working capital equal to 150% of the outstanding funded debt.

It would appear to be sound theory to require regularly some protective provisions on the score of working capital in the case of industrial

---

[4] Ashland Home Telephone First 4^1/2s, due 1961, are a *public-utility* issue with a peculiar, and rather weak, provision relating to net current assets.

bonds. We have already suggested that an adequate ratio of net current assets to funded debt be considered as one of the specific criteria in the selection of industrial bonds. This criterion should ordinarily be set up in the indenture itself, so that the bondholder will be entitled to the *maintenance* of a satisfactory ratio throughout the life of the issue and to an adequate remedy if the figure declines below the proper point.

The prohibition of dividend payments under such conditions is sound and practicable. But the more stringent penalty, which terms a deficiency of working capital "an event of default," is not likely to prove effective or beneficial to the bondholder. The objection that receivership harms rather than helps the creditors applies with particular force in this connection. Referring to the United States Radiator 5s, mentioned above, we may point out that the balance sheet of January 31, 1933, showed a default in the 150% working-capital requirement. (The net current assets were $2,735,000, or only 109% of the $2,518,000 bond issue.) Nevertheless, the trustee took no steps to declare the principal due, nor was it asked to do so by the required number of bondholders. In all probability a receivership invoked for this reason would have been considered as highly injurious to the bondholders' interests. But this attitude would mean that the provision in question should never have been included in the indenture.[5]

Voting Control as a Remedy. We have previously advanced and discussed the suggestion that the bondholders' right to the appointment of trustees in the event of any default might well be replaced by a right to receive *voting control* over the enterprise. Whatever the reader's view as to the soundness of this suggestion as applied to default in payment of interest or principal, we imagine that he will agree with us that it has merit in the case of "secondary" defaults, *e.g.*, failure to maintain working capital as agreed or to make sinking-fund payments; for the present alternatives—either to precipitate insolvency or to do nothing at all—are alike completely unsatisfactory.

---

[5] Similar situations existed in 1933 with respect to G. R. Kinney (shoe) Company 7$\frac{1}{2}$s, due 1936, and Budd Manufacturing Company First 6s, due 1935. Early in 1934, the United States Radiator Corporation asked the debenture holders to modify the provisions respecting both working-capital maintenance and sinking-fund payments. No substantial *quid pro quo* was offered for these concessions. Characteristically, the reason given by the company itself for this move was not that the bondholders were entitled to some remedial action but that the "technical default under the indenture" interfered with projected bank borrowings by the company.

Protective Provisions for Investment-trust Issues. Investment-trust bonds belong in a special category, we believe, because by their nature they lend themselves to the application of stringent remedial provisions. Such bonds are essentially similar to the collateral loans made by banks on marketable securities. As a protection for these bank loans, it is required that the market value of the collateral be maintained at a certain percentage in excess of the amount owed. In the same way the lenders of money to an investment trust should be entitled to demand that the value of the portfolio continuously exceed the amount of the loans by an adequate percentage, *e.g.*, 25%. If the market value should decline below this figure, the investment trust should be required to take the same action as any other borrower against marketable securities. It should either put up more money (*i.e.*, raise more capital from the stockholders) or sell out securities and retire debt with the proceeds, in an amount sufficient to restore the proper margin.

The disadvantages that inhere in bond investment generally justify the bond buyer in insisting upon every possible safeguard. In the case of investment-trust bonds, a very effective measure of protection may be assured by means of the covenant to maintain the market value of the portfolio above the bonded debt. Hence investors in investment-trust issues should demand this type of protective provision, and—what is equally important—they should require its strict enforcement. Although this stand will inflict hardship upon the stockholders when market prices fall, this is part of the original bargain, in which the stockholders agreed to take most of the risk in exchange for the surplus profits.[6]

A survey of bond indentures of investment trusts discloses a signal lack of uniformity in the matter of these protective provisions. Most of them do require a certain margin of asset value over debt as a condition to the sale

---

[6] If the market value of the assets falls below 100% of the funded debt, a condition of insolvency would seem to be created which entitles the bondholders to insist upon immediate remedial action. For otherwise the stockholders would be permitted to speculate on the future with what is entirely the bondholders' capital. But even this apparently simple point is not without its difficulties. In 1938, holders of Reynolds Investing Company 5s endeavored to have a trustee appointed on grounds of insolvency, but stockholders claimed that the market price of certain large security holdings was less than their real value. After considerable delay, trustees were appointed, pursuant to an agreement among the various interests. Note that Guardian Investors Corporation 5s, due 1948, have been "under water" nearly all the time since 1932 and sold as low as 24, without any remedial steps being taken.

of additional bonds. The required ratio of net assets to funded debt varies from 120% (*e.g.*, General American Investors) to 250% (*e.g.*, Niagara Shares Corporation). The more usual figures are 125 or 150%. A similar restriction is placed upon the payment of cash dividends. The ratio required for this purpose varies from 125% (*e.g.*, Domestic and Foreign Investors) to 175% (which must be shown to permit cash dividends on Central States Electric Corporation common). The modal figure is probably 140 or 150%.

But the majority of issues do not require at all times and unconditionally the maintenance of a minimum excess of asset value above bonded indebtedness. Examples of such a covenant may indeed be given, *e.g.*, General Public Service Corporation Convertible Debenture 5s, due 1953; American European Securities Company Collateral 5s, due 1958; and Affiliated Fund, Inc., Secured Convertible Debenture 4^1/$_2$s and 4s, due 1949, all of which require maintenance of a 125% ratio of asset value at market to funded debt. In the case of Affiliated Fund, the remedy provided is the immediate sale by the trustee of pledged collateral and the retirement of bonds until the required ratio is restored. In the other cases more elaborate machinery is invoked to declare the entire issue due and payable. We would suggest that provisions of this type—preferably those most simple of application—be a standard requirement for investment-trust bond issues.[7]

SINKING FUNDS

In its modern form a sinking fund provides for the periodic retirement of a certain portion of a senior issue through payments made by the corporation. The sinking fund acquires the security by call, by means of sealed tenders, or by open-market purchases made by the trustee or the corporation. In the latter case the corporation turns in the bonds to the sinking fund in lieu of cash. The sinking fund usually operates once or

---

[7] Another type of remedy appeared in the indenture securing the Reynolds Investing Company 5s, which provided that if at any time the net value of the assets should fall below 110% of the bond issue, the latter should be due and payable on the next interest date. The same difficulty arose in applying this provision as in the case of the solvency question discussed above.

Note also the case of Alleghany Corporation Collateral Trust 5s, due 1949. The offering circular indicated that a coverage of 150% would be compulsory. Yet the indenture provided that failure to maintain this margin would not constitute an event of default but would result only in the prohibition of dividends and in the impounding by the trustee of the income from the pledged collateral.

twice a year, but provisions for quarterly and even monthly payments are by no means unusual. In the case of many bond issues, the bonds acquired by the sinking fund are not actually retired but are "kept alive," *i.e.*, they draw interest, and these interest sums are also used for sinking-fund purchases, thus increasing the latter at a compounded rate.

Example: An important instance of this arrangement was supplied by the two issues of United States Steel Sinking Fund 5s, originally totaling $504,000,000. Bonds of the junior issue, listed on the New York Stock Exchange, were familiarly known in the bond market as "Steel Sinkers." By adding the interest on bonds in the fund, the annual payments grew from $3,040,000 in 1902 to $11,616,000 in 1928. (The following year the entire outstanding amounts of these issues were retired or provided for.)

Benefits. The benefits of a sinking fund are of a twofold nature. The continuous reduction in the size of the issue makes for increasing safety and the easier repayment of the balance at maturity. Also important is the support given to the market for the issue through the repeated appearance of a substantial buying demand. Nearly all industrial bond issues have sinking funds; the public-utility group shows about as many with as without; in the railroad list sinking funds are exceptional. But in recent years increasing emphasis has been laid upon the desirability of a sinking fund, and few long-term senior issues of any type are now offered without such a provision.[8]

Indispensable in Some Cases. Under some circumstances a sinking fund is absolutely necessary for the protection of a bond. This is true in general when the chief backing of the issue consists of a wasting asset. Bonds on mining properties invariably have a sinking fund, usually of substantial proportions and based upon the tonnage mined. A sinking fund of smaller relative size is regularly provided for real estate mortgage bonds. In all these cases the theory is that the annual depletion or depreciation allowances should be applied to the reduction of the funded debt.

Examples: A special example of importance was the large Interborough Rapid Transit Company First and Refunding 5% issue, due 1966, which was secured mainly by a lease on properties that belong to the City

---

[8] During 1933 the Interstate Commerce Commission strongly recommended that railways adopt sinking funds to amortize their existing debt. The Chicago and North Western Railway thereupon announced a plan of this kind, the details of which were not particularly impressive.

of New York. Obviously it was essential to provide through a sinking fund for the retirement of the entire issue by the time the lease expired in 1967, since the corporation would then be deprived of most of its assets and earning power. Similarly with Tobacco Products 6¹/2s, due in 2022, which depended for their value entirely upon the annual payments of $2,500,000 made by American Tobacco Company under a lease expiring in 2022.

The absence of a sinking fund under conditions of this kind invariably leads to trouble.

Examples: Federal Mining and Smelting Company supplied the unusual spectacle of a mining enterprise with a large preferred-stock issue ($12,000,000); and furthermore the preferred stock had no sinking fund. Declaration of a $10 dividend on the common in 1926 led to court action to protect the preferred stock against the threatened breakdown of its position through depletion of the mines coupled with the distribution of cash earnings to the junior shares. As a result of the litigation the company refrained from further common dividends until 1937 and devoted its surplus profits to reducing the preferred issue, which was completely retired in 1939.

Iron Steamboat Company General Mortgage 4s, due 1932, had no sinking fund, although the boats on which they were a lien were obviously subject to a constant loss in value. These bonds to the amount of $500,000 were issued in 1902 and were a second lien on the entire property of the company (consisting mainly of seven small steamboats operating between New York City and Coney Island), junior to $100,000 of first-mortgage bonds. During the years 1909 to 1925, inclusive, the company paid dividends on the common stock aggregating in excess of $700,000 and by 1922 had retired all of the first-mortgage bonds through the operation of the sinking fund for that issue. At this point the 4s, due 1932, became a first lien upon the entire property. In 1932, when the company went into bankruptcy, the entire issue was still outstanding. The mortgaged property was sold at auction in February 1933 for $15,050, a figure resulting in payment of less than 1 cent on the dollar to the bondholders. An adequate sinking fund might have retired the entire issue out of the earnings which were distributed to the stockholders.

When the enterprise may be regarded as permanent, the absence of a sinking fund does not necessarily condemn the issue. This is true not only of most high-grade railroad bonds and of many high-grade utility bonds but also of most of the select group of old-line industrial preferred stocks that merit an investment rating, *e.g.*, National Biscuit Preferred, which has no sinking fund. From the broader standpoint, therefore, sinking funds may be characterized as invariably desirable and sometimes but not always indispensable.

Serial Maturities as an Alternative. The general object sought by a sinking fund may be obtained by the use of serial maturities. The retirement of a portion of the issue each year by reason of maturity corresponds to the reduction by means of sinking-fund purchases. Serial maturities are relatively infrequent, their chief objection resting probably in the numerous separate market quotations that they entail. In the equipment-trust field, however, they are the general rule. This exception may be explained by the fact that insurance companies and other financial institutions are the chief buyers of equipment obligations, and for their special needs the variety of maturity dates proves a convenience. Serial maturities are also frequently employed in state and municipal financing.

Problems of Enforcement. The enforcement of sinking-fund provisions of a bond issue presents the same problem as in the case of covenants for the maintenance of working capital. Failure to make a sinking-fund payment is regularly characterized in the indenture as an event of default, which will permit the trustee to declare the principal due and thus bring about receivership. The objections to this "remedy" are obvious, and we can recall no instance in which the omission of sinking-fund payments, unaccompanied by default of interest, was actually followed by enforcement of the indenture provisions. When the company continues to pay interest but claims to be unable to meet the sinking fund, it is not unusual for the trustee and the bondholders to withhold action and merely to permit arrears to accumulate. More customary is the making of a formal request to the bondholders by the corporation for the postponement of the sinking-fund payments. Such a request is almost invariably acceded to by the great majority of bondholders, since the alternative is always pictured as insolvency. This was true even in the case of Interborough Rapid Transit 5s, for which—as we have pointed out—the sinking fund was an essential element of protection.[9]

---

[9] The plan of voluntary readjustment proposed in 1922 postponed sinking-fund payments on these bonds for a five-year period. About 75% of the issue accepted this modification.

The suggestion made in respect to the working-capital covenants, *viz.*, that voting control be transferred to the bondholders in the event of default, is equally applicable to the sinking-fund provision. In our view that would be distinctly preferable to the present arrangement under which the bondholder must either do nothing to protect himself or else take the drastic and calamitous step of compelling bankruptcy.

The emphasis we have laid upon the proper kind of protective provisions for industrial bonds should not lead the reader to believe that the presence of such provisions carries an assurance of safety. This is far from the case. The success of a bond investment depends primarily upon the success of the enterprise and only to a very secondary degree upon the terms of the indenture. Hence the seeming paradox that the senior securities that have fared best in the depression have on the whole quite unsatisfactory indenture or charter provisions. The explanation is that the best issues as a class have been the oldest issues, and these date from times when less attention was paid than now to protective covenants.

In Appendix Note 34 on accompanying CD, we present two examples of the opposite kind (Willys-Overland Company First $6^1/_2$s, due 1933, and Berkey and Gay Furniture Company First 6s, due 1941) wherein a combination of a strong statistical showing with all the standard protective provisions failed to safeguard the holders against a huge subsequent loss. But while the protective covenants we have been discussing do not *guarantee* the safety of the issue, they nevertheless *add* to the safety and are therefore worth insisting upon.

Sinking-fund payments have been suspended without penalty in the case of numerous real estate issues, under the provisions of various state mortgage moratorium laws. *Example:* Harriman Building First 6s, due 1951. No sinking-fund payments were made between 1934 and 1939 by virtue of the New York Moratorium Law.

See accompanying CD for Chapter 20, "Preferred-stock Protective Provisions. Maintenance of Junior Capital."

Chapter 21

SUPERVISION OF
INVESTMENT HOLDINGS

Traditional Concept of "Permanent Investment." A generation ago "permanent investment" was one of the stock phrases of finance. It was applied to the typical purchase by a conservative investor and may be said to have embraced three constituent ideas: (1) intention to hold for an indefinite period; (2) interest solely in annual income, without reference to fluctuations in the value of principal; and (3) freedom from concern over future developments affecting the company. A sound investment was by definition one that could be bought, put away, and forgotten except on coupon or dividend dates.

This traditional view of high-grade investments was first seriously called into question by the unsatisfactory experiences of the 1920–1922 depression. Large losses were taken on securities that their owners had considered safe beyond the need of examination. The ensuing seven years, although generally prosperous, affected different groups of investment issues in such divergent ways that the old sense of complete security—with which the term "gilt-edged securities" was identified—suffered an ever-increasing impairment. Hence even before the market collapse of 1929, the danger ensuing from neglect of investments previously made, and the need for periodic scrutiny or supervision of all holdings, had been recognized as a new canon in Wall Street. This principle, directly opposed to the former practice, is frequently summed up in the dictum, "There are no permanent investments."

Periodic Inspection of Holdings Necessary—but Troublesome. That the newer view is justified by the realities of fixed-value investment can scarcely be questioned. But it must be frankly recognized also that this same necessity for supervision of all security holdings implies a rather serious indictment of the whole concept of fixed-value investment. If risk of loss can be minimized only by the exercise of constant supervisory care, in addition to the painstaking process of initial choice, has not such investment become more trouble than it is worth? Let it be assumed that the typical investor, following the conservative standards of selection herein recommended, will average a yield of $3^1/2$% on a diversified list of corporate securities. This $3^1/2$% return appears substantially higher than the $2^1/2$% obtainable from long-term United States government bonds and also more attractive than the 2 or $2^1/2$% offered by savings banks. Nevertheless, if we take into account not only the effort required to make a proper selection but also the greater efforts entailed by the subsequent repeated check-ups, and if we then add thereto the still inescapable risk of depreciation or definite loss, it must be confessed that a rather plausible argument can be constructed against the advisability of fixed-value investments in general. The old idea of permanent, trouble-free holdings was grounded on the not illogical feeling that if a limited-return investment could not be regarded as trouble-free it was not worth making at all.

Superiority of United States Savings Bonds. Objectively considered, investment experience of the last decade undoubtedly points away from the fixed-value security field and into the direction of (1) United States government bonds or savings-bank deposits; or (2) admittedly speculative operations, with endeavors to reduce risk and increase profits by means of skillful effort; or (3) a search for the exceptional combination of safety of principal with a chance for substantial profit. For all people of moderate means United States Savings Bonds undoubtedly offer the most suitable medium for fixed-value investment. In fact we are inclined to state categorically that, on the basis of 1940 interest yields, their superiority to other issues makes them the *only* sensible purchase of this type. The reason is, of course, that it is not possible to obtain a significantly higher return on investment issues (save for a few obscure exceptions) without injecting an element of principal risk which makes the commitment unsound. In addition the holder's redemption right before maturity is a very valuable feature of the bonds. If only small investors as a class would resolutely reject the various types of "savings plans," with their multifarious titles, now being offered to them with an ostensible "sure income return" of 4 to 6%, and thankfully take advantage of the 2.90% available on United States Savings Bonds, we are convinced that they would save in the aggregate an enormous amount of money, trouble and heartbreak.

But even if the ordinary investment problems of most investors could be thus simply disposed of, many investors would remain who must consider other types of fixed-value investment. These include: (1) institutional investors of all kinds, *e.g.*, savings and commercial banks, insurance companies, educational and philanthropic agencies; (2) other large investors, *e.g.*, corporations and wealthy individuals; (3) those with moderate income derived wholly from investments, since the maximum annual return ultimately obtainable from United States Savings Bonds is limited to $2,500 per annum.[1] It is true also that many smaller investors will for one reason or another prefer to place part of their funds in other types of fixed-value investment.

The second alternative, *viz.*, to speculate instead of investing, is entirely too dangerous for the typical person who is building up his capital out of savings or business profits. The disadvantages of ignorance, of human greed, of mob psychology, of trading costs, of weighting of the dice by insiders and manipulators,[2] will in the aggregate far overbalance the purely theoretical superiority of speculation in that it offers profit possibilities in return for the assumption of risk. We have, it is true, repeatedly argued against the acceptance of an admitted risk to principal without the presence of a compensating chance for profit. In so doing, however, we have not advocated speculation in place of investment but only intelligent speculation in preference to obviously unsound and ill-advised forms of investment. We are convinced that the public generally will derive far better results from fixed-value investments, if selected with exceeding care, than from speculative operations, even though these may be aided by considerable education in financial matters. It may well be that the results of investment will prove disappointing; but if so, the results of speculation would have been disastrous.

The third alternative—to look for investment merit combined with an opportunity for profit—presents, we believe, a suitable field for the talents of the securities analyst. But it is a dangerous objective to hold before the untrained investor. He can readily be persuaded that safety exists

---

[1] This is based on the maximum $7,500 permitted each year to one individual. After the tenth year of continued investment, an annual income of $2,500 would accrue via the maturity of a $10,000 unit each year and its replacement by a new $7,500 subscription.

[2] This factor has been greatly reduced by the operation of the Securities Exchange Act of 1934.

where there is only promise or, conversely, that an attractive statistical showing is alone sufficient to warrant purchase.

Having thus considered the three alternative policies open to those with capital funds, we see that fixed-value investment in the traditional field of high-grade bonds and preferred stocks remains a necessary and desirable activity for many individuals and corporate bodies. It is quite clear also that periodic reexamination of investment holdings is necessary to reduce the risk of loss. What principles and practical methods can be followed in such supervision?

Principles and Problems of Systematic Supervision; Switching.

It is generally understood that the investor should examine his holdings at intervals to see whether or not all of them may still be regarded as entirely safe and that if the soundness of any issue has become questionable, he should exchange it for a better one. In making such a "switch" the investor must be prepared to accept a moderate loss on the holding he sells out, which loss he must charge against his aggregate investment income.

In the early years of systematic investment supervision, this policy worked out extremely well. Seasoned securities of the high-grade type tended to cling rather tenaciously to their established price levels and frequently failed to reflect a progressive deterioration of their intrinsic position until some time after this impairment was discoverable by analysis. It was possible, therefore, for the alert investor to sell out such holdings to some heedless and unsuspecting victim, who was attracted by the reputation of the issue and the slight discount at which it was obtainable in comparison with other issues of its class. The impersonal character of the securities market relieves this procedure of any ethical stigma, and it is considered merely as establishing a proper premium for shrewdness and a deserved penalty for lack of care.

Increased Sensitivity of Security Prices. In more recent years, however, investment issues have lost what may have been called their "price inertia," and their quotations have come to reflect promptly any materially adverse development. This fact creates a serious difficulty in the way of effective switching to maintain investment quality. By the time that any real impairment of security is manifest, the issue may have fallen in price not only to a speculative level but to a level even lower than the decline in earnings would seem to justify.[3] (One reason for this excessive price decline is that an unfavorable apparent *trend* has come to influence prices even more severely than the absolute earnings figures.) The owner's natural reluctance to accept a large loss is reinforced by the reasonable belief that he would be selling the issue at an unduly low price, and he is likely to find himself compelled almost unavoidably to assume a speculative position with respect to that security.

Exceptional Margins of Safety as Insurance against Doubt. The only effective means of meeting this difficulty lies in following counsels of perfection in making the original investment. The degree of safety enjoyed by the issue, as shown by quantitative measures, must be so far in *excess* of the minimum standards that a large shrinkage can be suffered before its position need be called into question. Such a policy should reduce to a very small figure the proportion of holdings about which the investor will subsequently find himself in doubt. It would also permit him to make his exchanges when the showing of the issue is still comparatively strong and while, therefore, there is a better chance that the market price will have been maintained.

Example and Conclusion. As a concrete example, let us assume that the investor buys an issue such as the Liggett and Myers Tobacco Company Debenture 5s, due 1951, which earned their interest an average of nearly twenty times in 1934–1938, as compared with the minimum requirement of three times. If a decline in profits should reduce the coverage to four times, he might prefer to switch into some other issue (if one can be found) that is earning its interest eight to ten times. On these assumptions he would have a fair chance of obtaining a full price for the Liggett and Myers issue, since it would still be making an impressive exhibit. But if the influence of the downward trend of earnings has depressed the quotation to a large discount, then he could decide to retain the issue rather than accept an appreciable loss. In so doing he would have the great advantage of being able to feel that the safety of investment was still not in any real danger.

---

[3] Many railroad bonds have proved an exception to this statement since 1933. Note, for example, that Baltimore and Ohio Railroad First 4s, due 1948, sold at $109^1/_2$ in 1936, although the margin over total interest charges had long been much too small. In 1938 these bonds sold at $34^1/_4$.

Such a policy of demanding very high safety margins would obviously prove especially beneficial if a period of acute depression and market unsettlement should supervene. It is not practicable, however, to recommend this as a standard practice for all investors, because the supply of such strongly buttressed issues is too limited, and because, further, it is contrary to human nature for investors to take *extreme* precautions against future collapse when current conditions make for optimism.[4]

Policy in Depression. Assuming that the investor has exercised merely reasonable caution in the choice of his fixed-value holdings, how will he fare and what policy should he follow in a period of depression? If the depression is a moderate one, his investments should be only mildly affected marketwise and still less in their intrinsic position. If conditions should approximate those of 1930–1933, he could not hope to escape a severe shrinkage in the quotations and considerable uneasiness over the safety of his holdings. But any reasoned policy of fixed-value investment requires the assumption that disturbances of the 1930–1933 amplitude are nonrecurring in their nature and need not be specifically guarded against in the future. If the 1921–1922 and the 1937–1938 experiences are accepted instead as typical of the "recurrent severe depression," a carefully selected investment list should give a reasonably good account of itself in such a period. The investor should not be stampeded into selling out holdings with a strong past record because of a current decline in earnings. He is likely, however, to pay more attention than usual to the question of improving the quality of his securities, and in many cases it should be possible to gain some benefits through carefully considered switches.

The experiences of the 1937–1938 "recession" offer strong corroboration of the foregoing analysis. Practically all senior securities that would have met our stringent requirements at the end of 1936 came through the ensuing setback without serious damage marketwise. But bonds that have sold at high levels despite an inadequate over-all earnings coverage—particularly a large number of railroad issues—suffered an enormous shrinkage in value. (See our discussion in Chap. 7 and also Appendix Notes 11 and 13, pages 740 and 742 on accompanying CD.)

---

[4] We must caution the reader, however, against assuming that very large coverage of interest charges is, in itself, a complete assurance of safety. An operating loss eliminates the margin of safety, however high it may have been. Hence, inherent stability is an essential requirement, as we emphasize in our Studebaker example given in Chap. 2.

Sources of Investment Advice and Supervision. Supervision of securities involves the question of who should do it as well as how to do it. Investors have the choice of various agencies for this purpose, of which the more important are the following:

1. The investor himself.
2. His commercial bank.
3. An investment banking (or underwriting) house.
4. A New York Stock Exchange firm.
5. The advisory department of a large trust company.
6. Independent investment counsel or supervisory service.

The last two agencies charge fees for their service, whereas the three preceding supply advice and information gratis.[5]

Advice from Commercial Bankers. The investor should not be his own sole consultant unless he has training and experience sufficient to qualify him to advise others professionally. In most cases he should at least supplement his own judgment by conference with others. The practice of consulting one's bank about investments is widespread, and it is undeniably of great benefit, especially to the smaller investor. If followed consistently it would afford almost complete protection against the hypnotic wiles of the high-pressure stock salesman and his worthless "blue sky" flotations.[6] It is doubtful, however, if the commercial banker is the most suitable adviser to an investor of means. Although his judgment is usually sound, his knowledge of securities is likely to be somewhat superficial, and he cannot be expected to spare the time necessary for a thoroughgoing analysis of his clients' holdings and problems.

Advice from Investment Banking Houses. There are objections of another kind to the advisory service of an investment banking house. An institution with securities of its own to sell cannot be looked to for entirely impartial guidance. However ethical its aims may be, the compelling force of self-interest is bound to affect its judgment. This is particularly true

---

[5] A growing number of Stock Exchange firms now supply investment advice on a fee basis.

[6] Under S.E.C. supervision the "blue-sky flotation" of the old school has largely disappeared from interstate commerce, its place being taken by small but presumably legitimate enterprises which are sold to the public at excessively high prices. Numerous other types of fraud are still fairly prevalent, as can be seen from the 1938 report of the Better Business Bureau of New York City.

when the advice is supplied by a bond salesman whose livelihood depends upon persuading his customers to buy the securities that his firm has "on its shelves." It is true that the reputable underwriting houses consider themselves as bound in some degree by a fiduciary responsibility toward their clients. The endeavor to give them sound advice and to sell them suitable securities arises not only from the dictates of good business practice but more compellingly from the obligations of a professional code of ethics.

Nevertheless, the sale of securities is not a profession but a business and is necessarily carried on as such. Although in the typical transaction it is to the advantage of the seller to give the buyer full value and satisfaction, conditions may arise in which their interests are in serious conflict. Hence it is impracticable, and in a sense unfair, to require investment banking houses to act as impartial advisers to buyers of securities; and, broadly speaking, it is unwise for the investor to rely primarily upon the advice of sellers of securities.

Advice from New York Stock Exchange Firms. The investment departments of the large Stock Exchange firms present a somewhat different picture. Although they also have a pecuniary interest in the transactions of their customers, their advice is much more likely to be painstaking and thoroughly impartial. Stock Exchange houses do not ordinarily own securities for sale. Although at times they participate in selling operations, which carry larger allowances than the ordinary market commission, their interest in pushing such individual issues is less vital than that of the underwriting houses who actually own them. At bottom, the investment business or bond department of Stock Exchange firms is perhaps more important to them as a badge of respectability than for the profits it yields. Attacks made upon them as agencies of speculation may be answered in part by pointing to the necessary services that they render to conservative investors. Consequently, the investor who consults a large Stock Exchange firm regarding a small bond purchase is likely to receive time and attention out of all proportion to the commission involved. Admittedly this practice is found profitable in the end, as a cold business proposition, because a certain proportion of the bond customers later develop into active stock traders. In behalf of the Stock Exchange houses it should be said that they make no effort to persuade their bond clients to speculate in stocks, but the atmosphere of a brokerage office is perhaps not without its seductive influence.

Advice from Investment Counsel. Although the idea of giving investment advice on a fee basis is not a new one, it has only recently developed into an important financial activity. The work is now being done by special departments of large trust companies, by a division of the statistical services, and by private firms designating themselves as investment counsel or investment consultants. The advantage of such agencies is that they can be entirely impartial, having no interest in the sale of any securities or in any commission on their client's transactions. The chief disadvantage is the cost of the service, which averages about $1/2\%$ per annum on the principal involved. As applied strictly to investment funds this charge would amount to about $1/7$ or $1/8$ of the annual income, which must be considered substantial.

In order to make their fees appear less burdensome, some of the private investment consultants endeavor to forecast the general course of the bond market and to advise their clients as to when to buy or sell. It is doubtful if trading in bonds, to catch the market swings, can be carried on successfully by the investor. If the course of the bond market can be predicted, it should be possible to predict that of the stock market as well, and there would be undoubted technical advantages in trading in stocks rather than in bonds. We are sceptical of the ability of any paid agency to provide reliable forecasts of the market action of either bonds or stocks. Furthermore we are convinced that any combined effort to advise upon the choice of individual high-grade investments and upon the course of bond *prices* is fundamentally illogical and confusing. Much as the investor would like to be able to buy at just the right time and to sell out when prices are about to fall, experience shows that he is not likely to be brilliantly successful in such efforts and that by injecting the trading element into his investment operations he will disrupt the income return on his capital and inevitably shift his interest into speculative directions.

It is not clear as yet whether or not advice on a fee basis will work out satisfactorily in the field of standard high-grade investments, because of their relatively small income return. In the purely speculative field the objection to paying for advice is that if the adviser *knew* whereof he spoke he would not need to bother with a consultant's duties. It may be that the profession of adviser on securities will find its most practicable field in the intermediate region, where the adviser will deal with problems arising from depreciated investments, and where he will propose advantageous exchanges and recommend bargain issues selling considerably below their intrinsic value.

PART III

SENIOR SECURITIES WITH SPECULATIVE FEATURES

"Blood and Judgement"

by J. Ezra Merkin

If the names of Graham and Dodd are a talisman for value investors, they are practically a sacrament for those who focus on bankrupt companies. After all, bankruptcy, or distressed, investing is perhaps the purest form of value investing, the natural home for those who take Graham and Dodd seriously. In effect, distressed investing is a form of value investing at a substantial discount. The former astronaut and airline CEO Frank Borman has opined that "capitalism without bankruptcy is like Christianity without hell." Not only is bankruptcy an inherent feature of the landscape of risk, but the term "distressed investing" might ultimately be redundant for the true disciple of Graham and Dodd. Because the average observer does not view the securities of bankrupt or nearly bankrupt companies as a classic safe haven, we need to understand a bit more about the authors' understanding of "investing" and how that matches up with the characteristics of distressed investing. In that light, it will become apparent that distressed investing is a classic Graham and Dodd discipline.

Today, you can easily go online and buy 100 shares of Microsoft or Apple, and we would say that those who do so have invested in those companies. Graham and Dodd would demur. They view *investment* as "a convenient omnibus word, with perhaps an admixture of euphemism— that is, a desire to lend a certain respectability to financial dealings of

I am deeply grateful for the assistance of Jerome Balsam, general counsel at Gabriel Capital Group, in preparing this introduction.

miscellaneous character." (p. 100) For the authors, *investment* is to be contrasted with *speculation*, and they argue: "It should be essential, therefore, for anyone engaging in financial operations to know whether he is investing or speculating and, if the latter, to make sure that his speculation is a justifiable one." (p. 101)

Thus, the authors caution that "bonds should be bought on a depression basis" because an investment cannot be sound unless it can withstand true adversity. (p. 154) Think about that!—on a *depression* basis. Moreover, while Graham and Dodd favor the reader with 727 pages of analysis, examples, charts, and advice, they caution that "stock speculation," that is, probably the majority of security purchases and sales made by Americans today, "does not come within the scope of this volume." (p. 29) At nearly seven decades' remove from Graham and Dodd's second edition, and even further from the Great Crash of 1929, the language, let alone the permanent frame of mind, of disciplined austerity does not come easily to the contemporary investor (let alone speculator). Many repeat the mantras of value investing; few—even among those who appreciate their wisdom—practice them consistently. It is easy to get caught up with the crowd when the market is booming, harder to think about what securities are really worth.

The temptation to speculate recurs regularly, as animal spirits send markets soaring beyond valuations that the fundamentals would justify. It is not easy to stay on the sidelines while others are busy getting rich. In our generation, perhaps the ultimate example of speculation for the sake of speculation came with the dot-com boom. It is then that prudence and caution give way to excitement, and propositions that would ordinarily sound ridiculous become strangely plausible. It's just like when Big Julie, in the classic Broadway musical *Guys and Dolls*, challenged Nathan Detroit to a game of craps played with dice that had no dots, other than those Big Julie claimed he could see.

Early in 2000, near the top of the market, Arthur J. Samberg, head of
the well-regarded hedge fund Pequot Capital Management and a top-
notch technology investor, shared his four favorite stocks with the *Barron's* Roundtable. (They were Critical Path, Double Click, Kana
Communications, and Message Media.) The Graham and Dodd who cautioned that "the notion that the desirability of a common stock was
entirely independent of its price seems inherently absurd" (p. 359) would
have blanched when Samberg said:

> I'll give you no numbers. I'll give you no prices. I am not going to tell you
> which ones are going to succeed or fail. I think they are all pretty good
> companies, and if you bought a package of these stocks over the next
> three to four years, you would do very well. . . . I hear this stuff all the time,
> about how it is a bubble, it's ridiculous. If you just use the numbers to do
> this stuff, number one, you won't buy them, which is probably a good
> thing for some people. But you will never understand the amount of
> change that's going on, and how much is still ahead of us.

How the authors would have protested! *I'll give you no numbers?* But
numbers are the raw material of the Graham and Dodd search for value.
I'll give you no prices? Whether a security is a good buy or not is a function of its price relative to its value. Almost any security, regardless of its
characteristics, can be cheap or dear: it all depends how much you have
to pay for it.[1]

Distressed investors inevitably declare their allegiance to Graham and
Dodd. They take comfort with the authors' ascetic posture and believe in
their mantras. They do not dream of "ten-baggers," though, on rare occasions, they may come. The idea is to find valuable assets or inherently

---

[1] Mason Hawkins and Staley Cates of the Longleaf family of funds, among the most successful Graham and Dodd acolytes of our era, emphasize what they call the price-to-value ratio of the stocks
they buy. They "talk so frequently about buying companies at '60% of intrinsic value or less' it sounds
almost like a religious chant. But their method works." Steven Goldberg, "Want to Win at Fund Investing? Learn from Longleaf," Kiplinger.com, May 22, 2007.

profitable companies that have nonetheless leveraged themselves up to levels of debt unsustainable by their cash flows.[2]

Graham and Dodd's margin of safety sends investors to scrutinize the balance sheet and projected earnings. They perform the analytical function that the authors endorse, apply the same skills, study the same documents. For them, the balance sheet is the main thing, far more than earnings, if for no other reason than necessity, as most bankrupt companies no longer have earnings. Graham and Dodd devote Part VI of the 1940 edition, nearly 70 pages, to balance sheet analysis. In the context of equity investing, the authors prize stocks that sell below their current asset, or liquidating, value. They preach: *"When a common stock sells persistently below its liquidating value, then either the price is too low or the company should be liquidated."* (p. 563) If you buy a security below liquidation value, you should not get hurt, even if liquidation is in the offing. This is true for shareholders; how much more so for creditors, who precede shareholders in the hierarchy of claims.

The Varieties of Bankruptcy

I would like to suggest a typology of bankruptcy investing, consistent, I believe, with Graham and Dodd's approach. We will find that there are two types of bankruptcies, which are, in effect, three. First, there are (1) *liquidations*, which are the purest Graham and Dodd exercise of all, as the investor buys a security to create a workout that is entirely (or nearly entirely) cash. It is a rate-of-return play, as the investor makes a judgment that the balance sheet will support cash distributions above those implied by the current prices of the securities. What's more, these distributions will be received soon enough to create a rate of return that justifies the risk involved. Second, there are *reorganizations*, which come in two flavors: (2) those producing a mélange of cash and securities and (3) those in which

---

[2] This is especially true for reorganizations, more so than for liquidations, a distinction on which I shall elaborate presently.

the investor's goal is control of the reorganized company. In the second type of bankruptcy, "cash and securities" can consist of a bewildering array of paper: senior debt, senior subordinated debt, mezzanine debt, junior debt, preferred stock, and equity. The third type of bankruptcy, in which the investor seeks control, is a polar opposite of a liquidation, in that the hope is to achieve profit from seizing control of a going concern rather than reaping the proceeds of the sale of its parts. The first and third types of bankruptcy are conceptually simpler to structure, unlike the cash and securities reorganizations, which have an intermediate goal (get some cash out of the business at the outset and then hope it will prove profitable going forward) but the greatest structural complexity.

In almost all cases of distressed investing, holding periods start at a year or two and can stretch longer—considerably longer when the investor takes a controlling position in the company. Whereas Charles Dickens once wrote to a friend that the character he most enjoyed portraying was "the rogue who transforms himself in a blink of an eye and thereby instantly earns his eternal reward," it is not the nature of a distressed investment to realize its goals in the blink of an eye or even in the turn of a quarter or two. The process is necessarily drawn out, and investors cannot easily wait till the end of the process to buy because the product is often illiquid, all the more so when the investor wishes to accumulate enough securities to achieve control.

In effect, the bankruptcy investor acts as the incubator, buying tadpoles and selling frogs. In liquidations, the frogs are very green: the investor receives cash and, sometimes, a small amount of senior debt; in reorganizations, on the other hand, the investor may receive a mélange, or what I like to call a "grab bag," of cash, senior debt, junior debt, and new equity in a reorganized company. At the extreme, where the frogs are greenest—in a liquidation—the investor is essentially creating cash at a discount, weighted for time and risk. As the investor moves from liquidation to reorganization to control reorganization, he or she moves away from classic Graham and Dodd balance sheet analysis toward more speculative endeavors.

Distressed investors combine a financial analysis of a company's capital structure with a legal analysis of the rights and prerogatives of bondholders at each level of the capital structure. As the authors noted, litigation can be necessary "to cut the Gordian knot" when "creditors . . . belong to several classes with conflicting interests." (p. 234) Blending the financial and legal analysis is crucial. As distressed investors contemplate an investment, their financial flexibility is defined and limited by the legal remedies made available by specific covenants and broader contract and bankruptcy law; simultaneously, their legal rights are circumscribed by what is financially achievable.[3] In other words, distressed investors cross-reference the legally permissible with the financially doable. When they find the desired fit, they invest.

A few examples of recent (and not so recent) coups in distressed investing give an idea of what takes place in the field. These examples also suggest that, while individual investors may have success picking stocks, it is far more difficult for them to partake in distressed investing. Doing well in the bankruptcy process often entails expenditures of time and resources that are beyond their capabilities.

Liquidations

Texaco: A Quasi-bankruptcy

In the standard liquidation, senior creditors are paid off as best as the company's assets will allow; sometimes, unsecured creditors are fortu-

---

[3] When Graham and Dodd wrote *Security Analysis*, the Bankruptcy Act of 1898, also known as the "Nelson Act," was the law of the land. While bankruptcy procedure has since changed, with the 1978 adoption of the Bankruptcy Code and some subsequent amendments, most recently the Bankruptcy Abuse Prevention and Consumer Protection Act of 2005, these legal changes do not undermine the general principles laid out by the authors.

nate enough to receive a meaningful distribution too. In the rare cases when even unsecured creditors are paid in full, the equity is not wiped out. The very unusual story of Texaco—founded in 1901 as Texas Fuel Company, eventually merged into Chevron a century later—offers useful lessons about liquidations, even though Texaco was not liquidated and, notwithstanding its bankruptcy filings, was never insolvent. Ultimately, Texaco is most significant as an example of the use of the Bankruptcy Code as an escape hatch, to evade legal or contractual liabilities.[4]

Distressed investing generally involves buying debt instruments of a troubled company, because in most bankruptcies the equity is wiped out. That is not always the case, however, and sometimes an astute investor can find riches in the equity of a distressed company, as demonstrated by Carl Icahn in the case of Texaco. Here's what led the oil giant to bankruptcy.

In 1984, Texaco acquired Getty Oil Company, but it was sued by Pennzoil, which contended that Texaco had interfered with its prior contract to buy part of Getty. The following year, a jury determined Texaco was wrong and awarded Pennzoil $10.3 billion. To appeal the judgment, Texaco would have had to post a multi-billion-dollar security bond, which it could not do. Therefore, in 1987, Texaco filed for protection from its creditors under Chapter 11 of the Bankruptcy Code. This was not a real bankruptcy but rather a nearly *sui generis* use of bankruptcy law to fend off legal obligations. Although Texaco was legally bankrupt, it was never insolvent. Upon the heels of the filing, Texaco's stock fell from nearly $32 to $28.50 before rebounding to $31.25. As an oil analyst put it at the time, "While Texaco will be in bankruptcy, Texaco won't be a bankrupt company."[5] *Time* magazine summarized the benefits to Texaco of this unconventional bankruptcy:

---

[4] *Time*, "Bankruptcy as an Escape Hatch," March 5, 1984.

[5] Janice Castro, "A Break in the Action," *Time*, April 27, 1987.

Taking advantage of liberalized bankruptcy laws enacted in 1978, which no longer require corporations to demonstrate that they are insolvent,[6] the oil giant is immune, for the moment, from far more than the debilitating bond judgment. Pennzoil can no longer slap liens, as it was reportedly preparing to do, on up to $8 billion in Texaco assets. With $3 billion already in reserve, Texaco no longer has to pay $630 million worth of annual interest on $7 billion in normal business debts. Nor is it required to pay dividends on 242.3 million outstanding common shares, an estimated saving this year of nearly $727 million.[7]

Eventually, Texaco was able to settle with Pennzoil for a massive, but at least manageable, $3 billion, and it emerged from bankruptcy.[8] Most of the distressed investing community focused on Texaco's senior securities, such as preferred stock and bonds. Icahn, who had owned Texaco stock before the bankruptcy, increased his holdings dramatically after the Chapter 11 filing, eventually raising his stake to 16.6% of the company. Obviously, he was banking that the reorganization of Texaco would not wipe out the equity. It was a very good call. After conducting an unsuccessful proxy fight and making a play for the entire company, Icahn successfully negotiated for a special dividend of $8 per share to stockholders, for a total of $1.9 billion. In addition, Texaco announced a $500 million stock buyback. At the end, Icahn had made $1.1 billion, or a return of over 75%.[9]

---

[6] Texaco is but one example of how the Bankruptcy Code may be used as an escape hatch. Crucially, in *NLRB v. Bildisco & Bildisco*, 465 U.S. 513 (1984), the Supreme Court held that a company may use section 365(a) of the code, which permits the bankruptcy trustee to assume or reject executory contracts, to escape from the terms of a collective-bargaining agreement by which it had been bound.

[7] Ibid.

[8] For an overview of the Texaco bankruptcy and Icahn's subsequent jousting with the company, see Mark Potts, "With Icahn Agreement, Texaco Emerges from Years of Trying Times," *Washington Post*, February 5, 1989, p. H2.

[9] Michael Arndt, "Texaco, Icahn Make a Deal," *Chicago Tribune*, January 30, 1989, p. C3. Maybe the best bankruptcy investment of all is to try the case that sends the company into bankruptcy. *Forbes* pegs the net worth of Joseph Jamail, Jr., the plaintiff's lawyer in *Pennzoil v. Texaco*, at $1.5 billion.

Texaco's unusual situation can be summarized in one sentence, often repeated by Graham and Dodd disciple Warren Buffett: A great investment opportunity occurs when a marvelous business encounters a one-time huge, but solvable, problem. The tale also serves as an example of how perceptions had changed since Graham and Dodd's day. Here was a bankruptcy in which the equity was not wiped out—and no one expected it to be wiped out—whereas Graham and Dodd had argued that bondholders would be best off not enforcing their rights to the hilt because "receivership" (to say nothing of "bankruptcy") was so dreaded a word on Wall Street that "its advent means ordinarily a drastic shrinkage in the price of all the company's securities, including the bonds for the 'benefit' of which the receivership was instituted." (p. 230) By illuminating bankruptcy, they made it not so scary. This change in perceptions is not to the discredit of the authors. Indeed, they probably were indispensable to the shift, in light of their role in educating the investing public. Call it the Graham and Dodd Heisenberg effect. In light of Graham and Dodd, the game shifted, all the way to Carl Icahn. The effect may be similarly present in the authors' relatively concise discussion of distressed investing. Their brevity is readily understandable not only because the field has grown since Graham and Dodd published but because the themes sounded throughout their work are inherently applicable to this mode, such that dedicating a chapter to distressed investing as such would have been nearly superfluous.

Grab Bag Reorganizations

In Graham and Dodd's terminology, we move away from investment toward speculation when we shift focus from liquidations to reorganizations that include cash plus a bag of securities. At the end of the reorganization process, the investor may hold several kinds of paper, each of which may be valued differently.

Adelphia Communications

Because companies often issue different classes of debt, bankruptcy litigation commonly involves a battle among the different classes of creditors. The bankruptcy of Adelphia Communications offers an example of
intercreditor strife and of how an accurate projection of the outcome can
lead to outsize returns.

John Rigas, the son of Greek immigrants, founded Adelphia in 1952,
which rose to become one of the largest cable companies in the United
States. Rigas was a pioneer in the industry, inducted into the Cable Television Hall of Fame in 2001. He also became a billionaire, owner of the
Buffalo Sabres, and philanthropic hero of Coudersport, Pennsylvania,
where his business empire got started. As the company grew, Rigas did
not run a tight ship. At one point, Adelphia's debt reached 11 times its
market capitalization, compared to ratios of 1.28 for Comcast and 0.45
for Cox Communications.[10] The whole edifice unraveled when an investment analyst figured out that the company was liable for $2.3 billion in
off-balance-sheet loans to Rigas family members, which they used to
buy Adelphia stock. Eventually, Adelphia filed for Chapter 11, and, in
August 2007, Rigas went to federal prison for conspiracy, securities fraud,
and bank fraud.

Adelphia's bankruptcy featured intercreditor disputes over the proceeds. Even after the company's assets had been sold to Time Warner
and Comcast—this being a reorganization, not a liquidation—there was
still intense litigation between the bondholders of the holding company,
Adelphia, and of a large subsidiary, Century Communications. Eventually,
the Century bondholders agreed to a 3% decrease in their recovery in
exchange for the support of several large bondholders for the plan of
reorganization. For the most part, the plan maintained the structural

---

[10] These figures, and certain other details, come from Devin Leonard, "The Adelphia Story," *Fortune*,
August 12, 2002.

integrity of the Century bonds, while enabling Adelphia to emerge from bankruptcy. The plan was eventually approved, notwithstanding some remaining opposition from Adelphia bondholders. A contemporaneous increase in cable valuations, as well as strong results from industry leaders Time Warner and Comcast, helped Adelphia to garner the votes it needed in support of the plan. Those who bought Century bonds at the bottom and held them through a contentious and protracted legal process enjoyed a return of over 400%. In general, creditors received a combination of cash and Time Warner Cable Class A common stock, with percentage recoveries as of August 31, 2007, varying from 100% for certain trade claims to 99.6% for senior subordinated notes, 94.7% for some senior notes, 83.7% for senior discount notes, 70.7% for other senior notes, and a variety of other percentages down to 0% for Adelphia common stock, preferred stock, and convertible preferred stock.[11]

Winn-Dixie Stores

As it filed for bankruptcy in February 2005, Winn-Dixie was the eighth-largest food retailer in the United States, with revenues of $9.9 billion. The company was founded by William Milton Davis in 1914, and at the time of the bankruptcy Davis's heirs still owned 35% of the common stock. Winn-Dixie's Chapter 11 filing was precipitated by overexpansion and severe competition, primarily fueled by Publix Super Markets and Wal-Mart Stores. There was doubt whether the Florida-based company could emerge, but there were also reasons for optimism. The new CEO was the well-respected Peter Lynch, formerly the president and COO of Albertson's. As he asserted his leadership and operations stabilized, vendors cautiously supported the reorganization plan. The company closed or sold a third of its stores, downsizing distribution operations and headcount.

---

[11] Information on Distribution to Certain Classes of Claims (available at www.adelphiarestructuring.com).

Still, vendors were reluctant to extend credit to Winn-Dixie, so the company was unable to enjoy the "float" available to grocery stores that turn over inventory before they have to pay for it. Some investors concluded that the company was likely to receive credit, unwind pent-up working capital, and once again take advantage of the float as it emerged from bankruptcy. In addition, they looked forward to the company's ability, as part of the supermarket industry, to operate with negative working capital and receive significant fees for shelf space. Moreover, Winn-Dixie had long-term leases at below-market rents. Management's strategy, which included leasing space to Boston Markets rather than operating its own roasted chicken counters, made sense to investors. Thus, those who invested in Winn-Dixie were less concerned than much of Wall Street that the company would fritter away its cash. During the second quarter of 2006, Winn-Dixie bonds were available at under 60 cents on the dollar, as the company was then effectively valued at under $450 million, or approximately 5% of revenue. This was a rare contemporary example of being able to buy a company for net working capital, or one whose mark-to-market enterprise value was under 10% of revenue. Graham and Dodd surely would have approved. Winn-Dixie emerged from bankruptcy in December 2006. By the end of the second quarter of 2007, on the heels of its emergence, the company's enterprise value had tripled to $1.4 billion.

Bradlees

At the conclusion of a grab bag reorganization, creditors may find themselves in a very different position from the one they occupied at the outset. As Graham and Dodd note, voting control over the corporation can pass in bankruptcy to the bondholders, who will then become equity holders in the new entity that enjoys a statutory fresh start. (p. 238) Thus, even though most distressed investments are made in debt rather than equity, there is an important equity component to the bankruptcy process. (The authors point out that debt may, of course, be exchanged for equity under voluntary reorganization plans too. [pp. 236–237])

An example was Bradlees, a retailer that emerged from bankruptcy in early 1999. Bondholders received cash, new notes, and equity. The stock was hammered in the aftermath of the diminution in demand for all distressed securities at the end of 1998. At the bottom, Bradlees had nearly $138 of sales per share of common stock, in contrast with the concededly more successful Wal-Mart's $31. In the second quarter of 1999, Wall Street woke up to the disparity, and Bradlees was the best-performing over-the-counter stock of that three-month period. The new bonds shot up in value too. By July, the total Bradlees postbankruptcy securities package had reached an aggregate value of $1.55 (see table), in contrast with a March low of 62 cents. By August 1999, Bradlees' stocks alone were worth far more than the old bonds. As the table shows, the equity portion of these grab bags can be volatile, but they can be rewarding to the patient investor.

Bradlees' Grab Bag

Date	6/30/98	12/31/98	2/5/99	3/15/99	3/31/99	5/6/99	5/21/99	5/26/99	6/3/99	6/23/99	6/30/99	7/8/99
Old Bonds	0.78	0.50	-	-	-	-	-	-	-	-	-	-
Cash	-	-	0.20	0.20	0.20	0.20	0.20	0.20	0.20	0.20	0.20	0.20
Certificates	-	-	0.06	0.06	0.06	0.06	0.06	0.06	0.06	0.06	0.06	0.06
New Notes	-	-	0.22	0.22	0.22	0.22	0.26	0.26	0.26	0.27	0.27	0.27
Stock	-	-	0.26	0.14	0.20	0.53	0.58	0.51	0.57	0.84	0.86	1.02
Total	**0.78**	**0.50**	**0.74**	**0.62**	**0.68**	**1.01**	**1.10**	**1.03**	**1.09**	**1.37**	**1.39**	**1.55**

Most distressed investors did not hold on for the entire ride because they knew Bradlees was no Wal-Mart but they could not predict when Wall Street would recognize Bradlees' deficiencies. As the masters taught, it is difficult to hold a stock for more than a 200% gain "without a dangerous surrender to 'bull-market psychology.'" (p. 324) Stated otherwise, be an investor, not a speculator. Eventually, competition caught up with

Bradlees, which filed a second bankruptcy petition in December 2000 and, this time around, was liquidated.[12]

Reorganization as Avenue to Control

As we move further down the ladder from classic Graham and Dodd investing to something approaching speculation, we look at reorganizations that lead to control of the company. Warren Buffett has often bought debt for a rate of return rather than for the creation of equity and obtaining of control. He seems reluctant to complete the trip and become a completely integrated bankruptcy investor. Others, however, have pushed on for ownership and control.

Guinness Peat Aviation

For Graham and Dodd, low-grade bonds, together with preferred stock, were Wall Street's orphans. "The investor [in the Graham and Dodd sense of the term] must not buy them, and the speculator generally prefers to devote his attention to common stocks." (p. 323) And yet, the authors note, the large supply of these securities and the lack of demand may make their price attractive.

An example of an attractive low-grade bond, and a fascinating case study of the evolution of distressed investing, is Guinness Peat Aviation (GPA), which served as a precursor of today's common prepackaged bankruptcies, or "prepacks." That's an arrangement in which the debtor and creditors agree upon a reorganization plan *before* the bankruptcy filing, thereby making it much easier and more cost-efficient to file a bankruptcy petition and obtain confirmation in court. In GPA's case, the bankruptcy filing never proved necessary.

GPA was an Ireland-based commercial aircraft sales and leasing company founded in 1975. At its peak, it had 280 aircraft on lease to 83 air-

---

[12] Reuters, "Bradlees Files for Bankruptcy," December 26, 2000.

lines. In 1990, the company placed a stunning order for 700 new aircraft, valued at $17 billion. GPA, however, was a victim of bad timing. It floated an IPO in 1992, during the downturn in the airline industry that followed the 1991 Gulf War. The IPO failed to close, and GPA, with some $10 billion in debt thanks to the huge order, was in serious trouble. Its debt cratered to about half its face value, which is the point at which distressed investors became involved. They snapped up bonds at yields 700 to 950 basis points over Treasuries because they liked the value of the airplane collateral. Eventually, GPA was rescued by its larger competitor GE Commercial Aviation Services. It was a great deal for the rescuer because it could refinance GPA's debt with the benefit of General Electric's AAA rating. It was a great deal for distressed investors because once GE assumed GPA's obligations, GPA's bonds became unsecured debt at the bottom of GE's balance sheet and still traded nearly at par. Overnight, the bonds nearly doubled in value.

MCI WorldCom

One of the spectacular corporate collapses early in this century occurred at WorldCom, the once and future MCI. From at least as early as 1999 and going into 2002, financial officers at the telecommunications company booked routine business costs as capital expenditures, which understated expenses and thus resulted in an overstatement of income by at least $9 billion. "In just a few years WorldCom erased $200 billion in market value and shed thousands of jobs. By July 2002, the fraud and lax supervision forced WorldCom into bankruptcy."[13]

In December 2002, Michael Capellas was hired as the new CEO of the company as it sought to reorganize. A federal court overseeing the Securities and Exchange Commission's case against MCI WorldCom appointed a former SEC chairman, Richard Breeden, as the company's "corporate

[13] Stephanie N. Mehta, "MCI: Is Being Good Good Enough?" *Fortune*, October 27, 2003.

monitor." Thus, Capellas and his management team needed to simultaneously deal with regulatory constraints, clean up the errors and fraud of
their predecessors, and try to do business in a highly competitive market.

Mark Neporent, the chief operating officer of Cerberus Capital Management, one of the distressed investors involved in the bankruptcy,
served as cochairman of the Official Creditors' Committee.[14] With competitors of the reorganizing MCI seeking to exclude the company from
federal contracts, Neporent testified to the Senate Judiciary Committee
with respect to the benefits of the reorganization process:

> It is beyond doubt that MCI's reorganization plan provides creditors with
> a much greater chance of recovery than does liquidation, which would
> literally throw away billions of dollars of value. MCI's going-concern value
> is estimated to be approximately $12 billion to $15 billion, while its liqui-
> dation value is only $4 billion. Not surprisingly, representatives of 90% of
> MCI's debt have quickly and efficiently resolved their internecine differ-
> ences—exactly as contemplated by the Bankruptcy Code—and have
> given their support to MCI's proposed reorganization plan.[15]

By 2005, the reorganized MCI was back on its feet again, and its postbankruptcy owners sold the company to Verizon for about $8.4 billion,
comfortably more than the liquidation value averted by reorganization.
MCI was a case in which reorganization as a means of obtaining control
helped to unlock the value of the company's assets.

Distressed Investing

A fundamental question about value investing in general, and distressed
investing in particular, is why should bargains be available? If the market is

<hr>

[14] Graham and Dodd were concerned that protective committees organized by investment bankers
may fail to protect investor interests impartially. They saluted the 1938 bankruptcy legislation that
subjected the activities and compensation of protective committees to court scrutiny. (pp. 240–241)
Today, of course, the activities of creditors' committees, which play a major role in reorganizations,
are closely supervised.

[15] Neporent's testimony is available at judiciary.senate.gov.

efficient, as academic theory would hold, why is today's price not necessarily the very best guess at a security's true value? Even though they were professors, Graham and Dodd looked at reality rather than theory, and they rejected the Efficient Market Hypothesis (EMH) developed at the University of Chicago before it had a name, let alone an acronym. They famously analogized the market to a *voting machine*, producing results that are the product partly of reason and partly of emotion, rather than an exact and impersonal *weighing machine*. (p. 70) The authors relied on a "twofold assumption: first, that the market price is frequently out of line with the true value; and, second, that there is an inherent tendency for these disparities to correct themselves." (pp. 69–70) Before anyone from the Chicago School has a coronary, let's hear some more from Graham and Dodd on the first assumption: "As to the truth of the former statement, there can be very little doubt—even though Wall Street often speaks glibly of the 'infallible judgment of the market' and asserts that 'a stock is worth what you can sell it for—neither more nor less.'" (p. 70)

If the market gets the "correct" price "wrong" in ordinary investing, such error occurs even more frequently in distressed investing. As implied by the very name *distressed investing*, purchasers of distressed securities search for bargains made available by the unhappiness of sellers who bought those securities in happier times. In Graham and Dodd's day, when a stock stopped paying dividends, many institutional holders were compelled by their charters to sell. (pp. 127–128 on accompanying CD) Today, the same is true of bonds when the issuer stops paying the coupon. Thus, when a company experiences distress, there are many forced sellers clamoring for the narrow exit doors, and there are not enough buyers to widen the door and hold up the "correct" price. Even the institutions that are not legally bound to sell when a coupon is missed will often do so anyway. At many institutions, the idea of a workout department is the telephone: pick it up and sell the security. Against this background, the distressed specialist is making a judgment that the securities retain value greater than that ascribed to them by the market or even their current owners.

Wall Street, moreover, is constitutionally predisposed to overdo things. The stereotype imagines a Wall Street populated by bulls and bears. In reality, the Street itself is neither bull nor bear but shark, constantly shifting direction in an eternal search for food. This feeding process involves massive shifts of capital, which, inevitably, is sometimes misallocated. As Sir John Templeton reportedly put it, "Bull markets are born in pessimism, grow on skepticism, mature on optimism, and die on euphoria."[16] The bankruptcy investor lives off these misallocations. He or she is long the downstream product of what the Wall Street shark wants to sell. In good times, Wall Street permits the raising of debt and thereby the retirement of stock, leading to an acquisition boom. Euphoria in Wall Street's debt-creation machine leads to a crash, and that is when the bankruptcy investor supplies fresh equity and retires debt, frequently at a discount.

To be sure, things have changed since Graham and Dodd's time. Technological advances and the democratization of finance arguably make the market more efficient. After all, in 1940, you could not instantaneously track the prices of myriad securities via a Bloomberg terminal or the Internet. You could not construct elaborate Excel spreadsheets and instantaneously adjust all the figures by changing one number. You could not receive e-mail alerts whenever there was news about the companies you followed. And there were not thousands of professionals hunched over computer terminals all day competing for investment bargains. The late, legendary Leon Levy advised novices in the business to assume that the decisions they are making today are simultaneously being made by others at hundreds of offices around the country. As a

---

[16] Bill Miller, "Good Times Are Coming!" *Time*, March 8, 2005.

result, there is a good argument to be made that the markets are more rational today than when Graham and Dodd wrote. In fact, Graham himself made that argument, during the final year of his life. "In the old days any well-trained security analyst could do a good professional job of selecting undervalued securities through detailed studies," he told an interviewer in 1976, "but in the light of the enormous amount of research now being carried on, I doubt whether in most cases such extensive efforts will generate sufficiently superior selections to justify their cost."[17] In other words, Professor Graham feared that his work had been so successful as to render itself obsolete. Not quite. Little did the professor know that he was just getting started.

Graham and Dodd Today

Graham and Dodd recognized that things change. In the opening paragraph of their preface to the second edition, six years after the first edition, they observed that "things happen too fast in the economic world to permit the authors to rest comfortably for long." (p. xli) Sometimes the authors were restless, appearing to be decades ahead of their time.

The Risk Insight

A prime example of Graham and Dodd's prescience has found practical application in an important sector of modern securities markets. Though the authors, skeptical as always of the rationality of markets, said that "security prices and yields are not determined by any exact mathematical calculation of the expected risk, but they depend rather upon the *popularity* of the issue" (p. 164), they also laid the theoretical foundation, upon which the edifice was constructed decades later, for high yield investing. It was the authors who said, "If we assume that a fairly large

---

[17] Kenneth L. Fisher, *100 Minds That Made the Market* (New York: Wiley, 2007), p. 61. Fisher goes on to observe of this late-in-life conversion: "Ironically, Graham's adoption of 'the efficient market' was just before computer backtests would poke all kind of holes in that theory."

proportion of a group of carefully selected low-priced bonds will escape default, the income received on the group as a whole over a period of time will undoubtedly far exceed the dividend return on similarly priced common stocks." (p. 327)

Others appropriated that idea to help sell junk bonds, especially the low-grade original issue bonds that took Wall Street by storm in the 1980s. But there is little doubt that Graham and Dodd would have disapproved of such bonds. It's one thing to buy fallen angels—once investment-grade bonds whose issuers had fallen on hard times. Those were usually senior securities that even in the case of a bankruptcy could lay claim to some assets. Original issue junk had no such backing. Should those bonds falter, there may not be any recovery at all.

During the 1980s, a significant percentage of the high yield bond market consisted of securities that had never been sold directly to investors but were parts of packages of securities and cash given to selling shareholders in acquisitions. The investment bank Drexel Burnham Lambert perfected this strategy, creating such instruments as zero-coupon bonds (paying no interest for, say, five years) or "pay-in-kind (PIK) preferreds," which, instead of paying cash interest, just issued more preferred stock. Almost no one thought these securities were worth their nominal value, but selling shareholders generally approved the transactions. As the decade ended, however, the junk bond market collapsed and so did several of Drexel's deals. These problems, coupled with Drexel's legal difficulties with the SEC and prosecutors, led to the firm's bankruptcy filing in 1990. Jeffrey Lane, former president of Shearson Lehman Hutton, observed: "This is the nature of the financial service business. You go into a steady decline, and then you fall off a cliff."

It is one thing to buy fallen angels, former investment-grade bonds whose issues had fallen on hard times, and quite another to issue an angel that never took wing. Fallen angels were usually senior securities

that could always lay claim to some assets, even in the case of a bankruptcy. The Drexel-designed securities that were exchanged lacked even
this saving grace. They were probably very good examples of what Graham and Dodd most disapproved of in the financial markets. In the
ensuing collapse, most of them had no recovery at all.

Graham and Dodd had the insight that the difference between the
risk-free rate of return and the yields offered by securities of varying risk
created investment opportunities, especially if a diversified portfolio
could lock in high returns while reducing the overall risk. In almost any
kind of investing, returns have at least *some* (if not a mathematically
exact) connection to the risk-free rate of return, with investors demanding higher returns for greater risk. The premium that investors demand
for high yield bonds over the safety of Fed Funds offers a good snapshot
for the market's appetite for risk, as seen in this two-decade survey:

Are You Getting Paid to Take Risk?

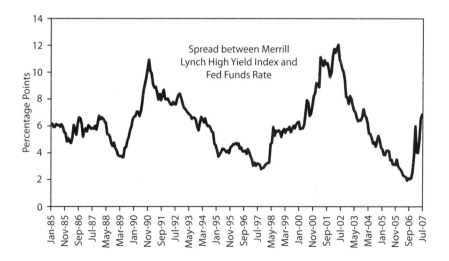

A two-decade survey of the spread between the Merrill Lynch High Yield (MLHY) Index and
the Fed Funds Rate. When the spread is high, high yield bonds are said to be cheap.

The chart shows this spread over time by subtracting the risk-free Fed Funds rate from the riskier Merrill Lynch High Yield (MLHY) Index. The spread serves as a proxy *for the returns available for opportunistic capital, including in the field of distressed investing.* Unlike, say, venture capital, with which the investor is seeking a pot of gold (albeit with some diversification so that the occasional winner offsets the losers), the chart is relevant to the large segment of any portfolio designed to create a rate of return for opportunistic capital. That rate of return available is effectively tethered to the risk-free rate, and the spread shown in the chart is the simplest, and perhaps best, measure of where markets have priced it over the last two decades.

The yields move in tandem most of the time, but the real opportunities come when they move in opposite directions—that is, when the spread expands, it is time to buy; when it compresses, to sell. Note the vast expansion in the spread from 1989 to 1991, which reflected some weakness in the economy and led to the reelection defeat of George H. W. Bush even though things had begun to improve before Election Day 1992. The spread was very narrow during the stock market boom of 1998, began to expand as the dot-com bubble reached its peak, and exploded after the bubble burst. The spread, which had expanded to under 1,200 basis points by the end of 2002, had shrunk to about 700 basis points by the end of 2003, less than 400 by the start of 2006, and under 200 in early 2007. This powerful compression of yields served as a springboard for a revaluation for all asset classes for which the High Yield Index is a proxy.

When the spread is at its widest, as in 1991 or 2002, investors are paid handsomely for risk. When the spread is at its narrowest, as in early 2007, the market is too sanguine about risk, and it becomes time to sell. Of course, it is very difficult to predict where the spread will move tomorrow or next week, but opportunistic investors recognize diversions from the norm. When the spread is particularly wide, they go fishing; when it is particularly narrow, they stay close to home and mend their nets.

The way life works, of course, is that at times of wide spreads, with huge opportunities available for alternative investment, it is extremely difficult to raise capital in the area. Thus, once the spread narrows and opportunities are fewer, money flows into alternatives. As Leon Levy was wont to say: When you have the ideas, you can't get the money; when you can get the money, you don't have the ideas. In this respect, investors in the distressed investing sector do not behave so differently from retail stock market investors.

First Principles and Paradigm Shifts

It is easy to acknowledge that seemingly immutable rules can become obsolete, but difficult to know when that is the case. In the spring of 1951, the Dow Jones Industrial Average stood at about 250. Professor Graham told his class at Columbia University Business School that the Dow had traded below 200 at some time during every full year since its inception in 1896. With Professor Graham's best student ever—supposedly, the only one ever to receive an A+ from the master—about to graduate that summer, the professor suggested that maybe the student would benefit from delaying his investing career until after the Dow had completed its predictable decline to under 200, which had yet to happen in 1951. Showing how richly he deserved the A+, Warren Buffett declined the advice, and a good thing it was because the Dow did not return to 200 that year or in any year since.[18] "I had about ten thousand bucks" when Professor Graham gave his advice, Buffett told the *Wall Street Journal*. "If I had taken his advice, I would probably still have about ten thousand bucks."[19]

A few years later, in 1958, equity dividend yields fell below bond yields for the first time. A sensible investor putting money to work at the

---

[18] Kenneth Lee, *Trouncing the Dow: A Value-Based Method for Making Huge Profits* (New York: McGraw-Hill, 1998), pp. 1–2.

[19] In Berkshire Hathaway's 2000 annual report, Buffett said of his experience in Graham's class that "a few hours at the feet of the master proved far more valuable to me than had ten years of supposedly original thinking."

time could hardly credit the change as part of a permanent new reality. To the contrary, it must have seemed a mandate to short the stock market. Think of all the money lost over all the years by the true believers who have argued: "This time is different." Yet the seasoned professionals of that time were cautious and wrong, and the irreverent optimists were right. This time, it really was different. From the safe perspective of a half century, it seems incontrovertible that a new valuation benchmark had been established.

So when can one safely conclude that "this time is different," especially in light of all the times that it really is *not* different? In 1951, Professor Graham's rule of 200 had held for 55 years. Once breached, it never again proved true, but who would have had Buffett's foresight and audacity to conclude that it could safely be ignored? The 1958 investor who waited for the century-old relationship between dividend yields and bond market yields to reassert itself is still waiting too. Once reversed, that relationship has moved ever farther apart.

Still, if Graham and Dodd's bible cannot be understood today without commentary, the *attitude* embodied in this work is timeless. As long as investors remain human, and thus subject to greed, fear, pressure, doubt, and the entire range of human emotions, there will be money to be made by those who steel themselves to overcome emotion. As long as the human tendency to march in herds persists, there will be opportunities for contrarians who are unafraid to stand alone. Think of Graham and Dodd as embodying the spirit of Hamlet, Prince of Denmark, who declared: "Blest are those/Whose blood and judgement are so well commingled,/That they are not a pipe for Fortune's finger/To sound what stop she please."[20]

---

[20] *Hamlet*, Act III, Scene 2.

Chapter 22

PRIVILEGED ISSUES

WE COME now to the second major division of our revised classification of securities, *viz.*, bonds and preferred stocks presumed by the buyer to be subject to substantial change in principal value. In our introductory discussion (Chap. 5) we subdivided this group under two heads: those issues which are speculative because of inadequate safety, and those which are speculative because they possess a conversion or similar privilege which makes possible substantial variations in market price.[1]

SENIOR ISSUES WITH SPECULATIVE PRIVILEGES

In addition to enjoying a prior claim for a fixed amount of principal and income, a bond or preferred stock may also be given the right to share in benefits accruing to the common stock. These privileges are of three kinds, designated as follows:

1. Convertible—conferring the right to exchange the senior issue for common stock on stipulated terms.

2. Participating—under which additional income may be paid to the senior security holder, dependent usually upon the amount of common dividends declared.

3. Subscription—by which holders of the bond or preferred stock may purchase common shares, at prices, in amounts, and during periods, stipulated.[2]

---

[1] In the 1934 edition we had here a section on investment-quality senior issues obtainable at bargain levels. Although these were plentiful in the 1931–1933 period, they have since grown very scarce—even in the market decline of 1937–1938. To save space, therefore, we are now omitting this section.

[2] There is still a fourth type of profit-sharing arrangement, of less importance than the three just described, which made its first appearance in the 1928–1929 bull market. This is the so-called "optional" bond or preferred stock. The option consists of taking interest or dividend payments in a fixed amount of common stock (*i.e.*, at a fixed price per share) in lieu of cash.

Since the conversion privilege is the most familiar of the three, we shall frequently use the term "convertible issues" to refer to privileged issues in general.

Such Issues Attractive in Form. By means of any one of these three provisions a senior security can be given virtually all the profit possibilities that attach to the common stock of the enterprise. Such issues must therefore be considered as the most attractive of all in point of *form*, since they permit the combination of maximum safety with the chance of unlimited appreciation in value. A bond that meets all the requirements of a sound investment and in addition possesses an interesting conversion privilege would undoubtedly constitute a highly desirable purchase.

Their Investment Record Unenviable: Reasons. Despite this impressive argument in favor of privileged senior issues as a *form* of investment, we must recognize that actual experience with this class has not been generally satisfactory. For this discrepancy between promise and performance, reasons of two different kinds may be advanced.

The first is that only a small fraction of the privileged issues have actually met the rigorous requirements of a sound investment. The conversion feature has most often been offered to compensate for inadequate security.[3] This weakness was most pronounced during the period of greatest

---

For example, Commercial Investment Trust $6 Convertible Preference, Optional Series of 1929, gave the holder the option to take his dividend at the annual rate of one-thirteenth share of common instead of $6 in cash. This was equivalent to a price of $78 per share for the common, which meant that the option would be valuable whenever the stock was selling above 78. Similarly, Warner Brothers Pictures, Inc., Optional 6% Convertible Debentures, due 1939, issued in 1929, gave the owner the option to take his interest payments at the annual rate of one share of common stock instead of $60 in cash.

It may be said that this optional arrangement is a modified form of conversion privilege, under which the interest or dividend amounts are made separately convertible into common stock. In most, possibly all, of these issues, the principal is convertible as well. The separate convertibility of the income payments adds somewhat, but not a great deal, to the attractiveness of the privilege.

[3] The *Report of the Industrial Securities Committee of the Investment Bankers Association of America* for 1927 quotes, presumably with approval, a suggestion that since a certain percentage of the senior securities of moderate-sized industrial companies "are liable to show substantial losses over a period of five or ten years," investors therein should be given a participation in future earnings through a conversion or other privilege to compensate for this risk. See *Proceedings of the Sixteenth Annual Convention of the Investment Bankers Association of America*, pp. 144–145, 1927.

vogue for convertible issues, between 1926 and 1929.[4] During these years it was broadly true that the strongly entrenched industrial enterprises raised money through sales of common stock, whereas the weaker—or weakly capitalized—undertakings resorted to privileged senior securities.

The second reason is related to the conditions under which profit may accrue from the conversion privilege. Although there is indeed no upper limit to the price that a convertible bond may reach, there is a very real limitation on the amount of profit that the holder may realize while still maintaining an *investment position*. After a privileged issue has advanced with the common stock, its price soon becomes dependent *in both directions* upon changes in the stock quotation, and to that extent the continued holding of the senior issue becomes a *speculative* operation. An example will make this clear:

Let us assume the purchase of a high-grade $3^1/2\%$ bond at par, convertible into two shares of common for each $100 bond (*i.e.*, convertible into common stock at 50). The common stock is selling at 45 when the bond is bought.

First stage: (1) If the stock declines to 35, the bond may remain close to par. This illustrates the pronounced technical advantage of a convertible issue over the common stock. (2) If the stock advances to 55, the price of the bond will probably rise to 115 or more. (Its "immediate conversion value" would be 110, but a premium would be justified because of its advantage over the stock.) This illustrates the undoubted speculative possibilities of such a convertible issue.

Second stage: The stock advances further to 65. The conversion value of the bond is now 130, and it will sell at that figure, or slightly higher. At this point the original purchaser is faced with a problem. Within wide limits, the future price of his bond depends entirely upon the course of the common stock. In order to seek a larger profit he must risk the loss of the profit in hand, which in fact constitutes a substantial part of the present market value of his security. (A drop in the price of the common

---

[4] Prior to the appearance on Feb. 16, 1939, of *Release No.* 208 (*Statistical Series*) of the S.E.C., no comprehensive compilation of the dollar volume of privileged issues has been made and regularly maintained. That release gave data on a quarterly basis for the period from Apr. 1, 1937, through Dec. 31, 1938, and additional data have since been published quarterly by the S.E.C. Further evidence of the volume of this type of financing over a much longer period is presented in Appendix Note 35, p. 770 on accompanying CD.

could readily induce a decline in the bond from 130 to 110.) If he elects to hold the issue, he places himself to a considerable degree in the position of the stockholders, and this similarity increases rapidly as the price advances further. If, for example, he is still holding the bond at a level say of 180 (90 for the stock), he has for all practical purposes assumed the status and risks of a stockholder.

Unlimited Profit in Such Issues Identified with Stockholder's Position. The unlimited profit possibilities of a privileged issue are thus in an important sense illusory. They must be identified not with the ownership of a bond or preferred stock but with the assumption of a common stockholder's position—which any holder of a nonconvertible may effect by exchanging his bond for a stock. Practically speaking, the range of profit possibilities for a convertible issue, *although still maintaining the advantage of an investment holding*, must usually be limited to somewhere between 25 and 35% of its face value. For this reason original purchasers of privileged issues do not ordinarily hold them for more than a small fraction of the maximum market gains scored by the most successful among them, and consequently they do not actually realize these very large possible profits. Thus the profits taken may not offset the losses occasioned by unsound commitments in this field.

Examples of Attractive Issues. The two objections just discussed must considerably temper our enthusiasm for privileged senior issues as a class, but they by no means destroy their inherent advantages nor the possibilities of exploiting them with reasonable success. Although *most* new convertible offerings may have been inadequately secured,[5] there are fairly frequent exceptions to the rule, and these exceptions should be of prime interest to the alert investor. We append three leading examples of such opportunities, taken from the utility, the railroad, and the industrial fields.

1. *Commonwealth Edison Company Convertible Debenture 3¹/₂s, Due 1958.* These bonds were offered to shareholders in June and September 1938 at par. The statistical exhibit of the company gave every assurance that the debentures were a sound commitment at that price. They were convertible into 40 shares of common stock until maturity or prior redemption.

---

[5] This criticism does not apply to convertible bonds issued from 1933 to date, the majority of which meet our investment standards.

In September 1938 the debentures could have been bought on the New York Stock Exchange at par when the stock was selling at 24^1/$_2$. At these prices the bonds and stock were selling very close to a parity, and a slight advance in the price of the stock would enable the holder of the bond to sell at a profit. Less than a year later (July 1939) the stock had risen to 31^3/$_8$, and the bonds to 124^3/$_4$.

2. *Chesapeake and Ohio Railway Company Convertible 5s, Due 1946.* These bonds were originally offered to shareholders in June 1916. They were convertible into common stock at 75 until April 1, 1920; at 80 from the latter date until April 1, 1923; at 90 from the latter date until April 1, 1926; and at 100 from the latter date until April 1, 1936.

Late in 1924 they could have been bought on a parity basis (*i.e.*, without payment of a premium for the conversion privilege) at prices close to par. Specifically, they sold on November 28, 1924, at 101 when the stock sold at 91. At that time the company's earnings were showing continued improvement and indicated that the bonds were adequately secured. (Fixed charges were covered twice in 1924.) The value of the conversion privilege was shown by the fact that the stock sold at 131 in the next year, making the bonds worth 145.

3. *Rand Kardex Bureau, Inc., 5^1/$_2$s, Due 1931.* These bonds were originally offered in December 1925 at 99^1/$_2$. They carried stock-purchase warrants (detachable after January 1, 1927) entitling the holder to purchase 22^1/$_2$ shares of Class *A* common at $40 per share during 1926, at $42.50 per share during 1927, at $45 per share during 1928, at $47.50 per share during 1929, and at $50 per share during 1930. (The Class *A* stock was in reality a participating preferred issue.) The bonds could be turned in at par in payment for the stock purchased under the warrants, a provision that virtually made the bonds convertible into the stock.

The bonds appeared to be adequately secured. The previous exhibit (based on the earnings of the predecessor companies) showed the following coverage for the interest on the new bond issue:

Year	Number of Times Interest Covered
1921 (depression year)	1.7
1922 (depression year)	2.3
1923	6.7
1924	7.2
1925 (9 months)	12.2

Net current assets exceed twice the face value of the bond issue.

When the bonds were offered to the public, the Class *A* stock was quoted at about 42, indicating an immediate value for the stock-purchase warrants. The following year the stock advanced to 53, and the bonds to 130$^1/_2$. In 1927 (when Rand Kardex merged with Remington Typewriter) the stock advanced to 76, and the bonds to 190.

Example of an Unattractive Issue. By way of contrast with these examples we shall supply an illustration of a superficially attractive but basically unsound convertible offering, such as characterized the 1928–1929 period.

National Trade Journals, Inc., 6% Convertible Notes, Due 1938. The company was organized in February 1928 to acquire and publish about a dozen trade journals. In November 1928 it sold $2,800,000 of the foregoing notes at 97$^1/_2$. The notes were initially convertible into 27 shares of common stock (at $37.03 per share) until November 1, 1930; into 25 shares (at $40 a share) from the latter date until November 1, 1932; and at prices that progressively increased to $52.63 a share during the last two years of the life of the bonds.

These bonds could have been purchased at the time of issuance and for several months thereafter at prices only slightly above their parity value as compared with the market value of the equivalent stock. Specifically, they could have been bought at 97$^1/_2$ on November 30, when the stock sold at 34$^1/_8$, which meant that the stock needed to advance only two points to assure a profit on conversion.

However, at no time did the bonds appear to be adequately secured, despite the attractive picture presented in the offering circular. The circular exhibited "estimated" earnings of the predecessor enterprise based on the 3$^1/_2$ years preceding, which averaged 4.16 times the charges on the bond issue. But close to half of these estimated earnings were expected to be derived from economies predicted to result from the consolidation in the way of reduction of salaries, etc. The conservative investor would not be justified in taking these "earnings" for granted, particularly in a hazardous and competitive business of this type, with a relatively small amount of tangible assets.

Eliminating the estimated "earnings" mentioned in the preceding paragraph the exhibit at the time of issuance and thereafter was as follows:

Year	Price range of bonds	Price range of stock	Prevailing conversion price	Times interest earned	Earned per share on common
1925				1.73*	$0.78*
1926				2.52*	1.84*
1927				2.80*	2.20*
1928	100 −97¹/₂	35⁷/₈−30	$37.03	1.69†	1.95
1929	99 −50	34⁵/₈− 5	37.03	1.86†	1.04
1930	42 −10	6³/₈− ¹/₂	37.03−$40	0.09†	1.68(d)
1931	10¹/₂− 5	1	40.00	Receivership	

* Predecessor enterprise. Pre-share figures are after estimating federal taxes.
† Actual earnings for last 10 months of 1928 and succeeding calendar years.

Receivers were appointed in June 1931. The properties were sold in August of that year, and bondholders later received about 8¹/₂ cents on the dollar.

Principle Derived. From these contrasting instances an investment principle may be developed that should afford a valuable guide to the selection of privileged senior issues. The principle is as follows: *A privileged senior issue, selling close to or above face value, must meet the requirements either of a straight fixed-value investment or of a straight common-stock speculation, and it must be bought with one or the other qualification clearly in view.*

The alternative given supplies two different approaches to the purchase of a privileged security. It may be bought as a sound investment with an *incidental* chance of profit through an enhancement of principal, or it may be bought *primarily* as an attractive form of speculation in the common stock. Generally speaking, there should be no middle ground. The *investor* interested in safety of principal should not abate his requirements in return for a conversion privilege; the *speculator* should not be attracted to an enterprise of mediocre promise because of the pseudo-security provided by the bond contract.

Our opposition to any compromise between the purely investment and the admittedly speculative attitude is based primarily on subjective grounds. Where an intermediate stand is taken, the result is usually confusion, clouded thinking, and self-deception. The investor who relaxes his safety requirements to obtain a profit-sharing privilege is frequently not prepared, financially or mentally, for the inevitable loss if fortune should frown on the venture. The speculator who wants to reduce his risk by operating in convertible issues is likely to find his primary interest divided between the enterprise itself and the terms of the privilege, and he will probably be uncertain in his own mind as to whether he is at bottom a stockholder or a bondholder. (Privileged issues *selling at substantial discounts from par* are not in general subject to this principle, since they belong to the second category of speculative senior securities to be considered later.)

Reverting to our examples, it will be seen at once that the Commonwealth Edison $3^1/_2$s could properly have been purchased as an investment without any regard to the conversion feature. The strong possibility that this privilege would be of value made the bond almost uniquely attractive at the time of issuance. Somewhat similar statements could be made with respect to the Chesapeake and Ohio and the Rand Kardex bonds. Any of these three securities should also have been attractive to a speculator who was persuaded that the related common stock was due for an advance in price.

On the other hand the National Trade Journals Debentures could not have passed stringent qualitative and quantitative tests of safety. Hence they should properly have been of interest only to a person who had full confidence in the future value of the stock. It is hardly likely, however, that most of the buying of this issue was motivated by the primary desire to invest or speculate in the National Trade Journals common stock, but it was based rather on the attractive terms of the conversion privilege and on the feeling that the issue was "fairly safe" as a bond investment. It is precisely this compromise between true investment and true speculation that we disapprove, chiefly because the purchaser has no clear-cut idea of the purpose of his commitment or of the risk that he is incurring.

Rules Regarding Retention or Sale. Having stated a basic principle to guide the *selection* of privileged issues, we ask next what rules can be established regarding their subsequent retention or sale. Convertibles bought primarily as a form of commitment in the common stock may be held for a larger profit than those acquired from the investment standpoint. If a bond of the former class advances from 100 to 150, the large premium need not in itself be a controlling reason for selling out; the owner must be guided rather by his views as to whether or not the common stock has advanced enough to justify taking his profit. But when the purchase is made primarily as a safe bond investment, then the limitation on the amount of profit that can conservatively be waited for comes directly into play. For the reasons explained in detail above, the conservative buyer of privileged issues will not ordinarily hold them for more than a 25 to 35% advance. This means that a really successful investment operation in the convertible field does not cover a long period of time. Hence such issues should be bought with the *possibility* of long-term holding in mind but with the *hope* that the potential profit will be realized fairly soon.

The foregoing discussion leads to the statement of another investment rule, *viz.:*

> In the typical case, a convertible bond should not be converted by the investor. It should be either held or sold.

It is true that the object of the privilege is to bring about such conversion when it seems advantageous. If the price of the bond advances substantially, its current yield will shrink to an unattractive figure, and there is ordinarily a substantial gain in income to be realized through the exchange into stock. Nevertheless when the investor does exchange his bond into the stock, he abandons the priority and the unqualified claim to principal and interest upon which the purchase was originally premised. If after the conversion is made things should go badly, his shares may decline in value far below the original cost of his bond, and he will lose not only his profit but part of his principal as well.

Moreover he is running the risk of transforming himself—generally, as well as in the specific instances—from a bond investor into a stock speculator. It must be recognized that there is something insidious about even a good convertible bond; it can easily prove a costly snare to the unwary. To avoid this danger the investor must cling determinedly to a conservative viewpoint. When the price of his bond has passed out of the investment range, he must sell it; most important of all, he must not consider his judgment impugned if the bond subsequently rises to a much higher level. The market behavior of the issue, once it has entered the speculative range, is no more the investor's affair than the price gyrations of any speculative stock about which he knows nothing.

If the course of action here recommended is followed by investors generally, the conversion of bonds would be brought about only through their purchase for this specific purpose by persons who have decided independently to acquire the shares for either speculation or supposed investment.[6] The arguments against the investor's converting convertible issues apply with equal force against his exercising stock-purchase warrants attached to bonds bought for investment purposes.

A continued policy of investment in privileged issues would, under favorable conditions, require rather frequent taking of profits and replacement by new securities not selling at an excessive premium. More concretely, a bond bought at 100 would be sold, say, at 125 and be replaced by another good convertible issue purchasable at about par. It is not likely that satisfactory opportunities of this kind will be continuously available or that the investor would have the means of locating all those that are at hand. But the trend of financing in recent years offers some promise that a fair number of really attractive convertibles may again make their appearance. Following the 1926–1929 period, marked by a flood of privileged issues generally of poor quality, and the 1930–1934 period, in which the emphasis on safety caused the virtual disappearance of conversion privileges from new bond offerings, there has been a definite swing of the pendulum towards a middle point, where participating features are at times employed to facilitate the sale of sound bond offerings.[7] Most of those sold between 1934 and 1939 either carried very low coupon rates or immediately jumped to a prohibitive premium. But we incline to the view that the discriminating and careful investor is again likely to find a reasonable number of attractive opportunities presented in this field.

---

[6] In actual practice, conversions often result also from arbitrage operations involving the purchase of the bond and the simultaneous sale of the stock at a price slightly higher than the "conversion parity."

[7] For data regarding the relative frequency of privilege issues between 1925 and 1938, see Appendix Note 35, p. 770 on accompanying CD, and the S.E.C. statistical releases referred to in a footnote on page 291.

Chapter 23

TECHNICAL CHARACTERISTICS OF PRIVILEGED SENIOR SECURITIES

IN THE PRECEDING chapter privileged senior issues were considered in their relationship to the broader principles of investment and speculation. To arrive at an adequate knowledge of this group of securities from their practical side, a more intensive discussion of their characteristics is now in order. Such a study may conveniently be carried on from three successive viewpoints: (1) considerations common to all three types of privilege—conversion, participation, and subscription (*i.e.*, "warrant"); (2) the relative merits of each type, as compared with the others; (3) technical aspects of each type, considered by itself.[1]

CONSIDERATIONS GENERALLY APPLICABLE TO PRIVILEGED ISSUES

The attractiveness of a profit-sharing feature depends upon two major but entirely unrelated factors: (1) the *terms* of the arrangement and (2) the *prospects* of profits to share. To use a simple illustration:

Company *A*	Company *B*
4% bond selling at 100	4% bond selling at 100
Convertible into stock at 50 (*i.e.*, two shares of stock for a $100 bond)	Convertible into stock at 33^1/$_3$ (*i.e.*, three shares of stock for a $100 bond)
Stock selling at 30	Stock selling at 30

---

[1] This subject is treated at what may appear to be disproportionate length because of the growing importance of privileged issues and the absence of thoroughgoing discussion thereof in the standard descriptive textbooks.

Terms of the Privilege vs. Prospects for the Enterprise. The *terms* of the conversion privilege are evidently more attractive in the case of Bond *B*; for the stock need advance only a little more than 3 points to assure a profit, whereas Stock *A* must advance over 20 points to make conversion profitable. Nevertheless, it is quite possible that Bond *A* may turn out to be the more advantageous purchase. For conceivably Stock *B* may fail to advance at all while Stock *A* may double or triple in price.

As between the two factors, it is undoubtedly true that it is more profitable to select the right *company* than to select the issue with the most desirable *terms*. There is certainly no mathematical basis on which the attractiveness of the enterprise may be offset against the terms of the privilege, and a balance struck between these two entirely dissociated elements of value. But in analyzing privileged issues of the investment grade, the *terms* of the privilege must receive the greater attention, not because they are more important but because they can be more definitely dealt with. It may seem a comparatively easy matter to determine that one enterprise is more promising than another. But it is by no means so easy to establish that one common stock at a given price is clearly preferable to another stock at its current price.

Reverting to our example, if it were quite certain, or even reasonably probable, that Stock *A* is more likely to advance to 50 than Stock *B* to advance to 33, then both issues would not be quoted at 30. Stock *A*, of course, would be selling higher. The point we make is that the market price in general *reflects already* any superiority that one enterprise has demonstrated over another. The investor who prefers Bond *A* because he expects its related stock to rise a great deal faster than Stock *B*, is exercising independent judgment in a field where certainty is lacking and where mistakes are necessarily frequent. For this reason we doubt that a successful policy of buying privileged issues *from the investment approach* can be based primarily upon the purchaser's view regarding the future expansion of the profits of the enterprise. (In stating this point we are merely repeating a principle previously laid down in the field of fixed-value investment.)

Where the speculative approach is followed, *i.e.*, where the issue is bought primarily as a desirable method of acquiring an interest in the stock, it would be quite logical, of course, to assign dominant weight to the buyer's judgment as to the future of the company.

Three Important Elements. *1. Extent of the Privilege.* In examining the *terms* of a profit-sharing privilege, three component elements are seen to enter. These are:

a. The *extent* of the profit-sharing or speculative interest per dollar of investment.
b. The *closeness* of the privilege to a realizable profit at the time of purchase.
c. The *duration* of the privilege.

The amount of speculative interest attaching to a convertible or warrant-bearing senior security is equal to the current market value of the number of shares of stock covered by the privilege. Other things being equal, the larger the amount of the speculative interest per dollar of investment the more attractive the privilege.

Examples: Rand Kardex $5^{1}/_{2}$s, previously described, carried warrants to buy $22^{1}/_{2}$ shares of Class *A* stock initially at 40. Current price of Class *A* stock was 42. The "speculative interest" amounted to $22^{1}/_{2} \times 42$, or $945 per $1,000 bond.

Reliable Stores Corporation 6s, offered in 1927, carried warrants to buy only 5 shares of common stock initially at 10. Current price of the common was 12. Hence the "speculative interest" amounted to 5×12, or only $60 per $1,000 bond.

Intercontinental Rubber Products Co. 7s offered an extraordinary example of a large speculative interest attaching to a bond. As a result of peculiar provisions surrounding their issuance in 1922, each $1,000 note was convertible into 100 shares of stock and also carried the right to purchase 400 additional shares at 10. When the stock sold at 10 in 1925, the speculative interest per $1,000 note amounted to 500×10, or $5,000. If the notes were then selling, say, at 120, the speculative interest would have equalled 417% of the bond investment—or 70 *times* as great as in the case of the Reliable Stores offering.

The practical importance of the amount of speculative interest can be illustrated by the following comparison, covering the three examples above given.

Item	Reliable Stores 6s	Rand Kardex 5¹/₂s	Intercontinental Rubber 7s
Number of shares covered by each $1,000 bond	5	22¹/₂	500
Base price	$10.00	$40.00	$10.00
Increase in value of bond when stock advances:			
25% above base price	12.50	225.00	1,250.00
50% above base price	25.00	450.00	2,500.00
100% above base price	50.00	900.00	5,000.00

In the case of convertible bonds the speculative interest always amounts to 100% of the bond at par when the stock sells at the conversion price. Hence in these issues our first and second component elements express the same fact. If a bond selling at par is convertible into stock at 50, and if the stock sells at 30, then the speculative interest amounts to 60% of the commitment, which is the same thing as saying that the current price of the stock is 60% of that needed before conversion would be profitable. Stock-purchase-warrant issues disclose no such fixed relationship between the amount of the speculative interest and the proximity of this interest to a realizable profit. In the case of the Reliable Stores 6s, the speculative interest was very small, but it showed an actual profit at the time of issuance, since the stock was selling *above* the subscription price.

Significance of Call on Large Number of Shares at Low Price. It may be said parenthetically that a speculative interest in a large number of shares selling at a low price is technically more attractive than one in a smaller number of shares selling at a high price. This is because low-priced shares are apt to fluctuate over a wider range *percentagewise* than higher priced stocks. Hence if a bond is both well secured and convertible into many shares at a low price, it will have an excellent chance for very large profit without being subject to the offsetting risk of greater loss through a speculative dip in the price of the stock.

For example, as a matter of *form* of privilege, the Ohio Copper Company 7s, due 1931, convertible into 1,000 shares of stock selling at $1, had better possibilities than the Atchison, Topeka and Santa Fe Convertible 4¹/₂s, due 1948, convertible into 6 shares of common, selling at 166²/₃, although in each case the amount of speculative interest equalled $1,000 per bond. As it turned out, Ohio Copper stock advanced from less than $1 a share in 1928 to $4^7/8$ in 1929, making the bond worth close to 500% of par. It would have required a rise in the price of Atchison from 166 to 800 to yield the same profit on the convertible $4^1/2$s, but the highest price reached in 1929 was under 300.

In the case of *participating issues*, the extent of the profit-sharing interest would ordinarily be considered in terms of the amount of extra income that may conceivably be obtained as a result of the privilege. A limited extra payment (*e.g.*, Bayuk Cigars, Inc., 7% Preferred, which may receive not more than 1% additional) is of course less attractive than an unlimited participation (*e.g.*, White Rock Mineral Springs Company 5% Second Preferred, which received a total of $26^1/4$% in 1930).

2 and 3. Closeness and Duration of the Privilege. The implications of the second and third factors in valuing a privilege are readily apparent. A privilege having a long period to run is in that respect more desirable than one expiring in a short time. The nearer the current price of the stock to the level at which conversion or subscription becomes profitable the more attractive does the privilege become. In the case of a participation feature, it is similarly desirable that the current dividends or earnings on the common stock should be close to the figure at which the extra distribution on the senior issue commences.

By "conversion price" is meant the price of the common stock equivalent to a price of 100 for the convertible issue. If a preferred stock is convertible into $1^2/3$ as many shares of common, the conversion price of the common is therefore 60. The term "conversion parity," or "conversion level," may be used to designate that price of the common which is equivalent to a given quotation for the convertible issue, or *vice versa*. It can be found by multiplying the price of the convertible issue by the conversion price of the common. If the preferred stock just mentioned is selling at 90, the conversion parity of the common becomes $60 \times 90\% = 54$. This means that to a buyer of the preferred at 90 an advance in the common above 54 will create a realizable profit. Conversely, if the common sold at 66, one might say that the conversion parity of the preferred is 110.

The "closeness" of the privilege may be stated arithmetically as the ratio between the market price and the conversion parity of the common stock. In the foregoing example, if the common is selling at 54 and the preferred at 110 (equivalent to 66 for the common), the "index of closeness" becomes 54 ÷ 66, or 0.82.

COMPARATIVE MERITS OF THE THREE TYPES OF PRIVILEGES

From the theoretical standpoint, a participating feature—unlimited in time and possible amount—is the most desirable type of profit-sharing privilege. This arrangement enables the investor to derive the specific benefit of participation in profits (*viz.*, increased income) without modifying his original position as a senior-security holder. These benefits may be received over a long period of years. By contrast, a conversion privilege can result in higher income only through actual exchange into the stock and consequent surrender of the senior position. Its real advantage consists, therefore, only of the opportunity to make a profit through the sale of the convertible issue at the right time. Similarly the benefits from a subscription privilege may conservatively be realized only through sale of the warrants (or by the subscription to and prompt sale of the stock). If the common stock is purchased and held for permanent income, the operation involves the risking of additional money on a basis entirely different from the original purchase of the senior issue.

Example of Advantage of Unlimited Participation Privilege.
An excellent practical example of the theoretical advantages attaching to a well-entrenched participating security is afforded by Westinghouse Electric and Manufacturing Company Preferred. This issue is entitled to cumulative prior dividends of $3.50 per annum (7% on $50 par) and in addition participates equally per share with the common in any dividends paid on the latter in excess of $3.50. As far back as 1917 Westinghouse Preferred could have been bought at 52$^{1}/_{2}$, representing an attractive straight investment with additional possibilities through its participating feature. In the ensuing 15 years to 1932 a total of about $7 per share was disbursed in extra dividends above the basic 7%. In the meantime an opportunity arose to sell out at a large profit (the high price being 284 in 1929), which corresponded to the enhancement possibilities of a convertible or subscription-warrant issue. If the stock was not sold, the profit was naturally lost in the ensuing market decline. But the investor's original position remained unimpaired, for at the low point of 1932 the issue was

still paying the 7% dividend and selling at 52 $1/2$—although the common had passed its dividend and had fallen to 15 $5/8$.

In this instance the investor was able to participate in the surplus profits of the common stock in good years while maintaining his preferred position, so that, when the bad years came, he lost only his temporary *profit*. Had the issue been convertible instead of participating, the investor could have received the higher dividends only through converting and would later have found the dividend omitted on his common shares and their value fallen far below his original investment.

Participating Issues at Disadvantage, Marketwise. Although from the standpoint of long-pull-investment holding, participating issues are theoretically the most desirable, they may behave somewhat less satisfactorily in a major market upswing than do convertible or subscription-warrant issues. During such a period a participating senior security may regularly sell below its proper comparative price. In the case of Westinghouse Preferred, for example, its price during 1929 was usually from 5 to 10 points lower than that of the common, although its intrinsic value per share could not be less than that of the junior stock.[2]

The reason for this phenomenon is as follows: The price of the common stock is made largely by speculators interested chiefly in quick profits, to secure which they need an active market. The preferred stock, being closely held, is relatively inactive. Consequently the speculators are willing to pay several points more for the inferior common issue simply because it can be bought and sold more readily and because other speculators are likely to be willing to pay more for it also.

The same anomaly arises in the case of closely held common stocks with voting power, compared with the more active nonvoting issue of the same company. American Tobacco *B* and Liggett and Myers Tobacco *B* (both nonvoting) have for years sold higher than the voting stock. A similar situation formerly existed in the two common issues of Bethlehem

---

[2] A much greater price discrepancy of this kind existed in the case of White Rock Mineral Springs Participating Preferred and common during 1929 and 1930. Because of this market situation, holders of nearly all the participating preferred shares accepted an offer to exchange into common stock, although this meant no gain in income and the loss of their senior position.

Steel, Pan American Petroleum and others.[3] The paradoxical principle holds true for the securities market generally that *in the absence of a special demand* relative scarcity is likely to make for a lower rather than a higher price.

In cases such as Westinghouse and American Tobacco the proper corporate policy would be to extend to the holder of the intrinsically more valuable issue the privilege of exchanging it for the more active but intrinsically inferior issue. The White Rock company actually took this step. Although the holders of the participating preferred might make a mistake in accepting such an offer, they cannot object to its being made to them, and the common stockholders may gain but cannot lose through its acceptance.

Relative Price Behavior of Convertible and Warrant-bearing Issues. From the standpoint of price behavior under favorable market conditions the best results are obtained by holders of senior securities with detachable stock-purchase warrants.

To illustrate this point we shall compare certain price relationships shown in 1929 between four privileged issues and the corresponding common stocks. The issues are as follows:

1. Mohawk Hudson Power Corporation 7% Second Preferred, carrying warrants to buy 2 shares of common at 50 for each share of preferred.

2. White Sewing Machine Corporation 6% Debentures, due 1936, carrying warrants to buy $2^{1}/_{2}$ shares of common stock for each $100 bond.

3. Central States Electric Corporation 6% Preferred, convertible into common stock at $118 per share.

4. Independent Oil and Gas Company Debentures 6s, due 1939, convertible into common stock at $32 per share.

The following table shows in striking fashion that in speculative markets issues with purchase warrants have a tendency to sell at large premiums in relation to the common-stock price and that these premiums are much greater than in the case of similarly situated convertible issues.

---

[3] The persistently wide spread between the market prices for R. J. Reynolds Tobacco Company common and Class *B* stocks rests on the special circumstance that officers and employees of the company who own the common stock enjoy certain profit-sharing benefits not accorded to holders of the Class *B* stock. The New York Stock Exchange will no longer list nonvoting common stocks, nor are these permitted to be issued in reorganizations effected under Chap. X of the 1938 Bankruptcy Act.

Senior issue	Market price of common	Conversion or subscrip- tion price of common	Price of senior issue	Realizable value of senior issue based on privilege (conversion or subscrip- tion parity)	Amount by which senior issue sold above parity, ("pre- mium"), points
Mohawk Hudson 2d Pfd	52$\frac{1}{2}$	50	163*	105	58
White Sewing Machine 6s	39	40	123$\frac{1}{2}$†	97$\frac{1}{2}$	26
Central States Electric Pfd	116	118	97	98	−1
Independent Oil & Gas 6s	31	32	105	97	8

* Consisting of 107 for the preferred stock, ex-warrants, plus 56 for the warrants.
† Consisting of 98$\frac{1}{2}$ for the bonds, ex-warrants, plus 25 for the warrants.

Advantage of Separability of Speculative Component. This advantage of subscription-warrant issues is due largely to the fact that their speculative component (*i.e.*, the subscription warrant itself) can be entirely separated from their investment component (*i.e.*, the bond or preferred stock ex-warrants). Speculators are always looking for a chance to make large profits on a small cash commitment. This is a distinguishing characteristic of stock option warrants, as will be shown in detail in our later discussion of these instruments. In an advancing market, therefore, speculators bid for the warrants attached to these privileged issues, and hence they sell separately at a substantial price even though they may have no immediate exercisable value. These speculators greatly prefer buying the option warrants to buying a corresponding *convertible bond*, because the latter requires a much larger cash investment per share of common stock involved.[4] It follows, therefore, that the separate market

[4] Note that the Independent Oil and Gas bonds represented a commitment of $33.60 per share of common, whereas the White Sewing Machine warrants involved a commitment of only $10 per share of common. But the former meant *ownership* of either a fixed claim or a share of stock, whereas the latter meant only the *right to buy* a share of stock at a price above the market.

values of the bond plus the option warrant (which combine to make the price of the bond "with warrants") may considerably exceed the single quotation for a closely similar convertible issue.

Second Advantage of Warrant-bearing Issues. Subscription-warrant issues have a second point of superiority, in respect to callable provisions. A right reserved by the corporation to redeem an issue prior to maturity must in general be considered as a disadvantage to the holder; for presumably it will be exercised only when it is to the benefit of the issuer to do so, which means usually that the security would otherwise sell for more than the call price.[5] A callable provision, unless at a very high premium, might entirely vitiate the value of a participating privilege. For with such a provision there would be danger of redemption as soon as the company grew prosperous enough to place the issue in line for extra distributions.[6] In some cases participating issues that are callable are made convertible as well, in order to give them a chance to benefit from any large advance in the market price of the common that may have taken place up to the time of call. (See for examples: National Distillers Products Corporation $2.50 Cumulative Participating Convertible Preferred;[7] Kelsey-Hayes Wheel Company $1.50 Participating Convertible Class A stock.) Participating *bonds* are generally limited in their right to participate in surplus earnings and are commonly callable. (See White Sewing Machine Corporation Participating Debenture 6s, due 1940;

---

[5] The callable feature may be—and recently has been—an unfavorable element of great importance even in "straight" nonconvertible bonds.

In a few cases a callable feature works out to the advantage of the holder, by facilitating new financing which involves the redemption of the old issue at a price above the previous market. But the same result could be obtained, if there were no right to call, by an offer to "buy in" the security. This was done in the case of United States Steel Corporation 5s, due 1951, which were not callable but were bought in at 110.

[6] Dewing cites the case of Union Pacific Railroad—Oregon Short Line Participating 4s, issued in 1903, which were secured by the pledge of Northern Securities Company stock. The bondholders had the right to participate in any dividends in excess of 4% declared on the deposited collateral. The bonds were called at 102$\frac{1}{2}$ just at the time when participating distributions seemed likely to occur. See Arthur S. Dewing, *A Study of Corporation Securities*, p. 328, New York, 1934.

[7] Coincident with the rise of the common stock from 16$\frac{7}{8}$ to 124$\frac{7}{8}$ in 1933, all the National Distillers Preferred Stock was converted in that year. Nearly all the conversions were precipitated by a change in the conversion rate after June 30, 1933. The small balance was converted as a result of the calling of issue at 40 and dividend in August.

United Steel Works Corporation Participating 6^1/$_2$s, Series *A*, due 1947; neither of which is convertible.) Sometimes participating issues are protected against loss of the privilege through redemption by setting the call price at a very high figure. Something of this sort was apparently attempted in the case of San Francisco Toll-Bridge Company Participating 7s, due 1942, which were callable at 120 through November 1, 1933, and at lower prices thereafter. Celluloid Corporation Participating Second Preferred is callable at 150, whereas Celanese Corporation Participating First Preferred is noncallable.

Another device to prevent vitiating the participating privilege through redemption is to make the issue callable at a price that may be directly dependent upon the value of the participating privilege. For example, Siemens and Halske Participating Debentures, due in 1930, are callable after April 1, 1942, *at the average market price for the issue during the six months preceding notice of redemption but at not less than the original issue price* (which was over 230% of the par value). The Kreuger and Toll 5% Participating Debentures had similar provisions.

Even in the case of a *convertible* issue a callable feature is technically a serious drawback because it may operate to reduce the duration of the privilege. Conceivably a convertible bond may be called just when the privilege is about to acquire real value.[8]

But in the case of issues with stock-purchase warrants, the subscription privilege almost invariably runs its full time even though the senior issue itself may be called prior to maturity. If the warrant is detachable, it simply continues its separate existence until its own expiration date. Frequently, the subscription privilege is made "nondetachable"; *i.e.*, it can be exercised only by presentation of the senior security. But even in these

---

[8] This danger was avoided in the case of Atchison, Topeka and Santa Fe Railway Convertible 4^1/$_2$s, due 1948, by permitting the issue to be called only after the conversion privilege expired in 1938. (On the other hand, Affiliated Fund Secured Convertible Debentures are callable at par at any time on 30 days' notice, in effect allowing the company to destroy any chance of profiting from the conversion privilege.)

Another protective device recently employed is to give the holder of a convertible issue a stock-purchase warrant, at the time the issue is redeemed, entitling the holder to buy the number of shares of common stock that would have been received upon conversion if the senior issue had not been redeemed. See Freeport Texas Company 6% Cumulative Convertible Preferred, issued in January 1933. United Biscuit 7% Preferred, convertible into 2^1/$_2$ shares of common, is callable at 110; but if called before Dec. 31, 1935, the holder had the option to take $100 in cash, plus a warrant to buy 2^1/$_2$ shares of common at 40 until Jan. 1, 1936.

instances, if the issue should be redeemed prior to the expiration of the purchase-option period, it is customary to give the holder a separate warrant running for the balance of the time originally provided.

Example: Prior to January 1, 1934, United Aircraft and Transport Corporation had outstanding 150,000 shares of 6% Cumulative Preferred stock. These shares carried nondetachable warrants for one share of common stock at $30 a share for each two shares of preferred stock held. The subscription privilege was to run to November 1, 1938, and was protected by a provision for the issuance of a detached warrant evidencing the same privilege per share in case the preferred stock was redeemed prior to November 1, 1938. Some of the preferred stock was called for redemption on January 1, 1933, and detached warrants were accordingly issued to the holders thereof. (A year later the remainder of the issue was called and additional warrants issued.)

Third Advantage of Warrant-bearing Issues. Subscription-warrant issues have still a third advantage over other privileged securities, and this is in a practical sense probably the most important of all. Let us consider what courses of conduct are open to holders of each type in the favorable event that the company prospers, that a high dividend is paid on the common, and that the common sells at a high price.

1. Holder of a participating issue:
   a. May sell at a profit.
   b. May hold and receive participating income.
2. Holder of a convertible issue:
   a. May sell at a profit.
   b. May hold but will receive no benefit from high common dividend.
   c. May convert to secure larger income but sacrifices his senior position.
3. Holder of an issue with stock-purchase warrants:
   a. May sell at a profit.
   b. May hold but will receive no benefit from high common dividend.
   c. May subscribe to common to receive high dividend. He may invest new capital, or he may sell or apply his security ex-warrants to provide funds to pay for the common. In either case he undertakes the risks of a common stockholder in order to receive the high dividend income.

d. May dispose of his warrants at a cash profit and retain his original security, ex-warrants. (The warrant may be sold directly, or he may subscribe to the stock and immediately sell it at the current indicated profit.)

The fourth option listed above is peculiar to a subscription-warrant issue and has no counterpart in convertible or participating securities. It permits the holder to cash his profit from the speculative component of the issue and still maintain his original *investment* position. Since the typical buyer of a privileged senior issue should be interested primarily in making a sound investment—with a secondary opportunity to profit from the privilege—this fourth optional course of conduct may prove a great convenience. He is not under the necessity of selling the entire commitment, as he would be if he owned a convertible, which would then require him to find some new medium for the funds involved. The reluctance to sell one good thing and buy another, which characterizes the typical investor, is one of the reasons that holders of high-priced convertibles are prone to convert them rather than to dispose of them. In the case of participating issues also, the owner can protect his *principal* profit only by selling out and thus creating a reinvestment problem.

Example: The theoretical and practical advantage of subscription-warrant issues in this respect may be illustrated in the case of Commercial Investment Trust Corporation $6^{1}/_{2}\%$ Preferred. This was issued in 1925 and carried warrants to buy common stock at an initial price of $80 per share. In 1929 the warrants sold as high as $69.50 per share of preferred. The holder of this issue was therefore enabled to sell out its speculative component at a high price and to retain his original preferred-stock commitment, which maintained an investment status throughout the depression until it was finally called for redemption at 110 on April 1, 1933. At the time of the redemption call the common stock was selling at the equivalent of about $50 per old share. If the preferred stock had been convertible, instead of carrying warrants, many of the holders would undoubtedly have been led to convert and to retain the common shares. Instead of netting a large profit they would have been faced with a substantial loss.

Summary. To summarize this section, it may be said that, for *long-pull holding*, a sound participating issue represents the best form of profit-sharing privilege. From the standpoint of maximum *price advance* under favorable market conditions, a senior issue with detachable stock-purchase warrants is likely to show the best results. Furthermore, subscription-warrant issues as a class have definite advantages in that the privilege is ordinarily not subject to curtailment through early redemption of the security, and they permit the realization of a speculative profit while retaining the original investment position.

Chapter 24

TECHNICAL ASPECTS OF
CONVERTIBLE ISSUES

THE THIRD DIVISION of the subject of privileged issues relates to technical aspects of each type, separately considered. We shall first discuss convertible issues.

The effective terms of a conversion privilege are frequently subject to change during the life of the issue. These changes are of two kinds: (1) a decrease in the conversion price, to protect the holder against "dilution"; and (2) an increase in the conversion price (in accordance usually with a "sliding-scale" arrangement) for the benefit of the company.

Dilution, and Antidilution Clauses. The value of a common stock is said to be diluted if there is an increase in the number of shares without a corresponding increase in assets and earning power. Dilution may arise through split-ups, stock dividends, offers of subscription rights at a low price, and issuance of stock for property or services at a low valuation per share. The standard "antidilution" provisions of a convertible issue endeavor to reduce the conversion price proportionately to any decrease in the per-share value arising through any act of dilution.

The method may be expressed in a formula, as follows: Let C be the conversion price, O be the number of shares now outstanding, N be the number of new shares to be issued, and P be the price at which they are to be issued.

Then

$$C' \text{ (the new conversion price)} = \frac{CO + NP}{O + N}$$

The application of this formula to Chesapeake Corporation Convertible Collateral 5s, due 1947, is given in Appendix Note 36, page 770 on accompanying CD. A simpler example of an antidilution adjustment is afforded by the Central States Electric Corporation 6% Convertible Preferred previously referred to (page 306). After its issuance in 1928, the common stock received successive stock dividends of 100 and 200%. The conversion price was accordingly first cut in half (from $118 to $59 per share) and then again reduced by two-thirds (to $19.66 per share).

A much less frequent provision merely reduces the conversion price to any lower figure at which new shares may be issued. This is, of course, more favorable to the holder of the convertible issue.[1]

Protection against Dilution Not Complete. Although practically all convertibles now have antidilution provisions, there have been exceptions.[2] As a matter of course, a prospective buyer should make certain that such protection exists for the issue he is considering.

It should be borne in mind that the effect of these provisions is to preserve only the principal or par value of the privileged issue against dilution. If a convertible is selling considerably above par, the *premium* will still be subject to impairment through additional stock issues or a special dividend. A simple illustration will make this clear.

A bond is convertible into stock, par for par. The usual antidilution clauses are present. Both bond and stock are selling at 200.

Stockholders are given the right to buy new stock, share for share, at par ($100). These rights will be worth $50 per share, and the new stock (or the old stock "ex-rights") will be worth 150. No change will be made in the conversion basis, because the new stock is not issued below the old conversion price. However, the effect of offering these rights must be to compel immediate conversion of the bonds, since otherwise they would lose 25% of their value. As the stock will be worth only 150 "ex-rights," instead of 200, the value of the unconverted bonds would drop proportionately.

The foregoing discussion indicates that, when a large premium or market profit is created for a privileged issue, the situation is vulnerable to sudden change. Although prompt action will always prevent loss through such changes, their effect is always to terminate the effective life of the

---

[1] See Appendix Note 37, p. 772 on accompanying CD, for example (Consolidated Textile Corporation 7s, due 1923).

[2] See Appendix Note 38, p. 772 on accompanying CD, for example (American Telephone and Telegraph Company Convertible 4$^{1}/_{2}$s, due 1933).

privilege.[3] The same result will follow, of course, from the calling of a privileged issue for redemption at a price below its then conversion value.

Where the number of shares is *reduced* through recapitalization, it is customary to *increase* the conversion price proportionately. Such recapitalization measures include increases in par value, "reverse split-ups" (*e.g.*, issuance of 1 no-par share in place of, say, 5 old shares), and exchanges of the old stock for fewer new shares through consolidation with another company.[4]

Sliding Scales Designed to Accelerate Conversion.

The provisions just discussed are intended to maintain equitably the original basis of conversion in the event of subsequent capitalization changes. On the other hand, a "sliding-scale" arrangement is intended definitely to reduce the value of the privilege as time goes on. The underlying purpose is to accelerate conversion, in other words, to curtail the effective duration and hence the real value of the option. Obviously, any diminution of the worth of the privilege to its recipients must correspondingly benefit the donors of the privilege, who are the company's common shareholders.

The more usual terms of a sliding scale prescribe a series of increases in the conversion price in successive periods of time. A more recent variation makes the conversion price increase as soon as a certain portion of the issue has been exchanged.

Examples: American Telephone and Telegraph Company Ten-year Debenture 4^1/2s, due 1939, issued in 1929, were made convertible into common at $180 per share during 1930, at $190 per share during 1931 and 1932, and at $200 per share during 1933 to 1937, inclusive. These prices were later reduced through the issuance of additional stock at $100, in accordance with the standard antidilution provision.

---

[3] To guard against this form of dilution, holders of convertible issues are sometimes given the right to subscribe to any new offerings of common stock on the same basis as if they owned the amount of common shares into which their holdings are convertible. See the indentures securing New York, New Haven and Hartford Railroad Company, Convertible Debenture 6s, due 1948, and Commercial Investment Trust Corporation Convertible Debenture 5^1/2s, due 1949.

[4] See Appendix Note 39, p. 773 on accompanying CD, for example of Dodge Brothers, Inc., Convertible Debenture 6s, due 1940.

Anaconda Copper Mining Company Debenture 7s, due 1938, were issued in the amount of $50,000,000. The first $10,000,000 presented were convertible into common stock at $53 per share; the second $10,000,000 were convertible at $56; the third at $59; the fourth at $62, and the final lot at $65. An $8,000,000 issue of Hiram Walker-Goderham and Worts 4¹/₄s, due 1945, was convertible as follows: at $40 per share for the first $2,000,000 block of bonds; at $45 per share for the next block of $2,000,000; the third block at $55; and the final block at $60 per share.

Sliding Scale Based on Time Intervals. The former type of sliding scale, based on time intervals, is a readily understandable method of reducing the liberality of a conversion privilege. Its effect can be shown in the case of Porto Rican-American Tobacco Company 6s, due 1942. These were convertible into pledged Congress Cigar Company, Inc., stock at $80 per share prior to January 2, 1929, at $85 during the next three years and at $90 thereafter. During 1928 the highest price reached by Congress Cigar was 87¹/₄, which was only a moderate premium above the conversion price. Nevertheless a number of holders were induced to convert before the year-end, because of the impending rise in the conversion basis. These conversions proved very ill-advised, since the price of the common fell to 43 in 1929, against a low of 89 for the bonds. In this instance, the adverse change in the conversion basis not only meant a smaller potential profit for those who delayed conversion until after 1928 but also involved a risk of serious loss through inducing conversion at the wrong time.

Sliding Scale Based on Extent Privilege Is Exercised. The second method, however, based on the quantities converted, is not so simple in its implications. Since it gives the first lot of bonds converted an advantage over the next, it evidently provides a *competitive* stimulus to early conversion. By so doing it creates a conflict in the minds of the holder between the desire to retain his senior position and the fear of losing the more favorable basis of conversion through prior action by other bondholders. This fear of being forestalled will ordinarily result in large-scale conversions as soon as the stock advances moderately above the initial conversion price, *i.e.*, as soon as the bond is worth slightly more than the original cost. Accordingly, the price of the senior issue should oscillate over a relatively narrow range while the common stock is advancing and while successive blocks of bonds are being converted.

Example: The sequence of events normally to be expected is shown fairly well by the market action of Hiram Walker-Goderham and Worts Convertible 4¹/₄s described on page 312. The bonds, issued in 1936 at par, ranged in price between 100 and 111¹/₄ during 1936–1939. In the same period the stock ranged between 26¹/₈ and 54. If the initial conversion price of 40 for the stock had prevailed throughout the period, the bonds should have sold for at least 135 when the stock sold at 54. But meanwhile, as the price of the stock rose, successive blocks of the bonds were converted (partly under the impetus supplied by successive calls for redemption of parts of the issue), thus tipping off higher conversion prices until the $55 bracket was reached in 1937. In consequence the bonds did not appreciate commensurately with the rise in the price of the stock.[5]

When the last block under such a sliding scale is reached, the *competitive* element disappears, and the bond or preferred stock is then in the position of an ordinary convertible, free to advance indefinitely with the stock.

It should be pointed out that issues with such a sliding-scale provision do not always follow this theoretical behavior pattern. The Anaconda Copper Company Convertible 7s, for example, actually sold at a high premium (30%) in 1928, before the first block was exhausted. This seems to have been one of the anomalous incidents of the highly speculative atmosphere at the time.[6] From the standpoint of critical analysis, a convertible of this type must be considered as having very limited possibilities of enhancement until the common stock approaches the last and highest conversion price.[7]

The sliding-scale privilege on a "block" basis belongs to the objectionable category of devices that tend to mislead the holder of securities as

---

[5] See pp. 266–267 of the 1934 edition of this work for a more detailed exhibit of a similar record in Engineers Public Service Company $5 Convertible Preferred in 1928–1929.

[6] The size of the premium was due in part to the high coupon rate. The bonds were, however, callable at 110, a point that the market ignored.

[7] In some cases (*e.g.*, Porto Rican-American 6s, already mentioned, and International Paper and Power Company First Preferred) the conversion privilege ceases entirely after a certain fraction of the issue has been converted. This maintains the competitive factor throughout the life of the privilege and in theory should prevent it from ever having any substantial value.

to the real nature and value of what he owns. The competitive pressure to take advantage of a limited opportunity introduces an element of compulsion into the exercise of the conversion right which is directly opposed to that freedom of choice for a reasonable time which is the essential merit of such a privilege. There seems no reason why investment bankers should inject so confusing and contradictory a feature into a security issue. Sound practice would dictate its complete abandonment or in any event the avoidance of such issues by intelligent investors.

Issues Convertible into Preferred Stock. Many bond issues were formerly made convertible into preferred stock. Ordinarily some increase in income was offered to make the provision appear attractive. (For examples, see Missouri-Kansas-Texas Railroad Company Adjustment 5s, due 1967, convertible prior to January 1, 1932 into $7 preferred stock; Central States Electric Corporation Debenture 5s, due 1948, convertible into $6 preferred stock; G. R. Kinney Company Secured $7^1/2$s, due 1936, convertible into $8 preferred stock; American Electric Power Corporation 6s, due 1957, convertible into $7 preferred stock.)

There have been instances in which a fair-sized profit has been realized through such a conversion right, but the upper limitation on the market value of the ordinary preferred stock is likely to keep down the maximum benefits from such a privilege to a modest figure. Moreover, since developments in recent years have made preferred stocks in general appear far less desirable than formerly, the right to convert, say, from a 4% bond into a 5% preferred is likely to constitute more of a danger to the unwary than an inducement to the alert investor. If the latter is looking for convertibles, he should canvass the market thoroughly and endeavor to find a suitably secured issue convertible into common stock. In a few cases where bonds are convertible into preferred stock, the latter is in turn convertible into common or participates therewith, and this double arrangement may be equivalent to convertibility of the bond into common stock. For example, International Hydro-Electric System 6s, due 1944, are convertible into Class *A* stock, which is in reality a participating second preferred.

There are also bond issues convertible into either preferred or common or into a combination of certain amounts of each.[8] Although any individual issue of this sort may turn out well, in general it may be said that complicated provisions of this sort should be avoided (both by issuing companies and by security buyers) because they tend to create confusion.

Bonds Convertible at the Option of the Company. The unending flood of variations in the terms of conversion and other privileges that developed during the 1920's made it difficult for the untrained investor to distinguish between the attractive, the merely harmless, and the positively harmful. Hence he proved an easy victim to unsound financing practices which in former times might have stood out as questionable because of their departure from the standard. As an example of this sort we cite the various Associated Gas and Electric Company "Convertible Obligations" which were made convertible by their terms into preferred or Class *A* stock *at the option of the company.* Such a contraption was nothing more than a preferred stock masquerading as a bond. If the purchasers were entirely aware of this fact and were willing to invest in the preferred stock, they would presumably have no cause to complain. But it goes without saying that an artifice of this kind lends itself far too readily to concealment and possible misrepresentation.[9]

---

[8] See, for example, the Chicago, Milwaukee, St. Paul and Pacific Railroad Company Convertible Adjustment Mortgage 5s, Series *A*, due Jan. 1, 2000, which are convertible into 5 shares of the preferred and 5 shares of common. For other examples see p. 623 in the Appendix of the 1934 edition of this work.

[9] These anomalous securities were variously entitled "investment certificates," "convertible debenture certificates," "interest-bearing allotment certificates," and "convertible obligations." In 1932 the company compelled the conversion of the large majority of them, but the holder was given an option (in addition to those already granted by the terms of the issues) of converting into equally anomalous "Convertible Obligations, Series *A* and *B*, due 2022," which are likewise convertible into stock at the option of the company. The company was deterred from compelling the conversion of some $17,000,000 "5$1/2$% Investment Certificates" after Nov. 15, 1933, by a provision in the indenture for that issue prohibiting the exercise of the company's option in case dividends on the $5.50 Dividend Series Preferred were in arrears (no dividends having been paid thereon since June 15, 1932).

It is interesting to note that the Pennsylvania Securities Commission prohibited the sale of these "Convertible Obligations" in December 1932 because of their objectionable provisions. The company resisted the Commission's order in the Federal District Court of

Bonds Convertible into Other Bonds. Some bonds are convertible into other bonds. The usual case is that of a short-term issue, the holder of which is given the right to exchange into a long-term bond of the same company. Frequently the long-term bond is deposited as collateral security for the note. (For example, Interborough Rapid Transit Company 7s, due 1932, were secured by deposit of $1,736 of the same company's First and Refunding 5s, due 1966, for each $1,000 note, and they were also convertible into the deposited collateral, the final rate being $1,000 of 5s for $900 of 7% notes.) The holder thus has an option either to demand repayment at an early date or to make a long-term commitment in the enterprise. In practice, this amounts merely to the chance of a moderate profit at or before maturity, in the event that the company prospers, or interest rates fall, or both.

Unlike the case of a bond convertible into a preferred stock, there is usually a *reduction* in the coupon rate when a short-term note is converted into a long-term bond. The reason is that short-term notes are ordinarily issued when interest rates, either in general or for the specific company, are regarded as abnormally high, so that the company is unwilling to incur so steep a rate for a long-term bond. It is thus expected that, when normal conditions return, long-term bonds can be floated at a much lower rate; and hence the right to exchange the note for a long-term bond, even on a basis involving some reduction in income, may prove to be valuable.[10]

Convertible Bonds with an Original Market Value in Excess of Par. One of the extraordinary developments of the 1928–1929 financial

---

Philadelphia but later dropped its suit (see 135 *Chronicle* 4383, 4559; 136 *Chronicle* 326, 1011).

[10] See the following issues taken from the 1920–1921 period: Shawinigan Water and Power Company 7^{1}/2% Gold Notes, issued in 1920 and due in 1926, convertible into First and Refunding 6s, Series B, due 1950, which were pledged as security; San Joaquin Light and Power Corporation Convertible Collateral Trust 8s, issued in 1920 and due in 1935, convertible into the pledged Series C First and Refunding 6s, due 1950; Great Western Power Company of California Convertible Gold 8s, issued in 1920 and due in 1930, convertible into pledged First and Refunding 7s, Series B, due in 1950.

Another type of bond-for-bond conversion is represented by Dawson Railway and Coal 5s, due 1951, which are convertible into El Paso and Southwestern Railroad Company First 5s, due 1965 (the parent company, which in turn is a subsidiary of the Southern Pacific). Such examples are rare and do not invite generalization.

pyrotechnics was the offering of convertible issues with an original market value greatly in excess of par. This is illustrated by Atchison, Topeka and Santa Fe Railway Company Convertible 4¹/2s, due 1948, and by American Telephone and Telegraph Company Convertible 4¹/2s, due 1939. Initial trading in the former on the New York Curb Market (on a "when issued" basis) in November 1928 was around 125, and initial trading in the latter on the New York Stock Exchange (on a "when issued" basis) on May 1, 1929, was at 142. Obviously investment in the bonds at these levels represented primarily a commitment in the common stock, since they were immediately subject to the danger of a substantial loss of principal value if the stock declined. Furthermore the income return was entirely too low to come under our definition of investment. Although it may be thought that the stockholders were acquiring a normal investment through the exercise of their subscription right to purchase the issues at par, the essential nature of their commitment was determined by the initial market value of the security to which they were subscribing. For this reason we think such financing should be condemned, because under the guise of an attractive investment it created a basically speculative form of security.

A Technical Feature of Some Convertible Issues. A technical feature of the American Telephone and Telegraph convertible issue deserves mention. The bonds were made convertible at 180, but, instead of presenting $180 of bonds to obtain a share of stock, the holder might present $100 of bonds and $80 in cash. The effect of such an option is to make the bond more valuable whenever the stock sells above 180 (*i.e.*, whenever the conversion value of the bond exceeds 100). This is illustrated as follows:

If the stock sells at 360, a straight conversion basis of 180 would make the bond worth 200. But by the provision accepting $80 per share in cash, the value of the bond becomes $360 - 80 = 280$.

This arrangement may be characterized as a combination of a conversion privilege at 180 with a stock purchase right at 100.

Delayed Conversion Privilege. The privilege of converting is sometimes not operative immediately upon issuance of the obligation.

Examples: This was true, for example, of Brooklyn Union Gas Company Convertible 5¹/2s, discussed in Note 38 of the Appendix on accompanying CD. Although they were issued in December 1925, the right to convert did not accrue until January 1, 1929. Similarly, New York, New Haven, and Hartford Railroad Company Convertible Debenture 6s, due in 1948, although issued in 1907, were not convertible until January 15, 1923; Chesapeake Corporation Convertible 5s, due 1947, were issued in 1927 but did not become convertible until May 15, 1932.

More commonly the suspension of the conversion privilege does not last so long as these examples indicate, but in any event this practice introduces an additional factor of uncertainty and tends to render the privilege less valuable than it would be otherwise. This feature may account in part for the spread, indicated in Note 38, page 772, of the Appendix on accompanying CD, which existed during 1926, 1927, and the early part of 1928 between the Brooklyn Union Gas Company 5$^{1}/_{2}$s and the related common stock.

See accompanying CD for Chapter 25, "Senior Securities with Warrants. Participating Issues. Switching and Hedging."

Chapter 26

SENIOR SECURITIES OF
QUESTIONABLE SAFETY

AT THE LOW point of the 1932 securities market the safety of at least 80% of all corporate bonds and preferred stocks was open to some appreciable degree of doubt.[1] Even prior to the 1929 crash the number of speculative senior securities was very large, and it must inevitably be still larger for some years to come. The financial world is faced, therefore, with the unpleasant fact that a considerable proportion of American securities belong to what may be called a misfit category. A low-grade bond or preferred stock constitutes a relatively unpopular form of commitment. The investor must not buy them, and the speculator generally prefers to devote his attention to common stocks. There seems to be much logic to the view that if one decides to speculate he should choose a thoroughly speculative medium and not subject himself to the upper limitations of market value and income return, or to the possibility of confusion between speculation and investment, which attach to the lower priced bonds and preferred stocks.

Limitation of Profit on Low-priced Bonds Not a Real Drawback. But however impressive may be the objection to these nondescript securities, the fact remains that they exist in enormous quantities, that they are owned by innumerable security holders, and that hence they must be taken seriously into account in any survey of security analysis. It is reasonable to conclude that the large supply of such issues, coupled with the lack of a natural demand for them, will make for a level of prices below their intrinsic value. Even if an inherent unattractiveness in the *form* of such securities be admitted, this may be more than offset by the attractive *price* at which they may be purchased. Furthermore, the limitations

---

[1] See Appendix Note 42, p. 776 on accompanying CD, for data on bond prices in 1931–1934 and 1939.

of principal profit in the case of a low-priced bond, as compared with a common stock, may be of only minor practical importance, because the profit actually *realized* by the common-stock buyer is ordinarily no greater than that obtainable from a speculative senior security. If, for example, we are considering a 4% bond selling at 35, its maximum possible price appreciation is about 70 points, or 200%. The average common-stock purchase at 35 cannot be held for a greater profit than this without a dangerous surrender to "bull-market psychology."

Two Viewpoints with Respect to Speculative Bonds. There are two directly opposite angles from which a speculative bond may be viewed. It may be considered in its relation to investment standards and yields, in which case the leading question is whether or not the low price and higher income return will compensate for the concession made in the safety factor. Or it may be thought of in terms of a common-stock commitment, in which event the contrary question arises; *viz.*, "Does the *smaller* risk of loss involved in this low-priced bond, as compared with a common stock, compensate for the smaller possibilities of profit?" The nearer a bond comes to meeting investment requirements—and the closer it sells to an investment price—the more likely are those interested to regard it from the investment viewpoint. The opposite approach is evidently suggested in the case of a bond in default or selling at an extremely low price. We are faced here with the familiar difficulty of classification arising from the absence of definite lines of demarcation. Some issues can always be found reflecting any conceivable status in the gamut between complete worthlessness and absolute safety.

Common-stock Approach Preferable. We believe, however, that the sounder and more fruitful approach to the field of speculative senior securities lies from the direction of common stocks. This will carry with it a more thorough appreciation of the risk involved and therefore a greater insistence upon either reasonable assurance of safety or especially attractive possibilities of profit or both. It induces also—among intelligent security buyers at least—a more intensive examination of the corporate picture than would ordinarily be made in viewing a security from the investment angle.

Such an approach would be distinctly unfavorable to the purchase of slightly substandard bonds selling at moderate discounts from par. These, together with high-coupon bonds of second grade, belong in the category of "business men's investments" which we considered and decided against in Chap. 7. It may be objected that a general adoption of this attitude would result in wide and sudden fluctuations in the price of many issues. Assuming that a 4% bond deserves to sell at par as long as it meets strict investment standards, then as soon as it falls slightly below these standards its price would suffer a precipitous decline, say, to 70; and, conversely, a slight improvement in its exhibit would warrant its jumping suddenly back to par. Apparently there would be no justification for intermediate quotations between 70 and 100.

The real situation is not so simple as this, however. Differences of opinion may properly exist in the minds of investors as to whether or not a given issue is adequately secured, particularly since the standards are qualitative and personal as well as arithmetical and objective. The range between 70 and 100 may therefore logically reflect a greater or lesser agreement concerning the safety of the issue. This would mean that an investor would be justified in buying such a bond, say, at 85, if his own considered judgment regarded it as sound, although he would recognize that there was doubt on this score in the minds of other investors that would account for its appreciable discount from a prime investment price. According to this view, the levels between 70 and 100, approximately, may be designated as the range of "subjective variations" in the status of the issue.

The field of speculative values proper would therefore commence somewhere near the 70 level (for bonds with a coupon rate of 4% or larger) and would offer maximum possibilities of appreciation of at least 50% of the cost. (In the case of other senior issues, 70% of *normal value* might be taken as the dividing line.) In making such commitments, it is recommended that the same general attitude be taken as in the careful purchase of a common stock; in other words, that the income account and the balance sheet be submitted to the same intensive analysis and that the same effort be made to evaluate future possibilities—favorable and unfavorable.

Important Distinctions between Common Stocks and Speculative Senior Issues. We shall not seek, therefore, to set up standards of selection for speculative senior issues in any sense corresponding to the quantitative tests applicable to fixed-value securities. On the other hand, although they should preferably be considered in their relationship to the common-stock approach and technique, it is necessary to appreciate certain rather important points of difference that exist between common stocks as a class and speculative senior issues.

Low-priced Bonds Associated with Corporate Weakness. The limitation on the profit possibilities of senior securities has already been referred to. Its significance varies with the individual case, but in general we do not consider it a controlling disadvantage. A more emphatic objection is made against low-priced bonds and preferred stocks on the ground that they are associated with corporate weakness, retrogression, or depression. Obviously the enterprise behind such a security is not highly successful, and furthermore, it must have been following a downward course, since the issue originally sold at a much higher level. In 1928 and 1929 this consideration was enough to condemn all such issues absolutely in the eyes of the general public. Businesses were divided into two groups: those which were successful and progressing, and those which were on the downgrade or making no headway. The common shares of the first group were desirable no matter how high the price; but no security belonging to the second group was attractive, irrespective of how low it sold.

This concept of permanently strong and permanently weak corporations has been pretty well dissipated by the subsequent depression, and we are back to the older realization that time brings unpredictable changes in the fortunes of business undertakings.[2] The fact that the low price of a bond or preferred stock results from a decline in earnings need not signify that the company's outlook is hopeless and that there is nothing ahead but still poorer results. Many of the companies that fared very badly in 1931–1933 regained a good part of their former earning power, and their senior securities recovered from exceedingly low prices to investment levels. It turned out, therefore, that there was just as much reason to expect substantial recoveries in the quotations of depressed senior securities as in the price of common stocks generally.

Many Undervalued in Relation to Their Status and Contractual Position. We have already mentioned that the unpopularity of speculative senior securities tends to make them sell at lower prices than common stocks, in relation to their intrinsic value. From the standpoint of the intelligent buyer this must be considered a point in their favor. With

---

[2] But see later references to *The Ebb and Flow of Investment Value,* by Mead and Grodinski, published in 1939, which strongly espouses the thesis stated in the previous paragraph (*infra,* p. 371 and Appendix Note 71, p. 845 on accompanying CD).

respect to their intrinsic position, speculative bonds—and, to a lesser degree, preferred stocks—derive important advantages from their contractual rights. The fixed obligation to pay bond interest will usually result in the continuation of such payments as long as they are in any way possible. If we assume that a fairly large proportion of a group of carefully selected low-priced bonds will escape default, the income received on the group as a whole over a period of time will undoubtedly far exceed the dividend return on similarly priced common stocks.

Preferred shares occupy an immeasurably weaker position in this regard, but even here the provisions transferring voting control to the senior shares in the event of suspension of dividends will be found in some cases to impel their continuance. Where the cash resources are ample, the desire to maintain an unbroken record and to avoid accumulations will frequently result in paying preferred dividends even though poor earnings have depressed the market price.

Examples: Century Ribbon Mills, Inc., failed to earn its 7% preferred dividend in eight out of the thirteen years from 1926 to 1938, inclusive, and the price repeatedly declined to about 50. Yet the preferred dividend was continued without interruption during this entire period, while the common received a total of but 50 cents. Similarly, a purchaser of Universal Pictures Company First Preferred at about 30 in 1929 would have received the 8% dividend during three years of depression before the payment was finally suspended.

Contrasting Importance of Contractual Terms in Speculation and Investment. The reader should appreciate the distinction between the *investment* and the *speculative* qualities of preferred stocks in this matter of dividend continuance. From the investment standpoint, *i.e.*, the *dependability* of the dividend, the absence of an enforceable claim is a disadvantage as compared with bonds. From the speculative standpoint, *i.e.*, the possibility of dividends' being continued under unfavorable conditions, preferred stocks have certain semicontractual claims to consideration by the directors that undoubtedly give them an advantage over common stocks.

Bearing of Working-capital and Sinking-fund Factors on Safety of Speculative Senior Issues.

A large working capital, which has been characteristic of even nonprosperous industrials for some years past, is much more directly advantageous to the senior securities than to the common stock. Not only does it make possible the continuance of interest or preferred-dividend payments, but it has an important bearing also on the retirement of the principal, either at maturity or by sinking-fund operations or by voluntary repurchase. Sinking-fund provisions, for bonds as well as preferred stocks, contribute to the improvement of both the market quotation and the intrinsic position of the issue. This advantage is not found in the case of common stocks.

Examples: Francis H. Leggett Company, manufacturers and wholesalers of food products, issued $2,000,000 of 7% preferred stock carrying a sinking-fund provision which retired 3% of the issue annually. By June 30, 1932, the amount outstanding had been reduced to $608,500, and, because of the small balance remaining, the issue was called for redemption at 110, *in the depth of the depression.* Similarly, Century Ribbon Mills Preferred was reduced from $2,000,000 to $544,000 between 1922 and 1938; and Lawrence Portland Cement Company Debenture $5^1/2$s were reduced from $2,000,000 to $650,000 on December 31, 1938, the balance being called for redemption on April 1, 1939.

Importance of Large Net-current-asset Coverage. Where a low-priced bond is covered several times over by net current assets, it presents a special type of opportunity, because experience shows that the chances of repayment are good, even though the earnings may be poor or irregular.

Examples: Electric Refrigeration Corporation (Kelvinator) 6s, due 1936, sold at 66 in November 1929 when the net current assets of the company according to its latest statement amounted to $6,008,900 for the $2,528,500 of bonds outstanding. It is true that the company had operated at a deficit in 1927 and 1928, but fixed charges were earned nearly nine times in the year ended September 30, 1929, and the net current assets were nearly four times the market value of the bond issue. The bonds recovered to a price close to par in 1930 and were redeemed at 105 in 1931. Similarly, Electric Refrigeration Building Corporation First 6s, due 1936, which were in effect guaranteed by Kelvinator Corporation under a lease, sold at 70 in July 1932 when the net current assets of the parent company amounted to about six times the $1,073,000 of bonds outstanding and over eight times the total market value of the issue. The bonds were called at $101^1/2$ in 1933.

Other examples that may be cited in this connection are Murray Corporation First $6^1/2$s, due 1934, which sold at 68 in 1932 (because of current operating deficits) although the company had net current assets of over 2¹/₂ times the par value of the issue and nearly four times their market value at that price; Sidney Blumenthal and Company 7% Notes, due 1936, which sold at 70 in 1926 when the company had net current assets of twice the par value of the issue and nearly three times the total market value thereof (they were called at 103 in 1930); Belding, Heminway Company 6s, due 1936, which sold at 67 in 1930 when the company had net current assets of nearly three times the par value of the issue and over four times its market value. In the latter case drastic liquidation of inventories occurred in 1930 and 1931, proceeds from which were used to retire about 80% of the bond issue through purchases in the market. The balance of the issue was called for payment at 101 early in 1934.

In the typical case of this kind the chance of profit will exceed the chance of loss, and the probable amount of profit will exceed the probable amount of loss. It may well be that the risk involved in each individual case is still so considerable as to preclude us from applying the term "investment" to such a commitment. Nevertheless, we suggest that if the insurance principle of diversification of risk be followed by making a number of such commitments at the same time, the net result should be sufficiently dependable to warrant our calling the group purchase an *investment operation*. This was one of the possibilities envisaged in our broadened definition of investment as given in Chap. 4.

Limitations upon Importance of Current-asset Position. It is clear that considerable weight attaches to the working-capital exhibit in selecting speculative bonds. This importance must not be exaggerated, however, to the point of assuming that, whenever a bond is fully covered by net current assets, its safety is thereby assured. The current assets shown in any balance sheet may be greatly reduced by subsequent operating losses; more important still, the stated values frequently prove entirely undependable in the event of insolvency.[3]

Of the many examples of this point which can be given, we shall mention R. Hoe and Company 7% Notes and Ajax Rubber Company First 8s. Although these obligations were covered by net working capital in 1929, they subsequently sold as low as 2 cents on the dollar. (See also our

---

[3] The comparative reliability of the various components in the current-assets figure (cash assets, receivables, inventories) will receive detailed treatment in a discussion of balance-sheet analysis in Part VI.

discussion of Willys-Overland Company First 6¹/₂s and Berkey and Gay Furniture Company First 6s in Note 34 of the Appendix on accompanying CD.[4])

EXAMPLES OF LOW-PRICED INDUSTRIAL BONDS COVERED BY NET CURRENT ASSETS, 1932*

Name of issue	Due	Low price 1932	Date of balance sheet	Net current assets†	Funded debt at part†	Normal interest coverage	
						Period	Times earned‡
American Seating 6s	1936	17	Sept. 1932	$ 3,826	$ 3,056	1924–1930	5.2
Crucible Steel 5s	1940	39	June 1932	16,163	13,250	1924–1930	9.4
McKesson & Robbins 5¹/₂s	1950	25	June 1932	42,885	20,848	1925–1930	4.1
Marion Steam Shovel 6s	1947	21	June 1932	4,598	2,417	1922–1930	3.9
National Acme 6s	1942	54	Dec. 1931	4,327	1,963	1922–1930	5.5

* See Appendix Note 43, p. 777 on accompanying CD, for a brief discussion of the sequel to these examples first given in the 1934 edition of this work.
† 000 omitted.
‡ Coverage for 1931 charges, adjusted where necessary.

We must distinguish, therefore, between the mere fact that the working capital, as reported, covers the funded debt and the more significant fact that it exceeds the bond issue *many times over*. The former statement is always interesting, but by no means conclusive. If added to other favorable factors, such as a good earnings coverage in normal years and a generally satisfactory qualitative showing, it might make the issue quite attractive but preferably as part of a group-purchase in the field.

Speculative Preferred Stocks. *Stages in Their Price History.* Speculative preferred stocks are more subject than speculative bonds to irrational activity, so that from time to time such preferred shares are overvalued in the market in the same way as common stocks. We thus have three possible stages in the price history of a preferred issue, in each of which the market quotation tends to be out of line with the value:

1. The first stage is that of original issuance, when investors are persuaded to buy the offering at a full investment price not justified by its intrinsic merit.

---

[4] Perhaps it should be added that three of the four issues mentioned in this paragraph had spectacular recoveries from the low prices of the depression (*e.g.*, the new Hoe 7s, which were exchanged for the old 7s, sold at 100 in 1937).

2. In the second stage the lack of investment merit has become manifest, and the price drops to a speculative level. During this period the decline is likely to be overdone, for reasons previously discussed.

3. A third stage sometimes appears in which the issue advances speculatively in the same fashion as common stocks. On such occasions certain factors of questionable importance—such as the amount of dividend accumulations—are overemphasized.

An example of this third or irrational stage will be given a little later.

The Rule of "Maximum Valuation for Senior Issues." Both as a safeguard against being led astray by the propaganda that is characteristic of the third stage and also as a general guide in dealing with speculative senior issues, the following principle of security analysis is presented, which we shall call "the rule of maximum valuation for senior issues."

> *A senior issue cannot be worth, intrinsically, any more than a common stock would be worth if it occupied the position of that senior issue, with no junior securities outstanding.*

This statement may be understood more readily by means of an example.

Company *X* and Company *Y* have the same value. Company *X* has 80,000 shares of preferred and 200,000 shares of common. Company *Y* has only 80,000 shares of common and no preferred. Then our principle states that a share of Company *X* preferred cannot be worth more than a share of Company *Y* common. This is true because Company *Y* common represents the same value that lies behind *both* the preferred and common of Company *X*.

Instead of comparing two equivalent companies such as *X* and *Y*, we may assume that Company *X* is recapitalized so that the old common is eliminated and the preferred becomes the sole stock issue, *i.e.*, the new common stock. (To coin a term, we may call such an assumed change the "communizing" of a preferred stock.) Then our principle merely states the obvious fact that the value of such a hypothetical common stock cannot be *less* than the value of the preferred stock it replaces, because it is equivalent to the preferred *plus* the old common. The same idea may be applied to a speculative bond, followed either by common stock only or by both preferred and common. If the bond is "commonized," *i.e.*, if it is assumed to be turned into a common stock, with the old stock issues eliminated, then the value of the new common stock thus created cannot be less than the present value of the bond.

This relationship must hold true regardless of how high the coupon or dividend rate, the par value or the redemption price of the senior issue may be and, particularly, regardless of what amount of unpaid interest or dividends may have accumulated. For if we had a preferred stock with accumulations of $1,000 per share, the value of the issue could be no greater than if it were a common stock (without dividend accumulations) representing complete ownership of the business. The unpaid dividends cannot create any additional value for the company's securities in the aggregate; they merely affect the division of the total value between the preferred and the common.

Excessive Emphasis Placed on Amount of Accrued Dividends. Although a very small amount of analysis will show the above statements to be almost self-evident truths, the public fails to observe the simplest rules of logic when once it is in a gambling mood. Hence preferred shares with large dividend accruals have lent themselves readily to market manipulation in which the accumulations are made the basis for a large advance in the price of both the preferred and common. An excellent example of such a performance was provided by American Zinc, Lead, and Smelting Company shares in 1928.

American Zinc preferred stock was created in 1916 as a stock dividend on the common, the transaction thus amounting to a split-up of old common into preferred and new common. The preferred was given a stated par of $25 but had all the attributes of a $100-par stock ($6 cumulative dividends, redemption and liquidating value of $100). This arrangement was evidently a device to permit carrying the preferred issue in the balance sheet as a much smaller liability than it actually represented. Between 1920 and 1927 the company reported continuous deficits (except for a negligible profit in 1922); preferred dividends were suspended in 1921, and by 1928 about $40 per share had accumulated.

In 1928 the company benefited moderately from the prevailing prosperity and barely earned $6 per share on the preferred. However, the company's issues were subjected to manipulation that advanced the price of the preferred from 35 in 1927 to 118 in 1928, while the common rose even more spectacularly from 6 to 57. These advances were accompanied by rumors of a plan to pay off the accumulated dividends—exactly how, not being stated. Naturally enough, this development failed to materialize.[5]

The irrationality of the gambling spirit is well shown here by the absurd acceptance of unpaid preferred dividends *as a source of value for both the preferred and the common.* The speculative argument in behalf of the common stock ran as follows: "The accumulated preferred dividends are going to be paid off. This will be good for the common. Therefore let us buy the common." According to this topsy-turvy reasoning, if there were no unpaid preferred dividends ahead of the common it would be less attractive (even at the same price), because there would then be in prospect no wonderful plan for clearing up the accumulations.

We may use the American Zinc example to demonstrate the practical application of our "rule of maximum valuation for senior issues." Was American Zinc Preferred too high at 118 in 1928? Assuming the preferred stockholders owned the company completely, this would then mean a price of 118 for a *common* stock earning $6 per share in 1928 after eight years of deficits. Even in the hectic days of 1928 speculators would not have been at all attracted to such a common stock at that price, so that the application of our rule should have prevented the purchase of the preferred stock at its inflated value.

The quotation of 57 reached by American Zinc common was evidently the height of absurdity, since it represented the following valuation for the company:

Preferred stock, 80,000 sh. @ 118	$ 9,440,000
Common stock, 200,000 sh. @ 57	11,400,000
Total valuation	$20,840,000
Earnings, 1928	481,000
Average earnings, 1920–1927	*188,000(d)*

In order to equal the above valuation for the American Zinc Company the hypothetical common stock (80,000 shares basis) would have had to sell at $260 *per share*, earning a bare $6 and paying no dividend.

---

[5] But years later, in 1936, accumulated preferred dividends were taken care of by a recapitalization plan which gave the preferred stockholders the bulk of the enlarged common issue.

This figure indicates the extent to which the heedless public was led astray in this case by the exploitation of unpaid dividends.

American Hide and Leather Company offers another, but less striking, example of this point. In no year between 1922 and 1928, inclusive, did the company earn more than $4.41 on the preferred, and the average profits were very small. Yet in each of these seven years, the preferred stock sold as high as 66 or higher. This recurring strength was based largely on the speculative appeal of the enormous accumulated preferred dividends which grew from about $120 to $175 per share during this period.

Applying our rule, we may consider American Hide and Leather Preferred as representing complete ownership of the business, which to all intents and purposes it did. We should then have a common stock which had paid no dividends for many years and with average earnings at best (using the 1922–1927 period) of barely $2 per share. Evidently a price of above 65 for such a common stock would be far too high. Consequently this price was excessive for American Hide and Leather Preferred, nor could the existence of accumulated dividends, however large, affect this conclusion in the slightest.

Variation in Capital Structure Affects Total Market Value of Securities.

From the foregoing discussion it might be inferred that the value of a single capital-stock issue must always be equivalent to the combined values of any preferred and common stock issues into which it might be split. In a theoretical sense this is entirely true, but in practice it may not be true at all, because a division of capitalization into senior securities and common stock may have a real advantage over a single common-stock issue. This subject will receive extended treatment under the heading of "Capitalization Structure" in Chap. 40.

The distinction between the idea just suggested and our "rule of maximum valuation" may be clarified as follows:

1. Assume Company X = Company Y
2. Company X has preferred (P) and common (C); Company Y has common only (C')
3. Then it *would appear* that

$$\text{Value of } P + \text{value of } C = \text{value of } C'$$

since each side of the equation represents equal things, namely the total value of each company.

But this apparent relationship may not hold good in practice because the preferred-and-common capitalization method may have real advantages over a single common-stock issue.

On the other hand, our "rule of maximum valuation" merely states that the value of *P alone* cannot exceed value of C'. This should hold true in practice as well as in theory, except in so far as manipulative or heedlessly speculative activity brushes aside all rational considerations.

Our rule is stated in negative form and is therefore essentially negative in its application. It is most useful in detecting instances where preferred stocks or bonds are *not worth* their market price. To apply it positively it would be necessary, first, to arrive at a value for the preferred on a "communized" basis (*i.e.*, representing complete ownership of the business) and then to determine what deduction from this value should be made to reflect the part of the ownership fairly ascribable to the existing common stock. At times this approach will be found useful in establishing the fact that a given senior issue is worth more than its market price. But such a procedure brings us far outside the range of mathematical formulas and into the difficult and indefinite field of common-stock valuation, with which we have next to deal.

PART IV

THEORY OF COMMON-STOCK INVESTMENT. THE DIVIDEND FACTOR

GO WITH THE FLOW

BY BRUCE BERKOWITZ

In the urban, melting-pot neighborhood where I grew up, one of the most popular retail establishments was the corner variety store. Area residents frequented the place for small, everyday needs—a newspaper or magazine or a quart of milk. We kids showed up constantly with what change we had cajoled from family members or earned by running errands, eager to spend it on candy bars, chewing gum, and soft drinks.

The owner had one cash register, seated on a countertop near the front door. Into it went the cash from customers' purchases. The proprietor took out what he needed to stock the shelves, pay the rent, maintain the store, and meet his small payroll. If there was anything left after that, the proprietor had the choice of using the remaining cash to invest in the business's growth, pay down debts, or meet personal living expenses.

Years later, after I had started working in the investment business, I began reading the annual reports written by Berkshire Hathaway chairman Warren Buffett, which led me to the works of Benjamin Graham and David Dodd. I soon realized that the financial operations of this simple variety store represented a good example of free cash flow. Graham and Dodd referred to that excess cash as "earnings power" or "owner earnings." That's the amount of cash an owner can pocket after paying all expenses and making whatever investments are necessary to maintain the business. This free cash flow is the well from which all returns are drawn, whether they are dividends, stock buybacks, or investments capable of enhancing future returns.

Graham and Dodd were among the first to apply careful financial analysis to common stocks. Until then, most serious investment analysis had focused on fixed income securities. Graham and Dodd argued that stocks, like bonds, have a well-defined value based on a stream of future returns. With bonds, the returns consist of specific payments made under contractual commitments. With stocks, the returns consist of dividends that are paid from the earnings of the business, or cash that could have been used to pay dividends that was instead reinvested in the business.

By examining the assets of a business and their earnings (or cash flow) power, Graham and Dodd argued that the value of future returns could be calculated with reasonable accuracy. Once determined, this value helps you decide whether to purchase a particular stock. A calculated value of $20 for a stock trading at $10 per share would allow for a profit even if your estimate was off by a few dollars. But if you estimated a $12 value for a stock trading at $10 per share, it would fail to make the buy list; even though the stock was somewhat undervalued, there would not be a sufficient margin for error.

Sharpen Your Pencil

The fundamental problem of equity investing is how to value a company. In the 1930s, that was done by measuring tangible assets. The reason: much of the stock market's capitalization in that era was based on raw materials (mainly mining companies), transportation (railroads), utilities, and manufacturing. All of those industries had significant amounts of plant, equipment, and inventory. Today, service firms dominate the economy, and, even in manufacturing, much of a firm's capital comes from intangibles— software, acquired brands, customers, product portfolios—that do not appear explicitly on the balance sheet. For example, relatively little of the value of software companies like Oracle and Microsoft or a business services firm like Automated Data Processing is captured by tangible assets.

To value equities, we at Fairholme begin by calculating free cash flow. We start with net income as defined under Generally Accepted Accounting Principles (GAAP). Then we add back noncash charges such as depreciation and amortization, which are formulaic calculations based on historical costs (depreciation for tangible assets, amortization for intangibles) and may not reflect a reduction in those assets' true worth.

Even so, most assets deteriorate in value over time, and we have to account for that. So we subtract an estimate of the company's cost of maintaining tangible assets such as the office, plant, inventory, and equipment; and intangible assets like customer traffic and brand identity. Investment at this level, properly deployed, should keep the profits of the business in a steady state.

That is only the beginning. For instance, companies often misstate the costs of employees' pension and postretirement medical benefits. They also overestimate their benefit plans' future investment returns or underestimate future medical costs, so in a free cash flow analysis, you need to adjust the numbers to reflect those biases.

Companies often lowball what they pay management. For instance, until the last several years, most companies did not count the costs of stock option grants as employee compensation, nor did the costs show up in any other line item. Some went so far as to try to mask this options expense by repurchasing large quantities of shares in the open market to offset the stock options exercised by employees. The problem: companies were often paying much more on the open market than they received from employees exercising options granted years before. This difference was rarely reported as an official cost of doing business.

Another source of accounting-derived profits comes from long-term supply contracts. For instance, when now-defunct Enron entered into a long-term trading or supply arrangement, the company very optimistically estimated the net present value of future profits from the deal and put that into the current year's earnings even though no cash was received. Enron is gone, but not the practice. Insurance companies and banks still have considerable leeway in how they estimate the future losses arising from insured events or loan defaults. And for any company, gains and losses on derivative contracts are difficult to nail down with precision since the markets for such instruments are thin.

Some companies understate free cash flow because they expense the cost of what are really investments in their growth. For instance, adding new auto insurance customers may cost as much as 20% to 30% more than the cash received from new policyholders in their first year. Some of this excess cost goes to replace customers who did not renew their policies. But if the number of policyholders is growing, a portion of the expense represents investment in growth. Berkshire Hathaway's GEICO subsidiary does just this, and as a result, accounting earnings understate free cash flow assuming a steady-state business. When Microsoft sells a Windows program, the company recognizes that future servicing costs are part of that sale. Microsoft accounts for these costs by spreading the revenues and expenses over a number of years. The result is to defer profits to future periods and provide the company with a cushion against future adverse developments.

All of these noncash accounting conventions illustrate the difficulty of identifying a company's current free cash flow. Still, we are far from done. My associates and I next want to know (a) how representative is current cash flow of average past flow, and (b) is it increasing or decreasing—that is, does the company face headwinds or ride on tailwinds?

Cash Flow Where You Least Expect It

Certainly one company facing stiff headwinds in 2008 was Mohawk Industries, a carpeting and flooring firm we first purchased in 2006 at prices in the low $60s. At the time, the company reported GAAP earnings of $6.70 per share, but our analysis showed free cash flow of $9 per share. Why was free cash flow so much greater than earnings? First, Mohawk had been growing by acquiring some of the smaller players as part of an industrywide consolidation, so it gained economies of scale that allowed the company to reduce capital spending and lower its working capital needs. Even more important, the use of GAAP required Mohawk to take significant charges against its earnings to amortize the intangible assets it had picked up in its buying spree. (The difference between what a company pays for an acquisition and the acquired company's book value goes on the balance sheet as an intangible asset called "goodwill.") These charges reduced net income but did not take any cash out of the business. All told, we calculated that Mohawk was selling at less than seven times its free cash flow, an attractive valuation. It was akin to buying a bond yielding 14%, with a decent chance that the coupon payments would rise over time.

In 2008, in the midst of a seriously depressed new housing market (most carpeting and flooring go into new construction), Mohawk Industries was still generating $6 to $7 a share of free cash flow. The stock at $75 a share was trading at around 11 to 12 times free cash flow, still an attractive multiple for a company in a cyclical downswing. True, revenues were slumping, but industry consolidation had largely eliminated once-rampant price-cutting competition among manufacturers. In fact, manufacturers were able to pass along increased raw materials costs to customers. That has helped to preserve profit margins and cash flow. While the carpeting and flooring industry will continue to fluctuate with the economy, Mohawk's management has been able to keep its free cash flow generation fairly steady.

Not surprisingly, investors who search for companies with good free cash flow often find them in mature industries, such as the flooring business. Capital required for growth is limited and financing demands are modest, so free cash is plentiful. That's not usually the case with high-growth companies, but sometimes meticulous analysis will uncover one, such as EchoStar Corp., parent of the DISH satellite TV business.

That company went public in June 1995, on the premise that there was room for another pay-TV provider. By 2000, at the peak of Wall Street's infatuation with all things tech, EchoStar had 3.4 million subscribers, an enterprise value (market value of equity, plus net debt) of approximately $30 billion, and a reported annual loss of nearly $800 million. Worse yet, the company was consuming cash like crazy as it sought to build its infrastructure and customer base—and that alone would take it off many value investors' radar.

Fast forward five years, and the subscriber count topped 12 million. With many of the start-up costs behind it, free cash was flowing and growing—monthly subscriber fees are a pretty reliable income stream. Yet at that time, in 2005, EchoStar's enterprise value was just $17 billion. Clearly, the market was not giving the company much credit for its cash-generating abilities. That allowed Fairholme to purchase shares in an excellent franchise business with a double-digit free cash flow yield while risk-free investments were paying 5%.

Some companies produce plentiful cash flow, but their corporate structures mask it. That's the case with Leucadia National, a holding company with an eclectic mix of businesses. Leucadia's portfolio of businesses resembles that of Buffett's Berkshire Hathaway. While these companies in aggregate do not necessarily produce steady cash flow for the holding company, at the subsidiary level cash flow can be very good, and ultimately that value will benefit the parent company. Leucadia's free cash flow is quite variable and unpredictable, mainly because its managers are always buying and selling businesses in its portfolio. But management has proven skillful at deploying the company's cash. Its net worth has compounded at close to 25% per annum for almost three decades. If you invest in a company such as Leucadia or Berkshire Hathaway, you are banking on management's ability to identify investments with high free cash flow.

Leucadia and Berkshire Hathaway point to another important aspect of evaluating free cash flow: how management deploys cash and whether those decisions enhance shareholder value. As mentioned earlier, free cash flow can either be returned to shareholders via dividends or share repurchases, or it can be reinvested in the business. Graham and Dodd equated cash returns to shareholders with dividends. The tax advantages of stock buybacks were hardly considered in capital allocation decisions, and in fact, they are of little interest to the institutional investors who dominate today's markets.

Today, share buybacks at discounted prices are clearly preferable to dividends. The qualifying factor here is the price. If the company buys back undervalued stock, selling shareholders suffer while long-term shareholders benefit. If the company buys its stock at inflated prices, sellers benefit and long-term holders lose out. Value investors, having a long-term orientation, generally look for companies that consistently repurchase their stocks during periods of undervaluation.

Management must decide when to return cash to shareholders and when to invest it. Earnings intelligently invested will generate higher future levels of free cash flow. On the other hand, poorly invested earnings destroy value. Warren Buffett has been an undisputed genius of capital allocation for over 50 years, and no one minds that his Berkshire Hathaway does not pay a dividend. On the other hand, some managements, especially those in struggling industries, would benefit their investors by returning capital to them rather than reinvesting in the business at low rates of return.

Dividends as Signals

Traditionally, corporate boards have tended to set dividend payouts at levels that are comfortably covered by earnings. That way, a greater share of earnings is retained in good times. In bad times, dividends are often maintained even if they exceed free cash flow. A board might do that to express its long-term confidence in the business. If earnings are growing, a board will steadily increase the dividends, though usually at a slower pace than earnings.

Now, investors scrutinize companies' dividend policies as a window into management's thinking about the durability of the free cash flow. If changes in cash flow were considered temporary, companies presumably would not adjust dividends. If management believed the changes were likely to be permanent, it would adjust dividends accordingly. If management regarded new investment opportunities as relatively low risk, those opportunities could be financed with debt, allowing dividends to remain untouched. If new opportunities were viewed as relatively risky, they might have to be financed through a reduction in the dividend. If these strategies were honestly executed, they would help investors extrapolate from current to likely future cash flow and hence, to equity value. In this context, a high dividend level would be a positive factor in equity valuation.

The danger here is that management may be tempted to manipulate the dividend to create an inappropriately favorable picture of future cash flow. Companies under stress, such as General Motors or Citigroup have been, are almost always late to cut their dividends. In such cases investors who buy stocks with unusually rich dividend yields and deteriorating fundamentals are asking for trouble. These dividends are likely to be sliced. Companies that pay dividends with the proceeds of newly issued equity rather than free cash flow are similarly likely to be manipulating investors through false signals. Real estate investment trusts and income trusts, which must pay out virtually all their income to shareholders, are similarly reluctant to reduce their stated distributions.

On the other hand, companies that have free cash to distribute and poor investment prospects should make higher dividend payouts. Also, companies like Dell Computer and Amazon.com that operate with significantly negative working capital—they collect from purchasers before they have to pay suppliers—and little fixed investment have minimal need to reinvest earnings. Yet they stubbornly pay no dividends and accumulate large amounts of cash.

Whose Cash Is It Anyway?

Identifying a company with a big cash stash and the ability to generate more is a great start. But the cash doesn't do the shareholder any good unless management makes smart investments with it, or returns it to its owners via dividends or share buybacks. Management talent and intentions are crucial.

Sometimes there is just too much cash to ignore, even if it is under the control of folks who won't invest it or distribute it. In those cases activist investors often take large stakes and pressure managers to "unlock the value" in the company; failing that, they try to replace those managers. One way or another, if there's enough money in the cash register, somebody will find a way to get it out.

Chapter 27

THE THEORY OF COMMON-
STOCK INVESTMENT

IN OUR INTRODUCTORY discussion we set forth the difficulties inherent in efforts to apply the analytical technique to speculative situations. Since the speculative factors bulk particularly large in common stocks, it follows that analysis of such issues is likely to prove inconclusive and unsatisfactory; and even where it appears to be conclusive, there is danger that it may be misleading. At this point it is necessary to consider the function of common-stock analysis in greater detail. We must begin with three realistic premises. The first is that common stocks are of basic importance in our financial scheme and of fascinating interest to many people; the second is that owners and buyers of common stocks are generally anxious to arrive at an intelligent idea of their value; the third is that, even when the underlying motive of purchase is mere speculative greed, human nature desires to conceal this unlovely impulse behind a screen of apparent logic and good sense. To adapt the aphorism of Voltaire, it may be said that if there were no such thing as common-stock analysis, it would be necessary to counterfeit it.

Broad Merits of Common-stock Analysis. We are thus led to the question: "To what extent is common-stock analysis a valid and truly valuable exercise, and to what extent is it an empty but indispensable ceremony attending the wagering of money on the future of business and of the stock market?" We shall ultimately find the answer to run somewhat as follows: "As far as the *typical* common stock is concerned—an issue picked at random from the list—an analysis, however elaborate, is unlikely to yield a dependable conclusion as to its attractiveness or its real value. But in individual cases, the exhibit may be such as to permit reasonably confident conclusions to be drawn from the processes of analysis." It would follow that analysis is of positive or scientific value only in the case of the exceptional common stock, and that for common stocks in general it must be regarded either as a somewhat questionable aid to speculative judgment or as a highly illusory method of aiming at values that defy calculation and that must somehow be calculated none the less.

Perhaps the most effective way of clarifying the subject is through the historical approach. Such a survey will throw light not only upon the changing status of common-stock analysis but also upon a closely related subject of major importance, *viz.*, the theory of common-stock investment. We shall encounter at first a set of old established and seemingly logical principles for common-stock investment. Through the advent of new conditions, we shall find the validity of these principles impaired. Their insufficiency will give rise to an entirely different concept of common-stock selection, the so-called "new-era theory," which beneath its superficial plausibility will hold possibilities of untold mischief in store. With the prewar theory obsolete and the new-era theory exploded, we must finally make the attempt to establish a new set of logically sound and reasonably dependable principles of common-stock investment.

History of Common-stock Analysis. Turning first to the history of common-stock *analysis*, we shall find that two conflicting factors have been at work during the past 30 years. On the one hand there has been an increase in the *investment prestige* of common stocks as a class, due chiefly to the enlarged number that have shown substantial earnings, continued dividends, and a strong financial condition. Accompanying this progress was a considerable advance in the frequency and adequacy of corporate statements, thus supplying the public and the securities analyst with a wealth of statistical data. Finally, an impressive theory was constructed asserting the preeminence of common stocks as long-term investments. But at the time that the interest in common stocks reached its height, in the period between 1927 and 1929, the *basis of valuation* employed by the stock-buying public departed more and more from the factual approach and technique of security analysis and concerned itself increasingly with the elements of potentiality and prophecy. Moreover, the heightened instability in the affairs of industrial companies and groups of enterprises, which has undermined the investment quality of bonds in general, has of course been still more hostile to the maintenance of true investment quality in common stocks.

Analysis Vitiated by Two Types of Instability. The extent to which common-stock analysis has been vitiated by these two developments, (1) the instability of tangibles and (2) the dominant importance of intangibles, may be better realized by a contrast of specific common stocks prior to 1920 and in more recent times. Let us consider four typical examples: Pennsylvania Railroad; Atchison, Topeka, and Santa Fe Railway; National Biscuit; and American Can.

PENNSYLVANIA RAILROAD COMPANY

Year	Range for stock	Earned per share	Paid per share
1904	70–56	$4.63	$3.00
1905	74–66	4.98	3.00
1906	74–61	5.83	3.25
1907	71–52	5.32	3.50
1908	68–52	4.46	3.00
1909	76–63	4.37	3.00
1910	69–61	4.60	3.00
1911	65–59	4.14	3.00
1912	63–60	4.64	3.00
1913	62–53	4.20	3.00
1923	48–41	5.16	3.00
1924	50–42	3.82	3.00
1925	55–43	6.23	3.00
1926	57–49	6.77	3.125
1927	68–57	6.83	3.50
1928	77–62	7.34	3.50
1929	110–73	8.82	3.875
1930	87–53	5.28	4.00
1931	64–16	1.48	3.25
1932	23–7	1.03	0.50
1933	42–14	1.46	0.50
1934	38–20	1.43	1.00
1935	33–27	1.81	0.50
1936	45–28	2.94	2.00
1937	50–20	2.07	1.25
1938	25–14	0.84	0.50

ATCHISON, TOPEKA, AND SANTA FE RAILWAY COMPANY

Year	Range of stock	Earned per share	Paid per share
1904	89–64	$ 9.47*	$ 4.00
1905	93–78	5.92*	4.00
1906	111–85	12.31*	4.50
1907	108–66	15.02*	6.00
1908	101–66	7.74*	5.00
1909	125–98	12.10*	5.50
1910	124–91	8.89*	6.00
1911	117–100	9.30*	6.00
1912	112–103	8.19*	6.00
1913	106–90	8.62*	6.00
1923	105–94	15.48	6.00
1924	121–97	15.47	6.00
1925	141–116	17.19	7.00
1926	172–122	23.42	7.00
1927	200–162	18.74	10.00
1928	204–183	18.09	10.00
1929	299–195	22.69	10.00
1930	243–168	12.86	10.00
1931	203–79	6.96	10.00
1932	94–18	0.55	2.50
1933	80–35	*1.03(d)*	Nil
1934	74–45	0.33	2.00
1935	60–36	1.38	2.00
1936	89–59	1.56	2.00
1937	95–33	0.60	2.00
1938	45–22	0.83	Nil

* Fiscal years ended June 30.

American Can was a typical example of a prewar speculative stock. It was speculative for three good and sufficient reasons: (1) It paid no dividend; (2) its earnings were small and irregular; (3) the issue was "watered," *i.e.*, a substantial part of its stated value represented no actual investment in the business. By contrast, Pennsylvania, Atchison, and National Biscuit were regarded as investment common stocks—also for three good and sufficient reasons: (1) They showed a satisfactory record of continued dividends; (2) the earnings were reasonably stable and averaged substantially in excess of the dividends paid; and (3) each dollar of stock was backed by a dollar or more of actual investment in the business.

NATIONAL BISCUIT COMPANY

Year	Range for stock	Earned per share	Paid per share
1909	120–97	$ 7.67*	$ 5.75
1910	120–100	9.86*	6.00
1911	144–117	10.05*	8.75
1912	161–114	9.59*	7.00
1913	130–104	11.73*	7.00
1914	139–120	9.52*	7.00
1915	132–116	8.20*	7.00
1916	131–118	9.72*	7.00
1917	123–80	9.87†	7.00
1918	111–90	11.63	7.00
	(old basis)‡	(old basis)‡	(old basis)‡
1923	370–266	$35.42	$21.00
1924	541–352	38.15	28.00
1925	553–455	40.53	28.00
1926	714–518	44.24	35.00
1927	1,309–663	49.77	42.00
1928	1,367–1,117	51.17	49.00
1929	1,657–980	57.40	52.50
1930	1,628–1,148	59.68	56.00
1931	1,466–637	50.05	49.00
1932	820–354	42.70	49.00
1933	1,061–569	36.93	49.00
1934	866–453	27.48	42.00
1935	637–389	22.93	31.50
1936	678–503	30.28	35.00
1937	584–298	28.35	28.00
1938	490–271	30.80	28.00

* Earnings for the year ended Jan. 31 of the following year.

† Eleven months ending Dec. 31, 1917.

‡ Stock was split 4 for 1 in 1922, followed by a 75% stock dividend. In 1930 it was again split $2\frac{1}{2}$ for 1. Published figures applicable to new stock were one-seventh of those given above for 1923–1929. Likewise the foregoing figures for 1930–1938 are $17\frac{1}{2}$ times the published figures for those years.

If we study the range of market price of these issues during the decade preceding the World War (or the 1909–1918 period for National Biscuit), we note that American Can fluctuated widely from year to year in the fashion regularly associated with speculative media but that Pennsylvania, Atchison, and National Biscuit showed much narrower variations and evidently tended to oscillate about a base price (*i.e.*, 97 for Atchison, 64 for Pennsylvania, and 120 for National Biscuit) that seemed to represent a well-defined view of their investment or intrinsic value.

AMERICAN CAN COMPANY

Year	Range for stock	Earned per share	Paid per share
1904	....	$ 0.51*	0
1905	....	*1.39(d)*†	0
1906	....	*1.30(d)*‡	0
1907	8–3	*0.57(d)*	0
1908	10–4	*0.44(d)*	0
1909	15–8	*0.32(d)*	0
1910	14–7	*0.15(d)*	0
1911	13–9	0.07	0
1912	47–11	8.86	0
1913	47–21	5.21	0
1923	108–74	19.64	$ 5.00
1924	164–96	20.51	6.00
1925	297–158	32.75	7.00
	(old basis)§	(old basis)§	(old basis)§
1926	379–233	26.34	13.25
1927	466–262	24.66	12.00
1928	705–423	41.16	12.00
1929	1,107–516	48.12	30.00
1930	940–628	48.48	30.00
1931	779–349	30.66	30.00
1932	443–178	19.56	24.00
1933	603–297	30.24	24.00
1934	689–542	50.32	24.00
1935	898–660	34.98	30.00
1936	825–660	34.80	36.00
1937	726–414	36.48	24.00
1938	631–425	26.10	24.00

* Fiscal year ended Mar. 31, 1905.
† Nine months ended Dec. 31, 1905.
‡ Excluding fire losses of 58 cents a share.
§ Stock was split 6 for 1 in 1926. Published figures applicable to new stock were one-sixth of those given for 1926–1938.

Prewar Conception of Investment in Common Stocks. Hence the prewar relationship between analysis and investment on the one hand and price changes and speculation on the other may be set forth as follows: Investment in common stocks was confined to those showing stable dividends and fairly stable earnings; and such issues in turn were expected to maintain a fairly stable market level. The function of analysis was primarily to search for elements of *weakness* in the picture. If the earnings were not properly stated; if the balance sheet revealed a poor current position, or the funded debt was growing too rapidly; if the physical plant was not properly maintained; if dangerous new competition was threatening, or if the company was losing ground in the industry; if the management was deteriorating or was likely to change for the worse; if there was reason to fear for the future of the industry as a whole—any of these defects or some other one might be sufficient to condemn the issue from the standpoint of the cautious investor.

On the positive side, analysis was concerned with finding those issues which met all the requirements of investment and *in addition* offered the best chance for future enhancement. The process was largely a matter of comparing similar issues in the investment class, *e.g.*, the group of dividend-paying Northwestern railroads. Chief emphasis would be laid upon the relative showing for past years, in particular the average earnings in relation to price and the stability and the trend of earnings. To a lesser extent, the analyst sought to look into the future and to select the industries or the individual companies that were likely to show the most rapid growth.

Speculation Characterized by Emphasis on Future Prospects. In the prewar period it was the well-considered view that when *prime emphasis* was laid upon what was expected of the future, instead of what had been accomplished in the past, a speculative attitude was thereby taken. Speculation, in its etymology, meant looking forward; investment was allied to "vested interests"—to property rights and values taking root in the *past*. The future was uncertain, therefore speculative; the past was known, therefore the source of safety. Let us consider a buyer of American Can common in 1910. He may have bought it believing that its price was going to advance or be "put up" or that its earnings were going to increase or that it was soon going to pay a dividend or possibly that it was destined to develop into one of the country's strongest industrials. From the prewar standpoint, although one of these reasons may have been more intelligent or creditable than another, each of them constituted a *speculative* motive for the purchase.

Technique of Investing in Common Stocks Resembled That for Bonds. Evidently there was a close similarity between the technique of investing in common stocks and that of investing in bonds. The common-stock investor, also, wanted a stable business and one showing an adequate margin of earnings over dividend requirements. Naturally he had to content himself with a smaller margin of safety than he would demand of a bond, a disadvantage that was offset by a larger income return (6% was standard on a good common stock compared with $4\frac{1}{2}\%$ on a high-grade bond), by the chance of an increased dividend if the business continued to prosper, and—generally of least importance in his eyes—by the possibility of a profit. A common-stock investor was likely to consider himself as in no very different position from that of a purchaser of second-grade bonds; essentially his venture amounted to sacrificing a certain *degree* of safety in return for larger income. The Pennsylvania and Atchison examples during the 1904–1913 decade will supply specific confirmation of the foregoing description.

Buying Common Stocks Viewed as Taking a Share in a Business. Another useful approach to the attitude of the prewar common-stock investor is from the standpoint of taking an interest in a private business. The typical common-stock investor was a business man, and it seemed sensible to him to value any corporate enterprise in much the same manner as he would value his own business. This meant that he gave at least as much attention to the asset values behind the shares as he did to their earnings records. It is essential to bear in mind the fact that a private business has always been valued primarily on the basis of the "net worth" as shown by its statement. A man contemplating the purchase of a partnership or stock interest in a private undertaking will always start with the value of that interest as shown "on the books," *i.e.*, the balance sheet, and will then consider whether or not the record and prospects are good enough to make such a commitment attractive. An interest in a private business may of course be sold for more or less than its proportionate asset value; but the book value is still invariably the starting point of the calculation, and the deal is finally made and viewed in terms of the premium or discount from book value involved.

Broadly speaking, the same attitude was formerly taken in an investment purchase of a marketable common stock. The first point of departure was the par value, presumably representing the amount of cash or property originally paid into the business; the second basal figure was the book value, representing the par value plus a ratable interest in the accumulated surplus. Hence in considering a common stock, investors asked themselves: "Is this issue a desirable purchase at the premium above book value, or the discount below book value, represented by the market price?" "Watered stock" was repeatedly inveighed against as a deception practiced upon the stock-buying public, who were misled by a fictitious statement of the asset values existing behind the shares. Hence one of the protective functions of security analysis was to discover whether or not the value of the fixed assets, as stated on the balance sheet of a company, fairly represented the actual cost or reasonable worth of the properties.

Investment in Common Stocks Based on Threefold Concept. We thus see that investment in common stocks was formerly based upon the threefold concept of: (1) a suitable and established dividend return, (2) a stable and adequate earnings record, and (3) a satisfactory backing of tangible assets. Each of these three elements could be made the subject of careful analytical study, viewing the issue both by itself and in comparison with others of its class. Common-stock commitments motivated by any other viewpoint were characterized as speculative, and it was not expected that they should be justified by a serious analysis.

THE NEW-ERA THEORY

During the postwar period, and particularly during the latter stage of the bull market culminating in 1929, the public acquired a completely different attitude towards the investment merits of common stocks. Two of the three elements above stated lost nearly all their significance, and the third, the earnings record, took on an entirely novel complexion. The new theory or principle may be summed up in the sentence: "The value of a common stock depends entirely upon what it will earn in the future."

From this dictum the following corollaries were drawn:

1. That the dividend rate should have slight bearing upon the value.

2. That since no relationship apparently existed between assets and earning power, the asset value was entirely devoid of importance.

3. That past earnings were significant only to the extent that they indicated what *changes* in the earnings were likely to take place in the future.

This complete revolution in the philosophy of common-stock investment took place virtually without realization by the stock-buying public and with only the most superficial recognition by financial observers. An effort must be made to reach a thorough comprehension of what this changed viewpoint really signifies. To do so we must consider it from three angles: its causes, its consequences and its logical validity.

Causes for This Changed Viewpoint. Why did the *investing* public turn its attention from dividends, from asset values, and from average earnings to transfer it almost exclusively to the earnings *trend, i.e.,* to the *changes* in earnings expected in the future? The answer was, first, that the records of the past were proving an undependable guide to investment; and, second, that the rewards offered by the future had become irresistibly alluring.

The new-era concepts had their root first of all in the obsolescence of the old-established standards. During the last generation the tempo of economic change has been speeded up to such a degree that the fact of being *long established* has ceased to be, as once it was, a warranty of *stability.* Corporations enjoying decade-long prosperity have been precipitated into insolvency within a few years. Other enterprises, which had been small or unsuccessful or in doubtful repute, have just as quickly acquired dominant size, impressive earnings, and the highest rating. The major group upon which investment interest was chiefly concentrated, *viz.,* the railroads, failed signally to participate in the expansion of national wealth and income and showed repeated signs of definite retrogression. The street railways, another important medium of investment prior to 1914, rapidly lost the greater portion of their value as the result of the development of new transportation agencies. The electric and gas companies followed an irregular course during this period, since they were harmed rather than helped by the war and postwar inflation, and their impressive growth was a relatively recent phenomenon. The history of industrial companies was a hodge-podge of violent changes, in which the benefits of prosperity were so unequally and so impermanently distributed as to bring about the most unexpected failures alongside of the most dazzling successes.

In the face of all this instability it was inevitable that the threefold basis of common-stock investment should prove totally inadequate. Past earnings and dividends could no longer be considered, in themselves, an index of future earnings and dividends. Furthermore, these future earn-

ings showed no tendency whatever to be controlled by the amount of the
actual investment in the business—the asset values—but instead
depended entirely upon a favorable industrial position and upon capable
or fortunate managerial policies. In numerous cases of receivership, the
current assets dwindled, and the fixed assets proved almost worthless.
Because of this absence of any connection between both assets and earnings and between assets and realizable values in bankruptcy, less and less
attention came to be paid either by financial writers or by the general public to the formerly important question of "net worth," or "book value";
and it may be said that by 1929 book value had practically disappeared
as an element in determining the attractiveness of a security issue. It is a
significant confirmation of this point that "watered stock," once so burn-
ing an issue, is now a forgotten phrase.

Attention Shifted to the Trend of Earnings. Thus the prewar
approach to investment, based upon past records and tangible facts,
became outworn and was discarded. Could anything be put in its place?
A new conception was given central importance—that of *trend of earnings*. The past was important only in so far as it showed the direction in
which the future could be expected to move. A continuous increase in
profits proved that the company was on the upgrade and promised still
better results in the future than had been accomplished to date. Conversely, if the earnings had declined or even remained stationary during
a prosperous period, the future must be thought unpromising, and the
issue was certainly to be avoided.

The Common-stocks-as-long-term-investments Doctrine.
Along with this idea as to what constituted the basis for common-stock
selection emerged a companion theory that common stocks represented
the most profitable and therefore the most desirable media for long-term
investment. This gospel was based upon a certain amount of research,
showing that diversified lists of common stocks had regularly increased
in value over stated intervals of time for many years past. The figures
indicated that such diversified common-stock holdings yielded both a
higher income return and a greater principal profit than purchases of
standard bonds.

The combination of these two ideas supplied the "investment theory"
upon which the 1927–1929 stock market proceeded. Amplifying the principle stated on page 356, the theory ran as follows:

1. "The value of a common stock depends on what it can earn in the future."
2. "Good common stocks are those which have shown a rising trend of earnings."
3. "Good common stocks will prove sound and profitable investments."

These statements sound innocent and plausible. Yet they concealed two theoretical weaknesses that could and did result in untold mischief. The first of these defects was that they abolished the fundamental distinctions between investment and speculation. The second was that they ignored the *price* of a stock in determining whether or not it was a desirable purchase.

New-era Investment Equivalent to Prewar Speculation. A moment's thought will show that "new-era investment," as practiced by the public and the investment trusts, was almost identical with speculation as popularly defined in preboom days. Such "investment" meant buying common stocks instead of bonds, emphasizing enhancement of principal instead of income, and stressing the changes of the future instead of the facts of the established past. It would not be inaccurate to state that new-era investment was simply old-style speculation confined to common stocks with a satisfactory trend of earnings. The impressive new concept underlying the greatest stock-market boom in history appears to be no more than a thinly disguised version of the old cynical epigram: "Investment is successful speculation."

Stocks Regarded as Attractive Irrespective of Their Prices. The notion that the desirability of a common stock was entirely independent of its price seems incredibly absurd. Yet the new-era theory led directly to this thesis. If a public-utility stock was selling at 35 times its *maximum* recorded earnings, instead of 10 times its *average* earnings, which was the preboom standard, the conclusion to be drawn was not that the stock was now too high but merely that the standard of value had been raised. Instead of judging the market price by established standards of value, the new era based its standards of value upon the market price. Hence all upper limits disappeared, not only upon the price at which a stock *could* sell but even upon the price at which it would *deserve* to sell. This fantastic reasoning actually led to the purchase at $100 per share of common stocks earning $2.50 per share. The identical reasoning would support the purchase of these same shares at $200, at $1,000, or at any conceivable price.

An alluring corollary of this principle was that making money in the stock market was now the easiest thing in the world. It was only necessary to buy "good" stocks, regardless of price, and then to let nature take her upward course. The results of such a doctrine could not fail to be tragic. Countless people asked themselves, "Why work for a living when a fortune can be made in Wall Street without working?" The ensuing migration from business into the financial district resembled the famous gold rush to the Klondike, except that gold was brought to Wall Street instead of taken from it.

Investment Trusts Adopted This New Doctrine. An ironical sidelight is thrown on this 1928–1929 theory by the practice of the investment trusts. These were formed for the purpose of giving the untrained public the benefit of expert administration of its funds—a plausible idea and one that had been working reasonably well in England. The earliest American investment trusts laid considerable emphasis upon certain time-tried principles of successful investment, which they were much better qualified to follow than the typical individual. The most important of these principles were:

1. To buy in times of depression and low prices and to sell out in times of prosperity and high prices.
2. To diversify holdings in many fields and probably in many countries.
3. To discover and acquire undervalued individual securities as the result of comprehensive and expert statistical investigations.

The rapidity and completeness with which these traditional principles disappeared from investment-trust technique is one of the many marvels of the period. The idea of buying in times of depression was obviously inapplicable. It suffered from the fatal weakness that investment trusts could be organized only in good times, so that they were virtually compelled to make their initial commitments in bull markets. The idea of world-wide geographical distribution had never exerted a powerful appeal upon the provincially minded Americans (who possibly were right in this respect), and with things going so much better here than abroad this principle was dropped by common consent.

Analysis Abandoned by Investment Trusts. But most paradoxical was the early abandonment of research and analysis in guiding investment-trust policies. However, since these financial institutions owed their existence to the new-era philosophy, it was natural and perhaps only just that they should adhere closely to it. Under its canons investment had now become so beautifully simple that research was unnecessary and elaborate statistical data a mere incumbrance. The investment process consisted merely of finding prominent companies with a rising trend of earnings and then buying their shares regardless of price. Hence the sound policy was to buy only what every one else was buying—a select list of highly popular and exceedingly expensive issues, appropriately known as the "blue chips." The original idea of searching for the undervalued and neglected issues dropped completely out of sight. Investment trusts actually boasted that their portfolios consisted exclusively of the active and standard (*i.e.*, the most popular and highest priced) common stocks. With but slight exaggeration, it might be asserted that under this convenient technique of investment, the affairs of a ten-million-dollar investment trust could be administered by the intelligence, the training and the actual labors of a single thirty-dollar-a-week clerk.

The man in the street, having been urged to entrust his funds to the superior skill of investment experts—for substantial compensation—was soon reassuringly told that the trusts would be careful to buy nothing except what the man in the street was buying himself.

The Justification Offered. Irrationality could go no further; yet it is important to note that mass speculation can flourish only in such an atmosphere of illogic and unreality. The self-deception of the mass speculator must, however, have its element of justification. This is usually some generalized statement, sound enough within its proper field, but twisted to fit the speculative mania. In real estate booms, the "reasoning" is usually based upon the inherent permanence and growth of land values. In the new-era bull market, the "rational" basis was the record of long-term improvement shown by diversified common-stock holdings.

A Sound Premise Used to Support an Unsound Conclusion.
There was, however, a radical fallacy involved in the new-era application of this historical fact. This should be apparent from even a superficial examination of the data contained in the small and rather sketchy volume from which the new-era theory may be said to have sprung. The book is entitled *Common Stocks as Long Term Investments*, by Edgar

Lawrence Smith, published in 1924.[1] Common stocks were shown to have a tendency to increase in value with the years, for the simple reason that they earned more than they paid out in dividends and thus the reinvested earnings added to their worth. In a representative case, the company would earn an average of 9%, pay 6% in dividends, and add 3% to surplus. With good management and reasonable luck the fair value of the stock would increase with its book value, at the annual rate of 3% *compounded*. This was, of course, a theoretical rather than a standard pattern, but the numerous instances of results poorer than "normal" might be offset by examples of more rapid growth.

The attractiveness of common stocks for the long pull thus lay essentially in the fact that they earned more than the bond-interest rate upon their cost. This would be true, typically, of a stock earning $10 and selling at 100. But as soon as the price was advanced to a much higher price in relation to earnings, this advantage disappeared, *and with it disappeared the entire theoretical basis for investment purchases of common stocks.* When in 1929 investors paid $200 per share for a stock earning $8, they were buying an earning power no greater than the bond-interest rate, without the extra protection afforded by a prior claim. Hence in using the past performances of common stocks as the reason for paying prices 20 to 40 times their earnings, the new-era exponents were starting with a sound premise and twisting it into a woefully unsound conclusion.

In fact their rush to take advantage of the inherent attractiveness of common stocks itself produced conditions entirely different from those which had given rise to this attractiveness and upon which it basically depended, *viz.*, the fact that earnings had averaged some 10% on market price. As we have seen, Edgar Lawrence Smith plausibly explained the growth of common-stock values as arising from the building up of asset values through the reinvestment of surplus earnings. Paradoxically enough, the new-era theory that exploited this finding refused to accord the slightest importance to the asset values behind the stocks it favored. Furthermore, the validity of Mr. Smith's conclusions rested necessarily upon the assumption that common stocks could be counted on to behave

---

[1] The reader is referred to Chelcie C. Bosland, *The Common Stock Theory of Investment, Its Development and Significance*, New York, 1937, for a survey of the literature on the common-stock theory. *Common Stock Indexes* by Alfred Cowles 3d and associates, Bloomington, Ind., 1939, is a significant work on this subject which has appeared since publication of Professor Bosland's book.

in the future about as they had in the past. Yet the new-era theory threw out of account the past earnings of corporations except in so far as they were regarded as pointing to a *trend* for the future.

Examples Showing Emphasis on Trend of Earnings. Take three companies with the following exhibits:

EARNINGS PER SHARE

Year	Company *A* (Electric Power & Light)	Company *B* (Bangor & Aroostook R. R.)	Company *C* (Chicago Yellow Cab)
1925	$1.01	$6.22	$5.52
1926	1.45	8.69	5.60
1927	2.09	8.41	4.54
1928	2.37	6.94	4.58
1929	2.98	8.30	4.47
5-year average	$1.98	$7.71	$4.94
High price, 1929	86⅝	90⅜	35

The 1929 high prices for these three companies show that the new-era attitude was enthusiastically favorable to Company *A*, unimpressed by Company *B*, and definitely hostile to Company *C*. The market considered Company *A* shares worth more than twice as much as Company *C* shares, although the latter earned 50% more per share than Company *A* in 1929 and its average earnings were 150% greater.[2]

Average vs. Trend of Earnings. These relationships between price and earnings in 1929 show definitely that the past exhibit was no longer a measure of normal earning power but merely a weathervane to show which way the winds of profit were blowing. That the *average earnings* had ceased to be a dependable measure of future earnings must indeed be admitted, because of the greater instability of the typical business to which we have previously alluded. But it did not follow at all that the *trend of earnings* must therefore be a more dependable guide than the *average;* and even if it were more dependable, it would not necessarily provide a safe basis, entirely by itself, for investment.

---

[2] See Appendix Note 44, p. 778 on accompanying CD, for a discussion of the subsequent performance of these three companies.

The accepted assumption that because earnings have moved in a certain direction for some years past they will continue to move in that direction is fundamentally no different from the discarded assumption that because earnings averaged a certain amount in the past they will continue to average about that amount in the future. It may well be that the earnings trend offers a more dependable clue to the future than does the earnings average. But at best such an indication of future results is far from certain, and, more important still, there is no method of establishing a logical relationship between trend and price.[3] This means that the value placed upon a satisfactory trend must be wholly arbitrary, and hence speculative, and hence inevitably subject to exaggeration and later collapse.

Danger in Projecting Trends into the Future. There are several reasons why we cannot be sure that a trend of profits shown in the past will continue in the future. In the broad economic sense, there is the law of diminishing returns and of increasing competition which must finally flatten out any sharply upward curve of growth. There is also the flow and ebb of the business cycle, from which the particular danger arises that the earnings curve will look most impressive on the very eve of a serious setback. Considering the 1927–1929 period we observe that since the trend-of-earnings theory was at bottom only a pretext to excuse rank speculation under the guise of "investment," the profit-mad public was quite willing to accept the flimsiest evidence of the existence of a favorable trend. Rising earnings for a period of five, or four, or even three years only, were regarded as an assurance of uninterrupted future growth and a warrant for projecting the curve of profits indefinitely upward.

---

[3] The new-era investment theory was conspicuously reticent on the mathematical side. The relationship between price and earnings, or price and trend of earnings was anything that the market pleased to make it (note the price of Electric Power and Light compared with its earnings record given on p. 363). If an attempt were to be made to give a mathematical expression to the underlying idea of valuation, it might be said that it was based on the *derivative* of the earnings, stated in terms of time. In recent years more serious efforts have been made to establish a mathematical basis for discounting expected future earnings or dividends. See Gabriel Preinreich, *The Theory of Dividends*, New York, 1935; and J. B. Williams, *The Theory of Investment Value*, Cambridge, Mass., 1938. The latter work is built on the premise that the value of a common stock is equal to the present value of all future dividends. This principle gives rise to an elaborate series of mathematical equations designed to calculate exactly what a common stock is worth, *assuming* certain vital facts about future earnings, distribution policy and interest rates.

Example: The prevalent heedlessness on this score was most evident in connection with the numerous common-stock flotations during this period. The craze for a showing of rising profits resulted in the promotion of many industrial enterprises that had been favored by temporary good fortune and were just approaching, or had already reached, the peak of their prosperity. A typical example of this practice is found in the offering of preferred and common stock of Schletter and Zander, Inc., a manufacturer of hosiery (name changed later to Signature Hosiery Company). The company was organized in 1929, to succeed a company organized in 1922, and the financing was effected by the sale of 44,810 shares of $3.50 convertible preferred shares at $50 per share and 261,349 voting-trust certificates for common stock at $26 per share. The offering circular presented the following exhibit of earnings from the constituent properties:

Year	Net after federal taxes	Per share of preferred	Per share of common
1925	$ 172,058	$ 3.84	$0.06
1926	339,920	7.58	0.70
1927	563,856	12.58	1.56
1928	1,021,308	22.79	3.31

The subsequent record was as follows:

1929	812,136	18.13	2.51
1930	*179,875(d)*	*4.01(d)*	*1.81(d)*

In 1931 liquidation of the company's assets was begun, and a total of $17 per share in liquidating dividends on the preferred had been paid up to the end of 1933. (Assets then remaining for liquidation were negligible.) The common was wiped out.

This example illustrates one of the paradoxes of financial history, *viz.,* that at the very period when the increasing instability of individual companies had made the purchase of common stocks far more precarious than before, the gospel of common stocks as safe and satisfactory investments was preached to and avidly accepted by the American public.

Chapter 28

NEWER CANONS OF COMMON-STOCK INVESTMENT

OUR EXTENDED discussion of the theory of common-stock investment has thus far led only to negative conclusions. The older approach, centering upon the conception of a stable average earning power, appears to have been vitiated by the increasing instability of the typical business. As for the new-era view, which turned upon the earnings trend as the sole criterion of value, whatever truth may lurk in this generalization, its blind adoption as a basis for common-stock purchases, without calculation or restraint, was certain to end in an appalling debacle. Is there anything at all left, then, of the idea of sound investment in common stocks?

A careful review of the preceding criticism will show that it need not be so destructive to the notion of investment in common stocks as a first impression would suggest. The instability of individual companies may conceivably be offset by means of thoroughgoing diversification. Moreover, the trend of earnings, although most dangerous as a *sole* basis for selection, may prove a useful *indication* of investment merit. If this approach is a sound one, there may be formulated an acceptable canon of common-stock investment, containing the following elements:

1. Investment is conceived as a *group* operation, in which diversification of risk is depended upon to yield a favorable average result.

2. The individual issues are selected by means of qualitative and quantitative tests corresponding to those employed in the choice of fixed-value investments.

3. A greater effort is made, than in the case of bond selection, to determine the future outlook of the issues considered.

Whether or not a policy of common-stock acquisition based upon the foregoing principles deserves the title of investment is undoubtedly open to debate. The importance of the question, and the lack of well-defined and authoritative views thereon, compel us to weigh here the leading arguments for and against this proposition.

THREE GENERAL APPROACHES

Secular Expansion as Basis. May the ownership of a carefully selected, diversified group of common stocks, purchased at reasonable prices, be characterized as a sound investment policy? An affirmative answer may be developed from any one of three different kinds of assumptions relating to the future of American business and the policy of selection that is followed. The first will posit that certain basic and long-established elements in this country's economic experience may still be counted upon. These are (1) that our national wealth and earning power will increase, (2) that such increase will reflect itself in the increased resources and profits of our important corporations, and (3) that such increases will in the main take place through the normal process of investment of new capital and reinvestment of undistributed earnings. The third part of this assumption signifies that a broad causal connection exists between accumulating surplus and future earning power, so that common-stock selection is not a matter purely of chance or guesswork but should be governed by an analysis of past records in relation to current market prices.

If these fundamental conditions still obtain, then common stocks with suitable exhibits should on the whole present the same favorable opportunities in the future as they have for generations past. The cardinal defect of instability may not be regarded, therefore, as menacing the long-range development of common stocks as a whole. It does indeed exert a powerful temporary effect upon all business through the variations of the economic cycle, and it has permanently adverse effects upon individual enterprises and single industries. But of these two dangers, the latter may be offset in part by careful selection and chiefly by wide diversification; the former may be guarded against by unvarying insistence upon the reasonableness of the price paid for each purchase.

They would be rash authors who would express themselves unequivocably for or against this basic assumption that American business will develop in the future pretty much as in the past. In our Introduction we point out that the experience of the last fifteen years weighs against this proposition. Without seeking to prophesy the future, may it not suffice to declare that the *investor* cannot safely rely upon a *general* growth of earnings to provide both safety and profit over the long pull? In this respect it would seem that we are back to the investor's attitude in 1913—with the difference that his caution *then* seemed needlessly blind to the powerful evidences of secular growth inherent in our economy. Our caution today would appear, at least, to be based on bitter experience and on the recognition of some newer and less promising factors in the whole business picture.

Individual Growth as Basis of Selection. Those who would reject the suggestion that common-stock investment may be founded securely on a *general* secular expansion may be attracted to a second approach. This stresses the element of selectivity and is based on the premise that *certain favored companies* may be relied on to grow steadily. Hence such companies, when located, can be bought with confidence as long-term investments. This philosophy of investment is set forth at some length in the 1938 report of National Investors Corporation, an investment trust, from which we quote as follows:

> The studies by this organization, directed specifically toward improved procedure in selection, afford evidence that the common stocks of growth companies—that is, companies whose earnings move forward from cycle to cycle, and are only temporarily interrupted by periodic business depressions—offer the most effective medium of investment in the field of common stocks, either in terms of dividend return or longer term capital appreciation. We believe that this general conclusion can be demonstrated statistically and is supported by economic analysis and practical reasoning.

In considering this statement critically, we must start with the emphatic but rather obvious assertion that the investor who can successfully identify such "growth companies" *when their shares are available at reasonable prices* is certain to do superlatively well with his capital. Nor can it be denied that there have been investors capable of making such selections with a high degree of accuracy and that they have benefited hugely from their foresight and good judgment. But the real question is whether or not *all* careful and intelligent investors can follow this policy with fair success.

Three Aspects of the Problem. Actually the problem falls into three parts: First, what is meant by a "growth company"? Second, can the investor identify such concerns with reasonable accuracy? Third, to what extent does the price paid for such stocks affect the success of the program?

1. *What Are Growth Companies?* The National Investors Corporation discussion defined growth companies as those "whose earnings move forward from cycle to cycle." How many cycles are needed to meet this definition? The fact of the matter seems to be that prior to 1930 a large proportion of *all* publicly owned American businesses grew from cycle to cycle. The distinguishing characteristic of growth companies, as now understood, developed only in the period between 1929 and 1936–1937. In this *one* cycle we find that most companies failed to regain their full depression losses. The minority that did so stand out from the rest, and it is these which are now given the complimentary title of "growth companies." But since this distinction is in reality based on performance during a single cycle, how sure can the investor be that it will be maintained over the longer future?

It is true, from what we have previously said, that many of the companies that expanded from 1929 to 1937 had participated in the general record of growth prior to 1929, so that they combine the advantages of a long period of upbuilding and an *exceptional* ability to expand in the last decade. The following are examples of large and well-known companies of this class:

Air Reduction	Monsanto Chemical
Allis Chalmers	Owens-Illinois Glass
Coca-Cola	J. C. Penney
Commercial Credit	Procter & Gamble
Dow Chemical	Sherwin-Williams Paint
Du Pont	Standard Oil of New Jersey
International Business Machines	Scott Paper
International Nickel	Union Carbide and Carbon
Libbey-Owens-Ford	

2. *Can the Investor Identify Them?* But our natural enthusiasm for such excellent records is tempered somewhat by a sobering consideration. This is the fact that, viewed historically, most successful companies

of the past are found to have pursued a well-defined life cycle, consisting first of a series of struggles and setbacks; second, of a halcyon period of prosperity and persistent growth; which in turn passes over into a final phase of supermaturity—characterized by a slackening of expansion and perhaps an actual loss of leadership or even profitability.[1] It follows that a business that has enjoyed a very long period of increasing earnings may *ipso facto* be nearing its own "saturation point." Hence the seeker for growth stocks really faces a dilemma; for if he chooses newer companies with a short record of expansion, he runs the risk of being deceived by a temporary prosperity; and if he chooses enterprises that have advanced through several business cycles, he may find this apparent strength to be the harbinger of coming weakness.

We see, therefore, that the identification of a growth company is not so simple a matter as it may at first appear. It cannot be accomplished solely by an examination of the statistics and records but requires a considerable supplement of special investigation and of business judgment. Proponents of the growth-company principle of investment are wont currently to lay great emphasis on the element of industrial research. In the absence of *general* business expansion, exceptional gains are likely to be made by companies supplying new products or processes. These in turn are likely to emerge from research laboratories. The profits realized from cellophane, ethyl gas and various plastics, and from advances in the arts of radio, photography, refrigeration, aeronautics, etc., have created a natural enthusiasm for research as a business asset and a natural tendency to consider the possession of research facilities as the *sine qua non* of industrial progress.

Still here, too, caution is needed. If the mere ownership of a research laboratory could guarantee a successful future, every company in the land would have one. Hence, the investor must pay heed to the kind of facilities owned, the abilities of the researchers and the potentialities of the field under investigation. It is not impossible to study these points successfully, but the task is not easy, and the chance of error is great.

3. *Does the Price Discount Potential Growth?* The third source of difficulty is perhaps the greatest. Assuming a fair degree of confidence on

---

[1] This characteristic pattern of successful enterprise is discussed at length in the 1938 report of National Investors Corporation, pp. 4–6.

the part of the investor that the company will expand in the future, what *price* is he justified in paying for this attractive element? Obviously, if he can get a good future for *nothing, i.e.,* if the price reflects only the past record, he is making a sound investment. But this is not the case, of course, *if the market itself is counting on future growth.* Characteristically, stocks thought to have good prospects sell at relatively high prices. How can the investor tell whether or not the price is *too* high? We think that there is no good answer to this question—in fact we are inclined to think that even if one knew for a certainty just what a company is fated to earn over a long period of years, it would still be impossible to tell what is a fair price to pay for it today. It follows that *once the investor pays a substantial amount for the growth factor,* he is inevitably assuming certain kinds of risk; *viz.,* that the growth will be less than he anticipates, that over the long pull he will have paid too much for what he gets, that for a considerable period the market will value the stock less optimistically than he does.

On the other hand, assume that the investor strives to avoid paying a high premium for future prospects by choosing companies about which he is personally optimistic, although they are not favorites of the stock market. No doubt this is the type of judgment that, if sound, will prove most remunerative. But, by the very nature of the case, it must represent the activity of strong-minded and daring individuals rather than investment in accordance with accepted rules and standards.[2]

May Such Purchases Be Described as Investment Commitments? This has been a longish discussion because the subject is important and not too well comprehended in Wall Street. Our emphasis has been laid more on the pitfalls of investing for future growth than on its advantages. But we repeat that this method may be followed successfully if it is pursued with skill, intelligence and diligent study. If so, is it appropriate to call such purchases by the name of "investment"? Our answer is "yes," provided that two factors are present: the first, already mentioned, that the elements affecting the future are examined with real care and a wholesome

---

[2] The "expanding-industry" criterion of common-stock investment is vigorously championed in an arresting book *The Ebb and Flow of Investment Values,* New York, 1939, by Edward S. Mead and J. Grodinsky. For a consideration of their views in some detail see Appendix Note 71, p. 845 on accompanying CD.

scepticism, rather than accepted quickly via some easy generalization; the second, that the price paid be not substantially different from what a prudent business man would be willing to pay for a similar opportunity presented to him to invest in a private undertaking over which he could exercise control.

We believe that the second criterion will supply a useful touchstone to determine whether the buyer is making a well-considered and legitimate commitment in an enterprise with an attractive future, or instead, under the guise of "investment," he is really taking a flier in a popular stock or else letting his private enthusiasm run away with his judgment.

It will be argued, perhaps, that common-stock investments such as we have been discussing may properly be made at a considerably higher price than would be justified in the case of a private business, first, because of the great advantage of marketability that attaches to listed stocks and, second, because the large size and financial power of publicly owned companies make them inherently more attractive than any private enterprise could be. As to the second point, the price to be paid should suitably reflect any advantages accruing by reason of size and financial strength, but this criterion does not really depend on whether the company is publicly or privately owned. On the first point, there is room for some difference of opinion whether or not the ability to *control* a private business affords a full counterweight (in value analysis) to the advantage of marketability enjoyed by a listed stock. To those who believe marketability is more valuable than control, we might suggest that in any event the premium to be paid for this advantage cannot well be placed above, say, 20% of the value otherwise justified without danger of introducing a definitely speculative element into the picture.

Selection Based on Margin-of-safety Principle. The third approach to common-stock investment is based on the margin-of-safety principle. If the analyst is convinced that a stock is *worth more* than he pays for it, and if he is *reasonably optimistic* as to the company's future, he would regard the issue as a suitable component of a group investment in common stocks. This attack on the problem lends itself to two possible techniques. One is to buy *at times when the general market is low*, measured by quantitative standards of value. Presumably the purchases would then be confined to representative and fairly active issues. The other technique would be employed to discover undervalued *individual* common stocks, which presumably are available even when the general market is not particularly low. In either case the "margin of safety" resides in the discount at which the stock is selling below its minimum intrinsic value, as measured by the analyst. But with respect to the hazards and the psychological factors involved, the two approaches differ considerably. Let us discuss them in their order.

Factors Complicating Efforts to Exploit General Market Swings. A glance at the chart on page 26, showing the fluctuations of common-stock prices since 1900, would suggest that prices are recurrently too high and too low and that consequently there should be repeated opportunities to buy stocks at less than their value and to sell them out later at fair value or higher. A crude method of doing this—but one apparently encouraged by the chart itself—would consist simply of drawing a straight line through the approximate midpoints of past market swings and then planning to buy somewhere below this line and to sell somewhere above it.

Perhaps such a "system" would be as practical as any, but the analyst is likely to insist on a more scientific approach. One possible refinement would operate as follows:

1. Select a diversified list of leading industrial common stocks.

2. Determine a base or "normal" value for the group by capitalizing their average earnings at some suitable figure, related to the going long-term interest rate.

3. Determine a buying point at some percentage below this normal value and a selling point above it. (Or buying and selling may be done "on a scale down" and "on a scale up.")

A method of this kind has plausible logic to recommend it, and it is favored also by an age-old tradition that success in the stock market is gained by buying at depressed levels and selling out when the public is optimistic. But the reader will suspect at once that there is a catch to it somewhere. What are its drawbacks?

As we see it, the difficulties attending this idea are threefold: First, although the *general* pattern of the market's behavior may be properly anticipated, the specific buying and selling points may turn out to have been badly chosen, and the operator may miss his opportunity at one extreme or the other. Second, there is always a chance that the character of the market's behavior may change significantly, so that a scheme of operation that would have worked well in the past will cease to be practicable. Third, the method itself requires a considerable amount of human fortitude. It generally involves buying and selling when the prevalent psychology favors the opposite course, watching one's shares go lower after purchase and higher after sale and often staying out of the market for long periods (*e.g.,* 1927–1930) when most people are actively interested in stocks. But despite these disadvantages, which we do not minimize, it is our view that this method has a good deal to commend it to those temperamentally qualified to follow it.

The Undervalued-individual-issue Approach. The other application of the principle of investing in undervalued common stocks is directed at individual issues, which upon analysis appear to be worth substantially more than they are selling for. It is rare that a common stock will appear satisfactory *from every qualitative angle* and at the same time will be found to be selling at a low price by such quantitative standards as earnings, dividends, and assets. Issues of this type would undoubtedly be eligible for a group purchase that would fulfill our supplementary criterion of "investment" given in Chap. 4. ("An investment operation is one that can be justified on both qualitative and quantitative grounds.")

Of more practical importance is the question whether or not investment can be successfully carried on in common stocks that appear cheap from the quantitative angle and that—upon study—seem to have *average* prospects for the future. Securities of this type can be found in reasonable abundance, as a result of the stock market's obsession with companies considered to have *unusually good prospects of growth.* Because of this emphasis on the growth factor, quite a number of enterprises that are long established, well financed, important in their industries and presumably destined to stay in business and make profits indefinitely in the future, but that have no speculative or growth appeal, tend to be discriminated against by the stock market—especially in years of subnormal profits—and to sell *for considerably less than the business would be worth to a private owner.*[3]

---

[3] Note that we have applied the touchstone of "value to a private investor" to justify *two* different types of *investment* in common stocks: (1) purchase of issues thought to have exceptional prospects at no higher price than would be paid for a corresponding interest in a private business, and (2) purchase of issues with good records and *average* prospects at a much *lower* price than the business is worth to a private owner. See Appendix Note 45, p. 778 on accompanying CD, for the exhibit of an issue of the latter type (Swift and Company).

We incline strongly to the belief that this last criterion—a price far less than value to a private owner—will constitute a sound touchstone for the discovery of true investment opportunities in common stocks. This view runs counter to the convictions and practice of most people seeking to invest in equities, including practically all the investment trusts. Their emphasis is mainly on long-term growth, prospects for the next year, or the indicated trend of the stock market itself. Undoubtedly any of these three viewpoints may be followed successfully by those especially well equipped by experience and native ability to exploit them. But we are not so sure that any of these approaches can be developed into a system or technique that can be confidently followed by everyone of sound intelligence who has studied it with care. Hence we must raise our solitary voice against the use of the term *investment* to characterize these methods of operating in common stocks, however profitable they may be to the truly skillful. Trading in the market, forecasting next year's results for various businesses, selecting the best media for long-term expansion—all these have a useful place in Wall Street. But we think that the interests of investors and of Wall Street as an institution would be better served if operations based primarily on these factors were called by some other name than investment.

Whether or not our own concept of common-stock investment is a valid one may be more intelligently considered after we have given extended treatment to the chief factors that enter into a statistical analysis of a stock issue. The need for such analysis is quite independent of our investment philosophy. After all, common stocks exist and are actively dealt in by the public. Those who buy and sell will properly seek to arm themselves with an adequate knowledge of financial practice and with the tools and technique necessary for an intelligent analysis of corporate statements.

Such information and equipment for the common-stock investor form the subject matter of the following chapters.

Chapter 29

THE DIVIDEND FACTOR IN COMMON-STOCK ANALYSIS

A NATURAL classification of the elements entering into the valuation of a common stock would be under the three headings:

1. The dividend rate and record.
2. Income-account factors (earning power).
3. Balance-sheet factors (asset value).

The dividend rate is a simple fact and requires no analysis, but its exact significance is exceedingly difficult to appraise. From one point of view the dividend rate is all-important, but from another and equally valid standpoint it must be considered an accidental and minor factor. A basic confusion has grown up in the minds of managements and stockholders alike as to what constitutes a proper dividend policy. The result has been to create a definite conflict between two aspects of common-stock ownership: one being the possession of a marketable security, and the other being the assumption of a partnership interest in a business. Let us consider the matter in detail from this twofold approach.

Dividend Return as a Factor in Common-stock Investment.
Until recent years the dividend return was the overshadowing factor in common-stock investment. This point of view was based on simple logic. The prime purpose of a business corporation is to pay dividends to its owners. A successful company is one that can pay dividends regularly and presumably increase the rate as time goes on. Since the idea of investment is closely bound up with that of dependable income, it follows that investment in common stocks would ordinarily be confined to those with a well-established dividend. It would follow also that the *price* paid for an investment common stock would be determined chiefly by the amount of the dividend.

We have seen that the traditional common-stock investor sought to place himself as nearly as possible in the position of an investor in a bond or a preferred stock. He aimed primarily at a steady income return, which in general would be both somewhat larger and somewhat less certain than that provided by good senior securities. Excellent illustrations of the effect of this attitude upon the price of common stocks are afforded by the records of the earnings, dividends and annual price variations of American Sugar Refining between 1907 and 1913 and of Atchison, Topeka, and Santa Fe Railway between 1916 and 1925 presented herewith.

AMERICAN SUGAR REFINING COMPANY

Year	Range for stock	Earned per share	Paid per share
1907	138–93	$10.22	$7.00
1908	138–99	7.45	7.00
1909	136–115	14.20	7.00
1910	128–112	5.38	7.00
1911	123–113	18.92	7.00
1912	134–114	5.34	7.00
1913	118–100	*0.02(d)*	7.00

ATCHISON, TOPEKA, AND SANTA FE RAILWAY COMPANY

Year	Range for stock	Earned per share	Paid per share
1916	109–100	$14.74	$6
1917	108–75	14.50	6
1918	100–81	10.59*	6
1919	104–81	15.41*	6
1920	90–76	12.54*	6
1921	94–76	14.69†	6
1922	109–92	12.41	6
1923	105–94	15.48	6
1924	121–97	15.47	6
1925	141–116	17.19	7

* Results for these years based on actual operations. Results of federal operation were: 1918—$9.98; 1919—$16.55; 1920—$13.98.
† Includes nonrecurrent income. Excluding the latter the figure for 1921 would have been $11.29.

The market range of both issues is surprisingly narrow, considering the continuous gyrations of the stock market generally during those periods. The most striking feature of the exhibit is the slight influence exercised both by the irregular earnings of American Sugar and by the exceptionally well-maintained and increasing earning power on the part of Atchison. It is clear that the price of American Sugar was dominated throughout by its $7 rate and that of Atchison by its $6 rate, even though the earnings records would apparently have justified an entirely different range of relative market values.

Established Principle of Withholding Dividends. We have, therefore, on the one hand an ingrained and powerfully motivated tradition which centers investment interest upon the present and past dividend rate. But on the other hand we have an equally authoritative and well-established principle of *corporate management* which subordinates the current dividend to the future welfare of the company and its shareholders. It is considered proper managerial policy to withhold current earnings from stockholders, for the sake of any of the following advantages:

1. To strengthen the financial (working-capital) position.
2. To increase productive capacity.
3. To eliminate an original overcapitalization.

When a management withholds and reinvests profits, thus building up an accumulated surplus, it claims confidently to be acting for the best interests of the shareholders. For by this policy the continuance of the established dividend rate is undoubtedly better assured, and furthermore a gradual but continuous increase in the regular payment is thereby made possible. The rank and file of stockholders will give such policies their support, either because they are individually convinced that this procedure redounds to their advantage or because they accept uncritically the authority of the managements and bankers who recommend it.

But this approval by stockholders of what is called a "conservative dividend policy" has about it a peculiar element of the perfunctory and even the reluctant. The typical investor would most certainly prefer to have his dividend today and let tomorrow take care of itself. No instances are on record in which the withholding of dividends for the sake of future profits has been hailed with such enthusiasm as to advance the price of the stock. The direct opposite has invariably been true. *Given two companies in the same general position and with the same earning power, the one paying the larger dividend will always sell at the higher price.*

Policy of Withholding Dividends Questionable. This is an arresting fact, and it should serve to call into question the traditional theory of corporate finance that the smaller the percentage of earnings paid out in dividends the better for the company and its stockholders. Although investors have been taught to pay lip service to this theory, their instincts—and perhaps their better judgment—are in revolt against it. If we try to bring a fresh and critical viewpoint to bear upon this subject, we shall find that weighty objections may be leveled against the accepted dividend policy of American corporations.

Examining this policy more closely, we see that it rests upon two quite distinct assumptions. The first is that it is advantageous to the stockholders to leave a substantial part of the annual earnings in the business; the second is that it is desirable to maintain a steady dividend rate in the face of fluctuations in profits. As to the second point, there would be no question at all, provided the dividend *stability* is achieved without too great sacrifice in the *amount* of the dividend. Assume that the earnings vary between $5 and $15 annually over a period of years, averaging $10. No doubt the stockholder's advantage would be best served by maintaining a stable dividend rate of $8, sometimes drawing upon the surplus to maintain it, but on the average increasing the surplus at the rate of $2 per share annually.

This would be an ideal arrangement. But in practice it is rarely followed. We find that stability of dividends is usually accomplished by the simple expedient of paying out a *small part* of the average earnings. By a *reductio ad absurdum* it is clear that any company that earned $10 per share on the average could readily stabilize its dividend at $1. The question arises very properly if the shareholders might not prefer a much larger aggregate dividend, even with some irregularity. This point is well illustrated in the case of Atchison.

The Case of Atchison. Atchison maintained its dividend at the annual rate of $6 for the 15 years between 1910 and 1924. During this time the average earnings were in excess of $12 per share, so that the stability was attained by withholding over half the earnings from the stockholders. Eventually this policy bore fruit in an advance of the dividend to $10, which rate was paid between 1927 and 1931, and was accompanied by a rise in the market price to nearly $300 per share in 1929. Within six months after the last payment at the $10 rate (in December 1931) the dividend was omitted entirely. Viewed critically, the stability of the Atchison dividend between 1910 and 1924 must be considered as of dubious benefit to the stockholders. During its continuance they received an unduly small return in relation to the earnings; when the rate was finally advanced, the importance attached to such a move promoted excessive speculation in the shares; finally, the reinvestment of the enormous sums out of earnings failed to protect the shareholders from a complete loss of income in 1932. Allowance must be made, of course, for the unprecedented character of the depression in 1932. But the fact remains that the actual operating losses in dollars per share up to the passing of the dividend were entirely insignificant in comparison with the surplus accumulated out of the profits of previous years.

United States Steel, Another Example. The Atchison case illustrates the two major objections to what is characterized and generally approved of as a "conservative dividend policy." The first objection is that stockholders receive *both currently and ultimately* too low a return in relation to the earnings of their property; the second is that the "saving up of profits for a rainy day" often fails to safeguard even the moderate dividend rate when the rainy day actually arrives. A similarly striking example of the ineffectiveness of a large accumulated surplus is shown by that leading industrial enterprise, United States Steel.

The following figures tell a remarkable story:

Profits available for the common stock, 1901–1930 ....$2,344,000,000
    Dividends paid:
      Cash 891,000,000
      Stock 203,000,000
    Undistributed earnings..1,250,000,000
    Loss after preferred dividends Jan. 1, 1931–June 30, 1932 59,000,000
    Common dividend passed June 30, 1932.

A year and a half of declining business was sufficient to outweigh the beneficial influence of 30 years of practically continuous reinvestment of profits.

The Merits of "Plowing-back" Earnings. These examples serve to direct our critical attention to the other assumption on which American dividend policies are based, *viz.*, that it is advantageous to the stockholders if a large portion of the annual earnings are retained in the business. This may well be true, but in determining its truth a number of factors must be considered that are usually left out of account. The customary reasoning on this point may be stated in the form of a syllogism, as follows:

> Major premise—Whatever benefits the company benefits the stockholders.
> Minor premise—A company is benefited if its earnings are retained rather than paid out in dividends.
> Conclusion—Stockholders are benefited by the withholding of corporate earnings.

The weakness of the foregoing reasoning rests of course in the major premise. Whatever benefits a business benefits its owners, *provided* the benefit is not conferred upon the corporation at the *expense* of the stockholders. Taking money away from the stockholders and presenting it to the company will undoubtedly strengthen the enterprise, but whether or not it is to the owners' advantage is an entirely different question. It is customary to commend managements for "plowing earnings back into the property"; but, in measuring the benefits from such a policy, the time element is usually left out of account. It stands to reason that, if a business paid out only a small part of its earnings in dividends, the value of the stock should increase over a period of years, but it is by no means so certain that this increase will compensate the stockholders for the dividends withheld from them, *particularly if interest on these amounts is compounded.*

An inductive study would undoubtedly show that the earning power of corporations does not in general expand proportionately with increases in accumulated surplus. *Assuming that the reported earnings were actually available for distribution,* then stockholders in general would certainly fare better in dollars and cents if they drew out practically all of these earnings in dividends. An unconscious realization of this fact has much to do with the tendency of common stocks paying liberal dividends to sell higher than others with the same earning power but paying out only a small part thereof.

Dividend Policies Arbitrary and Sometimes Selfishly Determined. One of the obstacles in the way of an intelligent understanding by stockholders of the dividend question is the accepted notion that the determination of dividend policies is entirely a managerial function, in the same way as the general running of the business. This is legally true, and the courts will not interfere with the dividend action or inaction except upon an exceedingly convincing showing of unfairness. But if stockholders' opinions were properly informed, it would insist upon curtailing the despotic powers given the directorate over the dividend policy. Experience shows that these unrestricted powers are likely to be abused for various reasons. Boards of directors usually consist largely of executive officers and their friends. The officers are naturally desirous of retaining as much cash as possible in the treasury, in order to simplify their financial problems; they are also inclined to expand the business persistently for the sake of personal aggrandizement and to secure higher salaries. This is a leading cause of the unwise increase of manufacturing facilities which has proved recurrently one of the chief unsettling factors in our economic situation.

The discretionary power over the dividend policy may also be abused in more sinister fashion, sometimes to permit the acquisition of shares at an unduly low price, at other times to facilitate unloading at a high quotation. The heavy surtaxes imposed upon large incomes frequently make it undesirable from the standpoint of the large stockholders that earnings be paid out in dividends. Hence dividend policies may be determined at times from the standpoint of the taxable status of the large stockholders who control the directorate. This is particularly true in cases where these dominant stockholders receive substantial salaries as executives. In such cases they are perfectly willing to leave their share of the earnings in the corporate treasury, since the latter is under their control and since by so doing they retain control over the earnings accruing to the other stockholders as well.

Arbitrary Control of Dividend Policy Complicates Analysis of Common Stocks. Viewing American corporate dividend policies as a whole, it cannot be said that the virtually unlimited power given the management on this score has redounded to the benefit of the stockholders. In entirely too many cases the right to pay out or withhold earnings at will is exercised in an unintelligent or inequitable manner. Dividend policies are often so arbitrarily managed as to introduce an additional uncertainty in the analysis of a common stock. Besides the difficulty of judging the earning power, there is the second difficulty of predicting what part of the earnings the directors will see fit to disburse in dividends.

It is important to note that this feature is peculiar to American corporate finance and has no close counterpart in the other important countries. The typical English, French, or German company pays out practically all the earnings of each year, except those carried to reserves.[1] Hence they do not build up large profit-and-loss surpluses, such as are common in the United States. Capital for expansion purposes is provided abroad not out of undistributed earnings but through the sale of additional stock. To some extent, perhaps, the reserve accounts shown in foreign balance sheets will serve the same purpose as an American surplus account, but these reserve accounts rarely attain a comparable magnitude.

Plowing Back Due to Watered Stock. The American theory of "plowing back" earnings appears to have grown out of the stock-watering practices of prewar days. Many of our large industrial companies made their initial appearance with no tangible assets behind their common shares and with inadequate protection for their preferred issues. Hence it was natural that the management should seek to make good these deficiencies out of subsequent earnings. This was particularly true because additional stock could not be sold at its par value, and it was difficult therefore to obtain new capital for expansion except through undistributed profits.[2]

Examples: Concrete examples of the relation between overcapitalization and dividend policies are afforded by the outstanding cases of Woolworth and United States Steel Corporation.

In the original sale of F. W. Woolworth Company shares to the public, made in 1911, the company issued preferred stock to represent all the tangible assets and common stock to represent the good-will. The balance sheet accordingly carried a good-will item of $50,000,000 among the assets, offsetting a corresponding liability for 500,000 shares of common, par $100.[3] As Woolworth prospered, a large surplus was built up out of

---

[1] See Appendix Note 46, p. 781 on accompanying CD, for discussion and examples.

[2] The no-par-value device is largely a post-1918 development.

[3] This was for many years a standard scheme for financing of industrial companies. It was followed by Sears Roebuck, Cluett Peabody, National Cloak and Suit, and others.

earnings, and amounts were charged against this surplus to reduce the good-will account, until finally it was written down to $1.[4]

In the case of United States Steel Corporation, the original capitalization exceeded tangible assets by no less than $768,000,000, representing all the common and more than half the preferred stock. This "water" in the balance sheet was not shown as a good-will item, as in the case of Woolworth, but was concealed by an overvaluation of the fixed assets (*i.e.*, of the "Property Investment Accounts"). Through various accounting methods, however, the management applied earnings from operations to the writing off of these intangible or fictitious assets. By the end of 1929 a total of $508,000,000—equal to the entire original common-stock issue—had been taken from earnings or surplus and deducted from the property account. The balance of $260,000,000 was set up separately as an intangible asset in the 1937 report and then written off entirely in 1938 by means of a reduction in the stated value of the common stock.

Some of the accounting policies above referred to will be discussed again, with respect to their influence on investment values, in our chapters on Analysis of the Income Account and Balance-sheet Analysis. From the dividend standpoint it is clear that in both of these examples the decision to retain large amounts of earnings, instead of paying them out to the stockholders, was due in part to the desire to eliminate intangible items from the asset accounts.

Conclusions from the Foregoing. From the foregoing discussion certain conclusions may be drawn. These bear, first on the very practical question of what significance should be accorded the dividend rate as compared with the reported earnings and, secondly, upon the more theoretical but exceedingly important question of what dividend policies should be considered as most desirable from the standpoint of the stockholders' interest.

Experience would confirm the established verdict of the stock market that a dollar of earnings is worth more to the stockholder if paid him in dividends than when carried to surplus. The common-stock investor should ordinarily require both an adequate earning power and an adequate

---

[4] It should be noted that when the good-will of Woolworth was originally listed in the balance sheet at $50,000,000, its actual value (as measured by the market price of the shares) was only some $20,000,000. But when the good-will was written down to $1, in 1925, its real value was apparently many times $50,000,000.

dividend. If the dividend is disproportionately small, an investment purchase will be justified only on an exceptionally impressive showing of earnings (or by a very special situation with respect to liquid assets). On the
other hand, of course, an extra-liberal dividend policy cannot compensate
for inadequate earnings, since with such a showing the dividend rate must
necessarily be undependable.

To aid in developing these ideas quantitatively, we submit the following definitions:

> The *dividend rate* is the amount of annual dividends paid per share,
> expressed either in dollars or as a percentage of a $100 par value. (If the
> par value is less than $100, it is inadvisable to refer to the dividend rate
> as a percentage figure since this may lead to confusion.)
>
> The *earnings rate* is the amount of annual earnings per share, expressed
> either in dollars or as a percentage of a $100 par value.
>
> The *dividend ratio*, *dividend return* or *dividend yield*, is the ratio of the
> dividend paid to the market price (*e.g.*, a stock paying $6 annually and
> selling at 120 has a dividend ratio of 5%).
>
> The *earnings ratio*, *earnings return* or *earnings yield*, is the ratio of the
> annual earnings to the market price (*e.g.*, a stock earning $6 and selling
> at 50 shows an earnings yield of 12%).[5]

Let us assume that a common stock *A*, with average prospects, earning $7 and paying $5 should sell at 100. This is a 7% earnings ratio and
5% dividend return. Then a similar common stock, *B*, earning $7 but
paying only $4, should sell lower than 100. Its price evidently should be
somewhere between 80 (representing a 5% dividend yield) and 100 (representing a 7% earnings yield). In general the price should tend to be
established nearer to the lower limit than to the upper limit. A fair
approximation of the proper relative price would be about 90, at which
level the dividend yield is 4.44%, and the earnings ratio is 7.78%. If the
investor makes a small concession in dividend yield below the standard,
he is entitled to demand a more than corresponding increase in the earning power above standard.

In the opposite case a similar stock, *C*, may earn $7 but pay $6. Here
the investor is justified in paying some premium above 100 because of

---

[5] The term *earnings basis* has the same meaning as *earnings ratio*. However, the term *dividend
basis* is ambiguous, since it is used sometimes to denote the rate and sometimes the ratio.

the larger dividend. The upper limit, of course, would be 120 at which price the dividend ratio would be the standard 5%, but the earnings ratio would be only 5.83%. Here again the proper price should be closer to the lower than to the upper limit, say, 108, at which figure the dividend yield would be 5.56% and the earnings ratio 6.48%.

Suggested Principle for Dividend Payments. Although these figures are arbitrarily taken, they correspond fairly well with the actualities of investment values under what seem now to be reasonably normal conditions in the stock market. The dividend *rate* is seen to be important, apart from the earnings, not only because the investor naturally wants cash income from his capital but also because the earnings that are *not* paid out in dividends have a tendency to lose part of their effective value for the stockholder. Because of this fact American shareholders would do well to adopt a different attitude than hitherto with respect to corporate dividend policies. We should suggest the following principle as a desirable modification of the traditional viewpoint:

Principle: Stockholders are entitled to receive the earnings on their capital except to the extent they decide to reinvest them in the business. The management should retain or reinvest earnings only with the specific approval of the stockholders. Such "earnings" as must be retained to protect the company's position are not true earnings at all. They should not be reported as profits but should be deducted in the income statement as necessary reserves, with an adequate explanation thereof. *A compulsory surplus is an imaginary surplus.*[6]

Were this principle to be generally accepted, the withholding of earnings would not be taken as a matter of course and of arbitrary determination by the management, but it would require justification corresponding to that now expected in the case of changes in capitalization and of the sale of additional stock. The result would be to subject dividend policies to greater scrutiny and more intelligent criticism than they now receive, thus imposing a salutary check upon the tendency of managements to expand unwisely and to accumulate excessive working capital.[7]

---

[6] We refer here to a surplus which *had to be accumulated* in order to *maintain* the company's status, and not to a surplus accumulated as a part of good management.

[7] The suggested procedure under the British Companies Act of 1929 requires that dividend payments be approved by the shareholders at their annual meeting but prohibits the

If it should become the standard policy to disburse the major portion of each year's earnings (as is done abroad), then the rate of dividend will vary with business conditions. This would apparently introduce an added factor of instability into stock values. But the objection to the present practice is that it *fails* to produce the stable dividend rate which is its avowed purpose and the justification for the sacrifice it imposes. Hence instead of a dependable dividend that mitigates the uncertainty of earnings we have a frequently arbitrary and unaccountable dividend policy that aggravates the earnings hazard. The sensible remedy would be to transfer to the stockholder the task of averaging out his own annual income return. Since the common-stock investor must form some fairly satisfactory opinion of average earning power, which transcends the annual fluctuations, he may as readily accustom himself to forming a similar idea of average *income*. As in fact the two ideas are substantially identical, dividend fluctuations *of this kind* would not make matters more difficult for the common-stock investor. In the end such fluctuations will work out more to his advantage than the present method of attempting, usually unsuccessfully, to stabilize the dividend by large additions to the surplus account.[8] On the former basis, the stockholder's average income would probably be considerably larger.

A Paradox. Although we have concluded that the payment of a liberal portion of the earnings in dividends adds definitely to the attractiveness of a common stock, it must be recognized that this conclusion involves a curious paradox. Value is increased by taking away value. The more the stockholder subtracts in dividends from the capital and surplus fund the larger value he places upon what is left. It is like the famous legend of the Sibylline Books, except that here the price of the remainder is *increased* because part has been taken away.

---

approval of a rate greater than that recommended by the directors. Despite the latter proviso, the mere fact that the dividend policy is submitted to the stockholders for their specific approval or criticism carries an exceedingly valuable reminder to the management of its responsibilities, and to the owners of their rights, on this important question.

Although this procedure is not required by the Companies Act in all cases, it is generally followed in England. See Companies Act of 1929, Sections 6–10; Table A to the Companies Act of 1929, pars. 89–93; *Palmer's Company Law*, pp. 222–224, 13th ed., 1929.

[8] For a comprehensive study of the effects of withholding earnings on the regularity of dividend payments, see O. J. Curry, *Utilization of Corporate Profits in Prosperity and Depression*, Ann Arbor, 1941.

This point is well illustrated by a comparison of Atchison and Union Pacific—two railroads of similar standing—over the ten-year period between January 1, 1915, and December 31, 1924.

Item	Per share of common	
	Union Pacific	Atchison
Earned, 10 years 1915–1924	$142.00	$137
Net adjustments in surplus account	dr. 1.50*	cr. 13
Total available for stockholders	$140.50	$150
Dividends paid	$97.50	$60
Increase in market price	33.00	25
Total realizable by stockholders	$130.50	$85
Increase in earnings, 1924 over 1914	9%†	109%†
Increase in book value, 1924 over 1914	25%	70%
Increase in dividend rate, 1924 over 1914	25%	none
Increase in market price, 1924 over 1914	28%	27%
Market price, Dec. 31, 1914	116	93
Market price, Dec. 31, 1924	149	118
Earnings, year ended June 30, 1914	$13.10	$7.40
Earnings, calendar year 1924	14.30	15.45

* Excluding about $7 per share transferred from reserves to surplus.
† Calendar year 1924 compared with year ended June 30, 1914.

It is to be noted that because Atchison failed to increase its dividend the market price of the shares failed to reflect adequately the large increase both in earning power and in book value. The more liberal dividend policy of Union Pacific produced the opposite result.

This anomaly of the stock market is explained in good part by the underlying conflict of the two prevailing ideas regarding dividends which we have discussed in this chapter. In the following brief summary of the situation we endeavor to indicate the relation between the theoretical and the practical aspects of the dividend question.

Summary

1. In some cases the stockholders derive positive benefits from an ultraconservative dividend policy, *i.e.*, through much larger eventual earnings and dividends. In such instances the market's judgment proves to be wrong in penalizing the shares because of their small dividend. The price of these shares should be higher rather than lower on account of the fact that profits have been added to surplus instead of having been paid out in dividends.

2. Far more frequently, however, the stockholders derive much greater benefits from dividend payments than from additions to surplus. This happens because either: (*a*) the reinvested profits fail to add proportionately to the earning power or (*b*) they are not true "profits" at all but reserves that *had* to be retained merely to protect the business. In this majority of cases the market's disposition to emphasize the dividend and to ignore the additions to surplus turns out to be sound.

3. The confusion of thought arises from the fact that the stockholder votes in accordance with the first premise and invests on the basis of the second. If the stockholders asserted themselves intelligently, this paradox would tend to disappear. For in that case the withholding of a large percentage of the earnings would become an exceptional practice, subject to close scrutiny by the stockholders and presumably approved by them from a considered conviction that such retention would be beneficial to the owners of the shares. Such a ceremonious endorsement of a low dividend rate would probably and properly dispel the stock market's scepticism on this point and permit the price to reflect the earnings that are accumulating as well as those which were paid out.

The foregoing discussion may appear to conflict with the suggestion, advanced in the previous chapter, that long-term increases in common-stock values are often due to the reinvestment of undistributed profits. We must distinguish here between the two lines of argument. Taking our standard case of a company earning $10 per share and paying dividends of $7, we have pointed out that the repeated annual additions of $3 per share to surplus should serve to increase the value of the stock over a period of years. This may very well be true, and at the same time the rate of increase in value may be substantially less than $3 per annum compounded. If we take the reverse case, *viz.*, $3 paid in dividends and $7 added to surplus, the distinction is clearer. Undoubtedly the large addition to surplus will expand the value of the stock, but quite probably also this value will fail to increase at the annual rate of $7 compounded. Hence the argument against reinvesting large proportions of the yearly earnings would remain perfectly valid. Our criticism is advanced against the latter type of policy, *e.g.*, the retention of 70% of the earnings, and not against the normal reinvestment of some 30% of the profits.

Dividend Policies since 1934. If the dividend practice of American corporations were to be judged solely by the record during 1934–1939, the criticism expressed in this chapter would have to be softened considerably. In these recent years there has been a definite tendency towards greater liberality in dividend payments, particularly by companies that do not have clearly defined opportunities for profitable expansion. Retention of earnings by rapidly growing enterprises, *e.g.*, airplane manufacturers, is hardly open to objection. Since the end of 1932, on the other hand, General Motors Corporation has disbursed about 80% of earnings to common-stock holders, with no wide deviation in any year through 1939. In 1939 the Treasury Department announced that it would use 70% as a rough or preliminary test to decide whether or not a company is subject to the penalty taxes for improper accumulation of surplus.

As far as stock prices are concerned, it can hardly be said that they have been unduly influenced by arbitrary dividend policies in these recent years. For not only have the policies themselves been far less arbitrary than in former times, but there has been a definite tendency in the stock market to subordinate the dividend factor to the reported and prospective earnings.

The Undistributed-profits Tax. The more liberal dividends of recent years have been due in part to the highly controversial tax on undistributed profits. This was imposed by Congress in 1936, on a graduated scale running from 7 to 27%. Following violent criticism, the tax was reduced to a vestigial $2^1/2$% in 1938 and repealed entirely the following year. Its main object was to compel companies to distribute their earnings, so that they might be subject to personal income taxes levied against the stockholders. A secondary objective appears to have been to restrict the accumulation of corporate surpluses, which were thought by some to be injurious, either because they withheld purchasing power from individuals or because they were conducive to unwise expansion. But the tax was widely and violently condemned, chiefly on the ground that it prevented the creation of surplus or reserve funds essential to meet future losses or emergencies or expansion needs. It was said to lay a heavy penalty on corporate thrift and prudence and to bear with particular severity on small or new corporations which must rely largely on retained profits for their growth.

Law Objectionable but Criticized on Wrong Grounds. In our own opinion the law was a very bad one, but it has been criticized largely on the wrong grounds. Its objective, as first announced, was to tax corporations exactly as if they were partnerships and hence to equalize the taxation basis of corporate and unincorporated businesses. Much could be said in favor of this aim. But as the bill was finally passed it effectively superposed partnership taxation on top of corporate taxation, thus heavily discriminating against the corporate form and especially against small stockholders. Nor was it a practicable tax as far as wealthy holders were concerned, because the extremely high personal tax rates, combined with the corporation taxes (state and federal), created an over-all burden undoubtedly hostile to individual initiative. Fully as bad were the technical details of the tax law, which compelled distributions in excess of actual accounting profits, disregarded very real capital losses and allowed no flexibility in the treatment of inventory values.

Despite the almost universal opinion to the contrary, we do not believe that the undistributed profits tax really prevented the reinvestment of earnings, except to the extent that these were diminished by personal income taxes—as they would be in an unincorporated business. Corporations had available a number of methods for retaining or recovering these earnings, without subjecting them to the penalty tax. These devices included (1) declaration of taxable stock dividends (*e.g.*, in preferred stock); (2) payment of "optional" dividends, so contrived as to impel the stockholders to take stock rather than cash; (3) offering of additional stock on attractive terms at the time of payment of cash dividends. Critics of the tax have asserted that these methods are inconvenient or impracticable. Our own observation is that they were quite practicable and were resorted to by a fair number of corporations in 1936 and 1937,[9] but that they were

---

[9] See Rolbein, David L., "Noncash Dividends and Stock Rights as Methods for Avoidance of the Undistributed Profits Tax," XII *The Journal of Business of the University of Chicago* 221–264,

avoided by the majority, either from unfamiliarity or from a desire to throw as harsh a light as possible upon the law.

Proper Dividend Policy. In view of the scepticism that we have expressed as to whether or not stockholders are really benefited by dividend-withholding policies, we may be thought sympathetic to the idea of preventing reinvestment of profits by imposing penalty taxes thereon. This is far from true. Dividend and reinvestment policies should be controlled not by law but by the intelligent decision of stockholders. Individual cases may well justify retention of earnings to an extent far greater than is ordinarily desirable. The practice should vary with the circumstances; the policy should be determined and proposed in the first instance by the management; but it should be subject to independent consideration and appraisal by stockholders in their own interest, as distinguished from that of the corporation as a separate entity or the management as a special group.

July, 1939. For more comprehensive surveys of this tax see Alfred G. Buehler, *The Undistributed Profits Tax*, New York, 1937 (an adverse appraisal), and Graham, Benjamin, "The Undistributed Profits Tax and the Investor," LXVI *Yale Law Journal* 1–18, November, 1936, elaborating the views expressed above.

See accompanying CD for Chapter 30, "Stock Dividends."

PART V

ANALYSIS OF THE INCOME ACCOUNT. THE EARNINGS FACTOR IN COMMON-STOCK VALUATION

THE QUEST FOR RATIONAL INVESTING

BY GLENN H. GREENBERG

Thue confession: I never read *Security Analysis* while at Columbia Business School. Never even took a securities analysis course. Instead, some invisible hand guided me into stock research and later money management, where I have labored for the past 33 years. It wasn't until perhaps the middle of my investment career that I decided it was time to pick up Graham and Dodd and see what all the buzz was about. The first 300 pages dealt with fixed income securities, which I have seldom owned and were of little interest to me. The equity section seemed dated: topics such as determining the earnings power of industrial cyclicals and the appropriate depreciation of utility plant and equipment conjured up sepia-tone images of a bygone era. I was running my own investment business and in need of immediate investment ideas. Could this book help me find my next winner? Not likely, I decided. So imagine my reaction years later when an editor from McGraw-Hill called to ask me to write this introduction. After a long, long silence I asked if he could send me a copy.

Rereading Graham and Dodd felt a little bit like reading Polonius's charge to his son in *Hamlet* as he departs to pursue his studies abroad ("neither a borrower nor a lender be" and "to thine own self be true"). Yes, the advice was sound, but it seemed so obvious. In Part V, we are counseled against placing too much emphasis on near-term earnings and warned not to trust unscrupulous management. We are cautioned about

manipulation of financial statements and urged to appreciate the qualitative aspects of a business we invest in. A bright line is drawn for us separating speculation from investment. The appropriate level of debt in the
capital structure, how to think about commodity-based investments, and
the manic-depressive nature of markets are all addressed—well of course
these ideas sound familiar because they have been interwoven through
so many annual letters by Warren Buffett and cited by other great
investors who credit Graham and Dodd for some portion of their investment success. As implied by the title of this part, Graham and Dodd do
present detailed discussion and analysis of the income statement
accounts, but it is the more general investment precepts that I and others
treasure. This work is the more remarkable because it was written during
the uniquely depressed circumstances of 1934, a nation of 25% unemployment with most businesses struggling to survive. Yet Graham and
Dodd were able to codify the principles that have inspired great investors
through 75 years of remarkable prosperity. Their insights are as applicable now as ever.

The purpose of Part V is to explore analysis of the income accounts in
order to estimate the earnings power of the business and thereby determine if the stock is undervalued. There is no magic formula for this task:
the future may resemble the past—or it may not! Virtually every page of
this part is filled with useful analysis of company financials and great clar-
ity of thought on a wide variety of industries. Financial analysis, not the
CEO's letter, is key to assessing a business. There is a total absence of
terms like "story," "concept," "paradigm," or "trend" to justify an investment. We all want to buy low and sell high, but first we must develop
confidence in the sustainability of a business in order to arrive at a sound
judgment about what constitutes "low" and "high."

Estimating average future earnings is not easy. In the 1930s there was
tremendous volatility in earnings because of the operating leverage inher-

ent in manufacturing and resource businesses. The challenge in determining earnings power in today's more stable economy is different but no less daunting. There are global competitors and disruptive new technologies. Financial companies have developed extraordinary new products, which have been profitable to date but now face testing. Technology firms have to constantly reinvent themselves. Even the most stable businesses may surprise. I recall visiting Coca-Cola in late 1993. It was generally hailed as the finest business in the world because of its pricing power and boundless international growth opportunities. Valued at 18 times earnings, it was a bargain provided that earnings could grow over 15% annually for an extended period of time. It never occurred to anyone that this incredible franchise would have flattish earnings from 1996 through 2002.

How We Invest

At my firm, Chieftain Capital Management, we evaluate an investment opportunity based on the predictability of the business and a dispassionate calculation of its expected rate of return. We read all of a company's public filings, we analyze its industry and competitors (of which, ideally, there should not be many), we talk to its management team and industry experts, and we gather any other relevant data we can find, distilling it all into a historical analysis of the performance of the business. Obvious questions arise: Can margins continue to rise? Is the business becoming more capital intensive? Why are sales slowing? And so on. This analysis becomes the basis for further discussions with management and ultimately our projections of future results.

We and other investors today tend to focus on cash flow after capital expenditures (free cash flow), instead of earnings, to evaluate the investment merits of a business. One advantage of this approach is that it helps shortcut a good many games that management can play in reporting profits. Moreover, earnings are seldom synonymous with cash available for shareholders, and it is the latter that should matter to investors. It has always struck me as curious that the first questions asked by a private investor are, how much money must I put up, how much cash will I get back, and how fast? Why should investors in publicly traded stocks ask different questions?

Finally, we calculate the rate of return implied by the free cash flows we expect the business to generate, in perpetuity, taking into account the investments the company needs to make to continue its growth. We generally will not buy a stock unless it is priced to give us at least a 15% rate of return. Obviously, there is much judgment involved in determining such a hurdle rate, and it must be refined to reflect the quality of the business and expected returns from alternative investment opportunities. In 1974 our investment hurdle would have been much higher—perhaps 25%—because there were so many undervalued stocks to choose from and interest rates were higher. By insisting on a very high rate of return, compared to the high-single-digit return we calculate to be offered by the broader market, we give ourselves significant margin for error. Our goal is to set the bar very high knowing that there will be few times when we find a great business selling at a price that will also give us a great rate of return. We seldom find a stock meeting these criteria, so when we do, we build a large position: never less than 5% of our assets and often as much as 25%. We sell a stock when the return in our model drops to 10%—even though our alternative may be cash earning less than 5%. At all times we are mindful that our approach is only as good as our assumptions about the future, and small changes in our assumptions, such as the growth rate of cash flows over the long term, can dramatically alter prospective returns.

A recent reminder of the importance of assumptions is a purchase we made in early 2007 of Ryanair, the world's largest airline as measured by passengers. The Irish company sports by far the lowest fares of anyone in the short-haul business in the European markets it serves. In 10 years, it has grown its passengers tenfold and yet it has only a 7% share of the market. Last year its average fare was 44 euros, which compares with 66 euros for easyJet, 91 for Aer Lingus, and well over 100 euros for all the flag carriers. Even so, Ryanair has averaged 20% net margins over the past decade, versus low single digits for its rivals. We paid 16 times the current year's earnings estimates and felt this price was justified by Ryanair's huge cost advantages and growth prospects. Then the price of oil doubled again. The shares have declined 30% since our initial investment, and the profit outlook has dimmed.

Still, the business franchise is intact. Nothing has happened that makes us believe the long-term value of our investment has diminished. In fact, during this period of adversity, other low-cost carriers are expected to cease operations. Lenders are likely to be cautious in funding possible new entrants, and consumers may wish to trade down to take advantage of Ryanair's low fares. Over time, a company with this kind of cost advantage must take market share and earn attractive returns.

The process I have just described is our attempt to cover the bases outlined by the authors of *Security Analysis*. For Graham and Dodd, step 1 is careful quantitative analysis with particular attention to identifying real, not accounting, earnings. Accounting has always presented management with opportunities to misrepresent results. In 1934, companies ran nonrecurring gains through the profit-and-loss statement and stretched out depreciation schedules to make earnings look better than they were. Managers would charge certain losses directly to shareholders' equity, bypassing (and inflating) net income in the process. In addition to earnings, Graham and Dodd were also attuned to the importance of free cash flow, as in their discussion of the Eureka Pipe Line (Chapter 36 on accompanying CD). Just as Graham and Dodd illustratively juxtapose the perspectives of the private businessperson and the public investor, my partners and I often ask ourselves the question: If this were a private business, how would we measure its value?

Accounting Challenges

Today, the accounting challenges for the investor are far more difficult. The Financial Accounting Standards Board (FASB) has issued any number of accounting mandates that muddy the waters. For example, while I certainly oppose excessive granting of stock options to management and employees, there are numerous difficulties in accounting for them as a current expense as prescribed by the recent FASB statement 123R. First off, stock options are a noncash obligation and may never cost the shareholder a penny—but under 123R even a deeply out-of-the-money option will still result in an expense years after being awarded to an employee. Second, stock options are already reflected in the diluted share base used to calculate the earnings-per-share (EPS) figures most investors focus on; by further burdening net income with an expense for options, diluted EPS under today's accounting clearly reflects double counting. Finally, valuing options requires numerous assumptions and thus opens the door to manipulation. By the way, the previous approach to accounting for stock options was even odder: options granted with a strike price equal to the market price had no expense impact, but those granted below market would, in some cases, result in an expense every year thereafter that the underlying stock rose. There is equal confusion to be found in the FASB approach to accounting for derivatives, hedging, pensions, leases, and recognition of profits for carried interests, to name a few. Now companies can even record a profit if their debt gets downgraded. Sometimes accounting rules seem designed to carry us *very* far from economic reality, and some managers are quite amenable to taking investors on such a journey.

Having analyzed the historical record, the second and far greater challenge is to determine "the utility of this past record as an indication of future earnings." Graham and Dodd call it a "qualitative survey of the enterprise." Is the future of the business adequately predictable so as to permit a long-term investment? Is the business growing so rapidly as to attract numerous competitors? Is it subject to being undermined by a new technology or changing consumer taste? Will it be squashed by imports or Wal-Mart or by a business model enabled by the Internet? In other words, how predictable are future cash flows? And how do we feel about the corporate culture and management leadership? Can they be relied on to be shrewd, rational, and motivated to maximize the value of our investment? Or do they have a different agenda? Will management *itself* follow the Graham and Dodd principles in investing the shareholders' money?

Whose Company Is It?

This last point is particularly important. Often managers get confused and believe that it is *their* company, which they can run to satisfy their personal needs—and few such managers would acknowledge that this applies to them. We spend a lot of time getting to know the stewards of the companies in which we invest to ascertain their personal priorities. Small observations can sometimes provide a clue. A CEO who won't answer tough questions directly is a warning sign. A deeply tanned CEO wearing a lot of gold jewelry is not likely to be someone we feel we can trust.

Worse yet is a CEO who undervalues his stock by offering it in exchange for shares of a company with less attractive business prospects than his own. This happened in 2004 when Comcast CEO Brian Roberts made a surprise offer to purchase Disney in an all-stock deal that would have been hugely dilutive to free cash flow and would have radically changed the nature of the company. Clearly the motivation of the management was to build an empire by owning an American icon rather than to build the value of its own business, on a per share basis, for the investors. We sold a large portion of our Comcast shares upon learning of the offer. Worried about dilution of the value of the company, others did the same, driving down the stock price by over 20%. Roberts subsequently withdrew the Disney offer since he no longer had a sufficiently valuable stock with which to make the acquisition.

Similarly, it can be disheartening to discuss the concept of share repurchases with some managers. If we ask whether the cash return on a capital project is as good as the return from buying back stock, they generally look at us as though we're speaking in a foreign tongue.

This qualitative assessment allows the discriminating investor to single out truly *good* businesses. Few investors active today lived as I did through the bear market of 1973 to 1974 or the crash of 1987, when the market lost 30% of its value in only a few days. As I watched the disasters around me, I made a promise to myself to avoid any stock that I would not feel comfortable holding through another 1987-like crash. The reason is simple: in the aftermath of a collapse, much wealth has evaporated and confidence is circling the drain. Wild rumors are flying—and many may just be true. Without confidence in the staying power of a business, the overwhelming tendency is simply to follow the crowd and sell. Many who do sell are so shell-shocked that they are afraid to buy again until well after a recovery has occurred. Trading on emotions is nearly always the wrong thing to do, especially for those investors who have carefully done their homework. Certainly a good business can hit a rough patch, but it is not unusual for such a business to regain its footing. Sometimes huge stock declines occur for no apparent reason.

I recall that shortly after making a new investment in LabCorp in August 2002, the company reported quarterly earnings that were 6% shy of Street estimates. The stock, for which we had paid $34, or 12 times the next year's free cash flow, fell as low as $18 in October 2002. Of course, we were horrified at the sudden loss, but after checking our research and confirming our understanding of the favorable characteristics of the business, we tripled our position at what proved to be bargain prices. At $18, the stock was trading at less than 7 times expected free cash flow.

LabCorp met all our definitions for an outstanding business. It was very profitable and had low capital requirements. The industry had consolidated from seven national competitors to two with only modest regional overlap, LabCorp being one of them. More importantly, it was difficult to enter the business because of the third-party medical payment system that we have in our country. A new entrant would have trouble getting reimbursed by health insurance companies, which want to send business to only the lowest-cost labs. LabCorp has continued to prosper due in part to the aging of the population, and it is now on the cusp of benefiting from the introduction of early cancer detection blood tests, such as one for ovarian cancer. All of this leads to the question of why it collapsed in the fall of 2002. Who knows? But only through careful research can one develop the confidence to take advantage of such a bargain.

After completing the quantitative and qualitative analyses, Graham and Dodd address the issue of valuation. They emphasize the importance of looking at *average* earnings, so as not to be misled by a recent year of abnormal performance, and of applying a conservative valuation multiple to such earnings. The authors admit that money can be made buying a stock with a high price-to-earnings (P/E) multiple but that such an investment must be deemed "speculative"—a gamble no different from a bet on a commodity future or a roll of the dice. A successful speculation is simply luck, and few investors are lucky for long. Probably the most important principle from this book is that stock investing is a risky business. The future is unknowable. Not only are earnings subject to many uncertainties, but P/E multiples can change drastically based on uncontrollable factors such as interest rates, investor sentiment, or government actions. Foreign investing can be particularly speculative. While the growth in developing countries is faster than in our own, there are serious imponderables: Will regulations change in a way that handicaps the foreign investor? What are the chances the business will be nationalized? Will a contract with a foreign government be honored? And there are more mundane risks such as currency fluctuations, the accuracy of local accounting practices, and management corruption.

A Daunting Challenge

If Graham and Dodd are so widely read and respected, why are there so few disciplined practitioners of their advice? I believe the answer lies in three human traits: aversion to boredom, a tendency for emotions to overwhelm reason, and greed. Careful research takes time and seldom results in a clear case for buying a large position. It is tedious to review company after company, only to find that most are neither really special nor greatly undervalued. It is equally tedious to hold shares in a good company for an extended period. Even if the investment does well, most of the time it *feels* like the stock is treading water or even going down. Part of the problem is that the value of the business is quoted $6^{1}/_{2}$ hours a day, 5 days a week, 52 weeks a year, and market liquidity tempts us to trade from one stock to another.

The second challenge to rational investing is to maintain one's logical convictions in the face of excess gloom or euphoria as reflected in stock prices. I doubt many owners of private companies are preoccupied with the value of their business on a short-term basis—how different from the public markets, where a rising stock price makes us feel smart and a falling one makes us feel dumb. In my office, when one of our businesses is floundering and the stock is getting pounded, my partners and I start to doubt the reasoned basis upon which we made the investment. Our self-doubts and fears of failure cause us to glimpse catastrophe where once we envisioned opportunity. Or if you prefer the Graham and Dodd condensed version: "Obviously it requires strength of character in order to think and act in opposite fashion from the crowd and also patience to wait for opportunities that may be spaced *years* apart."

The third factor, greed, has always distorted investors' behavior, but it is especially present in markets today given the proliferation of hedge funds. Investors in these funds keep jumping from fund to fund, trying to latch on to the latest hot manager. The high fees encourage these managers to pursue "get-rich-quick" trading strategies. The more money they make, the more money they attract, and investors have been sold on the promise of unsustainably high returns. A cycle ensues as hedge fund investors quickly move their money from fund to fund, and hedge fund managers try to swing for the fences every month. I once attended the U.S. Open and sat near two hedge fund managers whom I did not know. They were talking shop during the match, and much to my surprise, their discussion focused exclusively on assets under management and fees. I kept waiting for them to mention an investment idea, but it never happened.

Today the crowd focuses on isolated data points, the latest wiggles in the business outlook, or the opinion expressed in the most recent research report. With so much information available, there is a tendency to act too quickly to buy and sell in haste, and to substitute the views of others for the hard work necessary to come to one's own conclusions. Perhaps this is why so many market participants can be described only as "traders" and "speculators," unafraid of using debt to turbocharge returns. Their method requires frequent profitable trades, *after* transaction costs, and incurs far higher taxes than the long-term investor pays. They also pay a heavy price in terms of emotional wear and tear. It is easy to vacation or enjoy family if one owns great businesses—and it's impossible if

one is tracking a flock of trading positions about which one has little conviction. Most importantly, a fast-moving, leveraged approach is likely to
fail spectacularly at some point over a lifetime, which is an unacceptable
risk for those of us who invest our own money alongside our clients'.

Few investors these days seem to take the time to truly understand
the quality and motivation of top management. This book clearly emphasizes the importance of unflinching intellectual honesty on the part of an
investor while preparing an analysis—matched by similar integrity in the
management of the enterprise in which the investor places client capital.
Slick managers, who always have an infallible business plan and dismiss
all past mistakes as nonrecurring anomalies, will do everything they can
to prevent you from peering behind Oz's curtain to see the true outlook
for the business.

A recurring theme of *Security Analysis* is the importance of gathering
as much information as possible, but then making judgments, which are
subject to being wildly off the mark. One will not find any claims of a
"surefire" way to pick stocks. There is recognition that even the most
exhaustive analysis can fail to bring investment success. Graham and
Dodd don't make security analysis seem easy or a guarantee of profits.
During my initial reading of the book many years ago, I wish I had
digested the short preface to the first edition: "We are concerned chiefly
with concepts, methods, standards, principles and, above all, with *logical
reasoning*." The authors were not trying to write "Investing for Dummies"
or a chronicle of stock tips. They were trying to help the thoughtful
investor develop a successful approach to long-term wealth creation
"which will stand the test of the ever enigmatic future." I have come to
believe that it may require a bit of experience on the part of the reader to
fully appreciate the power of this book to remain relevant. Perhaps this
wisdom, like youth, is wasted on the young.

Another fascinating element of Part V is the discussion of optimal
capital structure, because it speaks to the current media frenzy over pri-

vate equity investors. First prevalent in the 1980s and more dramatically today, investment groups have applied leverage in order to enhance equity returns in taking companies private. The book refers to such levered, option-like-equity holders as having a situation in which "heads I win, tails you lose." This seems particularly apt for the general partners of today's private equity firms. Indeed, high leverage can lead to outsized returns, but it is another form of speculation, much like buying stock at a very high P/E ratio.

I will presume a little to imagine how Graham and Dodd would analyze the likely investment results for those limited partners only now allocating huge sums to the private equity "megafunds." Pioneering institutional investors in private equity funds blazed the alternative investment trail 20 years ago. Now that Yale's investment approach and success are widely celebrated, endowment and state retirement fund managers want to join a party that is close to ending. Buyout prices have never been higher, strategic buyers are regularly outbid by ravenous financial buyers, and remaining opportunities for operational improvement are few. Expected returns, in short, are driven almost solely by maximizing leverage. With many buyouts thus priced and levered for only clear skies and smooth waters, a general rise in interest rates or a business downturn could be disastrous. The equity in these deals—that is, the limited partners' capital—could easily be wiped out. One wonders if the stewards of capital pouring money into private equity today have any concept of the risks they are taking as fiduciaries. Interestingly, the private equity firms themselves are going public at generous valuations even though they have little permanent capital, the lifeblood of their businesses. What if their limited partners are not satisfied with results and don't re-up? What is the correct P/E for a business model facing such risk of destruction? Investment in these companies would seem the very embodiment of the term "speculation."

Similarly, what would Graham and Dodd make of today's collateralized debt obligations that have been bought, not based on due diligence but on the AAA rubber stamp from a credit rating agency? Or lenders rushing to scoop up "covenant-light," "pay-in-kind" loans used in 90%-levered capital structures? Institutional appetite for hedge funds and "2-and-20" fees? Investment theses built around ever-rising valuations and continued "global liquidity"? There's no need to wonder—*Security Analysis,* timely as ever, has much to say on speculative excess.

Yes, we have heard this speech before: The stock market is a voting machine, not a weighing machine. Future prices fall outside the realm of sound prediction. Even the best companies can be speculations at the wrong price. One must understand the nature of a business to assess the inherent permanence of earning power. While it is easy to say, it is hard to actually "buy low and sell high" because human nature programs us to take comfort in the company of others. There is a distinction between investment and speculation. Never invest with unscrupulous management. Earnings must be understood in the absence of nonrecurring items. Debt in the capital structure enhances returns, but there are limits. The market shoots first and finds reasons later.

If it all seems self-evident, like Polonius's speech, that's because such wisdom has stood the test of time and it has become part of our lexicon as investors. Yet few people endeavor to walk the walk by researching businesses intensively, sifting through many dozens to find those worthy of their capital. Few people are willing to concentrate their investments in a small number of businesses that they know thoroughly and believe will grow their net worth at an attractive rate over the long term. Many days this work is just plain boring. Other days (and sometimes months), the market totally ignores your handful of precious stocks. A portfolio of predictable, reliable businesses does not make you the most exciting person at the cocktail party, nor does it give you flashy sales promotion material. I have come to believe the quest for rational investing is appealing only to a handful of us. But at least we sleep well at night and live well by day—and our clients do as well.

Chapter 31

ANALYSIS OF THE INCOME ACCOUNT

IN OUR HISTORICAL DISCUSSION of the theory of investment in common stocks we traced the transfer of emphasis from the net worth of an enterprise to its capitalized earning power. Although there are sound and compelling reasons behind this development, it is none the less one that has removed much of the firm ground that formerly lay—or seemed to lie—beneath investment analysis and has subjected it to a multiplicity of added hazards. When an investor was able to take very much the same attitude in valuing shares of stock as in valuing his own business, he was dealing with concepts familiar to his individual experience and matured judgment. Given sufficient information, he was not likely to go far astray, except perhaps in his estimate of future earning power. The interrelations of balance sheet and income statement gave him a double check on intrinsic values, which corresponded to the formulas of banks or credit agencies in appraising the eligibility of the enterprise for credit.

Disadvantages of Sole Emphasis on Earning Power. Now that common-stock values have come to depend exclusively upon the earnings exhibit, a gulf has been created between the concepts of private business and the guiding rules of investment. When the business man lays down his own statement and picks up the report of a large corporation, he apparently enters a new and entirely different world of values. For certainly he does not appraise his own business solely on the basis of its recent operating results without reference to its financial resources. When in his capacity as investor or speculator the business man elects to pay no attention whatever to corporate balance sheets, he is placing himself at a serious disadvantage in several different respects: In the first place, he is embracing a *new* set of ideas that are alien to his everyday business experience. In the second place, instead of the twofold test of value afforded by both earnings and assets, he is relying upon a *single* and therefore less dependable criterion. In the third place, these earnings statements on which he relies exclusively are subject to more rapid and radical *changes* than those which occur in balance sheets. Hence an exaggerated degree of instability is introduced into his concept of stock values. In the fourth place, the earnings statements are far more subject to *misleading* presentation and mistaken inferences than is the typical balance sheet when scrutinized by an investor of experience.

Warning against Sole Reliance upon Earnings Exhibit.

In approaching the analysis of earnings statements we must, therefore, utter an emphatic warning against exclusive preoccupation with this factor in dealing with investment values. With due recognition of the greatly restricted importance of the asset picture, it must nevertheless be asserted that a company's resources still have some significance and require some attention. This is particularly true, as will be seen later on, because the meaning of any income statement cannot properly be understood except with reference to the balance sheet at the beginning and the end of the period.

Simplified Statement of Wall Street's Method of Appraising Common Stocks.

Viewing the subject from another angle, we may say that the Wall-Street method of appraising common stocks has been simplified to the following standard formula:

1. Find out what the stock is earning. (This usually means the earnings per share as shown in the last report.)

2. Multiply these per-share earnings by some suitable "coefficient of quality" which will reflect:

> *a.* The dividend rate and record.
>
> *b.* The standing of the company—its size, reputation, financial position, and prospects.
>
> *c.* The type of business (*e.g.*, a cigarette manufacturer will sell at a higher multiple of earnings than a cigar company).
>
> *d.* The temper of the general market. (Bull-market multipliers are larger than those used in bear markets.)

The foregoing may be summarized in the following formula:

Price = current earnings per share $\times$ quality coefficient.[1]

The result of this procedure is that in most cases the "earnings per share" have attained a weight in determining value that is equivalent to the *weight of all the other factors taken together.* The truth of this is evident if it be remembered that the "quality coefficient" is itself largely determined by the *earnings trend*, which in turn is taken from the stated earnings over a period.

Earnings Not Only Fluctuate but Are Subject to Arbitrary Determination.

But these earnings per share, on which the entire edifice of value has come to be built, are not only highly fluctuating but are subject also in extraordinary degree to arbitrary determination and manipulation. It will be illuminating if we summarize at this point the various devices, legitimate and otherwise, by which the per-share earnings may *at the choice of those in control* be made to appear either larger or smaller.

1. By allocating items to surplus instead of to income, or *vice versa.*

2. By over-or understating amortization and other reserve charges.

3. By varying the capital structure, as between senior securities and common stock. (Such moves are decided upon by managements and ratified by the stockholders as a matter of course.)

4. By the use made of large capital funds not employed in the conduct of the business.

Significance of the Foregoing to the Analyst.

These intricacies of corporate accounting and financial policies undoubtedly provide a broad field for the activities of the securities analyst. There are unbounded opportunities for shrewd detective work, for critical comparisons, for discovering and pointing out a state of affairs quite different from that indicated by the publicized "per-share earnings."

---

[1] Where there are no earnings or where the amount is recognized as being far below "normal," Wall Street is reluctantly compelled to apply what is at bottom a more rational method of valuation, *i.e.*, one ascribing greater weight to *average* earning power, working capital, etc. But this is the *exceptional* procedure.

That this work may be of exceeding value cannot be denied. In a number of cases it will lead to a convincing conclusion that the market price is far out of line with intrinsic or comparative worth and hence to profitable action based upon this sound foundation. But it is necessary to caution the analyst against overconfidence in the practical utility of his findings. It is always good to know the truth, but it may not always be wise to act upon it, particularly in Wall Street. And it must always be remembered that the truth that the analyst uncovers is first of all not the *whole* truth and, secondly, not the *immutable* truth. The result of his study is only a *more nearly correct version of the past*. His information may have lost its relevance by the time he acquires it, or in any event by the time the market place is finally ready to respond to it.

With full allowance for these pitfalls, it goes without saying, none the less, that security analysis must devote thoroughgoing study to corporate income accounts. It will aid our exposition if we classify this study under three headings, *viz.:*

1. The accounting aspect. Leading question: What are the true earnings for the period studied?

2. The business aspect. Leading question: What indications does the earnings record carry as to the *future* earning power of the company?

3. The aspect of investment finance. Leading question: What elements in the earnings exhibit must be taken into account, and what standards followed, in endeavoring to arrive at a reasonable *valuation* of the shares?

CRITICISM AND RESTATEMENT OF THE INCOME ACCOUNT

If an income statement is to be informing in any true sense, it must at least present a fair and undistorted picture of the year's operating results. Direct misstatement of the figures in the case of publicly owned companies is a rare occurrence. The Ivar Kreuger frauds, revealed in 1932, partook of this character, but these were quite unique in the baldness as well as in the extent of the deception. The statements of most important companies are audited by independent public accountants, and their reports are reasonably dependable within the rather limited sphere of accounting accuracy.[2] But from the standpoint of common-stock analysis these

---

[2] In recent years several instances of gross overstatements of earnings and current assets in audited statements have come to light—notably the case of McKesson and Robbins

audited statements may require critical interpretation and adjustment, especially with respect to three important elements:

1. Nonrecurrent profits and losses.
2. Operations of subsidiaries or affiliates.
3. Reserves.

General Observations on the Income Account. Accounting procedure allows considerable leeway to the management in the method of treating nonrecurrent items. It is a standard and proper rule that transactions applicable to past years should be excluded from current income and entered as a charge or credit direct to the surplus account. Yet there are many kinds of entries that may technically be considered part of the current year's results but that are none the less of a special and nonrecurrent nature. Accounting rules permit the management to decide whether to show these operations as part of the *income* or to report them as adjustments of *surplus*. Following are a number of examples of entries of this type:

1. Profit or loss on sale of fixed assets.
2. Profit or loss on sale of marketable securities.
3. Discount or premium on retirement of capital obligations.
4. Proceeds of life insurance policies.
5. Tax refunds and interest thereon.
6. Gain or loss as result of litigation.
7. Extraordinary write-downs of inventory.
8. Extraordinary write-downs of receivables.
9. Cost of maintaining nonoperating properties.

Wide variations will be found in corporate practice respecting items such as the foregoing. Under each heading examples may be given of either inclusion in or exclusion from the income account. Which is the better accounting procedure in some of these cases may be a rather controversial question, but, as far as the analyst is concerned, his object requires that all these items be segregated from the *ordinary operating results* of the year. For what the investor chiefly wants to learn from an annual report is the *indicated earning power* under the given set of

---

Company in 1938. (Interstate Hosiery Mills and Illinois Zinc Corporation are other examples also uncovered in 1938.) Despite the sensational impression caused by the McKesson and Robbins scandal, it must be recognized that over a long period of years only an infinitesimal percentage of publicly owned companies have been involved in frauds of this character.

conditions, *i.e.*, what the company might be expected to earn year after year if the business conditions prevailing during the period were to continue unchanged. (On the other hand, as we shall point out later, all these extraordinary items enter properly into the calculation of earning power as actually shown over a *period of years* in the past.)

The analyst must endeavor also to adjust the reported earnings so as to reflect as accurately as possible the company's interest in results of controlled or affiliated companies. In most cases consolidated reports are made, so that such adjustments are unnecessary. But numerous instances have occurred in which the statements are incomplete or misleading because either: (1) they fail to reflect any part of the profits or losses of important subsidiaries or (2) they include as income dividends from subsidiaries that are substantially less or greater than the current earnings of the controlled enterprises.

The third aspect of the income account to which the analyst must give critical attention is the matter of reserves for depreciation and other amortization, and reserves for future losses and other contingencies. These reserves are subject in good part to arbitrary determination by the management. Hence they may readily be overstated or understated, in which case the final figure of reported earnings will be correspondingly distorted. With respect to amortization charges, another and more subtle element enters which may at times be of considerable importance, and that is the fact that the deductions from income, as calculated by the management based on the book cost of the property, may not properly reflect the amortization that the *individual investor* should charge against his own commitment in the enterprise.

Nonrecurrent Items: Profits or Losses from Sale of Fixed Assets.

We shall proceed to a more detailed discussion of these three types of adjustment of the reported income account, beginning with the subject of nonrecurrent items.[3] Profits or losses from the sale of fixed assets belong quite obviously to this category, and they should be

---

[3] The Securities Act of 1933 and the Securities Exchange Act of 1934 specifically empower the Commission to prescribe the methods to be followed in differentiating between recurrent and nonrecurrent items in the reports of registered companies which must be filed with the S.E.C. and with the exchanges [Sec. 19(a) of the 1933 act and Sec. 13(b) of the 1934 act]. The initial registration forms (A-1, A-2 and 10) and the annual report form (10-K) require separation of nonrecurrent profit-and-loss items within the income account.

excluded from the year's result in order to gain an idea of the "indicated earning power" based on the assumed continuance of the business conditions existing then. Approved accounting practice recommends that profit on sales of capital assets be shown only as a credit to the surplus account. In numerous instances, however, such profits are reported by the company as part of its current net income, creating a distorted picture of the earnings for the period.

Examples: A glaring example of this practice is presented by the report of the Manhattan Electrical Supply Company for 1926. This showed earnings of $882,000, or $10.25 per share, which was regarded as a very favorable exhibit. But a subsequent application to list additional shares on the New York Stock Exchange revealed that out of this $882,000 reported as earned, no less than $586,700 had been realized through the sale of the company's battery business. Hence the earnings from ordinary operations were only $295,300, or about $3.40 per share. The inclusion of this special profit in income was particularly objectionable because in the very same year the company had charged to surplus extraordinary *losses* amounting to $544,000. Obviously the special losses belonged to the same category as the special profits, and the two items should have been grouped together. The effect of including the one in income and charging the other to surplus was misleading in the highest degree. Still more discreditable was the failure to make any clear reference to the profit from the battery sale either in the income account itself or in the extended remarks that accompanied it in the annual report.[4]

During 1931 the United States Steel Corporation reported "special income" of some $19,300,000, the greater part of which was due to "profit on sale of fixed property"—understood to be certain public-utility holdings in Gary, Indiana. This item was included in the year's earnings and resulted in a final "net income" of $13,000,000. But since this credit was definitely of a nonrecurring nature, the analyst would be compelled to eliminate it from his consideration of the 1931 operating results, which would accordingly register a *loss* of $6,300,000 before preferred dividends. United States Steel's accounting method in 1931 is at variance with its previous

---

[4] The president's remarks contained only the following in respect to this transaction: "After several years of unprofitable experience in the battery business the directors arranged a sale of same on satisfactory terms." In 1930 a scandal developed by reason of the president's manipulation of this company's shares on the New York Stock Exchange.

policy, as shown by its treatment of the large sums received in the form of income-tax refunds in the three preceding years. These receipts were not reported as current income but were credited directly to surplus.

Profits from Sale of Marketable Securities. Profits realized by a business corporation from the sale of marketable securities are also of a special character and must be separated from the ordinary operating results.

Examples: The report of National Transit Company, a former Standard Oil subsidiary, for the year 1928 illustrates the distorting effect due to the inclusion in the income account of profits from this source. The method of presenting the story to the stockholders is also open to serious criticism. The consolidated income account for 1927 and 1928 was stated in approximately the following terms:

Item	1927	1928
Operating revenues	$3,432,000	$3,419,000
Dividends, interest, and miscella-		
neous income	463,000	370,000
Total revenues	$3,895,000	$3,789,000
"Operating expenses, including depreciation		
and profit and loss direct items" (in 1928		
"including profits from sale of securities")	3,264,000	2,599,000
Net income	$631,000	$1,190,000
(Earned per share)	($1.24)	($2.34)

The increase in the earnings per share appeared quite impressive. But a study of the detailed figures of the parent company alone, as submitted to the Interstate Commerce Commission, would have revealed that $560,000 of the 1928 income was due to its profits from the sale of securities. This happens to be almost exactly equal to the increase in consolidated net earnings over the previous year. Allowing on the one hand for income tax and other offsets against these special profits but on the other hand for probable additional profits from the sale of securities by the manufacturing subsidiary, it seems likely that all or nearly all of the apparent improvement in earnings for 1928 was due to nonoperating items. Such gains must clearly be eliminated from any comparison or calculation of *earning power*. The form of statement resorted to by National Transit, in which such profits are applied to *reduce operating expenses*, is bizarre to say the least.

The sale by the New York, Chicago, and St. Louis Railroad Company, through a subsidiary, of its holdings of Pere Marquette stock in 1929 gave rise later to an even more extraordinary form of bookkeeping manipulation. We shall describe these transactions in connection with our treatment of items involving nonconsolidated subsidiaries. During 1931 F.W. Woolworth Company included in its income a profit of nearly $10,000,000 on the sale of a part interest in its British subsidiary. The effect of this inclusion was to make the per-share earnings appear larger than any previous year, when in fact they had experienced a recession. It is somewhat surprising to note that in the same year the company charged against *surplus* an additional tax accrual of $2,000,000 which seemed to be closely related to the special profit included in *income*.

Reduction in the market value of securities should be considered as a nonrecurring item in the same way as losses from the sale of such securities. The same would be true of shrinkage in the value of foreign exchange. In most cases corporations charge such write-downs, when made, against surplus. The General Motors report for 1931 included both such adjustments, totaling $20,575,000 as deductions from *income*, but was careful to designate them as "extraordinary and nonrecurring losses."

Methods Used by Investment Trusts in Reporting Sale of Marketable Securities. Investment-trust statements raise special questions with respect to the treatment of profits or losses realized from the sale of securities and changes in security values. Prior to 1930 most of these companies reported profits from the sale of securities as part of their regular income, but they showed the appreciation on *unsold* securities in the form of a memorandum or footnote to the balance sheet. But when large losses were taken in 1930 and subsequently, they were shown in most cases not in the income account but as charges against capital, surplus, or reserves. The *unrealized* depreciation was still recorded by most companies in the form of an explanatory comment on the balance sheet, which continued to carry the securities owned at original cost. A minority of investment trusts reduced the carrying price of their portfolio to the market by means of charges against capital and surplus.

It may logically be contended that, since dealing in securities is an integral part of the investment-trust business, the results from sales and even the changes in portfolio values should be regarded as ordinary rather than extraordinary elements in the year's report. Certainly a study confined to the interest and dividend receipts less expenses would prove of negligible value. If *any* useful results can be expected from an analysis of investment-trust exhibits, such analysis must clearly be based on the three items: investment income, profits or losses on the sale of securities and changes in market values. It is equally obvious that the gain or shrinkage, so computed, in any one year is no indication whatever of *earning power* in the recurrent sense. Nor can an average taken over several years have any significance for the future unless the results are first compared with some appropriate measure of general market performance. Assuming that an investment trust has done substantially better than the relevant "average," this is of course a *prima facie* indication of capable management. But even here it would be difficult to distinguish confidently between superior ability and luckier guesses on the market.

The gist of this critique is twofold: (1) the over-all change in principal value is the only available measure of investment-trust performance, but (2) this measure cannot be regarded as an index of "normal earning power" in any sense analogous to the recorded earnings of a well-entrenched industrial business.[5]

Similar Problem in the Case of Banks and Insurance Companies. A like problem is involved in analyzing the results shown by insurance companies and by banks. Public interest in insurance securities is concentrated largely upon the shares of fire insurance companies. These enterprises represent a combination of the insurance business and the investment-trust business. They have available for investment their capital funds plus substantial amounts received as premiums paid in advance. Generally speaking, only a small portion of these funds is subject to legal restrictions as regards investment, and the balance is handled in much the same way as the resources of the investment trusts. The underwriting business as such has rarely proved highly profitable. Frequently it shows a deficit, which is offset, however, by interest and dividend income. The profits or losses shown on security operations, including changes in their market value, exert a predominant influence upon the public's attitude toward

---

[5] See Appendix Note 47, p. 782 on accompanying CD, for a summary of the findings of the S.E.C. in its investigation of management investment-trust performance and for further comment by the authors concerning the record and practices of management investment trusts.

fire-insurance-company stocks. The same has been true of bank stocks to a smaller, but none the less significant, degree. The tremendous over-speculation in these issues during the late 1920's was stimulated largely by the participation of the banks, directly or through affiliates, in the fabulous profits made in the securities markets.

Since 1933 banks have been required to divorce themselves from their affiliates, and their operations in securities other than government issues have been more carefully supervised and restricted. But in view of the large portion of their resources invested in bonds, substantial changes in bond prices are still likely to exert a pronounced effect upon their reported earnings.

The fact that the operations of financial institutions generally—such as investment trusts, banks and insurance companies—must necessarily reflect changes in security values makes their shares a dangerous medium for widespread public dealings. Since in these enterprises an increase in security values may be held to be part of the year's profits, there is an inevitable tendency to regard the gains made in good times as part of the "earning power" and to value the shares accordingly. This results of course in an absurd overvaluation, to be followed by collapse and a correspond-ingly excessive depreciation. Such violent fluctuations are particularly harmful in the case of financial institutions because they may affect public confidence. It is true also that rampant speculation (called "investment") in bank and insurance-company stocks leads to the ill-advised launching of new enterprises, to the unwise expansion of old ones and to a general relaxation of established standards of conservatism and even of probity.

The securities analyst, in discharging his function of investment coun-sellor, should do his best to discourage the purchase of stocks of banking and insurance institutions by the ordinary small investor. Prior to the boom of the 1920's such securities were owned almost exclusively by those having or commanding large financial experience and matured judgment. These qualities are needed to avoid the special danger of mis-judging values in this field by reason of the dependence of their reported earnings upon fluctuations in security prices.

Herein lies also a paradoxical difficulty of the investment-trust move-ment. Given a proper technique of management, these organizations may well prove a logical vehicle for the placing of small investor's funds. But considered as a marketable security dealt in by small investors, the invest-ment-trust stock itself is a dangerously volatile instrument. Apparently this troublesome factor can be held in check only be educating or by effectively cautioning the general public on the interpretation of investment-trust reports. The prospects of accomplishing this are none too bright.

Profits through Repurchase of Senior Securities at a Discount.

At times a substantial profit is realized by corporations through the repurchase of their own senior securities at less than par value. The inclusion of such gains in current income is certainly a misleading practice, first, because they are obviously nonrecurring and, second, because this is at best a questionable sort of profit, since it is made at the expense of the company's own security holders.

Example: A peculiar example of this accounting practice was furnished as long ago as 1915 by Utah Securities Corporation, a holding company controlling Utah Power and Light Company. The following income account illustrates this point:

YEAR ENDED MARCH 31, 1915

Earnings of Utah Securities Corporation	
including surplus of subsidiaries accruing to it	$ 771,299
Expenses and taxes	30,288
Net earnings	$ 741,011
Profit on redemption of 6% notes	1,309,657
Income from all sources accruing to Utah	
Securities Corporation	$ 2,050,668
Deduct interest charges on 6% notes	1,063,009
Combined net income for the year	$ 987,659

The foregoing income account shows that the chief "earnings" of Utah Securities were derived from the repurchase of its own obligations at a discount. Had it not been for this extraordinary item the company would have failed to cover its interest charges.

The widespread repurchases of senior securities at a substantial discount constituted one of the unique features of the 1931–1933 depression years. It was made possible by the disproportion that existed between the strong cash positions and the poor earnings of many enterprises. Because of the latter influence the senior securities sold at low prices, and because of the former the issuing companies were able to buy them back in large amounts. This practice was most in evidence among the investment trusts.

Examples: The International Securities Corporation of America, to use an outstanding example, repurchased in the fiscal year ending November 30, 1932, no less than $12,684,000 of its 5% bonds, representing nearly half of the issue. The average price paid was about 55, and the operation showed a profit of about $6,000,000, which served to offset the shrinkage in the value of the investment portfolio.

In the industrial field we note the report of Armour and Company for 1932. This showed net earnings of $1,633,000 but only after including in income a profit of $5,520,000 on bonds bought in at a heavy discount. Similarly, more than all of the 1933 net of Goodrich Rubber, United Drug, Bush Terminal Building Company and others was ascribable to this nonrecurring source. A like condition was disclosed in the report of United Cigar-Whelan Stores for the first half of 1938.[6] (Observe, on the other hand, that some companies, *e.g.*, Gulf States Steel Corporation in 1933, have followed the better practice of crediting this profit direct to surplus.)

A contrary result appears when senior securities are retired at a cost exceeding the face or stated value. When this premium involves a large amount, it is always charged against surplus and not against current income.

Examples: As prominent illustrations of this practice, we cite the charge of $40,600,000 against surplus made by United States Steel Corporation in 1929, in connection with the retirement at 110 of $307,000,000 of its own and subsidiaries' bonds, also the charge of $9,600,000 made against surplus in 1927 by Goodyear Tire and Rubber Company, growing out of the retirement at a premium of various bond and preferred-stock issues and their replacement by new securities bearing lower coupon and dividend rates. From the analyst's standpoint, either profit or expense in such special transactions involving the company's own securities should be regarded as nonrecurring and excluded from the operating results in studying a single year's performance.

A Comprehensive Example. American Machine and Metals, Inc. (successor to Manhattan Electrical Supply Company mentioned earlier in this chapter), included in its current *income* for 1932 a profit realized from the repurchase of its own bonds at a discount. Because the reports for 1931 and 1932 illustrate to an unusual degree the arbitrary nature of

---

[6] The report for the full year 1938 credited this profit to *surplus.*

REPORT OF AMERICAN MACHINE AND METALS, INC., FOR 1931 AND 1932

Item	1932	1931
Income account:		
Net before depreciation and interest	Loss $ 136,885	Profit $101,534
Add profit on bonds repurchased	174,278	270,701
Profit, including bonds repurchased	37,393	372,236
Depreciation	87,918	184,562
Bond interest	119,273	140,658
Final net profit or loss	Loss 169,798	Profit 47,015
Charges against capital, capital surplus and earned surplus:		
Deferred moving expense and mine development	111,014	
Provision for losses on:		
Doubtful notes, interest thereon, and claims	600,000	
Inventories	385,000	
Investments	54,999	
Liquidation of subsidiary	39,298	
Depletion of ore reserves	28,406	32,515
Write-down of fixed assets (net)	557,578	
Reduction of ore reserves and mineral rights	681,742	
Federal tax refund, etc	cr. 7,198	cr. 12,269
Total charges not shown in income account	$2,450,839	$20,246
Result shown in income account	dr. 169,798	cr. 47,015
Received from sale of additional stock	cr. 44,000	
Combined change in capital and surplus	dr. $2,576,637	cr. $26,769

much corporate accounting, we reproduce herewith in full the income account and the appended capital and surplus adjustments.

We find again in 1932, as in 1926, the highly objectionable practice of including extraordinary profits in income while charging special losses to surplus. It does not make much difference that in the later year the nature of the special profit—gain through repurchase of bonds at less than par—is disclosed in the report. Stockholders and stock buyers for the most part pay attention only to the final figure of earnings per share, as presented by the company; nor are they likely to inquire carefully into the manner in which it is determined. The significance of some of the charges made by this company against surplus in 1932 will be taken up later under the appropriate headings.

Other Nonrecurrent Items. The remaining group of nonrecurrent profit items is not important enough to merit detailed discussion. In most cases it is of minor consequence whether they appear as part of the year's earnings or are credited to surplus where they properly belong.

Examples: Gimbel Brothers included the sum of $167,660, proceeds of life insurance policies, in income for 1938, designating it as a "nontrading item." On the other hand, United Merchants and Manufacturers, receiving a similar payment of $1,579,000 in its 1938 fiscal year, more soundly credited it to surplus—although it had sustained a large loss from operations.

Bendix Aviation Corporation reported as income for the year 1929 the sum of $901,282 received in settlement of a patent suit, and again in 1931 it included in current earnings an amount $242,656 paid to it as back royalties collected through litigation. The 1932 earnings of Gulf Oil Corporation included the sum of $5,512,000 representing the value of oil previously in litigation. By means of this item, designated as nonrecurrent, it was able to turn a loss of $2,768,000 into a profit of $2,743,000. Although tax refunds are regularly shown as credits to surplus only, the accumulated interest received thereon sometimes appears as part of the income account, *e.g.*, $2,000,000 reported by E. I. du Pont de Nemours and Company in 1926 and an unstated but apparently much larger sum included in the earnings of United States Steel for 1930.

Chapter 32

EXTRAORDINARY LOSSES AND OTHER SPECIAL ITEMS IN THE INCOME ACCOUNT

THE QUESTION OF NONRECURRENT LOSSES is likely to create peculiar difficulties in the analysis of income accounts. To what extent should writedowns of inventories and receivables be regarded as extraordinary deductions not fairly chargeable against the year's operating results? In the disastrous year 1932 such charge-offs were made by nearly every business. The accounting methods used showed wide divergences, but the majority of companies spared their income accounts as much as possible and subtracted these losses from surplus. On the other hand the milder inventory losses of the 1937–1938 recession were almost universally charged into the earnings statement.

Inventory losses are directly related to the conduct of the business and are, therefore, by no means extraordinary in their general character. The collapse of inventory values in 1931–1932 might be considered extraordinary in its *extent*, in the same way as the business results as a whole were exceptional. It follows from this reasoning that if the 1931–1932 results are taken into account at all, *e.g.*, in computing a long-term average, all losses on inventories and receivables must be considered part of the operating deficit of those years even though charged to surplus. In Chap. 37 we shall consider the role of extraordinary years in determining the average earning power.

Manufactured Earnings. An examination of the wholesale charges made against surplus in 1932 by American Machine and Metals, detailed on page 422, suggests the possibility that *excessive* provision for losses may have been made in that year with the intention of benefiting future income accounts. If the receivables and inventories were written down to an unduly low figure on December 31, 1932, this artificially low "cost price" would give rise to a correspondingly inflated profit in the following years. This point may be made clear by the use of hypothetical figures as follows:

Assume fair value of inventory and receivables on Dec. 31, 1932 to be	$2,000,000
Assume profit for 1933 based on such fair value	200,000
But assume that, by special and excessive charges to surplus, the inventory and receivables had been written down to	1,600,000
Then the amounts realized therefrom will show a correspondingly greater profit for 1933, which might mean *reported* earnings for 1933 of	600,000
This would be three times the proper figure.	

The foregoing example illustrates a whole set of practices that constitute perhaps the most vicious type of accounting manipulation. They consist, in brief, of taking sums out of surplus (or even capital) and then reporting these same sums as income. The charge to surplus goes unnoticed; the credit to income may have a determining influence upon the market price of the securities of the company.[1] We shall later point out that the "conservative" writing down of the property account has precisely this result, in that it permits a decreased depreciation charge and hence an increase in the apparent earnings. The dangers inherent in accounting methods of this sort are the more serious because they are so little realized by the public, so difficult to detect even by the expert analyst and so impervious to legislative or stock-exchange correction.

The basing of common-stock values on reported per-share earnings has made it much easier for managements to exercise an arbitrary and

---

[1] The United States Industrial Alcohol Company reports for 1932 and subsequent years reflect a situation somewhat similar to that here suggested. This company departed from its usual practice in 1932 by setting up a reserve for $1,500,000 out of surplus to reduce molasses inventory to estimated current market value. (Previously this item had regularly been carried at cost.) Later reports state that earnings for 1933, 1934 and 1935 had benefited by this reserve to the extent of $772,000, $677,000 and $51,000 respectively. Significantly, income tax for 1934 was based on $677,000 less than the reported profit. (See pp. 626–627 for a broad summary of the effect of this company's accounting methods on its reported per-share earnings for the years 1929–1938.)

unwholesome control over the price level of their shares. Whereas it should be emphasized that the overwhelming majority of managements are honest, it must be emphasized also that loose or "purposive" accounting is a highly contagious disease.

Reserves for Inventory Losses. The accounting for inventory losses is frequently complicated by the use of reserves set up before the loss is actually realized. These reserves are usually created by a charge to surplus, on the theory that it is a function of the surplus account to act as a sort of contingency reserve to absorb unusual future losses. If later the inventory shrinkage actually takes place, it is naturally charged against the reserve already created to meet it. The result is that in *no year* does the income account reflect the inventory loss, although it is just as much a hazard of operations as a decline in selling prices. When a company charges inventory losses to surplus—whether directly or through the intermediary of a reserve device—the analyst must take this practice carefully into account, especially in comparing the published results with those of other companies. A good illustration of this rule is afforded by a comparison of the reports submitted by United States Rubber Company and by Goodyear Tire and Rubber Company for the years 1925–1927, during which time rubber prices were subject to wide fluctuations.

In these three years Goodyear charged against *earnings* a total of $11,500,000 as reserves against decline of raw-material prices. Of this amount one-half was used to absorb actual losses sustained and the other half was carried forward into 1928 (and eventually used up in 1930).

United States Rubber during this period charged a total of $20,446,000 for inventory reserves and write-downs, all of which was absorbed by actual losses taken. But the form of annual statement, as submitted to the stockholders, excluded these deductions from income and made them appear as special adjustments of surplus. (In 1927, moreover, the inventory loss of $8,910,000 was apparently offset by a special credit of $8,000,000 from the transfer of *past* earnings of the crude-rubber producing subsidiary.)

The result of these divergent bases of reporting annual income was that the per-share earnings of the two companies, as compiled by the statistical manuals, made an entirely misleading comparative exhibit. The following per-share earnings are taken from *Poor's Manual* for 1928:

Year	U.S. Rubber	Goodyear
1925	$14.92	$9.45
1926	10.54	3.79
1927	1.26	9.02
3-year average	$ 8.91	$7.42

For proper comparative purposes the statements must manifestly be considered on an identical basis, or as close thereto as possible. Such a comparison might be made by three possible methods, *viz.:*

1. As reported by United States Rubber, *i.e.*, excluding inventory reserves and losses from the current income account.

2. As reported by Goodyear, *i.e.*, reducing the earnings of the period of high prices for crude rubber by a reserve for future losses and using this reserve to absorb the later shrinkage.

3. Eliminating such reserves, as an arbitrary effort of the management to level out the earnings. On this basis the inventory losses would be deducted from the results of the year in which they were actually sustained. (The Standard Statistics Company's analysis of Goodyear includes a revision of the reported earnings in conformity with this approach.)

We have then, for comparative purposes, three statements of the per-share earnings for the period:

Year	1. Omitting adjustments of inventory		2. Allowing for inventory adjustments, as made by the companies		3. Excluding *reserves* and charging losses to the year in which decline occurred	
	U.S. Rubber	Goodyear	U.S. Rubber	Goodyear	U.S. Rubber	Goodyear
1925	$14.92	$18.48	$11.21	$9.45	$14.92	$18.48
1926	10.54	3.79	0.00	3.79	14.71(d)	2.53(d)
1927	1.26*	13.24	9.73(d)*	9.02	1.26*	13.24
3-year average	$8.91	$12.17	$0.49	$7.42	$0.49	$9.73

* Excluding credit for profits made prior to 1926 by United States Rubber Plantations, Inc.

The range of market prices for the two common issues during this period suggests that the accounting methods followed by United States

Rubber served rather effectively to obscure the unsatisfactory nature of its results for these years.

Year	U.S. Rubber common		Goodyear common	
	High	Low	High	Low
1925	97	33	50	25
1926	88	50	40	27
1927	67	37	69	29
Average of highs and lows	62		40	

More recently United States Rubber has followed the Goodyear practice of taking out of the earnings of prosperous years a reserve for future inventory shrinkage. As a result of this policy, the company somewhat understated its earnings for 1935 and 1936 but overstated them for 1937.

A More Recent Contrast. The packing industry supplies us with a more extreme divergence in the method used by two companies to handle the matter of probable future inventory losses.

Wilson and Company set up a reserve of $750,000 prior to the beginning of its 1934 fiscal year, for "Fluctuation in Inventory Valuation." This was taken partly from surplus and partly from income. In 1934 it reduced its opening inventory by this reserve, thus increasing the year's reported profit by $750,000. The S.E.C., however, required it to amend its registration statement so as to credit this amount to surplus and not to income.

On the other hand, Swift and Company reduced its reported earnings in the fiscal years 1933–1935 by $16,767,000, which was set up as a reserve for future inventory decline. In 1938 the expected decline occurred; but instead of drawing on this reserve to spare the income account, the company charged the full loss against the year's operations and then transferred $11,000,000 of the reserve directly to surplus. In this exceptional case the net income for the six-year period 1933–1938 was *understated*, since amounts were actually taken out of income and turned over to surplus.[2]

Other Elements in Inventory Accounting. The student of corporate reports must familiarize himself with two permissible variations from

---

[2] Standard Statistics has restated the Swift annual reports by listing the 1933–1935 deductions for inventory declines as charges to *surplus*.

the usual accounting practice in handling inventories. As is well known, the standard procedure consists of taking inventory at the close of the year at the lower of cost or market. The "cost of goods sold" is then found by adding purchases to the opening inventory and subtracting the closing inventory, valued as described.

Last-In, First-Out. The first variation from this method consists of taking as the cost of goods sold the actual amount paid for the *most recently acquired* lots. The theory behind this method is that a merchant's selling price is related mainly to the current replacement price or the recent cost of the article sold. The point is of importance only when there are substantial changes in unit values from year to year; it cannot affect the aggregate reported profits over a long period but only the division of results from one year to another; it may be useful in reducing income tax by avoiding alternations of loss and profit due to inventory fluctuations.[3]

The Normal-stock or Basic-stock Inventory Method. A more radical method of minimizing fluctuations due to inventory values has been followed by a considerable number of companies for some years past. This method is based on the theory that the company must regularly carry a certain physical stock of materials and that there is no more reason to vary the value of this "normal stock" from year to year—because of market changes—than there would be to vary the value of the manufacturing plant as the price index rises or falls and to reflect this change in the year's operations. In order to permit the base inventory to be carried at an unchanging figure, the practice is to mark it down to a very low unit price level—so low that it should never be necessary to reduce it further to get it down to current market.

As long ago as 1913 National Lead Company applied this method to the three principal constituents of its inventory, *viz.*, lead, tin and antimony. The method was subsequently adopted also by American Smelting and Refining Company and American Metals Company. Some of the New England cotton mills had followed a like policy, prior to the collapse in the cotton market in 1930, by carrying their raw cotton and work in process at very low base prices. In 1936 the Plymouth Cordage Company

---

[3] Corporations were first permitted to use this so-called "last-in, first-out" method by the terms of the Revenue Acts of 1938 and 1939, applying to 1939 and subsequent years. A hypothetical example to illustrate the difference between the two inventory methods is given in Appendix Note 48, p. 784 on accompanying CD.

adopted the normal-stock inventory method, after following a somewhat similar policy in 1933–1935; and for purpose of concrete illustration we supply the relevant data for this company, covering the years 1930–1939, in Appendix Note 49, page 785 on accompanying CD.

Idle-plant Expense. The cost of carrying nonoperating properties is almost always charged against income. Many statements for 1932 earmarked substantial deductions under this heading.

Examples: Youngstown Sheet and Tube Company reported a charge of $2,759,000 for "Maintenance Expense, Insurance and Taxes of Plants, Mines, and Other Properties that were Idle." Stewart Warner Corporation followed the exceptional policy of charging against *surplus* in 1932, instead of income, the sum of $309,000 for "Depreciation of Plant Facilities not used in current year's production." The 1938 report of Botany Worsted Mills contained a charge against income of $166,732, picturesquely termed "cost of idleness."

The analyst may properly consider idle-plant expense as belonging to a somewhat different category from ordinary charges against income. In theory, at least, these expenses should be of a temporary and therefore nonrecurring type. Presumably the management can terminate these losses at any time by disposing of or abandoning the property. If, for the time being, the company elects to spend money to carry these assets along in the expectation that future value will justify the outlay, it does not seem logical to consider these assets as equivalent to a permanent liability, *i.e.*, as a permanent drag upon the company's earning power, which makes the stock worth considerably less than it would be if these "assets" did not exist.

Example: The practical implications of this point are illustrated by the case of New York Transit Company, a carrier of oil by pipe line. In 1926, owing to new competitive conditions, it lost all the business formerly carried by its principal line, which thereupon became "idle plant." The depreciation, taxes and other expenses of this property were so heavy as to absorb the earnings of the company's other profitable assets (consisting of a smaller pipe line and high-grade-bond investments). This created an apparent net loss and caused the dividend to be passed. The price of the stock accordingly declined to a figure far less than the company's holdings of cash and marketable securities alone. In this uncritical appraisal by the stock market, the idle asset was considered equivalent to a serious and permanent liability.

In 1928, however, the directors determined to put an end to these heavy carrying charges and succeeded in selling the unused pipe line for a substantial sum of money. Thereafter, the stockholders received special cash distributions aggregating $72 per share (nearly twice the average market price for 1926 and 1927), and they still retained ownership of a profitable business which resumed regular dividends. Even if no money had been realized from the idle property, its mere abandonment would have led to a considerable increase in the value of the shares.

This is an impressive, if somewhat extreme, example of the practical utility of security analysis in detecting discrepancies between intrinsic value and market price. It is customary to refer with great respect to the "bloodless verdict of the market place," as though it represented invariably the composite judgment of countless shrewd, informed and calculating minds. Very frequently, however, these appraisals are based on mob psychology, on faulty reasoning, and on the most superficial examination of inadequate information. The analyst, on his side, is usually unable to apply his technique effectively to correcting or taking advantage of these popular errors, for the reason that surrounding conditions change so rapidly that his own conclusions may become inapplicable before he can profit by them. But in the exceptional case, as illustrated by our last example, the facts and the logic of the case may be sharply enough defined to warrant a high degree of confidence in the practical value of his analysis.

Deferred Charges. A business sometimes incurs expenses that may fairly be considered as applicable to a number of years following rather than to the single 12-month period in which the outlay was made. Under this heading might be included the following:

> Organization expense (legal fees, etc.).
> Moving expenses.
> Development expenses (for new products or processes, also for opening up a mine, etc.).
> Discount on obligations sold.

Under approved accounting methods such costs are spread over an appropriate period of years. The amount involved is entered upon the balance sheet as a Deferred Charge, which is written off by annual charges against earnings. In the case of bond-discount the period is fixed by the life of the issue; mine development expenses are similarly prorated on the basis of the tonnage mined. For most other items the number of years must be arbitrarily taken, five years being a customary figure.

In order to relieve the reported earnings of these annual deductions it has become common practice to write off such expense applicable to future years by a single charge against surplus. In theory this practice is improper, because it results in the understatement of operating expenses for a succeeding period of years and hence in the exaggeration of the net income. If, to take a simple example, the president's salary were paid for ten years in advance and the entire outlay charged against surplus as a "special expense," it is clear that the profits of the ensuing period would thereby be overstated.[4] There is the danger also that expenses of a character frequently repeated, *e.g.*, advertising campaigns, or cost of developing new automobile models, might be omitted from the income account by designating them as deferred charges and then writing them off against surplus.[5]

Ordinarily the amounts involved in such accounting transactions are not large enough to warrant the analyst's making an issue of them. Security analysis is a severely practical activity, and it must not linger over matters that are not likely to affect the ultimate judgment. At times however, these items may assume appreciable importance.

Examples: The Kraft Cheese Company for example, during some years prior to 1927 carried a substantial part of its advertising outlays as a deferred charge to be absorbed in the operations of subsequent years. In 1926 it spent about $1,000,000 for advertising and charged only one-half of this amount against current income. But in the same year the balance of this expenditure was deducted from surplus, and furthermore an additional $480,000 was similarly written off against surplus to cancel the balance carried forward from prior years as a deferred charge. By this means the company was able to report to its stockholders the sum of $1,071,000 as earned for 1926. But when in the following year it applied to list additional shares, it found it necessary to adopt a less questionable basis of

---

[4] See Appendix Note 50, p. 786 on accompanying CD, for details of accounting methods followed by Interstate Department Stores in 1934–1936, which resembled somewhat the hypothetical case given above.

[5] A similar objection lies against the practice of charging against surplus the loss incurred in closing chain-store units. *Example:* The charge of $326,000 made by F. G. Shattuck Company for this purpose in 1935. This would seem to be a recurrent expense of chain-store enterprises, which frequently add and close down units.

reporting its income to the New York Stock Exchange, so that its profit for 1926 was restated to read $461,296, instead of $1,071,000.

The 1932 report of International Telephone and Telegraph Company showed various charges *against surplus* aggregating $35,817,000, which included the following: "Write-off of certain deferred charges that have today no tangible value although originally set up to be amortized over a period of years in accordance with accepted accounting principles, $4,655,696."

Hudson Motor Car Company charged against surplus instead of income the following items (among others) during 1930–1931.

1930	Special adjustment of tools and materials due to development of new models	$2,266,000
1931	Reserve for special tools	2,000,000
	Rearrangement of plant equipment	633,000
	Special advertising	1,400,000

In 1933 Hecker Products (then called Gold Dust Corporation) appropriated out of surplus the sum of $2,000,000 as a reserve for the "net cost of introduction and exploitation of new products." About three-quarters of this amount was expended in years 1933–1936, and the balance then transferred to "General and Contingency Reserves."

The effect of these accounting practices is to relieve the reported earnings of expenditures that most companies charge currently thereagainst, and that in any event should be charged against earnings in installments over a short period of years.

Amortization of Bond Discount. Bonds are usually floated by corporations at a price to net the treasury less than par. The discount suffered is part of the cost of borrowing the money, *i.e.*, part of the interest burden, and it should be amortized over the life of the bond issue by an annual charge against earnings, included with the statement of interest paid. It was formerly considered "conservative" to write off such bond discounts by a single charge against surplus, in order not to show so intangible an item among the assets on the balance sheet. More recently these write-offs against surplus have become popular for the opposite reason, *viz.*, to eliminate future annual deductions from earnings and in that way to make the shares more "valuable."

Example: Associated Gas and Electric Company charged against surplus in 1932 the sum of $5,892,000 for "debt discount and expense" written off.

This practice has aroused considerable criticism in recent years both from the New York Stock Exchange and from the S.E.C. As a result of these objections a number of companies have reversed their previous charge to surplus and are again charging amortization of bond discounts annually against earnings.[6]

---

[6] See the changed accounting practice of Northern States Power Company (Minnesota) following a controversy over this point in connection with the registration of a bond issue in 1984. (The total amount involved here was over $8,000,000.) It is noteworthy, also, that *even on called bonds* companies have been required to carry forward the unamortized discount to be written off by an annual charge against earnings during the life of the refunding issue. (See the report of Columbia Gas and Electric Company for 1936, p. 17.)

Some of the bond refundings in recent years seem to have involved a surprisingly small net saving of interest when the premium paid to retire the old issue is taken into account. Perhaps an explanation of some of these operations lies in the fact that (1) the company has been able to charge both the premium paid and the balance of the original discount against surplus, thus relieving future earnings of this very real burden; and (2) both these items have been chargeable to profits subject to *income tax*, thus reducing this tax substantially and increasing the *apparent* profits for the year.

Chapter 33

MISLEADING ARTIFICES IN THE INCOME ACCOUNT. EARNINGS OF SUBSIDIARIES

Flagrant Example of Padded Income Account. On comparatively rare occasions, managements resort to padding their income account by including items in earnings that have no real existence. Perhaps the most flagrant instance of this kind that has come to our knowledge occurred in the 1929–1930 reports of Park and Tilford, Inc., an enterprise with shares listed on the New York Stock Exchange. For these years the company reported net income as follows:

$$1929—\$1,001,130 = \$4.72 \text{ per share.}$$
$$1930— \quad 124,563 = \quad 0.57 \text{ per share.}$$

An examination of the balance sheets discloses that during these two years the item of Good-will and Trade-marks was written up successively from $1,000,000 to $1,600,000 and then to $2,000,000, and these increases *deducted* from the expenses for the period. The extraordinary character of the bookkeeping employed will be apparent from a study of the condensed balance sheets as of three dates, shown on page 436.

These figures show a reduction of $1,600,000 in net current assets in 15 months, or $1,000,000 more than the cash dividends paid. This shrinkage was concealed by a $1,000,000 write-up of Good-will and Trade-marks. No statement relating to these amazing entries was vouchsafed to the stockholders in the annual reports or to the New York Stock Exchange in subsequent listing applications. In answer to an individual inquiry, however, the company stated that these additions to Good-will and Trade-marks represented expenditures for advertising and other sales efforts to develop the business of Tintex Company, Inc., a subsidiary.[1]

---

[1] In the 1930 report the wording in the balance sheet was changed from "Good-will and Trade-marks" to "Tintex Good-will and Trade-marks." In 1939 the Good-will item was written off, and the $1,000,000 write-up of 1929–1930 deducted from earned surplus.

PARK AND TILFORD, INC.

Balance sheet	Sept. 30, 1929	Dec. 31, 1929	Dec. 31, 1930
Assets:			
Fixed assets	$1,250,000	$1,250,000	$1,250,000
Deferred charges	132,000	163,000	32,000
Good-will and Trade-marks	1,000,000	1,600,000	2,000,000
Net current assets	4,797,000	4,080,000	3,154,000
Liabilities:			
Bonds and mortgages	2,195,000	2,195,000	2,095,000
Capital and surplus	4,984,000	4,898,000	4,341,000
Total of assets and liabilities	$7,179,000	$7,093,000	$6,436,000

Adjusted earnings	First 9 months, 1929	Last 3 months, 1929	Year, 1929	Year, 1930
Earnings for stock as reported	$929,000	$ 72,000	$1,001,000	$125,000
Cash dividends paid	463,000	158,000	621,000	453,000
Charges against surplus				229,000
Added to capital and surplus	466,000	*decrease* 86,000	380,000	*decrease* 557,000
Earnings for stock as corrected (excluding increase in intangibles and deducting charges to surplus)	929,000	528,000(d)	401,000	504,000(d)

The charging of current advertising expense to the good-will account is inadmissible under all canons of sound accounting. To do so without any disclosure to the stockholders is still more discreditable. It is difficult to believe, moreover, that the sum of $600,000 could have been expended for this purpose by Park and Tilford in the *three months* between September 30 and December 31, 1929. The entry appears therefore to have included a recrediting to *current* income of expenditures made in a *previous period*, and to that extent the results for the fourth quarter of 1929 may have been flagrantly distorted. Needless to say, no accountants' certificate accompanied the annual statements of this enterprise.

Balance-sheet and Income-tax Checks upon the Published Earnings Statements. The Park and Tilford case illustrates the necessity of relating an analysis of income accounts to an examination of the appurtenant balance sheets. This is a point that cannot be stressed too strongly, in view of Wall Street's naïve acceptance of reported income and reported earnings per share. Our example suggests also a further check upon the reliability of the published earnings statements, *viz.,* by the amount of the federal income tax accrued. The taxable profit can be calculated fairly readily from the income-tax accrual, and this profit compared in turn with the earnings reported to stockholders. The two figures should not necessarily be the same, since the intricacies of the tax laws may give rise to a number of divergences.[2] We do not suggest that any effort be made to reconcile the amounts absolutely but only that very wide differences be noted and made the subject of further inquiry.

The Park and Tilford figures analyzed from this viewpoint supply the suggestive results as shown in the table on page 438.

The close correspondence of the tax accrual with the reported income during the earlier period makes the later discrepancy appear the more striking. These figures eloquently cast suspicion upon the truthfulness of the reports made to the stockholders during 1927–1929, at which time considerable manipulation was apparently going on in the shares.

This and other examples discussed herein point strongly to the need for independent audits of corporate statements by certified public accountants. It may be suggested also that annual reports should include a detailed reconcilement of the net earnings reported to the shareholders with the

---

[2] See Appendix Note 51, p. 787 on accompanying CD, for a brief résumé of these divergences.

net income upon which the federal tax is paid. In our opinion a good deal
of the information relative to minor matters that appears in registration
statements and prospectuses might be dispensed with to general advantage; but if, in lieu thereof, the S.E.C. were to require such a reconcilement,
the cause of security analysis would be greatly advanced.

| Period | Federal income tax accrued | Rate of tax, per cent | Net income before federal tax | |
			A. As indicated by the tax accrued	B. As reported to the stockholders
5 mo. to Dec. 1925	$36,881	13	$283,000	$ 297,000
1926	66,624	13¹/₂	493,000	533,000
1927	51,319	13¹/₂	380,000	792,000
1928	79,852	12	665,000	1,315,000
1929	81,623*	11	744,000	1,076,000

* Including $6,623 additional paid in 1931.

Another Extraordinary Case of Manipulated Accounting. An
accounting vagary fully as extraordinary as that of Park and Tilford, though
exercising a smaller influence on the reported earnings, was indulged
in by United Cigar Stores Company of America, from 1924–1927. The "theory" behind the entries was explained by the company for the first time in
May 1927 in a listing application that contained the following paragraphs:[3]

> The Company owns several hundred long-term leaseholds on business build-
> ings in the principal cities of the United States, which up until May, 1924, were
> not set up on the books. Accordingly, at that time they were appraised by the
> Company and Messrs. F. W. Lafrentz and Company, certified public account-
> ants of New York City, in excess of $20,000,000.
> The Board of Directors have, since that time, authorized every three months
> the setting up among the assets of the Company a portion of this valuation
> and the capitalization thereof, in the form of dividends, payable in Common
> Stock at par on the Common Stock on the quarterly basis of 1¹/₄% on the
> Common Stock issued and outstanding.

[3] See application to list 6% Cumulative Preferred Stock of United Cigar Stores Company of
America on the New York Stock Exchange, dated May 18, 1927 (Application #A-7552).

The entire capital surplus created in this manner has been absorbed by the issuance of Common Stock at par for an equal amount and accordingly is not a part of the existing surplus of the Company. No cash dividends have been declared out of such capital surplus so created.

The present estimated value of such leaseholds, using the same basis of appraisal as in 1924, is more than twice the present value shown on the books of the Company.

The effect of the inclusion of "Appreciation of Leaseholds" in earnings is shown herewith:

Year	Net earnings as reported	Earned per share of common ($25-par basis)	Market range ($25-par basis)	Amount of "Leasehold Appreciation" included in earnings	Earned per share of common excluding lease appreciation
1924	$6,697,000	$4.69	64–43	$1,248,000	$3.77
1925	8,813,000	5.95	116–60	1,295,000*	5.05
1926	9,855,000	5.02	110–83	2,302,000	3.81
1927	9,952,000†	4.63	100–81	2,437,000	3.43

* The 5% stock dividend paid in 1925 amounted to $1,737,770. There is an unexplained difference between the two figures, which in the other years are identical.
† Excluding refund of federal taxes of $229,017 applicable to prior years.

In passing judgment on the inclusion of leasehold appreciation in the current earnings of United Cigar Stores, a number of considerations might well be borne in mind.

1. Leaseholds are essentially as much a liability as they are an asset. They are an obligation to pay rent for premises occupied. Ironically enough, these very leaseholds of United Cigar Stores eventually plunged it into bankruptcy.

2. Assuming leaseholds may acquire a capital value to the occupant, such value is highly intangible, and it is contrary to accounting principles to mark up above actual cost the value of such intangibles in a balance sheet.

3. If the value of any capital asset is to be marked up, such enhancement must be credited to Capital Surplus. By no stretch of the imagination can it be considered as *income*.

4. The $20,000,000 appreciation of the United Cigar Stores leases took place prior to May 1924, but it was *treated as income in subsequent years*. There was thus no connection between the $2,437,000 appreciation included in the profits of 1927 and the operations or developments of that year.

5. If the leaseholds had really increased in value, the effect should be visible in *larger earnings* realized from these favorable locations. Any other recognition given this enhancement would mean counting the same value twice. In fact, however, allowing for extensions of the business financed by additional capitalization, the per-share earnings of United Cigar Stores showed no advancing trend.

6. Whatever value is given to leaseholds must be amortized over the life of the lease. If the United Cigar Stores investors were paying a high price for the shares because of earnings produced by these valuable leases, then they should *deduct* from earnings an allowance to write off this capital value by the time it disappears through the expiration of the leases.[4] The United Cigar Stores Company continued to amortize its leaseholds on the basis of *original cost*, which apparently was practically nothing.

The surprising truth of the matter, therefore, is that the effect of the appreciation of leasehold values—if it had occurred—should have been to *reduce* the subsequent operating profits by an increased amortization charge.

7. The padding of the United Cigar Stores income for 1924–1927 was made the more reprehensible by the failure to reveal the facts clearly in the annual reports to shareholders.[5] Disclosure of the essential facts to the New York Stock Exchange was made nearly three years after the practice was initiated. It may have been compelled by legal considerations growing out of the sale to the public at that time of a new issue of preferred stock, underwritten by large financial institutions. The following year the policy of including leasehold appreciation in earnings was discontinued.

These accounting maneuvers of United Cigar Stores may be fairly described, therefore, as the *unexplained* inclusion in current earnings of an

---

[4] This subject is treated fully in a succeeding chapter.

[5] The reports stated the "Net Profit for the year, including Enhancement of Leasehold Values" (giving amount of the latter), but no indication was afforded that this enhancement was arbitrarily computed and had taken place in previous years.

imaginary appreciation of an *intangible* asset—the asset being in reality a *liability*, the enhancement being related to a *previous* period and the proper effect of the appreciation, if it had occurred, being to *reduce* the subsequent realized earnings by virtue of higher amortization charges.

The federal-income-tax check, described in the Park and Tilford example, will also give interesting results if applied to United Cigar Stores as shown in the table below.

Moral Drawn from Foregoing Examples. A moral of considerable practical utility may be drawn from the United Cigar Stores example. When an enterprise pursues questionable accounting policies, *all* its securities must be shunned by the investor, no matter how safe or attractive some of them may appear. This is well illustrated by United Cigar Stores Preferred, which made an exceedingly impressive statistical showing for many successive years but later narrowly escaped complete extinction. Investors confronted with the strange bookkeeping detailed above might have reasoned that the issue was still perfectly sound, because, when the overstatement of earnings was corrected, the margin of safety remained more than ample. Such reasoning is fallacious. You cannot make a quantitative deduction to allow for an unscrupulous management; the only way to deal with such situations is to avoid them.

Year	Federal tax reserve	Income before tax		
		A. Indicated by tax reserve	B. Reported to stockholders	C. Reported to stockholders less leasehold appreciation
1924	$700,000	$5,600,000	$7,397,000	$6,149,000
1925	825,000	6,346,000	9,638,000	8,343,000
1926	900,000	6,667,000	10,755,000	8,453,000
1927	900,000	6,667,000	10,852,000*	8,415,000*
1928	700,000	5,833,000	9,053,000	9,053,000
1929	13,000	118,000	3,132,000†	3,132,000†
1930	none	none	1,552,000	1,552,000

* Eliminating tax refund of $229,000 evidently applicable to prior years.
† This is also reported as $2,947,000, after an adjustment.

Fictitious Value Placed on Stock Dividends Received. From 1922 on most of the United Cigar Stores common shares were held by Tobacco Products Corporation, an enterprise controlled by the same interests. This was an important company, the market value of its shares averaging more than $100,000,000 in 1926 and 1927. The accounting practice of Tobacco Products introduced still another way of padding the income account, *viz.*, by placing a fictitious valuation upon stock dividends received.

For the year 1926 the company's earnings statement read as follows:

Net income	$10,790,000
Income tax	400,000
Class *A* dividend	3,136,000
Balance for common stock	7,254,000
Earned per share	11
Market range for common	117–95

Detailed information regarding the company's affairs during that period has never been published (the New York Stock Exchange having been unaccountably willing to list new shares on submission of an extremely sketchy exhibit). Sufficient information is available, however, to indicate that the net income was made up substantially as follows:

Rental received from lease of assets to American Tobacco Co.	$ 2,500,000
Cash dividends on United Cigar Stores common (80% of total paid)	2,950,000
Stock dividends on United Cigar Stores common	
(par value $1,840,000), less expenses	5,340,000
	$10,790,000

It is to be noted that Tobacco Products must have valued the stock dividends received from United Cigar Stores at about three times their face value, *i.e.*, at three times the value at which United Cigar charged them against surplus. Presumably the basis of this valuation by Tobacco Products was the market price of United Cigar Stores shares, which price was easily manipulated due to the small amount of stock not owned by Tobacco Products.

When a holding company takes into its income account stock dividends received at a higher value than that assigned them by the subsidiary that pays them, we have a particularly dangerous form of pyramiding of earnings. The New York Stock Exchange, beginning in 1929, has made stringent regulations forbidding this practice. (The point was discussed in Chap. 30, which is on accompanying CD.) In the case of Tobacco Products the device was especially objectionable because the stock dividend was issued in the first instance to represent a fictitious element of earnings, *i.e.*, the appreciation of leasehold values. By unscrupulous exploitation of the holding-company mechanism these imaginary profits were effectively multiplied by three.

On a consolidated earnings basis, the report of Tobacco Products for 1926 would read as follows:

American Tobacco Co. lease income, less income tax, etc.	$2,100,000
80% of earnings on United Cigar Stores common	6,828,000*
	$8,928,000
Class A dividend	3,136,000
Balance for common	$5,792,000
Earned per share	$7.27

* Excluding leasehold appreciation.

The reported earnings for Tobacco Products common given as $11 per share are seen to have been overstated by about 50%.

It may be stated as a Wall-Street maxim that where manipulation of accounts is found, stock juggling will be found also in some form or other. Familiarity with the methods of questionable finance should assist the analyst and perhaps even the public, in detecting such practices when they are perpetrated.[6]

SUBSIDIARY COMPANIES AND CONSOLIDATED REPORTS

This title introduces our second general type of adjustment of reported earnings. When an enterprise controls one or more important subsidiaries, a *consolidated* income account is necessary to supply a true picture of the year's operations. Figures showing the parent company's

---

[6] To avoid an implication of inconsistency, because of our favorable comments on Tobacco Products Corporation 6$^{1}/_{2}$s, due 2022, in a previous chapter, we must point out that a complete change of management took place in this situation during 1930. There have also been two complete changes in the management of United Cigar Stores and its successor.

results only are incomplete and may be quite misleading. As previously remarked, they may either understate the earnings by not showing all the current profits made by the subsidiaries, or they may overstate the earnings by failure to deduct subsidiaries' losses or by including dividends from subsidiaries in excess of their actual income for the year.

Former and Current Practices. In earlier years disclosure of subsidiaries' results was a matter of arbitrary election by management, and in many cases important data of this kind were kept secret.[7] For some time prior to 1933 the New York Stock Exchange had insisted in connection with *new* listings that the results of subsidiaries be presented either in a consolidated statement or separately. But since passage of the 1934 act, all registered companies are required to supply this information in their annual reports to the Commission, and therefore practically all follow the same procedure in their statements to stockholders.

Degree of Consolidation. Even in so-called "consolidated statements" the degree of consolidation varies considerably. Woolworth consolidates its domestic and Canadian subsidiaries but not its foreign affiliates. American Tobacco consolidates only its wholly owned domestic subsidiaries. Most utilities now issue consolidated reports including all companies controlled by them (by ownership of a majority of the voting stock) and deduct the portion of the earnings applicable to others under the heading of "minority interest."[8] In the railroad field results are rarely consolidated unless the subsidiary is both 100% owned and also operated as an integral part of the system. Hence, Atlantic Coast Line does not reflect its share of the results after dividends of Louisville and Nashville, which is 51% owned but separately operated. The same is true with respect to the 53% voting control of Wheeling and Lake Erie held by the Nickel Plate (New York, Chicago, and St. Louis Railroad Company).

---

[7] For a discussion of the misleading effect of such policies in former years, see references to Reading Company, Consolidated Gas Company (now Consolidated Edison Company), and Warren Brothers Company, on pp. 380–381 of the first edition of this work. Prior to the S.E.C. legislation, most railroad companies failed to supply any information regarding the earnings of their nontransportation subsidiaries, some of which were of substantial importance. *Examples:* Northern Pacific, Atchison.

[8] North American Company has been somewhat exceptional in that it consolidates only subsidiaries at least 75% owned and thus excludes two important companies in which its interest in 1939 was 73.5 and 51%, respectively.

Allowance for Nonconsolidated Profits and Losses. It is now frequent procedure for industrial companies to indicate either in the income account or in a footnote thereto their equity in the profits or losses of nonconsolidated subsidiaries after allowance for dividends.

Examples: The 1938 report of American Tobacco Company showed by way of footnote that dividends received from nonconsolidated subsidiaries exceeded their earnings by $427,000. Hercules Powder reported a similar figure of $257,514 for that year, in footnote form, whereas prior to 1937 it had included its share of the undistributed earnings of such affiliates under the heading "Other Income." Railroad companies handle this matter differently. The Atchison, for example, now supplies full balance sheet and income account data of affiliates in an Appendix to its own report, which continues to reflect only the dividends received from these companies.

The analyst should adjust the reported earnings for the results of nonconsolidated affiliates, if this has not already been done in the income account and if the amounts involved are significant. The criterion here is not the technical question of control but the *importance* of the holdings.

Examples: On the one hand it is not customary, nor does it seem worth while, to make such calculations with respect to the holdings of Union Pacific in Illinois Central and other railroads. These holdings, although substantial, do not bulk large enough to affect the Union Pacific common stock materially. On the other hand, the adjustment is clearly indicated in the case of the ownership of Chicago, Burlington, and Quincy stock by Northern Pacific and Great Northern, each holding less than a controlling interest (48.6%).

Year	Du Pont earnings per share	Adjustments to reflect Du Pont's interest in operating results of General Motors	Earnings per share of Du Pont as adjusted
1929	$6.99	+$2.07	$9.06
1930	4.52	+ 0.04	4.56
1931	4.30	− 0.51	3.79
1932	1.81	− 1.35	0.46
1933	2.93	+ 0.43	3.36
1934	3.63	+ 0.44	4.07
1935	5.02	+ 1.30	6.32
1936	7.53	+ 0.77	8.30
1937	7.25	+ 0.57	7.82
1938	3.74	+ 0.61	4.35

Similarly, the interest of Du Pont in General Motors, representing about 23% of the total issue, is undoubtedly significant enough in its effect on the owning company to warrant adjustment of its earnings to reflect the results of General Motors. This is actually done by Du Pont each year in the form of an adjustment of *surplus* to reflect the previous year's change in the book value of its General Motors holdings. The analyst would prefer, however, to make the adjustment concurrently and to include it in the calculated earnings of Du Pont. The effect of such adjustments on the earnings of Du Pont for 1929–1938 is shown in the table on p. 445.

The report of General Motors Corporation for 1931 is worthy of appreciative attention because it includes a supplementary calculation of the kind suggested in this and the previous chapter *i.e.*, exclusive of special and nonrecurring profits or losses and inclusive of General Motors' interest in the results of nonconsolidated subsidiaries. The report contains the following statement of per-share earnings for 1931 and 1930:

EARNINGS PER SHARE, INCLUDING THE EQUITY IN UNDIVIDED PROFITS OR
LOSSES OF NONCONSOLIDATED SUBSIDIARIES

Year	Including nonrecurrent items	Excluding nonrecurrent items
1931	$2.01	$2.43
1930	3.25	3.04

Suggested Procedure for Statistical Agencies.

Although this procedure may seem to complicate a report, it is in fact a salutary antidote against the oversimplification of common-stock analysis which resulted from exclusive preoccupation with the single figure of per-share earnings. The statistical manuals and agencies have naturally come to feature the per-share earnings in their analyses of corporations. They might, however, perform a more useful service if they omitted a calculation of the per-share earnings in all cases where the company's reports appear to contain irregularities or complications in any of the following directions and where a satisfactory correction is not practicable:

1. By reason of nonrecurrent items included in income or because of charges to surplus that might properly belong in the income account.

2. Because current results of subsidiaries are not accurately reflected in the parent company's statements.

3. Because the depreciation and other amortization charges are irregularly computed.[9]

Special Dividends Paid by Subsidiaries. When earnings of nonconsolidated subsidiaries are allowed to accumulate in their surplus accounts, they may be used later to bolster up the results of a poor year by means of a large special dividend paid over to the parent company.

Examples: Such dividends, amounting to $11,000,000, were taken by the Erie Railroad Company in 1922 from the Pennsylvania Coal Company and Hillside Coal and Iron Company. The Northern Pacific Railway Company similarly eked out its depleted earnings in 1930 and 1931 by means of large sums taken as special dividends from the Chicago, Burlington, and Quincy Railroad Company, the Northern Express Company, and the Northwestern Improvement Company, the last being a real-estate, coal and iron-ore subsidiary. The 1931 earnings of the New York, Chicago, and St. Louis Railroad Company included a back dividend of some $1,600,000 on its holdings of Wheeling and Lake Erie Railway Company Prior Preferred Stock, only a part of which was earned in that year by the Wheeling road.

This device of concealing a subsidiary's profits in good years and drawing upon them in bad ones may seem quite praise-worthy as a method of stabilizing the reported earning power. But such benevolent deceptions are frowned upon by enlightened opinion, as illustrated by the more recent regulations of the New York Stock Exchange which insist upon full disclosure of subsidiaries' earnings. It is the duty of management to disclose the truth and the whole truth about the results of each period; it is the function of the stockholders to deduce the "normal earning power" of their company by averaging out the earnings of prosperity and depression. Manipulation of the reported earnings by the management even for the desirable purpose of maintaining them on an even keel is objectionable none the less because it may too readily lead to manipulation for more sinister reasons.

Distorted Earnings through Parent-subsidiary Relationships. Examples are available of the use of the parent-subsidiary relationship to produce astonishing distortions in the reported income. We shall give two illustrations taken from the railroad field. These instances are the more impressive because the stringent accounting regulations of the Interstate

---

[9] Standard Statistics does not calculate per-share earnings if depreciation has not been deducted.

Commerce Commission might be expected to prevent any misrepresentation of earnings.

Examples: In 1925 Western Pacific Railroad *Corporation* paid dividends of $7.56 upon its preferred stock and $5 upon its common stock. Its income account showed earnings slightly exceeding the dividends paid. These earnings consisted almost entirely of dividends aggregating $4,450,000 received from its operating subsidiary, the Western Pacific Railroad *Company*. The year's earnings of the railroad, itself, however, were only $2,450,000. Furthermore its accumulated surplus was insufficient to permit the larger dividend that the parent company desired to report as its income for the year. To achieve this end, the parent company went to the extraordinary lengths of *donating* the sum of $1,500,000 to the operating company, and it immediately took the same money back as a *dividend* from its subsidiary. The donation it charged against its *surplus;* the receipt of the same money as dividends it reported as *earnings.* In this devious fashion it was able to report $5 "earned" upon its common stock, when in fact the applicable earnings were only about $2 per share.

In support of our previous statement that bad accounting practices are contagious, we may point out that the Western Pacific example of 1925 was followed by the New York, Chicago, and St. Louis Railroad Company ("Nickel Plate") in 1930 and 1931. The details are briefly as follows:

In 1929 Nickel Plate sold, through a subsidiary, its holdings of Pere Marquette stock to Chesapeake and Ohio, which was under the same control. A profit of $10,665,000 was realized on this sale, which gain was properly credited to surplus. In 1930 Nickel Plate needed to increase its income; whereupon it took the $10,665,000 profit out of its surplus, returned it to the subsidiary's treasury and then took $3,000,000 thereof in the form of a "dividend" from this subsidiary, which it included in its 1930 *income.* A similar dividend of $2,100,000 was included in the income account for 1931.

These extraordinary devices may have been resorted to for what was considered the necessary purpose of establishing a net income large enough to keep the company's bonds legal for trust-fund investments.[10]

---

[10] For an extreme example of this kind see the annual reports of Wabash Railway Company and Ann Arbor Railroad Company for 1930 and the comment thereon at p. 1022 of *Moody's*

The result, however, was the same as that from all other misleading accounting practices, *viz.*, to lead the public astray and to give those "on the inside" an unfair advantage.

Broader Significance of Subsidiaries' Losses. We have suggested in this chapter that security analysis must make full allowance for the results of subsidiaries, whether they be profits or losses. But the question may well be raised: Is the loss of a subsidiary necessarily a direct offset against the parent company's earnings? Why should a company be worth *less* because it owns something—in this case, an unprofitable interest? Could it not at any time put an end to the loss by selling, liquidating or even abandoning the subsidiary? Hence, if good management is assumed, must we not also assume that the subsidiary losses are at most temporary and therefore to be regarded as nonrecurring items rather than as deductions from normal earnings?

This point is similar to that discussed in the previous chapter relative to idle-plant expense and similar also to the matter of unprofitable *divisions* of a business, to be touched upon later. There is no one, simple answer to the questions that we have raised. Actually, if the subsidiary could be wound up *without an adverse effect upon the rest of the business*, it would be logical to view such losses as temporary—since good sense would dictate that in a short time the subsidiary must either become profitable or be disposed of. But if there are important business relations between the parent company and the subsidiary, *e.g.*, if the latter affords an outlet for goods or supplies cheap materials or absorbs an important share of the overhead, then the termination of its losses is not so simple a matter. It may turn out, upon further analysis, that all or a good part of the subsidiary's loss is a necessary factor in the parent company's profit. It is not an easy task to determine just what business relationships are

---

Manual of Investments (Steam Railroads), 1931. The Wabash owned 99% of both the preferred and the common stock of the Ann Arbor. In December 1930 the Ann Arbor directors declared a $5 dividend per share on the preferred and a $27 dividend per share on the common. This action was taken in the face of a working-capital deficit and net earnings available of little over 10% of the dividends thus declared. Neither dividend was ever paid. This maneuver, however, enabled the Wabash to credit its share of the dividends declared to its income account as "dividend income" to the extent of $1,073,455, which was sufficient to raise the fixed-charge coverage of the Wabash from about 1.3 times to a figure slightly in excess of 1.5 times.

involved in each instance. Like so many other elements in analysis, this point usually requires an investigation going well beyond the reported figures. The following examples will illustrate the type of situation and analysis with which we have been dealing.

Example A: Purity Bakeries Corporation. This large maker of bread and cake operates through a number of subsidiaries, of which one of the largest is Cushman's Sons, Inc., of New York. Cushman's has outstanding $7 and $8 cumulative preferred stock, not guaranteed by Purity. The annual reports of Purity are on a consolidated basis and show earnings after deduction of full dividends on those Cushman's preferred shares not owned by Purity, whether earned or paid. The separate reports of Cushman's reveal that between 1934 and 1937 its operations resulted in a considerable loss to Purity, on its accounting basis, *viz.:*

(000 OMITTED)

Year	Purity net income as reported	Loss of Cushman's after full preferred dividends	Purity earnings excluding Cushman's operations
1937	$463	$426	$889
1936	690	620	1,310
1935	225 (d.)	930	678
1934	209	173	382
Average 4 years	278	537	815
Per share of Purity	0.36	0.71	1.06

The earnings are thus seen to be three times as large excluding Cushman's as they were including Cushman's. Could the analyst have reasoned that the former provides the truer measure of Purity's earning power, since the company can be expected either again to earn money from that subsidiary (as it had earned it in the past up to 1934) or to drop it? The question of inter-corporate relationships would have to be considered. A note in the 1937 report of Cushman's indicated that Purity was making a fairly large service charge in connection with its subsidiaries' operations, which suggests that Cushman's might be of some extra value in absorbing overhead. This matter would call for a careful inquiry.

But the report for the next year, 1938, showed, first, that Cushman's had earned the preferred dividend deduction, and secondly, that two unprofitable retail plants (in Philadelphia and Chicago) had been closed. Subject to further investigation, therefore, the analyst might well infer that the subsidiary's losses were nonpermanent in nature and that the reported results for 1934–1937 are to be viewed with this point in mind.

Example B: Lehigh Coal and Navigation Company. This enterprise has derived its income from various sources, chief of which has been the lease of its railroad property to the Central Railroad of New Jersey for an annual rental of $2,268,000. Its next largest holding consists of anthracite coal mines, which since 1930 have been operated at a loss. In 1937 this loss was equivalent to about 90 cents per share of Lehigh stock. As a result the company reported a *consolidated* net loss of $306,000 for the year, as contrasted with a profit on a parent-company basis only of $1,125,000, or 64 cents per share.

But in this case the analyst could not safely make the assumption that the Lehigh stock was not worth *less* by reason of its ownership of the mining properties than it would be worth without them. Operation of the mines supplied an important tonnage to the railroad division. If the mines were shut down, the ability of the Jersey Central to pay the annual rental might have been critically impaired, especially since the lessee road had been doing poorly for some years past. (In fact the claim was later made by the Jersey Central that the Lehigh Coal and Navigation was obligated in connection with the lease to supply a certain tonnage from its coal properties). Hence, in this rather complicated set-up the investor could not safely go behind the consolidated results, including the losses of the anthracite subsidiary.

Example C: Barnsdall Oil Company. We have here a situation opposite from the other two. Barnsdall Oil owned both refining and producing properties, the latter profitable, the former unprofitable. In 1935 it segregated the refineries (and marketing units) in a separate company, of which it distributed the common stock to its own stockholders, retaining, however, the preferred stock and substantial claims against the new company. In 1936–1938 the refineries and stations continued to lose; Barnsdall Oil advanced considerable sums to cover these losses and wrote them off by charges first against capital surplus and then against earned surplus. On the other hand, its *income account*, freed from the burden of these refining losses, showed profits from producing operations at a steady rate from June 1, 1933, to the end of 1938.

In 1939, however, the New York Stock Exchange called upon the company to correct its statements to stockholders by advising them of the effect upon the reported profits of charging there-against the write-downs of the investment in the refining company. These losses would have reduced the indicated profits by more than one-third.

It is clear, from the standpoint of proper accounting, *that as long as a company continues to control an unprofitable division*, its losses must be shown as deductions from its other earnings. The analyst must decide what the chances are of terminating the losses in the future, and view the current price of the stock accordingly. The method followed by the Barnsdall Oil Company appears therefore clearly open to criticism, since it served merely to terminate the *reporting* of its refining losses without really terminating the losses themselves. (At the end of 1939 the company set steps into motion for an apparent complete divorcement and sale of the refining and marketing divisions.)

Summary. To avoid leaving this point in confusion, we shall summarize our treatment by suggesting:

1. In the first instance, subsidiary losses are to be deducted in every analysis.

2. If the amount involved is significant, the analyst should investigate whether or not the losses may be subject to early termination.

3. If the result of this examination is favorable, the analyst may consider all or part of the subsidiary's loss as the equivalent of a nonrecurring item.

Chapter 34

THE RELATION OF DEPRECIATION AND SIMILAR CHARGES TO EARNING POWER

A CRITICAL analysis of an income account must pay particular attention to the amounts deducted for depreciation and kindred charges. These items differ from ordinary operating expenses in that they do not signify a current and corresponding outlay of cash. They represent the estimated shrinkage in the value of the fixed or capital assets, due to wearing out, to using up or to their approaching extinction for whatever cause. The important charges of this character may be classified as follows:

1. Depreciation (and obsolescence), replacements, renewals or retirements.
2. Depletion or exhaustion.
3. Amortization of leaseholds, leasehold improvements, licenses, etc.
4. Amortization of patents.

All these items may properly be embraced under the title "amortization," but we shall sometimes refer to them generically as "depreciation items," or simply as "depreciation," because the latter is a more familiar term.

Leading Questions Relative to Depreciation. The accounting theory that governs depreciation charges is simple enough. If a capital asset has a limited life, provision must be made to write off the cost of that asset by charges against earnings distributed over the period of its life. But behind this innocent statement lie complications of a threefold character. First we find that accounting rules themselves may permit a value other than cost as the base for the amortization charge. Second, we find many ways in which companies fail to follow accepted accounting practice in stating their depreciation deduction in the income account. Third, there are occasions when an allowance that may be justified from an accounting standpoint will fail to meet the situation properly from an investment standpoint. These problems will engage our attention in this and the next two chapters. Our discussion will be directed first towards industrial companies generally, following which we shall consider special aspects having to do with oil companies, mining companies and public utilities.[1]

THE DEPRECIATION BASE

Depreciation Base Other than Cost. There is support in accounting circles for the theory that the function of the depreciation allowance is to provide for the *replacement* of the asset at the end of its life rather than merely to write off its *cost*. If this idea were actually followed, the current or expected future replacement cost would be the basis for the depreciation charge, and it would vary not only with the value of the identical asset but also with changes in the character of the item that is expected to replace the one worn out.

Whatever may be said for or against this theory,[2] it is virtually never followed in the form stated. But we do meet in practice with a variant of the idea, *viz.*, the substitution of the replacement value of all the fixed assets *as of a given date* in place of cost on the balance sheet, followed usually by annual depreciation charges based on the new value.

Since 1914 there have been two waves of such revaluations. The first, taking place in the 1920's, marked up prewar costs to the higher values currently prevailing. The second, appearing in 1931–1933, marked down property accounts to the much lower valuations associated with the depression.[3]

Examples: In 1926 American Ice Company wrote up its fixed assets by $7,868,000, and in 1935 it wrote them down correspondingly to restore the valuations to a cost basis. The 1926 write-up resulted in larger depreciation charges thereafter against income, and the 1935 reduction resulted in lower depreciation charges. In 1933 American Locomotive Company

---

[1] With a very few exceptions the *railroads* charge depreciation only on their equipment (including this item in the maintenance charges). For the year 1937 Class I railroads charged a total of $191,798,000 for depreciation of equipment and only $5,236,000 for depreciation of way and structures.

[2] In our view it is at once simpler and more logical to base depreciation on original cost. Replacement cost should affect the accounts *after* replacement takes place (which may never happen) rather than before.

[3] See Fabricant, Solomon, "Revaluations of Fixed Assets, 1925–1934" (*National Bureau of Economic Research Bulletin* 62, 1936), and *Capital Consumption and Adjustment*, National Bureau of Economic Research, Chap. XII, 1938.

reduced the stated value of its stock from $50 to $5 a share and utilized most of the capital surplus thus created to write down fixed properties by nearly $26,000,000 and its investment in General Steel Castings Corporation by about $6,200,000. The net effect on the income account was to reduce depreciation charges to about 40% of their former level.

There is some criticism in accounting circles of the propriety of such sporadic changes in the depreciation base from original cost. In our opinion they are not objectionable *provided:*

1. The new values are set up in the *bona fide* conviction that they represent existing realities more fairly than the old values.
2. Proper depreciation against these new values is charged in the income account.

In many cases, however, we find that companies revaluing their fixed assets fail to observe one or the other of these conditions.

Mark-downs to Reduce Depreciation Charges.

Perhaps the most striking phenomenon in the field of depreciation accounting is the recent marking down of the fixed assets, not in the interests of conservatism but with the precisely opposite intent of making a better earnings exhibit and thereby *increasing* the apparent value of the shares.

We believe that it will be more convenient for the reader if we defer consideration of the significance to security analysis of these devices until our chapter devoted to "Amortization Charges from the Investor's Standpoint." At this time, since we are dealing with accounting methods, we shall merely remark that in our opinion excessive write-downs of fixed assets, for the avowed or obvious purpose of decreasing depreciation and increasing reported earnings, constitute an inexcusable subterfuge and should not be condoned by the accounting profession. Registration statements submitted to the S.E.C. include a statement of how much lower the earnings would have been if the former plant values had been retained. We think that such information should also appear as a footnote to the income account in the annual reports to stockholders, but it would be better practice still if accountants refused to certify a report containing such mark-downs and insisted on restoration of the proper figures to the company's accounts.

Balance Sheet–Income Account Discrepancies.

Many corporations that have marked up their fixed assets fail to increase correspondingly their depreciation charges against the income account. They are in effect attempting to get the benefit of the higher valuation in their balance sheet without accepting the burden of consequently higher depreciation charges against earnings. This practice has been especially prevalent in the case of mining and oil companies. Two examples drawn from the general industrial field are given here:

Examples: Hall Printing Company wrote up its property account by $6,222,000 in 1926 and 1931, crediting this "appraisal increment" to capital surplus. Depreciation on this appreciated value was then charged to capital surplus, instead of to income; *e.g.,* typically, in the year ended March 1938 the company charged $406,000 for such depreciation against surplus and $864,000 for "regular" depreciation against income. In April 1938 the balance of the appraisal increment was eliminated by writing down both property account and capital surplus; and the special depreciation charge was then discontinued.

Borg Warner has been charging about $102,000 per annum since 1935 (and various amounts in prior years) to "Appreciation Surplus," instead of to income, to amortize a write-up of fixed assets made in 1927.

It should be obvious that no company should use one set of values for its balance sheet and another for its income account. The more recent tendency is to correct these disparities by eliminating the previous write-up from the balance sheet, thus returning to original cost.

THE RATE OF DEPRECIATION. STANDARD AND NONSTANDARD PRACTICE

1. As Shown by Listing Statements. The vast majority of industrial companies follow the standard policy of charging an appropriate depreciation rate against each class of depreciable asset. The analyst can readily check this fact by reference to New York Stock Exchange listing applications or to a prospectus or registration statement.

Examples: If standard methods are followed, they are likely to be announced in somewhat the following manner:

(From listing application of Electric Storage Battery Company, dated December 17, 1928.)

> The policy of this Company in regard to depreciation ... is as follows: On buildings the term of life is twenty to thirty-three years, depending upon the character of construction. Machinery, tools and fixtures are written off at the rate of one to ten years, depending upon the character of the equipment.

Office furniture and fixtures are written off in ten years. On all depreciable properties rates are determined by actual experience and engineers' estimates as to the productive life of the equipment. In respect to depreciation of current assets, a reserve is set aside to cover probable loss from bad debts.

(From the listing application of Midland Steel Products Company, dated February 11, 1930.)

The following are the rates of depreciation used:

	Rate of depreciation per year, %
Buildings	2
Grounds, driveways and walks	2
Machinery	7
Furniture and fixtures	10
Railroad sidings	2
Automobiles and trucks	.25

Tools and dies—amortized over life of job when number of units required can be determined, otherwise written off at close of each fiscal year.

These rates have been used by the Company for several years, being standard practice in the industry.

The rates are based upon the estimated life of the respective property involved. Thus, with respect to buildings, the cost is depreciated, over 50 years; grounds, driveways, and walks, over 50 years; machinery over 14 years; furniture and fixtures, over 10 years; railroad sidings, over 50 years. No residual value at the expiration of said periods is considered in determining the rates used.

In contrast with this standard policy, now all but universally followed, we may point to the questionable practice on this important point formerly resorted to by such important companies as American Car and Foundry, American Sugar Refining and Baldwin Locomotive Works.

The American Sugar Refining Company's listing application, dated December 6, 1923, contained the following statement:

The Company maintains a very liberal policy as to depreciation as shown by the annual profit and loss statement of past years. The value of its properties is at all times fully maintained by the making of all needful and proper repairs thereto and renewals and replacements thereof.

This declaration sounds reassuring, but it is far too indefinite to satisfy the analyst. The actual depreciation charges, as shown in the following record, disclose an unusually arbitrary and erratic policy.

ANNUAL CHARGES BY AMERICAN SUGAR REFINING COMPANY FOR DEPRECIATION

Year	Charged to income	Charged to surplus
1916–1920	$2,000,000	None
1921	None	None
1922–1923	1,000,000	None
1924	None	None
1925	1,000,000	None
1926	1,000,000	$2,000,000
1927	1,000,000	1,000,000
1928	1,250,000	500,000
1929	1,000,000	500,000
1930	1,000,000	542,631
1931	1,000,000	None
1932	1,000,000	None

The additional charges to surplus made in the years 1926–1930, inclusive, appear to strengthen our contention that American Sugar's depreciation allowances have been both arbitrary and inadequate.

The American Car and Foundry's application, dated April 2, 1925, contains the following:

The Company has no depreciation account as such. However, its equivalent is found in the policy and the practice of the Company to maintain at all times its plants and properties in first class physical condition and in a high state of efficiency by repairing, renewing and replacing equipment and buildings as their physical conditions may require, and by replacing facilities with those of more modern type, when such action results in more economical production. This procedure amply covers depreciation and obsolescence and the cost is charged to Operating Expenses.

Here again a sceptical attitude on the part of the analyst is "amply" warranted. The same is true in respect of American Can which managed—inexplicably—to avoid all reference to its depreciation policy in its listing application dated February 26, 1926, although it did mention that the company had spent approximately $50,000,000 on extensions and improvement of properties since February 1907 and that "during this period properties have been depreciated by at least $20,000,000."

Baldwin Locomotive Works, in its listing application dated October 3, 1929, makes the following rather astonishing statement on depreciation:

> The amount of the depreciation upon plant and equipment as determined by the Federal Government for the five years 1924 to 1928 inclusive has totaled $5,112,258.09 which has been deducted either from income or surplus as follows:

Year	From income	From surplus	Total depreciation
1924	$600,000	None	$600,000.00
1925	None	None	None
1926	None	None	None
1927	1,000,000	$2,637,881.01	3,637,881.01
1928	600,000	274,377.08	874,377.08
	$2,200,000	$2,912,258.09	$5,112,258.09

> It is expected that in future years the amount of depreciation based upon the estimated useful life of depreciable properties as determined by the Federal Government, allowed by the Commissioner of Taxes as a proper deduction from income and agreed to by our engineers, will govern the amount to be used by the Works in its calculation of depreciation.

Evidently the income statements of Baldwin for this period were anything but accurate. The average annual earnings per share of common stock for 1924–1928, as reported to the stockholders, were strikingly higher than the correct figure, as shown at the top of page 460.

2. As Shown by Comparisons of Two Companies. When the analyst knows that a company's depreciation policy differs from the standard, there is special reason to check the adequacy of the allowance. Comparison with a single company in the same field may yield significant results, as is shown by the table in the middle of page 460 respecting American Sugar and American Car and Foundry.

EARNINGS PER SHARE OF COMMON

Year	As reported	As corrected for annual depreciation charge of $1,022,000
1924	$0.40(d)	$2.51(d)
1925	6.02(d)	11.13(d)
1926	22.42	17.31
1927	5.21	5.10
1928	5.34(d)	7.45(d)
5-year average	$3.33	$0.06

Company	Average property account (net) 1928–1932	Average depreciation charge 1928–1932	% of depreciation charge to property account
American Sugar Refining	$60,665,000	$1,050,000*	1.73†
National Sugar Refining	19,250,000‡	922,000‡	4.79‡
American Car and Foundry	72,000,000	1,186,000§	1.65
American Steel Foundries	31,000,000	1,136,000	3.66

* Exclusive of depreciation charged to surplus. Including the latter, this figure would be $1,358,500.
† Including depreciation charged to surplus this figure would be 2.24%.
‡ Based on the four years 1929–1932, inclusive. Figure for 1928 unavailable.
§ Estimated at one-half of the expenditures for renewals and repairs. In the case of United States Steel for the period 1901–1933, the charge for depreciation averaged about 40% of the total allowances for both maintenance and depreciation.

Both comparatively and absolutely the depreciation allowances made by American Sugar and American Car and Foundry appear to have been inadequate.[4]

---

[4] For examples of insufficient charges and charges less than income tax deductions by industrial companies see: Harbison-Walker Refractories Company charge of $296,000 in 1936, termed "grossly inadequate" by new management and revised to $472,000; McKeesport Tin Plate Corporation report for 1937 stating that the charge on the income tax return was $803,000 vs. $425,000 in statement to stockholders. Similarly, National Enameling and Stamping Company for each year 1935–1937 charged about $185,000 in its income account as contrasted with about $280,000 on its tax return. In 1938 insufficient depreciation for 1933–1937 was cured by a charge of $443,000 to surplus. The auditors for the Cudahy Packing Company stated in the certificate accompanying the 1939 report that in their opinion the reserves for depreciation set up by the company in years prior to Oct. 29, 1938, were inadequate.

Depreciation Charges Often an Issue in Mergers. Comparative depreciation charges at times become quite an issue in determining the fairness of proposed terms of consolidation.

Example: In 1924 a merger plan was announced embracing the Chesapeake and Ohio, Hocking Valley, Pere Marquette, "Nickel Plate," and Erie railroads. Some Chesapeake and Ohio stockholders dissented, and they convinced the Interstate Commerce Commission that the terms of the consolidation were highly unfair to their road. Among other matters they pointed out that the earnings of Chesapeake and Ohio in the preceding three years had in reality been much higher than stated, due to the unusually heavy charges made against them for depreciation and retirement of equipment.[5] A similar objection was made in connection with the projected merger of Bethlehem Steel and Youngstown Sheet and Tube in 1929, which plan was also defeated. Some figures on these two steel producers are given as shown in the table on p. 462.

Concealed Depreciation. That nothing can be taken for granted in security analysis is shown by the strange case of American Can, which until 1937 had failed to reveal details of its depreciation policy to its shareholders. During the years 1922–1936 it deducted annually a flat $2,000,000 for this purpose. A comparison with Continental Can—which charged about the same amount against a much smaller plant investment—would have suggested that American Can's earning power had been overstated. But the annual report for 1934 disclosed to stockholders for the first time that the company had also been charging sums to operating expenses for "replacements," without giving the amount. The fact (but not the amounts) that such charges had been made in 1935 and 1936 was also revealed in those years. Meanwhile Form 10-K for 1935, filed with the S.E.C., revealed that the amount of these extra

---

Conversely, for cases of excessive depreciation, note: Depreciation charges of Acme Steel for 1932–1935 were found by the federal government to have been $555,000 too high. This amount, less income tax thereon of $104,000, was credited to surplus in 1936. (This is almost the exact opposite of the National Enameling case.) Chicago Yellow Cab Company in 1938 credited to surplus $483,000 for excess depreciation in former years.

[5] Large expenditures made by Chesapeake and Ohio upon its equipment in 1926–1928 and charged to operating expense were later claimed by the Interstate Commerce Commission to represent *capital* outlays. In 1933 this controversy was taken into the courts, and the Interstate Commerce Commission was sustained.

charges was about $2,400,000. Finally the annual report for 1937 advised the stockholders that the corresponding extra charge-off amounted to approximately $3,275,000 for the year 1936. Beginning with 1937 the company made "regular" depreciation charges, amounting to $5,702,000 in that year and to $6,085,000 in 1938. Thus, by easy stages, the owners of the business were told the facts of life bearing on their property.

1928	Bethlehem Steel	Youngstown Sheet & Tube
Property account, Dec. 31, 1927	$673,000,000	$204,000,000
Sales	295,000,000	141,000,00
Depreciation, depletion, and obsolescence	13,658,000	8,321,000
Ratio: depreciation to property account	2.03%	4.08%
Ratio: depreciation to sales	4.63%	5.90%

In the light of this later disclosure, the earlier inference[6] that American Can had understated its depreciation charges must give way to the remark that the company had failed to reveal the facts.

A Case of Excessive Depreciation Charges Concealed by Accounting Methods. The American Can example suggests comparison with the earlier practice of National Biscuit Company, an enterprise controlled largely by the same interests. For many years prior to 1922 the company was constantly adding to the number of its factories, but its property account failed to show any appreciable increase, except in the single year 1920. The reports to stockholders were supremely ambiguous on the matter of depreciation charges,[7] but according to the financial manuals the company's policy was as follows: "Depreciation is $300,000 per annum, and all items of replacement and building alterations are charged direct to operating expense."

It is difficult to avoid the conclusion, however, that the capital investments in additional plants were actually being charged against the profits

---

[6] Drawn in the 1934 edition of this book.

[7] Prior to 1919, the company's balance sheet each year stated its fixed assets "Less Depreciation Account—$300,000." Evidently this was the deduction for the current year and not the amount accumulated.

NATIONAL BISCUIT COMPANY

Year ended	Earnings for common stock	Net plant account at end of year
Jan. 31, 1911	$2,883,000	$53,159,000
1912	2,937,000	53,464,000
1913	2,803,000	53,740,000
1914	3,432,000	54,777,000
1915	2,784,000	54,886,000
1916	2,393,000	55,207,000
1917	2,843,000	55,484,000
Dec. 31, 1917	2,886,000 (11 mo.)	53,231,000
1918	3,400,000	52,678,000
1919	3,614,000	53,955,000
1920	3,807,000	57,788,000
1921	3,941,000	57,925,000
1922	9,289,000	61,700,000
1923	10,357,000	64,400,000
1924	11,145,000	67,292,000
1925	11,845,000	69,745,000

and that the real earnings were in all probability much larger than those reported to the public. Coincident with the issuance of seven shares of stock for one and the tripling of the cash-dividend rate in 1922, this policy of understating earnings was terminated. The result was a sudden doubling of the apparent earning power, accompanied by an equally sudden expansion in the plant account. The contrast between the two periods is shown forcibly in the table on this page.

Failure to State Depreciation Charges. Prior to the S.E.C. regulation some of the important companies reported earnings after depreciation but failed to state the amount deducted for this purpose. Fortunately, this information must now be supplied in the case of every registered company.[8]

---

[8] Allied Chemical and Dye Corporation endeavored to have this and other data held confidential, but after considerable delay it was made public (in 1938). This company, like a few others, still excludes its sales and depreciation figures from its reports to stockholders, but this important information is available in the annual reports to the S.E.C. (Form 10-K).

AMORTIZATION CHARGES OF OIL
AND MINING COMPANIES

These important sectors of the industrial field are subject to special factors bearing on amortization. In addition to depreciation in the ordinary sense—which they usually calculate in the same way as do other companies[9] they must allow for depletion of their ore or oil reserves. In the case of mining concerns there is also the factor of development expense. Oil producers, on the other hand, have additional charges for intangible drilling costs and for unproductive leases. These items are important in their bearing on the true profits, and they are troublesome because of the varying methods that are followed by different enterprises.

Depletion Charges of Mining Companies. Depletion represents the using up of capital assets by turning them into products for sale. It applies to companies producing metals, oil and gas, sulphur, timber, etc. As the holdings, or reserves, of these products are exhausted, their value must gradually be written off through charges against earnings. In the case of the older mining companies (including particularly the copper and sulphur producers) the depletion charges are determined by certain technical requirements of the federal income tax law, which rest upon the amount and value of the reserves as they were supposed to exist on March 1, 1913, or by applying certain percentages to the value of the product. Because of the artificial base used in these computations, many companies have omitted the depletion charge from their reports to stockholders.

Independent Calculation by Investor Necessary. As we shall show later, the investor in a mining concern must ordinarily compute his own depletion allowance, based upon the *amount that he has paid* for his share of the mining property. Consequently a depletion charge based either on the company's original book cost or on the special figure set up for income-tax purposes would be confusing rather than helpful. The omission of the depletion charge of mining companies is not to be criticized, therefore; but the stockholder in such enterprises must be well aware of the fact in studying their reports. Furthermore, in any comparison of

---

[9] However, the cost of equipment and materials on *oil-producing properties* is often written off through the depletion charge (which is based on the barrels produced) instead of the depreciation account (which is based on the *time* elapsing).

mining companies a proper distinction must be drawn between those which do and those which do not deduct their depletion charges in reporting their earnings. Following are some examples of companies that pursue one or the other policy:

Companies That Report Earnings without Deduction for Depletion:
- Alaska Juneau Gold Mining Co.
- Anaconda Copper Mining Co.
- Dome Mines, Ltd. (gold)
- Kennecott Copper Corp.
- Noranda Mines, Ltd. (copper and gold)
- Texas Gulf Sulphur Co.

Companies That Report Earnings after Deduction for Depletion:
- Cerro de Pasco Copper Corp.
- Granby Consolidated Mining, etc., Co. (copper)
- Homestake Mining Co. (gold)
- International Nickel Co. of Canada, Ltd.
- Patino Mines, etc. (tin)
- Phelps Dodge Corp. (copper)
- St. Joseph Lead Co.

Depletion and Similar Charges in the Oil Industry.

In the oil industry depletion charges are more closely related to the actual cost of doing business than in the case of mining enterprises. The latter ordinarily invest in a single property or group of properties, the cost of which is then written off over a fairly long period of years. But the typical large oil producer normally spends substantial sums each year on new leases and new wells. These additional holdings are needed to make up for the shrinkage of reserves through production. The depletion charge corresponds in some measure, therefore, to a current cash outlay for the purpose of maintaining reserves and production. New wells may yield as high as 80% of their total output during the first year. Hence nearly all the cost of such "flush production" must be written off in a single fiscal period, and most of the "earnings" from this source are in reality a return of the capital expended thereon. If the investment is not written off rapidly through depletion and other charges, the profit and the value of the property account will both be grossly overstated. In the case of an oil company actively engaged in development work, the various headings under which write-offs must be made include the following:

1. *Depreciation* of tangible assets.

2. *Depletion* of oil and gas reserves, based upon the cost of the leases.

3. *Unprofitable leases* written off. Part of the acquisitions and exploration will always prove totally valueless and must be charged against the revenue from the productive leases.

4. *Intangible drilling costs.* These are either written off at one time, as equivalent to an operating expense, or amortized over the life of the well.

Example: The case of Marland Oil in 1926 illustrates the extent to which reported earnings of oil companies are dependent upon the accounting policies with respect to amortization. This company spent large sums annually on new leases and wells to maintain its rate of production. Prior to 1926 it charged the so-called "intangible drilling costs" to capital account and then wrote them off against earnings through an annual amortization charge. In 1926 Marland adopted the more conservative policy of charging off all these "intangible costs" currently against earnings. The effect on profits is shown in the following table.

MARLAND OIL COMPANY

Item	1925	1926	1927
Gross earnings and miscellaneous income	$73,231,000	$87,360,000	$58,980,000
Net before reserves	24,495,000	30,303,000	9,808,000
Amortization charges	9,696,000	18,612,000	17,499,000
Balance for stock	14,799,000	11,691,000	7,691,000(d)

In the past ten years significant changes have occurred in the policies followed by the important oil companies. Prior to the depression the general tendency was towards charging the "intangible drilling costs" to earnings—as shown in the change made by Marland in 1926. But since the depression many of the large companies have switched over to the less conservative basis of capitalizing these costs, subject to annual amortization.[10] This change seems justified in good part by the wide adoption of state proration laws, which effectively spread out the total production of a new well over many years instead of concentrating it within a relatively few months. This makes an oil well a fairly long-term capital asset, so that charging off a good part of its cost (now often running to very high figures) against a single year's profits would be unduly severe.

The companies have also aided their earnings by large write-downs of fixed assets, with corresponding reductions in the annual amortization

---

[10] Companies making this change since 1930 include Standard Oil of Indiana and New Jersey, Gulf Oil, Tidewater Associated, Consolidated Oil.

charges against them. This practice has perhaps been more widespread among oil companies than in any other industrial group. Some producers have also switched their charges for property *retirements* from earnings to the depreciation reserve. Finally, we have examples of a reduction in amortization charge being brought about by adoption of an "over-all basis" instead of a lease basis for depletion. By this means, oil produced from high-cost leases is written off not at its actual cost but at the average cost of all the oil reserves owned.

The significance of these changes in accounting policy is illustrated by the following:[11]

Examples: Gulf Oil Corporation increased its 1932 earnings by $3,621,000, by capitalizing intangible drilling costs instead of charging them off, as formerly.

Socony-Vacuum increased its 1932 earnings by $6,095,000 (and subsequent earnings correspondingly) as a result of a write-down of fixed assets with consequent reduction in depreciation charges. In 1935 its profits were increased $1,376,000 by charging this sum—representing losses on certain retired property—to depreciation reserve instead of to income, as theretofore. In 1936 it began to capitalize intangible drilling costs, adding about $8,850,000 to profits in that year through this change. In 1937 the company made a further revision in its depreciation policy (apparently intended to place it on the standard basis), which added some $2,500,000 to that year's profits.

Pure Oil Company reduced its 1934 depletion charges and increased its earnings by $1,698,000 through adoption of the "over-all" basis.

The Meaning of These Variations to the Analyst and the Investor.
These differences of accounting methods are highly confusing and may arouse some resentment in the investor. We must recognize, however, that most of them are technically admissible, in that they represent choices between the ordinary and the more conservative basis of amortizing the fixed assets. What is called for, in consequence, is not so much censure as sound interpretation.

Suggested Standards. The analyst should seek to apply a uniform and reasonably conservative rate of amortization to a property base that

---

[11] These examples are drawn largely from Alfred Braunthal, "Are Oil Earnings Reports Fictitious?" *Barron's*, Mar. 8, 1937.

reflects the realities of the proposed investment. We suggest the following standards, in so far as it may be feasible to apply them:

1. *Depreciation on Tangible Assets.* This should always be taken at the well-established rates, applied to cost—or to a figure substantially less than cost only if the facts clearly justify the write-down.

2. *Intangible Drilling Costs.* We believe that capitalizing these costs, and then writing them off as oil is produced—although less "conservative"—is the preferable basis both for comparative purposes and to supply a fair reflection of current earnings. In comparing companies that use one and the other method, the analyst must make the best allowance he can for the understatement of earnings by the companies that charge off 100% the first year.

Example: The difficulty of making this adjustment in practice may be shown by comparing the 1938 reports of Continental Oil Company and Ohio Oil Company. These two concerns are roughly similar in their set-up. Both produced about 20 million barrels in 1938; Continental Oil refined about two-thirds, and Ohio Oil about one-third its output. Continental charges all its intangible drilling costs direct to income, while Ohio capitalizes these costs and writes them off over the life of the wells.

It might be expected that the total amortization charges of Continental, including drilling expense on the 100% basis, would be relatively higher than those of Ohio. Yet in 1938 Ohio charged off $11,602,000, or $21^1/2$% of its $54 million sales; while Continental charged off $14,038,000, or 17.6% of its $80 million gross. Apparently no adjustment would be needed by the analyst to equalize the two accounting methods. The reasons may be found in several circumstances; *e.g.,* (*a*) after a number of years the gradual write-off method approximates the 100% method, since amortization of old drilling expense becomes continuously greater. (*b*) In the case of Continental, this concern wrote down its property account in 1932 by some $45,000,000 and thus reduced its normal depreciation and depletion charges considerably in succeeding years.

3. *Property Retirement and Abandoned Leases.* We think that loss on property retired (in excess of depreciation already accrued) should be charged against the year's earnings, rather than against surplus as is done by most companies in other fields. The reason is that property retirements are likely to be a normal and recurrent factor in the business of a large,

integrated oil company, instead of happening only sporadically as in other lines. Abandoned leases come under this general heading, and the loss thereon should be charged to earnings.

4. *Depletion of Oil Reserves.* The proper *theoretical* principle here is that the analyst should allow for depletion on the basis at which the oil reserves are valued in the market. This point, as applied to amortization generally, will be discussed in the next chapter. It implies, as we shall see, that what may be the correct *accounting* basis for computing depletion may not be the most suitable basis for the analysis of investment values.

Unfortunately, business practice in the oil industry has been such as to make the sound application of this principle exceedingly difficult. The oil-producing part of the industry has apparently accounted for most of the profits; the refining and marketing divisions have earned little, if anything, on their investment. If *earnings* were the criterion of value here, most of the market price of a typical oil stock would be ascribable to the producing division, and on this basis a comparatively high depletion charge against each barrel taken out would be called for. On the other hand, if the division were made in proportion to *book values*, the refining and marketing sections would loom large, the oil reserves would have a much smaller value, and the depletion charge would be proportionately smaller.

We do not see any really satisfactory answer to the dilemma that we have posed—for it seems to us that the partition of earning power in the industry between production and the other branches is an essentially artificial one and cannot be viewed as permanent. We therefore are led to suggest the following *practical compromise* with the problem:

1. In the case of *integrated* oil companies, accept the company's depletion figure as the best available. (This includes acceptance of the "overall" basis, if used, since this method would seem to reflect the facts fairly.) However, any charges for depletion made against an "appreciation" account in the balance sheet should be deducted from income.

2. In the case of companies that are solely oil producers, or virtually so, the analyst can compute *what the market is paying* for the total developed oil reserves (if an estimate of these is published). Hence he can make his own depletion calculation, for the particular purpose of his analysis, in such an instance in the same manner as in the case of a mining proposition. (For a calculation of this kind applied to Texas Gulf Producing Company see p. 502 on accompanying CD.)

OTHER TYPES OF AMORTIZATION
OF CAPITAL ASSETS

Leaseholds and Leasehold Improvements. The ordinary lease involves no capital investment by the lessee, who merely undertakes to pay rent in return for the use of property. But if the rental payments are considerably less than the use of the property is worth, and if the arrangement has a considerable period to run, the leasehold—as it is called—may have a substantial value. Oil lands are leased on a standard basis for a royalty amounting usually to one-eighth of the production. Leaseholds on which a substantial output is developed or assured are worth a large bonus above the rental payments involved, and they are bought and sold in the same way as the fee ownership of the property. Similar bonuses are paid—in boom times usually—for long-term leases on urban real estate.

If a company has paid money for a leasehold, the cost is regarded as a capital investment that should be written off during the life of the lease. (In the case of an oil lease the write-off is made against each barrel produced, rather than on a time basis, since the output declines rapidly from the initial flush figure.) These charges are in reality part of the rent paid for the property and must obviously be included in current operating expense.

When structures are built on leased property or alterations made or fixtures installed, they are designated as "leasehold improvements." Hence their cost must be written down to nothing during the life of the lease, since they belong to the landlord when the lease expires. The annual charge-off for this purpose is called "amortization of leasehold improvements." It partakes to some extent of the nature of a depreciation charge. Chain-store enterprises frequently invest considerable sums in such leasehold improvements, and consequently the annual write-offs thereof may be of appreciable importance in their income accounts.

Example: The December 31, 1938, balance sheet of F.W. Woolworth Company carried "Buildings Owned and Improvements on Leased Premises to be amortized over periods of leases" at a net valuation of $46,717,000. The charge against 1938 earnings for amortization of these buildings and leasehold improvements amounted to $3,925,283.

Since these items belong to the amortization group, they lend themselves to the same kind of arbitrary treatment as do the others. By making the annual charge against surplus instead of income or by writing down the entire capital investment to $1 and thus eliminating the annual charge entirely, a corporation can exclude these items of operating cost from its reported per-share earnings and thus make the latter appear deceptively large.

Amortization of Patents. In theory, a patent should be dealt with in exactly the same way as a mining property; *i.e.*, its cost to the investor should be written off against earnings during its remaining life. It is obvious, therefore, that charges made against earnings by the company— which are based on the *book value* of the patent—have ordinarily little relevance to the real situation. Consideration of this question belongs chiefly to a later chapter on amortization from the investor's standpoint, and to avoid dividing our treatment we shall postpone to the same place our brief discussion of the accounting methods relative to patents encountered in corporate reports.

Amortization of Good-will. This is a matter of very minor importance. A few companies have followed the rather extraordinary policy of charging off their good-will account against earnings in a number of annual installments.

Examples: Radio Corporation of America charged $310,000 a year for this purpose between 1934 and 1937. This was applicable to the good-will account of its subsidiary National Broadcasting Company and was discontinued in 1938, although $1,876,000 remained unamortized.

Obviously, this practice has no factual basis, since good-will has no duration of life apart from that of the business as a whole. Where the item is of any size, the analyst should adjust the earnings by canceling the charge.

See accompanying CD for Chapter 35, "Public-utility Depreciation Policies," and Chapter 36, "Amortization Charges from the Investor's Standpoint."

Chapter 37

SIGNIFICANCE OF THE
EARNINGS RECORD

IN THE LAST SIX CHAPTERS our attention was devoted to a critical examination of the income account for the purpose of arriving at a fair and informing statement of the results for the period covered. The second main
question confronting the analyst is concerned with the utility of this past
record as an indicator of future earnings. This is at once the most important
and the least satisfactory aspect of security analysis. It is the most important
because the sole practical value of our laborious study of the past lies in the
clue it may offer to the future; it is the least satisfactory because this clue is
never thoroughly reliable and it frequently turns out to be quite valueless.
These shortcomings detract seriously from the value of the analyst's work,
but they do not destroy it. The past exhibit remains a sufficiently dependable guide, in a sufficient proportion of cases, to warrant its continued use
as the chief point of departure in the valuation and selection of securities.

The Concept of Earning Power. The concept of *earning power* has a
definite and important place in investment theory. It combines a statement
of actual earnings, shown over a period of years, with a reasonable expectation that these will be approximated in the future, unless extraordinary conditions supervene. The record must cover a number of years, first because a
continued or repeated performance is always more impressive than a single
occurrence and secondly because the average of a fairly long period will tend
to absorb and equalize the distorting influences of the business cycle.

A distinction must be drawn, however, between an average that is the
mere arithmetical resultant of an assortment of disconnected figures and
an average that is "normal" or "modal," in the sense that the annual results
show a definite tendency to approximate the average. The contrast
between one type of earning power and the other may be clearer from
the following examples:

ADJUSTED EARNINGS PER SHARE 1923–1932

Year	S. H. Kress	Hudson Motors
1932	$2.80	*$3.54(d)*
1931	4.19	*1.25(d)*
1930	4.49	0.20
1929	5.92	7.26
1928	5.76	8.43
1927	5.26	9.04
1926	4.65	3.37
1925	4.12	13.39
1924	3.06	5.09
1923	3.39	5.56
10-year average	$4.36	$ 4.75

The average earnings of about $4.50 per share shown by S. H. Kress and Company can truly be called its "indicated earning power," for the reason that the figures of each separate year show only moderate variations from this norm. On the other hand the Hudson Motors average of $4.75 per share is merely an abstraction from ten widely varying figures, and there was no convincing reason to believe that the earnings from 1933 onward would bear a recognizable relationship to this average. A similar conclusion was drawn from our discussion of the exhibit of J. I. Case Company on page 65.

These conclusions, reached in 1933, are supported by the results of the six years following:

EARNINGS PER SHARE

Year	S. H. Kress[1]	Hudson Motors	J. I. Case
1933	$4.23	*$2.87(d)*	*$14.66(d)*
1934	4.76	*2.10(d)*	*7.38(d)*
1935	4.63	0.38	5.70
1936	4.62	2.14	12.37
1937	4.62	0.42	19.20
1938	2.76	*2.94(d)*	8.89
1939	3.86	*0.86(d)*	*1.87(d)*

[1] Stated on basis of old capitalization, before 2-for-1 split-up in 1936.

Quantitative Analysis Should Be Supplemented by Qualitative Considerations.
In studying earnings records an important principle of security analysis must be borne in mind:

Quantitative data are useful only to the extent that they are supported by a qualitative survey of the enterprise.

In order for a company's business to be regarded as reasonably stable, it does not suffice that the past record should show stability. The nature of the undertaking, considered apart from any figures, must be such as to indicate an inherent permanence of earning power. The importance of this additional criterion was well illustrated by the case of the Studebaker Corporation which was used as an example in our discussion of qualitative factors in analysis on page 87. It is possible, on the other hand, that there may be considerable variation in yearly earnings, but there is a reasonable basis nevertheless for taking the average as a rough index at least of future performance. In 1934 we cited United States Steel Corporation as a leading case in point. The text of our discussion was as follows:

The annual earnings for 1923–1932 are given below.

UNITED STATES STEEL CORPORATION, 1923–1932

Year	Earnings per share of common*	Output of finished steel, tons	% of total output of country	Net per ton before deprec.
1932	$11.08(d)	3,591,000	34.4	$3.54(d)
1931	1.40(d)	7,196,000	37.5	5.71
1930	9.12	11,609,000	39.3	13.10
1929	21.19	15,303,000	37.3	16.90
1928	12.50	13,972,000	37.1	13.83
1927	8.81	12,979,000	39.5	12.66
1926	12.85	14,334,000	40.4	13.89
1925	9.19	13,271,000	39.7	12.49
1924	8.41	11,723,000	41.7	13.05
1923	11.73	14,721,000	44.2	12.20
10-year average	$ 8.13	11,870,000	39.1	11.03

* Adjusted for changes in capitalization.

If compared with those of Studebaker for 1920–1929, the foregoing earnings show much greater instability. Yet the average of about $8 per share for the ten-year period has far more significance as a guide to the future than had Studebaker's indicated earning power of about $6.75 per share. This greater dependability arises from the entrenched position of United States Steel in its industry; and also from the relatively narrow fluctuations in both the annual output and the profit per ton over most of this period. These two elements may be used as a basis for calculating approximate "normal earnings" of U. S. Steel, somewhat as follows:

Normal or usual annual production of finished goods	13,000,000 tons
Gross receipts per ton of finished products	$100.00
Net earnings per ton before depreciation	$12.50
Net earnings on 13,000,000 tons	$160,000,000.00
Depreciation, bond interest, and preferred dividends	90,000,000.00
Balance for 8,700,000 shares of common	70,000,000.00
Normal earnings per share	$8.00

The average earnings for the 1923–1932 decade are thus seen to approximate a theoretical figure based upon a fairly well-defined "normal" output and profit margin. (The increase in number of shares outstanding prevents this normal figure from exceeding the ten-year average.) Although a substantial margin of error must be allowed for in such a computation, it at least supplies a starting point for an intelligent estimate of future probabilities.

Examining this analysis six years later, we may draw some conflicting conclusions as to its value. United States Steel's earnings did recover to $7.88 per share in 1937 ($8.31 before the surtax on undistributed profits). The price advanced from the 1933 average of 45$\frac{1}{2}$ to a high of 126 in March 1937. Hence our implication that the company had a better earning power than the 1932 results and stock prices reflected would seem to have been amply justified by the event.

But actually the average earnings for 1934–1939 have been quite disappointing (amounting to no more than 14 cents per share). If these results have as much validity for the steel industry as they have for most lines of business, we should have to admit that the analysis based on 1923–1932 was not really useful, because the underlying conditions in steel have changed for the worse. (The change consists chiefly in much higher unit costs and a lower average output, selling prices on the whole having been well maintained.[1])

Current Earnings Should Not Be the Primary Basis of Appraisal. The *market level* of common stocks is governed more by their current earnings than by their long-term average. This fact accounts in good part for the wide fluctuations in common-stock prices, which largely (though by no means invariably) parallel the changes in their earnings between good years and bad. Obviously the stock market is quite irrational in thus varying its valuation of a company proportionately with the temporary changes in its reported profits.[2] A private business might easily earn twice as much in a boom year as in poor times, but its owner would never think of correspondingly marking up or down the value of his capital investment.

This is one of the most important lines of cleavage between Wall Street practice and the canons of ordinary business. Because the speculative public is clearly wrong in its attitude on this point, it would seem that its errors should afford profitable opportunities to the more logically minded to buy common stocks at the low prices occasioned by temporarily reduced earnings and to sell them at inflated levels created by abnormal prosperity.

The Classical Formula for "Beating the Stock Market." We have here the long-accepted and classical formula for "beating the stock market." Obviously it requires strength of character in order to think and to act in opposite fashion from the crowd and also patience to wait for opportunities that may be spaced years apart. But there are still other considerations that greatly complicate this apparently simple rule for successful

---

[1] It may be interesting to note that our 1933 conclusions as to the earning power of United States Steel are quite similar to those reached by J. B. Williams in his elaborate study of this company contained in his book *The Theory of Investment Value*, pp. 409–462. But note also, as against the foregoing indication of normal earning power, the rather pessimistic implications of the longer range study of United States Steel's position on pp. 607–611 below. The company's failure to reestablish this earning power in 1934–1939 might suggest that the latter analysis deserved the greater weight.

[2] The rise of United States Steel to 126 in March 1937, already mentioned, is a striking example of this folly of the stock market. It was based on a single good year, following six bad or mediocre ones. Within twelve months the price had declined to 42—a loss of two-thirds of its quotation, and over $730,000,000 in aggregate market value for this single issue. The range of Youngstown Sheet and Tube and Jones and Laughlin Steel in that period was even wider.

operations in stocks. In actual practice the selection of suitable buying and selling levels becomes a difficult matter. Taking the long market cycle of 1921–1933, an investor might well have sold out at the end of 1925 and remained out of the market in 1926–1930 and bought again in the depression year 1931. The first of these moves would later have seemed a bad mistake of judgment, and the last would have had most disturbing consequences. In other market cycles of lesser amplitude such serious miscalculations are not so likely to occur, but there is always a good deal of doubt with regard to the correct time for applying the simple principle of "buy low and sell high."

It is true also that underlying values may change substantially from one market cycle to another, more so, of course, in the case of individual issues than for the market as a whole. Hence if a common stock is sold at what seems to be a generous price in relation to the average of past earnings, it may later so improve its position as to justify a still higher quotation even in the next depression. The converse may occur in the purchase of securities at subnormal prices. If such permanent changes did not frequently develop, it is doubtful if the market would respond so vigorously to current variations in the business picture. The mistake of the market lies in its assumption that *in every case* changes of this sort are likely to go farther, or at least to persist, whereas experience shows that such developments are exceptional and that the *probabilities* favor a swing of the pendulum in the opposite direction.

The analyst cannot follow the stock market in its indiscriminate tendency to value issues on the basis of current earnings. He may on occasion attach predominant weight to the recent figures rather than to the average, but only when persuasive evidence is at hand pointing to the continuance of these current results.

Average vs. Trend of Earnings. In addition to emphasizing strongly the current showing of a company, the stock market attaches great weight to the indicated *trend of earnings.* In Chap. 27 we pointed out the twofold danger inhering in this magnification of the trend—the first being that the supposed trend might prove deceptive, and the second being that valuations based upon trend obey no arithmetical rules and therefore may too easily be exaggerated. There is indeed a fundamental conflict between the concepts of the *average* and of the *trend*, as applied to an earnings record. This may be illustrated by the following simplified example:

Company	Earned per share in successive years						7th (current)	Average of 7 years	Trend
	1st	2nd	3d	4th	5th	6th			
A	$1	$2	$3	$4	$5	$6	$7	$4	Excellent
B	7	7	7	7	7	7	7	7	Neutral
C	13	12	11	10	9	8	7	10	Bad

On the basis of these figures the better the trend, when compared with the same current earnings (in this case $7 per share), the poorer the average and the higher the average the poorer the trend. They suggest an important question respecting the theoretical and practical interpretation of earnings records: Is not the trend at least as significant for the future as the average? Concretely, in judging the probable performance of Companies A and C over the next five years, would not there be more reason to think in terms of a sequence of $8, $9, $10, $11, and $12 for A and a sequence of $7, $6, $5, $4, and $3 for C rather than in terms of the past average of $4 for A and $10 for C?

The answer to this problem derives from common sense rather than from formal or *a priori* logic. The favorable trend of Company A's results must certainly be taken into account, but not by a mere automatic projection of the line of growth into the distant future. On the contrary, it must be remembered that the automatic or normal economic forces militate *against* the indefinite continuance of a given trend.[3] Competition, regulation, the law of diminishing returns, etc., are powerful foes to unlimited expansion, and in smaller degree opposite elements may operate to check a continued decline. Hence instead of taking the maintenance of a favorable trend for granted—as the stock market is wont to do—the analyst must approach the matter with caution, seeking to determine the causes of the superior showing and to weigh the specific elements of strength in the company's position against the general obstacles in the way of continued growth.

Attitude of Analyst Where Trend Is Upward. If such a *qualitative* study leads to a favorable verdict—as frequently it should—the analyst's philosophy must still impel him to base his investment valuation on an assumed earning power no larger than the company has already achieved in a

---

[3] See our discussion of the Schletter and Zander example in Chap. 27.

period of normal business. This is suggested because, in our opinion, investment values can be related only to demonstrated performance; so that neither expected increases nor even past results under conditions of abnormal business activity may be taken as a basis. As we shall point out in the next chapter, this assumed earning power may properly be capitalized more liberally when the prospects appear excellent than in the ordinary case, but we shall also suggest that the maximum multiplier be held to a conservative figure (say, 20, under the conditions of 1940) if the valuation reached is to be kept within strictly *investment* limits. On this basis, assuming that general business conditions in the current year are not unusually good, the earning power of Company A might be taken at $7 per share, and its investment value might be set as high as 140.[4] The divergence in method between the stock market and the analyst—as we define his viewpoint—would mean in general that the price levels ruling for the so-called "good stocks" under normal market conditions are likely to appear overgenerous to the conservative student. This does not mean that the analyst is convinced that the market valuation is wrong but rather that he is not convinced that its valuation is right. He would call a substantial part of the price a "speculative component," in the sense that it is paid not for *demonstrated* but for expected results. (This subject is discussed further in Chap. 39.)

Attitude of Analyst Where Trend Is Downward. Where the trend has been definitely downward, as that of Company C, the analyst will assign great weight to this unfavorable factor. He will not assume that the downcurve *must* presently turn upward, nor can he accept the past average—which is much higher than the current figure—as a normal index of future earnings. But he will be equally chary about any hasty conclusions to the effect that the company's outlook is hopeless, that its earnings are certain to disappear entirely and that the stock is therefore without merit or value. Here again a qualitative study of the company's situation and prospects is essential to forming an opinion whether *at some price*, relatively low, of course, the issue may not be a bargain, despite its declining earnings trend. Once more we identify the viewpoint of the analyst with that of a sensible business man looking into the pros and cons of some privately owned enterprise.

---

[4] See Appendix Note 53, p. 790 on accompanying CD, for a reference to the more conservative viewpoint on this matter expressed by us in the 1934 edition of this work and the reasons for the change.

To illustrate this reasoning, we append the record of net earnings for 1925–1933 of Continental Baking Corporation and American Laundry Machinery Company.

Year	Continental Baking	American Laundry Machinery
1933	$2,788,000	$1,187,000(d)
1932	2,759,000	986,000(d)
1931	4,243,000	772,000
1930	6,114,000	1,849,000
1929	6,671,000	3,542,000
1928	5,273,000	4,128,000
1927	5,570,000	4,221,000
1926	6,547,000	4,807,000
1925	8,794,000	5,101,000

The profits of American Laundry Machinery reveal an uninterrupted decline, and the trend shown by Continental Baking is almost as bad. It will be noted that in 1929—the peak of prosperity for most companies—the profits of these concerns were substantially less than they were four years earlier.

Wall Street reasoning would be prone to conclude from this exhibit that both enterprises are definitely on the downward path. But such extreme pessimism would be far from logical. A study of these two businesses from the qualitative standpoint would indicate first that the respective industries are permanent and reasonably stable and secondly that each company occupies a leading position in its industry and is well fortified financially. The inference would properly follow that the unfavorable tendency shown during 1925–1932 was probably due to accidental or nonpermanent conditions and that in gaging the future earning power more enlightenment will be derived from the substantial *average* than from the seemingly disastrous trend.[5]

Deficits a Qualitative, Not a Quantitative Factor. When a company reports a deficit for the year, it is customary to calculate the amount in dollars per share or in relation to interest requirements. The statistical

---

[5] The results since 1933 would tend to bear out this earlier conclusion, at least in part.

manuals will state, for example, that in 1932 United States Steel Corporation earned its bond-interest "deficit 12.40 times" and that it showed a deficit of $11.08 per share on its common stock. It should be recognized that such figures, when taken by themselves, *have no quantitative significance* and that their value in forming an *average* may often be open to serious question.

Let us assume that Company A lost $5 per share of common in the last year and Company B lost $7 per share. Both issues sell at 25. Is this an indication of any sort that Company A stock is preferable to Company B stock? Obviously not; for assuming it were so, it would mean that the more shares there were outstanding the more valuable each share would be. If Company B issues 2 shares for 1, the loss would be reduced to $3.50 per share, and on the assumption just made, each new share would then be worth more than an old one. The same reasoning applies to bond interest. Suppose that Company A and Company B each lost $1,000,000 in 1932. Company A has $4,000,000 of 5% bonds and Company B has $10,000,000 of 5% bonds. Company A would then show interest earned "deficit 5 times" and Company B would earn its interest "deficit 2 times." These figures should not be construed as an indication of any kind that Company A's bonds are less secure than Company B's bonds. For, if so, it would mean that the smaller the bond issue the poorer its position—a manifest absurdity.

When an *average* is taken over a period that includes a number of deficits, some question must arise as to whether or not the resultant figure is really indicative of the *earning power*. For the wide variation in the individual figures must detract from the representative character of the average. This point is of considerable importance in view of the prevalence of deficits during the depression of the 1930's. In the case of most companies the average of the years since 1933 may now be thought more representative of indicated earning power than, say, a ten-year average 1930–1939.[6]

Intuition Not a Part of the Analyst's Stock in Trade.

In the absence of indications to the contrary we accept the past record as a basis for judging the future. But the analyst must be on the lookout for any such

---

[6] It is an open question whether or not either the ten-year period 1930–1939 or the six years 1934–1939 fairly reflect the future earning power of companies in the heavy industries, *e.g.*, United States Steel, Bethlehem Steel, American Locomotive.

indications to the contrary. Here we must distinguish between vision or intuition on the one hand, and ordinary sound reasoning on the other. The ability to see what is coming is of inestimable value, but it cannot be expected to be part of the analyst's stock in trade. (If he had it, he could dispense with analysis.) He can be asked to show only that moderate degree of foresight which springs from logic and from experience intelligently pondered. It was not to be demanded of the securities statistician, for example, that he foretell the enormous increase in cigarette consumption since 1915 or the decline in the cigar business or the astonishing stability of the snuff industry; nor could he have predicted—to use another example—that the two large can companies would be permitted to enjoy the full benefits from the increasing demand for their product, without the intrusion of that demoralizing competition which ruined the profits of even faster growing industries, *e.g.*, radio.

Analysis of the Future Should Be Penetrating Rather than Prophetic. Analytical reasoning with regard to the future is of a somewhat different character, being penetrating rather than prophetic.[7]

Example: Let us take the situation presented by Intertype Corporation in March-July 1939, when the stock was selling at $8 per share. This old, established company was one of the leaders in a relatively small industry (line-casting machines, etc., for the printing trade). Its recent earnings had not been favorable, nor did there seem to be any particular reason for optimistic expectations as to the near-term outlook. The analyst, however, could not fail to be impressed by the balance sheet, which showed net current assets available for the stock amounting to close to $20 per share. The ten-year earnings, dividend and price record of the common stock was as shown in the table on p. 483.

Certainly there is nothing attractive in this record, marked as it is by irregularity and the absence of a favorable trend. But although these facts would undoubtedly condemn the issue in the eyes of the speculator, the reasoning of the analyst might conceivably run along different lines.

The essential question for him would be whether or not the company can be counted on to remain in business and to participate about as before in good times and bad. On this point consideration of the industry, the

---

[7] See Appendix Note 54, p. 790 on accompanying CD, for an example (Mack Trucks, Inc.) used in the first edition of this work, together with its sequel.

Year	Earned per share	Dividend paid	Price range
1938	$0.57	0.45	$12^3/_4$–8
1937	1.41	0.80	$26^1/_2$–9
1936	1.42	0.75	$22^3/_4$–15
1935	0.75	0.40	16–$6^1/_8$
1934	0.21		10–$5^5/_8$
1933	0.77(d)		$11^1/_4$–$1^7/_8$
1932	1.82(d)		7–$2^1/_2$
1931	0.56	1.00	$18^1/_2$–$4^5/_8$
1930	1.46	2.00	32–12
1929	3.05	1.75	$38^7/_8$–17
Average 1934–1938	0.87		
Average 1929–1938	0.68		

company's prominent position in it and the strong financial set-up would clearly suggest an affirmative answer. If this were granted, the analyst would then point out that the shares could be bought at 8 with very small chance of ultimate loss and with every indication that under the next set of favorable conditions the value of the stock would double. Note that in 3 years out of the past 5 and in 6 out of the past 10, the stock sold between 2 and 4 times the July 1939 price.

This type of reasoning, it will be noted, lays emphasis not upon an accurate prediction of future trends but rather on reaching the general conclusion that the company will continue to do business pretty much as before.

Wall Street is inclined to doubt that any such presumption may be applied to companies with an irregular trend, and to consider that it is just as difficult and hazardous to reach a conclusion of this kind as to determine that a "growing company" will continue to grow. But in our view the Intertype form of reasoning has two definite advantages over the customary attitude, *e.g.*, that which would prefer a company such as Coca-Cola, at 22 times recent earnings and 35 times its asset value, because of the virtually uninterrupted expansion of its profits for more than 15 years.

The first advantage is that, after all, private business is conducted and investments made therein on the same kind of assumptions that we have made with respect to Intertype. The second is that reasoning of this kind can be *conservative* in that it allows for a liberal margin of safety in case of error or disappointment. It runs considerably less risk of confusion between "confidence in the future" and mere speculative enthusiasm.

Large Profits Frequently Transitory. More frequently we have the opposite type of situation from that just discussed. Here the analyst finds reason to question the indefinite continuance of past prosperity.

Examples: Consider a company like J. W. Watson ("Stabilator") Company, engaged chiefly in the manufacture of a single type of automotive accessory. The success of such a "gadget" is normally short-lived; competition and changes in the art are an ever present threat to the stability of earning power. Hence in such a case the student could have pointed out that the market price, bearing the usual ratio to current and average earnings, reflected a quite unwarranted confidence in the permanence of profits that by their nature were likely to be transitory. Some of the pertinent data relative to this judgment are given in the table below, with respect to this company.[8]

THE J. W. WATSON COMPANY

Year	Net for common	Per share	Price range for common	Dividend
1932	$214,026(d)	$1.07(d)	$3/8-1/8$	None
1931	240,149(d)	1.20(d)	$2-1/8$	None
1930	264,269(d)	1.32(d)	6–1	None
1929	323,137(d)	1.61(d)	$14^7/8-1^5/8$	None
1928	348,930(d)	1.74(d)	$20-5^1/4$	50 cents
1927	503,725	2.16	$25^3/4-18^7/8$	50 cents
1926	577,450*	2.88*	(Issue not quoted prior to 1927)	
1925	502,593*	2.51*		
1924	29,285*	0.15*		
1923	173,907*	0.86*		
1922	142,701*	0.71*		

* Earnings are for predecessor companies, applied to 1932 capitalization.

---

[8] The common stock of the company was originally offered in September 1927 at $24.50 per share, a price 17.3 times the average earnings of the predecessor companies during the preceding five years. This relatively high price was accounted for in part by the apparently

A similar consideration would apply to the exhibit of Coty, Inc., in 1928. Here was a company with an excellent earnings record, but the earnings were derived from the popularity of a trade-marked line of cosmetics. This was a field in which the variable tastes of femininity could readily destroy profits as well as build them up. The inference that rapidly rising profits in previous years meant much larger profits in the future was thus especially fallacious in this case, because *by the nature of the business* a peak of popularity was likely to be reached at some not distant point, after which a substantial falling off would be, if not inevitable, at least highly probable. Some of the data appearing on the Coty exhibit are as follows:

Year	Net income	Earned per share (adjusted)
1923	$1,070,000	$0.86
1924	2,046,000	1.66
1925	2,505,000	2.02
1926	2,943,000	2.38
1927	3,341,000	2.70
1928	4,047,000	3.09
1929	4,058,000	2.73

At the high price of 82 in 1929, Coty, Inc., was selling in the market for about $120,000,000, or thirty times its *maximum* earnings. The actual investment in the business (capital and surplus) amounted to about $14,000,000.

Subsequent earnings were as shown in the table following.

COTY, INC.

Year	Net income	Earned per share
1930	$1,318,000	$0.86
1931	991,000	0.65
1932	521,000	0.34 (low price in 1932–1$^1/_2$)

favorable "trend" of earnings, in part by the high recent and current earnings and in part by the reckless standards of appraisal beginning to prevail at the time.

See pp. 438–440 of the 1934 edition of this work for a companion case—The Gabriel Company.

A third variety of this kind of reasoning could be applied to the brew-ery-stock flotations in 1933. These issues showed substantial current or prospective earnings based upon capacity operations and the indicated profit per barrel. Without claiming the gift of second sight, an analyst could confidently predict that the flood of capital being poured into this new industry would ultimately result in overcapacity and keen competition.

Hence a continued large return on the actual cash investment was scarcely probable; it was likely, moreover, that many of the individual companies would prove financial failures, and most of the others would be unable to earn enough to justify the optimistic price quotations engen-dered by their initial success.[9]

---

[9] See Appendix Note 55, p. 792 on accompanying CD, for brief comments on the subsequent performance of the brewery issues of 1933.

Chapter 38

SPECIFIC REASONS FOR QUESTIONING OR REJECTING THE PAST RECORD

IN ANALYZING AN INDIVIDUAL company, each of the governing elements in the operating results must be scrutinized for signs of possible unfavorable changes in the future. This procedure may be illustrated by various examples drawn from the mining field. The four governing elements in such situations would be: (1) life of the mine, (2) annual output, (3) production costs and (4) selling price. The significance of the first factor has already been discussed in connection with charges against earnings for depletion. Both the output and the costs may be affected adversely if the ore to be mined in the future differs from that previously mined in location, character or grade.[1]

Rate of Output and Operating Costs. *Examples: Calumet and Hecla Consolidated Copper Company.* The reports of this copper producer for 1936 and previous years illustrate various questions with respect to ore reserves. The income account for 1936 may be summarized as follows:

Copper produced	78,500,000 lb.
Copper sold	95,200,000 lb. @ 9.80 cents
Profit before depreciation and depletion	$3,855,000
Depreciation	1,276,000
Depletion	1,726,000
Earned per share after depreciation but before depletion on 2,006,000 shares	$1.29

---

[1] When ore reserves are stated only as so many tons, or so many years of life, these data may be misleading in the absence of assurance regarding the *quality* of ore remaining. *Example:* The depletion charges of Alaska Juneau Gold Mining Company suggested a remaining life of some 85 years from 1934. The registration statement however, claimed only some 25 years of life from 1934. The implication (confirmed upon inquiry) is that the longer "life" included much low-grade ore of noncommercial character.

Early in 1937 the stock sold at $20 per share, a valuation of $40,000,000 for the company, or $30,000,000 for the mining properties plus $10,000,000 for the working capital.

A detailed analysis of the make-up of the 1936 earnings would have shown them to be derived from four separate sources, approximately as follows:

Source of copper	Number of pounds, millions	Profit before depreciation and depletion	
		Cents per pound (approximate)	Total (approximate)
Copper previously produced	17.3	4.5	$ 775,000
Conglomerate mine	36.3	3.6	1,305,000
Ahmeek mine	23.0	3.3	760,000
Reclamation plants	19.2	5.3	1,015,000
	95.8	4.0	$3,855,000

Of these four sources of profit, all but the smallest were definitely limited in life. The sale of copper produced in prior years was obviously nonrecurring. The mainstay of the company's production for 70 years—the Conglomerate Branch—was facing exhaustion "in the course of 12 or 14 months." The reclamation-plant copper, recovered by reworking old tailings and providing the cheapest metal, was limited to a life of 5 to 7 years. There remained as the only more permanent source of future output the Ahmeek Mine, which was the highest cost operation and which had therefore been shut down from April 1932 through 1935. (There were also certain other high-cost properties that were still shut down in 1936.)

Analysis would indicate, therefore, that probably not more than a total of some 7 to 8 millions in profit could be expected in the future from the Conglomerate and the reclamation operations. Hence, aside from new developments of a speculative character, the greater part of the 40 millions of valuation for the company would have to be supported by earnings from higher cost properties *which had contributed only a minor part of the 1936 results.*[2]

---

[2] In the 1934 edition of this book we discussed a similar situation existing in this company in 1927, at which time the largest part of the profits were being contributed by the reclamation-plant operations, which were known to have a limited life.

Freeport Sulphur Company. The exhibit of the then Freeport Texas Company in 1933 supplies the same type of problem for the analyst, and it also raises the question of the propriety of the use, under such circumstances, of the past earnings record to support the sale of new securities. An issue of $2,500,000 of 6% cumulative convertible preferred stock was sold at $100 per share in January 1933 in order to raise funds to equip a new sulphur property leased from certain other companies.

The offering circular stated among other things:

1. That the sulphur reserves had an estimated life of at least 25 years based upon the average annual sales for 1928–1932;
2. That the earnings for the period 1928–1932 averaged $2,952,500, or 19.6 times the preferred-dividend requirement.

The implication of these statements would be that, assuming no change in the price received for sulphur, the company could confidently be expected to earn over the next 25 years approximately the amounts earned in the past.

The facts in the case, however, did not warrant any such deduction. The company's past earnings were derived from the operation of two properties, at Bryanmound and at Hoskins Mound, respectively. The Bryanmound area was owned by the company and had contributed the bulk of the profits. But by 1933 its life was "definitely limited" (in the words of the listing application); *in fact the reserves were not likely to last more than about three years.* The Hoskins Mound was leased from the Texas Company. After paying $1.06 per ton fixed royalty, no less than 70% of the remaining profits were payable to Texas Company as rental.[3] One half of Freeport's sales were required to be made from sulphur produced at Hoskins. The new property at Grande Ecaille, La., now to be developed, would require royalty payments amounting to some 40% of the net earnings.

When these facts are studied, it will be seen that the earnings of Freeport Texas for 1928–1932 had no direct bearing on the results to be expected from future operations. The sulphur reserves, stated to be good for 25 years, represented mineral located in an entirely different place and

---

[3] The rate had been 50% until Freeport recouped its capital expenditures on the property. Illustrative of the general theme of this chapter is the break in Freeport's price from 109¼ to 65⅝ in January-February 1928 coincident with the change in the royalty rate. The student may examine a similar development in the case of Texas Gulf Sulphur, occurring in 1934–1935.

to be extracted under entirely different conditions from those obtaining in the past. A large profit-sharing royalty would be payable on the sulphur produced from the new project, whereas the old Bryanmound was owned outright by Freeport and hence its profits accrued 100% to the company.

In addition to this known element of higher cost, great stress must be laid also upon the fact that the major future profits of Freeport were now expected from a *new project*. The Grande Ecaille property was not yet equipped and in operation, and hence it was subject to the many hazards that attach to enterprises in the development stage. The cost of production at the new mine might conceivably be much higher, or much lower, than at Bryanmound. From the standpoint of security analysis the important point is that, where two quite different properties are involved, you have two virtually separate enterprises. Hence the 1928–1932 record of Freeport Texas was hardly more relevant to its future history than were the figures of some entirely different sulphur company, *e.g.*, Texas Gulf Sulphur.

Returning once more to the business man's viewpoint on security values, the Freeport Texas exhibit suggests the following interesting line of reasoning. In June 1933 this enterprise was selling in the market for about $32,000,000 (25,000 shares of preferred at 125 and 730,000 shares of common at 40). The major portion of its future profits were expected to be derived from an investment of $3,000,000 to equip a new property leased from three large oil companies. Presumably these oil companies drove as good a bargain for themselves as possible in the terms of the lease. The market was in effect placing a valuation of some $20,000,000, or more, upon a new enterprise in which only $3,000,000 was to be invested. It was possible, of course, that this enterprise would prove to be worth much more than six times the money put into it. But from the standpoint of ordinary business procedure the payment of such an enormous premium for anticipated future results would appear imprudent in the extreme.[4]

Evidently the stock market—like the heart, in the French proverb—has reasons all its own. In the writers' view, where these reasons depart

---

[4] Since the Freeport Texas preferred issue was relatively small, representing less than one-tenth of the total market value of the company, this analysis would not call into question the safety of the senior issue, but reflects only upon the soundness of the valuation accorded the common stock—judged by investment standards. After 1933 the company did in fact encounter serious problems of production, which held down the earnings and depressed the market price, but these problems were later solved. Yet the maximum earnings attained by 1940—$3.30 per share in 1937—could scarcely justify the price of 49 paid by speculators in 1933.

violently from sound sense and business experience, common-stock buyers must inevitably lose money in the end, even though large speculative gains may temporarily accrue, and even though certain fortunate purchases may turn out to be permanently profitable.

The Future Price of the Product. The three preceding examples related to the future continuance of the rate of output and the operating costs upon which the past record of earnings was predicted. We must also consider such indications as may be available in regard to the *future selling price* of the product. Here we must ordinarily enter into the field of surmise or of prophecy. The analyst can truthfully say very little about future prices, except that they fall outside the realm of sound prediction. Now and then a more illuminating statement may be justified by the facts. Adhering to the mining field for our examples, we may mention the enormous profits made by zinc producers during the Great War, because of the high price of spelter. Butte and Superior Mining Company earned no less than $64 per share before depreciation and depletion in the two years 1915–1916, as the result of obtaining about 13 cents per pound for its output of zinc, against a prewar average of about $5^{1}/_{4}$ cents. Obviously the future earning power of this company was almost certain to shrink far below the war-time figures, nor could these properly be taken together with the results of any other years in order to arrive at the average or supposedly "normal" earnings.[5]

Change in Status of Low-cost Producers. The copper-mining industry offers an example of wider significance. An analysis of companies in this field must take into account the fact that since 1914 a substantial number of new low-cost producers have been developed and that other companies have succeeded in reducing extraction costs through metallurgical improvements. This means that there has been a definite lowering of the "center of gravity" of production costs for the entire industry. Other things being equal, this would make for a lower selling price in the future than obtained in the past. (Such a development is more strikingly illustrated by the crude-rubber industry.) Differently stated, mines that formerly rated as low-cost producers, *i.e.*, as having costs well below the average, may have lost this advantage, unless they have also greatly improved their technique

---

[5] The same type of reasoning clearly applies to the *volume of business* due to war conditions, as well illustrated by the exhibits of airplane companies in 1939–1940.

of production. The analyst would have to allow for these developments in his calculations, by taking a cautious view of future copper prices—at least as compared with the prewar or the predepression average.[6]

Anomalous Prices and Price Relationships in the History of the I.R.T. System.

The checkered history of the Interborough Rapid Transit System in New York City has presented a great variety of divergences between market prices and the real or relative values ascertainable by analysis. Two of these discrepancies turn upon the fact that *for specific reasons* the then current and past earnings should not have been accepted as indicative of future earning power. In abbreviated form the details of these two situations are as follows:

For a number of years prior to 1918 the Interborough Rapid Transit Company was very prosperous. In the 12 months ended June 30, 1917, it earned $26 per share on its capital stock and paid dividends of $20 per share. Nearly all of this stock was owned by Interborough Consolidated Corporation, a holding concern (previously called Interborough-Metropolitan Corporation) which in turn had outstanding collateral trust bonds, 6% preferred stock and common stock. Including its share of the undistributed earnings of the operating company it earned about $11.50 per share on its preferred stock and about $2.50 on the common. The preferred sold in the market at 60, and the common at 10. These issues were actively traded in, and they were highly recommended to the public by various financial agencies which stressed the phenomenal growth of the subway traffic.

A modicum of analysis would have shown that the real picture was entirely different from what appeared on the surface. New rapid transit facilities were being constructed under contract between the City of New York and the Interborough (as well as others under contract between the City and the Brooklyn Rapid Transit Company). As soon as the new lines were placed in operation, which was to be the following year, the earnings available for Interborough were to be limited under this contract to the figure prevailing in 1911–1913, *which was far less than the current*

---

[6] On the other hand, the rise in the price of gold in 1933 invalidated *for statistical purposes* previous earnings of gold producers based on $20.67 gold. Whether or not the future price of gold will remain at $35 is anyone's guess, but there seems no reason to make any calculations based on the old value.

profits. The City would then be entitled to receive a high return on its enormous investment in the new lines. If and after all such payments were made in full, including back accruals, the City and the Interborough would then share equally in surplus profits. However, the preferential payments due the City would be so heavy that experts had testified that under the most favorable conditions it would be *more than 30 years* before there could be any surplus income to divide with the company.

The subjoined brief table shows the significance of these facts.

INTERBOROUGH RAPID TRANSIT SYSTEM

Item	Actual earnings 1917	*Maximum* earnings when contract with City became operative
Balance for I.R.T. stock	$9,100,000	$5,200,000
Share applicable to Interborough Consolidated Corp.	8,800,000	5,000,000
Interest on Inter. Consol. bonds	3,520,000	3,520,000
Balance for Inter. Consol. pfd.	5,280,000	1,480,000
Preferred dividend requirements	2,740,000	2,740,000
Balance for Inter. Consol. common	2,540,000	*1,260,000(d)*
Earned per share, Inter. Consol. pfd.	$11.50	$3.25
Earned per share, Inter. Consol. common	2.50	nil

The underlying facts proved beyond question, therefore, that instead of a brilliant future being in store for Interborough, it was destined to suffer a severe loss of earning power within a year's time. It would then be quite impossible to maintain the $6 dividend on the holding company's preferred stock, and no earnings at all would be available for the common for a generation or more. On this showing it was mathematically certain that both Interborough Consolidated stock issues were worth far less than their current selling prices.[7]

---

[7] Indications pointed strongly to manipulative efforts by insiders in 1916–1917 to foist these shares upon the public at high prices before the period of lower earnings began. The payment of full dividends on the preferred stock, during an interlude of large earnings known to be temporary, was inexcusable from the standpoint of corporate policy but understandable as a

The sequel not only bore out this criticism, which it was bound to do, but demonstrated also that where an *upper limit* of earnings or value is fixed, there is usually danger that the actual figure will be less than the maximum. The opening of the new subway lines coincided with a large increase in operating costs, due to war-time inflation; and also, as was to be expected, it diminished the profits of the older routes. Interborough Rapid Transit Company was promptly compelled to reduce its dividend, and it was omitted entirely in 1919. In consequence the holding company, Interborough Consolidated, suspended its preferred dividends in 1918. The next year it defaulted the interest on its bonds, became bankrupt and disappeared from the scene, *with the complete extinction of both its preferred and common stock.* Two years later Interborough Rapid Transit Company, recently so prosperous, barely escaped an imminent receivership by means of a "voluntary" reorganization which extended a maturing note issue. When this extended issue matured in 1932, the company was again unable to pay, and this time receivers took over the property.

During the ten-year period between the two receivership applications another earnings situation developed, somewhat similar to that of 1917.[8] In 1928 the Interborough reported earnings of $3,000,000, or $8.50 per share for its common stock, and the shares sold as high as 62. But these earnings included $4,000,000 of "back preferential" from the subway division. The latter represented a limited amount due the Interborough Rapid Transit out of subway earnings to make good a deficiency in the profits of the early years of operating the new lines. On June 30, 1928 the amount of back preferential remaining to be paid the company was only

---

device to aid in unloading stock. These dividend distributions were not only unfair to the $4^1/2\%$ bondholders, but, because of certain prior developments, they were probably illegal as well. (Reference to this aspect of the case was made in Chap. 20 on accompanying CD).

[8] See Appendix Note 56, p. 792 on accompanying CD, for a concise discussion of the numerous anomalies in price between various Interborough System securities, *viz.*:

1. Between Interborough Metropolitan $4^1/2$s and Interborough Consolidated Preferred in 1919.
2. Between I.R.T. 5s and I.R.T. 7s in 1920.
3. Between I.R.T. stock and Manhattan "Modified" stock in 1929.
4. Between I.R.T. 5s and I.R.T. 7s in 1933.
5. Between Manhattan "Modified" and Manhattan "Unmodified" stock in 1933.

$1,413,000. *Hence all the profits available for Interborough stock were due to a special source of revenue that could continue for only a few months longer.* Heedless speculators, however, were capitalizing as permanent an earning power of Interborough stock which analysis would show was of entirely nonrecurrent and temporary character.

Chapter 39

PRICE-EARNINGS RATIOS FOR COMMON STOCKS. ADJUSTMENTS FOR CHANGES IN CAPITALIZATION

IN PREVIOUS CHAPTERS various references have been made to Wall Street's ideas on the relation of earnings to values. A given common stock is generally considered to be worth a certain number of times its current earnings. This number of times, or multiplier, depends partly on the prevailing psychology and partly on the nature and record of the enterprise. Prior to the 1927–1929 bull market ten times earnings was the accepted standard of measurement. More accurately speaking, it was the common point of departure for valuing common stocks, so that an issue would have to be considered exceptionally desirable to justify a higher ratio, and conversely.

Beginning about 1927 the ten-times-earnings standard was superseded by a rather confusing set of new yardsticks. On the one hand, there was a tendency to value common stocks in general more liberally than before. This was summarized in a famous dictum of a financial leader implying that good stocks were worth fifteen times their earnings.[1] There was also the tendency to make more sweeping distinctions in the valuations of different kinds of common stocks. Companies in especially favored groups, *e.g.*, public utilities and chain stores, in 1928–1929, sold at a very high multiple of current earnings, say, twenty-five to forty times. This was true also of the "blue chip" issues, which comprised leading units in miscellaneous fields. As pointed out before, these generous valuations

---

[1] The wording of this statement, as quoted in the *Wall Street Journal* of March 26, 1928, was as follows: " 'General Motors shares, according to the Dow, Jones & Co. averages,' Mr. Raskob remarked, 'should sell at fifteen times earning power, or in the neighborhood of $225 per share, whereas at the present level of $180 they sell at approximately only twelve times current earnings.' "

were based upon the assumed continuance of the upward trend shown over a longer or shorter period in the past. Subsequent to 1932 there developed a tendency for prices to rule higher in relation to earnings because of the sharp drop in long-term interest rates.

Exact Appraisal Impossible. Security analysis cannot presume to lay down general rules as to the "proper value" of any given common stock. Practically speaking, there is no such thing. The bases of value are too shifting to admit of any formulation that could claim to be even reasonably accurate. The whole idea of basing the value upon current earnings seems inherently absurd, since we know that the current earnings are constantly changing. And whether the multiplier should be ten or fifteen or thirty would seem at bottom a matter of purely arbitrary choice.

But the stock market itself has no time for such scientific scruples. It must make its values first and find its reasons afterwards. Its position is much like that of a jury in a breach-of-promise suit; there is no sound way of measuring the values involved, and yet they must be measured somehow and a verdict rendered. Hence the prices of common stocks are not carefully thought out computations but the resultants of a welter of human reactions. The stock market is a voting machine rather than a weighing machine. It responds to factual data not directly but only as they affect the decisions of buyers and sellers.

Limited Functions of the Analyst in Field of Appraisal of Stock Prices. Confronted by this mixture of changing facts and fluctuating human fancies, the securities analyst is clearly incapable of passing judgment on common-stock prices generally. There are, however, some concrete, if limited, functions that he may carry on in this field, of which the following are representative:

1. He may set up a basis for *conservative* or *investment* valuation of common stocks, as distinguished from speculative valuations.
2. He may point out the significance of: (*a*) the capitalization structure; and (*b*) the source of income, as bearing upon the valuation of a given stock issue.
3. He may find unusual elements in the balance sheet which affect the implications of the earnings picture.

A Suggested Basis of Maximum Appraisal for Investment. The investor in common stocks, equally with the speculator, is dependent on future rather than past earnings. His fundamental basis of appraisal must be an intelligent and conservative estimate of the future earning power. But his *measure* of future earnings can be conservative only if it is limited by actual performance over a period of time. We have suggested, however, that the profits of the most recent year, taken singly, might be accepted as the gage of future earnings, *if* (1) general business conditions in that year were not exceptionally good, (2) the company has shown an upward trend of earnings for some years past and (3) the investor's study of the industry gives him confidence in its continued growth. In a very exceptional case, the investor may be justified in counting on higher earnings in the future than at any time in the past. This might follow from developments involving a patent or the discovery of new ore in a mine or some similar specific and significant occurrence. But in most instances he will derive the investment value of a common stock from the average earnings of a period between five and ten years. This does not mean that all common stocks with the same average earnings should have the same value. The common-stock investor (*i.e.*, the *conservative* buyer) will properly accord a more liberal valuation to those issues which have current earnings above the average or which may reasonably be considered to possess better than average prospects or an inherently stable earning power. But it is the essence of our viewpoint that some moderate upper limit must *in every case* be placed on the multiplier in order to stay within the bounds of conservative valuation. We would suggest that *about 20 times average earnings* is as high a price as can be paid in an *investment* purchase of a common stock.

Although this rule is of necessity arbitrary in its nature, it is not entirely so. Investment presupposes demonstrable value, and the typical common stock's value can be demonstrated only by means of an established, *i.e.*, an average, earning power. But it is difficult to see how average earnings of *less than* 5% upon the market price could ever be considered as vindicating that price. Clearly such a price-earnings ratio could not provide that *margin of safety* which we have associated with the investor's position. It might be accepted by a purchaser in the expectation that future earnings will be larger than in the past. But in the original and most useful sense of the term such a basis of valuation is *speculative*.[2] It falls outside the purview of common-stock investment.

---

[2] See Appendix Note 57, p. 794 on accompanying CD, for a discussion of the relationship between bond-interest rates and the "multiplier" for common stocks.

Higher Prices May Prevail for Speculative Commitments. The intent of this distinction must be clearly understood. We do not imply that it is a mistake to pay more than 20 times average earnings for any common stock. We do suggest that such a price would be speculative. The purchase may easily turn out to be highly profitable, but in that case it will have proved a wise or fortunate speculation. It is proper to remark, moreover, that very few people are consistently wise or fortunate in their speculative operations. Hence we may submit, as a corollary of no small practical importance, *that people who habitually purchase common stocks at more than about 20 times their average earnings are likely to lose considerable money in the long run.* This is the more probable because, in the absence of such a mechanical check, they are prone to succumb recurrently to the lure of bull markets, which always find some specious argument to justify paying extravagant prices for common stocks.

Other Requisites for Common Stocks of Investment Grade and a Corollary Therefrom. It should be pointed out that if 20 times average earnings is taken as the *upper limit* of price for an investment purchase, then ordinarily the price paid should be substantially less than this maximum. This suggests that about 12 or 12$^1/_2$ times average earnings may be suitable for the typical case of a company with neutral prospects. We must emphasize also that a reasonable ratio of market price to average earnings is not the only requisite for a common-stock investment. It is a necessary but not a sufficient condition. The company must be satisfactory also in its financial set-up and management, and not unsatisfactory in its prospects.

From this principle there follows another important corollary, *viz.: An attractive common-stock investment is an attractive speculation.* This is true because, if a common stock can meet the demand of a conservative investor that he get full value for his money *plus* not unsatisfactory future prospects, then such an issue must also have a fair chance of appreciating in market value.

Examples of Speculative and Investment Common Stocks. Our definition of an investment basis for common-stock purchases is at variance with the Wall Street practice in respect to common stocks of high rating. For such issues a price of considerably more than 20 times average earnings is held to be warranted, and furthermore these stocks are designated as "investment issues" regardless of the price at which they sell. According to our view, the high prices paid for "the best common stocks" make these purchases essentially speculative, because they require future growth to justify them. Hence common-stock investment operations, as we define them, will occupy a middle ground in the market, lying between low-price issues that are speculative because of doubtful quality and well-entrenched issues that are speculative, none the less, because of their high price.

GROUP A: COMMON STOCKS SPECULATIVE IN DECEMBER 1938 BECAUSE OF THEIR HIGH PRICE (FIGURES ADJUSTED TO REFLECT CHANGES IN CAPITALIZATION)

Item	Group A		
	General Electric	Coca Cola	Johns-Manville
Amount Earned per Share of Common:			
1938	$0.96	$5.95	$1.09
1937	2.20	5.73	5.80
1936	1.52	4.66	5.13
1935	0.97	3.48	2.17
1934	0.59	3.12	0.22
1933	0.38	2.20	0.64(d)
1932	0.41	2.17	4.47(d)
1931	1.33	2.96	0.45
1930	1.90	2.79	3.66
1929	2.24	2.56	8.09
10-yr. average	$1.25	$3.56	$2.15
5-yr. average (1934–1938)	$1.25	$4.59	$2.88
Bonds	None	None	None
Pfd. Stock	None	600,000 sh. @ 60	75,000 sh. @ 130
		$36,000,000	$9,750,000
Common Stock	28,784,000 sh. @ $43^{1}/_{2}$	3,992,000 sh. @ $132^{1}/_{4}$	850,000 sh. @ 105
	$1,250,000,000	$529,500,000	$89,300,000
Total capitalization	$1,250,000,000	$565,500,000	$99,050,000
Net tangible assets, 12/31/38	$335,182,000	$43,486,000	$48,001,000
Net current assets, 12/31/38	$155,023,000	$25,094,000	$17,418,000
Average earnings on common-stock price, 1929–1938	2.9%	2.7%	2.0%
Maximum earnings on common-stock price, 1929–1938	5.1%	4.5%	7.7%
Minimum earnings on common-stock price, 1929–1938	0.9%	1.6%	(d)
Average earnings on common-stock price, 1934–1938	2.9%	3.5%	2.7%

These distinctions are illustrated by[3] the accompanying nine examples, taken as of December 31, 1938.

Comments on the Various Groups. The companies listed in Group *A* are representative of the so-called "first-grade" or "blue chip" industrials, which

GROUP B: COMMON STOCKS SPECULATIVE IN DECEMBER 1938 BECAUSE OF
THEIR IRREGULAR RECORD

Item	Group B		
	Goodyear Tire and Rubber	Simmons	Youngstown Sheet and Tube
Amount earned per share of common:			
1938	$1.34	$1.42	$0.89(d)
1937	1.95	2.88	6.79
1936	3.90	3.53	7.03
1935	0.12	1.14	0.64
1934	0.66(d)	0.84(d)	2.95(d)
1933	0.79(d)	0.04	7.76(d)
1932	4.24(d)	2.57(d)	11.75(d)
1931	0.04	0.79(d)	6.55(d)
1930	0.37(d)	1.05(d)	5.17
1929	10.23	4.15	17.28
10-yr. average	$1.15	$0.79	$0.70
5-yr. average (1934–1938)	$ 1.35	$1.63	$2.12
Bonds	$50,235,000	$10,000,000	$87,000,000
Pfd. stock	650,000 sh. @ 108	None	150,000 sh. @ 81
	70,250,000		12,165,000
Common stock	2,059,000 sh. @ 37⁵/₈	1,158,000 sh. @ 32	1,675,000 sh. @ 54¹/₄
	$77,500,000	$37,050,000	$90,900,000
Total capitalization	$197,985,000	$47,050,000	$190,065,000
Net tangible assets, 12/31/38	$170,322,000	$28,446,000	$224,678,000
Net current assets, 12/31/38	$96,979,000	$14,788,000	$83,375,000
Average earnings on common-stock price, 1929–1938	3.1%	2.5%	1.3%
Maximum earnings on common-stock price, 1929–1938	27.2%	13.0%	31.8%
Minimum earnings on common-stock price, 1929–1938	(d)	(d)	(d)
Average earnings on common-stock price, 1934–1938	3.6%	5.1%	3.9%

---

[3] See Appendix Note 58, p. 795 on accompanying CD, for the examples given in the 1934 edition, and their later performance.

were particularly favored in the great speculation of 1928–1929 and in the markets of ensuing years. They are characterized by a strong financial position, by presumably excellent prospects and in most cases by relatively stable or growing earnings in the past. *The market price* of the shares, however, was higher than would be justified by their average earnings. In fact the profits of the *best* year in the 1929–1938 decade were less than 8% of the

GROUP C: COMMON STOCKS MEETING INVESTMENT TESTS IN DECEMBER 1938 FROM THE QUANTITATIVE STANDPOINT

Item	Group C		
	Adams-Millis	American Safety Razor	J. J. Newberry
Amount earned per share of common:			
1938	$3.21	$1.48	$4.05
1937	2.77	2.47	5.27
1936	2.55	2.70	6.03
1935	2.93	2.42	4.94
1934	3.41	2.03	5.38
1933	2.63	1.40	3.06
1932	1.03	1.14	1.07
1931	4.72	1.58	1.73
1930	4.83	2.50	2.27
1929	4.83	2.57	3.15
10-yr. average	$3.29	$2.03	$3.70
5-yr. average (1934–1938)	$2.97	$2.22	$5.13
Bonds	None	None	$5,587,000
Pfd. stock	None	None	51,000 sh. @ 106 $5,405,000
Common stock	156,000 sh. @ 21 $3,280,000	524,000 sh. @ 14⁷/₈ $7,800,000	380,000 sh. @ 34¹/₂ $13,110,000
Total capitalization	$3,280,000	$7,800,000	$24,102,000
Net tangible assets, 12/31/38	$3,320,000	$6,484,000	$25,551,000
Net current assets, 12/31/38	$926,000	$3,649,000	$8,745,000
Average earnings on common-stock price, 1929–1938	15.7%	13.7%	10.7%
Maximum earnings on common-stock price, 1929–1938	23.0%	18.2%	17.5%
Minimum earnings on common-stock price, 1929–1938	4.9%	7.7%	3.1%
Average earnings on common-stock price, 1934–1938	14.1%	14.9%	14.9%

December 1938 market price. It is also characteristic of such issues that they sell for enormous premiums above the actual capital invested.

The companies analyzed in Group *B* are obviously speculative, because of the great instability of their earnings records. They show varying relationships of market price to average earnings, maximum earnings, and asset values.

The common stocks shown in Group *C* are examples of those which meet specific and quantitative tests of investment quality. These tests include the following:

1. The earnings have been reasonably stable, allowing for the tremendous fluctuations in business conditions during the ten-year period.
2. The average earnings bear a satisfactory ratio to market price.[4]
3. The financial set-up is sufficiently conservative, and the working-capital position is strong.

Although we do not suggest that a common stock bought for investment be *required* to show asset values equal to the price paid, it is none the less characteristic of issues in Group *C* that, as a whole, they will not sell for a huge premium above the companies' actual resources.

Common-stock *investment*, as we envisage it, will confine itself to issues making exhibits of the kind illustrated by Group *C*. But the actual purchase of any such issues must require *also* that the purchaser be satisfied in his own mind that the prospects of the enterprise are at least reasonably favorable.

ALLOWANCES FOR CHANGES IN CAPITALIZATION

In dealing with the past record of earnings, when given on a per-share basis, it is elementary that the figures must be adjusted to reflect any important changes in the capitalization which have taken place during the period. In the simplest case these will involve a change only in the number of shares of common stock due to stock dividends, split-ups, etc. All that is necessary then is to restate the capitalization throughout the period on the basis of the current number of shares. (Such recalculations are made by some of the statistical services but not by others.)

---

[4] Note that the *average* earnings of the three companies in Group *C* were nearly two and one-half times as large relative to market price as the *maximum* earnings of the companies in Group *A*.

When the change in capitalization has been due to the sale of additional stock at a comparatively low price (usually through the exercise of subscription rights or warrants) or to the conversion of senior securities, the adjustment is more difficult. In such cases the earnings available for the common during the earlier period must be increased by whatever gain would have followed from the issuance of the additional shares. When bonds or preferred stocks have been converted into common, the charges formerly paid thereon are to be added back to the earnings and the new figure then applied to the larger number of shares. If stock has been sold at a relatively low price, a proper adjustment would allow earnings of, say, 5 to 8% on the proceeds of the sale. (Such recalculations need not be made unless the changes indicated thereby are substantial.)

A corresponding adjustment of the per-share earnings must be made at times to reflect the possible *future* increase in the number of shares outstanding as a result of conversions or exercise of option warrants. When other security holders have a choice of any kind, sound analysis must allow for the possible adverse effect upon the per-share earnings of the common stock that would follow from the exercise of the option.

Examples: This type of adjustment must be made in analyzing the reported earnings of American Airlines, Inc., for the 12 months ended September 30, 1939.

Earnings as reported	$1,128,000
Per share on about 300,000 shares outstanding.	$3.76
	(Price December 1939 about 37)

But there were outstanding $2,600,000 of 4$^{1}/_{2}$% debentures, convertible into common stock at $12.50 per share. The analyst must *assume* conversion of the bonds, giving the following adjusted result:

Earnings, adding back $117,000 interest	$1,245,000
Per share on 508,000 shares	$2.45

More than one-third of the reported earnings per share are lost when the necessary adjustment is made.

American Water Works and Electric Company can be used to illustrate both types of adjustment. (See page 505.)

Adjustment *A* reflects the payment of stock dividends in 1928, 1929 and 1930.

Adjustment *B* assumes conversion of the $15,000,000 of convertible 5s, issued in 1934, thus increasing the earnings by the amount of the interest charges but also increasing the common-stock issue by 750,000 shares. (The foregoing adjustments are independent of any possible modifications in the reported earnings arising from the questioning of the depreciation charges, etc., as previously discussed.)

	Earnings* for common as reported			Adjustment *A*		Adjustment *B*		
Year	Amount of shares	Number	Per share	Number of shares	Earned per share	Amount	Number of shares	Earned per share
1933	$2,392	1,751	$1.37	1,751	$1.37	$3,140	2,501	$1.26
1932	2,491	1,751	1.42	1,751	1.42	3,240	2,501	1.30
1931	4,904	1,751	2.80	1,751	2.80	5,650	2,501	2.26
1930	5,424	1,751	3.10	1,751	3.10	6,170	2,501	2.47
1929	6,621	1,657	4.00	1,741	3.80	7,370	2,491	2.95
1928	5,009	1,432	3.49	1,739	2.88	5,760	2,489	2.30
1927	3,660	1,361	2.69	1,737	2.11	4,410	2,487	1.76
7-year average			$2.70		$2.50			$2.04

* Number of shares and earnings in thousands.

Corresponding adjustments in book values or current-asset values per share of common stock should be made in analyzing the balance sheet. This technique is followed in our discussion of the Baldwin Locomotive Works exhibit in Appendix Note 70, page 838 on accompanying CD, in which outstanding warrants are allowed for.

ALLOWANCES FOR PARTICIPATING INTERESTS

In calculating the earnings available for the common, full recognition must be given to the rights of holders of participating issues, whether or not the amounts involved are actually being paid thereon. Similar allowances must be made for the effect of management contracts providing for a substantial percentage of the profits as compensation, as in the case of investment trusts. Unusual cases sometimes arise involving "restricted shares," dividends on which are contingent upon earnings or other considerations.

Example: Trico Products Corporation, a large manufacturer of automobile accessories, is capitalized at 675,000 shares of common stock, of which 450,000 shares (owned by the president) were originally "restricted" as to dividends. The unrestricted stock is first entitled to dividends of $2.50 per share, after which both classes share equally in further dividends. In addition, successive blocks of the restricted stock were to be released from the restriction according as the earnings for 1925 and successive years reached certain stipulated figures. (To the end of 1938, a total of 239,951 shares had been thus released.)

ADJUSTED EARNINGS: TRICO PRODUCTS CORPORATION[1]

Year	Earnings for common	Earned per share on unrestricted stock		
		A. Ignoring restricted shares	B. Maximum distribution on unrestricted shares	C. Allowing for release of restricted shares (i.e., on total capitalization)
1929	$2,250,000	$6.67	$4.58	$3.33
1930	1,908,000	5.09	3.94	2.83
1931	1,763,000	4.70	3.72	2.61
1932	965,000	2.57	2.54	1.44
1933	1,418,000	3.78	3.21	2.10
1934	1,772,000	4.72	3.74	2.62
1935	3,567,000	9.84	6.52	5.38
1936	4,185,000	9.75	7.25	6.39
1937	3,792,000	8.97	6.82	5.99
1938	2,320,000	5.56	4.53	3.70
10-year average	$3,394,000	$6.17	$4.69	$3.64

[1] The calculations for the years 1935–1938 have been affected by repurchases of unrestricted shares by the corporation.

In the above table Column C supplies the soundest measure of the earning power shown for the unrestricted shares. Column A is irrelevant.

A situation similar to that in Trico Products Corporation obtained in the case of Montana Power Company stock prior to June 1921.

General Rule. The material in the last few pages may be summarized in the following general rule:

The intrinsic value of a common stock preceded by convertible securities, or subject to dilution through the exercise of stock options or through participating privileges enjoyed by other security holders, cannot reasonably be appraised at a higher figure than would be justified if all such privileges were exercised in full.

Chapter 40

CAPITALIZATION STRUCTURE

THE DIVISION of a company's total capitalization between senior securities and common stock has an important bearing upon the significance of the earning power per share. A set of hypothetical examples will help make this point clear. For this purpose we shall postulate three industrial companies, A, B and C, each with an earning power (*i.e.*, with average and recent earnings) of $1,000,000. They are identical in all respects save capitalization structure. Company A is capitalized solely at 100,000 shares of common stock. Company B has outstanding $6,000,000 of 4% bonds and 100,000 shares of common stock. Company C has outstanding $12,000,000 of 4% bonds and 100,000 shares of common stock.

We shall assume that the bonds are worth par and that the common stocks are worth about 12 times their per-share earnings. Then the value of the three companies will work out as follows:

Company	Earnings for common stock	Value of common stock	Value of bonds	Total value of company
A	$1,000,000	$12,000,000		$12,000,000
B	760,000	9,000,000	$6,000,000	15,000,000
C	520,000	6,000,000	12,000,000	18,000,000

These results challenge attention. Companies with identical earning power appear to have widely differing values, due solely to the arrangement of their capitalization. But the capitalization structure is itself a matter of voluntary determination by those in control. Does this mean that the fair value of an enterprise can be arbitrarily increased or decreased by changing around the relative proportions of senior securities and common stock?

Can the Value of an Enterprise Be Altered through Arbitrary Variations in Capital Structure? To answer this question properly we must scrutinize our examples with greater care. In working out the value of the three companies we assumed that the bonds would be worth par and that the stocks would be worth twelve times their earnings. Are these assumptions tenable? Let us consider first the case of Company B. If there are no unfavorable elements in the picture, the bonds might well sell at about 100, since the interest is earned four times. Nor would the presence of this funded debt ordinarily prevent the common stock from selling at 12 times its established earning power.

It will be urged however, that, if Company B shares are worth 12 times their earnings, Company A shares should be worth more than this multiple because they have no debt ahead of them. The risk is therefore smaller, and they are less vulnerable to the effect of a shrinkage in earnings than is the stock of Company B. This is obviously true, and yet it is equally true that Company B shares will be more responsive to an *increase* in earnings. The following figures bring this point out clearly:

	Earned per share		Change in earnings per share from base	
Assumed earnings	Co. A	Co. B	Co. A	Co. B
$1,000,000	$10.00	$ 7.60	(Base)	(Base)
750,000	7.50	5.10	−25%	−33%
1,250,000	12.50	10.10	+25%	+33%

Would it not be fair to assume that the greater sensitivity of Company B to a possible decline in profits is offset by its greater sensitivity to a possible increase? Furthermore, if the investor expects higher earnings in the future—and presumably he selects his common stocks with this in mind—would he not be justified in selecting the issue that will benefit more from a given degree of improvement? We are thus led back to the original conclusions that Company B may be worth $3,000,000, or 25% more than Company A due solely to its distribution of capitalization between bonds and stock.

Principle of Optimum Capitalization Structure. Paradoxical as this conclusion may seem, it is supported by the actual behavior of common stocks in the market. If we subject this contradiction to closer analysis, we shall find that it arises from what may be called an *oversimplification* of Company *A*'s capital structure. Company *A*'s common stock evidently contains the two elements represented by the bonds and stock of Company *B*. Part of Company *A*'s stock is at bottom equivalent to Company *B*'s bonds and should *in theory* be valued on the same basis, *i.e.*, 4%. The remainder of Company *A*'s stock should then be valued at 12 times earnings. This theoretical reasoning would give us a combined value of $15,000,000, *i.e.*, an average 6²/₃% basis, for the two components of Company *A* stock, which, of course, is the same as that of Company *B* bonds and stock taken together.

But this $15,000,000 value for Company *A* stock would not ordinarily be realized *in practice*. The obvious reason is that the common-stock buyer will rarely recognize the existence of a "bond component" in a common-stock issue, and in any event, not wanting such a bond component, he is unwilling to pay extra for it.[1] This fact leads us to an important principle, both for the security buyer and for corporate management, *viz.*:

The optimum capitalization structure for any enterprise includes senior securities to the extent that they may safely be issued and bought for investment.

Concretely this means that the capitalization arrangement of Company *B* is preferable to that of Company *A* from the stockholder's standpoint, assuming that in both cases the $6,000,000 bond issue would constitute a sound investment. (This might require, among other things, that the companies show a net working capital of not less than $6,000,000 in accordance with the stringent tests for sound industrial issues recommended in Chap. 13, which is on accompanying CD.) Under such conditions the contribution of the entire capital by the common stockholders may be called an *overconservative set-up*, as it tends generally to make the stockholder's dollar less productive to him than if a reasonable part of the capital were borrowed. An analogous situation holds true in most private businesses, where it is

---

[1] See our discussion of American Laundry Machinery Company on pp. 505–507 of the 1934 edition of this work for an illustration of the possible effect of a change of capital structure from an all-stock to a stock-and-bond combination. Actual changes of this kind were made by American Zinc (through a dividend in preferred stock in 1916) and by Maytag Company through similar distributions in 1928. The usual method of introducing a speculative capitalization structure into a company with a conservative set-up is through formation of a holding company that issues its own senior securities and common stock against acquisition of the operating company's common. *Examples:* Chesapeake Corporation in 1927, Kaufmann Department Stores Securities Corporation in 1925.

recognized as profitable and proper policy to use a conservative amount of banking accommodation for seasonal needs rather than to finance operations entirely by owners' capital.

Corporate Practices Resulting in Shortage of Sound Industrial Bonds. Furthermore, just as it is desirable from the bank's standpoint that sound businesses borrow seasonally, it is also desirable from the standpoint of investors generally that strong industrial corporations raise an appropriate part of their capital through the sale of bonds. Such a policy would increase the number of high-grade bond issues on the market, giving the bond investor a wider range of choice and making it deservedly difficult to sell unsound bonds. Unfortunately the practice of industrial corporations in recent years has tended to produce a shortage of good industrial bond issues. Strong enterprises have in general refrained from floating new bonds and in many cases have retired old ones. But this avoidance of bonded debt by the strongest industrial companies has in fact produced results demoralizing to investors and investment policies in a number of ways. The following observations on this point, written in 1934, are still applicable in good part:

1. It has tended to restrict new industrial-bond financing to companies of weaker standing. The relative scarcity of good bonds impelled investment houses to sell and investors to buy inferior issues, with inevitably disastrous results.

2. The shortage of good bonds also tended to drive investors into the preferred-stock field. For reasons previously detailed (in Chap. XIV) straight preferred stocks are unsound in theory, and they are therefore likely to prove unsatisfactory investment media as a class.

3. The elimination (or virtual elimination) of senior securities in the set-up of many large corporations has, of course, added somewhat to the investment quality of their common stocks, but it has added even more to the investor's demand for these common stocks. This in turn has resulted in a good deal of common-stock buying by people whose circumstances required that they purchase sound bonds. Furthermore it has supplied a superficial justification for the creation of excessive prices for these common stocks; and finally it contributed powerfully to that confusion between investment motives and speculative motives which during 1927–1929 served to debauch so large a proportion of the country's erstwhile careful investors.

Appraisal of Earnings Where Capital Structure Is Top-heavy. In order to carry this theory of capitalization structure a step further, let us examine the case of Company C. We arrived at a valuation of $18,000,000 for this enterprise by assuming that its $12,000,000 bond issue would sell at par and the stock would sell for 12 times its earnings of $5.20 per share. But this assumption as to the price of the bonds is clearly fallacious. Earnings of twice interest charges are not sufficient protection for an industrial bond, and hence investors would be unwise to purchase such an issue at par. In fact this very example supplies a useful demonstration of our contention that a coverage of two times interest is inadequate. If it were ample—as some investors seem to believe—the owners of any reasonably prosperous business, earning 8% on the money invested, could get back their entire capital by selling a 4% bond issue, and they would still have control of the business together with one-half of its earnings. Such an arrangement would be exceedingly attractive for the proprietors but idiotic from the standpoint of those who buy the bonds.

Our Company C example also sheds some light on the effect of the rate of interest on the apparent safety of the senior security. If the $12,000,000 bond issue had carried a 6% coupon, the interest charges of $720,000 would then be earned less than $1^{1}/_{2}$ times. Let us assume that Company D had such a bond issue. An unwary investor, looking at the two exhibits, might reject Company D's 6% bonds as unsafe because their interest coverage was only 1.39 but yet accept the Company C bonds at par because he was satisfied with earnings of twice fixed charges. Such discrimination would be scarcely intelligent. Our investor would be rejecting a bond *merely because* it pays him a generous coupon rate, and he would be accepting another bond *merely because* it pays him a low interest rate. The real point, however, is that the minimum margin of safety behind bond issues must be set high enough to avoid the possibility that safety may even *appear* to be achieved by a mere lowering of the interest rate. The same reasoning would apply of course to the dividend rate on preferred stocks.

Since Company C bonds are not safe, because of the excessive size of the issue, they are likely to sell at a considerable discount from par. We cannot suggest the proper price level for such an issue, but we have indicated in Chap. 26 that a bond speculative because of inadequate safety should not ordinarily be purchased above 70. It is also quite possible that the presence of this excessive bond issue might prevent the stock from selling at 12 times its earnings, because conservative stock buyers would avoid Company C as subject to too great hazard of financial difficulties in the event of untoward developments. The result may well be that, instead of being worth $18,000,000 in the market as originally assumed, the combined bond and stock issues of Company C will sell for less than $15,000,000 (the Company B valuation), or even for less than $12,000,000 (the value of Company A).

As a matter of cold fact, it should be recognized that this unfavorable result may not necessarily follow. If investors are sufficiently careless and if speculators are sufficiently enthusiastic, the securities of Company C may conceivably sell in the market for $18,000,000 or even more. But such a situation would be unwarranted and unsound.[2] Our theory of capitalization structure could not admit a Company C arrangement as in any sense standard or suitable. This indicates that there are definite limits upon the advantages to be gained by the use of senior securities. We have already expressed this fact in our principle of the optimum capitalization structure, for senior securities cease to be an advantage at the point where their amount becomes larger than can safely be issued or bought for investment.

We have characterized the Company A type of capitalization arrangement as "overconservative"; the Company C type may be termed "speculative," whereas that of Company B may well be called "suitable" or "appropriate."

The Factor of Leverage in Speculative Capitalization Structure.
Although a speculative capitalization structure throws all the company's securities outside the pale of investment, it may give the common stock a definite speculative advantage. A 25% increase in the earnings of Company C (from $1,000,000 to $1,250,000) will mean about a 50% increase in the earnings per share of common (from $5.20 to $7.70). Because of this fact there is some tendency for speculatively capitalized enterprises

---

[2] In 1925 Dodge Brothers (motor) securities were sold to the public on the basis of $160,000,000 principal value of bonds and preferred stock and about $50,000,000 market value of common. Net tangible assets were only $80,000,000, and average earnings about $16,000,000. This obviously top-heavy capitalization structure did not militate against the security values at first, but a severe decline in earnings in 1927 soon revealed the unsoundness of the financial setup. (In 1928 the company was taken over by Chrysler.)

to sell at relatively high values in the aggregate during good times or good markets. Conversely, of course, they may be subject to a greater degree of undervaluation in depression. There is, however, a real advantage in the fact that such issues, when selling on a deflated basis, can advance much further than they can decline.

AMERICAN WATER WORKS AND ELECTRIC COMPANY

Item	1921	1923	1924	1929	Ratio of 1929 figures to 1921 figures
Gross earnings*	$20,574	$36,380	$38,356	$54,119	2.63 :1
Net for charges*	6,692	12,684	13,770	22,776	3.44 :1
Fixed charges and preferred dividends*	6,353	11,315	12,780	16,154	2.54 :1
Balance for common*	339	1,369	990	6,622	19.53 :1
1921 basis:†					
Number of shares of common	92,000	100,000	100,000	130,000	1.41 :1
Earned per share	$3.68	$13.69	$9.90	$51.00	13.86 :1
High price of common	6$^1/_2$	44$^3/_4$	209	about 2500	385.00 :1
% earned on high price of common	56.6%	30.6%	4.7%	2.04%	0.037 :1
As reported:					
Number of shares of common	92,000	100,000	500,000	1,657,000	
Earned per share	$3.68	$13.69	$1.98	$4.00	
High price of common	6$^1/_2$	44$^3/_4$	41$^7/_8$	199	

* In thousands.
† Number of shares and price adjusted to eliminate effect of stock dividends and split-ups.

The record of American Water Works and Electric Company common stock between 1921 and 1929 presents an almost fabulous picture of enhancement in value, a great part of which was due to the influence of a highly speculative capitalization structure. Four annual exhibits during this period are summarized in the table above.

The purchaser of 1 share of American Water Works common stock at the high price of 6$^1/_2$ in 1921, if he retained the distributions made in

stock, would have owned about 12^1/$_2$ shares when the common sold at its
high price of 199 in 1929. His $6.50 would have grown to about $2,500.
While the market value of the common shares was thus increasing some
400-fold, the gross earnings had expanded to only 2.6 times the earlier
figure. The tremendously disproportionate rise in the common-stock
value was due to the following elements, in order of importance:

1. A much higher valuation placed upon the per-share earnings of this
issue. In 1921 the company's capitalization was recognized as top-heavy;
its bonds sold at a low price, and the earnings per share of common were
not taken seriously, especially since no dividends were being paid on the
second preferred. In 1929 the general enthusiasm for public-utility shares
resulted in a price for the common issue of nearly 50 times its highest
recorded earnings.

2. The speculative capitalization structure allowed the common
stock to gain an enormous advantage from the expansion of the company's properties and earnings. Nearly all the additional funds needed
were raised by the sale of senior securities. It will be observed that
whereas the gross revenues increased about 160% from 1921 to 1929,
the balance per share of old common stock grew 14-fold during the
same period.

3. The margin of profit improved during these years, as shown by the
higher ratio of net to gross. The speculative capital structure greatly
accentuated the benefit to the common stock from the additional net
profits so derived.[3]

Other Examples: The behavior of speculatively capitalized enterprises
under varying business conditions is well illustrated by the appended
analysis of A. E. Staley Manufacturing Company, manufacturers of corn
products. For comparison there is given also a corresponding analysis of
American Maize Products Company, a conservatively capitalized enterprise in the same field.

The most striking aspect of the Staley exhibit is the extraordinary fluctuation in the yearly earnings per share of common stock. The business
itself is evidently subject to wide variations in net profit, and the effect of

---

[3] See Appendix Note 59, p. 799 on accompanying CD, for data illustrating the reverse
process applied to American Water Works from 1929 through 1938; also for a similar speculative opportunity in United Light and Power Company Preferred Stock in 1935.

these variations on the common stock is immensely magnified by reason of the small amount of common stock in comparison with the senior securities.[4] The large depreciation allowance acts also as the equivalent of a heavy fixed charge. Hence a decline in net before depreciation from $3,266,000 in 1929 to $1,540,000 the next year, somewhat over 50%, resulted in a drop in earnings *per share of common* from $84 to only $3.74. The net profits of American Maize Products were fully as variable, but the small amount of prior charges made the fluctuations in common-stock earnings far less spectacular.

A. E. STALEY

Year	Net before depreciation*	Depreciation*	Fixed charges and pfd. dividends*	Balance for common*	Earned per share
1933	$2,563	$743	$652	$1,168	$55.63
1932	1,546	753	678	114	5.43
1931	892	696	692	496(d)	23.60(d)
1930	1,540	753	708	79	3.74
1929	3,266	743	757	1,766	84.09
1928	1,491	641	696	154	7.35
1927	1,303	531	541	231	11.01
1926	2,433	495	430	1,507	71.77
1925	792	452	358	18(d)	0.87(d)
1924	1,339	419	439	481	22.89

* 000 omitted.

---

[4] In 1934 the company declared a 100% stock dividend, thus doubling the number of shares of common, and in 1937 split the stock 10 for 1 and changed the par value from $100 to $10. These two developments multiplied the outstanding shares by 20. Persistence of the variable factor in the earnings for the common stock is shown by the following per-share figures, based on the 1933 capitalization:

1934	$28.46
1935	2.76(d)
1936	52.88
1937	18.40(d)
1938	38.80
1939	68.00

AMERICAN MAIZE PRODUCTS

Year	Net before depreciation*	Depreciation*	Fixed charges and pfd. dividends*	Balance for common*	Earned per share
1933	$1,022	$301		$721	$2.40
1932	687	299		388	1.29
1931	460	299		161	0.54
1930	1,246	306	22	918	3.06
1929	1,835	312	80	1,443	4.81
1928	906	317	105	484	1.61
1927	400	318	105	23(d)	0.08(d)

* 000 omitted.

CAPITALIZATION (AS OF JANUARY 1933)

Item	A. E. Staley	American Maize Products
6% bonds	($4,000,000* @ 75) $3,000,000	
$7 pfd. stock	(50,000 sh. @ 44) 2,200,000	
Common stock	(21,000 sh. @ 45) 950,000	(300,000 sh. @ 20) $6,000,000
Total capitalization	$6,150,000	$6,000,000
Average earnings, 1927–1932, about	900,000	615,000
% of these earning on 1933 capitalization	14.6%	10.3%†
Average earnings per sh. of common	$14.76	$1.87
% earned on price of common	32.8%	9.4%†
Working capital, Dec. 31, 1932	$3,664,000	$2,843,000
Net assets, Dec. 31, 1932	$15,000,000	$4,827,000

* Deducting estimated amount of bonds in treasury.
† The difference between these two figures is due to the varying treatment of the preferred stock outstanding during 1927–1930. A very small amount of preferred stock remaining in 1931–1933 is ignored in the above calculations.

Speculative Capitalization May Cause Valuation of Total Enterprise at an Unduly Low Figure. The market situation of the Staley securities in January 1933 presents a practical confirmation of our theoretical analysis of Company *C* above. The top-heavy capitalization structure

resulted in a low price for the bonds and the preferred stock, the latter being affected particularly by the temporary suspension of its dividend in 1931. The result was that, instead of showing an increased total value by reason of the presence of senior securities, the company sold in the market at a much lower relative price than the conservatively capitalized American Maize Products. (The latter company showed a normal relationship between average earnings and market value. It should not properly be termed *overconservatively* capitalized because the variations in its annual earnings would constitute a good reason for avoiding any substantial amount of senior securities. A bond or preferred stock issue of very small size, on the other hand, would be of no particular advantage or disadvantage.)

The indication that the A. E. Staley Company was undervalued in January 1933 in comparison with American Maize Products is strengthened by reference to the relative current-asset positions and total resources. Per dollar of net asset values the Staley company was selling only one-third as high as American Maize.

The overdeflation of a speculative issue like Staley common in unfavorable markets creates the possibility of an amazing price advance when conditions improve, because the earnings per share then show so violent an increase. Note that at the beginning of 1927 Staley common was quoted at about 75, and a year later it sold close to 300. Similarly the shares advanced from a low of 33 in 1932 to the equivalent of 320 in 1939.

A Corresponding Example. A more spectacular instance of tremendous price changes for the same reason is supplied by Mohawk Rubber. In 1927 the common sold at 15, representing a valuation of only $300,000 for the junior issue, which followed $1,960,000 of preferred. The company had lost $610,000 in 1926 on $6,400,000 of sales. In 1927 sales dropped to $5,700,000, but there was a net profit of $630,000. This amounted to over $23 per share on the small amount of common stock. The price consequently advanced from its low of 15 in 1927 to a high of 251 in 1928. In 1930 the company again lost $669,000, and the next year the price declined to the equivalent of only $4.

In a speculatively capitalized enterprise, the common stockholders benefit—or have the possibility of benefiting—at the expense of the senior security holders. The common stockholder is operating with a little of his own money and with a great deal of the senior security holder's money; as between him and them it is a case of "Heads I win, tails you lose." This strategic position of the common stockholder with relatively small commitment is an extreme form of what is called "trading on the equity." Using another expression, he may be said to have a "cheap call" on the future profits of the enterprise.

Speculative Attractiveness of "Shoe-string" Common Stocks Considered.

Our discussion of fixed-value investment has emphasized as strongly as possible the disadvantage (amounting to unfairness) that attaches to the senior security holder's position where the junior capital is proportionately slight. The question would logically arise if there are not corresponding *advantages* to the common stock in such an arrangement, from which it gains a very high degree of speculative attractiveness. This inquiry would obviously take us entirely outside the field of common-stock *investment* but would represent an expedition into the realm of intelligent or even scientific speculation.

We have already seen from our A. E. Staley example that in bad times a speculative capitalization structure may react adversely on the market price of both the senior securities and the common stock. During such a period, then, the common stockholders do not derive a present benefit at the expense of the bondholder. This fact clearly detracts from the speculative advantage inherent in such common stocks. It is easy to suggest that these issues be purchased only when they are selling at abnormally low levels due to temporarily unfavorable conditions. But this is really begging the question, because it assumes that the intelligent speculator can consistently detect and wait for these abnormal and temporary conditions. If this were so, he could make a great deal of money regardless of what type of common stock he buys, and under such conditions he might be better advised to select high-grade common stocks at bargain prices rather than these more speculative issues.

Practical Aspects of the Foregoing. To view the matter in a practical light, the purchase of speculatively capitalized common stocks must be considered under general or market conditions that are supposedly normal, *i.e.*, under those which are not obviously inflated or deflated. Assuming (1) diversification, and (2) reasonably good judgment in selecting companies with satisfactory prospects, it would seem that the speculator should be able to profit rather substantially in the long run from commitments of this kind. In making such purchases, partiality should evidently be shown to those companies in which most of the senior capital is in the form of preferred stock rather than bonds. Such an arrangement removes or minimizes the danger of extinction of the junior equity through default in bad times and thus permits the shoe-string common stockholder to maintain his position until prosperity returns. (But just because the preferred-stock contract benefits the common shareholder in this way, it is clearly disadvantageous to the preferred stockholder himself.)

We must not forget, however, the peculiar practical difficulty in the way of realizing the full amount of prospective gain in any one of the purchases. As we pointed out in the analogous case of convertible bonds, as soon as a substantial profit appears the holder is in a dilemma, because he can hold for a further gain only by risking that already accrued. Just as a convertible bond loses its distinctive advantages when the price rises to a point that carries it clearly outside of the straight investment class, so a shoe-string common-stock commitment is transformed into a more and more substantial commitment as the price continues to rise. In our Mohawk Rubber example the intelligent purchaser at 15 could not have expected to hold it beyond 100—even though its quotation did reach 250—because at 100, or before, the shares had lost the distinctive characteristics of a speculatively capitalized junior issue.

Chapter 41

LOW-PRICED COMMON STOCKS. ANALYSIS OF THE SOURCE OF INCOME

LOW-PRICED STOCKS

The characteristics discussed in the preceding chapter are generally thought of by the public in connection with *low-priced stocks*. The majority of issues of the speculatively capitalized type do sell within the low-priced range. The definition of "low-priced" must, of course, be somewhat arbitrary. Prices below $10 per share belong to this category beyond question; those above $20 are ordinarily excluded; so that the dividing line would be set somewhere between $10 and $20.

Arithmetical Advantage of Low-priced Issues. Low-priced common stocks appear to possess an inherent arithmetical advantage arising from the fact they can advance so much more than they can decline. It is a commonplace of the securities market that an issue will rise more readily from 10 to 40 than from 100 to 400. This fact is due in part to the preferences of the speculative public, which generally is much more partial to issues in the 10-to-40 range than to those selling above 100. But it is also true that in many cases low-price common stocks give the owner the advantage of an interest in, or "call" upon, a relatively large enterprise at relatively small expense.

A statistical study of the relative price behavior of industrial stocks in various price groups was presented in the April 1936 issue of *The Journal of Business of the University of Chicago.*[1] The study was devoted to the period 1926–1935[2] and revealed a continuous superiority of diversified,

---

[1] Fritzemeier, Louis H., "Relative Price Fluctuations of Industrial Stocks in Different Price Groups," *loc. cit.*, pp. 133–154.

[2] See pp. 473–474 of the 1934 edition of this work for reference to an earlier study devoted to the relative behavior of low-priced and high-priced issues when purchased at or near the

low-priced issues over diversified, high-priced issues as speculative media. The following quotation from the study summarizes the results and conclusions reached by the author:

> Unless there are serious uncompensated errors in the statistical work here presented, this investigation would seem to establish the existence of certain relationships between price level and price fluctuations which have hitherto gone unreported by students of stock-market phenomena. These relationships may be briefly stated as follows:
>
> 1. Low-price stocks tend to fluctuate relatively more than high-price stocks.
>
> 2. In a "bull" market the low-price stocks tend to go up relatively more than high-price stocks, and they do not lose these superior gains in the recessions which follow. In other words, the downward movement of low-price stocks is less than proportional to their upward movement, when compared with the upward and downward movement of high-price stocks.
>
> *********
>
> Assuming (1) that the future behavior of the various price groups will be similar to their past behavior and (2) that the selection of stocks on the basis of the activity for the current year does not account completely, if at all, for the superior performance of the stocks in the low-price groups, it seems logical to conclude the following:
>
> 1. Low-price industrial stocks offer greater opportunities for speculative profits than high-price industrial stocks.
>
> 2. In case two or more issues of industrial stocks seem to offer equal prospective profits, the speculator should purchase the shares selling at the lowest price.

Some Reasons Why Most Buyers of Low-priced Issues Lose Money.

The pronounced liking of the public for "cheap stocks" would therefore seem to have a sound basis in logic. Yet it is undoubtedly true that most people who buy low-priced stocks lose money on their purchases. Why is this so? The underlying reason is that the public buys issues that are *sold* to it, and the sales effort is put forward to benefit the seller and not the buyer. In consequence the bulk of the low-priced purchases made by the public are of the wrong kind; *i.e.*, they do not provide

---

bottoms of depressions in 1897, 1907, 1914 and 1921. Within its more limited scope this study, published in 1931 by J. H. Holmes and Company, led to conclusions similar to those of Fritzemeier.

the real advantages of this security type. The reason may be either because the companies are in bad financial condition or because the common stock is low-priced in appearance only and actually represents a full or excessive commitment in relation to the size of the enterprise. The latter is preponderantly true of *new* security offerings in the low-priced range. In such cases, a *pseudo*-low price is accomplished by the simple artifice of creating so large a number of shares that even at a few dollars per share the total value of the common issue is excessive. This has been true of mining-stock flotations from of old and was encountered again in the liquor-stock offerings of 1933 and in the airplane issues in 1938–1939.

A *genuinely* low-priced common stock will show an aggregate value for the issue which is small in relation to the company's assets, sales and past or prospective profits. The examples shown herewith will illustrate the difference between a "genuine" and "pseudo-low" price.

Item	Wright-Hargreaves Mines, Ltd. (gold mining)	Barker Bros. Corp. (retail store)
July 1933:		
Price of common stock	7	5
Number of shares outstanding	5,500,000	148,500
Total value of common	$38,500,000	$ 743,000
Preferred stock at par		2,815,000
Preferred stock at market		500,000
Year 1932:		
Sales	$ 3,983,000	$ 8,154,000
Net earnings	2,001,000*	703,000(d)
Period 1924–1932:		
Maximum sales	$ 3,983,000	$16,261,000
Maximum net earnings	2,001,000*	1,100,000
Maximum earnings per share of common	$0.36*	$7.59
Working capital, Dec. 1932	$ 1,930,000	$ 5,010,000
Net tangible assets, Dec. 1932	4,544,000	7,200,000

* Before depletion.

The Wright-Hargreaves issue was low-priced in appearance only, for in fact the price registered a very high valuation for the company as compared with all parts of its financial exhibit. The opposite was true of Barker Brothers because here the $743,000 valuation represented by the common stock was exceedingly small in relation to the size of the enterprise. (Note also that the same statement could be applied to Barker Brothers Preferred, which at its quotation of 18 partook of the qualities of a low-priced common stock.)[3]

Observation of the stock market will show that the stocks of companies facing receivership are likely to be more active than those which are very low in price merely because of poor current earnings. This phenomenon is caused by the desire of insiders to dispose of their holdings before the receivership wipes them out, thus accounting for a large supply of these shares at a low level and also sometimes for unscrupulous efforts to persuade the unwary public to buy them. But where a low-priced stock fulfills our conditions of speculative attractiveness, there is apt to be no pressure to sell and no effort to create buying. Hence the issue is inactive and attracts little public attention. This analysis may explain why the public almost always buys the wrong low-priced issues and ignores the really promising opportunities in this field.

Low Price Coupled with Speculative Capitalization. Speculatively capitalized enterprises, according to our definition, are marked by a relatively large amount of senior securities and a comparatively small issue of common stock. Although in most cases the common stock will sell at a low price per share, it need not necessarily do so if the number of shares is small. In the Staley case, for example (referred to on pp. 515–516) even at $50 per share for the common in 1933 the capitalization structure would still have been speculative, since the bonds and preferred at par would represent over 90% of the total. It is also true that even where there are no senior securities the common stock may have possibilities equivalent to those in a speculatively capitalized enterprise. These possibilities will occur wherever the market value of the common issue-represents a small

---

[3] See Appendix Note 60, p. 800 on accompanying CD, for the sequel to these examples. For a more recent contrast along the same lines the student is invited to compare the showing of Continental Motors Corporation and Gilchrist Company when both were selling at $5 near the close of 1939. Beyond our basic distinction, founded on the relationship between the valuation of the company and its assets and sales, there is here a striking contrast in the earnings record and working-capital position.

amount of money in relation to the size of the business, regardless of how it is capitalized.

To illustrate this point we append a condensed analysis of Mandel Brothers, Inc., and Gimbel Brothers, Inc., two department-store enterprises, as of September 1939.

Item	Gimbel Bros.	Mandel Bros.
September 1939:		
Bonds at par	$26,753,000	
Preferred stock	197,000 sh. @ 50	
	$9,850,000	
Common stock	977,000 sh. @ 8	297,000 sh. @ 5
	$7,816,000	$1,485,000
Total capitalization	$44,419,000	$1,485,000
Results for 12 months to July 31, 1939:		
Sales	$87,963,000	$17,883,000
Net before interest	1,073	155,000
Balance for common	*1,105(d)*	155,000
Earned per share	*1.13(d)*	0.52
Period 1934–1938*:		
Maximum sales (1937)	$100,081,000	$19,378,000
Maximum net earnings (1937) for common	2,032,000	414,000
Maximum earnings per share of common (1937)	2.08	1.33
High price of common	29³/₈ (1937)	18 (1936)
Average earnings per share of common	0.23	0.46
Jan. 31, 1939:		
Net current assets	$22,916,000	$ 4,043,000
Net tangible assets	75,614,000	6,001,000
Rents paid 1937	1,401,000	867,000

* Based on report for succeeding Jan. 31.

Gimbel Brothers presents a typical picture of a speculatively capitalized enterprise. On the other hand Mandel Brothers has no senior securities ahead of the common, but despite this fact the relatively small market value of the entire issue imparts to the shares the same sort of speculative possibilities (though in somewhat lesser degree) as are found in the Gimbel Brothers set-up. Note, however, that the rental payments of Mandel Brothers are proportionately much higher than those of Gimbel Brothers and that these rental charges are equivalent in good part to senior securities.

Large Volume and High Production Cost Equivalent to Speculative Capital Structure. This example should lead us to widen our conception of a speculatively situated common stock. The speculative or *marginal* position may arise from any cause that reduces the percentage of gross available for the common to a subnormal figure and that therefore serves to create a subnormal value for the common stock in relation to the volume of business. Unusually high operating or production costs have the identical effect as excessive senior charges in cutting down the percentage of gross available for common. The following hypothetical examples of three copper producers will make this point more intelligible and also lead to some conclusions on the subject of large output versus low operating costs.

Item	Company A	Company B	Company C
Capitalization:			
6% Bonds		$50,000,000	
Common stock	1,000,000 sh.	1,000,000 sh.	1,000,000 sh.
Output	100,000,000 lb.	150,000,000 lb.	150,000,000 lb.
Cost of production (before interest)	7¢	7¢	9¢
Interest charge per pound		2¢	
Total cost per pound	7¢	9¢	9¢
A			
Assumed price of copper	10¢	10¢	
Profit per pound	3¢	1¢	
Output per share	100 lb.	150 lb.	
Profit per share	$3	$1.50	
Value of stock at 10 times earnings	$30	$15	
Output per $1 of market value of stock	3¹/₃ lb.	10 lb.	
B			
Assumed price of copper	13¢	13¢	
Profit per pound	6¢	4¢	
Profit per share	$6	$6	
Value per share at ten times earnings	$60	$60	
Output per $1 of market price of stock	1²/₃ lb.	2¹/₂ lb.	

It is scarcely necessary to point out that the higher production cost of Company C will have exactly the same effect as the bond-interest requirement of Company B (assuming output and production costs to continue as stated).

General Principle Derived. The foregoing table is perhaps more useful in showing concretely the inverse relationship that usually exists between profit per unit and output per dollar of stock value.

The general principle may be stated that the lower the unit cost the lower the production per dollar of market value of stock and *vice versa.* Since Company A has a 7-cent cost, its stock naturally sells at a higher price *per pound of output* than Company C with its 9-cent cost. Conversely, Company C produces more pounds per dollar of stock value than Company A. This fact is not without significance from the standpoint of speculative technique. When a rise in the price of the commodity occurs, there will ordinarily be a larger advance, percentagewise, in the shares of high-cost producers than in the shares of low-cost producers. The foregoing table indicates that a rise in the price of copper from 10 to 13 cents would increase the value of Company A shares by 100% and the value of Company B and C shares by 300%. Contrary to the general impression in Wall Street, the stocks of high-cost producers are more logical commitments than those of the low-cost producers when the buyer is convinced that a rise in the price of the product is imminent and he wishes to exploit this conviction to the utmost.[4] Exactly the same advantage attaches to the purchase of speculatively capitalized common stocks when a pronounced improvement in sales and profits is confidently anticipated.

THE SOURCES OF INCOME

The "source of income" will ordinarily be thought of as meaning the same thing as the "type of business." This consideration enters very largely into the basis on which the public will value the earnings per share shown by a given common stock. Different "multipliers" are used for different sorts of enterprise, but we must point out that these distinctions are themselves subject to

---

[4] The action of the market in advancing Company B shares from 15 to 60 because copper rises from 10 to 13 cents is in itself extremely illogical, for there is ordinarily no warrant for supposing that the higher metal price will be *permanent.* However, since the market does in fact behave in this irrational fashion, the speculator must recognize this behavior in his calculation.

change with the changing times.[5] Prior to the World War the railroad stocks were valued most generously of all, because of their supposed stability. In 1927–1929 the public-utility group sold at the highest ratio to earnings, because of their record of steady growth. Between 1933 and 1939 adverse legislation and, in particular, the fear of government competition greatly reduced the relative popularity of the utility stocks. The most liberal valuations have recently been accorded to the large and well-entrenched industrial enterprises which were able to maintain substantial earnings during the depression and are considered to possess favorable long-term prospects. Because of these repeated variations in relative behavior and popularity, security analysis must hesitate to prescribe any definitive rules for valuing one type of business as against another. It is a truism to say that the more impressive the record and the more promising the prospects of stability and growth the more liberally the per-share earnings should be valued, subject always to our principle that a multiplier higher than about 20 (*i.e.*, an "earnings basis" of less than 5%) will carry the issue out of the *investment* price range.

A Special Phase: Three Examples. A more fruitful field for the technique of analysis is found in those cases where the source of income must be studied in relation to specific assets owned by the company, instead of in relation merely to the general nature of the business. This point may be quite important when a substantial portion of the income accrues from investment holdings or from some other fixed and dependable source. Three examples will be used to illuminate this rather subtle aspect of common-stock analysis.

1. *Northern Pipe Line Company.* For the years 1923–1925 the Northern Pipe Line Company reported earnings and dividends as follows:

Year	Net earnings	Earned per share*	Dividend paid
1923	$308,000	$7.70	$10, plus $15 extra
1924	214,000	5.35	8
1925	311,000	7.77	6

* Capitalization, 40,000 shares of common stock.

---

[5] See Cowles, Alfred, 3d, and associates (*Common Stock Indexes*, 1871–1937), pp. 43–46, 404–418, Bloomington, Ind., 1938, for a study of earnings-price ratios for different industrial groups in successive years from 1871 through 1937. Ratios for 1934–1938 and for 1936–1938 are supplied in our analysis of the New York Stock Exchange industrial list in Appendix Note 61, p. 800 on accompanying CD.

In 1924 the shares sold as low as 72, in 1925 as low as 67$^1/_2$ and in 1926 as low as 64. These prices were on the whole somewhat less than ten times the reported earnings and reflected a lack of enthusiasm for the shares, due to a pronounced decline in profits from the figures of preceding years and also to the reductions in the dividend.

Analysis of the income account however, would have revealed the following division of the *sources of income:*[6]

Income	1923		1924		1925	
	Total	Per share	Total	Per share	Total	Per share
Earned from:						
Pipe-line operations	$179,000	$4.48	$ 69,000	$1.71	$103,000	$2.57
Interest and rents	164,000	4.10	159,000	3.99	170,000	4.25
Nonrecurrent items	dr. 35,000	dr. 0.88	dr. 14,000	0.35	cr. 38,000	cr. 0.95
	$308,000	$7.70	$214,000	$5.35	$311,000	$7.77

This income account is exceptional in that the greater part of the profits were derived from sources other than the pipe-line business itself. About $4 per share were regularly received in interest on investments and rentals. The balance sheet showed holdings of nearly $3,200,000 (or $80 per share) in Liberty Bonds and other gilt-edged marketable securities, on which the interest income was about 4%.

This fact meant that a special basis of valuation must be applied to the per-share earnings, inasmuch as the usual "ten-times-earnings" basis would result in a nonsensical conclusion. Gilt-edged investments of $80 per share would yield an income of $3.20 per share, and at ten times earnings this $80 would be "worth" only $32 per share, a *reductio ad absurdum*. Obviously, that part of the Northern Pipe Line income that was derived from its bond holdings should logically be valued at a higher basis than the portion derived from the fluctuating pipe-line business. A sound valuation of Northern Pipe Line stock would therefore have to proceed along the lines suggested below. The pipe-line earnings would have to be valued at a low basis because of their unsatisfactory trend. The interest

---

[6] Although the company's reports to its stockholders contained very little information, complete financial and operating data were on file with the Interstate Commerce Commission and open to public inspection.

and rental income must presumably be valued on a basis corresponding with the actual value of the assets producing the income. This analysis indicated clearly that, at the price of 64 in 1926, Northern Pipe Line stock was selling considerably below its intrinsic value.[7]

Average 1923–1925*		Valuation basis	Value per share
Earned per share from pipe line.	$2.92	15% (6²/₃ times earnings)	$ 20
Earned per share from interest and rentals	4.10	5% (20 times earnings)	80
Total	$7.02		$100

* The nonrecurrent profits and losses are not taken into account.

2. *Lackawanna Securities Company.* This company was organized to hold a large block of Glen Alden Coal Company 4% bonds formerly owned by the Delaware, Lackawanna and Western Railroad Company, and its shares were distributed pro rata to the Delaware, Lackawanna and Western stockholders. The Securities Company had outstanding 844,000 shares of common stock. On December 31, 1931 its sole asset—other than about $1 per share in cash—consisted of $51,000,000 face value of Glen Alden 4% first mortgage bonds. For the year 1931, the income account was as follows:

Interest received on Glen Alden bonds $2,084,000
Less:
    Expenses 17,000
    Federal taxes 250,000
Balance for stock 1,817,000
Earned per share $2.15

Superficially, the price of 23 in 1932 for a stock earning $2.15 did not appear out of line. But these earnings were derived, not from ordinary commercial or manufacturing operations, but from the holding of a bond

---

[7] A parallel situation existed in the case of Davis Coal and Coke Company prior to the distribution of $50 per share to stockholders out of its large holdings of government bonds in 1937–1938. Shortly prior to this action the stock had sold at 35. The student can see from the annual reports that the average earnings of $2.06 per share and average dividends of $2.56 in 1934–1937 came entirely from sources other than the coal business.

issue which presumably constituted a high-grade investment. (In 1931
the Glen Alden Coal Company earned $9,550,000 available for interest
charges of $2,151,000, thus covering the bond requirements 4¹/₂ times.)
By valuing this interest income on about a 10% basis the market was in
fact valuing the Glen Alden bonds at only 37 cents on the dollar. (The
price of 23 for a share of Lackawanna Securities was equivalent to $60
face value of Glen Alden bonds at 37, plus $1 in cash)

Here again, as in the Northern Pipe Line example, analysis would
show convincingly that the customary ten-times-earnings basis resulted
in a glaring undervaluation of this specially situated issue.

TOBACCO PRODUCTS CORPORATION

Item	Price: December 1931	Market value
Capitalization		
2,240,000 shares of 7% Class A (par $20)	$6	$13,440,000
3,300,000 shares common	2¹/₄	7,425,000
Total		$20,825,000
Net income for the year 1931		about $2,200,000
Earned per share of Class A		about $1
Earned for common after Class A dividends		nil
Dividend paid on Class A		$0.80

3. *Tobacco Products Corporation of Virginia.* In this example, as in the
other two, the company was selling in the market for about ten times the
latest reported earnings. But the 1931 earnings of Tobacco Products were
derived entirely from a lease of certain of its assets to American Tobacco
Company, which provided for an annual rental of $2,500,000 for 99 years
from 1923. Since the American Tobacco Company was able to meet its
obligation without question, this annual rental income was equivalent to
interest on a high-grade investment. Its value was therefore much more
than ten times the income therefrom. This meant that the market valuation of the Tobacco Products stock issues in December 1931 was far less
than was justified by the actual position of the company. (The value of
the lease was in fact calculated to be about $35,600,000 on an amortized
basis. The company also owned a large amount of United Cigar Stores'

stock, which later proved to be practically worthless, but these additional holdings did not, of course, detract from the value of its American Tobacco lease.)

Relative Importance of Situations of This Kind. The field of study represented by the foregoing examples is not important quantitatively, because, after all, only a very small percentage of the companies examined will fall within this group. Situations of this kind arise with sufficient frequency, however, to give this discussion practical value. It should be useful also in illustrating again the wide technical difference between the critical approach of security analysis and the highly superficial reactions and valuations of the stock market.

Two Lines of Conduct Suggested. When it can be shown that certain conditions, such as those last discussed, tend to give rise to undervaluations in the market, two different lines of conduct are thereby suggested. We have first an opportunity for the securities analyst to detect these undervaluations and eventually to profit from them. But there is also the indication that the financial set-up that causes this undervaluation is erroneous and that the stockholders' interests require the correction of this error. The very fact that a company constituted like Northern Pipe Line or Lackawanna Securities tends to sell in the market far below its true value proves as strongly as possible that the whole arrangement is wrong from the stand-point of the owners of the business.

At the bottom of these cases there is a basic principle of consistency involved. It is inconsistent for most of the capital of a pipe-line enterprise actually to be employed in the ownership of gilt-edged bonds. The whole set-up of Lackawanna Securities was also inconsistent, because it replaced a presumably high-grade bond issue, which investors might be willing to buy at a fair price, by a nondescript stock issue which no one would purchase except at an exceptionally low price. (In addition a heavy and needless burden of corporate income tax was involved, as was true in the Tobacco Products case.)

Illogical arrangements of this kind should be recognized by the real parties in interest, *i.e.*, the stockholders, and they should insist that the anomaly be rectified. This was finally done in the three examples just given. In the case of Northern Pipe Line the capital not needed in the pipe-line business was returned to the stockholders by means of special distributions aggregating $70 per share. The Lackawanna Securities Company was entirely dissolved and the Glen Alden bonds in its treasury distributed pro rata to the stockholders in lieu of their stock. Finally, the Tobacco Products Corporation was recapitalized on a basis by which $6^{1}/_{2}\%$ bonds were issued against the American Tobacco lease, so that this asset of fixed value was represented by a fixed-value security (which later were redeemed at par) instead of by shares of stock in a corporation subject to highly speculative influences. By means of these corporate rearrangements the real values were speedily established in the market price.[8]

The situations that we have just analyzed required a transfer of attention from the income account figures to certain related features revealed in the balance sheet. Hence the foregoing topic—Sources of Income— carries us over into our next field of inquiry: The Balance Sheet.

---

[8] The student is invited to consider two further examples illustrating this point in 1939, *viz.*

1. Westmoreland Coal Company, selling at 8 although the company held some $18 per share in cash assets alone. This case is broadly similar to our Davis Coal and Coke example, although there were some differences. See discussion of this company on pp. 588–589.

2. American Cigarette and Cigar. In this case there is also a long-term lease to American Tobacco Company (as in the Tobacco Products example), but the situation is complicated by the company's own operations, which have produced losses, and by ownership of other assets.

Attention is drawn also to our discussion of Lehigh Coal and Navigation Company on p. 451, in which we suggested that the mining losses were perhaps inseparable from the large income from lease of the railroad.

PART VI

BALANCE-SHEET ANALYSIS. IMPLICATIONS OF ASSET VALUES

DECONSTRUCTING THE BALANCE SHEET

BY BRUCE GREENWALD

The enduring value of *Security Analysis* rests on certain critical ideas developed by Graham and Dodd that were then, and remain, fundamental to any well-conceived investment strategy. The first of these is the distinction between "investment" and "speculation" as defined by Graham and Dodd:

> An investment operation is one which, upon thorough analysis, promises safety of principal and a satisfactory return. Operations not meeting these requirements are speculative. (p. 106)

The critical parts of this definition are "thorough analysis" and "safety of principal and a satisfactory return." Nothing about these requirements has changed since 1934.

A second related idea is that of focusing on the intrinsic value of a security. It is, according to Graham and Dodd,

> that value which is justified by the facts, e.g., the assets, earnings, dividends, [and] definite prospects, as distinct, let us say, from market quotations established by market manipulation or distorted by psychological excesses. (p. 64)

In an ideal world, intrinsic value would be the true value of a security; in today's language it would be the present discounted value of the expected future cash flows it generates. If these expected cash flows and an appropriate discount rate could be calculated perfectly from the available facts, then the intrinsic and true values would be the same. However, Graham and Dodd recognized that this was never possible. "Inadequate or incorrect data and [the] uncertainties of the future" meant that intrinsic value would always be "an elusive concept."

Nevertheless, thorough investigation of intrinsic value was, in this view, central to any investment process worthy of the name. It served first of all to organize examination and use of the available information, ensuring that the relevant facts would be brought to bear and irrelevant noise ignored. Second, it would produce an appreciation of the range of uncertainty associated with any particular intrinsic value calculation. Graham and Dodd recognized that even a very imperfect intrinsic value would be useful in making investment decisions. In their words,

> It needs only to establish that the value is adequate—e.g., to protect a bond or justify a stock purchase—or else that the value is considerably higher or considerably lower than the market price . . . [and] the degree of indistinctness may be expressed by a very hypothetical "range of approximate value," which would grow wider as the uncertainty of the picture increased. (pp. 66–67)

The purchase of securities should then be made only at prices far enough below the intrinsic value to provide a margin of safety that would offer appropriate protection against this "indistinctness" in the calculated intrinsic value. In essence, what Graham and Dodd required was that an investor, as opposed to a speculator, should know as far as possible the value of any security purchased and also the degree of uncertainty attached to that value. An investment would be made only at a price that provided a sufficient margin of safety to compensate for the uncertainty involved. As a prescription for obtaining "protection of principal and a satisfactory return," this approach has obvious advantages over almost any conceivable alternative.

The compelling logic of these foundations is one source of the continuing relevance of *Security Analysis*. But the book also provides a detailed roadmap of what a "thorough analysis" looks like that is exemplary in its completeness.

With regard to common stock investments, Graham and Dodd examine the roles of both present and future prospects (with an appropriately skeptical view of the latter). They consider the implications of the quantitative analyses of financial statements and qualitative appreciations of less easily quantifiable factors, like management. In the key area of quantitative analysis, they look comprehensively at all financial statements, including most notably a firm's balance sheet.

In this they were at odds with their contemporaries. In describing those practices, Graham and Dodd noted,

> We find little beyond the rather indefinite concept that "a good stock is a good investment." "Good" stocks are those of either (1) leading companies with satisfactory records, . . . or (2) any well-financed enterprise believed to have especially attractive prospects of increased future earnings. . . . Balance-sheet values are considered to be entirely out of the picture. Average [historical] earnings have little significance when there is a marked trend. The so-called "price-earnings ratio" is applied variously, sometimes to the past, sometimes to the present, and sometimes to the near future. (p. 29)

This description might have been written today. So-called price-earnings ratios continue to dominate valuation discussions. They are applied even more "variously" than in the past; now they include the ratio of a stock's price to its earnings before interest and taxes (EBIT) and/or more perniciously the ratio of a stock's price to its earnings before interest, taxes, depreciation, and amortization (EBITDA). Balance sheets are once again almost "entirely out of the picture." Today, as in 1934, a "thorough" analysis of intrinsic value encompassing all the relevant information remains the exception rather than the rule.

With respect to the balance sheet, Graham and Dodd describe four fundamental areas of usefulness. First, the balance sheet identifies the quantity and nature of resources tied up in a business. For an economically viable enterprise, these resources are the basis of its returns. In a competitive environment, a firm without resources cannot generally expect to earn any significant profits. If an enterprise is not economically viable, then the balance sheet can be used to identify the resources that can be recovered in liquidation and how much cash the resources might return.

Second, the resources on a balance sheet provide a basis for analyzing the nature and stability of sources of income. As Graham and Dodd note,

> There are indeed certain presumptions in favor of purchases far below asset value and against those made at a high premium above it. . . . A business that sells at a premium does so because it earns a large return upon its capital; this large return attracts competition, and, generally speaking, it is not likely to continue indefinitely. Conversely, in the case of a business selling at a large discount because of abnormally low earnings. The absence of new competition, the withdrawal of old competition from the field and other natural economic forces may tend eventually to improve the situation and restore a normal rate of profit on the investment. (pp. 557–558)

Here, they recognize that earnings on assets that are well in excess of a company's cost of capital will be sustainable only under special circumstances. Thus, earnings estimates will be more realistic and accurate if they are supported by appropriate asset values. Earnings without such support are likely to be of short duration and, thus, of less value than earnings protected by the necessary returns on assets in place.

Third, the liabilities side of the balance sheet, which identifies sources of funding, describes the financial condition of the firm. A high level of short-term debt (or long-term debt that expires in the near future) indi-

cates a possibility of debilitating financial distress. Under these circumstances, even a slight impairment in profits may lead to significant permanent loss in the value of a business.

Fourth, the evolution of the balance sheet over time provides a check
on the quality of earnings. Today, this is covered, in principle, by the
statement of cash flows, which should reconcile revenue and cost flows
with changes in overall financial position. However, it remains true, as
Graham and Dodd noted, that

> the form of the balance sheet is better standardized than the income
> statement [or the statement of cash flows] and it does not offer such fre-
> quent grounds for criticism. (p. 93)

A balance sheet is a snapshot of a company's assets and liabilities at
a particular time. It can be checked for accuracy and value at that
moment. This places significant constraints on the degree to which the
assets and liabilities can be manipulated. In contrast, flow variables such
as revenue and earnings measure changes over time that by their nature
are evanescent. If they are to be monitored, they must be monitored
over an extended period. In 1934, and today, this fundamental difference
accounts for the superior reliability (in theory) of balance sheet figures.
Indeed, as we will discuss later, while the stock market was celebrating
WorldCom's earnings growth in the late 1990s, signs of financial stress
were already showing up in the balance sheet, stresses that would eventually lead to one of the largest bankruptcies in history as measured by
the face value of the company's debts.

Thorough Analysis

The special importance that Graham and Dodd placed on balance sheet
valuations remains one of their most important contributions to the idea
of what constitutes a "thorough" analysis of intrinsic value. It is also,

unfortunately, one of their most frequently overlooked contributions outside the relatively small community of value investors.

The reason that the balance sheet is often ignored goes back to the times that produced *Security Analysis*. Back then, the economy and businesses were operating under severely depressed conditions. As a result, Graham and Dodd went to balance sheets to determine liquidation values or, as a proxy for these, current assets minus all liabilities. The logic behind this predisposition was compelling and conservative. If a company could be bought at a price well below its liquidation value, then it seemed unambiguously to be a bargain. Earnings could pick up because of either an improvement in a firm's industry environment (competition eases or demand recovers) or better management. If the earnings improvement produced a market value above liquidation value, all well and good. On the other hand, if such positive earnings developments failed to materialize and if this happened before the liquidation value of the firm was significantly damaged, then the company could be liquidated and the proceeds distributed to its shareholders. In either case, the shareholders who bought below liquidation value would earn a "satisfactory return" on their investment.

The only risk, of which Graham and Dodd were well aware, was that management would continue to operate the firm unprofitably and, in the process, dissipate the value of the assets. Thus, they advocated their own version of shareholder activism as a necessary complement to this kind of investing. As they wrote,

> The choice of a common stock is a single act; its ownership is a continuing process. Certainly there is just as much reason to exercise care and judgment in *being* a stockholder as in *becoming* a stockholder. It is a notorious fact, however, that the typical American stockholder is the most docile and apathetic animal in captivity. (p. 575)

Taken as a whole, this approach was unimpeachable and, in its time, successful in practice.

Since then the practice of buying below liquidation value has been undermined by two factors. First, the rapid rise in tax rates post-1940 has meant that strategies like this one, which have often involved realizing short-term gains over relatively short periods, have incurred high tax costs. Second, and more importantly, opportunities to buy stocks at prices below liquidation value, which were abundant in the 1930s, have effectively disappeared in the long-term prosperity that has followed. Relatively few industries in recent times have become economically non-viable and hence candidates for liquidation. This reality has been embodied in the general level of stock prices, with the result that Graham and Dodd's much beloved "net nets"—that is, companies selling below the value of their current assets less all liabilities—are rare. And, when net nets are available, their second requirement—namely, that management not be dissipating those assets at a rapid rate—is seldom met.

However, the broader lessons that led Graham and Dodd to focus on the balance sheets of firms continue to apply, with extensions that are much within the spirit of their original approach. First, it is now recognized that for economically viable firms, assets wear out or become obsolete and have to be replaced. Thus, replacement value—the lowest possible cost of reproducing a firm's net assets by the competitors who are best positioned to do it—continues to serve the role that Graham and Dodd recognized. If projected profit levels for a firm imply a return on assets well above the cost of capital, then competitors will be drawn in. That, in turn, will drive down profits and with them the value of the firm. Thus, earnings power unsupported by asset values—measured as reproduction values—will, absent special circumstances, always be at risk from erosion due to competition. Both "safety of principal" and the promise of "a satisfactory return," therefore, require that "thorough" investors support their earnings projections with a careful assessment of the replacement values of a firm's assets. Investors who do this will have an advantage over those who do not, and they should outperform these less thorough investors in the long run.

What appears to have deterred Graham and Dodd from considering the replacement value of assets was the potential difficulty of calculating them. They chose to focus on the wealth of new financial information made available through the establishment of the Securities and Exchange Commission. With today's computers, that information can be obtained and digested almost instantaneously. Moreover, industry reports and trade publications, many of them available online, provide a wealth of information on asset values that was inconceivable to Graham and Dodd.

For example, the cost estimates of adding to existing reserves of oil and gas are widely available, at least for U.S. companies. So are estimates of recoverable deposits. As a result, investors today can calculate the values of resource companies' holdings with a precision that was unattainable in the authors' time. Physical property and equipment can also be valued with a higher degree of accuracy. For real estate, assessors with access to extensive transactions data can quickly and cheaply estimate the cost of purchasing comparable properties.

For other plant and equipment, consulting engineers and industry experts can provide this information. Using these sources, the cost of adding aluminum fabricating capacity to existing plants could be estimated at about $1,000 per ton per year. Existing capacity was available to handle any foreseeable demand. The then current earnings of aluminum fabricators lead to market valuations which implied that their existing capacity was worth well in excess of $1,000 per ton per year. The result: a race to build new capacity to take advantage of the potential earnings to be had in the fabricating business. This overexpansion resulted in falling earnings and lower stock prices. Such companies proved to be unsatisfactory investments. You could have anticipated this development only through a thorough analysis of the balance sheet.

Another area of difficulty that Graham and Dodd recognized was the valuation of intangible assets—product portfolios, customer relationships, trained workers, brand recognition—many of which do not even appear on a firm's balance sheet. But today available information sometimes allows these balance sheet items to be usefully estimated. Some of this information comes from financial statements. For example, the cost of replicating product portfolios, assuming these are not protected by patents, can be estimated using historical research and development data both from a company itself or other companies in its industry.

This analysis can be supplemented by expert information. Investment initiatives—whether new products, new store openings, or brand launches—are almost always based on detailed business plans. These plans identify the costs of such initiatives with reasonable accuracy and the benefits more fancifully. Investors can use these data to estimate the cost of producing intangible assets. Industry managers with substantial experience will be able to estimate such costs.

More importantly, many intangible assets trade just like real property. Cable franchises, clothing brands, new drug discoveries, store chains, and even music labels are bought by sophisticated buyers (usually larger companies) from sophisticated sellers (usually smaller companies). The prices paid in these private market transactions are presumably made with the alternative cost of internal development in mind. Thus, if a company like Liz Claiborne buys a brand that is similar to its own in-house brands for 50 cents per dollar of sales, then presumably this is reasonably close—but lower than—the cost of reproducing its own brands. These private market values are often used by sophisticated investors to price intangible assets.

Once a thorough analysis of asset and earnings power value is complete, there are three possible situations. The first is one in which the asset value of a company exceeds the value of its foreseeable earnings. That tells you the assets are not being used to full advantage by management. Here, the critical factor for value investors is the prospect of some catalyst that will alter either the behavior or identity of current management. Graham and Dodd were aware of this although they were not cognizant of the range of interventions available to activist investors today.

A second possibility is that earnings power may exceed the asset value of a company. To maintain those superior profits, there needs to be some economic factors to protect the firm from competition. Today, these factors are referred to as "moats," franchises, barriers to entry, or competitive advantages. What they look like and how they can be assessed is an essential part of modern income statement analysis. However, even in this case where asset values are least relevant, they do provide useful information about the value a firm will retain if the factors erode in the future.

The third case is one in which the earnings power and asset value of a firm are approximately equal. This is the circumstance that should hold with reasonable management and no special protections from competition. If qualitative judgments support such conclusions, then the asset value provides a critical check on the validity of earnings projections. A thorough asset valuation then helps to provide a complete picture of what an investor is getting for a security and helps that investor settle with confidence on an appropriate margin of safety.

Beyond these specific uses of asset valuations in current practice, there is one final inescapable area in which asset values must be used. Firms often have some assets—most notably cash—that are superfluous to the operation of their basic businesses. Such assets do not usually contribute to operating earnings, but they may represent an important part of the intrinsic value of a purchased security. The value of these assets must be added to any earnings-based value estimate (after appropriate subtraction of their interest income so as not to double count). Performing a comprehensive asset valuation ensures that they are not forgotten.

WorldCom: A Case Study

The financial statements of WorldCom, the telecom giant whose bankruptcy filing in the summer of 2002 was at its time the largest ever, illustrate the usefulness of a balance sheet analysis for tracking the financial condition of companies. Indeed, anyone who had been studying the balance sheet in the few years ahead of the bankruptcy would have suspected the company would come to no good end. For instance, in the middle of 1999, WorldCom had an equity market value of $125 billion. This compared to a year-end 1999 book value of $51.2 billion, which had been created almost entirely by issuing shares for acquisitions, notably $12 billion for MFS Communications in 1996 and $30 billion for MCI in 1997. Retained earnings over the company's 15-year history were negligible, so over 85% of the book value was goodwill and other intangibles. The ratio of market value to tangible net equity was in excess of 15. Such ratios will vary by industry, but in this case, 15 is ridiculously high.

How valuable were those intangibles? Not worth as much as the company said because they included neither significant patents nor developed process technologies. Even more important, WorldCom's business was characterized by high rates of customer churn and vigorous price competition for its telecommunications and data transmission services. Nor did there appear to be large barriers to entry that might have supported a market value significantly in excess of reproduction value, or what it would cost to reproduce the network. WorldCom's markets were characterized by many new entrants (including those companies acquired by WorldCom) and vigorous expansion by powerful existing competitors like AT&T. If anything, to the extent that economies of scale were relevant, WorldCom would have been operating at a significant competitive disadvantage to its larger competitor, AT&T.

However, what is more remarkable than the improbable market value placed on WorldCom's assets is the detailed story told by the evolution of its balance sheet. From year-end 1999 to year-end 2000, net property, plant, and equipment increased by 27%, or about $8 billion. In contrast, revenues increased by only 8%. That raised the question, why was such an aggressive investment program underway at the company? In fact, the investment figures turned out to have been fraudulently inflated by booking operating expenses as investments. However, even if they had not been fraudulent, the aggressive acceleration in property, plant, and equipment growth (up from about $5 billion in 1999) in the face of decelerating revenue growth should have raised questions about the management's judgment. The likelihood of a bad outcome from this insouciant attitude toward overexpansion should have been apparent.

Over the course of 2001, these consequences became clearly evident. During 2001, WorldCom's short-term debt almost entirely disappeared as current debt liabilities fell from $7.2 billion to $172 million. In marked contrast, long-term debt rose by about $12.5 billion. In fact, it actually increased by about $14 billion since an examination of the balance sheet footnotes indicated that more than $1 billion of additional long-term debt had disappeared by the accounting expedient of deconsolidating the subsidiary responsible for that debt. The fact that, in the face of now-declining revenues, WorldCom felt that it needed an additional $7 billion in debt financing—all of it long term—should have set off an alarm with any investor who bothered to look at the balance sheet.

What happened? In 2000, WorldCom's management lost control of its finances, making at best a highly risky bet on future revenue growth and at worst a calculated effort to disguise deteriorating operating margins by capitalizing expenses. In 2001, WorldCom scrambled for long-term financing, by which the company hoped to give management many years to solve problems. There was really no choice since attempting to sell equity in the face of a falling stock price would have sent a disastrous signal to the market. The primary vehicle WorldCom used was an

$11.9 billion debt sale to the public in May 2001, underwritten by financial institutions that justified the issue in terms of future earnings and cash flow.

If these institutions and their customers had followed Graham's advice to look carefully at the WorldCom balance sheet, they would have known better. They might not have fully anticipated the fraud and subsequent bankruptcy of WorldCom, but they would have seen enough to avoid both its stock and bonds as investments unlikely to provide either protection of principal or promise of a satisfactory return.

Chapter 42

BALANCE-SHEET ANALYSIS.
SIGNIFICANCE OF BOOK VALUE

ON NUMEROUS OCCASIONS prior to this point we have expressed our conviction that the balance sheet deserves more attention than Wall Street has been willing to accord it for many years past. By way of introduction to this section of our work, let us list five types of information and guidance that the investor may derive from a study of the balance sheet:

1. It shows how much capital is invested in the business.
2. It reveals the ease or stringency of the company's financial condition, *i.e.*, the working-capital position.
3. It contains the details of the capitalization structure.
4. It provides an important check upon the validity of the reported earnings.
5. It supplies the basis for analyzing the sources of income.

In dealing with the first of these functions of the balance sheet, we shall begin by presenting certain definitions. The *book value* of a stock is the value of the assets applicable thereto as shown in the balance sheet. It is customary to restrict this value to the tangible assets, *i.e.*, to eliminate from the calculation such items as good-will, trade names, patents, franchises, leaseholds. The book value is also referred to as the "asset value," and sometimes as the "tangible-asset value," to make clear that intangibles are not included. In the case of common stocks, it is also frequently termed the "equity."

Computation of Book Value. The *book value per share* of a common stock is found by adding up all the tangible assets, subtracting all liabilities and stock issues ahead of the common and then dividing by the number of shares.

In many cases the following formula will be found to furnish a short cut to the answer:

Book Value per share of common

$$= \frac{\text{Common Stock} + \text{Surplus Items} - \text{Intangibles}}{\text{Number of shares outstanding}}$$

By Surplus Items are meant not only items clearly marked as surplus but also premiums on capital stock and such reserves as are really part of the surplus. This would include, for example, reserves for preferred-stock retirement, for plant improvement, and for contingencies (unless known to be actually needed). Reserves of this character may be termed "Voluntary Reserves."

CALCULATION OF BOOK VALUE OF UNITED STATES STEEL COMMON ON DECEMBER 31, 1938
CONDENSED BALANCE SHEET DECEMBER 31, 1938 (IN MILLIONS)

Assets		Liabilities	
1. Property Investment Account		7. Common Stock	$653
(less depreciation)	$1,166	8. Preferred Stock	360
2. Mining Royalties	9	9. Subsidiary Stocks Publicly Held	5
3. Deferred Charges*	4	10. Bonded Debt	232
4. Miscellaneous Investments	19	11. Mining Royalty Notes	12
5. Miscellaneous Other Assets	3	12. Current Liabilities	79
6. Current Assets	510	13. Contingency and Other Reserves	39
		14. Insurance Reserves	46
		15. Capital Surplus	38
		16. Earned Surplus	247
	$1,711		$1,711

Tangible assets	$1,711,000,000
Less: All liabilities ahead of common (Sum of items 8–12)	688,000,000
Net assets for common stock	$1,023,000,000
Book value per share (on 8,700,000 shares).	$117.59

* Considerable argument could be staged over the question whether Deferred Charges are intangible or tangible assets, but as the amount involved is almost always small, the matter has no practical importance. It is more convenient, of course, to include the Deferred Charges with the other assets.

The alternative method of computation, which is usually shorter than the foregoing, is as follows:

Common stock	$653,000,000
Surplus and voluntary reserves (Sum of items 13–16)	370,000,000
Net assets for common stock	$1,023,000,000

Treatment of Preferred Stock When Calculating Book Value of Common.

In calculating the assets available for the common stock, care must be taken to subtract preferred stock at its proper valuation. Ordinarily, this will be the par or stated value of the preferred stock as it appears in the balance sheet. But there is a growing number of cases in which preferred stock is carried in the balance sheet at arbitrary values far lower than the real liability attaching thereto.

Island Creek Coal Company has a preferred stock of $1 par, which is entitled to annual dividends of $6 and to $120 per share in the event of dissolution. In 1939 the price of this issue ruled about 120. In the calculation of the asset value of Island Creek Coal Common the preferred stock should be deducted not at $1 per share but at $100 per share, its "true" or "effective" par, or else at 120. Capital Administration Company, Ltd., an investment trust, has outstanding preferred stock entitled to $3 cumulative dividends and to $50 or $55 in liquidation, but its par value is $10. It has also a Class A stock entitled to $20 in liquidation plus 70% of the assets remaining and to 70% of the earnings paid out after preferred dividends, but the par value of this issue is $1. Finally it has Class B stock, par 1 cent, entitled to the residue of earnings and assets. Obviously a balance sheet set up on the basis of par value is worse than meaningless in this case, and it must be corrected by the analyst somewhat as follows:

BALANCE SHEET DECEMBER 31, 1938

As published		As revised		
Total assets (at cost)	$5,335,300	(at mkt.)	$5,862,500
Payables and accruals	1,661,200		1,661,200
Preferred stock (at par $10)	434,000	(at 55*)	2,387,000
Class A stock (at par $1)	143,400	(at 20*)	2,868,000
Common stock (at par 1 cent)	2,400		*1,043,600(d)*
Surplus and reserves	3,094,300		
Total liabilities	$5,335,300		$5,862,600

* These approximate the effective par values of the issues.

Coca-Cola Company has outstanding a no-par Class *A* stock entitled to preferential dividends of $3 per share, cumulative, and redeemable at 55. The company carries this issue as a liability at its "stated value" of $5 per share. But the true par value is clearly $50.[1]

In all instances such as the above an "effective par value" must be set up for the preferred stock that will correspond properly to its dividend rate. A strong argument may be advanced in favor of valuing all preferred stocks on a uniform dividend basis, say 5%, unless callable at a lower figure. This would mean that a $1,000,000 five per cent issue would be valued at $1,000,000, a $1,000,000 four per cent issue would be given an effective value of $800,000 and a $1,000,000 seven per cent noncallable issue would be given an effective value of $1,400,000. But it is more convenient, of course, to use the par value, and in most cases the result will be sufficiently accurate.[2] A simpler method, which would work well for most practical purposes, is to value preferred issues at par (plus back dividends) or market, whichever is higher.

Calculation of Book Value of Preferred Stocks. In calculating the book value of a preferred stock issue it is treated as a common stock and the issues junior to it are left out of consideration. The following computations from the December 31, 1932, balance sheet of Tubize Chatillon Corporation will illustrate the principles involved.

---

[1] Amusingly enough, in 1929 the company carried *as an asset* 194,000 repurchased shares of Class *A* stock at their cost of $9,434,000, although the entire issue of 1,000,000 shares appeared as a liability of only $5,000,000. For a similar accounting absurdity applied to common stocks, see the June 1939 balance sheet of Hecker Products—on which its net stated liability for its capital stock works out as a *minus* figure.

[2] Standard Statistics Company, Inc., follows the practice of deducting preferred stock at its value *in case of involuntary liquidation*, when computing the book value of the common. This is scarcely logical, because dissolution or liquidation is almost always a remote contingency and would take place under conditions quite different from those obtaining at the time of analysis. The Standard Statistics Company method results in placing a "value" of $115 per share on Procter and Gamble Company $5 Second Preferred and a value of only $100 per share on the same company's $8 First Preferred. The real or practical value of the preferred stockholder's claims in this case would be much nearer in the proportion of 160 for the First Preferred against 100 for the Second Preferred, a 5% dividend yield basis for both. In the case of investment-trust issues, liquidation values of preferred issues are more relevant and should generally be used.

TUBIZE CHATILLON CORPORATION BALANCE SHEET, DECEMBER 31, 1932

Assets		Liabilities	
Property and		7% First Preferred Stock	
Equipment	$19,009,000	(par $100)	$ 2,500,000
Patents, Processes, etc........	802,000	$7 Second Preferred Stock	
Miscellaneous Assets	478,000	(par $1)	136,000
Current Assets	4,258,000	Common Stock (par $1)	294,000
		Bonded Debt	2,000,000
		Current Liabilities	613,000
		Reserve for Deprecia-	
		tion, etc.................	11,456,000
		Surplus	7,548,000
Total Assets	$24,547,000	Total Liabilities	$24,547,000

The book value of the First Preferred is computed as follows:

Total Assets...		$24,547,000
Less: Intangible Assets	802,000	
Reserve for Depreciation, etc	11,456,000	
Bonds...	2,000,000	
Current Liabilities	613,000	14,871,000
Net assets for First Preferred		$ 9,676,000
Book value per share.......................................		$387

Alternative method:

Capital Stock at par	$2,930,000
Surplus..	7,548,000
	$10,478,000
Less Intangible Assets	802,000
Net assets for First Preferred	$9,676,000

The Reserve for Depreciation and Miscellaneous Purposes was very large and might have included arbitrary allowances belonging in Surplus. But in the absence of details a reserve of this kind must be deducted from the assets. (It later transpired that a substantial part of the reserve was needed to absorb a write-off of plant abandoned owing to obsolescence.)

The book value of the Second Preferred stock is readily computed from the foregoing, as follows:

Net assets for First Preferred	$9,676,000
Less: First Preferred at par	2,500,000
Net assets for Second Preferred	$7,176,000
Book value per share	$52.75

In computing the book value of the common it would be an obvious error to deduct the Second Preferred at its nonrepresentative par value of $1. The "effective par" should be taken at not less than $100 per share, in view of the $7 dividend. Hence there are no assets available for the common stock, and its book value is nil.

Current-asset Value and Cash-asset Value. In addition to the well-known concept of book value, we wish to suggest two others of similar character, *viz.*, current-asset value and cash-asset value.

The current-asset value of a stock consists of the current assets alone, minus all liabilities and claims ahead of the issue. It excludes not only the intangible assets but the fixed and miscellaneous assets as well.

The cash-asset value of a stock consists of the cash assets alone, minus all liabilities and claims ahead of the issue.[3] Cash assets, other than cash itself, are defined as those directly equivalent to and held in place of cash. They include certificates of deposit, call loans, marketable securities at market value and cash-surrender value of insurance policies.

The following is an example of the computation of the three categories of asset value:

OTIS COMPANY (COTTON GOODS) BALANCE SHEET, JUNE 29, 1929

Assets		Liabilities	
1. Cash	$532,000	8. Accounts Payable	$79,000
2. Call Loans	1,200,000	9. Accrued Items, etc.	291,000
3. Accounts Receivable		10. Reserve for	
(less reserve)	1,090,000	Equipment, etc	210,000
4. Inventory (less reserve of		11. Preferred Stock	400,000
$425,000)*	1,648,000	12. Common Stock	4,079,000
5. Prepaid Items	108,000	13. Earned Surplus	1,944,000
6. Investments	15,000	14. Paid-in Surplus	1,154,000
7. Plant (less Depreciation)	3,564,000		
	$8,157,000		$8,157,000

* Inventories before reserves are valued at cost or market, whichever is lower.

[3] Cash assets per share of common are sometimes calculated without deduction of any liabilities. In our opinion this is a useful concept only when the other *current* assets exceed all liabilities ahead of the common.

A. Calculation of book value of common stock:

Total assets		$8,157,000
Less: Payables	$ 79,000	
Accrued items	291,000	
Preferred stock	400,000	770,000
		$7,387,000
Add voluntary reserve of $425,000		
subtracted from inventory		425,000
Net assets for common stock		$7,812,000
Book value per share (on 40,790 shares)		$191

B. Calculation of current-asset value of the common stock:

Total current assets (items 1,2,3, and 4).	$4,470,000
Add voluntary reserve against inventory	425,000
	$4,895,000
Less liabilities ahead of common (items 8, 9, and 11)	770,000
Current assets available for common	$4,125,000
Current-asset value per share	$101

C. Calculation of cash-asset value of the common stock:

Total cash assets (items 1 and 2)	$1,732,000
Less liabilities ahead of common (items 8, 9, and 11)	770,000
Cash assets available for common.	$ 962,000
Cash-asset value per share	$23.50

In these calculations it will be noted, first, that the inventory is increased by restoring the reserve of $425,000 subtracted therefrom in the balance sheet. This is done because the deduction taken by the company is clearly a reserve for contingent decline in value that has not yet taken place. As such it is entirely arbitrary or voluntary, and consistency of method would require the analyst to regard it as a surplus item. The same is true of the $210,000 "Reserve for Equipment and Other Expenses," which, as far as can be seen, represents neither an actual liability nor a necessary deduction from the value of any specific asset.

In June 1929 Otis Company common stock was selling at 35. The reader will observe an extraordinary divergence between this market price and the current-asset value of the shares. Its significance will engage our attention later.

Practical Significance of Book Value. The book value of a common stock was originally the most important element in its financial exhibit. It was supposed to show "the value" of the shares in the same way as a merchant's balance sheet shows him the value of his business. This idea has almost completely disappeared from the financial horizon. The value of a company's assets as carried in its balance sheet has lost practically all its significance. This change arose from the fact, first, that the value of the fixed assets, as stated, frequently bore no relationship to the actual cost and, secondly, that in an even larger proportion of cases these values bore no relationship to the figure at which they would be sold or the figure which would be justified by the earnings. The practice of inflating the book value of the fixed property is giving way to the opposite artifice of cutting it down to nothing in order to avoid depreciation charges, but both have the same consequence of depriving the book-value figures of any real significance. It is a bit strange, like a quaint survival from the past, that the leading statistical services still maintain the old procedure of calculating the book value per share of common stock from many, perhaps most, balance sheets that they publish.

Before we discard completely this time-honored conception of book value, let us ask if it may ever have practical significance for the analyst. In the ordinary case, probably not. But what of the extraordinary or extreme case? Let us consider the four exhibits shown on p. 556, as representative of extreme relationships between book value and market price.

No thoughtful observer could fail to be impressed by the disparities revealed in the examples given. In the case of General Electric and Commercial Solvents the figures proclaim more than the bare fact that the market was valuing the shares at many times their book value. The stock ticker seems here to register an aggregate valuation for these enterprises that is totally unrelated to their standing as ordinary business enterprises. In other words, these are in no sense *business valuations;* they are products of Wall Street's legerdemain, or possibly of its clairvoyance.

Financial Reasoning vs. Business Reasoning. We have here the point that brings home more strikingly perhaps than any other the widened rift between financial thought and ordinary business thought. It is an almost unbelievable fact that Wall Street never asks, "How much is the business selling for?" Yet this should be the first question in considering a stock purchase. If a business man were offered a 5% interest in some concern for $10,000, his first mental process would be to multiply the asked price by 20 and thus establish a proposed value of $200,000 for the entire undertaking. The rest of his calculation would turn about the question whether or not the business was a "good buy" at $200,000.

Item	General Electric	Pepperell Manufacturing
Price	(1930) 95	(1932) 18
Number of shares	28,850,000	97,600
Market value of common	$2,740,000,000	$ 1,760,000
Balance sheet	(Dec. 1929)	(June 1932)
Fixed assets (less depreciation)	$ 52,000,000	$ 7,830,000
Miscellaneous assets	183,000,000	230,000
Net current assets	206,000,000	9,120,000
Total net assets	$ 441,000,000	$17,180,000
Less bonds and preferred	45,000,000	
Book value of common	$ 396,000,000	$17,180,000
Book value per share	$13.75	$176

Item	Commercial Solvents	Pennsylvania Coal and Coke
Price	(July 1933) 57	(July 1933) 3
Number of shares	2,493,000	165,000
Market value of common	$142,000,000	$ 495,000
Balance sheet	(Dec. 1932)	(Dec. 1932)
Fixed assets (less depreciation)		6,500,000
Miscellaneous assets	2,600,000	990,000
Net current assets	6,000,000	740,000
Total assets for common	$ 8,600,000	$8,230,000
Book value per share	$3.50	$50

This elementary and indispensable approach has been practically abandoned by those who purchase stocks. Of the thousands who "invested" in General Electric in 1929–1930 probably only an infinitesimal number had any idea that they were paying on the basis of about $2\frac{1}{2}$ billions of dollars for the company, of which over two billions represented a premium above the money actually invested in the business. The price of 57 established for Commercial Solvents in July 1933 was more of a gambling phenomenon, induced by the expected repeal of prohibition. But the gamblers in this instance were acting no differently from those who call themselves investors, in their blithe disregard of the fact that they were paying 140 millions for an enterprise with about 10 millions of resources. (The fixed assets of Commercial Solvents, written down to nothing in the balance sheet, had real value, of course, but not in excess of a few millions.)

The contrast in the other direction shown by our examples is almost as impressive. A going but unsuccessful concern like Pennsylvania Coal and Coke can be valued in the market at about one-sixteenth of its stated resources almost on the same day as a speculatively attractive issue is bid for at sixteen times its net worth. The Pepperell example is perhaps more striking still, because of the unquestioned reality of the figures of book value and also because of the high reputation, large earnings, and liberal dividends of the enterprise covering a long stretch of years. Yet part owners of this business—under the stress of depression, it is true—were willing to sell out their interest at one-tenth of the value that a single private owner would have unhesitatingly placed upon it.

Recommendation. These examples, extreme as they are, suggest rather forcibly that the book value deserves at least a fleeting glance by the public before it buys or sells shares in a business undertaking. In any particular case the message that the book value conveys may well prove to be inconsequential and unworthy of attention. But this testimony should be examined before it is rejected. Let the stock buyer, if he lays any claim to intelligence, at least be able to tell himself, first, what value he is actually setting on the business and, second, what he is actually getting for his money in terms of tangible resources.

There are indeed certain presumptions in favor of purchases made far below asset value and against those made at a high premium above it. (It is assumed that in the ordinary case the book figures may be accepted as roughly indicative of the actual cash invested in the enterprise.) A business that sells at a premium does so because it earns a large return upon its capital; this large return attracts competition, and, generally speaking, it is not likely to continue indefinitely. Conversely in the case of a business selling at a large discount because of abnormally low earnings. The absence of new competition, the withdrawal of old competition from the field, and other natural economic forces may tend eventually to improve the situation and restore a normal rate of profit on the investment.

Although this is orthodox economic theory, and undoubtedly valid in a broad sense, we doubt if it applies with sufficient certainty and celerity to make it useful as a governing factor in common-stock selection. It may be pointed out that under modern conditions the so-called "intangibles," *e.g.*, good-will or even a highly efficient organization, are every whit as real from a dollars-and-cents standpoint as are buildings and machinery.[4] Earnings based on these intangibles may be even less vulnerable to competition than those which require only a cash investment in productive facilities. Furthermore, when conditions are favorable the enterprise with the relatively small capital investment is likely to show a more rapid rate of growth. Ordinarily it can expand its sales and profits at slight expense and therefore more rapidly and profitably for its stockholders than a business requiring a large plant investment per dollar of sales.

We do not think, therefore, that any rules may reasonably be laid down on the subject of book value in relation to market price, except the strong recommendation already made that the purchaser know what he is doing on this score and be satisfied in his own mind that he is acting sensibly.

---

[4] Judicial valuations of intangible assets (in the case of close corporations) still seem to adhere to the old concept that they are less "real" than tangible assets and thus need larger earnings, relatively, to support them. The divergence between the stock market's bases of valuation and those of business men and the courts, as applied to private enterprises, would provide excellent material for a critical study.

For a quantitative study leading to the conclusion that "good-will" has, on the whole, proved more profitable than tangible assets, see Lawrence N. Bloomberg, *The Investment Value of Goodwill*, Baltimore, 1938.

Chapter 43

SIGNIFICANCE OF THE
CURRENT-ASSET VALUE

THE CURRENT-ASSET VALUE of a common stock is more likely to be an important figure than the book value, which includes the fixed assets. Our discussion of this point will develop the following theses:

1. The current-asset value is generally a rough index of the *liquidating value*.

2. A large number of common stocks sell for less than their current-asset value and therefore sell below the amount realizable in liquidation.

3. The phenomenon of many stocks selling persistently below their liquidating value is fundamentally illogical. It means that a serious error is being committed, either: (*a*) in the judgment of the stock market, (*b*) in the policies of the company's management, or (*c*) in the attitude of the stockholders toward their property.

Liquidating Value. By the liquidating value of an enterprise we mean the money that the owners could get out of it if they wanted to give it up. They might sell all or part of it to some one else, on a going-concern basis. Or else they might turn the various kinds of assets into cash, in piecemeal fashion, taking whatever time is needed to obtain the best realization from each. Such liquidations are of everyday occurrence in the field of private business. By contrast, however, they are very rare indeed in the field of publicly owned corporations. It is true that one company often sells out to another, usually at a price well above liquidating value, also that insolvency will at times result in the piecemeal sale of the assets; but the voluntary withdrawal from an unprofitable business, accompanied by the careful liquidation of the assets, is an infinitely more frequent happening among private than among publicly owned concerns. This divergence is not without its cause and meaning, as we shall show later.

Realizable Value of Assets Varies with Their Character. A company's balance sheet does not convey exact information as to its value in liquidation, but it does supply clues or hints which may prove useful. The first rule in calculating liquidating value is that the liabilities are real but the value of the assets must be questioned. This means that all true liabilities shown on the books must be deducted at their face amount. The value to be ascribed to the assets, however, will vary according to their character. The following schedule indicates fairly well the relative dependability of various types of assets in liquidation.

Type of asset	% of liquidating value to book value	
	Normal range	Rough average
Current assets:		
Cash assets (including securities at market)	100	100
Receivables (less usual reserves)*	75–90	80
Inventories (at lower of cost or market)	50–75	$66^2/_3$
Fixed and miscellaneous assets:		
(Real estate, buildings, machinery, equipment,		
nonmarketable investments, intangibles, etc.)	1–50	15 (approx.)

* Note: Retail installment accounts must be valued for liquidation at a lower rate. Range about 30 to 60%. Average about 50%.

Calculation Illustrated. The calculation of approximate liquidating value in a specific case is illustrated as follows:

Example: White Motor Company. (See next page.)

Object of This Calculation. In studying this computation it must be borne in mind that our object is not to determine the exact liquidating value of White Motor but merely to form a rough idea of this liquidating value *in order to ascertain whether or not the shares are selling for less than the stockholders could actually take out of the business.* The latter question is answered very definitely in the affirmative. With full allowance for possible error, there was no doubt at all (in 1931) that White Motor would liquidate for a great deal more than $8 per share, or $5,200,000 for the company. The striking fact that the cash assets alone considerably exceed this figure, *after deducting all liabilities,* completely clinched the argument on this score.

Current-asset Value a Rough Measure of Liquidating Value. The estimated values in liquidation as given for White Motor are somewhat lower in respect of inventories and somewhat higher as regards the fixed and miscellaneous assets than one might be inclined to adopt in other examples. We are allowing for the fact that motor-truck inventories are likely to be less salable than the average. On the other hand some of the assets listed as non-current, in particular the investment in White Motor Securities Corporation,

WHITE MOTOR COMPANY

Capitalization: 650,000 shares of common stock.

Price in December 1931: $8 per share.

Total market value of the company: $5,200,000.

BALANCE SHEET, DECEMBER 31, 1931 (000 OMITTED)

		Estimated liquidating value	
Item	Book value	% of book value	Amount
Cash	$ 4,057 ⎫	100	
U.S. Govt. and New York City bonds	4,573 ⎬		$ 8,600
Receivables (less reserves)	5,611	80	4,500
Inventory (lower of cost or market)	9,219	50	4,600
Total current assets	$23,460		$17,700
Less current liabilities	1,353		1,400
Net current assets	$22,107		$16,300
Plant account	16,036 ⎫		
Less depreciation	7,491 ⎮		
Plant account, net	$ 8,545 ⎬	20	4,000
Investments in subsidiaries, etc.	4,996 ⎮		
Deferred charges	388 ⎮		
Good-will	5,389 ⎭		
Total net assets for common stock	$41,425		$20,300

Estimated liquidating value per share	$31
Book value per share	55
Current-asset value per share	34
Cash-asset value per share	$11
Market price per share	8

would be likely to yield a larger proportion of their book values than the ordinary property account. It will be seen that White Motor's estimated liquidating value (about $31 per share) was not far from the current-asset value ($34 per share). In the typical case it may be said that the noncurrent assets are likely to realize enough to make up most of the shrinkage suffered in the liquidation of the current assets. Hence our first thesis, *viz.*, that the current-asset value affords a rough measure of the liquidating value.

Prevalence of Stocks Selling below Liquidating Value. Our second point is that for some years past a considerable number of common stocks have been selling in the market well below their liquidating value. Naturally the percentage was largest during the depression. But even in the bull market of 1926–1929 instances of this kind were by no means rare. It will be noted that the striking case of Otis Company, presented in the last chapter, occurred during June 1929, at the very height of the boom. The Northern Pipe Line example, given in Chap. 41, dates from 1926. On the other hand, our Pepperell and White Motor illustrations were phenomena of the 1931–1933 collapse.

It seems to us that the most distinctive feature of the stock market of those three years was the large proportion of issues which sold below their liquidating value. Our computations indicate that over 40% of all the industrial companies listed on the New York Stock Exchange were quoted at some time in 1932 at less than their net current assets. A considerable number actually sold for less than their cash-asset value, as in the case of White Motor.[1] On reflection this must appear to be an extraordinary state of affairs. The typical American corporation was apparently worth more dead than alive. The owners of these great businesses could get more for their interest by shutting up shop than by selling out on a going-concern basis.

In the recession of 1937–1938 this situation was repeated on a smaller scale. Available data indicate that 20.5% of the industrial companies listed on the New York Stock Exchange sold in early 1938 at less than their net-current-asset value. (At the close of 1938, when the general price level was by no means abnormally low, a total of 54 companies out of 648 industrials studied sold for less than their net current assets.[2])

---

[1] See Appendix Note 62, p. 814 on accompanying CD, for a representative list of issues selling for less than liquidating value in 1932.

[2] See Appendix Note 61, p. 800 on accompanying CD, for other details on this point.

It is important to observe that these widespread discrepancies between price and current-asset value are a comparatively recent development. In the severe market depression of 1921 the proportion of industrial stocks in this class was quite small. Evidently the phenomena of 1932 (and 1938) were the direct out-growth of the new-era doctrine which transferred *all* the tests of value to the income account and completely ignored the balance-sheet picture. In consequence, a company without current earnings was regarded as having very little real value, and it was likely to sell in the market for the merest fraction of its realizable resources. Most of the sellers were not aware that they were disposing of their interest at far less than its scrap value. Many, however, who might have known the fact would have justified the low price on the ground that the liquidating value was of no practical importance, since the company had no intention of liquidating.

Logical Significance of This Phenomenon. This brings us to the third point, *viz.*, the logical significance of this "subliquidating-value" phenomenon from the standpoint of the market, of the managements and of the stockholders. The whole issue may be summarized in the form of a basic principle, *viz.*:

When a common stock sells persistently below its liquidating value, then either the price is too low or the company should be liquidated.

Two corollaries may be deduced from this principle:

Corollary I. Such a price should impel the stockholders to raise the question whether or not it is in their interest to continue the business.

Corollary II. Such a price should impel the management to take all proper steps to correct the obvious disparity between market quotation and intrinsic value, including a reconsideration of its own policies and a frank justification to the stockholders of its decision to continue the business.

The truth of the principle above stated should be self-evident. There can be no *sound* economic reason for a stock's selling continuously below its liquidation value. If the company is not worth more as a going concern than in liquidation, it should be liquidated. If it is worth more as a going concern, then the stock should sell for more than its liquidating value. Hence, on either premise, a price below liquidating value is unjustifiable.

Twofold Application of Foregoing Principle. Stated in the form of a logical alternative, our principle invites a twofold application. Stocks selling below liquidation value are in many cases too cheap and so offer an attractive medium for purchase. We have thus a profitable field here for the technique of security analysis. But in many cases also the fact that an issue sells below liquidating value is a signal that mistaken policies are being followed and that therefore the management should take corrective action—if not voluntarily, then under pressure from the stockholders. Let us consider these two lines of inquiry in order.

ATTRACTIVENESS OF SUCH ISSUES AS COMMITMENTS

Common stocks in this category practically always have an unsatisfactory trend of earnings. If the profits had been increasing steadily, it is obvious that the shares would not sell at so low a price. The objection to buying these issues lies in the probability, or at least the possibility, that earnings will decline or losses continue and that the resources will be dissipated and the intrinsic value ultimately become less than the price paid. It may not be denied that this does actually happen in individual cases. On the other hand, there is a much wider range of potential developments which may result in establishing a higher market price. These include the following:

1. The creation of an earning power commensurate with the company's assets. This may result from:
   a. General improvement in the industry.
   b. Favorable change in the company's operating policies, with or without a change in management. These changes include more efficient methods, new products, abandonment of unprofitable lines, etc.
2. A sale or merger, because some other concern is able to utilize the resources to better advantage and hence can pay at least liquidating value for the assets.
3. Complete or partial liquidation.

Examples of Effect of Favorable Developments on Such Issues.
General Improvement in the Industry. Examples already given, and certain others, will illustrate the operation of these various kinds of favorable developments. In the case of Pepperell the low price of $17^1/_2$ coincided with a large loss for the year ended June 30, 1932. In the following year conditions in the textile industry improved; Pepperell earned over $9 per share and resumed dividends; consequently the price of the stock advanced to 100 in January 1934 and to $149^3/_4$ in 1936.

Changes in Operating Policies. Hamilton Woolen Company, another example in the textile field, is a case of individual rather than of general improvement. For several years prior to 1928 the company had operated at substantial losses, which amounted to nearly $20 and $12 per share in 1926 and 1927, respectively. Late in 1927 the common stock sold at $13 per share, although the company had net current assets of $38.50 per share at that time. In 1928 and 1929 changes in management and in managerial policies were made, new lines of product and direct sales methods were introduced, and certain phases of production were reorganized. This resulted in greatly improved earnings which averaged about $5.50 per share during the succeeding four years, and within a single year the stock had risen to a price of about $40.[3]

Sale or Merger. The White Motor instance is typical of the genesis and immediate effect of a sale or merger, as applied to an issue selling for less than liquidating value. (The later developments, however, were quite unusual.) The heavy losses of White Motor in 1930–1932 impelled the management to seek a new alignment. Studebaker Corporation believed it could combine its own operations with those of White to mutual advantage, and it was greatly attracted by White's large holdings of cash. Hence in September 1932 Studebaker offered to purchase all White Motor's stock, paying for each share as follows:

$5 in cash.
$25 in 10-year 6% notes of Studebaker Corporation.
1 share of Studebaker common, selling for about $10.

It will be seen that these terms of purchase were based not on the recent market price of White—below $7 per share—but primarily upon the current-asset value. White Motor shares promptly advanced to 27 and later sold at the equivalent of 31$^{1}/_{2}$.[4]

An interesting example of the same kind, but of more recent date, is afforded by Standard Oil Company of Nebraska. The facts may be outlined as follows:

---

[3] For the later history of Hamilton Woolen Company, see pp. 584–585.

[4] An extraordinary sequel of this transaction was the receivership of Studebaker Corporation in April 1933, ostensibly caused by the opposition of minority stockholders of White Motor to a merger of the two companies. But this development is quite unrelated to our point of discussion, which turns upon the fact that in a sale or merger full recognition should always be, and is ordinarily, given to liquidating value, even though the current market price may be much lower.

Early in 1939 the stock was selling at about $6, representing a total valuation of $1,000,000 for 161,000 shares comprising the entire capitalization. The December 31, 1938, balance sheet is summarized in the appended table.

Assets		Liabilities	
Fixed and miscellaneous assets (net) ..	$2,794,000	Current liabilities	$176,000
Cash assets	1,155,000	Capital stock and surplus ..	4,734,000
Other current assets	961,000		$4,910,000
	$4,910,000		
(Net) Cash assets per share	$6.07		
Net current assets per share	12.05		
Net tangible assets per share	29.33		

The company was engaged in the distribution of petroleum products in Nebraska. It was carrying on an annual business of some $5,000,000 without appreciable profit. For the years 1935–1938 the reported earnings before depreciation averaged $0.69 per share; after "expended depreciation" there was an average profit of $0.39 per share; and after depreciation as taken by the company there was an average loss of $0.39 per share.

Here was a company clearly selling for much less than liquidating value, the reason being its unsatisfactory earnings record. There was good reason to believe, however, that the company was really worth more than bare liquidating value, because the outlet it provided for gasoline, etc., would make its numerous retail and bulk stations a desirable acquisition for some large refining company.

In April 1939 private interests offered to pay $12 per share for 66²/₃% of the outstanding stock. This bid failed of acceptance by a sufficient majority, but it was followed immediately by an offer to pay $17.50 per share, made by Standard Oil Company of Indiana, the refiner that had been supplying Standard Oil Company of Nebraska with its gasoline and that evidently was loath to lose this important outlet. The deal was promptly ratified; hence the stock of Standard Oil Company of Nebraska nearly tripled in value during a four-month's period in which the general market had suffered a decline.[5]

---

[5] See I. Benesch and Sons, and United Shipyards "A" in the table on p. 585 for other examples of a rise in price due to sale of properties.

Complete Liquidation. Mohawk Mining Company supplies an excellent example of a cash profit equivalent to a large advance in market value caused by the actual liquidation of the enterprise.

In December 1931 the stock sold at $11 per share, representing a total valuation of $1,230,000 for the 112,000 shares outstanding. The balance sheet at the end of 1931 showed the following:

Cash and marketable securities at market	$1,381,000
Receivables	9,000
Copper at market value, about	1,800,000
Supplies	71,000
	$3,261,000
Less current liabilities	68,000
Net current assets	$3,193,000
Fixed assets, less depreciation and depletion	2,460,000
Miscellaneous assets	168,000
Total assets for common stock	$5,821,000
Book value per share*	$52
Current-asset value per share*	28.50
Cash-asset value per share*	11.75
Market price per share	11

* After reducing securities and copper inventory to market value.

Shortly thereafter the management decided to liquidate the property. Within the years 1932–1934 regular and liquidating dividends were paid, aggregating $28.50 per share. It will be noted that the amount actually received in liquidation proved identical with the current-asset value just before the liquidation began, and it was $2^1/_2$ times the ruling market price at that time.

Partial Liquidation. Northern Pipe Line Company and Otis Company, already discussed, are examples of the establishment of a higher market value through partial liquidation. The two companies made the exhibits as shown in the table following.

In September 1929 Otis Company paid a special dividend of $4 per share, and in 1930 it made a distribution of $20 in partial liquidation, reducing the par value from $100 to $80. In April 1931 the shares sold at 45 and in April 1932 at 41. These prices were higher than the quotation in June 1929, despite the distributions of $24 per share made in the interim, and despite the fact also that the *general* market level had changed from fantastic inflation to equally fantastic deflation. Later the company went out of business altogether and paid its stockholders an additional $74 per share in liquidation—making the total received by them $102 per share since June 1929 (inclusive of other dividends in 1929–1934 amounting to $4 per share).[6]

Item	Northern Pipe Line	Otis Company
Date	1926	June 1929
Market price	$64	$35
Cash-asset value per share	79	$23^{1}/_{2}$
Current-asset value per share	82	101
Book value per share	116	191

Northern Pipe Line Company distributed $50 per share to its stockholders in 1928, as a return of capital, *i.e.*, partial liquidation. This development resulted in an approximate doubling of the market price between 1926 and 1928. Later a second distribution of $20 per share was made, so that the stockholders received more in cash than in the low market price of 1925 and 1926, and they also retained their full interest in the pipe-line business. Similar liberal distributions were made by most of the pipe-line companies of the so-called Standard Oil group. (Note also the partial liquidation of Davis Coal and Coke Company, described in the footnote on p. 529.)

Discrimination Required in Selecting Such Issues. There is scarcely any doubt that common stocks selling well below liquidating value represent on the whole a class of undervalued securities. They have declined in price more severely than the actual conditions justify. This must mean that *on the whole* these stocks afford profitable opportunities for purchase. Nevertheless, the securities analyst should exercise as much discrimination as possible in the choice of issues falling within this category. He will lean toward those for which he sees a fairly imminent prospect of some one of the favorable developments listed above. Or else he will be partial to such as reveal other attractive statistical features

---

[6] For other examples of liquidation bringing stockholders more than the previous market price see the table on p. 585.

besides their liquid-asset position, *e.g.*, satisfactory current earnings and dividends or a high average earning power in the past. The analyst will avoid issues that have been losing their current assets at a rapid rate and show no definite signs of ceasing to do so.

Examples: This latter point will be illustrated by the following comparison of two companies, the shares of which sold well below liquidating value early in 1933.

Item	Manhattan Shirt Company		Hupp Motor Car Corporation	
Price, January 1933	6		$2^1/_2$	
Total market value of Company	$1,476,000		$3,323,000	
Balance sheet	Nov. 30, 1932	Nov. 30, 1929	Dec. 31, 1932	Dec. 31, 1929
Preferred stock at par		$ 300,000		
Number of shares of common	246,000	281,000	1,329,000	1,475,000
Cash assets	$1,961,000	$ 885,000	$ 4,615,000	$10,156,000
Receivables	771,000	2,621,000	226,000	1,246,000
Inventories	1,289,000	4,330,000	2,115,000	8,481,000
Total current assets	$4,021,000	$7,836,000	$ 6,956,000	$19,883,000
Current liabilities	100,000	2,574,000	1,181,000	2,541,000
Net current assets	$3,921,000	$5,262,000	$ 5,775,000	$17,342,000
Other tangible assets	1,124,000	2,066,000	9,757,000	17,870,000
Total assets for common (and preferred)	$5,045,000	$7,328,000	$15,532,000	$35,212,000
Cash-asset value per share	$ 7.50	Nil	$2.625	$ 5.125
Current-asset value per share	16.00	$17.50	4.375	11.75

Both of these companies disclose an interesting relationship of current assets to market price at the close of 1932. But a comparison with the balance-sheet situation of three years previously will yield much more satisfactory indications for Manhattan Shirt than for Hupp Motors. The latter concern had lost more than half of its cash assets and more than 60% of its net current assets during the depression period. On the other hand, the current-asset value of Manhattan Shirt common was reduced by only 10% during these difficult times, and furthermore, its cash-asset position was greatly improved. The latter result was obtained through the liquidation of receivables and inventories, the proceeds of which paid off the 1929 bank loans and largely increased the cash resources.

From the viewpoint of past indications, therefore, the two companies must be placed in different categories. In the Hupp Motors case, we should have to take into account the possibility that the remaining excess of current assets over market price might soon be dissipated. This is not true so far as Manhattan Shirt is concerned, and in fact the achievement of the company in strengthening its cash position during the depression must be given favorable consideration. We shall recur later to this phase of security analysis, *viz.*, the comparison of balance sheets over a period in order to determine the true progress of an enterprise. The former point—that attention should be paid also to the past earnings record—may be brought home by a brief comparison of two companies in early 1939.

Item	Ely & Walker Dry Goods Co.		Pacific Mills	
Price, January, 1939	17		14	
Per share:	Dec. 31, 1932	Dec. 31, 1938	Dec. 31, 1932	Dec. 31, 1938
Net current assets	$30.00	$39.50	$26.95	$24.50
Net tangible assets	37.73	46.42	90.85	79.50
Average earnings, 1933–1938		1.82		2.41(d)
Average dividend, 1933–1938		1.25		0.50

The losses of Pacific Mills did not have a serious effect upon the balance-sheet position because they have come mainly out of the balance sheet via the depreciation allowance. But unless there were special reasons to expect a reversal of the operating results, the analyst would obviously prefer Ely & Walker as an investment purchase.

Bargains of This Type. Common stocks that (1) are selling below their liquid-asset value, (2) are apparently in no danger of dissipating these assets, and (3) have formerly shown a large earning power on the market price, may be said truthfully to constitute a class of *investment bargains*. They are indubitably *worth* considerably more than they are selling for, and there is a reasonably good chance that this greater worth will sooner or later reflect itself in the market price. At their low price these bargain stocks actually enjoy a high degree of safety, meaning by safety a relatively small risk of loss of principal.

It may be pointed out, however, that investment in such bargain issues needs to be carried on with some regard to general market conditions at the time. Strangely enough, this is a type of operation that fares best, relatively speaking, when price levels are neither extremely high nor extremely low. The purchase of "cheap stocks" when the market as a whole seems much higher than it should be, *e.g.*, in 1929 or early 1937, will not work out well, because the ensuing decline is likely to bear almost as severely on these neglected or unappreciated issues as on the general list. On the other hand, when all stocks are very cheap—as in 1932—there would seem to be fully as much reason to buy undervalued leading issues as to pick out less popular stocks, even though these may be selling at even lower prices by comparison.

A Common Stock Representing the Entire Business Cannot Be Less Safe than a Bond Having a Claim to Only a Part Thereof. In considering these issues it will be helpful to apply the converse of the proposition developed earlier in this book with reference to senior securities. We pointed out (Chap. 26) that a bond or preferred stock could not be worth more than its value would be if it represented full ownership of the company, *i.e.*, if it were a common stock without senior claims ahead of it. The converse is also true. A common stock cannot be *less safe* than it would be if it were a bond, *i.e.*, if instead of representing full ownership of the company it were given a fixed and limited claim, with some new common stock created to own what was left. This idea, which may appear somewhat abstract at first, may be clarified by a concrete comparison between a common stock and a bond issue of the types just described. Two companies in the investment-trust field are particularly well suited to illustrate our point, because they were both organized by the same banking interests, and they have identical officers.

Our table (p. 572) should make clear that Shawmut Association *stock* cannot be less safe intrinsically than the Investment Trust *senior debentures* at 85. For, with the same management behind them, the stock investment has behind it 180% in assets, whereas the bonds are protected by only 122% (of their market price) in assets. In addition to having this greater protection the Association stock represents the entire ownership of the company's assets, whereas the interest of the Investment Trust bonds is limited to their principal amount, the balance of the equity belonging to the junior holders. (In fact this junior equity can be fairly substantial, as measured by market price, even when the bonds are selling at a considerable discount.)

As of December 1939	Shawmut Association	Shawmut Bank Investment Trust
Bonds	None	$3,040,000 Senior Debenture 4¹/₂s and 5s @ 85 (average) = $2,585,000 $950,000 Junior Debenture 6s @ 50 (est) = $480,000
Stock	390,000 sh. @ 10¹/₄ $4,000,000	75,000 sh. @ 3¹/₂ 260,000
Total capitalization	$4,000,000	$3,325,000
Net asset value (September 1939)	7,201,000	(November 1939) 3,153,000
Ratio: Senior bonds at market to net assets		82%
Ratio: Total capitalization at market to net assets	55%	107%
12 months' investment income*	(To September 30) 198,000	(To November 30) 114,000
Per cent earned on capitalization at market	5.0	3.5

* Excluding gain or loss on security sales.

That the Shawmut *Association* stock is more attractive than the *Investment Trust* debentures at the prices quoted is scarcely open to challenge. Undoubtedly, also, the investor who would consider the bond issue to be "safer" than the Association shares is being misled by the *form* into overlooking the *essence*. Yet something remains to be said of the effect of these diverse forms upon the experience of the investor and consequently upon his attitude. The Investment Trust bonds do carry a certain assurance of continued income, because interest must be paid regularly or else the company faces insolvency. It is true for the same reason that special efforts will be made to pay them off at or before maturity in 1942 and 1952. Therefore we find that the company has a special inducement to buy in bonds at a discount—since they must ultimately be paid at par—and thus one-third of the issue has been reacquired. This policy has served to maintain the market price to an important extent and to improve the position of the remaining bonds.

None of this is true with respect to the Shawmut Association shares. They have in fact received continuous dividends since 1929, averaging 65 cents, or 6¹/₂% on the current price. But the rate has been variable, and the average stockholder feels that he is at the mercy of the management's decisions. (This is not entirely so in fact, since the penalty clauses in the Revenue Act virtually compel disbursement of the net income realized by investment trusts.) Nor has the market price been maintained by company repurchases at a reasonable discount from break-up value, so that the investor has been unable to look to the management to save him from the hard necessity of sacrificing his shares at as much as 50% below their intrinsic worth.

In the 1934 edition we illustrated this same point by considering American Laundry Machinery stock at its price of 7 in January 1933, which was equivalent to $4,300,000 for the entire company—as compared with over $4,000,000 in cash, $21,000,000 in net current assets, $27,000,000 in net tangible assets and 10-year average earnings of over $3,000,000 (including, however, a loss of $1,000,000 in 1932). The last two paragraphs of the chapter were as follows:

> Wall Street would have considered American Laundry Machinery stock "unsafe" at 7, but it would unquestionably have accepted a $4,500,000 bond issue of the same company. Its "reasoning" would have run that the interest on the bond was sure to be continued but that the 40-cent dividend then being paid on the stock was very insecure. In one case the directors had no choice but to pay interest and therefore would surely do so; in the other case the directors could pay or not as they saw fit and therefore would very likely suspend the dividend. But Wall Street is here confusing the temporary continuance of income with the more fundamental question of safety of principal. Dividends paid to common-stock holders do not in themselves make the stock any safer. The directors are merely turning over to the stockholders part of their own property; if the money were left in the treasury, it would still be the stockholder's property. There must therefore be an underlying fallacy in assuming that if the stockholders were given the power to compel payment of income—*i.e.*, if they were made bondholders in whole or in part—their position would thus be made intrinsically sounder. It is little short of idiocy to assume that the stockholders would be better off if they surrendered their complete ownership of the company in exchange for a limited claim against the same property at the rate of 5 or 6% on the investment. This is exactly what the public would do if it were willing to buy a $4,500,000 bond issue of American Laundry Machinery but would reject as "unsafe" the present common stock at $7 per share.

Nevertheless, Wall Street persists in thinking in these irrational terms, and it does so in part with practical justification. Somehow or other, common-stock ownership does not seem to give the public the same powers and possibilities—the same *values*, in short—as are vested in the private owners of a business. This brings us to the second line of reasoning on the subjects of stocks selling below liquidating value.

Chapter 44

IMPLICATIONS OF LIQUIDATING VALUE. STOCKHOLDER-MANAGEMENT RELATIONSHIPS

WALL STREET HOLDS THAT liquidating value is of slight importance because the typical company has no intention of liquidating. This view is logical, as far as it goes. When applied to a stock selling below break-up value, the Wall Street view may be amplified into the following: "Although this stock would liquidate for more than its market price, it is not worth buying because (1) the company cannot earn a satisfactory profit, and (2) it is not going to liquidate. In the previous chapter we suggested that the first assumption is likely to be wrong in a number of instances, for, although past earnings may have been disappointing, there is always a chance that through external or internal changes the concern may again earn a reasonable amount on its capital. But in a considerable proportion of cases the pessimism of the market will at least *appear* to be justified. We are led, therefore, to ask the question: "Why is it that no matter how poor a corporation's prospects may seem, its owners permit it to remain in business until its resources are exhausted?"

The answer to this question takes us into the heart of one of the strangest phenomena of American finance—the relations of stockholders to the businesses that they own. The subject transcends in its scope the narrow field of security analysis, but we shall discuss it here briefly because there is a distinct relationship between the value of securities and the intelligence and alertness of those who own them. The choice of a common stock is a single act; its ownership is a continuing process. Certainly there is just as much reason to exercise care and judgment in *being* as in *becoming* a stockholder.

Typical Stockholder Apathetic and Docile. It is a notorious fact, however, that the typical American stockholder is the most docile and apathetic animal in captivity. He does what the board of directors tell him to do and rarely thinks of asserting his individual rights as owner of the business and employer of its paid officers. The result is that the effective control of many, perhaps most, large American corporations is exercised not by those who together own a majority of the stock but by a small group known as "the management." This situation has been effectively described by Berle and Means in their significant work *The Modern Corporation and Private Property*. In Chap. I of Book IV the authors say:

> It is traditional that a corporation should be run for the benefit of its owners, the stockholders, and that to them should go any profits which are distributed. We now know, however, that a controlling group may hold the power to divert profits into their own pockets. There is no longer any certainty that a corporation will in fact be run primarily in the interests of the stockholders. The extensive separation of ownership and control, and the strengthening of the powers of control, raise a new situation calling for a decision whether social and legal pressure should be applied in an effort to insure corporate operation primarily in the interests of the owners or whether such pressure shall be applied in the interests of some other or wider group.

Again (on page 335) the authors restate this view in their concluding chapter as follows:

> ... A third possibility exists, however. On the one hand, the owners of passive property, by surrendering control and responsibility over the active property, have surrendered the right that the corporation should be operated in their sole interest—they have released the community from the obligation to protect them to the full extent implied in the doctrine of strict property rights. At the same time, the controlling groups, by means of the extension of corporate powers, have in their own interest broken the bars of tradition which require that the corporation be operated solely for the benefit of the owners of passive property. Eliminating the sole interest of the passive owner, however, does not necessarily lay a basis for the alternative claim that the new powers should be used in the interest of the controlling groups. The latter have not presented, in acts or words, any acceptable defense of the proposition that these powers should be so used. No tradition supports that proposition. The control groups have, rather, cleared the way for the claims of a group far wider than either the owners or the control. They have placed the community in a position to demand that the modern corporation serve not alone the owners or the control but all society.

Plausible but Partly Fallacious Assumptions by Stockholders.

Alert stockholders—if there are any such—are not likely to agree fully with the conclusion of Messrs. Berle and Means that they definitely have "surrendered the right that the corporation should be operated in their sole interest." After all, the American stockholder has abdicated not intentionally but by default. He can reassert the rights of control that inhere in ownership. Quite probably he would do so if he were properly informed and guided. In good part his docility and seeming apathy are results of certain traditional but unsound viewpoints which he seems to absorb by inheritance or by contagion. These cherished notions include the following:

1. The management knows more about the business than the stockholders do, and therefore its judgment on all matters of policy is to be accepted.

2. The management has no interest in or responsibility for the prices at which the company's securities sell.

3. If a stockholder disapproves of any major policy of the management, his proper move is to sell his stock.

Assumed Wisdom and Efficiency of Management Not Always Justified.

These statements sound plausible, but they are in fact only half truths—the more dangerous because they are not wholly false. It is nearly always true that the management is in the best position to judge which policies are most expedient. But it does not follow that it will always either recognize or adopt the course most beneficial to the shareholders. It may err grievously through incompetence. Stockholders of any given company appear to take it for granted that their management is capable. Yet the art of selecting stocks is said to turn largely on choosing the well-managed enterprise and rejecting others. This must imply that many companies are poorly directed. Should not this mean also that the stockholders of any company should be open-minded on the question whether its management is efficient or the reverse?

Interests of Stockholders and Officers Conflict at Certain Points.

But a second reason for not always accepting implicitly the decisions of the management is that *on certain points* the interests of the officers and the stockholders may be in conflict. This field includes the following:

1. Compensation to officers—Comprising salaries, bonuses, options to buy stock.

2. Expansion of the business—Involving the right to larger salaries and the acquisition of more power and prestige by the officers.

3. Payment of dividends—Should the money earned remain under the control of the management or pass into the hands of the stockholders?

4. Continuance of the stockholders' investment in the company—Should the business continue as before, although unprofitable, or should part of the capital be withdrawn, or should it be wound up completely?

5. Information to stockholders—Should those in control be able to benefit through having information not given to stockholders generally?

On all of these questions the decisions of the management are *interested* decisions, and for that reason they require scrutiny by the stockholders. We do not imply that corporate managements are not to be trusted. On the contrary, the officers of our large corporations constitute a group of men above the average in probity as well as in ability. But this does not mean that they should be given *carte blanche* in all matters affecting their own interests. A private employer hires only men he can trust, but he does not let these men fix their own salaries or decide how much capital he should place or leave in the business.

Directors Not Always Free from Self-interest in Connection with These Matters.

In publicly owned corporations these matters are passed on by the board of directors, whom the stockholders elect and to whom the officials are responsible. Theoretically, the directors will represent the stockholders' interests, when need be, as against the opposing interests of the officers. But this cannot be counted upon in practice. In many companies a majority, and in most companies a substantial part, of the board is composed of paid officials. The directors who are not officers are frequently joined by many close ties to the chief executives. It may be said in fact that the officers choose the directors more often than the directors choose the officers. Hence the necessity remains for the stockholders to exercise critical and independent judgments on all matters where the personal advantage of the officers may conceivably be opposed to their own. In other words, in this field the usual presumption of superior knowledge and judgment on the part of the management should not obtain, and any criticism offered in good faith deserves careful consideration by the stockholders.

Abuse of Managerial Compensation. Numerous cases have come to light in which the actions of the management in the matter of its own compensation have been open to serious question. Most of these relate to the years before 1933. In the case of Bethlehem Steel Corporation, cash bonuses clearly excessive in amount were paid. In the case of American Tobacco Company, rights to buy stock below the market price, of an enormous aggregate value, were allotted to the officers. These privileges to buy stock are readily subject to abuse. In the case of Electric Bond and Share Company, the management permitted itself to buy many shares of stock at far below market price. When later the price of the stock collapsed to a figure less than the subscription price, the obligation to pay for the shares was cancelled, and the sums already paid were returned to the officers. A similar procedure was followed in the case of White Motor Company, which will be more fully discussed later in this chapter.

Some of these transactions are explained, and partly justified, by the extraordinary conditions of 1928–1932. Others are inexcusable from any point of view. Nevertheless, human nature being what it is, such developments are not in the least surprising. They do not really reflect upon the character of corporate managements but rather on the patent unwisdom of leaving such matters within the virtually uncontrolled discretion of those who are to benefit by their own decisions.

The new regulations have done much to dispel the mist of secrecy that formerly shrouded the emoluments and stockholdings of corporate officials. Information on salaries, bonuses and stock options must be filed in connection with new security offerings, with the registration of issues on a national exchange, with the subsequent annual reports to the Commission and with the solicitation of proxies.[1] Although these data are not complete, they are sufficient for the practical purpose of advising the stockholders as to the cost of their management. Similarly, stockholdings of officers, directors and those owning 10% of a stock issue must be revealed monthly.

Since this information is not too readily accessible to the individual stockholder, the statistical agencies could further improve their already excellent service by subjoining the salary and stockholding data to their annual lists of officers and directors.

---

[1] Also, under provisions of the Revenue Act of 1936 the Treasury published the names and compensation of all corporate officers receiving over $15,000 in that year. The Revenue Act of 1938 requires these data for salaries of $75,000 or more, beginning with 1938.

In recent years the question of excessive compensation to management has excited considerable attention, and the public understands fairly well that here is a field where the officers' views do not necessarily represent the highest wisdom. It is not so clearly realized that to a considerable extent the same limitations apply in matters affecting the use of the stockholders' capital and surplus. We have alluded to certain aspects of this subject in our discussion of dividend policies (Chap. 29). It should be evident also that the matter of raising *new capital* for expansion is affected by the same reasoning as applies to the withholding of dividends for this purpose.

Wisdom of Continuing the Business Should Be Considered. A third question, *viz.*, that of retaining the stockholder's capital in the business, involves considerations that are basically identical. Managements are naturally loath to return any part of the capital to its owners, even though this capital may be far more useful—and therefore valuable—outside of the business than in it. Returning *a portion* of the capital (*e.g.*, excess cash holdings) means curtailing the resources of the enterprise, perhaps creating financial problems later on and certainly reducing somewhat the prestige of the officers. Complete liquidation means the loss of the job itself. It is scarcely to be expected, therefore, that the paid officers will consider the question of continuing or winding up the business from the standpoint solely of what is in the best interests of the owners. We must emphasize again that the directors are often so closely allied with the officers—who are themselves members of the board—that they too cannot be counted upon to consider such problems purely from the stockholders' point of view.

Thus it appears that the question whether or not a business should be continued is one that at times may deserve independent thought by its proprietors, the stockholders. (It should be pointed out also that this is, by its formal or legal nature, an *ownership problem* and not a *management problem*.) And a logical reason for devoting thought to this question would arise precisely from the fact that the stock has long been selling considerably below its liquidating value. After all, this situation *must* mean that either the market is wrong in its valuation or the management is wrong in keeping the enterprise alive. It is altogether proper that the stockholders should seek to determine which of these is wrong. In this determination the views and explanations of the management deserve the most appreciative attention, but the whole proceeding would be stultified if the management's opinion on this subject were to be accepted as final *per se.*

It is an unhappy fact that in many cases where a management's policies are attacked the critic has some personal axe to grind. This too is perhaps inevitable. There is very little altruism in finance. Wars against corporate managements take time, energy and money. It is hardly to be expected that individuals will expend all these merely to see the right thing done. In such matters the most impressive and creditable moves are those made by a group of substantial stockholders, having an important stake of their own to protect and impelled thereby to act in the interests of the shareholders generally. Representations from such a source, *in any matter where the interest of the officers and the owners may conceivably be opposed*, should gain a more respectful hearing from the rank and file of stockholders than has hitherto been accorded them in most cases.[2]

Broadcast criticisms initiated by stockholders, proxy battles, and various kinds of legal proceedings are exceedingly vexatious to managements, and in many cases they are unwisely or improperly motivated. Yet these should be regarded as one of the drawbacks of being a corporate official and as part of the price of a vigilant stock ownership. The public must learn to judge such controversies on their merits, as developed by statements of fact and by reasoned argument. It must not allow itself to be swayed by mere accusation or by irrelevant personalities.

The subject of liquidation must not be left without some reference to the employees' vital interest therein. It seems heartless in the extreme to discuss such a decision solely from the standpoint of what will be best for the stockholder's pocketbook. Yet nothing is to be gained by confusing the issue. If the reason for continuing the business is primarily to keep the workers employed, and if this means a real sacrifice by the owners, they are entitled to know and to face the fact. They should not be told that it would be unwise for them to liquidate, when in truth it would be profitable but inhumane. It is fair to point out that under our present economic system the owners of a business are not expected to dissipate their capital for the sake of continuing employment. In privately owned enterprises

---

[2] The proxy regulations of the S.E.C. seek to facilitate the presentation of viewpoints opposed to the management by requiring the company to send out requests for proxies (and covering letters) supplied by individual stockholders, postage to be paid by the latter.

such philanthropy is rare. Whether or not a sacrifice of capital for this purpose is conducive to the economic welfare of the country as a whole is a moot point also, but it is not within our province to discuss it here. Our object has been to clarify the issue and to stress the fact that a market price below liquidating value has special significance to the stockholders and should lead them to ask their management some searching questions.

Management May Properly Take Some Interest in Market Price for Shares. Managements have succeeded very well in avoiding these questions with the aid of the time-honored principle that market prices are no concern or responsibility of theirs. It is true, of course, that a company's officers are not responsible for fluctuations in the price of its securities. But this is very far from saying that market prices should *never* be a matter of concern to the management. This idea is not only basically wrong, but it has the added vice of being thoroughly hypocritical. It is wrong because the marketability of securities is one of the chief qualities considered in their purchase. But marketability must presuppose not only a place where they can be sold but also an opportunity to sell them at a *fair price*. It is at least as important to the stockholders that they be able to obtain a fair price for their shares as it is that the dividends, earnings and assets be conserved and increased. It follows that the responsibility of managements to act in the interest of their shareholders includes the obligation to prevent—in so far as they are able—the establishment of either absurdly high or unduly low prices for their securities.

It is difficult not to lose patience with the sanctimonious attitude of many corporate executives who profess not even to know the market price of their securities. In many cases they have a vital personal interest in these very market prices, and at times they use their inside knowledge to take advantage in the market of the outside public and of their own stockholders.[3] Not as a startling innovation but as a common-sense

---

[3] This reached such scandalous proportions "in the good old days" that the Securities Exchange Act of 1934 made "insiders" accountable to the corporation for profits realized on purchases and sales, or *vice versa*, completed within a six months' period. Enforcement must be through a stockholder's suit. This provision has been bitterly criticized in Wall Street as preventing legitimate activities of officers and directors, including support of the market price at critical times. Our own view is that, on balance, both logic and practicality are against the provision as it now stands. Publicity of operations—perhaps immediate rather than monthly—should supply a sufficient safeguard against fraud and a check upon questionable conduct.

recognition of things as they are, we recommend that directors be held to the duty of observing the market price of their securities and of using all proper efforts to correct patent discrepancies, in the same way as they would endeavor to remedy any other corporate condition inimical to the stockholders' interest.

Various Possible Moves for Correcting Market Prices for Shares. The forms that these proper efforts might take are various. In the first place the stockholders' attention may be called officially to the fact that the liquidating, and therefore the minimum, value of the shares is substantially higher than the market price. If, as will usually be the case, the directors are convinced that continuance is preferable to liquidation, the reasons leading to this conclusion should at the same time be supplied. A second line of action is in the direction of dividends. A special endeavor should be made to establish a dividend rate proportionate at least to the liquidating value, in order that the stockholders should not suffer a loss of income through keeping the business alive. This may be done even if current earnings are insufficient, provided there are accumulated profits and provided also the cash position is strong enough to permit such payments.

A third procedure consists of returning to the stockholders such cash capital as is not needed for the conduct of the business. This may be done through a pro rata distribution, accompanied usually by a reduction in par value or through an offer to purchase a certain number of shares pro rata at a fair price. Finally, a careful consideration by the directors of the discrepancy between earning power and liquidating value may lead them to conclude that a sale or winding up of the enterprise is the most sensible corrective step—in which case they should act accordingly.

Examples: Otis Company, 1929–1939. The course of action followed by the Otis Company management in 1929–1930 combined a number of these remedial moves. In July 1929 the president circularized the shareholders, presenting an intermediate balance sheet as of June 30 and emphasizing the disparity between the current bid price and the liquidating value. In September of that year—although earnings were no larger than before—dividend payments were resumed, a step permitted by the company's large cash holdings and substantial surplus. In 1930 a good part of the cash, apparently not needed in the business, was returned to the stockholders through the redemption of the small preferred issue and the repayment of $20 per share of common stock on account of capital.[4]

Subsequently the company embarked on a policy of piecemeal liquidation which resulted in a series of payments on capital account. From September 1929 to the final distribution in 1940 there was paid a total of $94 per share as return of capital, as well as $8 in the form of dividends. As we pointed out in our last chapter, these steps were highly effective in improving the status of the Otis stockholders during a period when most other issues were suffering a shrinkage in value, and ultimately gave them a far larger return than they were likely to receive through the continuance of the business.

Hamilton Woolen Company. The history of this enterprise since 1926 is even more interesting in this connection because it suggests a model technique for the handling by directors of problems affecting the stockholders' investment. In 1927 continued operating losses had resulted in a market price well below liquidating value. There was danger that the losses might continue and wipe out the capital. On the other hand, there was a possibility of much better results in the future, especially if new policies were adopted. A statement of the arguments for and against liquidation was forwarded to the stockholders, and they were asked to vote on the question. They voted to continue the business, with a new operating head; and the decision proved a wise one, since good earnings were realized, and the price advanced above liquidating value.

In 1934, however, the company again showed a large loss, occasioned in good part by serious labor difficulties. The management again submitted the question of liquidation to the stockholders, and this time a winding up of the business was voted. A sale of the business was promptly arranged, and the stockholders received somewhat more than the November 1934 current-asset value.

Particularly noteworthy were the details of the 1927 proceedings. The ultimate decision—to continue or to quit—was put up to the stockholders in whose province it lay; the management supplied information,

---

[4] Other examples of partial return of capital by companies continuing in business include: Cuban Atlantic Sugar Company (1938–1939), Great Southern Lumber Company (1927–1937), Keystone Watch Case Corporation (1932–1933) as well as Davis Coal and Coke Company and the several Standard Oil pipe line companies previously referred to (pp. 529, 568).

expressed its own opinion and permitted an adequate statement of the other side of the case.

Other Examples of Voluntary Liquidation. The subjoined partial list will demonstrate an obvious but fundamental fact, *viz.*, that the liquidation (or sale) of an unprofitable company holding substantial assets (particularly current) is almost certain to realize for the stockholders considerably more than the previously existing market price. The reason is, of course, that the market price is governed chiefly by the earnings, whereas the proceeds of liquidation depend upon the assets.

Company	Year liquidation or sale voted	Price shortly before vote to liquidate or sell	Amount realized for stock
American Glue	1930	$53	$139.00+
I. Benesch & Sons	1939	$2^1/4$	6.63
Federal Knitting Mills	1937	20	34.20
Lyman Mills	1927	112	220.25
Mohawk Mining	1933	11	28.50
Signature Hosiery Pfd	1931	$3^1/8$	17.00
Standard Oil of Nebraska	1939	6	17.50
United Shipyards *A*	1938	$2^1/4$	11.10*

* To Dec. 31, 1939.

Repurchase of Shares Pro Rata from Shareholders. The Hamilton Woolen management is also to be commended for its action during 1932 and 1933 in employing excess cash capital to repurchase pro rata a substantial number of shares at a reasonable price. This reversed the procedure followed in 1929 when additional shares were offered for subscription to the stockholders. The contraction in business that accompanied the depression made this additional capital no longer necessary, and it was therefore a logical move to give most of it back to the stockholders, to whom it was of greater benefit when in their own pockets than in the treasury of the corporation.[5]

---

[5] Hamilton Woolen sold 13,000 shares pro rata to stockholders at $50 per share in 1929. It repurchased, pro rata, 6,500 shares at $65 in 1932 and 1,200 shares at $50 in 1933. Faultless Rubber Company followed a similar procedure in 1934. Simms Petroleum Company reacquired stock both directly from the shareholders on a pro rata basis and in the open market. Its repurchases by both means between 1930 and 1933 aggregated nearly 45% of the shares outstanding at the end of 1929. Julian and Kokenge (Shoe) Company made pro rata repurchases of common stock in 1932, 1934 and 1939.

Abuse of Shareholders through Open-market Purchase of Shares.

During the 1930–1933 depression repurchases of their own shares were made by many industrial companies out of their surplus cash assets,[6] but the procedure generally followed was open to grave objection. The stock was bought in the open market without notice to the shareholders. This method introduced a number of unwholesome elements into the situation. It was thought to be "in the interest of the corporation" to acquire the stock at the lowest possible price. The consequence of this idea is that those stockholders who sell their shares back to the company are made to suffer as large a loss as possible, for the presumable benefit of those who hold on. Although this is a proper viewpoint to follow in purchasing other kinds of assets for the business, there is no warrant in logic or in ethics for applying it to the acquisition of shares of stock from the company's own stockholders. The management is the more obligated to act fairly toward the sellers because the company is itself on the buying side.

But, in fact, the desire to buy back shares cheaply may lead to a determination to reduce or pass the dividend, especially in times of general uncertainty. Such conduct would be injurious to nearly all the stockholders, whether they sell or not, and it is for that reason that we spoke of the repurchase of shares at an unconscionably low price as only *presumably* to the advantage of those who retained their interest.

Example: White Motor Company. In the previous chapter attention was called to the extraordinary discrepancy between the market level of White Motor's stock in 1931–1932 and the minimum liquidating value of the shares. It will be instructive to see how the policies followed by the management contributed mightily to the creation of a state of affairs so unfortunate for the stockholders.

White Motor Company paid dividends of $4 per share (8%) practically from its incorporation in 1916 through 1926. This period included the depression year 1921, in which the company reported a loss of nearly $5,000,000. It drew, however, upon its accumulated surplus to maintain the full dividend, a policy that prevented the price of the shares from declining below 29. With the return of prosperity the

---

[6] Figures published by the New York Stock Exchange in February 1934 revealed that 259 corporations with shares listed thereon had reacquired portions of their own stock.

quotation advanced to 72$^1/_2$ in 1924 and 104$^1/_2$ in 1925. In 1926 the stock-holders were offered 200,000 shares at par ($50), increasing the company's capital by $10,000,000. A stock dividend of 20% was paid at the same time.

Hardly had the owners of the business paid in this additional cash, when the earnings began to shrink, and the dividend was reduced. In 1928 about $3 were earned (consolidated basis), but only $1 was disbursed. In the 12 months ending June 30, 1931 the company lost about $2,500,000. The next dividend payment was omitted entirely, and the price of the stock collapsed to 7$^1/_2$.

The contrast between 1931 and 1921 is striking. In the earlier year the losses were larger, the profit-and-loss surplus was smaller and the cash holdings far lower than in 1931. But in 1921 the dividend was maintained, and the price thereby supported. A decade later, despite redundant holdings of cash and the presence of substantial undistributed profits, a single year's operating losses sufficed to persuade the management to suspend the dividend and permit the establishment of a grotesquely low market price for the shares.

During the period before and after the omission of the dividend the company was active in buying its own shares in the open market. These purchases began in 1929 under a plan adopted for the benefit of "those filling certain managerial positions." By June 1931 about 100,000 shares had been bought in at a cost of $2,800,000. With the passing of the dividend, the officers and employees were relieved of whatever obligations they had assumed to pay for these shares, and the plan was dropped. In the next six months, aided by the collapse in the market price, the company acquired 50,000 additional shares in the market at an average cost of about $11 per share. The total holdings of 150,000 shares were then retired and cancelled.

These facts, thus briefly stated, illustrate the vicious possibilities inherent in permitting managements to exercise discretionary powers to purchase shares with the company's funds. We note first the painful contrast between the treatment accorded to the White Motor managerial employees and to its stockholders. An extraordinarily large amount of stock was bought for the benefit of these employees at what seemed to be an attractive price. All the money to carry these shares was supplied by the stockholders. If the business had improved, the value of the stock would have advanced greatly, and all the benefits would have gone to the employees.

When things became worse, "those in managerial positions" were relieved of any loss, and the entire burden fell upon the stockholders.[7]

In its transactions *directly with its stockholders*, we see White Motor soliciting $10,000,000 in new capital in 1926. We see some of this additional capital (not needed to finance sales) employed to buy back many of these very shares at one-fifth of the subscription price. The passing of the dividend was a major factor in making possible these repurchases at such low quotations. The facts just related without further evidence might well raise a suspicion in the mind of a stockholder that the omission of the dividend was in some way related to a desire to depress the price of the shares. If the reason for the passing of the dividend was a desire to preserve cash, then it is not easy to see why, since there was money available to buy in stock, there was not money available to continue a dividend previously paid without interruption for 15 years.

The spectacle of a company overrich in cash passing its dividend, in order to impel desperate stockholders to sell out at a ruinous price, is not pleasant to contemplate.

Westmoreland Coal Company: Another Example. A more recent illustration of the dubious advantage accruing to stockholders from a policy of open-market repurchases of common stock is supplied by the case of Westmoreland Coal. In the ten years 1929–1938 this company reported a net loss in the aggregate amounting to $309,000, or $1.70 per share. However, these losses resulted after deduction of depreciation and depletion allowances totaling $2,658,000, which was largely in excess of new capital expenditures. Thus the company's cash position actually improved considerably during this period, despite payment of very irregular dividends aggregating $4.10 per share.

In 1935, according to its annual reports, the company began to repurchase its own stock in the open market. By the end of 1938 it had thus acquired 44,634 shares, which were more than 22% of the entire issue. The average price paid for this stock was $8.67 per share. Note here the extraordinary fact that this average price paid *was less than one-half the cash-asset holdings alone* per share, without counting the very large other

---

[7] In the sale to Studebaker in 1933 the directors set aside 15,000 shares of treasury stock as a donation to key men in the organization. Some White stockholders brought suit to set aside this donation, and the suit was settled by payment of 31 cents per share on White stock not acquired by Studebaker.

tangible assets. Note also that at no time between 1930 and 1939 did the stock sell so high as its cash assets alone. (At the end of 1938 the company reported cash and marketable securities totaling $2,772,000, while the entire stock issue was selling for $1,400,000.)

If this situation is analyzed, the following facts appear clear:

1. The low market price of the stock was due to the absence of earnings and the irregular dividend. Under such conditions the quoted price would not reflect the very large cash holding theoretically available for the shares. Stocks sell on earnings and dividends and not on cash-asset values—unless distribution of these cash assets is in prospect.

2. The true obligation of managements is to recognize the realities of such a situation and to do all in their power to protect every stockholder against unwarranted depreciation of his investment, and particularly against unnecessary sacrifice of a large part of the true value of his shares. Such sacrifices are likely to be widespread under conditions of this kind, because many stockholders will be moved by necessity or the desire for steady income or by a discouraged view of the coal industry to sell their shares for what they can get.

3. The anomaly presented by exceptionally large cash holdings and an absurdly low market price was obviously preventable. That the company had more cash than it needed is confessed by the fact that it had money available to buy in cheap stock—even if it were not evident from a study of the unusual relationship between cash holdings and annual business done.

4. All cash that could possibly be spared should have been returned to the stockholders on a pro rata basis. The use of some of it to buy in shares as cheaply as possible is unjust to the many stockholders induced by need or ignorance to sell. It favors those strong enough to hold their shares indefinitely. It particularly advantages those in control of the company, for *in their case* the company's cash applicable to their stock is readily available to them if they should need it (since they could then bring about a distribution). Just because this situation is distinctly not true of the rank and file of the stockholders, the market discounts so cruelly the value of their cash when held by the company instead of themselves.[8]

---

[8] Two additional factors in this situation deserve brief mention. The company had a rental obligation of 10 cents per ton, but not less than $189,000 annually, for mining coal from leased lands. This liability was an additional consideration, besides the ordinary ones, which argued

Summary and Conclusion. The relationship between stockholders and their managements, after undergoing many unsound developments during the hectic years from 1928 to 1933, have since been subjected to salutary controls—emanating both from S.E.C. regulation and from a more critical viewpoint generally. Certain elementary facts, once well-nigh forgotten, might well be emphasized here: Corporations are in law the mere creatures and property of the stockholders who own them; the officers are only the paid employees of the stockholders; the directors, however chosen, are virtually trustees, whose legal duty it is to act solely in behalf of the owners of the business.[9]

To make these general truths more effective in practice, it is necessary that the stock-owning public be educated to a clearer idea of what are the true interests of the stockholders in such matters as dividend policies, expansion policies, the use of corporate cash to repurchase shares, the various methods of compensating management, and the fundamental question of whether the owners' capital shall remain in the business or be taken out by them in whole or in part.

---

for maintenance of a comfortable cash position, but it could not justify the immobilizing of far more cash than the whole company appeared to be worth at any time between 1930 and 1939.

In October 1939 the company made application to the S.E.C. to terminate trading in its shares on the Philadelphia Stock Exchange and the New York Curb Exchange, intimating that the infrequency of transactions might be responsible for their unduly low price. The reader may judge whether or not, in the circumstances, the plight of the stockholders would be relieved in any wise by destroying the established market for their shares. (The application was later withdrawn.)

[9] The management of American Telephone and Telegraph Company has repeatedly asserted that it considers itself a trustee for the interests of stockholders, employees and the public, in equal measure. A policy of this kind, if frankly announced and sincerely followed, can scarcely be criticized in the case of a quasi-civic enterprise. But given the ordinary business company, the issue is more likely to be whether the management is acting as trustees for the stockholders or as trustees for the management.

Chapter 45

BALANCE-SHEET ANALYSIS (*Concluded*)

OUR DISCUSSION IN THE preceding chapters has related chiefly to situations in which the balance-sheet exhibit apparently justified a higher price than prevailed in the market. But the more usual purpose of balance-sheet analysis is to detect the opposite state of affairs, *viz.*, the presence of financial weaknesses that may detract from the investment or speculative merits of an issue. Careful buyers of securities scrutinize the balance sheet to see if the cash is adequate, if the current assets bear a suitable ratio to the current liabilities, and if there is any indebtedness of near maturity that may threaten to develop into a refinancing problem.

WORKING-CAPITAL POSITION AND DEBT MATURITIES

Basic Rules Concerning Working Capital. Nothing useful may be said here on the subject of how much cash a corporation should hold. The investor must form his own opinion as to what is needed in any particular case and also as to how seriously an apparent deficiency of cash should be regarded. On the subject of the *working-capital ratio*, a minimum of $2 of current assets for $1 of current liabilities was formerly regarded as a standard for industrial companies.

But since the late 1920's a tendency towards a stronger current position developed in most industries, and we find that the great majority of industrial corporations show a ratio well in excess of 2 to 1.[1] There is some tendency now to hold that a company falling below the average of its group

---

[1] See Appendix Note 61, p. 800 on accompanying CD, for comprehensive data with reference to industrial corporations listed on the New York Stock Exchanges at the end of 1938. See also the annual compilations in *Moody's Manual of Industrials*.

should be viewed with suspicion.[2] This idea seems to us to contain something of a logical fallacy, since it necessarily penalizes the lower half of any group, regardless of how satisfactory the showing may be, considered by itself. We are unable to suggest a better figure than the old 2-to-1 criterion to use as a *definite quantitative test* of a sufficiently comfortable financial position. Naturally the investor would favor companies that well exceed this minimum requirement, but the problem is whether or not a higher ratio *must* be exacted as a condition for purchase, so that an issue otherwise satisfactory would necessarily be rejected if the current assets are only twice current liabilities. We hesitate to suggest such a rule, nor do we know what new figure to prescribe.

A second measure of financial strength is the so-called "acid test," which requires that current assets *exclusive of inventories* be at least equal to current liabilities. Ordinarily the investor might well expect of a company that it meet *both* the 2-to-1 test and the acid test. If *neither* of these criteria is met it would in most cases reflect strongly upon the investment standing of a common-stock issue—as it would in the case of a bond or preferred stock—and it would supply an argument against the security from the speculative standpoint as well.

ARCHER-DANIELS-MIDLAND COMPANY

Item	June 30, 1933	June 30, 1932
Cash assets	$ 1,392,000	$3,230,000
Receivables	4,391,000	2,279,000
Inventories	12,184,000	4,081,000
Total current assets	$17,967,000	$9,590,000
Current liabilities	8,387,000	778,000
Working capital	$ 9,580,000	$8,812,000
Working capital excluding inventories	−2,604,000	+4,731,000

Exceptions and Examples. As in all arbitrary rules of this kind, exceptions must be allowed if justified by special circumstances. Consider, for example, the current position of Archer-Daniels-Midland Company on June 30, 1933, as compared with the previous year's figures.

---

[2] See Roy A. Foulke, *Signs of the Times*, pp. 17–19, 25 *et seq.*, New York 1938; and Alexander Wall, *How to Evaluate Financial Statements*, pp. 82–97, New York, 1936. Note, however, Wall's criticism of mere arithmetical averages as bases for comparison.

The position of this company on June 30, 1933, was evidently much less comfortable than a year before, and, judged by the usual standards, it might appear somewhat overextended. But in this case the increase in payables represented a return to the normal practice in the vegetable-oil industry, under which fairly large seasonal borrowings are regularly incurred to carry grain and flaxseed supplies. Upon investigation, therefore, the analyst would not consider the financial condition shown in the 1933 balance sheet as in any sense disturbing.

Contrasting examples on this point are supplied by Douglas Aircraft Company and Stokely Brothers and Company in 1936–1938.

A WORKING-CAPITAL COMPARISON (**000** OMITTED)

Item	Stokely Brothers and Company			Douglas Aircraft Company		
	May 31, 1936	May 31, 1937	May 31, 1938	Nov. 30, 1936	Nov. 30, 1937	Nov. 30, 1938
Current assets:						
Cash and receivables	$2,274	$2,176	$1,827	$2,885	$ 2,559	$4,673
Inventories	5,282	7,323	6,034	6,392	12,240	4,084
Total	$7,556	$9,499	$8,861	$9,277	$14,749	$8,757
Current liabilities:						
Notes payable	$2,000	$2,000	$2,500	$1,390	$ 5,230	
Other	1,527	1,286	1,320	1,179	3,183	2,129
Total	$3,527	$3,286	$3,820	$2,569	$ 8,413	$2,129
Bank loans due 1–3 years		3,000	3,000			
Total current liabilities plus 1–3 year notes	3,527	6,286	6,820	2,569	8,413	2,129
Net earnings for year	1,382	353(d)	713(d)	976	1,082	2,147

The situation in Douglas Aircraft in 1937 was not a seasonal matter, as in the case of Archer-Daniels-Midland, but grew out of the receipt of certain types of orders requiring considerable working capital. Upon inquiry the investor could have satisfied himself that the need for bank accommodation was likely to be temporary and that, in any event, the new business was sufficiently profitable to make any necessary financing an easy affair. The Stokely picture was quite different, since the large current debt had developed out of expanding inventories in an unprofitable market. Hence the May 1937 balance sheet of Stokely carried a serious warning for the preferred and common stockholder, as the table shows.

A year later Douglas Aircraft had paid off its bank loans and showed a current ratio of 4 to 1. Stokely suspended preferred dividends in October 1938, and in that year the price of the issue fell from 21 (par $25) to 10.

As we pointed out in our discussion of bond selection (Chap. 13 on accompanying CD), no standard requirements such as we have been discussing are recognized as applicable to railroads and public utilities. It must not be inferred therefrom that the working-capital exhibit of these companies is entirely unimportant—the contrary will soon be shown to be true—but only that it is not to be tested by any cut-and-dried formulas.

Large Bank Debt Frequently a Sign of Weakness. Financial difficulties are almost always heralded by the presence of bank loans or of other debt due in a short time. In other words, it is rare for a weak financial position to be created solely by ordinary trade accounts payable. This does not mean that bank debt is a bad sign in itself; the use of a reasonable amount of bank credit—particularly for seasonal needs—is not only legitimate but even desirable. But, whenever the statement shows Notes or Bills Payable, the analyst will subject the financial picture to a somewhat closer scrutiny than in cases where there is a "clean" balance sheet.

The postwar boom in 1919 was marked by an enormous expansion of industrial inventories carried at high prices and financed largely by bank loans. The 1920–1921 collapse of commodity prices made these industrial bank loans a major problem. But the depression of the 1930's had different characteristics. Industrial borrowings in 1929 had been remarkably small, due first to the absence of commodity or inventory speculation and secondly to the huge sales of stock to provide additional working capital. (Naturally there were exceptions, such as, notably, Anaconda Copper Mining Company which owed $35,000,000 to banks at the end of 1929, increased to $70,500,000 three years later.) The large bank borrowings were shown more frequently by the railroads and public utilities. These were contracted to pay for property additions or to meet maturing debt or—in the case of some railways—to carry unearned fixed charges. The expectation in all these cases was that the bank loans would be refunded by permanent financing; but in many instances such refinancing proved impossible, and receivership resulted. The collapse of the Insull system of public-utility holding companies was precipitated in this way.

Examples: It is difficult to say exactly how apprehensively the investor or speculator should have viewed the presence of $68,000,000 of bank loans in the New York Central balance sheet at the end of 1932 or the bills payable of $69,000,000 owned by Cities Service Company on December 31, 1931. But certainly this adverse sign should not have been ignored. The more conservatively minded would have taken it as a strong argument against any and all securities of companies in such a position, except possibly issues selling at so low a price as to constitute an admitted but attractive gamble. An improvement in conditions will, of course, permit such bank loans to be refunded, but logic requires us to recognize that the improvement is prospective whereas the bank loans themselves are very real and very menacing.[3]

When a company's earnings are substantial, it rarely becomes insolvent because of bank loans. But if refinancing is impracticable—as frequently it was in the 1931–1933 period—the lenders may require suspension of dividends in order to make all the profits available to reduce the debt. It is for this reason that the dividend on Brooklyn-Manhattan Transit Corporation common was passed in 1932 and the preferred dividend of New York Water Service Corporation was passed in 1931, although both companies were reporting earnings about as large as in previous years.

The 1937–1938 recession did not create corporate financial problems comparable with those arising out of the two previous depressions. In this respect there is a significant contrast between the stock markets of 1919–1921 and 1937–1938. For the decline in stock prices was actually greater—both in dollars and percentagewise—in the recent period than in the postwar collapse, although intrinsically the 1937–1938 downturn was of much smaller importance, since it had relatively slight effect upon the position of American corporations generally.[4] This may be taken as a rather disquieting sign that stock prices have been growing more irrationally sensitive to temporary fluctuations in business—a fact that we

---

[3] Improvement in general business, plus easy money rates (plus in the case of railroads a misguided optimism on the part of investors) enabled many companies to fund bank loans that looked dangerous in 1931–1933.

[4] The Stokely case is an exception to this statement, but there were surprisingly few of the kind.

are inclined to ascribe to the disappearance of the old-line distinctions between stock investors and stock speculators.

Intercorporate Indebtedness. Current debt to a parent or to an affiliated company is theoretically as serious as any other short-term liability, but in practice it is rarely made the basis of an embarrassing claim for payment.

Example: United Gas Corporation has owed $26,000,000 on open account to its parent Electric Bond and Share Company since 1930—so that it constantly reports a large excess of current liabilities over current assets. Yet this debt has not prevented it from paying first preferred dividends in 1936–1939. In 1932, however, with somewhat larger earnings than in 1939, it had been compelled to suspend the senior dividend because it had large bank loans in addition to its intercompany debt. The conservative buyer would naturally prefer to see the obligations to affiliates in some form other than a current liability.

The Danger of Early Maturing Funded Debt. A large bond issue coming due in a short time constitutes a critical financial problem when operating results are unfavorable. Investors and speculators should both give serious thought to such a situation when revealed by a balance sheet. Maturing funded debt is a frequent cause of insolvency.

Examples: Fisk Rubber Company was thrown into receivership by its inability to pay off an $8,000,000 note issue at the end of 1930. The insolvency of Colorado Fuel and Iron Company and of the Chicago, Rock Island and Pacific Railway Company in 1933 were both closely related to the fact that large bond issues fell due in 1934. The heedlessness of speculators is well shown by the price of $54 established for Colorado Fuel and Iron Preferred in June 1933, when its short-term bond issue (Colorado Industrial Company 5s, due 1934, guaranteed by the parent company) was selling at 45, *an indicated yield of well over 100% per annum.* This price for the bonds was an almost certain sign of trouble ahead. Failure to meet the maturity would in all likelihood mean insolvency (for a voluntary extension could by no means be counted upon) and the danger of complete extinction of the stock issues. It was typical of the speculator to ignore so obvious a hazard and typical also that he suffered a large loss for his carelessness. (Two months later, on announcement of the receivership, the price of the preferred stock dropped to 17$^1/_4$.)

New York, Chicago, and St. Louis Railroad Company has been faced with a continuous financial problem growing out of the sale of a three-year note issue in 1929. Since the first maturity in 1932 it was repeatedly extended under threat of receivership as an alternative. Typical of speculative disregard of financial problems was the advance of this company's preferred stock from $18^1/_2$ to $45^3/_4$ in 1939, against a low price that year of only 50 for the notes due in 1941.

Even when the maturing debt can probably be taken care of in some way, the possible cost of the refinancing must be taken into account.

Examples: This point is well illustrated by the $14,000,000 issue of American Rolling Mill Company $4^1/_2$% Notes, due November 1, 1933. In June 1933 the notes were selling at 80, which meant an annual yield basis of about 75%. At the same time the common stock had advanced from 3 to 24 and then represented a total valuation for the common stock of over $40,000,000. Speculators buying the stock because of improvement in the steel industry failed to consider the fact that, in order to refund the notes in the poor market than existing for new capital issues, a very attractive conversion privilege would have to be offered. This would necessarily react against the profit possibilities of the common stock. As it happened, a new 5% note issue, convertible into stock at 25, was offered in exchange for the $4^1/_2$% notes. The result was the establishment of a price of 101 for the notes in August 1933 against a coincident price of 21 for the common stock; and a price of 15 for the stock on November 1, 1933, when the notes were taken care of at par.

The impending maturity of a bond issue is of importance to the holders of all the company's securities, including mortgage debt ranking ahead of the maturing issue. For even the prior bonds will in all likelihood be seriously affected if the company is unable to take care of the junior issue. This point is illustrated in striking fashion by the Fisk Rubber Company First Mortgage 8s, due 1941. Although they were deemed to be superior in their position to the $5^1/_2$% unsecured notes, their holders suffered grievously from the receivership occasioned by the maturity of the $5^1/_2$s. The price of the 8s declined from 115 in 1929 to 16 in 1932.[5]

Bank Loans of Intermediate Maturity.

The combination of very low interest rates and the drying up of ordinary commercial bank loans has

---

[5] See other references to the two Fisk bond issues in Chaps. 6, 18, and 50.

produced a new phenomenon in recent years—the loaning of money to corporations by banks, repayable over a period of several years. Most of this money has been borrowed for the purpose of retiring bond issues (*e.g.*, Commercial Investment Trust Corporation in November 1939) and even preferred stock (*e.g.*, Archer-Daniels-Midland Company in 1939). In some cases such loans have been made for additional working capital (*e.g.*, Western Auto Supply Company in 1937) or to replace ordinary short-term bank credit (*e.g.*, American Commercial Alcohol, Stokely Brothers). In most cases it is stipulated or expected that the loans will be retired in annual installments.

From the standpoint of security analysis this bank credit resembles the short-term notes that used to be sold to the public as a familiar part of corporate financing. It must be considered partly equivalent to current liabilities and partly to early maturing debt. It is not dangerous if either the current-asset position is so strong that the loans could readily be taken care of as current liabilities or the earning power is so large and dependable as to make refinancing a simple problem. But if neither of these conditions is present (as in the Stokely example on page 593), the analyst must view the presence of a substantial amount of intermediate bank debt as a potential threat to dividends or even to solvency.

It should not be necessary to dilate further upon the prime necessity of examining the balance sheet for any possible adverse features in the nature of bank loans or other short-term debt.

COMPARISON OF BALANCE SHEETS OVER A PERIOD OF TIME

This important part of security analysis may be considered under three aspects, *viz.*:

1. As a check-up on the reported earnings per share.
2. To determine the effect of losses (or profits) on the financial position of the company.
3. To trace the relationship between the company's resources and its earning power over a long period.

Check-up on Reported Earnings per Share, Via the Balance Sheet. Some of this technique has already been used in connection with related phases of security analysis. In Chap. 36 (on accompanying CD), for instance, we gave an example of the first aspect, in checking the reported earnings of American Commercial Alcohol Corporation for 1931 and 1932. As an example covering a larger stretch of years we submit the following contrast between the average earnings of United States Industrial Alcohol Company for the ten years 1929–1938, as shown by the reported per-share figures and as indicated by the changes in its net worth in the balance sheet.

U. S. INDUSTRIAL ALCOHOL COMPANY, 1929–1938

1. NET EARNINGS AS REPORTED

1929	$4,721,000	*per share: $12.63
1930	1,105,000	2.95
1931	*1,834,000(d)*	*4.90(d)*
1932	176,000	0.47
1933	1,393,000	3.56
1934	1,580,000	4.03
1935	844,000	2.15
1936	78,000	0.20
1937	*456,000(d)*	*1.17(d)*
1938	*668,000(d)*	*1.71(d)*
Total for 10 years	$6,782,000	$18.21

* As stated in the company's annual reports.

2. DISCREPANCY BETWEEN EARNINGS AS ABOVE AND CHANGES IN THE SURPLUS ACCOUNT

Net earnings 1929–1938, as reported	$ 6,782,000
Less dividends paid	5,959,000
(*A*) Indicated balance to surplus.......................................	823,000
Earned surplus Dec. 31, 1928..	14,214,000
Less charge @ write-down of plant account to $1 in 1933................	455,000
Earned surplus Dec. 31, 1928, as adjusted	13,759,000
Earned surplus and contingency reserve, Dec. 31, 1938	5,736,000
(*B*) Decrease in surplus on balance sheet	8,023,000
Discrepancy between earnings shown in income accounts and those indicated by balance sheets	$ 8,846,000

3. EXPLANATION OF DISCREPANCY

Charges made to surplus and not deducted in income account from which earnings per share were computed by company:	
Mark-down of inventory	$4,500,000
Charge-off and write-down of various assets	3,969,000
Miscellaneous adjustments, net	377,000
	$8,846,000

In addition to the foregoing the company wrote down its fixed assets to $1 in 1933 by a charge of $19,301,000, of which $18,846,000 was taken out of capital account and the balance out of surplus. To the extent that depreciation charges since 1932 may have been insufficient because of this write-down (see p. 495 on accompanying CD), the reported earnings for the period were further overstated.

4. RESTATEMENT OF EARNINGS FOR 1929–1938

Earnings per income account	$6,782,000
Less charges made to surplus	8,846,000
Earnings for period as corrected	$2,064,000(d)

5. WORKING CAPITAL COMPARISON: 1938 VS. 1928

Net working capital Dec. 31,1928	$11,336,000
Net working capital Dec. 31, 1938	8,144,000
Decrease for ten years	3,192,000
Add proceeds of sales of capital stock	6,582,000
Real shrinkage in working capital for period	$9,774,000

The foregoing analysis does not require extended discussion, since most of the points involved were covered in Chaps. 31 to 36 (Chaps. 35–36 on accompanying CD). Virtually all the charges made to surplus between 1929 and 1938 (except for the write-down of the plant account to $1) represented a real diminution of the reported earning power of United States Industrial Alcohol during this ten-year period. It seems likely, also, that the surplus would have shrunk considerably farther if the plant account had been carried at a proper figure and appropriate depreciation charged against it since 1932. The fact that the company's working capital decreased by $3,192,000, despite receipt of $6,582,000 from the sale of additional stock, is further evidence that, instead of there being a surplus above dividends as reported, the company actually lost money before dividends during these ten years.[6]

Checking the Effect of Losses or Profits on the Financial Position of the Company. An example of the second aspect was given in

[6] An analysis of the exhibit of Stewart Warner Corporation for 1925–1932, leading to similar conclusions, appeared at this point in our 1934 edition. Cf. W. A. Hosmer, "The Effect of Direct Charges to Surplus on the Measurement of Income," *Business and Modern Society*, ed. by M.P. McNair and H. T. Lewis. pp. 113–151, Harvard University Press, 1938.

Chap. 43, in the comparison of the 1929–1932 balance sheets of Manhattan Shirt Company and Hupp Motor Car Corporation respectively. A similar comparison is shown below, covering the exhibit of Plymouth Cordage Company and H. R. Mallinson and Company during the same period, 1929–1932.

Examples:

Item	Plymouth Cordage Co.	H. R. Mallinson & Co.
Earnings reported:		
1930	$ 288,000	*$1,457,000(d)*
1931	25,000	*561,000(d)*
1932	*233,000(d)*	*200,000(d)*
Total (3 years) profit	$ 80,000	*$2,218,000(d)*
Dividends	1,348,000	66,000
Charges to surplus and reserves	2,733,000	116,000
Decrease in surplus and reserve for 3 years	$4,001,000	$2,400,000

COMPARATIVE BALANCE SHEETS (000 OMITTED)

	Plymouth Cordage		H. R. Mallinson	
Item	Sept. 30, 1929	Sept. 30, 1932	Dec. 31, 1929	Dec. 31, 1932
Fixed and miscellaneous assets (net)	$ 7,211	$ 5,157	$2,539	$2,224
Cash assets	1,721	3,784	526	20
Receivables	1,156	668	1,177	170
Inventories	8,059	3,150	3,060	621
Total assets	$18,147	$12,759	$7,302	$3,035
Current liabilities	$ 982	$ 309	$2,292	$ 486*
Preferred stock			1,342	1,281
Common stock	8,108	7,394	500	500
Surplus and miscellaneous reserves	9,057	5,056	3,168	768
Total liabilities	$18,147	$12,759	$7,302	$3,035
Net current assets	$ 9,954	$ 7,298	$2,471	$ 357
Net current assets excluding inventory	1,895	4,143	*589(d)*	*264(d)*

* Including $32,000 of "deferred liabilities."

Despite the large reduction in the surplus of Plymouth Cordage during these years, its financial position was even stronger at the end of the period than at the beginning, and the liquidating value per share (as distinct from book value) was probably somewhat higher. On the other hand, the losses of Mallinson almost denuded it of working capital and thereby created an extremely serious obstacle to a restoration of its former earning power.

Taking Losses on Inventories May Strengthen Financial Position. It is obvious that losses that are represented solely by a decline in the inventory account are not so serious as those which must be financed by an increase in current liabilities. If the shrinkage in the inventory exceeds the losses, so that there is an actual increase in cash or reduction in payables, it may then be proper to say—somewhat paradoxically—that the company's financial position has been strengthened even though it has been suffering losses. This reasoning has a concrete application in analyzing issues selling at less than liquidating value. It will be recalled that, in estimating break-up value, inventories are ordinarily taken at about 50 to 75% of the balance sheet figure, even though the latter is based on the lower of

MANHATTAN SHIRT COMPANY (000 OMITTED)

Item	Balance sheet, Nov. 30, 1929		Balance sheet, Nov. 30, 1932	
	Book value	Estimated liquidating value	Book value	Estimated liquidating value
Cash and bonds at market	$ 885	$ 885	$1,961	$1,961
Receivables	2,621	2,100	771	620
Inventories	4,330	2,900	1,289	850
Fixed and other assets	2,065*	500	1,124	300
Total assets	$9,901	$6,385	$5,145	$3,731
Current liabilities	2,574	2,574	100	100
Preferred stock	299	299		
Balance for common	$7,028	$3,513	$5,045	$3,631
Number of shares	281,000	281,000	246,000	246,000
Value per share	$25.00	$12.50	$20.50	$14.75

* Excluding good-will.

(*Continues*)

INCOME ACCOUNT 1930–1932

Balance after preferred dividends:

1930	*318,000(d)*
1931	93,000
1932	*139,000(d)*
3 years	*364,000(d)*
Charges to surplus	505,000*
Common dividends paid	723,000
	$1,592,000
Less discount on common stock bought	481,000
Decrease in surplus for period	$1,111,000*

* Eliminating transfer of $100,000 to Contingency Reserve.

cost or market. The result is that what appears as an operating loss in the company's statement may have the actual effect of a profit from the standpoint of the investor who has valued the inventory in his own mind at considerably less than the book figure. This idea is concretely illustrated in the Manhattan Shirt Company example beginning on p. 602.

If we consider only the company's figures there was evidently a loss for the period, with a consequent shrinkage in the value of the common stock. But if an investor had bought the stock, say, at $8 per share in 1930 (the low price in that year was 6$\frac{1}{8}$), he would more logically have appraised the stock in his own mind on the basis of its liquidating value rather than its book value. From his point of view, therefore, the intrinsic value of his holdings would have *increased* during the depression period from $12.50 to $14.75 per share, even after deducting the substantial dividends paid. What really happened was that Manhattan Shirt turned the larger portion of its assets into cash during these three years and sustained a much smaller loss in so doing than a conservative buyer of the stock would have anticipated. This accomplishment can be summarized in the table on p. 604.

We have here a direct contrast between the superficial indications of the income account and the truer story told by the successive balance sheets. Situations of this kind justify our repeated assertion that income-account analysis must be supplemented and confirmed by balance-sheet analysis.[7]

---

[7] The student will note a similar development in Manhattan Shirt, though on a smaller scale, between December 1937 and December 1938.

Assets turned into cash and application of proceeds	Amount	"Expected loss" thereon and application of difference
Reduction in inventory	$3,000,000	$1,000,000
Reduction in receivables	1,800,000	350,000
Reduction in plant, etc.	1,000,000	750,000
	$5,800,000	$2,100,000
Actual loss sustained	800,000	800,000
Net amount realized	$5,000,000	"Gain" on basis of liquidation values $1,300,000
Applied as follows:		Applied as follows:
To common dividends	$ 700,000	To common dividends $700,000
To payment of liabilities	2,500,000	To increase liquidating value $600,000
To redemption of preferred	300,000	
To retirement of common	500,000	
To increase in cash assets	1,000,000	
	$5,000,000	

Is Shrinkage in Value of Normal Inventory an Operating Loss? A further question may be raised with respect to changes in the inventory account, *i.e.*, whether or not a mere reduction in the *carrying price* should be regarded as creating an operating loss. In the case of Plymouth Cordage we note the following comparative figures:

Inventory Sept. 30, 1929 .... $8,059,000

Inventory Sept. 30, 1932 3,150,000

Decrease 60%

In the meantime the price of fibers had declined more than 50%, and there was good reason to believe that the actual number of pounds of fiber, rope and twine contained in the company's inventory was not very much smaller in 1932 than in 1929. At least half of the decline in the inventory account was therefore due solely to the fall in unit prices. Did this portion of the shrinkage in inventory values constitute an operating loss? Could it not be argued that its fixed assets had suffered a similar reduction in their appraisal value and that there was as much reason to charge this shrinkage against earnings as to charge the shrinkage in the carrying price of a certain physical amount of inventory?

We have already discussed this point in our exposition of the "normal-stock" basis of inventory valuation (in Chap. 32), a method adopted by Plymouth Cordage itself after 1932. In theory the analyst might attempt to put all companies on a normal-stock basis for the purpose of calculating their earning power exclusive of inventory fluctuations and for uniform comparisons. Actually, he has not the data necessary for such calculations. Hence he is reduced—here, as in many fields of analysis—to the necessity of making general rather than exact allowance for the distorting effect of inventory price changes.

Profits from Inventory Inflation. That the importance of inventory price changes is not confined to a depression period is emphatically shown by the events of 1919 and 1920. In 1919 the profits of industrial companies were very large; in 1920 the reported earnings were irregular but in the aggregate quite substantial. Yet the gains shown in these two years were in many cases the result of an *inventory inflation, i.e.,* a huge and speculative advance in commodity prices. Not only was the authenticity of these profits thereby made open to question, but the situation was replete with danger because of the large bank loans contracted to finance these overvalued inventories.

Examples: The following tabulation, which covers a number of the leading industrial companies, will bring out the significant contrast between the apparently satisfactory earnings developments and the

TWELVE INDUSTRIAL COMPANIES (AGGREGATE FIGURES)

	Year 1919	Year 1920	Years 1919–1920
Earned for common stock	$100,000,000	$ 48,000,000	$148,000,000
Dividends paid	35,000,000	68,000,000	103,000,000
Charges to surplus	5,000,000	10,000,000	15,000,000
Added to surplus	60,000,000	*30,000,000* (decr.)	30,000,000
Inventories increased	57,000,000	84,000,000	141,000,000
Change in other net current assets	+30,000,000	*131,000,000* (decr.)	*101,000,000* (decr.)
Plant, etc. increased	33,000,000	169,000,000	202,000,000
Capitalization increased	69,000,000	141,000,000	210,000,000
Reserve increased		12,000,000	12,000,000

undoubtedly disquieting balance-sheet developments between the end of 1918 and the end of 1920.

The companies included in the foregoing computation were American Can, American Smelting and Refining, American Woolen, Baldwin Locomotive Works, Central Leather, Corn Products Refining, General Electric, B. F. Goodrich, Lackawanna Steel, Republic Iron and Steel, Studebaker, United States Rubber.

We append also the individual figures for United States Rubber, in order to add concreteness to our illustration:

U. S. RUBBER (1919–1920)

Earned for common stock:

1919	$12,670,000	Per share: $17.60
1920	16,002,000	19.76
Total	$28,672,000	$37.36
Cash dividends paid	8,580,000	
Stock dividend paid	9,000,000	
Transferred to contingency reserve	6,000,000	
Adjustments of surplus and reserves	cr. 2,210,000	
Net increase in surplus and miscellaneous reserves	$7,300,000	

BALANCE SHEET (000 OMITTED)

Item	Dec. 31, 1918	Dec. 31, 1920	Increase
Plant and miscellaneous assets (net)	$131,000	$185,500	$54,500
Inventories	70,700	123,500	52,800
Cash and receivables	49,500	63,600	14,100
Total assets	$251,200	$372,600	$121,400
Current liabilities	$ 26,500	$ 74,300	$ 47,800
Bonds	68,600	87,000	18,400
Preferred and common stock	98,400	146,300	49,900
Surplus and miscellaneous reserves	57,700	65,000	7,300
Total liabilities	$251,200	$372,600	$121,400
Working capital	93,700	112,800	19,100
Working capital excluding inventory	23,000	10,700(d)	33,700(d)

The United States Rubber figures for 1919–1920 present the complete reverse of Manhattan Shirt's exhibit for 1930–1932. In the Rubber example we have large earnings but a coincident deterioration of the financial position due to heavy expenditures on plant and a dangerous expansion of inventory. The stock buyer would have been led astray completely had he confined his attention solely to United States Rubber's reported earnings of nearly $20 per share in 1920; and, conversely, the securities markets were equally mistaken in considering only the losses reported during 1930–1932, without reference to the favorable changes occurring at the same time in the balance-sheet position of many companies.

It will be noted from our discussion here and in Chap. 32 that the matter of inventory profits or losses belongs almost equally in the field of income account and of balance-sheet analysis.

Long-range Study of Earning Power and Resources. The third aspect of the comparison of successive balance sheets is of restricted interest because it comes into play only in an exhaustive study of a company's record and inherent characteristics. The purpose of this kind of analysis may best be conveyed by means of the following applications to the long-term exhibits of United States Steel Corporation and Corn Products Refining Company.

I. United States Steel Corporation: Analysis of Operating Results and Financial
Changes by Decades, 1903–1932
(Analysis was made in 1933)

The balance sheets are adjusted to exclude an intangible item ("water"), amounting to $508,000,000, originally added to the Fixed Property Account. This was subsequently written off between 1902 and 1929 by means of an annual sinking-fund charge (aggregating $182,000,000) and by special appropriations from surplus. The sinking-fund charges in question are also eliminated from the income account.

A. OPERATING RESULTS (IN MILLIONS)

Item	First decade 1903–1912	Second decade 1913–1922	Third decade 1923–1932	Total for 30 years
Finished goods produced	93.4 tons	123.3 tons	118.7 tons	335.4 tons
Gross sales (excluding inter-company items)	$4,583	$9,200	$9,185	$22,968
Net earnings*	979	1,674	1,096	3,749
Bond interest	303	301	184	788
Preferred dividends	257	252	252	761
Common dividends	140	356	609†	1,105†
Balance to surplus and "voluntary reserves"	279	765	51	1,095

* After depreciation, but eliminating parent company sinking-fund charges.
† Including $204,000,000 paid in stock.

B. RELATION OF EARNINGS TO AVERAGE CAPITAL (ALL DOLLAR FIGURES IN MILLIONS)

Item	First decade	Second decade	Third decade	Total for 30 years
Capital at beginning	$ 987	$1,416	$2,072	$ 987
Capital at end	1,416	2,072	2,112	2,112
Average capital about	1,200	1,750	2,100	1,700
% earned on average capital, per year	8.1%	9.6%	5.2%	7.4%
% paid per year in interest and dividends on average capital	5.8%	5.2%	4.0%*	5.2%*
Average common stock equity (common stock, surplus, and reserves)	$237	$620	$1,389	$816
% earned on common stock equity	17.7%	18.3%	4.8%	9.0%
% paid on common stock equity	5.9%	5.7%	2.9%*	3.7%*
Depreciation per year	$24	$34	$46	$35
Average fixed property account	1,000	1,320	1,600	1,300
Ratio of depreciation to fixed property	2.4%	2.6%	2.9%	2.7%

* Excluding stock dividend.

C. Balance-Sheet Changes (All figures in millions)

Item	Dec. 31, 1902	Dec. 31, 1912	Changes in first decade	Dec. 31, 1922	Changes in second decade	Dec. 31, 1932	Changes in third decade	Changes in 30 years
Assets:								
Fixed (less deprec.) and misc.*	$820	$1,160	+$340	$1,466	+$306	$1,741	+$275	+ $921
Net current assets	167	256	+ 89	606	+ 350	371	− 235	+ 204
Total	$987	$1,416	+$429	$2,072	+$656	$2,112	+ $40	+$1,125
Liabilities:								
Bonds	$380	$680	+$300	$571	−$109	$116	−$455	− $264
Preferred stock	510	360	− 150	360		360		− 150
Preferred dividends accrued						5	+ 5	+ 5
Common stock	508	508		508		952†	+ 444	+ 444
Surplus and "voluntary" reserves*	411(d)	132(d)	+ 279	633	+ 765	679	+ 46	+ 1,090
Total	$987	$1,416	+$429	$2,072	+$656	$2,112	+ $40	+$1,125

* Eliminating initial mark-up of $508,000,000, later written off.
† Including premiums of $81,000,000 and stock dividend of $204,000,000.

The Significance of the Foregoing Figures. The three decades had, superficially at least, a somewhat equal distribution of good years and bad. In the first decade 1904 and 1908 were depression years, while 1911 and 1912 were subnormal. The second period had three bad years, *viz.*, 1914, 1921 and 1922—the last due to high costs rather than to small volume. The third decade was made up of eight years of prosperity followed by two of unprecedented depression.

The figures show that the war period, which occurred in the middle decade, was a windfall for United States Steel and added more than 300 millions to profits, as compared with the rate established in the first ten years. On the other hand, the last ten years were marked by a drastic falling off in the rate of earnings on the invested capital. The difference between the 5.2% actually earned and the 8% that might be regarded as a satisfactory annual average amounted to close to 600 million dollars for the ten-year period.

Viewing the picture from another angle, we note that in the thirty years the actual investment in United States Steel Corporation was more than doubled and its productive capacity was increased threefold. Yet the average annual production was only 27% higher, and the average annual earnings before interest charges were only 12% higher, in 1923–1932 than in 1903–1912. This analysis would serve to raise the question: (1) if, since the end of the war, steel production has been transformed from a reasonably prosperous into a relatively unprofitable industry and (2) if this transformation is due in good part to excessive reinvestment of earnings in additional plant, thus creating a condition of overcapacity with resultant reduction in the margin of profit.

Postscript. The soundness of the foregoing analysis, made in 1933, may be judged by developments since then. It should be pointed out that both the plant account figures and the annual earnings should be adjusted downward in the light of the later disclosures, *viz.:* (1) segregation from plant account in 1937 of $269,000,000 (and write-off of this amount in 1938), representing intangible assets at organization in addition to the $508,000,000 written off to 1929; (2) a charge to surplus of $270,000,000 in 1935 for additional amortization of fixed assets, presumably applicable to the entire preceding period. These later revisions, however, do not affect in any essential degree the conclusions drawn above.

The showing of United States Steel in the years since 1932 would appear to bear out the pessimistic implications of the 1933 study. During the six years 1934–1939, which is most instances supply a fair test period for judging normal earning power, "Steel" common earned an average of but 14¢ per share. New developments in products, processes or other factors—including war profits—may change the picture for the better, but this has become a matter for speculative anticipation of future improvement rather than a reasonable expectation based on past performance.

II. SIMILAR ANALYSIS OF CORN PRODUCTS REFINING COMPANY
FEBRUARY 28, 1906 TO DEC. 31, 1935

A. AVERAGE ANNUAL INCOME ACCOUNT
(**000** OMITTED FROM DOLLAR FIGURES)

	1906–1915	1916–1925	1926–1935
Earned before depreciation	$3,798	$12,770	$14,220
Depreciation	811	2,538	2,557
Balance for interest and dividends	2,987	10,232	11,663
Bond interest	516	264	88
Preferred dividends (paid or accrued)	2,042	1,879	1,738
Balance for common	429	8,089	9,837
Common dividends		2,751	8,421
Balance to surplus	429	5,338	1,416
Balance to surplus for period	4,290	53,384	14,159
Adjustment of common stock, surplus and reserves	cr. 1,282	cr. 6,026	dr. 5,986
Increase in common stock, surplus and reserves	5,572	59,410	7,173

B. BALANCE SHEETS

	Feb. 28, 1906	Dec. 31, 1915	Dec. 31, 1925	Dec. 31, 1935
Plant (less depreciation) and miscellaneous assets	$49,000	$51,840	$ 47,865	$ 34,532
Investment in affiliates	2,000	4,706	16,203	33,141
Net current assets	1,000	11,091	42,528	43,192
Total	$52,000	$67,637	$106,596	$110,865
Bonds	9,571	12,763	2,474	
Preferred stock	28,293	29,873	25,004	24,574
Common stock, surplus and miscellaneous reserves	14,136	19,708	79,118	86,291
Preferred dividend accrued		5,293		
Total	$52,000	$67,637	$106,596	$110,865

C. PERCENTAGE EARNED[1] AND PAID ON TOTAL CAPITALIZATION
AND ON COMMON-STOCK EQUITY

Item	1906–1915	1916–1925	1926–1935	29⁵/₆ years
Average capitalization	$59,818	$87,116	$108,730	$81,432
Earned thereon	5.0%	11.8%	10.7%	10.2%
Paid thereon	4.2%	5.6%	9.4%	7.3%
Average common equity	$16,922	$49,413	$82,704	$50,213
Earned thereon	2.5%	16.4%	11.9%	12.2%
Paid thereon	nil	5.6%	10.2%	7.8%

[1] Adjustments to Surplus and Reserves are excluded from earnings.

NOTES ON FOREGOING COMPUTATION

1. The plant account and common-stock equity are corrected throughout to reflect a write-down of $36,000,000 made in 1922 and 1923.

2. Bonds outstanding are increased in 1906 and 1912 to reflect liability for issues of subsidiaries. Plant, etc., is increased in the same amounts.

3. Estimates considered to be sufficiently accurate are used in the initial balance sheet.

4. Deductions for bond interest are partly estimated for the first two periods.

5. The adjustments of Common Stock, Surplus, and Reserves represent chiefly changes in Miscellaneous Reserves and shrinkage of marketable securities.

Comment on the Corn Products Refining Company Exhibit. The early period was one of subnormal earnings, which would have been still poorer if more nearly adequate depreciation charges had been made. As in the case of United States Steel, the war period brought enormous earnings to Corn Products. The decade 1916–1925 was marked as a whole by a great increase in working capital and a substantial reduction in funded debt and preferred stock. Depreciation charges exceeded expenditures on new plant.

In the 1926–1935 period we note a striking divergence from the exhibit of United States Steel for 1923–1932. Despite inclusion of the depression years Corn Products was almost able to increase its earning power proportionately with its enlarged capital investment. Its annual profits (both before and after depreciation) were about four times as large in this decade as in the period ending in 1915. (If we use the same years for comparison, we shall find that United States Steel actually earned less in 1926–1935 than in 1906–1915.) The balance-sheet changes were marked by a further substantial shrinkage in the property account (due to the liberal depreciation charged) but by a larger increase in the investment in affiliated companies—indicating a broad expansion of the company's activities.

It is clear that the record of Corn Products Refining Company does not suggest the same questions or doubts as arise from an examination of the United States Steel Corporation's exhibit.

PART VII

ADDITIONAL ASPECTS OF SECURITY ANALYSIS. DISCREPANCIES BETWEEN PRICE AND VALUE

THE GREAT ILLUSION OF THE STOCK MARKET AND THE FUTURE OF VALUE INVESTING

BY DAVID ABRAMS

In value-investing circles, you meet many people who claim to have been inspired by what Benjamin Graham and David Dodd wrote in *Security Analysis*. Most are, at the very least, stretching the truth. A fair number of aspiring and practicing value investors may indeed have devoured *The Intelligent Investor*. But I would wager that few have actually dug deeply into *Security Analysis* and fewer still have read the classic cover to cover. I have to confess that although I had delved into various parts of *Security Analysis,* I had never read it from first page to last. So when I was asked to write an introduction to Part VII, which comprises the last hundred pages of the book, it was time to do my homework. After more than 20 years as an investment professional, I finally read the value investors' equivalent of Deuteronomy. Entitled "Additional Aspects of Security Analysis. Discrepancies between Price and Value," Part VII covers a lot of ground: the valuation of warrants; the potential decrease in the value of a company's common stock when it issues options to management; the shortcomings of relative value analysis; and the greed of investment bankers. In the 75 years since the original edition was published, both the world at large and the financial markets have undergone cataclysmic change. Yet, as Graham and Dodd understood, how markets work, how companies are run, and how people—both investors and corporate managers—tend to act in certain situations never change.

The world likes to categorize things, including investing styles, in neat little boxes. So it is that the financial media frequently label market participants as "value," "growth," or "momentum" investors. That's all fine, but I can tell you that I've observed a great many investors over the years, and I've never seen a consistently successful one whose strategy was *not* based on a value approach—paying less for something than it is worth, either today or in the future. True, some people like to buy things that will grow and others are drawn to assets that beckon from the bargain counter, while still others like to engage in arbitrage activities, buying one thing and selling another to profit on the price differential, or spread. But every successful investor I've ever known makes a calculation that compares an asset's purchase price to its present or future value.

Whatever their approach, countless investors have used the principles laid out in *Security Analysis* to uncover bargains. Scads of people have become wealthy doing so, including many of the contributors to this revised edition, not to mention all the people who were smart enough to buy Berkshire Hathaway years ago. Their success is a testament to value investing's glorious past. But what about its future? Is the road ahead bright and prosperous? Or is it bleak and beggarly? Are there more people practicing Ben Graham's underlying principles than there are bargains for them to find? Is there just too much money chasing a finite supply of bargains? Or might a serious security analyst still be able to prosper over time?

I am optimistic about the future of value investing. To be sure, there are many bright and savvy people in the financial markets employing Graham and Dodd's techniques, but the markets themselves have grown exponentially. The chunk of capital being invested by the value-investing crowd is a small percentage of the overall capitalization of global financial markets. Having observed the markets for more than two decades, my sense is that, rather than a glut of Graham and Dodd acolytes picking through scarce opportunities to find a place for their cash, money is ever more prone to sloshing around in giant waves, flowing from one fad to the next. If anything, it seems that the people controlling these mega-sums have become less intelligent and less sophisticated over time. The last decade alone has brought incredible extremes in valuation, starting in 1999 and 2000 with the high-altitude Internet bubble that was fol-lowed in short order by the utter collapse of the tech market. In the sum-mer of 2002, we witnessed a tremendous corporate debt meltdown. But soon, these excessively low valuations were pushed off the front pages by the most generous and lax lending standards of all time. Now, as I write this introduction, the mortgage market is imploding, creating per-haps yet another new set of opportunities. That we've seen the last of these extreme swings seems doubtful.

What is driving this manic phenomenon? The explanation is some-thing I call the "Great Illusion of the Stock Market." Investing looks easy, particularly in a world of inexpensive software and online trading. Buy-ing a stock is no more difficult than buying a book on Amazon.com. And because a great many people *have* gotten wealthy in the stock market, lots of others have come to believe that anyone can get rich with very little effort. They are wrong. All the people I know who've built wealth in the stock market have worked very hard at it. Graham and Dodd under-stood the effort it took to be successful in the market. They wrote:

> Since we have emphasized that analysis will lead to a positive conclusion
> only in the exceptional case, it follows that many securities must be
> examined before one is found that has real possibilities for the analyst.
> By what practical means does he proceed to make his discoveries?
> Mainly by hard and systematic work. (p. 669)

So, yes, you can get rich buying and selling stocks, but, as the authors well knew, it takes hard work and patience. Nevertheless, the Great Illu-sion persists, maybe because, like Woody Allen's film character Zelig, the market is a chameleon that changes its appearance to suit the times. Sometimes, it shows up as a tech stock bubble. Other times, it manifests itself as a ludicrously overvalued stock market as seen in the late 1980s in Japan. In a current incarnation, a raft of financial institutions across America are trying to emulate the success of David Swensen and his colleagues who manage Yale University's endowment by allocating large percentages of the capital to "alternative investment managers."

But the Great Illusion is just that—an illusion. If you want to get wealthy in the financial markets, you'll need to engage in "hard and systematic work." And for that, many sections of Part VII of *Security Analysis* are still essential. Given the drastic changes in the world since the book first appeared, it should come as no surprise that some of the material is no longer relevant for today's investor, and these shortcomings bear mentioning. So as we take a quick tour through this part, I'll point out some deficiencies along with the authors' nuggets of wisdom that still ring true.

One of the shortcomings shows up early in the first chapter of Part VII, in Chapter 46, "Stock-option Warrants," which is on the accompanying CD. This chapter may well be the most dated. When the book was first published, the derivatives market was still in its infancy. Fischer Black and Myron Scholes had not yet developed their famous formula for valuing stock options, and the products that now pervade the financial markets—options, interest rate futures, swaps, swaptions, and so on—were not fixtures in the financial markets. Chapter 46 homes in on stock warrants, one of the few derivative securities available at that time. The authors make some good points with their few specific examples, but their analysis is not sophisticated enough for today's world.

Take their example of Barnsdall Oil warrants. Graham and Dodd correctly conclude that these warrants were undervalued because the market priced them at their intrinsic value. It's not terribly relevant in today's world because such mispricing wouldn't last long. Besides pointing out the obvious—it's better to own a warrant trading at its intrinsic value than to own the underlying stock—Graham and Dodd note the leverage inherent in warrants and options. This analysis is good as far as it goes, but it just doesn't go far enough. The authors were able to identify that the Barnsdall Oil warrants were mispriced relative to the common stock, but they weren't able to provide the reader with an intellectual framework or the tools needed to value the warrants properly.

I should make it clear that just because an asset is overvalued or undervalued, it's not necessarily a good idea to try to capitalize on that mispricing. If the derivatives market fully understands the misvaluation of the underlying security, there is no particular edge to owning the derivative. However, if the market undervalues the derivatives on a mispriced security or group of securities, the odds to the derivative investor can be *very* favorable. In effect, the investor benefits from the double leverage of two mispriced securities—the underlying *and* the derivative. Although such a situation doesn't arise often, it can be particularly profitable. The ability to capture the compound mispricings can lead to extraordinary profits.

Perhaps the most famous example of this phenomenon occurred in the late 1980s, when the Japanese stock market rose to greater and greater heights, ultimately reaching an absurd level of overvaluation. While some believed that this was a "new era" in which Japan would economically dominate the world, value investors took a different view, believing instead that it was simply a case of a financial bubble that would ultimately correct itself. On Wall Street, there was a growing and widespread understanding that the Japanese stock market would eventually decline to more reasonable and rational levels, which spelled opportunity for those able to capitalize on what promised to be a dramatic price movement.

Against this backdrop, options sellers were, amazingly, willing to offer puts on the Nikkei Index at a remarkably cheap price. I remember asking the brokers who sold these options, "Who is taking the other side of these trades?" "European institutions," they said, which is the standard reply of Wall Street brokers who don't want to tell you what's really going on. In the end, it turned out that much of the exposure was held by Japanese financial institutions that were so confident their market would never go down that they wrote these multiyear contracts and took the entire premium into income immediately. Ultimately, the Japanese market collapsed, and my then employer, along with many other U.S. investors, profited handsomely as the puts soared in value.

More recently, the derivatives market in asset-backed securities of subprime mortgages offered a similarly distorted risk-reward equation in the form of credit default swaps (CDSs). These securities are a series of puts on bonds backed by subprime mortgages on residential property. When the bonds were issued, they were viewed by both investors and the rating agencies as safe (that is, investment grade) because of the assumptions about how these mortgages would perform. However, some astute investors realized that the underlying collateral was much riskier and subject to far more downside than the buyers originally assumed when they purchased CDSs on subprime bonds and indexes. When the subprime market collapsed in 2007, some of these securities increased in value more than 50 or 60 times the amount at risk. Every trade always has two sides, so it helps if you can figure out the thought process of the person on the opposite side of the trade. Warren Buffett once wrote: "If you've been in the poker game for 30 minutes and you don't know who the patsy is, you're the patsy."

"Work It Out"

Like Graham and Dodd, my own initial approach to the derivatives market was rather simplistic, and I well remember the day my young eyes were opened to the perils and pitfalls of my naiveté.

It was the early 1980s and I was just starting out on Wall Street. Derivatives were still a mostly nascent market, and stock options were among the first of these instruments to attract much attention. Like Graham and Dodd and many others on the Street, I grasped the leveraged nature of stock options and how they could be used to magnify the gains (or losses) of an individual stock position. But my knowledge beyond the basics was scant. I was working in the risk arbitrage department of a firm that did a lot of options arbitrage. And although I didn't yet understand what that meant, I did understand that the guys sitting next to me were making a lot of money doing it. What is more, they seemed to come in just before the market opened, left promptly right after the market closed, and never even glanced at the *Wall Street Journal,* preferring instead to read the gossipy *New York Post.* My curiosity was aroused. So one day I asked Ira, the head of the firm, to explain to me what he did. The two-minute conversation that followed forever changed the way I looked at derivatives and profoundly affected the way I've approached unfamiliar areas in finance and business ever since.

Ira pointed to a stock (I can't remember which one, although it could easily have been IBM since, in those days, the sun on Wall Street literally rose and set on whatever IBM was doing) and asked me this question: "What if you buy the $35 calls, sell the $40 calls, buy the $40 puts, and sell the $35 puts all at the same time?" My first thought was, "You've got a mess," but I didn't say that. I simply looked baffled. Seeing my confusion, he said, "Work it out. What's it worth at expiration?" After a few minutes with pencil and paper, I looked up, still a bit confused, and said, "It's always worth $5." "Right," he said. But still the light did not flicker in my brain until Ira asked, "What if you could buy it for $4.50?" Bingo! I finally got it. Even though I was new to Wall Street, I had done enough arbitrage to understand what Ira was saying. Typically, the most liquid option contracts are those with expiration dates relatively close by;

which means that if you could buy this "box," as it is called, consisting of two pairs of options for $4.50, you would make a guaranteed 11% on your money in less than six months.

It was my turn to pose a question. "Can you really buy them for $4.50?" I asked. "Sometimes," he said. And then I realized who had been the proverbial patsy in the poker game. It was me. By relying on Graham and Dodd's overly simplistic approach to the options market and not fully understanding the mathematics of the instruments in which I was investing, I didn't appreciate how the trade might look to the person on the other side. I was ripe for the picking, as they say. Perhaps my trades had been the other side of someone's buying a box for $4.50. I realized that, in all likelihood, the guy on the other side was probably smarter than I was. Embarrassed by my own ignorance, I vowed to wade into new situations with a greater respect for those on the other side of the trade and with more humility about the limits of my own knowledge. Never again would I be the patsy. That approach has served me well throughout my career.

Unlike the world in which Graham and Dodd lived and worked, today's security analyst is at a disadvantage without a good understanding of how option pricing models work and what their limitations are. Not only are derivatives pervasive in the financial markets but many corporations and investment entities use them for purposes both prudent and reckless.

As I continued to acquire experience and learned more about options and the models used to value them, I became aware of a major weakness in options theory. By and large, the academic work underpinning derivatives analysis, work that so many on Wall Street rely on, is predicated on the assumption that the markets are "efficient." The authors of *Security Analysis* would have had a good time arguing with these academics. They understood that the underlying premise of efficiency is not always true, writing:

Evidently the processes by which the securities market arrives at its appraisals are frequently illogical and erroneous. These processes, as we pointed out in our first chapter, are not automatic or mechanical but psychological, for they go on in the minds of people who buy and sell. (p. 669)

Ahead of their time when it came to the question of market efficiency, Graham and Dodd weren't able to foresee a need for the more complex mathematical relationships pointed out by my boss. They looked only at the relationship between the derivative security and the underlying instrument, which made for a somewhat primitive method of warrant analysis. Nevertheless, they did possess a keen understanding of how option and warrant issuance can affect the future value of the issuing company's common stock. In fact, they understood it better than many of today's accountants and Wall Street analysts. In a subsection entitled "A Dangerous Device for Diluting Stock Values," the authors write,

The public's failure to comprehend that all the value of option warrants is derived at the expense of the common stock has led to a practice that would be ridiculous if it were not so mischievous. (p. 653 on accompanying CD)

Those words could just as easily have been penned any time in the last decade, as some of the compensation schemes recently adopted at certain corporations have been shortchanging shareholders by masking the dilutive impact and inflating the income statement.

Until recently, companies recorded no expense on their income statements for the cost of options issued to management and directors. A couple of years ago, the rules were changed, and Generally Accepted Accounting Principles (GAAP) began requiring companies to use one of several methods to value the cost of their stock options. It's a big improvement over the prior practice of recording no expense, but the methods mandated by GAAP are the same as those used by analysts to value derivatives not issued by the company. Clearly, something is amiss. There is a huge difference between derivative contracts with third parties that do not result in more shares being issued and company-issued options that increase the number of its shares outstanding in the future, thereby diluting the interests of the current stockholders. Long-term shareholders need to fully appreciate the impact of these options issued by corporations to management; otherwise they'll find themselves shortchanged in the years to come.

Beware of the Investment Bankers!

Moving on to Chapter 47, "Cost of Financing and Management," Graham and Dodd might more aptly have named it, "Beware of the Investment Bankers!" As the saying goes, "The more things change, the more they stay the same." Or, as a friend once told me with regard to conflicts of interest on Wall Street, "Where there's no conflict, there's no interest." The reader will find it interesting to learn about ancient abuses at the hands of investment bankers, while the folks at Goldman Sachs and Morgan Stanley may shed a few tears of nostalgia when they read about the good old days of 20% underwriting spreads on the likes of American Bantam Car Corporation Convertible Preference Stock. But the last page of the chapter really stands out for its enduring relevance. Graham and Dodd wrote,

> The relaxation of investment bankers' standards in the late 1920s, and
> their use of ingenious means to enlarge their compensation, had
> unwholesome repercussions in the field of corporate management.
> Operating officials felt themselves entitled not only to handsome salaries
> but also to a substantial participation in the profits of the enterprise. . . .
> But it may not be denied that devious and questionable means were fre-
> quently employed to secure these large bonuses to the management
> without full disclosure of their extent to the stockholders. . . . With pub-

licity given to this compensation, we believe that the self-interest of stockholders may be relied on fairly well to prevent it from passing all reasonable limits. (p. 642)

So many of the recent excesses—from the Internet bubble to the leveraged buyout craze to the subprime mortgage fiasco—bear more than a passing resemblance to the shenanigans Graham and Dodd described years ago. And while the pair probably would not have been surprised at some of the excessive compensation at the corporate level, they likely would have been shocked that these excesses reached into the management of the New York Stock Exchange itself. Today's investors would do well to view Wall Street with at least the same degree of reproach and skepticism our authors exhibited in their writings.

Jumping ahead, Chapter 50, "Discrepancies between Price and Value," and Chapter 51, "Discrepancies between Price and Value (Continued)," are among the gems of Part VII, and anyone interested in investing should read them. They provide the reader with a useful list of dos and don'ts, places to look for value, and traps to avoid, illustrated by examples from the 1930s. Many of us have a tendency to romanticize the past, and when investors engage in such fond reminiscence, they often speak wistfully of Graham's era. Oh, for a return to the days when stocks sold at seven times earnings and less than working capital! And I must admit that when I read the Group A list in Chapter 50, I, too, felt a twinge of envy. How easy it must have been to be an investor in the late 1930s!

But wait a minute, I thought. I've encountered numerous opportunities in my own lifetime that would have made Graham green with envy. The truth is that, from time to time, financial markets present opportunities to buy assets that have remarkable risk-reward characteristics. It can be described only as the best of all worlds when an investor has the chance to make a decent amount of money in the worst case and oodles in the best case. My personal list begins with the Management Assistance Liquidating Trust—perhaps my first true value investment—and includes Public Service of New Hampshire 18% second mortgage bonds trading at par; Executive Life Muni GICs trading at 25 cents on the dollar in the wake of a trial court judge's decision later declared on appeal to have "no basis in law or reason"; and Gentiva common stock, a spin-off resulting from a merger that was trading at about a third of its working capital.

Around the same time Ira was enlightening me about the options market, my friend Chris Stavrou introduced me to Management Assistance Liquidating Trust when he faxed me the 10-Q, adorned with his handwritten notes. As he walked me through, I could see exactly what he saw: a stock trading at $2 that was worth $4. What's more, the company was now obligated to pay out to shareholders all the proceeds from the sale of its assets. Knowing that this was a certain double, I promptly sold all my other holdings and put 100% of my assets (all $10,000 worth) into this one stock. My only regret is that I didn't buy any for my company because I was afraid my boss, who was on vacation at the time, would disapprove of the investment.

One of the most recent and spectacular sets of opportunities occurred in mid-2002, amid the epic meltdown in the corporate bond market. Bargains were there for the taking—left, right, and center. Corporate bond market investors that year had stories galore. Mine was the AES 10.25% Senior Subordinated Notes, which traded as low as 15 cents on the dollar. At that price, the *current yield* was close to 66%. AES was a complex company with assets all over the world. Furthermore, it was financed in a nontraditional way with a combination of project-specific debt as well as corporate debt of different levels of seniority. The high degree of leverage combined with the complexity of the asset base caused the market to be concerned that the company would be forced into bankruptcy. Our analysis led us to the conclusion that there was more than sufficient value and cash flow to cover the debt. As it turned out, we were correct. These bonds never missed a payment and were called at par within a year of hitting their lows. Talk about a windfall! Surely, Ben Graham would have marveled at the bond market's temporary insanity in the summer of 2002.

As I continued reading through Part VII, I was particularly and delightedly struck by the authors' use of the English language. Their ability to express ideas cogently and clearly has seldom been matched in the field of finance, with the exception of perhaps their best and most famous student, Warren Buffett. After all, it was Graham and Dodd who created the parable of a manic Mr. Market, the gentleman who may be your friend or your enemy but who is someone whose advice you should never accept. A great example of their effective use of language is found in the discussion of the shortcomings of "market analysis."

It was also Graham and Dodd who coined the term "margin of safety," which has special relevance for the investment professionals who contributed to this edition of the book. All of us are fundamental analysts who examine securities one at a time, weighing the risk and reward characteristics of each investment at a particular price. While we may, from time to time, have views on where the stock market is headed, we generally do not make bets on its direction. Our reasons are many, but I think Graham and Dodd said it best when they wrote in Chapter 52:

> In market analysis there are no margins of safety; you are either right or wrong, and if you are wrong, you lose money. (p. 703)

That really sums it up nicely, doesn't it? Yet, all these years later, many investors are still consumed with formulating their own market view. Wall Street's finest firms employ market strategists, and many investors, professional and otherwise, are eager to hear those views. This, I submit, is simply more evidence that the Great Illusion persists.

In the very last chapter, Graham and Dodd offer advice to different groups of market participants, among them the small investor, the well-heeled investor, and the institutional investor. How has their advice held up?

For the small investor interested in income, the authors felt that the only suitable investment was U.S. government savings bonds. The securities performed as promised, of course, but there were a couple of developments that Graham and Dodd did not and could not foresee. First and foremost were the ravaging effects of inflation in the late 1970s and early 1980s. The inflationary spiral ultimately led to higher interest rates and large losses for bond investors. Second was the expansion of the fixed income markets and the proliferation of innumerable fixed income securities that created opportunities for value investing in the bond market for those willing to sift through vast numbers of similar instruments in search of anomalous pricing.

Graham and Dodd advised profit-seeking investors, both large and small, to purchase securities trading below their intrinsic value, and they suggested that investors submit their analytical work for critique by others. In essence, they were recommending that investors should all become part-time security analysts. Writing in the aftermath of the 1929 crash and ensuing Great Depression, the prospect of the kind of financial market profitability we've seen in recent years was unimaginable. In today's hypercompetitive world, it may be possible to succeed as a part-time investor, but it's not something I'd recommend. And if you don't want to devote yourself full-time to researching investments, you're probably better off engaging some professional assistance.

The prolific pair also advised institutions to invest solely in fixed income investments, if doing so would fulfill their needs. Fortunately, for universities such as Harvard, Yale, and Princeton, men such as Jack Meyer, David Swensen, and Andy Golden didn't follow that advice. And because of it, those institutions have far more resources at their disposal today than they would have otherwise. Thanks to the insight and independent thinking of these individuals, their respective institutions all have endowments measured in the tens of billions that give them a huge and perhaps permanent competitive advantage over many of their less wealthy peers. Beyond any specific advice that Graham and Dodd offered, the most important point investors should take away from *Security Analysis* is this: look at the numbers and think for yourself. All the great investors do, and that's what makes them great.

Interestingly enough, one group of investors was left out when Graham and Dodd were dispensing advice in the last chapter of *Security Analysis*. They had nary a word for all the young people starting out in financial careers that they undoubtedly hoped would bring them fortune and happiness, if not fame. To rectify that oversight, I offer a few last words of advice to this group. Many of my collaborators on this project are, like me, investment professionals who were once in your shoes— young, new to Wall Street, with little if any money in our bank accounts, but armed with energy, hope, and a good work ethic. We feel a particularly strong kinship with you. I think all of us would agree that we made a great career choice. And although we may initially have been motivated by the money, it's been a long time since the accumulation of wealth was the force that sends us into the office each day. We do what we do because we enjoy it. We relish the challenge, the stimulation, and the satisfaction that comes with finding the next bargain the market has to offer.

A number of years ago some professors at the University of Chicago concluded that Graham and Dodd had it all wrong. The market, they said, *was* efficient. In effect, they told aspiring analysts such as you: "Don't bother. Don't waste your time. The market is too efficient for you to be rewarded by your effort. Find something else to do with your life." For a long time, it was fashionable for people in financial circles to debate this topic, with the professors marshaling arguments in favor of their position and the practitioners insisting they were wrong, often pointing to the many aberrations that could not be explained by the academic theories.

Recently, the debate has died down, or perhaps it's just that the practitioners are too busy making money, too busy unearthing the next mispriced security, to find the time to argue anymore. As rewarding as our careers have been, I think all of us would tell you that it's been a constant intellectual challenge to understand an ever-changing and increasingly global financial world in a competition that draws many exceptionally talented, bright, and hardworking entrants. But it is just such rigorous competition among colleagues and friends that brings out the best in us. I, for one, feel fortunate to have met so many intellectually curious, hardworking, and motivated people during my time on Wall Street.

And so, to the aspiring young analyst, I can tell you that the answer to the question of the market's efficiency or lack thereof is clear: The market is inefficient enough. "Enough for what?" you ask. Inefficient enough for me—and you—to find some great opportunities from time to time. Not every day or every week, but often enough. The Great Illusion persists, leaving plenty of opportunities for those who wish to do the hard, sometimes boring, and often tedious work of value investing. Happy hunting!

See accompanying CD for Chapter 46, "Stock-option Warrants."

Chapter 47

COST OF FINANCING
AND MANAGEMENT

LET US CONSIDER IN MORE DETAIL the organization and financing of Petroleum Corporation of America, mentioned in the last chapter. This was a large investment company formed for the purpose of specializing in securities of enterprises in the oil industry. The public was offered 3,250,000 shares of capital stock at $34 per share. The company received therefore a net amount of $31 per share, or $100,750,000 in cash. It issued to unnamed recipients—presumably promoters, investment bankers and the management—warrants, good for five years, to buy 1,625,000 shares of additional stock, also at $34 per share.

This example is representative of the investment trust financing of the period. Moreover, as we shall see, the technique on this score that developed in boom years was carried over through the ensuing depression, and it threatened to be accepted as the standard practice for stock financing of all kinds of enterprises. But there is good reason to ask the real meaning of a set-up of this kind, first, with respect to what the buyer of the stock gets for his money, and second, with respect to the position occupied by the investment banking houses floating these issues.

Cost of Management; Three Items. A new investment trust—such as Petroleum Corporation in January 1929—starts with two assets: cash and management. Buyers of the stock at $34 per share were asked to pay for the management in three ways, *viz.*:

1. By the difference between what the stock cost them and the amount received by the corporation.

It is true that this difference of $3 per share was paid not to the management but to those underwriting and selling the shares. But from the standpoint of the stock buyer the only justification for paying more for the stock than the initial cash behind it would lie in his belief that the management was worth the difference.

2. By the value of the option warrants issued to the organizing interests.

These warrants in essence entitled the owners to receive one-third of whatever appreciation might take place in the value of the enterprise over the next five years. (From the 1929 view-point a five-year period gave ample opportunity to participate in the future success of the business.) This block of warrants had a real value, and that value in turn was taken out of the initial value of the common stock.

The price relationships usually obtaining between stock and warrants suggest that the 1,625,000 warrants would take about one-sixth of the value away from the common stock. On this basis, one-sixth of the $100,750,000 cash originally received by the company would be applicable to the warrants, and five-sixths to the stock.

3. By the salaries that the officers were to receive, and also by the extra taxes incurred through the use of the corporate form.

Summarizing the foregoing analysis, we find that buyers of Petroleum Corporation shares were paying the following price for the managerial skill to be applied to the investment of their money:

1. Cost of financing ($3 per share)	$9,750,000
2. Value of warrants (1/6th of remaining cash)	about 16,790,000
3. Future deductions for managerial salaries, etc	?
Total	$26,540,000+

The three items together may be said to absorb between 25 and 30% of the amount contributed by the public to the enterprise. By this we mean not merely a deduction of that percentage of future profits but an actual sacrifice of invested *principal* in return for management.

What Was Received for the Price Paid? Carrying the study a step farther, let us ask what kind of managerial skill this enterprise was to enjoy? The board of directors consisted of many men prominent in finance, and their judgment on investments was considered well worth having. But two serious limitations on the value of this judgment must here be noted. The first is that the directors were not obligated to devote themselves exclusively or even preponderantly to this enterprise. They were permitted, and seemingly intended, to multiply these activities indefinitely. Common sense would suggest that the value of their expert judgment to

Petroleum Corporation would be greatly diminished by the fact that so many other claims were being made upon it at the same time.

A more obvious limitation appears from the Corporation's projected activities. It proposed to devote itself to investments in a single field—petroleum. The scope for judgment and analysis was thereby greatly circumscribed. As it turned out, the funds were largely concentrated, first in two related companies—Prairie Pipe Line Company and Prairie Oil and Gas Company—and then in a single successor enterprise (Consolidated Oil Corporation). Thus Petroleum Corporation took on the complexion of a holding company, in which the exercise of managerial skill appears to be reduced to a minimum once the original acquisitions are made.[1]

We are forced to conclude that financial schemes of the kind illustrated by Petroleum Corporation of America are unsatisfactory from the standpoint of the stock buyer. This is true not only because the total cost to him for management is excessive in relation to the value of the services rendered but also because the cost is not clearly disclosed, being concealed in good measure by the use of the warrant artifice.[2] (The foregoing reasoning does not rest in any way upon the fact that Petroleum Corporation's investments proved unprofitable.[3])

Position of Investment Banking Firms in This Connection. The second line of inquiry suggested by this example is also of major importance. What is the position occupied by the investment banking firms floating an issue such as Petroleum Corporation of America, and how

---

[1] The same logical objection to the payment of a large "managerial bonus," in the form of option warrants to those organizing a holding company, may be urged against the set-up of Alleghany Corporation and United Corporation.

[2] In a series of "Notes" on the history of United Corporation financing by Sanford L. Schamus, in *Columbia Law Review* of May, June and November, 1937, the proposal was advanced that prospectuses issued under S.E.C. legislation should carry a tabulation showing the effect of the exercise of warrants on earnings and asset values. See November 1937 issue, pp. 1173–1174.

[3] A review of the operations of Petroleum Corporation, published by the S.E.C. in May 1939, criticizes severely a number of deals in which the management was interested on the other side. After 1933 a unique turn was given to the status of Petroleum Corporation through acquisition of a large interest (39.8%) therein by Consolidated Oil. The two companies thus became the largest stockholders of each other, an extraordinary and highly objectionable situation. See Part 3, Chap. II (2d sec.), of the *Report of the S.E.C. on Investment Trusts and Investment Companies.*

does this compare with the practice of former years? Prior to the late 1920's, the sale of stock to the public by reputable houses of issue was governed by the following three important principles:

1. The enterprise must be well established and offer a record and financial exhibit adequate to justify the purchase of the shares at the issue price.

2. The investment banker must act primarily as the representative of the buyers of the stock, and he must deal at arm's-length with the company's management. His duty includes protecting his clients against the payment of excessive compensation to the officers or any other policies inimical to the stockholders' interest.

3. The compensation taken by the investment banker must be reasonable. It represents a fee paid by the corporation for the service of raising capital.

These rules of conduct afforded a clear line of demarcation between responsible and disreputable stock financing. It was an established Wall Street maxim that capital for a new enterprise must be raised from private sources.[4] These private interests would be in a position to make their own investigation, work out their own deal and keep in close touch with the enterprise, all of which safeguards (in addition to the chance to make a large profit) were considered necessary to justify a commitment in any new venture. Hence the public sale of securities in a *new enterprise* was confined almost exclusively to "blue sky" promoters and small houses of questionable standing. The great majority of such flotations were either downright swindles or closely equivalent thereto by reason of the unconscionable financing charges taken out of the price paid by the public.

Investment-trust financing, by its very nature, was compelled to contravene these three established criteria of reputable stock flotations. The investment trusts were *new* enterprises; their management and their bankers were generally *identical;* the compensation for financing and management had to be determined solely by the recipients, without accepted standards of reasonableness to control them. In the absence of such standards, and in the absence also of the invaluable arm's-length bargaining

---

[4] An apparent exception might be made sometimes in a case such as Chile Copper Company where the demonstrated presence of huge bodies of ore was regarded as justifying public financing to bring the mine into production. The sale of stock of the Lincoln Motor Company in 1920 was one of the few real exceptions to the rule as here stated. In this instance an unusually high personal reputation was behind the enterprise, but it resulted in disastrous failure.

between corporation and banker, it was scarcely to be hoped that the interests of the security buyer would be adequately protected. Allowance must be made besides for the generally distorted and egotistical views prevalent in the financial world during 1928 and 1929.

Developments since 1929. For a time it appeared that the demoralizing influence of investment-trust financing was likely to spread to the entire field of common-stock flotations and that even the leading banking houses were prepared to sell shares of new or virtually new commercial enterprises, without past records and on the basis entirely of their expected future earnings. (There were definite signs of this tendency in the beer-and liquor-stock flotations of 1933.) Fortunately, a reversal of sentiment has since taken place, and we find that the relatively few common-stock issues sponsored by the first-line houses are now similar in character and arrangements to those of former days.[5]

However, there has been a fair amount of activity in the common-stock flotation field since 1933, carried on by houses of secondary size or standing. Most of these issues represent shares of new enterprises, which in turn tend to fall in whatever industrial group is easiest to exploit at the time. Thus in 1933 we had many gold-, liquor- and beer-stock flotations, and in 1938–1939 there was a deluge of airplane issues. The formation of new investment companies, on the other hand, appears to be a perennial industry. In surveying such common-stock flotations, the starting point must be the realization that the investment banker behind them is not acting primarily in behalf of his clients who buy the issue. For on the one side the new corporation is not an independent entity, which can negotiate at arm's-length with various bankers representing clients with money to invest, and on the other side, the banker is himself in part a promoter, in part a proprietor of the new business. In an important sense, he is raising funds from the public *for himself.*

New Role of Such Investment Bankers. More exactly stated, the investment banker who floats such issues is operating in a double guise. He makes a deal on his own behalf with the originators of the enterprise, and then he makes a separate deal with the public to raise from them the funds he has promised the business. He demands—and no doubt is

---

[5] See, for example, the offerings of New Idea Company common in 1937, General Shoe Company common in 1938, Julius Garfinckel and Company in 1939.

entitled to—a liberal reward for his pains. But the very size of his compensation introduces a significant change in his relationship to the public. For it makes a very real difference whether a stock buyer can consider the investment banker as essentially his agent and representative or must view the issuing house as a promoter-proprietor-manager of a business, endeavoring to raise funds to carry it on.

When investment banking becomes identified with the latter approach, the interests of the general public are certain to suffer. The Securities Act of 1933 aims to safeguard the security buyer by requiring full disclosure of the pertinent facts and by extending the previously existing liability for concealment or misrepresentation. Although full disclosure is undoubtedly desirable, it may not be of much practical help except to the skilled and shrewd investor or to the trained analyst. It is to be feared that the typical stock buyer will neither read the long prospectus carefully nor understand the implications of all it contains. Modern financing methods are not far different from a magician's bag of tricks; they can be executed in full view of the public without its being very much the wiser. The use of stock options as part of the underwriter-promoter's compensation is one of the newer and more deceptive tricks of the trade.

Two examples of new enterprise financing, in 1936 and 1939, will be discussed in some detail, with the object of illustrating both the character of these flotations and the technique of analysis required to appraise them.[6]

Example A: American Bantam Car Corporation, July 1936. This offering consisted of 100,000 shares of 6% Cumulative Convertible Preference stock, sold to the public at $10 per share, its par value. Each share was convertible into 3 shares of common stock. The "underwriters" received a gross commission of $2 per share, or 20% of the selling price; however, this compensation was for selling effort only, without any guarantee to take or place the shares.

The new company had acquired the plant of the American Austin Car Company, which had started out in 1929 with $3,692,000 in cash capital and had ended in bankruptcy. The organizers of the Bantam

---

[6] In the 1934 edition we analyzed, at this point, the offering of stock in Mouquin, Inc. (liquor importers) made in September 1933 at $6.75 per share. The facts showed that the public was asked to place a valuation of $1,670,000 on an enterprise with physical assets of $424,000 and no earnings record. The company passed out of existence in 1937, and the public's investment was wiped out.

enterprise bought in the Austin assets, subject to various liabilities, for only $5,000. They then turned over their purchase, plus $500 in cash, to the new company for 300,000 shares of its common stock. In other words, the entire common issue cost the promoters $5,500 cash plus their time and effort.

The prospectus stated—what was an obvious fact—that the preference stock was "offered as a speculation." That speculation could work out successfully only if the conversion privilege proved valuable, since the mere 6% return on a preferred stock was scarcely an adequate reward for the risk involved. (The character of the risk was shown clearly enough in the enormous losses of the predecessor company.) But note that before the conversion privilege could be worth anything, the common stock would have to sell for more than $3^1/$_3$ per share—and *in that case the* $5,500 *investment of the organizers would be worth over* $1,000,000. In other words, before the public could make *any* profit, the organizers would have to multiply their stake 180 *times*.

Sequel. By June 30, 1939, the company had accumulated a deficit of $750,000; it was compelled to borrow money from the R.F.C., and the preferred-stock holder no longer had any equity in current assets. The price of the preference stock declined to 3, but at the same time the common was quoted at ^{3}/$_4$ bid. This meant (if the quoted price could be trusted) that, although the public had lost 70% of its investment, the organizers' $5,500 contribution had still a nominal market value of $225,000.

Example B: Aeronautical Corporation of America, December 1939. This company offered to the public 60,000 shares of new common stock at $6.25 per share. The "underwriters," who made no firm commitment to take any shares, received on the sale of each share the following three kinds of compensation: (1) 90 cents in cash; (2) ^{1}/$_{20}$ of a share of stock, ostensibly worth 31 cents, donated by the principal stockholders; (3) a warrant to buy ^{1}/$_2$ share of stock at prices varying between $6.25 and $8.00 per share. If the common stock was fairly worth the $6.25 offering price, these warrants were undoubtedly worth at least $1 per share called for. This would mean an aggregate commission for selling effort of $2.34 per share, or more than one-third the amount paid over by the public.

The company had been in business since 1928 and had been manufacturing its light Aeronca planes since 1931. Its business had grown steadily from $124,000 sales in 1934 to about $850,000 sales in 1939.

However, the enterprise had been definitely unprofitable to the end of 1938, showing an aggregate deficit at that time of over $500,000 (including development expense written off). In $9^1/2$ months to October 15, 1939, it had earned $50,000. Prior to this offering of new shares to the public there were outstanding 66,000 shares of stock, which had a net asset value of only $1.28 per share. In addition to the warrants for 30,000 shares to be given the underwriters, there were like warrants for 15,000 shares in the hands of the officers.

There seemed strong reason to believe that the company occupied a favorable position in a growing industry. But analysis would show that the participation of the public in any future increase in earnings was seriously diluted in three different ways: by the cash selling expense subtracted from the price to be paid for the new stock, by the small tangible assets contributed by the original owners for their stock interest and by the warrants which would siphon off part of any increased value. To show the effect of this dilution, let us assume that the company proves so successful that its fair value is twice its tangible assets after completion of this financing—say, about $1,000,000 as compared with $484,000 of tangible assets. What could then be the value of the stock for which the public paid $6.25? If there were no warrants outstanding, this value would be about $8 per share on 126,000 shares. But allowing for a value of say $2.00 per share for the warrants, the stock itself would be worth only $7.25 per share. Hence even a very substantial degree of success on the part of this enterprise would add a mere 16% to the value of the public's purchase. Should things go the other way, a very large part of the investment would soon be dissipated.

Should the Public Finance New Ventures? Fairly complete observation of new-enterprise financing registered with the S.E.C. since 1933 has given us a pessimistic opinion as to its soundness and its economic value to the nation. The venturing of capital into new businesses is essential to American progress, but no substantial contribution to the upbuilding of the country has ever been made by *new* ventures *publicly* financed. Wall Street has always realized that the capital for such undertakings should properly be supplied on a private and personal basis—by the organizers themselves or people close to them. Hence the sale of shares in new businesses has never been a truly reputable pursuit, and the leading banking houses will not engage in it. The less fastidious channels through which such financing is done exact so high an over-all selling cost—*to the public*—that the chance of success of the new enterprise, small enough at best, is thereby greatly diminished.

It is our considered view that the nation's interest would be served by amending the Securities Act so as to prohibit the public offering of securities of new and definitely unseasoned ventures. It would not be easy to define precisely the criteria of "seasoning,"—*e.g.*, size, number of years' operation without loss—and it may be necessary to vest some discretion on this score with the S.E.C. We think, however, that borderline and difficult cases will be relatively few in number (although our second example above belongs, perhaps, in this category). We should be glad to see the powers and duties of the S.E.C. diminished in many details of minor significance; but on this point of protecting a public incapable of protecting itself, our view leans strongly towards more drastic legislation.

Blue-sky Promotions. In the "good old days" fraudulent stock promoters relied so largely upon high pressure salesmanship that they rarely bothered to give their proposition any semblance of serious merit. They could sell shares in a mine that was not even a "hole in the ground" or in an invention the chief recommendation for which was the enormous profit made by Henry Ford's early partners. The victim was in fact buying "blue sky" and nothing else. Any one with the slightest business sense could have detected the complete worthlessness of these ventures almost at a glance; in fact, the glossy paper used for the prospectus was in itself sufficient to identify the proposition as fraudulent.

The tightening of federal and state regulations against these swindles has led to a different type of security promotion. Instead of offering something entirely worthless, the promoter selects a real enterprise that he can sell at much more than its fair value. By this means the law can be obeyed and the public exploited just the same. Oil and mining ventures lend themselves best to such stock flotations, because it is easy to instill in the uninitiated an exaggerated notion of their true worth. The S.E.C. has been concerning itself more and more seriously with endeavors to defeat this type of semifraud. In theory a promoter may offer something worth $1 per share at $5, provided he discloses all the facts and adds no false representations. The Commission is not authorized to pass upon the soundness of new securities or the fairness of their price (except in the case of public-utility issues which come under the terms of the Public Utility Holding

Company Act of 1935). Actually, it appears to be doing its best, by various pressures, to discourage and even prevent the more grossly inequitable offerings. But it is essential that the public recognize that the Commission's powers in this respect are severely limited and that only a sceptical analysis by the intending buyer can assure him against exploitation.

Promotional activities are attracted especially to any new industry that is in the public eye. Profits made by those first in the field, or even currently by the enterprise floated, can be given a fictitious guise of permanence and of future enhancement. Hence gross overvaluations can be made plausible enough to sell. In the liquor flotations of 1933 the degree of overvaluation depended entirely upon the conscience of the sponsors. Accordingly, the list of stock offerings showed all gradations from the thoroughly legitimate down to the almost completely fraudulent.[7] A somewhat similar picture is presented by the aircraft flotations of 1938–1939. The public would do well to remember that whenever it becomes easy to raise capital for a particular industry, both the chances of unfair deals are magnified and the danger of overdevelopment of the industry itself becomes very real.

Repercussions of Unsound Investment Banking. The relaxation of investment bankers' standards in the late 1920's, and their use of ingenious means to enlarge their compensation, had unwholesome repercussions in the field of corporate management. Operating officials felt themselves entitled not only to handsome salaries but also to a substantial participation in the profits of the enterprise. In this respect the investment-trust arrangements, devised by the banking houses for their own benefit, set a stimulating example to the world of "big business."

Whether or not it is proper for executives of a large and prosperous concern to receive annual compensation running into hundreds of thousands or even millions of dollars is perhaps an open question. Its answer will depend upon the extent to which the corporation's success is due to their unique or surpassing ability, and this must be very difficult to determine with assurance. But it may not be denied that devious and questionable means were frequently employed to secure these large bonuses to the management without full disclosure of their extent to the stockholders.

---

[7] See Appendix Note 55, p. 792 on accompanying CD, relative to investors' experience with brewery-stock flotations of 1933.

Stock-option warrants (or long-term subscription rights) to buy shares at low prices, proved an excellent instrument for this purpose—as we have already pointed out in our discussion of stockholder-management relationships. In this field complete and continued publicity is not only theoretically desirable but of practical utility as well. The legislation of 1933–1934 marks an undeniable forward step in this regard, since the major facts of managerial compensation must now be disclosed in registration statements and in annual supplements thereto (Form 10-K). With publicity given to this compensation, we believe that the self-interest of stockholders may be relied on fairly well to prevent it from passing all reasonable limits.

Chapter 48

SOME ASPECTS OF
CORPORATE PYRAMIDING

PYRAMIDING IN CORPORATE finance is the creation of a speculative capital structure by means of a holding company or a series of holding companies. Usually the predominating purpose of such an arrangement is to enable the organizers to control a large business with the investment of little or no capital and also to secure to themselves the major part of its surplus profits and increased going-concern value. The device is most often utilized by dominant interests to "cash in" speculative profits on their holdings and at the same time to retain control. With the funds so provided, these successful captains of finance generally endeavor to extend their control over additional operating enterprises. The technique of pyramiding is well illustrated by the successive maneuvers of O. P. and M. J. Van Sweringen, which started with purchase of control of the then relatively unimportant New York, Chicago, and St. Louis Railroad and rapidly developed into a far-flung railroad "empire."[1]

Example: The Van Sweringen Pyramid. The original transaction of the Van Sweringens in the railroad field took place in 1916. It consisted of the

---

[1] The complete story of how this pyramiding was effected is told in the *Hearings before the Committee on Banking and Currency, United States Senate,* 73d Congress, 1st Session, on Senate Resolution 84 of the 72d Congress and Senate Resolution 56 of the 73d Congress, Part 2, pp. 563–777, June 5 to 8, 1933—on "Stock Exchange Practices." The story is also set forth in greater detail and with graphic portrayal in *Regulation of Stock Ownership in Railroads, Part* 2, pp. 820–1173 (House Report No. 2789, 71st Congress, 3d Session), especially the inserts at p. 878 thereof. For graphic and other presentation of the effects of pyramiding in the public-utility field see Utility Corporations (Sen. Doc. 92, 70th Congress, 1st Session, pt. 72-A), pp. 154–166.

The most notorious pyramided structure of recent years was the Insull set-up. An interesting example of a different type is presented by the United States and Foreign Securities Corporation—United States and International Securities Corporation relationship. These two situations are briefly described in Note 64 at p. 817 of the Appendix on accompanying CD.

purchase from the New York Central Railroad Company, for the sum of $8,500,000, of common and preferred stock constituting control of the New York, Chicago, and St. Louis Railroad Company (known as the "Nickel Plate"). This purchase was financed by giving a note to the seller for $6,500,000 and by a cash payment of $2,000,000, which in turn was borrowed from a Cleveland bank. Subsequent acquisitions of control of many other companies were effected by various means, including the following:

1. The formation of a private corporation for the purpose (*e.g.*, Western Corporation to acquire control of Lake Erie and Western Railroad Company, and Clover Leaf Corporation to acquire control of Toledo, St. Louis and Western Railroad Company—both in 1922).

2. The use of the resources of one controlled railroad to acquire control of others (*e.g.*, the New York, Chicago and St. Louis Railroad Company purchased large amounts of stock of Chesapeake and Ohio Railway and Pere Marquette Railway Company during 1923–1925).

3. The formation of a holding company to control an individual road, with sale of the holding company's securities to the public (*e.g.*, Chesapeake Corporation, which took over control of Chesapeake and Ohio Railway Company and sold its own bonds and stock to the public, in 1927).

4. Formation of a general holding company (*e.g.*, Alleghany Corporation, chartered in 1929. This ambitious project took over control of many railroad, coal, and miscellaneous enterprises).

The report on the "Van Sweringen Holding Companies" made to the House of Representatives in 1930[2] includes an interesting chart showing the contrast between the control exercised by the Van Sweringens and their relatively small equity or financial interest in the capital of the enterprises controlled. On page 646 we append a summary of these data. The figures in Column *A* show the percentage of voting securities held or controlled by the Van Sweringens; the figures in Column *B* show the proportion of the "contributed capital" (bonds, stock, and surplus) actually owned directly or indirectly by them.

It is worth recalling that similar use of the holding company for pyramiding control of railroad properties had been made before the war—notably in the case of the Rock Island Company. This enterprise was organized in 1902. Through an intermediate subsidiary it acquired nearly

---

[2] House Report 2789, 71st Congress, 3d Session, Part 2, pp. 820–1173.

all the common stock of the Chicago, Rock Island and Pacific Railway Company and about 60% of the capital stock of the St. Louis and San Francisco Railway Company. Against these shares the two holding companies issued large amounts of collateral trust bonds, preferred stock and common stock. In 1909 the stock of the St. Louis and San Francisco was sold. In 1915 the Rock Island Company and its intermediate subsidiary both went into bankruptcy; the stock of the operating company was taken over by the collateral trust bondholders; and the holding company stock issues were wiped out completely.

Companies	A. Control, %	B. Equity, %
Holding companies:		
The Vaness Co.	80.0	27.7
General Securities Corp.	90.0	51.8
Geneva Corp.	100.0	27.7
Alleghany Corp.	41.8	8.6
The Chesapeake Corp.	71.0	4.1
The Pere Marquette Corp.	100.0	0.7
Virginia Transportation Corp.	100.0	0.8
The Pittston Co.	81.8	4.3
Railroad Companies:		
The New York, Chicago and St. Louis R.R. Co.	49.6	0.7
The Chesapeake and Ohio Railway Co.	54.4	1.0
Pere Marquette Railway Co.	48.3	0.6
Erie Railroad Co.	30.8	0.6
Missouri Pacific Railroad Co.	50.5	1.7
The Hocking Valley Railway Co.	81.0	0.2
The Wheeling and Lake Erie Railway Co.	53.3	0.3
Kansas City Southern Railway Co.	20.8	0.9

The ignominious collapse of this venture was accepted at the time as marking the end of "high finance" in the railroad field. Yet some ten years later the same unsound practices were introduced once again, but on a larger scale and with correspondingly severer losses to investors. It remains to add that the Congressional investigation of railroad holding companies instituted in 1930 had its counterpart in a similar inquiry into the finances of the Rock Island Company made by the Interstate

Commerce Commission in 1914. The memory of the financial community is proverbially and distressingly short.

Evils of Corporate Pyramiding. The pyramiding device is harmful to the security-buying public from several standpoints. It results in the creation and sale to investors of large amounts of unsound senior securities. It produces common stocks of holding companies which are subject to deceptively rapid increases in earning power in favorable years and which are invariably made the vehicle of wild and disastrous public speculation. The possession of control by those who have no real capital investment (or a relatively minor one) is inequitable[3] and makes for irresponsible and unsound managerial policies. Finally the holding company device permits of financial practices that exaggerate the indicated earnings, dividend return, or "book value," during boom times, and thus intensify speculative fervor and facilitate market manipulation. Of these four objections to corporate pyramiding, the first three are plainly evident, but the last one requires a certain amount of analytical treatment in order to present its various implications.

Overstatement of Earnings. Holding companies can overstate their apparent earning power by valuing at an unduly high price the stock dividends they receive from subsidiaries or by including in their income profits made from the sale of stock of subsidiary companies.

Examples: The chief asset of Central States Electric Corporation was a large block of North American Company common on which regular stock dividends were paid. Prior to the end of 1929, these stock dividends were reported as income by Central States at the market value then current. As explained in our chapter on stock dividends, such market prices averaged far in excess of the value at which North American charged the stock dividends against its surplus and also far in excess of the distributable earnings on North American common. Hence the income account of Central States Electric gave a misleading impression of the earnings accruing to the company.

A transaction of somewhat different character but of similar effect to the foregoing was disclosed by the report of American Founders Trust for 1927. In November 1927 American Founders offered its shareholders the privilege of buying about 88,400 shares of International Securities Corporation

---

[3] See Appendix Note 65, p. 820 on accompanying CD, for examples on this point.

of America Class *B* Common at $16 per share. International Securities Corporation was a subsidiary of American Founders, and the latter had acquired the Class *B* stock of the former at a cash cost of $3.70 per share in 1926. American Founders reported net earnings for common stock in 1927 amounting to $1,316,488, most of which was created by its own stockholders through their purchase of shares of the subsidiary as indicated above.[4]

Distortion of Dividend Return. Just as a holding company's income may be exaggerated by reason of stock dividends received, so the dividend return on its shares may be distorted in the public's mind by payment of periodic stock dividends with a market value exceeding current earnings. People are readily persuaded also to regard the value of frequent subscription rights as equivalent to an income return on the common stock. Pyramided enterprises are prodigal with subscription rights, for they flow naturally from the succession of new acquisitions and new financing which both promote the ambitions of those in control and maintain speculative interest at fever heat—until the inevitable collapse.

The issuance of subscription rights sometimes gives the stock market an opportunity to indulge in that peculiar circular reasoning which is the joy of the manipulator and the despair of the analyst. Company *A*'s stock is apparently worth no more than 25. Speculation or pool activity has advanced it to 75. Rights are offered to buy additional shares at 25, and the rights have a market value of, say, $10 each. To the speculative fraternity these rights are practically equivalent to a special dividend of $10. It is a bonus that not only justifies the rise to 75 but warrants more optimism and a still higher price. To the analyst the whole proceeding is a delusion and a snare. Whatever value the rights command is manufactured solely out of speculators' misguided enthusiasm, yet this chimerical value is accepted as tangible income and as vindication of the enthusiasm that gave it birth. Thus, with the encouragement of the manipulator, the speculative public pulls itself up by its bootstraps to dizzier heights of irrationality.

---

[4] In the three years 1928–1930 the American Founders group reported total net investment profits of about $43,300,000; but all of this sum and more was derived from profits on intercompany transactions of the kind described above. See the S.E.C.'s Over-all Report on Investment Trusts, Part III, Chapter VI, Sections II and III, released February 12, 1940.

Example: Between August 1928 and February 1929 American and Foreign Power Company common stock advanced from 33 to 138⁷/₈, although paying no dividend. Rights were offered to the common stockholders (and other security holders) to buy second preferred stock with detached stock-purchase warrants. The offering of these rights, which had an initial market value of about $3 each, was construed by many as the equivalent of a dividend on the common stock.

Exaggeration of Book Value. The exaggeration of book value may be effected in cases where a holding company owns most of the shares of a subsidiary and where consequently an artificially high quotation may readily be established for the subsidiary issue by manipulating the small amount of stock remaining in the market. This high quotation is then taken as the basis of figuring the book value (sometimes called the "break-up value") of the share of the holding company. For an early example of these practices we may point to Tobacco Products Corporation (Va.) which owned about 80% of the common stock of United Cigar Stores Company of America. An unduly high market price seems to have been established in 1927 for the small amount of Cigar Stores stock available in the market, and this high price was used to make Tobacco Products shares appear attractive to the unwary buyer. The thoroughly objectionable accounting and stock dividend policies of United Cigar Stores, which we have previously discussed, were adjuncts to this manipulative campaign.

The most extraordinary example of such exaggeration of the book value is found, perhaps, in the case of Electric Bond and Share Company and was founded on its ownership of most of the American and Foreign Power Company warrants. The whole set-up seems to have been contrived to induce the public to pay absolutely fantastic prices without their complete absurdity being too apparent. A brief review of the various steps in this phantasmagoria of inflated values should be illuminating to the student of security analysis.

First, American and Foreign Power Company issued in all 1,600,000 shares of common and warrants to buy 7,100,000 more shares at $25. This permitted a price to be established for the common stock that generously capitalized its earnings and prospects but paid no attention to the existence of the warrants. The quotation of the common was aided by the issuance of rights, as explained above.

Second, the high price registered for the relatively small common-stock issue automatically created a correspondingly high value for the millions of warrants.

Third, Electric Bond and Share could apply these high values to its large holdings of American and Foreign Power common and its enormous block of warrants, thus setting up a correspondingly inflated value for its own common stock.

Exploitation of the Stock-purchase-warrant Device. The result of this process, at its farthest point in 1929, was almost incredible. The earnings available for American and Foreign Power common stock had shown the following rising trend (due in good part, however, to continuous new acquisitions):

Year	Earnings for common	Number of shares	Earned per share
1926	$216,000	1,243,988	0.17
1927	856,000	1,244,388	0.69
1928	1,528,000	1,248,930	1.22
1929	6,510,000	1,624,357	4.01

On the theory that a "good public-utility stock is worth up to 50 times its current earnings," a price of $199^1/4$ per share was recorded for American and Foreign Power common. This produced in turn a price of 174 for the warrants. Hence, by the insane magic of Wall Street, earnings of $6,500,000 were transmuted into a market value of $320,000,000 for the common shares and $1,240,000,000 for the warrants, a staggering total of $1,560,000,000.

Since over 80% of the warrants were owned by Electric Bond and Share Company, the effect of these absurd prices for American and Foreign Power junior securities was to establish a correspondingly absurd break-up value for Electric Bond and Share common. This break-up value was industriously exploited to justify higher and higher quotations for the latter issue. In March 1929 attention was called to the fact that the market value of this company's portfolio was equivalent to about $108 per share (of new stock), against a range of 91 to 97 for its own market quotation. The implication was that Electric Bond and Share stock was "undervalued." In September 1929 the price had advanced to $184^1/2$. It was then computed that the "break-up value" amounted to about 150, "allowing no value for the company's supervisory and construction business." The public did not stop to reflect that a considerable part of this "book value" was based upon an essentially fictitious market quotation for an asset that the company had received *for nothing* only a few years before (as a bonus with American and Foreign Power Second Preferred stock).

This exploitation of the warrants had a peculiar vitality which made itself felt even in the depth of the depression in 1932–1933. Time having brought its usual revenge, the once dazzling American and Foreign Power Company had trembled on the brink of receivership, as shown by a price of only $15^1/4$ for its 5% bonds. Nevertheless, in November 1933 the highly unsubstantial warrants still commanded an aggregate market quotation of nearly $50,000,000, a figure that bore a ridiculous relationship to the exceedingly low values placed upon the senior securities. The following table shows how absurd this situation was, the more so since it existed in a time of deflated stock prices, when relative values are presumably subjected to more critical appraisal.

(**000** OMITTED IN MARKET VALUE)

Issue	Amount outstanding	Price Nov. 1933	Total market value, 1933	Price Dec. 31, 1938	Total market value, 1938
5% Debentures	$50,000	40	$20,000	53	26,500
$7 First Preferred shares	480	21	10,100	$19^7/8$	9,300
$6 First Preferred shares	387	15	5,800	15	5,800
$7 Second Preferred shares	2,655	12	31,900	$9^1/4$	24,900
Common shares	1,850	10	18,500	$3^1/2$	6,500
Warrants shares	6,874	7	48,100	1	6,900

By the end of 1938, as the table indicates, a good part of the absurdity had been corrected.

Some Holding Companies Not Guilty of Excessive Pyramiding.

To avoid creating a false impression, we must point out that, although pyramiding is usually effected by means of holding companies, it does not follow that all holding companies are created for this purpose and are therefore reprehensible. The holding company is often utilized for entirely legitimate purposes, *e.g.*, to permit unified and economical operations of separate units, to diversify investment and risk and to gain certain technical advantages of flexibility and convenience. Many sound and important enterprises are in holding company form.

Examples: United States Steel Corporation is entirely a holding company; although originally there was some element of pyramiding in its capital set-up, this defect disappeared in later years. American Telephone and Telegraph Company is preponderantly a holding company, but its financial structure has never been subject to serious criticism. General Motors Corporation is largely a holding company.

A holding-company exhibit must therefore be considered on its merits. American Light and Traction Company is a typical example of the holding company organized entirely for legitimate purposes. On the other hand the acquisition of control of this enterprise by United Light and Railways Company (Del.) must be regarded as a pyramiding move on the part of the United Light and Power interests.

Speculative Capital Structure May Be Created in Other Ways.
It may be pointed out also that a speculative capital structure can be created without the use of a holding company.

Examples: The Maytag Company recapitalization, discussed in an earlier chapter, yielded results usually attained by the formation of a holding company and the sale of its senior securities. In the case of Continental Baking Corporation—to cite another example—the holding company form was not an essential part of the pyramided result there attained. The speculative structure was due entirely to the creation of large preferred issues by the parent company, and it would still have existed if Continental Baking had acquired all its properties directly, eliminating its subsidiaries. (As it happened, in 1938 this company took steps to acquire the assets of its chief subsidiaries, thus largely eliminating the holding-company form but retaining the speculative capital structure.)

Legislative Restraints on Pyramiding.
So spectacular were the disastrous effects of the public-utility pyramiding of the 1920's that Congress was moved to drastic action. The Public Utility Holding Company Act of 1935 includes the so-called "death sentence" for many of the existing systems, requiring them ultimately to simplify their capital structures and to dispose of subsidiaries operating in noncontiguous territory. Formation of new pyramids is effectively blocked by requiring Commission

approval for all acquisitions and all new financing. Similar steps are in prospect to regulate present railroad holding companies and to prevent creation of new ones.[5]

We may say with some confidence that the spectacle of the Van Sweringen debacle succeeding the Rock Island Company debacle is not likely to be duplicated in the future. The industrial field never offered the same romantic possibilities for high finance as were found among the rails and utilities, but it may well be that the ingenious talents of promoters and financial wizards will be directed towards the industrials in the future. The investor and the analyst should be on their guard against such new dazzlements.

---

[5] See Senate Resolution 71 of the 74th Congress and 21 volumes of hearings thereon which have appeared to date (December 1939). See also Senate Report No. 180, 75th Congress, 1st Session, and Senate Report No. 25, pts. 1, 4 and 5, 76th Congress, 1st Session.

Chapter 49

COMPARATIVE ANALYSIS OF COMPANIES IN THE SAME FIELD

STATISTICAL COMPARISONS of groups of concerns operating in a given industry are a more or less routine part of the analyst's work. Such tabulations permit each company's showing to be studied against a background of the industry as a whole. They frequently bring to light instances of undervaluation or overvaluation or lead to the conclusion that the securities of one enterprise should be replaced by those of another in the same field.

In this chapter we shall suggest standard forms for such comparative analyses, and we shall also discuss the significance of the various items included therein. Needless to say, these forms are called "standard" only in the sense that they can be used generally to good advantage; no claim of perfection is made for them, and the student is free to make any changes that he thinks will serve his particular purpose.

FORM I. RAILROAD COMPARISON

A. Capitalization:
   1. Fixed charges.*
   2. Effective debt (fixed charges* multiplied by 22).
   3. Preferred stock at market (number of shares × market price).
   4. Common stock at market (number of shares × market price).
   5. Total capitalization.
   6. Ratio of effective debt to total capitalization.
   7. Ratio of preferred stock to total capitalization.
   8. Ratio of common stock to total capitalization.
B. Income Account:
   9. Gross revenues.
   10. Ratio of maintenance to gross.

11. Ratio of railway operating income (net after taxes) to gross.
12. Ratio of fixed charges* to gross.
13. Ratio of preferred dividends to gross.
14. Ratio of balance for common to gross.

C. Calculations:

15. Number of times fixed charges* earned.
15. I.P.† Number of times fixed charges* plus preferred dividends earned.
16. Earned on common stock, per share.
17. Earned on common stock, % of market price.
18. Ratio of gross to aggregate market value of common stock (9 ÷ 4).
16. S.P.‡ Earned on preferred stock, per share.
17. S.P. Earned on preferred stock, % of market price.
18. S.P. Ratio of gross to aggregate market value of preferred stock (9 ÷ 3).
19. Credit or debit to earnings for undistributed profit or loss of subsidiaries (if important).

D. Seven-year average figures:

20. Earned on common stock, per share.
21. Earned on common stock, % of current market price of common.
20. S.P. Earned on preferred stock, per share.
21. S.P. Earned on preferred stock, % of current market price of preferred.
22. Number of times net deductions earned.
23. Number of times fixed charges earned.
22. I.P. Number of times net deductions plus preferred dividends earned.
23. I.P. Number of times fixed charges plus preferred dividends earned.

E. Trend figure:

24 to 30. Earned per share on common stock each year for past seven years. (Where necessary, earnings should be adjusted to present capitalization.)
24. S.P. to 30. S.P. Same data for speculative preferred stock, if wanted.

F. Dividends:

31. Dividend rate on common.
32. Dividend yield on common.
31. P. Dividend rate on preferred.
32. P. Dividend yield on preferred.

* Or net deductions if larger.
† I.P. = for studying an investment preferred stock.
‡ S.P. = for studying a speculative preferred stock.

Observations on the Railroad Comparison.[1] It has formerly been the custom to base earnings studies on the figures for the previous calendar years, with certain references to later interim reports. But since complete figures are now available month by month, it is more logical and effective practice to ignore the calendar-year division and to use instead the results for the twelve months to the latest date available. The simplest way to arrive at such a twelve months' figure is to apply the *change* shown for the current year to date to the results of the previous calendar year.

Example:

GROSS EARNINGS OF PENNSYLVANIA RAILROAD SYSTEM FOR
12 MONTHS ENDED JUNE, 1939

(1) 6 months to June 1939 (as reported)	$189,623,000
(2) 6 months to June 1938 (as reported)	167,524,000
(3) Difference	+22,099,000
(4) Calender year 1938	360,384,000
12 months to June 1939 (4 plus 3)	$382,483,000

Our table includes a few significant calculations based on the seven-year average. In an intensive study, average results should be scrutinized in more detail. To save time, it is suggested that additional average figures be computed only for those roads which the analyst selects for further investigation after he has studied the exhibits in the "standard form." Whether the period of averaging should cover seven years or a longer or shorter time is largely a matter for individual judgment. In theory it should be just long enough to cover a full cyclical fluctuation but not so long as to include factors or results that are totally out of date. The six years 1934–1939 might well be regarded as a somewhat better criterion, for example, than the longer period 1933–1939.

Figures relating to preferred stocks fall into two different classes, depending on whether the issue is considered for fixed-value investment or as a speculative commitment. (Usually the market price will indicate

---

[1] Reference is made to earlier chapters for explanation of the terminology and the critical tests referred to in this discussion.

clearly enough in which category a particular issue belongs.) The items marked "I.P." are to be used in studying an investment preferred stock, and those marked "S.P." in studying a speculative preferred. Where there are junior income bonds, the simplest and most satisfactory procedure will be to treat them in all respects as a preferred stock issue, with a footnote referring to their actual title. Such contingent bond interest will therefore be excluded from the net deductions or the fixed charges.

In this tabular comparison we follow the suggestion previously offered that the effective debt be computed by capitalizing the larger of net deductions or fixed charges. In using the table as an aid to the selection of senior issues for investment, chief attention will be paid to items 22 and 23 (or 22 "I.P." and 23 "I.P."), showing the average margin above interest (and preferred dividend) requirements. Consideration should be given also to items 6, 7 and 8, showing the division of total capitalization between senior securities and junior equity. (In dealing with bonds, the preferred stock is part of the junior equity; in considering a preferred stock for investment, it must be included with the effective debt.) Items 10 and 19 should also be examined to see if the earnings have been overstated by reason of inadequate maintenance or by the inclusion of unearned dividends from subsidiaries.

Speculative preferred stocks will ordinarily be analyzed in much the same way as common stocks, and the similarity becomes greater as the price of the preferred stock is lower. It should be remembered, however, that a preferred stock is always less attractive, logically considered, than a common stock making the same showing. For example, a $6 preferred earning $5 per share is intrinsically less desirable than a common stock earning $5 per share (and with the same prior charges), since the latter is entitled to all the present and future equity, whereas the preferred stock is strictly limited in its claim upon the future.

In comparing railroad common stocks (and preferred shares equivalent thereto), the point of departure is the percentage earned on the market price. This may be qualified, to an extent more or less important, by consideration of items 10 and 19. Items 12 and 18 will indicate at once whether the company is speculatively or conservatively capitalized, relatively speaking. A speculatively capitalized road will show a large ratio of net deductions to gross and (ordinarily) a small ratio of common stock at market value to gross. The converse will be true for a conservatively capitalized road.

Limitation upon Comparison of Speculatively and Conservatively Capitalized Companies in the Same Field. The analyst must beware of trying to draw conclusions as to the relative attractiveness of two railroad common stocks when one is speculatively and the other is conservatively capitalized. Two such issues will respond quite differently to changes for the better or the worse, so that an advantage possessed by one of them under current conditions may readily be lost if conditions should change.

Example: The example shown on p. 681 illustrates in a twofold fashion the fallacy of comparing a conservatively capitalized with a speculatively capitalized common stock. In 1922 the earnings of Union Pacific common were nearly four times as high in relation to market price as were those of Rock Island common. A conclusion that Union Pacific was "cheaper," based on these figures, would have been fallacious, because the relative capitalization structures were so different as to make the two companies noncomparable. This fact is shown graphically by the much larger expansion of the earnings and the market price of Rock Island common that accompanied the moderate rise in gross business during the five years following.

The situation in 1927 was substantially the opposite. At that time Rock Island common was earning proportionately more than Union Pacific common. But it would have been equally fallacious to conclude that Rock Island common was "intrinsically cheaper." The speculative capitalization structure of the latter road made it highly vulnerable to unfavorable development, so that it was unable to withstand the post-1929 depression.

Other Illustrations in Appendix. The practical approach to comparative analysis of railroad stocks (and bonds) may best be illustrated by the reproduction of several such comparisons made by one of the authors a number of years ago and published as part of the service rendered to clients by a New York Stock Exchange firm. These will be found in Appendix Note 66 on accompanying CD. It will be observed that the comparisons were made between roads in approximately the same class as regards capitalization structure, with the exception of the comparison between Atchison and New York Central, in which instance special reference was made to the greater sensitivity of New York Central to changes in either direction.

COMPARISON OF UNION PACIFIC AND ROCK ISLAND COMMON STOCKS

Item	Union Pacific R.R.	Chicago, Rock Island, & Pacific Ry.
A. Showing the effect of general improvement:		
Average price of common, 1922	140	40
Earned per share, 1922	$12.76	$0.96
% earned on market price, 1922	9.1%	2.4%
Fixed charges and preferred dividends earned, 1922	2.39 times	1.05 times
Ratio of gross to market value of common, 1922	62%	419%
Increase in gross, 1927 over 1922	5.7%	12.9%
Earned per share of common, 1927	$16.05	$12.08
Increase in earnings on common, 1927 over 1922	26%	1,158%
Average price of common, 1927	179	92
Increase in average price, 1927 over 1922	28%	130%
B. Showing the effect of a general decline in business:		
Earned on average price, 1927	9.0%	13.1%
Fixed charges and preferred dividends earned, 1927	2.64 times	1.58 times
Ratio of gross to market value of common, 1927	51%	204%
Decrease in gross, 1933 below 1927	46%	54%
Earned on common, 1933	$7.88	$20.40(d)
Decrease in earnings for common, 1933 below 1927	51%	269%
Average price of common, 1933	97	6
Decrease in average price, 1933 below 1927	46%	93%

Note: In June 1933 trustees in bankruptcy were appointed for the Rock Island.

FORM II.   PUBLIC-UTILITY COMPARISON

The public-utility comparison form is practically the same as that for railroads. The only changes are the following: Fixed charges (as mentioned in line 1 and elsewhere) should include subsidiary-preferred dividends. Line 2 should be called "Funded debt and subsidiary preferred stock," and these should be taken from the balance sheet. Items 22 and 22 I.P., relating to net deductions, are not needed. Item 10 becomes "ratio of depreciation to gross." An item, 10M, may be included to show "ratio of maintenance to gross" for the companies which publish this information.

Our observations regarding the use of the railroad comparison apply as well to the public-utility comparison. Variations in the depreciation rate are fully as important as variations in the railroad maintenance ratios. When a wide difference appears, it should not be taken for granted that one property is unduly conservative or the other not conservative enough, but a *presumption* to this effect does arise, and the question should be investigated as thoroughly as possible. A statistical indication that one utility stock is more attractive than another should not be acted upon until (among other qualitative matters) some study has been made of the rate situation and the relative prospects for favorable or unfavorable changes therein. In view of experience since 1933, careful attention should also be given to the dangers of municipal or federal competition.

FORM III.   INDUSTRIAL COMPARISON (FOR COMPANIES IN THE SAME FIELD)

Since this form differs in numerous respects from the two preceding, it is given in full herewith:

   A. Capitalization:

      1. Bonds at par.
      2. Preferred stock at market value
          (number of shares × market price).
      3. Common stock at market value
          (number of shares × market price).
      4. Total capitalization.
      5. Ratio of bonds to capitalization.
      6. Ratio of aggregate market value of preferred to capitalization.
      7. Ratio of aggregate market value of common to capitalization.

B.   Income Account (most recent year):

    8.   Gross sales.

    9.   Depreciation.

    10.   Net available for bond interest.

    11.   Bond interest.

    12.   Preferred dividend requirements.

    13.   Balance for common.

    14.   Margin of profit (ratio of 10 to 8).

    15.   % earned on total capitalization (ratio of 10 to 4).

C.   Calculations:

    16.   Number of times interest charges earned.

    16.   I.P. Number of times interest charges plus preferred dividends earned.

    17.   Earned on common, per share.

    18.   Earned on common, % of market price.

    17.   S.P. Earned on preferred, per share.

    18.   S.P. Earned on preferred, % of market price.

    19.   Ratio of gross to aggregate market value of common.

    19.   S.P. Ratio of gross to aggregate market value of preferred.

D.   Seven-year average:

    20.   Number of times interest charges earned.

    21.   Earned on common stock per share.

    22.   Earned on common stock, % of current market price. (20 I.P., 21 S.P. and 22 S.P.—Same calculation for preferred stock if wanted).

E.   Trend figure:

    23.   Earned per share of common stock each year for past seven years (adjustments in number of shares outstanding to be made where necessary).

    23.   S.P. Same data for speculative preferred issues, if wanted.

F.   Dividends:

    24.   Dividend rate on common.

    25.   Dividend yield on common.

24. P. Dividend rate on preferred.
25. P. Dividend yield on preferred.

G. Balance sheet:

26. Cash assets.
27. Receivables (less reserves).
28. Inventories (less proper reserves).
29. Total current assets.
30. Total current liabilities.
30. N. Notes Payable (Including "Bank Loans" and "Bills Payable")
31. Net current assets.
32. Ratio of current assets to current liabilities.
33. Ratio of inventory to sales.
34. Ratio of receivables to sales.
35. Net tangible assets available for total capitalization.
36. Cash-asset-value of common per share (deducting all prior obligations).
37. Net-current-asset-value of common per share (deducting all prior obligations).
38. Net-tangible-asset-value of common per share (deducting all prior obligations).

(36 S.P., 37 S.P., 38 S.P.—Same data for speculative preferred issues, if wanted).

H. Supplementary data (when available):

1. Physical output:
   Number of units; receipts per unit; cost per unit; profit per unit; total capitalization per unit; common stock valuation per unit.
2. Miscellaneous:
   For example: number of stores operated; sales per store; profit per store; ore reserves; life of mine at current (or average) rate of production.

Observations on the Industrial Comparison.

Some remarks regarding the use of this suggested form may be helpful. The net earnings figure must be corrected for any known distortions or omissions, including adjustments for undistributed earnings or losses of subsidiaries. If it appears to be misleading and cannot be adequately corrected, it should not be used as a basis of comparisons. (Inferences drawn from unreliable figures must themselves be unreliable.) No attempt should be made to subject the depreciation figures to exact comparisons; they are useful only in disclosing wide and obvious disparities in the rates used. The calculation of bond-interest-coverage is subject to the qualification discussed in Chap. 17, with respect to companies that may have important rental obligations equivalent to interest charges.

Whereas the percentage earned on the market price of the common (item 18) is a leading figure in all comparisons, almost equal attention must be given to item 15, showing the percentage earned on total capitalization. These figures, together with items 7 and 19 (ratio of aggregate market value of common stock to sales and to capitalization), will indicate the part played by conservative or speculative capitalization structures among the companies compared. (The theory of capitalization structure was considered in Chap. 40.)

As a matter of practical procedure it is not safe to rely upon the fact that the earnings ratio for the common stock (item 18) is higher than the average for the industry, unless the percentage earned on the total capitalization (item 15) is also higher. Furthermore, if the company with the poorer earnings exhibit shows much larger sales-per-dollar-of-common-stock (item 19), it may have better speculative possibilities in the event of general business improvement.

The balance-sheet computations do not have primary significance unless they indicate either definite financial weakness or a substantial excess of current-asset-value over the market price. The division of importance as between the current results, the seven-year average and the trend is something entirely for the analyst's judgment to decide. Naturally, he will have the more confidence in any suggested conclusion if it is confirmed on each of these counts.

Example of the Use of Standard Forms. An example of the use of the standard form to reach a conclusion concerning comparative values should be of interest. A survey of the common stocks of the listed steel producers in July 1938 indicated that Continental Steel had made a better exhibit than the average, whereas Granite City Steel had shown much smaller earning power. The two companies operated to some extent in the same branches of the steel industry; they were very similar in size, and the price of their common stocks was identical. In the tabulation presented on page 666 we supply comparative figures for these two enterprises, omitting some of the items on our standard form as immaterial to this analysis.

Comments on the Comparison. The use of five-year average figures for each item, presented along with those of the most recent twelve months, is suggested here because the subnormal business conditions in the year ended June 30, 1938 made it inadvisable to lay too great emphasis on the results for this single period. Granite City reports on calendar-year basis, whereas Continental used both a June 30 and a December 31 fiscal year during 1934–1938. However, the availability of quarterly or semiannual figures makes it a simple matter for the analyst to construct his average and 12 months' figures to end in the middle of the year.

Analysis of the data reveals only one point of superiority for Granite City Steel—the smaller amount of senior securities. But even this is not necessarily an advantage, since the relatively fewer shares of Continental common make them more sensitive to favorable as well as unfavorable developments. The exhibit for the June 1938 year, and five-year average, show a statistical superiority for Continental on each of the following important points:

> Earnings on market price of common stock.
> Earnings on total capitalization.
> Ratio of gross to market value of common.
> Margin of profit.
> Depreciation in relation to plant account.
> Working-capital position.
> Tangible asset values.
> Dividend return.
> Trend of earnings.

If the comparison is carried back prior to 1934, Granite City is found to have enjoyed a marked advantage in the depression years from mid-1930 to mid-1933. During this time it earned and paid dividends while Continental Steel was reporting moderate losses. It is curious to observe that in the more recent recession the tables were exactly turned, and Continental Steel did very well while Granite City fared badly. Obviously the 1937–1938 results would command more attention than those in the longer past. Nevertheless, the thorough analyst would endeavor to learn as much as possible about the basic reasons underlying the change in the relative performance of the two companies.

Study of Qualitative Factors Also Necessary. Our last observation leads to the more general remark that conclusions suggested by comparative tabulations of this sort should not be accepted until careful thought has been given to the qualitative factors. When one issue seems to be selling much too low on the basis of the exhibit in relation to that of another in the same field, there may be adequate reasons for this disparity that the statistics do not disclose. Among such valid reasons may be a definitely poorer outlook or a questionable management. A lower dividend return for a common stock should not ordinarily be considered as a strong offsetting factor, since the dividend is usually adjusted to the earning power within a reasonable time.

Although overconservative dividend policies are sometimes followed for a considerable period (a subject referred to in Chap. 29), there is a well-defined tendency even in these cases for the market price to reflect the earning power sooner or later.

Relative popularity and relative market activity are two elements not connected with intrinsic value that nevertheless exert a powerful and often a continuing effect upon the market quotation. The analyst must give these factors respectful heed, but his work would be stultified if he always favored the more active and the more popular issue.

The recommendation of an exchange of one security for another seems to involve a greater personal accountability on the part of the analyst than the selection of an issue for original purchase. The reason is that holders of securities for investment are loath to make changes, and thus they are particularly irritated if the subsequent market action makes the move appear to have been unwise. Speculative holders will naturally gage all advice by the test of market results—usually immediate results. Bearing these human-nature factors in mind, the analyst must avoid suggesting common-stock exchanges to speculators (except possibly if accompanied by an emphatic disclaimer of responsibility for subsequent market action), and he must hesitate to suggest such exchanges to holders for investment unless the statistical superiority of the issue recommended is quite impressive. As an arbitrary rule, we might say that there should be good reason to believe that by making the exchange the investor would be getting at least 50% more for his money.

Variations in Homogeneity Affect the Values of Comparative Analysis. The dependability of industrial comparisons will vary with

COMPARISON OF CONTINENTAL STEEL AND GRANITE CITY STEEL

(000 OMITTED, EXCEPT THOSE PER SHARE)

Item	Continental Steel	Granite City Steel
Market price of common, July 1938	17	17
1. Bonds at par	$1,202	$1,618
2. Preferred stock at market	2,450	
3. Common stock at market	3,410	6,494
4. Total capitalization	7,062	8,112
5. Ratio of common to total capitalization	48.3%	80.0%

	Average of 5 years ended 6/30/38	Year ended 6/30/38	Average of 5 years ended 6/30/38	Year ended 6/30/38
8. Gross sales	$15,049	$13,989	$8,715	$8,554
9. Depreciation	500	445	390	459
10. Net available for bond interest	704	559	336	287(d)
11. Bond interest	81	67	(Est.) 18	(Est.) 54
12. Preferred dividends	179	171		
13. Balance for common	444	321	318	341(d)
14. Margin of profit	4.7%	4.0%	3.9%	(def.)
15. % earned on total capitalization	10.0	7.9%	4.1%	(def.)
16. Interest charges earned	8.7 times	8.3 times	18.7 times	(def.)
17. Earned on common, per share	$2.29	$1.60	$1.20	$0.89(d)
18. Earned on common, % of market price	13.5	9.4	7.1	(d)
19. Ratio of gross to market value of common	441.5%	409.8%	134.3%	131.8%
Trend figures:				
23. Earned per share by years:				
Year ended June 30, 1938	$1.60		$0.89(d)	
Year ended June 30, 1937	3.83	1.31		
Year ended June 30, 1936	2.67		1.49	
Year ended June 30, 1935	1.69		1.45	
Year ended June 30, 1934	1.66		2.65	
Dividends:				
24. Dividend rate on common		$1.00		None
25. Dividend yield on common		5.9%		
Financial position (dates):		6/30/38		12/31/37
29. Total current assets		$6,467		$4,179
30. Total current liabilities		1,198		1,164
31. Net current assets		5,269		3,015
35. Net tangible assets for total capitalization		13,498		13,556

the nature of the industry considered. The basic question, of course, is whether future developments are likely to affect all the companies in the group similarly or dissimilarly. If similarly, then substantial weight may be accorded to the relative performance in the past, as shown by the statistical exhibit. An industrial group of this type may be called "homogeneous." But, if the individual companies in the field are likely to respond quite variously to new conditions, then the relative showing must be regarded as a much less reliable guide. A group of this kind may be termed "heterogeneous."

With certain exceptions for traffic and geographical variations, *e.g.*, in particular, the Pocohantas soft-coal carriers, the railroads must be considered a highly homogeneous group. The same is true of the larger light, heat and power utilities. In the industrial field the best examples of homogeneous groups are afforded by the producers of raw materials and of other standardized products in which the trade name is a minor factor. These would include producers of sugar, coal, metals, steel products, cement, cotton print cloths, etc. The larger oil companies may be considered as fairly homogeneous; the smaller concerns are not well suited to comparison because they are subject to sudden important changes in production, reserves and relative price received. The larger baking, dairy and packing companies fall into fairly homogeneous groups. The same is true of the larger chain-store enterprises when compared with other units in the same subgroups, *e.g.*, grocery, five-and-ten-cent, restaurant, etc. Department stores are less homogeneous, but comparisons in this field are by no means far-fetched.

Makers of manufactured goods sold under advertised trade-marks must generally be regarded as belonging to heterogeneous groups. In these fields one concern frequently prospers at the expense of its competitors, so that the units in the industry do not improve or decline together. Among automobile manufactures, for example, there have been continuous and pronounced variations in relative standing. Producers of all the various classes of machinery and equipment are subject to somewhat the same conditions. This is true also of the proprietary drug manufacturers. Intermediate positions from this point of view are occupied by such groups as the larger makers of tires, of tobacco products, of shoes, wherein changes of relative position are not so frequent.[2]

---

[2] But significant changes do occur, of course. Note, for example, the phenomenal growth of Philip Morris, relative to its large competitors, the somewhat less spectacular development of

The analyst must be most cautious about drawing comparative conclusions from the statistical data when dealing with companies in a heterogeneous group. No doubt preference may properly be accorded in
these fields to the companies making the best quantitative showing (if not
offset by known qualitative factors)—for this basis of selection would
seem sounder than any other—but the analyst and the investor should be
fully aware that such superiority may prove evanescent. As a general rule,
the less homogeneous the group the more attention must be paid to the
qualitative factors in making comparisons.

More General Limitations on the Value of Comparative Analysis.

It may be well once again to caution the student against being
deluded by the mathematical exactitude of his comparative tables into
believing that their indicated conclusions are equally exact. We have mentioned the need of considering qualitative factors and of allowing for lack
of homogeneity. But beyond these points lie all the various obstacles to
the success of the analyst that we presented in some detail in our first
chapter. The technique of comparative analysis may lessen some of the
hazards of his work, but it can never exempt him from the vicissitudes of
the future or the stubborness of the stock market itself or the consequences of his own failure—often unavoidable—to learn all the important facts. He must expect to appear wrong often and to be wrong on
occasion; but with intelligence and prudence his work should yield better over-all results than the guesses or the superficial judgments of the
typical stock buyer.

General Shoe and the exceptional comparative showing of Lee Tire, in the three fields mentioned. All three of these were relatively small enterprises.

Chapter 50

DISCREPANCIES BETWEEN
PRICE AND VALUE

OUR EXPOSITION OF THE TECHNIQUE of security analysis has included many different examples of overvaluation and undervaluation. Evidently the processes by which the securities market arrives at its appraisals are frequently illogical and erroneous. These processes, as we pointed out in our first chapter, are not automatic or mechanical but psychological, for they go on in the minds of people who buy or sell. The mistakes of the market are thus the mistakes of groups or masses of individuals. Most of them can be traced to one or more of three basic causes: exaggeration, oversimplification or neglect.

In this chapter and the next we shall attempt a concise review of the various aberrations of the securities market. We shall approach the subject from the standpoint of the practical activities of the analyst, seeking in each case to determine the extent to which it offers an opportunity for profitable action on his part. This inquiry will thus constitute an amplification of our early chapter on the scope and limitations of security analysis, drawing upon the material developed in the succeeding discussions, to which a number of references will be made.

General Procedure of the Analyst. Since we have emphasized that analysis will lead to a positive conclusion only in the exceptional case, it follows that many securities must be examined before one is found that has real possibilities for the analyst. By what practical means does he proceed to make his discoveries? Mainly by hard and systematic work. There are two broad methods that he may follow. The first consists of a series of comparative analyses by industrial groups along the lines described in the previous chapter. Such studies will give him a fair idea of the standard or usual characteristics of each group and also point out those companies which deviate widely from the modal exhibit. If, for example, he discovers that a certain steel common stock has been earning about twice as much on its market price as the industry as a whole, he has a clue to work on—or rather a suggestion to be pursued by dint of a thoroughgoing investigation of all the important qualitative and quantitative factors relating to the enterprise.

The same type of methodical inquiry may be applied to the field of bonds and preferred stocks. The wide area of receivership railroad bonds can best be explored by means of a comparative analysis of the showing of the bonds of roughly the same rank issued by, say, a dozen of the major carriers in trusteeship. Or a large number of public-utility preferred stocks could be listed according to: (1) their over-all dividend and interest coverage, (2) their stock-value ratio and (3) their price and yield. Such a simple grouping might indicate a few issues that either were well secured and returned more than the average or else were clearly selling too high in view of their inadequate statistical protection. And so on.

The second general method consists in scrutinizing corporate reports as they make their appearance and relating their showing to the market price of their bonds or stocks. These reports can be seen—in summary form, at least—in various daily papers; a more comprehensive presentation can be found in the daily corporation-report sheets of the financial services or weekly in the *Commercial and Financial Chronicle*. A quick glance at a hundred of such reports may reveal between five and ten that look interesting enough from the earnings or current-asset standpoint to warrant more intensive study.

Can Cyclical Swings of Prices Be Exploited? The best understood disparities between price and value are those which accompany the recurrent broad swings of the market through boom and depression. It is a mere truism that stocks sell too high in a bull market and too low in a bear market. For at bottom this is simply equivalent to saying that any upward or downward movement of prices must finally reach a limit, and since prices do not remain at such limits (or at any other level) permanently, it must turn out in retrospect that prices will have advanced or declined too far.

Can the analyst exploit successfully the repeated exaggerations of the general market? Experience suggests that a procedure somewhat like the following should turn out to be reasonably satisfactory:

1. Select a diversified list of leading common stocks, *e.g.*, those in the "Dow-Jones Industrial Average."

2. Determine an indicated "normal" value for this group by applying a suitable multiplier to average earnings. The multiplier might be equivalent to capitalizing the earnings at, say, twice the current interest rate on highest grade industrial bonds. The period for averaging earnings would ordinarily be seven to ten years, but exceptional conditions such as occurred in 1931–1933 might suggest a different method, *e.g.*, basing the average on the period beginning in 1934, when operating in 1939 or later.

3. Make composite purchases of the list when the shares can be bought at a substantial discount from normal value, say, at 2/3 such value. Or purchases may be made on a scale downwards, beginning say, at 80% of normal value.

4. Sell out such purchases when a price is reached substantially above normal value, say, 1/3 higher, or from 20% to 50% higher on a scale basis.

This was the general scheme of operations developed by Roger Babson many years ago. It yielded quite satisfactory results prior to 1925. But—as we pointed out in Chap. 37—during the 1921–1933 cycle (measuring from low point to low point) it would have called for purchasing during 1921, selling out probably in 1926, thus requiring complete abstinence from the market during the great boom of 1927–1929, and repurchasing in 1931, to be followed by a severe shrinkage in market values. A program of this character would have made far too heavy demands upon human fortitude.

The behavior of the market since 1933 has offered difficulties of a different sort in applying these mechanical formulas—particularly in determining normal earnings from which to compute normal values. It is scarcely to be expected that an idea as basically simple as this one can be utilized with any high degree of accuracy in catching the broad market swings. But for those who realize its inherent limitations it may have considerable utility, for at least it is likely on the average to result in purchases at intrinsically attractive levels—which is more than half the battle in common-stock investment.

"Catching the Swings" on a Marginal Basis Impracticable.

From the ordinary speculative standpoint, involving purchases on margin and short sales, this method of operation must be set down as impracticable. The outright owner can afford to buy too soon and to sell too soon. In fact he must expect to do both and to see the market decline farther after he buys and advance farther after he sells out. But the margin trader is necessarily concerned with immediate results; he swims with the tide, hoping to gage the exact moment when the tide will turn and to reverse his stroke the moment before. In this he rarely succeeds, so that his typical experience is temporary success ending in complete disaster. It is the essential character of the speculator that he buys because he thinks stocks are going up not because they are cheap, and conversely when he sells. Hence there is a fundamental cleavage of viewpoint between the speculator and the securities analyst, which militates strongly against any enduringly satisfactory association between them.

Bond prices tend undoubtedly to swing through cycles in somewhat the same way as stocks, and it is frequently suggested that bond investors follow the policy of selling their holdings near the top of these cycles and repurchasing them near the bottom. We are doubtful if this can be done with satisfactory results in the typical case. There are no well-defined standards as to when high-grade bond prices are cheap or dear corresponding to the earnings-ratio test for common stocks, and the operations have to be guided chiefly by a technique of gaging market moves that seems rather far removed from "investment." The loss of interest on funds between the time of sale and repurchase is a strong debit factor, and in our opinion the net advantage is not sufficient to warrant incurring the psychological dangers that inhere in any placing of emphasis by the investor upon market movements.

Opportunities in "Secondary" or Little-known Issues. Returning to common stocks, although overvaluation or undervaluation of leading issues occurs only at certain points in the stock-market cycle, the large field of "nonrepresentative" or "secondary" issues is likely to yield instances of undervaluation at all times. When the market leaders are cheap, some of the less prominent common stocks are likely to be a good deal cheaper. During 1932–1933, for example, stocks such as Plymouth Cordage, Pepperell Manufacturing, American Laundry Machinery and many others, sold at unbelievably low prices in relation to their past records and current financial exhibits. It is probably a matter for individual preference whether the investor should purchase an outstanding issue like General Motors at about 50% of its conservative valuation or a less prominent stock like Pepperell at about 25% of such value.

The Impermanence of Leadership. The composition of the market-leader group has varied greatly from year to year, especially in view of the recent shift of attention from past performance to assumed prospects. If we examine the list during the decline of 1937–1938, we shall find quite a number of once outstanding issues that sold at surprisingly low prices in relation to their statistical exhibits.

Example: A startling example of this sort is provided by Great Atlantic and Pacific Tea Company common, which in 1929 sold as high as 494 and in 1938 as low as 36. Salient data on this issue are as follows:

Year[1]	Sales (000 omitted)	Net (000 omitted)	Earned per share of common	Dividend paid on common	Price range of common
1938	$ 878,972	$15,834	$ 6.71	$4.00	72–36
1937	881,703	9,119	3.50	6.25	$117^{1}/_{2}$–$45^{1}/_{4}$
1936	907,371	17,085	7.31	7.00	$130^{1}/_{2}$–$110^{1}/_{2}$
1935	872,244	16,593	7.08	7.00	140 –121
1934	842,016	16,709	7.13	7.00	150–122
1933	819,617	20,478	8.94	7.00	$181^{1}/_{2}$–115
1932	863,048	22,733	10.02	7.00	168–$103^{1}/_{2}$
1931	1,008,325	29,793	13.40	6.50	260–130
1930	1,065,807	30,743	13.86	5.25	260–155
1929	1,053,693	26,220	11.77	4.50	494–162

[1] Year ended following Jan. 31, except price range.

The balance sheet of January 31, 1938, showed cash assets of 85 millions and net current assets of 134 millions. At the 1938 low prices, the preferred and common together were selling for 126 millions. Here, then, was a company whose spectacular growth was one of the great romances of American business, a company that was without doubt the largest retail enterprise in America and perhaps in the world, that had an uninterrupted record of earnings and dividends for many years—and yet was selling for less than its net current assets alone. Thus one of the outstanding businesses of the country was considered by Wall Street in 1938 to be worth less as a going concern than if it were liquidated. Why? First, because of chain-store tax threats; second, because of a recent decline in earnings; and, third, because the general market was depressed.

We doubt that a better illustration can be found of the real nature of the stock market, which does not aim to evaluate businesses with any exactitude but rather to express its likes and dislikes, its hopes and fears, in the form of daily changing quotations. There is indeed enough sound sense and selective judgment in the market's activities to create on most occasions some degree of correspondence between market price and ascertainable or intrinsic value. In particular, as was pointed out in Chap. 4, when we are dealing with something as elusive and nonmathematical as the evaluation of future prospects, we are generally led to accept the market's verdict as better than anything that the analyst can arrive at. But, on enough occasions to keep the analyst busy, the emotions of the stock market carry it in either direction beyond the limits of sound judgment.

Opportunities in Normal Markets. During the intermediate period, when average prices show no definite signs of being either too low or too high, common stocks may usually be found that seem definitely undervalued on a statistical basis. These generally fall into two classes: (1) Those showing high current and average earnings in relation to market price and (2) those making a reasonably satisfactory exhibit of earnings and selling at a low price in relation to net-current-asset value. Obviously, such companies will not be large and well known, or else the trend of

GROUP *A*. COMMON STOCKS SELLING AT THE END OF 1938 OR 1939 AT LESS THAN 7 TIMES PAST YEAR'S EARNINGS AND ALSO AT LESS THAN NET CURRENT ASSET VALUE

Company	Year taken	Price Dec. 31	Earnings for year per share	Average earnings 1934–1938 or 1934–1939 per share	Net current asset value per share	Net tangible asset value per share
J. D. Adams Mfg.	1938	8	$1.15	$1.20	$12.07	$14.38
American Seating	1939	10$^1/_4$	1.82	1.75	11.42	23.95
Bunte Bros.	1938	10	2.10	2.14	12.84	27.83
Grand Union	1939	10	1.80	1.25	13.60†	20.00†
International Silver	1939	26$^3/_4$	4.98	*def 0.10*	39.67	97.50
I. B. Kleinert	1938	8$^1/_2$	1.27	0.80	11.04	16.90
New Idea	1939	12$^1/_8$	2.18	1.78	13.44	16.02
*N. Y. Merchandise	1939	7$^3/_4$	1.44	1.44	11.66	14.05
*Pacific Commercial	1938	11$^1/_2$	2.31	2.77	24.18	27.74
Seton Leather	1938	6$^1/_4$	1.38	0.94	8.38	11.27

* These stocks belong also in Group *B*.
† Partly estimated.

earnings will not have been encouraging. In the appended table are given a number of companies falling in each group as of the end of 1938 or 1939, at which times the market level for industrial stocks did not appear to be especially high or especially low.

GROUP *B.* COMMON STOCKS SELLING AT THE END OF 1938 OR 1939 AT TWO-THIRDS, OR LESS, OF NET CURRENT ASSET VALUE AND ALSO AT LESS THAN 12 TIMES EITHER PAST YEAR'S OR AVERAGE EARNINGS

Company	Year taken	Price Dec. 31	Earnings for year per share	Average earnings 1934–1938 or 1934–1939 per share	Net current asset value per share	Net tangible asset value per share
Butler Bros.	1939	7	$0.83	$0.27	$12.75	$19.59
Ely & Walker	1939	18	2.30	1.83	41.60	48.51
Gilchrist	1939	4³/₄	0.70*	0.85*	13.85	17.39
Hale Bros. Stores	1939	14	1.81	2.00	22.13	28.14
Intertype	1939	8³/₄	0.55	0.82	19.77	22.35
Lee & Cady	1939	6	0.77	0.73	11.35	12.61
H. D. Lee Mercantile	1938	14	0.87	1.35	25.00	31.56
Manhattan Shirt	1938	11¹/₂	0.73	1.06	19.36	23.62
Reliance Mfg.	1939	12	1.69	0.94	18.97	22.21
S. Stroock	1939	9¹/₄	1.21	1.39	14.90	26.61

* Years ended following Jan 31.

It is not difficult for the assiduous analyst to find interesting statistical exhibits such as those presented in our table. Much more difficult is the task of determining whether or not the qualitative factors will justify following the quantitative indications—in other words, whether or not the investor may have sufficient confidence in the company's future to consider its shares a real bargain at the apparently subnormal price.

On this question the weight of financial opinion appears inclined to a generally pessimistic conclusion. The investment trusts, with all their facilities for discovering opportunities of this type, have paid little attention to them—partly, it is true, because they are difficult to buy and sell in the large quantities that the trusts prefer, but also because of their conviction that however good the statistical exhibit of a secondary company may be it is not likely to prove a profitable purchase *unless there is specific ground for optimism regarding its future.*

The main drawback of a typical smaller sized company is its vulnerability to a sudden and perhaps permanent loss of its earning power. Undoubtedly such adverse developments occur in a larger proportion of cases in this group than among the larger enterprises. As an offset to this we have the fact that the successful small company can multiply its value far more impressively than those which are already of enormous size. For example, the growth of Philip Morris, Inc., in market value from 5 millions in 1934 to 90 millions in 1939, accompanying a 1,200% increase in net earnings, would have been quite inconceivable in the case of American Tobacco. Similarly, the growth of Pepsi-Cola has far outstripped in percentage that of Coca-Cola; the same is true of General Shoe vs. International Shoe; etc.

But most students will try to locate the potential Philip Morris opportunities, by gaging future possibilities with greater or less care, and will then buy their shares even at a fairly high price—rather than make their commitments in a diversified group of "bargain issues" with only ordinary prospects. Our own experience leads us to favor the latter technique, although we cannot guarantee brilliant results therefrom under present-day conditions. Yet judging from observations made over a number of years, it would seem that investment in apparently undervalued common stocks can be carried on with a very fair degree of over-all success, provided average alertness and good judgment are used in passing on the future-prospect question—and provided also that commitments are avoided at times when the general market is statistically much too high. Two older examples of this type of opportunity are given here, to afford the reader some notion of former stock markets.

Florence Stove Common		Firestone Tire & Rubber Common	
Price in Jan. 1935	.35	Price in Nov. 1925	120
Dividend	$2	Dividend	$6
Earned per share:		Earned per share year ended Oct.:	
1934	$7.93	1925	$32.57*
1933	7.98	1924	16.92
1932	3.33	1923	14.06
1931	2.27	1922	17.08

* Earnings before contingency reserves were $40.95 per share.

In these cases the market price had failed to reflect adequately the indicated earning power.

Market Behavior of Standard and Nonstandard Issues. A close study of the market action of common stocks suggests the following further general observations:

1. Standard or leading issues almost always respond rapidly to changes in their reported profits—so much so that they tend regularly to exaggerate marketwise the significance of year-to-year fluctuations in earnings.

2. The action of the less familiar issues depends largely upon what attitude is taken towards them by professional market operators. If interest is lacking, the price may lag far behind the statistical showing. If interest is attracted to the issue, either manipulatively or more legitimately, the opposite result can readily be attained, and the price will respond in extreme fashion to changes in the company's exhibit.

Examples of Behavior of Nonstandard Issues. The following two examples will illustrate this diversity of behavior of nonrepresentative common stocks.

BUTTE AND SUPERIOR COPPER (ACTUALLY ZINC) COMPANY COMMON

Period	Earnings per share	Dividend per share	Price range
Year, 1914	$ 5.21	$ 2.25	44–24
1st quarter, 1915	4.27	0.75	50–36
2d quarter, 1915	7.73	3.25	80–45
3d quarter, 1915	10.13	5.75	73–57
4th quarter, 1915	11.34	8.25	75–59
Year 1915	$33.47	$18.00	80–36
Year 1916	30.58	34.00	105–42

These were extraordinarily large earnings and dividends. Even allowing for the fact that they were due to wartime prices for zinc, the market price showed none the less a striking disregard of the company's spectacular exhibit. The reason was lack of general interest or of individual market sponsorship.

Contrast the foregoing with the appended showing of the common stock of Mullins Body (later Mullins Manufacturing) Corporation.

Between 1924 and 1926 we note the characteristic market swings of a low-priced "secondary" common-stock issue. At the beginning of 1927 the shares were undoubtedly attractive, speculatively, at about 10, for the price was low in relation to the earnings of the three years previously. A substantial, but by no means spectacular, rise in profits during 1927–1928 resulted in a typical stock-market exploitation. The price advanced from 10 in 1927 to 95 in 1928 and fell back again to 10 in 1929.

Year	Earned per share	Dividend	Price range
1924	$1.91	None	18–9
1925	2.47	None	22–13
1926	1.97	None	20–8
1927	5.13	None	79–10
1928	6.53	None	95–69
1929	2.67	None	82–10

A contrast of another kind is afforded by the behavior of the aircraft-manufacturing stocks in 1938–1939, as compared with that of war beneficiaries in 1915–1918. The two following examples will illustrate the relationship between market price in 1938 and 1939 and actual performance at the time.

	Boeing Airplane Co.	Glenn L. Martin Co.
Date	December 1938	November 1939
Market value of company	$25,270,000	$49,413,000
	(722,000 sh. @ 35)	(1,092,000 sh. @ 45¼)
Sales 1938	2,006,000	12,417,000
Net 1938	555,000(*d*)	2,349,000
Sales, 9 months 1939	6,566,000	8,506,000
Net, 9 months 1939	2,606,000(*d*)	1,514,000
Tangible assets, Sept. 30, 1939	4,527,000	15,200,000

In these cases the market was evidently capitalizing the as yet unrealized profits from war orders as if they supplied a *permanent* basis of future earnings. The contrast between the Butte and Superior price-earnings ratio in 1915–1916 and that of these aircraft concerns in 1938–1939 is very striking.

Relationship of the Analyst to Such Situations. The analyst can deal intelligently and fairly successfully with situations such as Wright Aeronautical, Bangor and Aroostook, Firestone and Butte and Superior at the periods referred to. He could even have formed a worth-while opinion about Mullins early in 1927. But once this issue fell into market operators' hands it passed beyond the pale of analytical judgment. As far as Wall Street was concerned, Mullins had ceased to be a business and had become a symbol on the ticker tape. To buy it or to sell it was equally hazardous; the analyst could warn of the hazard, but he could have no idea of the limits of its rise or fall. (As it happened, however, the company issued a convertible preferred stock in 1928 which made possible a profitable hedging operation, consisting of the purchase of the preferred and the sale of the common.) Similarly with the airplane issues in 1939, the analyst could go no further than to indicate the obvious hazard that lay in treating as permanent a source of business that the whole world must necessarily hope was essentially temporary.

When the general market appears dangerously high to the analyst, he must be hesitant about recommending unfamiliar common stocks, even though they may seem to be of the bargain type. A severe decline in the general market will affect all stock prices adversely, and the less active issues may prove especially vulnerable to the effects of necessitous selling.

Market Exaggerations Due to Factors Other than Changes in Earnings: *Dividend Changes.*

The inveterate tendency of the stock market to exaggerate extends to factors other than changes in earnings. Overemphasis is laid upon such matters as dividend changes, stock split-ups, mergers and segregations. An increase in the cash dividend is a favorable development, but it is absurd to add $20 to the price of a stock just because the dividend rate is advanced from $5 to $6 annually. The buyer at the higher price is paying out in advance all the additional dividends that he will receive at the new rate *over the next 20 years.* The excited responses often made to stock dividends are even more illogical, since they are in essence nothing more than pieces of paper. The same is true of split-ups, which create more shares but give the stockholder nothing he did not have before—except the minor advantage of a possibly broader market due to the lower price level.[1]

Mergers and Segregations. Wall Street becomes easily enthusiastic over mergers and just as ebullient over segregations, which are the exact opposite. Putting two and two together frequently produces five in the stock market, and this five may later be split up into three and three. Such inductive studies as have been made of the results following mergers seem to cast considerable doubt upon the efficacy of consolidation as an aid to earning power.[2] There is also reason to believe that the personal element in corporate management often stands in the way of really advantageous consolidations and that those which are consummated are due sometimes to knowledge by those in control of unfavorable conditions ahead.

The exaggerated response made by the stock market to developments that seem relatively unimportant in themselves is readily explained in terms of the psychology of the speculator. He wants "action," first of all; and he is willing to contribute to this action if he can be given any pretext for bullish excitement. (Whether through hypocrisy or self-deception, brokerage-house customers generally refuse to admit they are merely gambling with ticker quotations and insist upon some ostensible "reason" for their purchases.) Stock dividends and other "favorable developments" of this character supply the desired pretexts, and they have been exploited by the professional market operators, sometimes with the connivance of the corporate officials. The whole thing would be childish if it were not so vicious. The securities analyst should understand how these absurdities of Wall Street come into being, but he would do well to avoid any form of contact with them.

---

[1] In the Atlas Tack manipulation of 1933 an effort was made to attract public buying by promising a split-up of the stock, 3 shares for 1. Obviously, such a move could make no real difference of any kind in the case of an issue selling in the 30s. The circumstances surrounding the rise of Atlas Tack from $1^1/2$ to $34^3/4$ in 1933 and its precipitous fall to 10 are worth studying as a perfect example of the manipulative pattern. It is illuminating to compare the price-earnings and the price-assets relationships of the same stock prior to 1929.

[2] See, for example, Arthur S. Dewing, "A Statistical Test of the Success of Consolidations," published in *Quarterly Journal of Economics*, November 1921 and reprinted in his *Financial Policy of Corporations*, pp. 885–898, New York, 1926. But see Henry R. Seager and Charles A. Gullick, *Trust and Corporation Problems*, pp. 659–661, New York, 1929, and *Report of the Committee on Recent Economic Changes*, Vol. I, pp. 194 *ff.*, New York, 1929.

Litigation. The tendency of Wall Street to go to extremes is illustrated in the opposite direction by its tremendous dislike of litigation. A lawsuit of any significance casts a damper on the securities affected, and the extent of the decline may be out of all proportion to the merits of the case. Developments of this kind may offer real opportunities to the analyst, though of course they are of a specialized nature. The aspect of broadest importance is that of receivership. Since the undervaluations resulting therefrom are almost always confined to bond issues, we shall discuss this subject later in the chapter in connection with senior securities.

Example: A rather striking example of the effect of litigation on common-stock values is afforded by the Reading Company case. In 1913 the United States government brought suit to compel separation of the company's railroad and coal properties. The stock market, having its own ideas of consistency, considered this move as a dangerous attack on Reading, despite the fact that the segregation would in itself ordinarily be considered as "bullish." A plan was later agreed upon (in 1921) under which the coal subsidiary's stock was in effect to be distributed pro rata among the Reading Company's common and preferred shareholders. This was hailed in turn as a favorable development, although in fact it constituted a victory for the government against the company.

Some common stockholders, however, objected to the participation of the preferred stock in the coal company "rights." Suit was brought to restrict these rights to the common stock. Amusingly, but not surprisingly, the effect of this move was to depress the price of Reading common. In logic, the common should have advanced, since, if the suit were successful, there would be more value for the junior shares, and, if it failed (as it did), there would be no less value than before. But the stock market reasoned merely that here was some new litigation and hence Reading common should be "let alone."

Situations involving litigation frequently permit the analyst to pursue to advantage his quantitative approach in contrast with the qualitative attitude of security holders in general. Assume that the assets of a bankrupt concern have been turned into cash and there is available for distribution to its bondholders the sum of, say, 50% net. But there is a suit pending, brought by others, to collect a good part of this money. It may be that the action is so far-fetched as to be almost absurd; it may be that it has been defeated in the lower courts, and even on appeal, and that it has now but a microscopic chance to be heard by the United States Supreme Court. Nevertheless, the mere pendency of this litigation will severely reduce the market value of the bonds. Under the conditions named, they are likely to sell as low as 35 instead of 50 cents on the dollar. The anomaly here is that a remote claim, which the plaintiff can regard as having scarcely any real value to him, is made the equivalent in the market to a heavy liability on the part of the defendant. We thus have a mathematically demonstrable case of undervaluations, and, taking these as a class, they lend themselves exceedingly well to exploitation by the securities analyst.

Examples: Island Oil and Transport 8% Notes. In June 1933 these notes were selling at 18. The receiver held a cash fund equivalent to about 45% on the issue, from which were deductible certain fees and allowances, indicating a net distributable balance of about 30 for the notes. The distribution was being delayed by a suit for damages that had been repeatedly unsuccessful in its various legal stages and was now approaching final determination. This suit was exerting an adverse effect upon the market value of the notes out of all proportion to its merits, a statement that is demonstrable from the fact that the litigation could have been settled by payment of a relatively small amount. After the earlier decisions were finally sustained by the higher courts, the noteholders received a distribution of $290 per $1,000 in April 1934. A small additional distribution was indicated.[3]

A similar situation arose in the case of United Shipyards Corporation stock after ratification of the sale of its properties to Bethlehem Steel Company in 1938. Dissenting holders brought suit to set the sale aside on the ground that the price was grossly inadequate. The effect of this litigation was to hold down the price of the Class *B* common to $1^1/_4$ in January 1939, as against a realizable value of between $2^1/_2$ to 3 if the sale was upheld. Obviously, if the suit had any merit, the stock should have been worth more rather than less than $2^1/_2$; alternatively, if it had no merit, as seemed

---

[3] A very similar situation existed in 1938 in connection with the various bond issues of National Bondholders Corporation, which was engaged in liquidating various properties and claims. These securities were selling at considerably less than the amount realizable for them in liquidation, chiefly because of certain suits involving a substantial cash fund. As in the Island Oil example, this litigation was in the last stages of appeal, and the decisions theretofore had all been favorable to the bondholders. Following the final decision the value of a typical issue advanced from 26 bid in 1938 to the equivalent of 41 bid in 1939.

clear, then the shares were clearly worth twice their selling price. (A similar disparity existed in connection with the price of the Class *A* stock.)

Undervalued Investment Issues. Undervalued bonds and preferred stocks of investment caliber may be discovered in any period by means of assiduous search. In many cases the low price of a bond or preferred stock is due to a poor market, which in turn results from the small size of the issue, but this very small size may make for greater inherent security. The Electric Refrigeration Building Corporation 6s, due 1936, described in Chap. 26, are a good example of this paradox.

At times some specific development greatly strengthens the position of a senior issue, but the price is slow to reflect this improvement, and thus a bargain situation is created. These developments relate usually to the capitalization structure or to corporate relationships. Several examples will illustrate our point.

Examples: In 1923 Youngstown Sheet and Tube Company purchased the properties of Steel and Tube Company of America and assumed liability for the latter's General Mortgage 7s, due 1951. Youngstown sold a 6% debenture issue at 99 to supply funds for this purchase. The following price relationship obtained at the time:

Company	Price	Yield, %
Youngstown Sheet and Tube Debenture 6s	99	6.02
Steel and Tube General 7s	102	6.85

The market failed to realize the altered status of the Steel and Tube bonds, and thus they sold illogically at a higher yield than the unsecured issue of the same obligor company. This presented a clear-cut opportunity to the analyst to recommend a purchase or an exchange.

In 1922 the City of Detroit purchased the urban lines of Detroit United Railway Company and agreed to pay therefor sums sufficient to retire the Detroit United Railway First $4^1/2$s, due 1932. Unusually strong protective provisions were inserted in the purchase contract which practically, if not technically, made the City of Detroit liable for the bonds. But, after the deal was consummated, the bonds sold at 82, yielding more than 7%. The bond market failed to recognize their true status as virtual obligations of the City of Detroit.

In 1924 Congoleum Company had outstanding $1,800,000 of 7% preferred stock junior to $2,890,000 of bonds and followed by 960,000 shares of common stock having an average market value of some $48,000,000. In October of that year the company issued 681,000 additional shares of common for the business of the Nairn Linoleum Company, a large unit in the same field, with $15,000,000 of tangible assets. The enormous equity thus created for the small senior issues made them safe beyond question, but the price of the preferred stock remained under par.

In 1927 Electric Refrigeration Corporation (now Kelvinator Corporation) sold 373,000 shares of common stock for $6,600,000, making a total of 1,000,000 shares of common stock, with average market value of about $21,000,000, coming behind only $2,880,000 of 6% notes, due in 1936. The notes sold at 74, however, to yield 11%. The low price was due to a large operating deficit incurred in 1927, but the market failed to take into account the fact that the receipt of a much greater amount of new cash from the sale of additional stock had established a very strong backing for the small note issue.

These four senior issues have all been paid off at par or higher. (The Congoleum-Nairn Preferred was called for payment at 107 in 1934.) Examples of this kind are convenient for the authors since they do not involve the risk of some later mischance casting doubt upon their judgment. To avoid loading the dice too heavily in our favor, we add another illustration which is current as this chapter is written.

A Current Example. Choctaw and Memphis Railroad Company First 5s, due 1949, were selling in 1939 at about 35, carrying more than 5 years' unpaid interest. They were a first lien on underlying mileage of the Chicago, Rock Island and Pacific System. The Rock Island had been reporting poor earnings since 1930, and all its obligations were in default. However, a segregation of the 1937 earnings by mortgage divisions showed that the Choctaw and Memphis mileage was very profitable and that its interest charges had been covered 2.6 times in that year even though the company had earned only $2,700,000 toward total interest of $14,080,000. Furthermore, the several reorganization plans presented up to 1939, including that of the I.C.C. examiner, had all provided for principal and back interest on this issue in full, although virtually the entire remaining bond structure was to be drastically cut down, and total interest charges were to be reduced to less than $2,500,000 annually.

Assuming, as seemed inevitable, that the company was to be reorganized along the lines proposed, it was clear that these Choctaw and Memphis bonds would enjoy a very strong position, whether they were to be left undisturbed with their lien on a valuable mileage and their back interest paid off, or were to be given par for par in a new, small first mortgage on the entire system. This conclusion would be inescapable unless it were true that a railroad with minimum gross earnings of 65 millions could not be counted on to meet charges of $2^1/_2$ millions annually—less than *one-fifth* its former burden.

Thus all the quantitative factors would seem to indicate strongly that the Choctaw and Memphis 5s were greatly undervalued at 35 and that *once the recapitalization was completed* the entrenched position of this issue should become manifest.[4]

Price-value Discrepancies in Receiverships.

In Chap. 18, dealing with reorganization procedure, we gave two diverse examples of disparities arising under a receivership: the Fisk Rubber case, in which the obligations sold at a ridiculously low price compared with the current assets available for them; and the Studebaker case, in which the price of the 6% notes was clearly out of line with that of the stock. A general statement may fairly be made that in cases where substantial values are ultimately realized out of a receivership, the senior securities will be found to have sold at much too low a price. This characteristic has a twofold consequence. It has previously led us to advise strongly against buying at investment levels *any* securities of a company that is likely to fall into financial difficulties; it now leads us to suggest that *after* these difficulties have arisen they may produce attractive analytical opportunities.

This will be true not only of issues so strongly entrenched as to come through reorganization unscathed (*e.g.*, Brooklyn Union Elevated 5s, as described in Chap. 2) but also of senior securities which are "scaled down" or otherwise affected in a readjustment plan. It seems to hold most

---

[4] See Appendix Note 67, p. 835 on accompanying CD, for text of the material in the 1934 edition relating to the Fox Film 6% Notes, due 1936, which in 1933 were selling at 75 to yield 20% to maturity.

Further Example: In 1938 Tung Sol Lamp Company 4% Notes, due 1941, were selling at 50. The very small size of this issue, in relation to the company's resources and earnings, made payment apparently certain. (In fact they were called in 1939 in advance of maturity.)

consistently in cases where liquidation or a sale to outside interests results ultimately in a cash distribution or its equivalent.

Examples: Three typical examples of such a consummation are given herewith.

1. *Ontario Power Service Corporation First 5^1/$_2$s, Due 1950.* This issue defaulted interest payment on July 1, 1932. About this time the bonds sold as low as 21. The Hydro-Electric Commission of Ontario purchased the property soon afterwards, on a basis that gave $900 of new debentures, fully guaranteed by the Province of Ontario, for each $1,000 Ontario Power Service bond. The new debentures were quoted at 90 in December 1933, equivalent to 81 for the old bonds. The small number of bondholders not making the exchange received 70% in cash.

2. *Amalgamated Laundries, Inc., 6^1/$_2$s, Due 1936.* Receivers were appointed in February 1932. The bonds were quoted at 4 in April 1932. In June 1932 the properties were sold to outside interests, and liquidating dividends of 12^1/$_2$% and 2% were paid in August 1932 and March 1933. In December 1933 the bonds were still quoted at 4, indicating expectation of at least that amount in further distributions.

3. *Fisk Rubber Company First 8s and Debenture 5^1/$_2$s, Due 1941 and 1931.* Information regarding these issues was given in Chap. 18. Receivership was announced in January 1931. In 1932 the 8s and 5^1/$_2$s sold as low as 16 and 10^1/$_2$ respectively. In 1933 a reorganization was effected, which distributed 40% in cash on the 8s and 37% on the 5^1/$_2$s, together with securities of two successor companies. The aggregate values of the cash and the new securities at the close of 1933 came close to 100% for the 8% bonds and 70% for the debenture 5^1/$_2$s.

Price Patterns Produced by Insolvency. Certain price patterns are likely to be followed during receivership or bankruptcy proceedings, especially if they are protracted. In the first place, there is often a tendency for the stock issues to sell too high, not only in relation to the price of the bond issues but also absolutely, *i.e.*, in relation to their probable ultimate value. This is due to the incidence of speculative interest, which is attracted by a seemingly low price range. In the case of senior issues, popular interest steadily decreases, and the price tends to decline accordingly, as the proceedings wear on. Consequently, the lowest levels are likely to be reached a short time before a reorganization plan is ready to be announced.

A profitable field of analytical activity should be found therefore in keeping in close touch with such situations, endeavoring to discover securities that appear to be selling far under their intrinsic value and to determine approximately the best time for making a commitment in them. But in these, as in all analytical situations, we must warn against an endeavor to gage too nicely the proper time to buy. An essential characteristic of security analysis, as we understand it, is that the time factor is a subordinate consideration. Hence our use of the qualifying word "approximately," which is intended to allow a leeway of several months and sometimes even longer, in judging the "right time" to enter upon the operation.

Opportunities in Railroad Trusteeships. In the years following 1932 a large part of the country's railroad mileage went into the hands of trustees. At the close of 1938 a total of 111 railway companies operating 78,016 miles (31% of the total railway mileage in the United States) were in the hands of receivers or trustees. This is the greatest mileage ever in the hands of the courts at any one time. Reorganization in every case has been long delayed, owing on the one hand to the complicated capital structures to be dealt with and on the other to the uncertainty as to future normal earnings. As a result the price of a great many issues fell to extremely low levels—which would undoubtedly have presented excellent opportunities for the shrewd investor, had it not been that the earnings of the railroads as a whole continued for some years to make disappointing showings as compared with general business.

Viewing the situation about the end of 1939, it appeared that many of the first-mortgage liens on important mileage had fallen to lower levels than were warranted by anything but a most pessimistic view of the future of the carriers. Certainly, these issues were cheaper than the bonds and stocks of solvent roads, which sold for the most part at liberal prices in relation to their current exhibits and which in many cases would be in danger of insolvency if future conditions turned out as badly as the low price of trusteeships issues seemed to anticipate. The technique of analyzing issues of the latter group is covered on accompanying CD in Chap. 12 and in Appendix Note 66, page 821.

Chapter 51

DISCREPANCIES BETWEEN PRICE
AND VALUE (*Continued*)

THE PRACTICAL DISTINCTIONS drawn in our last chapter between leading and secondary common stocks have their counterpart in the field of senior securities as between seasoned and unseasoned issues. A seasoned issue may be defined as an issue of a company long and favorably known to the investment public. (The security itself may be of recent creation so long as the company has a high reputation among investors.) Seasoned and unseasoned issues tend at times to follow divergent patterns of conduct in the market, *viz.*:

1. The price of seasoned issues is often maintained despite a considerable weakening of their investment position.
2. Unseasoned issues are very sensitive to adverse developments of any nature. Hence they often fall to prices far lower than seem to be warranted by their statistical exhibit.

Price Inertia of Seasoned Issues.   These opposite characteristics are due, in part at least, to the inertia and lack of penetration of the typical investor. He buys by reputation rather than by analysis and he holds tenaciously to what he has bought. Hence holders of long-established issues do not sell them readily, and even a small decline in price attracts buyers long familiar with the security.

Example: This trait of seasoned issues is well illustrated by the market history of the United States Rubber Company 8% Noncumulative Preferred. The issue received full dividends between 1905 and 1927. In each year of this period except 1924 there were investors who paid higher than par for this stock. Its popularity was based entirely upon its reputation and its dividend record, for the statistical exhibit of the company during most of the period was anything but impressive, even for an industrial bond, and hence ridiculously inadequate to justify the purchase of a noncumulative industrial preferred stock. Between the years 1922 and 1927, the following coverage was shown for interest charges and preferred dividends combined:

1922	1.20 times
1923	1.18 times
1924	1.32 times
1925	1.79 times
1926	1.00 times
1927	1.01 times

In 1928 the stock sold as high as 109. During that year the company sustained an enormous loss, and the preferred dividend was discontinued. Despite the miserable showing and the absence of any dividend, the issue actually sold at $92^1/_2$ in 1929. (In 1932 it sold at $3^1/_8$.)[1]

Vulnerability of Unseasoned Issues. Turning to unseasoned issues, we may point out that these belong almost entirely to the industrial field. The element of seasoning plays a very small part as between the various senior issues of the railroads; and in the public-utility group proper (*i.e.*, electric, manufactured gas, telephone and water companies) price variations will be found to follow the statistical showing fairly closely, without being strongly influenced by the factor of popularity or familiarity—except in the case of very small concerns.

Industrial financing has brought into the market a continuous stream of bond and preferred stock issues of companies new to the investment list. Investors have been persuaded to buy these offerings largely through the appeal of a yield moderately higher than the standard rate for seasoned securities of comparable grade. If the earning power is maintained uninterruptedly after issuance, the new security naturally proves a satisfactory commitment. But any adverse development will ordinarily induce a severe decline in the market price. This vulnerability of unseasoned issues gives rise to the practical conclusion that it is unwise to buy a *new* industrial bond or preferred stock for straight investment.

---

[1] A more recent example of the same kind is presented by Curtis Publishing 7% Preferred, which sold at 114 in 1936 and $109^1/_2$ in 1937, despite an exceedingly inadequate showing of earnings (and tangible assets). The high price of many railroad bonds in those years, notwithstanding their unsatisfactory earnings exhibit, illustrates this point more broadly.

Since such issues are unduly sensitive to unfavorable developments, it would seem that the price would often fall too low and in that case they would afford attractive opportunities to purchase. This is undoubtedly true, but there is great need of caution in endeavoring to take advantage of these disparities. In the first place, the disfavor accorded to unseasoned securities in the market is not merely a subjective matter, due to lack of knowledge. Seasoning is usually defined as an objective quality, arising from a demonstrated ability to weather business storms. Although this definition is not entirely accurate, there is enough truth in it to justify in good part the investor's preference for seasoned issues.

More important, perhaps, is the broad distinction of size and prominence that can be drawn between seasoned and unseasoned securities. The larger companies are generally the older companies, having senior issues long familiar to the public. Hence unseasoned bonds and preferred stocks are for the most part issues of concerns of secondary importance. But we have pointed out, in our discussion of industrial investments (Chap. 7), that in this field dominant size may reasonably be considered a most desirable trait. It follows, therefore, that in this respect unseasoned issues must suffer as a class from a not inconsiderable disadvantage.

Unseasoned Industrial Issues Rarely Deserve an Investment Rating. The logical and practical result is that unseasoned industrial issues can very rarely deserve an investment rating, and consequently they should only be bought on an admittedly speculative basis. This requires in turn that the market price be low enough to permit of a substantial rise; *e.g.*, the price must ordinarily be below 70.

It will be recalled that in our treatment of speculative senior issues (Chap. 26), we referred to the price sector of about 70 to 100 as the "range of subjective variation," in which an issue might properly sell because of a legitimate difference of opinion as to whether or not it was sound. It seems, however, that in the case of unseasoned industrial bonds or preferred stocks the analyst should not be attracted by a price level within this range, even though the quantitative showing be quite satisfactory. He should favor such issues only when they can be bought at a frankly speculative price.

Exception may be made to this rule when the statistical exhibit is extraordinarily strong, as perhaps in the case of the Fox Film 6% notes mentioned in the preceding chapter and described in Appendix Note 67, page 835 on accompanying CD. We doubt if such exceptions can prudently include any unseasoned industrial preferred stocks, because of the contractual weakness of such issues. (In the case of Congoleum preferred, described above, the company was of dominant size in its field, and the preferred stock was not so much "unseasoned" as it was inactive marketwise.)

Discrepancies in Comparative Prices. Comparisons may or may not be odious, but they hold a somewhat deceptive fascination for the analyst. It seems a much simpler process to decide that issue *A* is preferable to issue *B* than to determine that issue *A* is an attractive purchase in its own right. But in our chapter on comparative analysis we have alluded to the particular responsibility that attaches to the recommendation of security exchanges, and we have warned against an overready acceptance of a purely quantitative superiority. The future is often no respecter of statistical data. We may frame this caveat in another way by suggesting that the analyst should not urge a security exchange unless either (1) the issue to be bought is attractive, regarded by itself, or (2) there is a definite contractual relationship between the two issues in question. Let us illustrate consideration (1) by two examples of comparisons taken from our records.

Examples: I. Comparison Made in March 1932.

Item	Ward Baking First 6s, due 1937. Price 85¹/₄, yield 9.70%	Bethlehem Steel First & Ref. 5s, due 1942. Price 93, yield 5.90%
Total interest charges earned:		
1931	8.1 times	1.0 times
1930	8.2 times	4.3 times
1929	11.0 times	4.8 times
1928	11.2 times	2.7 times
1927	14.0 times	2.3 times
1926	14.5 times	2.6 times
1925	12.6 times	2.1 times
Seven-year average	11.4 times	2.8 times
Amount of bond issues	$ 4,546,000	$145,000,000*
Market value of stock issues (March '32 average)	12,200,000	116,000,000
Cash assets	3,438,000	50,300,000
Net working capital	3,494,000	116,300,000

* Including guaranteed stock.

In this comparison the Ward Baking issue made a far stronger statistical showing than the Bethlehem Steel bonds. Furthermore, it appeared sufficiently well protected to justify an investment rating, despite the high return. The qualitative factors, although not impressive, did not suggest any danger of collapse of the business. Hence the bonds could be recommended either as an original purchase or as an advantageous substitute for the Bethlehem Steel 5s.

II. Comparison Made in March 1929.

Item	Spear & Co. (Furniture Stores) 7% First Preferred. Price 77, yielding 9.09%	Republic Iron & Steel 7% Preferred. Price 112, yielding 6.25%
(Interest and) preferred dividends earned:		
1928	2.4 times	1.9 times
1927	4.0 times	1.5 times
1926	3.0 times	2.1 times
1925	2.5 times	1.7 times
1924	4.7 times	1.1 times
1923	6.5 times	2.5 times
1922	4.3 times	0.5 times
Seven-year average	3.9 times	1.6 times
Amount of bond issues	None	$32,700,000
Amount of (1st) preferred issue	$ 3,900,000	25,000,000
Market value of junior issues	3,200,000*	62,000,000
Net working capital	10,460,000	21,500,000

* Includes Second Preferred estimated at 50.

In this comparison the Spear and Company issue undoubtedly made a better statistical showing than Republic Iron and Steel Preferred. Taken by itself, however, its exhibit was not sufficiently impressive to carry conviction of investment merit, considering the type of business and the fact that we were dealing with a preferred stock. The price of the issue was not low enough to warrant recommendation on a fully speculative basis, *i.e.*, with prime emphasis on the opportunity for enhancement of principal. This meant in turn that it could not consistently be recommended in exchange for another issue, such as Republic Iron and Steel Preferred.

Comparison of Definitely Related Issues. When the issues examined are definitely related, a different situation obtains. An exchange can then be considered solely from the standpoint of the respective merits within the given situation; the responsibility for entering into or remaining in the situation need not be assumed by the analyst. In our previous chapters we have considered a number of cases in which relative prices were clearly out of line, permitting authoritative recommendations of exchange. These disparities arise from the frequent failure of the general market to recognize the effect of contractual provisions and often also from a tendency for speculative markets to concentrate attention on the common stocks and to neglect the senior securities. Examples of the first type were given in our discussion of price discrepancies involving guaranteed issues in Chap. 17. The price discrepancies between various Interborough Rapid Transit Company issues, discussed in Appendix Note 56 on accompanying CD, and between Brooklyn Union Elevated Railroad 5s and Brooklyn-Manhattan Transit Corporation 6s, referred to in Chap. 2, are other illustrations in this category.[2]

The illogical price relationships between a senior convertible issue and the common stock, discussed in Chap. 25 on accompanying CD, are examples of opportunities arising from the concentration of speculative interest on the more active junior shares. A different manifestation of the same general tendency is shown by the spread of 7 points existing in August 1933 between the price of American Water Works and Electric Company "free" common and the less active voting trust certificates for the same issue. Such phenomena invite not only direct exchanges but also hedging operations.

A similar comparison could be made in July 1933 between Southern Railway 5% Noncumulative Preferred, paying no dividend and selling at 49, and the Mobile and Ohio Stock Trust Certificates, which were an obligation of the same road, bearing a perpetual guaranty of a 4% dividend and selling concurrently at $39^3/_4$. Even if the preferred dividend had been immediately resumed and continued without interruption, the yield

---

[2] The student is invited to consider the price relationships between Pierce Petroleum and Pierce Oil preferred and common in 1929; between Central States Electric Corporation $5^1/_2$% bonds and North American Company common in 1934; between the common issues of Advance-Rumely Corporation and Allis-Chalmers Manufacturing Company in 1933; between Ventures, Ltd., and Falconbridge Nickel, and between Chesapeake Corporation and Chesapeake and Ohio Railway common stocks in 1939—as examples of disparities arising from ownership by one company of securities in another.

thereon would have been no higher than that obtainable from the senior fixed-interest obligation. (In 1939 Southern Railway Preferred, still paying no dividend, sold at 35 against a price of about 40 for the Mobile and Ohio 4% certificates. At these prices the advantage still appeared clearly on the side of the guaranteed issue.)

Other and Less Certain Discrepancies. In the foregoing examples the aberrations are mathematically demonstrable. There is a larger class of disparities between senior and junior securities that may not be proved quite so conclusively but are sufficiently certain for practical purposes. As an example of these, consider Colorado Industrial Company 5s, due August 1, 1934, guaranteed by Colorado Fuel and Iron Company, which in May 1933 sold at 43, while the Colorado Fuel and Iron 8% Preferred, paying no dividend, sold at 45. The bond issue had to be paid off in full within 14 months' time, or else the preferred stock was faced with the possibility of complete extinction through receivership. In order that the preferred stock might prove more valuable than the bonds bought at the same price, it would be necessary not only that the bonds be paid off at par in little over a year but that preferred dividends be resumed and back dividends discharged within that short time. This was almost, if not quite, inconceivable.

In comparing nonconvertible preferred stocks with common stocks of the same company, we find the same tendency for the latter to sell too high, relatively, when both issues are on a speculative basis. Comparisons of this kind can be safely drawn, however, only when the preferred stock bears cumulative dividends. (The reason for this restriction should be clear from our detailed discussion of the disabilities of noncumulative issues in Chap. 15.) A price of 10 for American and Foreign Power Company common when the $7 Cumulative Second Preferred was selling at 11 in April 1933 was clearly unwarranted. A similar remark may be made of the price of 21$^1/_2$ for Chicago Great Western Railroad Company common in February 1927, against 32$^1/_2$ for the 4% preferred stock on which dividends of $44 per share had accumulated.

It is true that if extraordinary prosperity should develop in situations of this kind, the common shares might eventually be worth substantially more than the preferred. But even if this should occur, the company is bound to pass through an intermediate period during which the improved situation permits it to resume preferred dividends and then to discharge the accumulations. Since such developments benefit the preferred stock directly, they are likely to establish (for a while at least) a market value for the senior issues far higher than that of the common stock. Hence, assuming any appreciable degree of improvement, a purchase of the preferred shares at the low levels should fare better than one made in the common stock.

Discrepancies Due to Special Supply and Demand Factors.

The illogical relationships that we have been considering grow out of supply and demand conditions that are, in turn, the product of unthinking speculative purchases. Sometimes discrepancies are occasioned by special and temporary causes affecting either demand or supply.

Examples: In the illogical relationship between the prices of Interboro Rapid Transit Company 5s and 7s in 1933, the operations of a substantial sinking fund, which purchased the 5s and not the 7s, were undoubtedly instrumental in raising the price of the former disproportionately. An outstanding example of this kind is found in the market action of United States Liberty $4^1/_4$s during the postwar readjustment of 1921–1922. Large amounts of these bonds had been bought during the war for patriotic reasons and financed by bank loans. A general desire to liquidate these loans later on induced a heavy volume of sales which drove the price down. This special selling pressure actually resulted in establishing a lower price basis for Liberty Bonds than for high-grade railroad issues, which were, of course, inferior in security and at a greater disadvantage also in the matter of taxation. Compare the following simultaneous prices in September 1920.

Issue	Price	Yield
United States Liberty Fourth $4^1/_4$s, due 1938	$84^1/_2$	5.64%*
Union Pacific First 4s, due 1947	80	5.42%

* Not allowing for tax exemption.

This situation supplied an excellent opportunity for the securities analyst to advise exchanges from the old-line railroad issues into Liberty Bonds.

A less striking disparity appeared a little later between the price of these Liberty Bonds and of United States Victory $4^3/_4$s, due 1923. This state of affairs is discussed in a circular, prepared by one of the authors and issued at that time, a copy of which is given in Appendix Note 68 on accompanying CD, as an additional example of "practical security analysis."

United States Savings Bonds Offer Similar Opportunity. For the investor of moderate means the disparity between United States government and corporate obligations has reappeared in recent years. The yield on United States Savings Bonds (available to any one individual to the extent of $10,000 principal amount each year) is 2.90% on the regular compound-interest basis of calculation and 3.33% on a simple-interest basis. This yield is definitely higher than that returned by best-rated public-utility and industrial issues.[3] In addition to their safety factor, which at present must clearly be set higher than that of any corporate issue, the United States Savings Bonds have the minor advantage of exemption from normal income tax and the major advantage of being redeemable *at the option of the holder* at any time, thus guaranteeing him against intermediate loss in market value.

---

[3] The average yields for such bonds for the first 3 months of 1940, carrying A1+ ratings of Standard Statistics Company, were only 2.62% and 2.44%, respectively.

Chapter 52

MARKET ANALYSIS AND SECURITY ANALYSIS

FORECASTING SECURITY PRICES is not properly a part of security analysis. However, the two activities are generally thought to be closely allied, and they are frequently carried on by the same individuals and organizations. Endeavors to predict the course of prices have a variety of objectives and a still greater variety of techniques. Most emphasis is laid in Wall Street upon the science, or art, or pastime, of prophesying the immediate action of the "general market," which is fairly represented by the various averages used in the financial press. Some of the services or experts confine their aim to predicting the longer term trend of the market, purporting to ignore day-to-day fluctuations and to consider the broader "swings" covering a period of, say, several months. A great deal of attention is given also to prophesying the market action of individual issues, as distinct from the market as a whole.

Market Analysis as a Substitute for or Adjunct to Security Analysis. Assuming that these activities are carried on with sufficient seriousness to represent more than mere guesses, we may refer to all or any of them by the designation of "market analysis." In this chapter we wish to consider the extent to which market analysis may seriously be considered as a substitute for or a supplement to security analysis. The question is important. If, as many believe, one can dependably foretell the movements of stock prices without any reference to the underlying values, then it would be sensible to confine security analysis to the selection of fixed-value investments only. For, when it comes to the common-stock type of issue, it would manifestly be more profitable to master the technique of determining when to buy or sell, or of selecting the issues that are going to have the greatest or quickest advance, than to devote painstaking efforts to forming conclusions about intrinsic value. Many

[697]

other people believe that the best results can be obtained by an analysis of the market position of a stock in conjunction with an analysis of its intrinsic value. If this is so, the securities analyst who ventures outside the fixed-value field must qualify as a market analyst as well and be prepared to view each situation from both standpoints at the same time.

It is not within our province to attempt a detailed criticism of the theories and the technique underlying all the different methods of market analysis. We shall confine ourselves to considering the broader lines of reasoning that are involved in the major premises of price forecasting. Even with this sketchy treatment it should be possible to reach some useful conclusions on the perplexing question of the relationship between market analysis and security analysis.

Two Kinds of Market Analysis. A distinction may be made between two kinds of market analysis. The first finds the material for its predictions exclusively in the past action of the stock market. The second considers all sorts of economic factors, *e.g.*, business conditions, general and specific; money rates; the political outlook. (The market's behavior is itself only one of these numerous elements of study.) The underlying theory of the first approach may be summed up in the declaration that "the market is its own best forecaster." The behavior of the market is generally studied by means of charts on which are plotted the movements of individual stocks or of "averages." Those who devote themselves primarily to a study of these price movements are known as "chartists," and their procedure is often called "chart reading."

But it must be pointed out that much present-day market analysis represents a combination of the two kinds described, in the sense that the market's action alone constitutes the predominant but not the exclusive field of study. General economic indications play a subordinate but still significant role. Considerable latitude is therefore left for individual judgment, not only in interpreting the technical indications of the market's action but also in reconciling such indications with outside factors. The "Dow theory," however, which is the best known method of market analysis, limits itself essentially to a study of the market's behavior. Hence we feel justified in dealing separately with chart reading as applied exclusively to stock prices.

Implication of the First Type of Market Analysis. It must be recognized that the vogue of such "technical study" has increased immensely during the past fifteen years. Whereas security analysis suffered a distinct loss of prestige beginning about 1927—from which it has not entirely recovered—chart reading apparently increased the number of its followers even during the long depression and in the years thereafter. Many sceptics, it is true, are inclined to dismiss the whole procedure as akin to astrology or necromancy, but the sheer weight of its importance in Wall Street requires that its pretensions be examined with some degree of care. In order to confine our discussion within the framework of logical reasoning, we shall purposely omit even a condensed summary of the main tenets of chart reading.[1] We wish to consider only the implications of the general idea that a study confined to past price movements can be availed of profitably to foretell the movements of the future.

Such consideration, we believe, should lead to the following conclusions:

1. Chart reading cannot possibly be a science.
2. It has not proved itself in the past to be a dependable method of making profits in the stock market.
3. Its theoretical basis rests upon faulty logic or else upon mere assertion.
4. Its vogue is due to certain advantages it possesses over haphazard speculation, but these advantages tend to diminish as the number of chart students increases.

1. *Chart Reading Not a Science and Its Practice Cannot Be Continuously Successful.* That chart reading cannot be a science is clearly demonstrable. If it were a science, its conclusions would be as a rule dependable. In that case everybody could predict tomorrow's or next week's price changes, and hence everyone could make money continuously by buying and selling at the right time. This is patently impossible. A moment's thought will show that there can be no such thing as a scientific prediction of economic events under human control. The very "dependability" of such a prediction will cause human actions that will invalidate it. Hence thoughtful chartists admit that continued success is dependent upon keeping the successful method known to only a few people.

---

[1] For detailed statements concerning the theory and practice of chart reading the student is referred to: R. W. Shabacker, *Stock Market Profits*, B. C. Forbes, New York, 1934; Robert Rhea, "The Dow Theory," *passim, Barron's*, New York, 1932; H. M. Gartley, "Analyzing the Stock Market," a series of articles in *Barron's* beginning with the issue of Sept. 19, 1932 and ending with the issue of Dec. 5, 1932. See Appendix Note 69, p. 837 on accompanying CD, for a brief statement of the main tenets of the Dow theory.

2. Because of this fact it follows that there is no generally known method of chart reading that has been continuously successful for a long period of time.[2] If it were known, it would be speedily adopted by numberless traders. This very following would bring its usefulness to an end.

3. *Theoretical Basis Open to Question.* The theoretical basis of chart reading runs somewhat as follows:

 a. The action of the market (or of a particular stock) reflects the activities and the attitude of those interested in it.
 b. Therefore, by studying the record of market action, we can tell what is going to happen next in the market.

The premise may well be true, but the conclusion does not necessarily follow. You may learn a great deal about the technical position of a stock by studying its chart, and yet you may not learn *enough* to permit you to operate profitably in the issue. A good analogy is provided by the "past performances" of race horses, which are so assiduously studied by the devotees of the race track. Undoubtedly these charts afford considerable information concerning the relative merits of the entries; they will often enable the student to pick the winner of a race; but the trouble is that they do not furnish that valuable information *often enough* to make betting on horse races a profitable diversion.

Coming nearer home, we have a similar situation in security analysis itself. The past earnings of a company supply a useful indication of its future earnings—useful, but not infallible. Security analysis and market analysis are alike, therefore, in the fact that they deal with data that are not conclusive as to the future. The difference, as we shall point out, is that the securities analyst can protect himself by a *margin of safety* that is denied to the market analyst.

Undoubtedly, there are times when the behavior of the market, as revealed on the charts, carries a definite and trustworthy meaning of particular value to those who are skilled in its interpretation. If reliance on chart indications were confined to those really convincing cases, a more positive argument could be made in favor of "technical study." But such

---

[2] Adherents of the Dow theory claim that it has been continuously successful for a great many years. We believe this statement to be open to much doubt—turning, in part, on certain disputed interpretations of what the theory indicated on various key occasions.

precise signals seem to occur only at wide intervals, and in the meantime human impatience plus the exigencies of the chart reader's profession impel him to draw more frequent conclusions from less convincing data.

4. *Other Theoretical and Practical Weaknesses.* The appeal of chart reading to the stock-market trader is something like that of a patent medicine to an incurable invalid. The stock speculator does suffer, in fact, from a well-nigh incurable ailment. The cure he seeks, however, is not abstinence from speculation but profits. Despite all experience, he persuades himself that these can be made and retained; he grasps greedily and uncritically at every plausible means to this end.

The plausibility of chart reading, in our opinion, derives largely from its insistence on the sound gambling maxim that losses should be cut short and profits allowed to run. This principle usually prevents sudden large losses, and at times it permits a large profit to be taken. The results are likely to be better, therefore, than those produced by the haphazard following of "market tips." Traders, noticing this advantage, are certain that by developing the technique of chart reading farther they will so increase its reliability as to assure themselves continued profits.

But in this conclusion there lurks a double fallacy. Many players at roulette follow a similar system, which limits their losses at any one session and permits them at times to realize a substantial gain. But in the end they always find that the aggregate of small losses exceeds the few large profits. (This must be so, since the mathematical odds against them are inexorable over a period of time.) The same is true of the stock trader, who will find that the expense of trading weights the dice heavily against him. A second difficulty is that, as the methods of chart reading gain in popularity, the amount of the loss taken in unprofitable trades tends to increase and the profits also tend to diminish. For as more and more people, following the same system, receive the signal to buy at about the same time, the result of this competitive buying must be that a higher average price is paid by the group. Conversely, when this larger group decides to sell out at the same time, either to cut short a loss or to protect a profit, the effect must again be that a lower average price is received. (The growth in the use of "stop-loss orders," formerly a helpful technical device of the trader, had this very effect of detracting greatly from their value as a protective measure.)

The more intelligent chart students recognize these theoretical weaknesses, we believe, and take the view that market forecasting is an *art* that requires talent, judgment, intuition and other personal qualities. They admit that no rules of procedure can be laid down, the automatic following of which will insure success. Hence the widespread tendency in Wall Street circles towards a composite or eclectic approach, in which a very thorough study of the market's performance is projected against the general economic background, and the whole is subjected to the appraisal of experienced judgment.

The Second Type of Mechanical Forecasting. Before considering the significance of this injection of the judgment factor, let us pass on to the other type of mechanical forecasting, which is based upon factors outside of the market itself. As far as the general market is concerned, the usual procedure is to construct indices representing various economic factors, *e.g.*, money rates, carloadings, steel production, and to deduce impending changes in the market from an observation of a recent change in these indices.[3] One of the earliest methods of the kind, and a very simple one, was based upon the percentage of blast furnaces in operation.

This theory was developed by Col. Leonard P. Ayres of the Cleveland Trust Company and ran to the effect that security prices usually reached a bottom when blast furnaces in operation declined through 60% of the total and that conversely they usually reached a top when blast furnaces in operation passed through the 60% mark on the upswing in use thereof.[4] A companion theory of Colonel Ayres was that the high point in bond prices is reached about 14 months subsequent to the low point in pig-iron production and that the peak in stock prices is reached about two years following the low point for pig-iron production.[5]

This simple method is representative of all mechanical forecasting systems, in that (1) it sounds vaguely *plausible* on the basis of *a priori*

---

[3] These indices may also be plotted on charts, in which case the forecasting takes on the aspect of chart reading. *Examples:* The *A, B,* and *C* lines of the *Harvard Economic Service* which were published in weekly letters from Jan. 3, 1922, to Dec. 26, 1931 (since continued through 1939 at less frequent intervals in *The Review of Economic Statistics*); also the single composite Index Line in the "Investment Timing Service" offered by Independence Fund of North America, Inc., in 1939.

[4] See *Bulletin of the Cleveland Trust Company,* July 15, 1924, cited by David F. Jordan, in *Practical Business Forecasting,* p. 203n, New York, 1927.

[5] See *Business Recovery Following Depression,* a pamphlet published by the Cleveland Trust Company in 1922. The conclusions of Colonel Ayres are summarized on p. 31 of the pamphlet.

reasoning and (2) it relies for its *convincingness* on the fact that it has "worked" for a number of years past. The necessary weakness of all these systems lies in the time element. It is easy and safe to prophesy, for example, that a period of high interest rates will lead to a sharp decline in the market. The question is, "How soon?" There is no scientific way of answering this question. Many of the forecasting services are therefore driven to a sort of pseudo-science, in which they take it for granted that certain time lags or certain coincidences that happened to occur several times in the past (or have been worked out laboriously by a process of trial and error), can be counted upon to occur in much the same way in the future.

Broadly speaking, therefore, the endeavor to forecast security-price changes by reference to mechanical indices is open to the same objections as the methods of the chart readers. They are not truly scientific, because there is no convincing reasoning to support them and because, furthermore, really scientific (*i.e.*, entirely dependable) forecasting in the economic field is a logical impossibility.

Disadvantages of Market Analysis as Compared with Security Analysis.

We return in consequence to our earlier conclusion that market analysis is an art for which special talent is needed in order to pursue it successfully. Security analysis is also an art; and it, too, will not yield satisfactory results unless the analyst has ability as well as knowledge. We think, however, that security analysis has several advantages over market analysis, which are likely to make the former a more successful field of activity for those with training and intelligence. In security analysis the prime stress is laid upon protection against untoward events. We obtain this protection by insisting upon margins of safety, or values well in excess of the price paid. The underlying idea is that even if the security turns out to be less attractive than it appeared, the commitment might still prove a satisfactory one. In market analysis there are no margins of safety; you are either right or wrong, and, if you are wrong, you lose money.[6]

---

[6] Viewing the two activities as possible professions, we are inclined to draw an analogous comparison between the law and the concert stage. A talented lawyer should be able to make a respectable living; a talented, *i.e.*, a "merely talented," musician faces heartbreaking obstacles to a successful concert career. Thus, as we see it, a thoroughly competent securities analyst should be able to obtain satisfactory results from his work, whereas permanent success as a market analyst requires unusual qualities—or unusual luck.

The cardinal rule of the market analyst that losses should be cut short and profits safeguarded (by selling when a decline commences) leads in the direction of active trading. This means in turn that the cost of buying and selling becomes a heavily adverse factor in aggregate results. Operations based on security analysis are ordinarily of the investment type and do not involve active trading.

A third disadvantage of market analysis is that it involves essentially a battle of wits. Profits made by trading in the market are for the most part realized at the expense of others who are trying to do the same thing. The trader necessarily favors the more active issues, and the price changes in these are the resultant of the activities of numerous operators of his own type. The market analyst can be hopeful of success only upon the assumption that he will be more clever or perhaps luckier than his competitors.

The work of the securities analyst, on the other hand, is in no similar sense competitive with that of his fellow analysts. In the typical case the issue that he elects to buy is not sold by some one who has made an equally painstaking analysis of its value. We must emphasize the point that the security analyst examines a far larger list of securities than does the market analyst. Out of this large list, he selects the exceptional cases in which the market price falls far short of reflecting intrinsic value, either through neglect or because of undue emphasis laid upon unfavorable factors that are probably temporary.

Market analysis seems easier than security analysis, and its rewards may be realized much more quickly. For these very reasons, it is likely to prove more disappointing in the long run. There are no dependable ways of making money easily and quickly, either in Wall Street or anywhere else.

Prophesies Based on Near-term Prospects. A good part of the analysis and advice supplied in the financial district rests upon the near-term business prospects of the company considered. It is assumed that, if the outlook favors increased earnings, the issue should be bought in the expectation of a higher price when the larger profits are actually reported. In this reasoning, security analysis and market analysis are made to coincide. The market prospect is thought to be identical with the business prospect.

But to our mind the theory of buying stocks chiefly upon the basis of their immediate outlook makes the selection of speculative securities entirely too simple a matter. Its weakness lies in the fact that the current market price already takes into account the consensus of opinion as to future prospects. And in many cases the prospects will have been given *more* than their just need of recognition. When a stock is recommended for the reason that next year's earnings are expected to show improvement, a twofold hazard is involved. First, the forecast of next year's results may prove incorrect; second, even if correct, it may have been discounted or even overdiscounted in the current price.

If markets generally reflected only this year's earnings, then a good estimate of next year's results would be of inestimable value. But the premise is not correct. Our table on page 707 shows on the one hand the annual earnings per share of United States Steel Corporation common and on the other hand the price range of that issue for the years 1902–1939. Excluding the 1928–1933 period (in which business changes were so extreme as necessarily to induce corresponding changes in stock prices), it is difficult to establish any definite correlation between fluctuations in earnings and fluctuations in market quotations.

In Appendix Note 70 (on accompanying CD), we reproduce significant parts of the analysis and recommendation concerning two common stocks made by an important statistical and advisory service in the latter part of 1933. The recommendations are seen to be based largely upon the apparent outlook for 1934. There is no indication of any endeavor to ascertain the fair value of the business and to compare this value with the current price. A thorough-going statistical analysis would point to the conclusion that the issue of which the sale is advised was selling below its intrinsic value, just because of the unfavorable immediate prospects, and that the opposite was true of the common stock recommended as worth holding because of its satisfactory outlook.

We are sceptical of the ability of the analyst to forecast with a fair degree of success the market behavior of individual issues over the near-term future—whether he base his predictions upon the technical position of the market or upon the general outlook for business or upon the specific outlook for the individual companies. More satisfactory results are to be obtained, in our opinion, by confining the positive conclusions of the analyst to the following fields of endeavor:

1. The selection of standard senior issues that meet exacting tests of safety.
2. The discovery of senior issues that merit an investment rating but that also have opportunities of an appreciable enhancement in value.

3. The discovery of common stocks, or speculative senior issues, that appear to be selling at far less than their intrinsic value.

4. The determination of definite price discrepancies existing between related securities, which situations may justify making exchanges or initiating hedging or arbitrage operations.

A SUMMARY OF OUR VIEWS ON INVESTMENT POLICIES

If we transfer our attention, finally, from the analyst to the owner of securities, we may briefly express our views on what he may soundly do and not do. The following résumé makes some allowance for different categories of investors.

A. The Investor of Small Means. *1. Investment for Income. In his case the only sensible investment for safety and accumulated income, under present conditions, is found in United States Savings Bonds.* Other good investments yield little if any more, and they have not equal protection against both ultimate and intermediate loss. Straight bonds and preferred stocks ostensibly offering a higher return are almost certain to involve an appreciable risk factor. The various types of "savings plans" and similar securities offered by salesmen are full of pitfalls; the investor persuaded by their promise of liberal income to prefer them to United States Savings Bonds is very, very likely to regret his choice.

2. Investment for Profit. Four approaches are open to both the small and the large investor:

a. Purchase of representative common stocks when the market level is clearly low as judged by objective, long-term standards. This policy requires patience and courage and is by no means free from the possibility of grave miscalculation. Over a long period we believe that it will show good results.

b. Purchase of individual issues with special growth possibilities, when these can be obtained at reasonable prices in relation to actual accomplishment.

Where growth is *generally* expected, the price is rarely reasonable. If the basis of purchase is a confidence in future growth not held by the public, the operation may prove sound and profitable; it may also prove ill-founded and costly.

c. Purchase of well-secured privileged senior issues. A combination of really adequate security with a promising conversion or similar right is a

UNITED STATES STEEL COMMON, 1901–1939

Year	Earned per share	Range of market price		
		High	Low	Average
1901	$ 9.1	55	24	40
1902	10.7	47	30	39
1903	4.9	40	10	25
1904	1.0	34	8	21
1905	8.5	43	25	34
1906	14.3	50	33	42
1907	15.6	50	22	36
1908	4.1	59	26	48
1909	10.6	95	41	68
1910	12.2	91	61	76
1911	5.9	82	50	66
1912	5.7	81	58	70
1913	11.0	69	50	60
1914	*0.3(d)*	67	48	58
1915	10.0	90	38	64
1916	48.5	130	80	105
1917	39.2	137	80	109
1918	22.1	117	87	102
1919	10.1	116	88	102
1920	16.6	109	76	93
1921	2.2	87	70	79
1922	2.8	112	82	97
1923	16.4	110	86	98
1924	11.8	121	94	108
1925	12.9	139	112	126
1926	18.0	161	117	139
1927*	12.3	246	155	201
1927†	8.8	176	111	144
1928	12.5	173	132	153
1929	21.2	262	150	206
1930	9.1	199	134	167
1931	*1.4(d)*	152	36	99
1932	*11.1(d)*	53	21	37
1933	*7.1(d)*	68	23	46
1934	*5.4(d)*	60	29	45
1935	*2.8(d)*	51	28	40
1936	2.9	80	46	63
1937	8.0	127	49	88
1938	*3.8(d)*	71	38	55
1939	1.84	83	41	62

* Before allowing for 40% stock dividend.
† After allowing for 40% stock dividend.

rare but by no means unknown phenomenon. A policy of careful selection in this field should bring good results, provided the investor has the patience and persistence needed to find his opportunities.

d. Purchase of securities selling well below intrinsic value. Intrinsic value takes into account not only past earnings and liquid asset values but also future earning power, conservatively estimated—in other words, qualitative as well as quantitative elements. We think that since a large percentage of *all* issues nowadays are relatively unpopular, there must be many cases in which the market goes clearly and crassly astray, thus creating real opportunities for the discriminating student. These may be found in bonds, preferred stocks and common stocks.

In our view, the search for and the recognition of security values of the types just discussed are not beyond the competence of the small investor who wishes to practice security analysis in a nonprofessional capacity, although he will undoubtedly need better than average intelligence and training. But we think it should be a necessary rule that the nonprofessional investor submit his ideas to the criticism of a professional analyst, such as the statistician of a New York Stock Exchange firm. Surely modesty is not incompatible with self-confidence; and there is logic in the thought that unless a man is qualified to advise others professionally, he should not, unaided, prescribe for himself.

3. *Speculation.* The investor of small means is privileged, of course, to step out of his role and become a speculator. (He is also privileged to regret his action afterwards.) There are various types of speculation, and they offer varying chances of success:

a. Buying stock in new or virtually new ventures. This we can condemn unhesitatingly and with emphasis. The odds are so strongly against the man who buys into these new flotations that he might as well throw three-quarters of the money out of the window and keep the rest in the bank.

b. Trading in the market. It is fortunate for Wall Street as an institution that a small minority of people can trade successfully and that many others think they can. The accepted view holds that stock trading is like anything else; *i.e.*, with intelligence and application, or with good professional guidance, profits can be realized. Our own opinion is sceptical, perhaps jaundiced. We think that, regardless of preparation and method, success in trading is either accidental and impermanent or else due to a highly uncommon talent. Hence the vast majority of stock traders are inevitably doomed to failure. We do not expect this conclusion to have much effect on the public. (Note our basic distinction between purchasing stocks at objectively low levels and selling them at high levels—which we term investment—and the popular practice of buying only when the market is "expected" to advance and selling when it is "due" to decline—which we call speculation.)

c. Purchase of "growth stocks" at generous prices. In calling this "speculation," we contravene most authoritative views. For reasons previously expressed, we consider this popular approach to be inherently dangerous and increasingly so as it becomes more popular. But the chances of individual success are much brighter here than in the other forms of speculation, and there is a better field for the exercise of foresight, judgment and moderation.

B. The Individual Investor of Large Means. Although he has obvious technical advantages over the small investor, he suffers from three special handicaps:

1. He cannot solve his straight investment problem simply by buying nothing but United States Savings Bonds, since the amount that any individual may purchase is limited. Hence he must, perforce, consider the broader field of fixed-value investment. We believe that strict application of quantitative tests, plus reasonably good judgment in the qualitative area, should afford a satisfactory end result.

2. However, the extraneous problem of possible inflation is more serious to him than to the small investor. Since 1932 there has been a strong common-sense argument for *some* common-stock holdings as a defensive measure. In addition, a substantial holding of common stocks corresponds with the traditional attitude and practice of the wealthy individual.

3. The size of his investment unit is more likely to induce the large investor to concentrate on the popular and active issues. To some extent, therefore, he is handicapped in the application of the undervalued-security technique. However, we imagine that a more serious obstacle thereto will be found in his preferences and prejudices.

C. Investment by Business Corporations. We believe that United States government bonds, carrying exemption from corporate income taxes, are almost the only logical medium for such business funds as may properly be invested for a term of years. (Under 1940 conditions short-time investment involves as much trouble as income.) It seems fairly evident, on the whole, that other types of investments by business enterprises—whether in bonds or in stocks—can offer an appreciably higher return only at risk of loss and of criticism.

D. Institutional Investment. We shall not presume to suggest policies for financial institutions whose business it is to be versed in the theory and practice of investment. The same might be said for philanthropic and educational institutions, since these generally have the benefit of experienced financiers in shaping their financial policies. But in order not to dodge completely a very difficult issue, we venture the following final observation: An institution that can manage to get along on the low income provided by high-grade fixed-value issues should, in our opinion, confine its holdings to this field. We doubt if the better performance of common-stock indexes over past periods will, in itself, warrant the heavy responsibilities and the recurring uncertainties that are inseparable from a common-stock investment program. This conclusion may perhaps be modified either if there is substantial unanimity of view that inflation must be guarded against or if the insufficiency of income compels search for a higher return. In such case those in charge may be warranted in setting aside a portion of the institution's funds for administration in other than fixed-value fields, in accordance with the canons and technique of security analysis.[7]

---

[7] Yale University now follows a policy of investing part of its funds in "equities"—defined as common stocks and nonpaying senior issues. The percentage varies in accordance with a fixed formula, somewhat as follows: The initial proportion is 30% of the total fund. Whenever a rise in the market level advances this figure to 40%, one-eighth of each stock holding is switched into bonds. Conversely, whenever a decline in the market reduces the proportion to 15%, bonds are sold and one-third additional of each stock is bought. See address of Laurence G. Tighe, Associate Treasurer of Yale University entitled "Present Day Investment Problems of Endowed Institutions," delivered on February 14, 1940 before the Trust Division of the American Bankers Association. It was summarized in the *New York Sun* of February 20, 1940.

PART VIII

GLOBAL VALUE INVESTING

GLOBETROTTING WITH GRAHAM AND DODD

BY THOMAS A. RUSSO

I have the privilege of introducing the part of *Security Analysis* that was never written, that on global investing. This was not a grievous omission by the authors. After all, other than in Great Britain and a few European countries, global securities markets were still fairly undeveloped when the second edition was published in 1940.

I first learned of global value investing from Professor Jack McDonald at Stanford Business School in the early 1980s. McDonald regaled us with "war stories" about his own experiences investing abroad. Even as recently as the 1980s, foreign investing was difficult. By U.S. standards, overseas markets were illiquid and trading costs high. Accounting practices were foreign, to say the least, and disclosure was less transparent than in the United States.

That was not all. Consider the challenges posed to the would-be global investor by local corporate governance and management practices; restrictions on capital movements; variations in taxation; differences in language, culture, and political stability; unusual hours at which trades are executed; complexity of foreign exchange transactions; currency risks; and logistics involved in managing custody of foreign securities. Why bother?

Oddly enough, it was Omaha, Nebraska's Warren Buffett who cleared a path for me through this minefield. A guest lecturer in Professor

McDonald's class, Buffett was not and still is not a specialist in global investing. Buffett, a student of Graham and Dodd's at Columbia in the 1950s, had, by the early 1980s, evolved from being purely a balance sheet investor to being an investor who was seeking companies with exceptional business franchises that were run by honest, capable, and shareholder-friendly managements. Such companies are rare, so why limit yourself to just the United States?

Because there is almost always a scarcity of great opportunity—Buffett says you are lucky to have 20 great ideas in your investing lifetime—a narrow search could result in less-than-optimal diversification. Investors can—and indeed, must—"compensate" for a sparse set of opportunities through a broad-based search. A deep and growing understanding of particular industries allows an investor to evaluate both domestic and foreign opportunities within a circle of competence. There may be local variations in tastes and laws, but the fundamental economics of producing, marketing, and distributing most goods and services transcend national boundaries.

Using a focus like Buffett's on the underlying economics of businesses also helps an investor cope with national differences in accounting and disclosure practices. Local accounting can be analyzed in the context of results of similarly situated companies in other countries. For example, if the implied returns of a German beer company appear to deviate from those of French, British, and Italian brewers, there is a reasonable chance that the nuances of financial statements were misunderstood and that further analysis of those numbers is required. Of course, discrepancies could also be explained by the local regulatory environment or divergent consumer preferences. When results for an important subsidiary are not fully identified in the income statement, the numbers can be better understood by studying similar businesses in other countries. For example, the profitability of brewing companies depends critically on local distribution networks and local market share. A brewery subsidiary with a small share in a distant market is not likely to represent significant value. Finally, focusing on underlying business operations leads an investor to develop a global network of industry contacts that may help fill in the gaps in financial reports.

Graham and Dodd—and Buffett—are properly concerned with the tendency of some managements to cling tightly to corporate assets, to withhold dividends, and to make acquisitions whose sole purpose seems to be to increase the prestige and salaries of management. That is why Buffett looks for managers who emphasize the long-term protection and enhancement of their business franchises and are primarily concerned with the effectiveness of a company's capital allocation process. When investing in foreign companies, you really need the kind of managers that Buffett covets because corporate governance rules and management practices are generally less responsive to shareholder concerns than they are in the United States. If management does not get it right, you cannot count on your fellow shareholders to make it happen.

Also, while cultural and language differences make it difficult to render judgments based on direct contact with overseas managers, management's long-term record is available. You can judge past decisions, based on your knowledge of the industry's best practices. Furthermore, as Buffett has frequently noted, simple businesses with strong franchises can be run by any idiot. Absent a track record, language and cultural differences make it difficult to identify, say, French, Czech, or Thai superstars from lesser lights. So Buffett's "simple business, strong franchise" approach offers an extra measure of protection when investing abroad.

Global Investing in Practice

Since embarking on my own course of investing abroad over 20 years ago, I have encountered challenges relating to currency fluctuations, accounting practices, corporate disclosure, trading, and execution as well as my share of administrative barriers. While each of these challenges has abated over the years as non-U.S. markets have become somewhat more oriented to global investors, they all remain obstacles for many investors seeking to go global.

Currency Risk

I have often been quizzed by prospective investors about how I planned to protect against the risk of adverse foreign currency fluctuations. While some American investors prefer to hedge all foreign currency exposure back to U.S. dollars, I believe investor interests are best served by diversifying currency holdings. Given that Americans are exposed to multiple currencies in the goods and services they purchase, it only makes sense to have some foreign currency exposure.

Gaining that exposure has not been easy. Prior to the euro's arrival in 1992, investing in European companies required conversion, for instance, into a host of currencies. Managing multiple currency positions is cumbersome and sometimes subject to high transaction costs. That is why I eventually gave up on, for instance, Figaro, Philip Morris's Slovakia-based confectionery subsidiary. Maintaining Slovak currency exposure was too costly.

Another factor is that, even if one were inclined to hedge, it would be surprisingly complicated to figure out a proper hedge. Most companies operate in multiple countries having different currencies. For example, investors who try to hedge away Nestlé's Swiss franc exposure (its shares are listed in Switzerland) will have trouble knowing what currency to hedge against, as less than 5% of Nestlé's revenues are in Swiss francs.

Moreover, sometimes the most compelling investment opportunities arise when currencies are reeling and, thus, costly to hedge. For instance, in the early 1990s I invested in the Norwegian stock market after prices had collapsed as a result of a shipping-industry crisis brought on by the Gulf War. The Scandinavian currencies were then under such pressure that a hedge—which was priced to build in further currency declines—would be prohibitively expensive. A strong argument could be made that not only were Norway's stocks undervalued, its currency was too. The very thing that would cause Norwegian shares to rise—the end of the Gulf War—would also be bullish for the currency.

Accounting Standards

When I first began to invest abroad, U.S. investors would ask, "Can you rely on foreign company accounting?" Even then my answer was, "Compared to what?" While there are many shortcomings in foreign accounting standards, in some cases they are actually more conservative than U.S. accounting rules. Meanwhile, our prized standards have not averted such accounting debacles as Enron's and WorldCom's frauds.

Nonetheless, early accounting standards in foreign markets did make investing abroad tricky. One area of difficulty involved unconsolidated subsidiaries. Often, you could find no reference to such partially owned subsidiaries either on the income statement or the balance sheet, even though they represented a considerable amount of a company's intrinsic value. Varied rules for treatment of goodwill, amortization, and depreciation made apples-to-apples comparisons difficult for companies based in different countries.

For instance, when I started investing in the Dutch brewer Heineken in the late 1980s, the company looked less profitable than its U.S. competitors. But Heineken logged what were effectively excessive depreciation charges because it used replacement cost accounting. Once adjusted under Generally Accepted Accounting Principles (GAAP), the brewer's profitability shined through. That was an easy adjustment, enabled by good financial disclosure in the Heineken reports.

Often, however, foreign companies fail to provide sufficient segment-level disclosures or worse yet they fail to disclose unconsolidated subsidiaries at all, and that makes these adjustments far more speculative. In such cases, investors have to insist on a wider margin of safety to protect against risks that arise from incomplete disclosure. Fortunately, worldwide accounting standards have improved over the years to require broader reporting of results by business segment and more disclosure of unconsolidated subsidiaries.

Information Unavailable

In some countries, information on public companies is often unavailable, and what is available is of poor quality. Some financial statements are not translated into English, especially in relatively small markets such as Norway and the Czech Republic. I have frequently hired translators to tell me what is in those reports. With the advent of Bloomberg and other data suppliers, more information is becoming available sooner and in English. However, news releases are often in the local language only.

It is also hard for U.S. investors to arrange meetings with management. I recall my first visit to Heineken in the late 1980s. When I was introduced to the vice chairman, he asked "What are you doing here?" in a way that showed he meant it. Indeed, he had likely never seen American investors before, and he could not quite imagine why they might have an interest in the company. Similarly, when initially investing in the U.K.-based breakfast cereal manufacturer Weetabix, only once was I able to meet with anyone from management.

Weetabix and Heineken were each controlled by their founding families, and there was little an investor could do to get management's ear. Nonetheless, a careful read of each company's reports showed that both were carefully run, shareholder-minded businesses.

I can live with investor-shy managements, but I require a greater margin of safety in making such investments. Still, there are limits. I recall visiting South Korea in the late 1990s following the Asian currency collapse. Meeting with senior management from one of South Korea's leading candy makers, Lotte Confectionery, I asked management about prospects for the next year's cash flow. The interpreter and management spoke for nearly 30 minutes, after which I got a one-word response: "Better." Lacking any insight into the discussion that led to that insufficient answer, I walked away from this otherwise promising company.

Who's Got Custody?

When I started investing abroad, few foreign companies had their shares listed in the United States in the form of now-common American Depositary Receipts (ADRs). That meant many American fiduciaries were effectively unable to invest abroad since they typically need to have domestic custody of shares. While I invest in both ADRs and local shares, some of my clients are able to hold only ADRs. Worse yet: some countries have restrictions that really handcuff foreign investors.

This was so in the mid-1980s when my investors who held shares in James Burroughs PLC (producer of Beefeater's Gin) were barred by law from accepting a stock swap offer by Whitbread. Instead, they could take only cash. As such, they were denied the chance to participate in subsequent acquisitions of Whitbread by Allied Domecq and of Allied Domecq by Pernod Ricard. Instead, they were forced to pay taxes on an unwillingly realized gain. Similarly, I have difficulty investing in some developing markets (for example, India and China) due to the local securities markets' regulations restricting foreign investments.

U.S.-based investors have also been limited in the types of instruments in which they can invest. For instance, when I first invested in Nestlé in the mid-1980s, as non-Swiss investors we could not buy actual shares, only "participation certificates." This was also true for both Weetabix and the Dutch-based media company De Telegraaf. Because a certificate holder would have fewer rights than a shareholder, I lowered the price I would pay to maintain a sufficient margin of safety in these situations.

Completing foreign trades and maintaining foreign holdings remains a challenge today, even with the tidal wave of funds flowing into overseas markets. Commissions remain fixed at high levels in most of them, and many of those markets levy fees and taxes atop the commissions. Finally, many U.S-based custodians charge extra fees for settling foreign trades; they also attempt to profit further on currency transactions. Collecting foreign dividends is typically delayed and subject to hefty commissions for converting dividends into dollars. Moreover, tax-exempt investors, such as pension funds and endowments, have a miserable time trying to recover taxes on foreign dividends that are withheld by local authorities. Taxable investors can solve this by claiming a credit on their U.S. taxes for foreign taxes paid. Finally, it is difficult to vote proxies for foreign holdings as custodians often are notified of corporate actions late or not at all by their foreign subcustodians.

Despite a litany of administrative and technical difficulties that remain even to this day, concerns regarding corporate governance and securities regulation are overblown. International corporate governance protections for investors, especially in Europe, increasingly resemble those in the United States. Nonexecutive board chairs exist in practice in many countries, a trend that is gaining steam in the United States. Additionally, although European markets lack new mandates for corporate board conduct such as those recently promulgated in the United States under Sarbanes-Oxley, the reality is that their principles-based systems of corporate governance provide every bit as much protection as our country's rules-based structure.

"Be Right Once": Weetabix

I always approach investing with a mindset that Warren Buffett once described as "being right once." Find businesses selling at reasonable prices with superior brands that possess genuine competitive advantage, conservative capital structures, and an owner-minded management team that has evidenced a history of respecting shareholder interests.

Let these owner-minded managements reinvest the abundant free cash flow their brands generate. Each business's intrinsic value should grow over time, ideally at a rate high enough to deliver attractive investor returns far into the future. An example of such a company is Weetabix.

I became aware of Weetabix about 20 years ago through my wife who, like everyone who spent their childhood in England, retains remarkable loyalty to its eponymous breakfast cereal, which is similar to Nabisco Shredded Wheat. It's not my taste. But, through market research into the breakfast-cereal industry and through conversations with Weetabix's global competitors, I discovered that Weetabix possesses not only intensely brand-loyal consumers but also a substantial share of the U.K. breakfast-cereal market. Could I invest in this company? I was impressed with the summary financials in a company handbook, but getting more detailed information was difficult.

What I discovered was that over the five years prior to my investment, Weetabix's revenues had grown by over 60%. More important, operating income had gone from 2.2 pence a share loss in 1982 to 38.6 pence a share profit in 1986. Nonetheless, Weetabix's operating margin, at just under 10%, was still modest by industry standards. That suggested further possible upside for margins. In addition, Weetabix's balance sheet was conservative, with cash balances of 7 million pounds, which amounted to over 10% of its market capitalization. What's more, the shares sold at a reasonable price-to-earnings ratio of 7, and a 14% free-cash-flow yield. On balance, Weetabix had a strongly branded product in its home market. Moreover, the company's performance was improving under the management of Sir Richard George, an heir to Weetabix's controlling family.

My first investment in Weetabix illustrates how difficult it can be to invest abroad. First and foremost, Weetabix voting shares were rarely, if ever, traded. The nonvoting certificates, which my clients owned, traded on a market called OFEX, which was not one of the main exchanges—

Weetabix shares indeed traded by appointment. The spreads between the bid and offer prices were enormous. On top of the wide spreads, transaction costs were high. Two brokers split the trading in Weetabix shares between them, so there was really no way to shop around for a better price. Despite these obstacles, the stock was such a bargain that I became a very large buyer of shares. But there were other frustrations: for about a decade, I had enormous difficulties perfecting settlement for the shares I purchased, and collecting dividends was excruciating.

Another reason Weetabix back then was so cheap was an investor bias against family-controlled companies. Investors often fear that family members in control of a public company may be indifferent to the share price or they may even divert assets to their personal benefit. Interestingly enough, I prefer to invest in family-controlled entities. Provided that you attach your interests to an honest clan, family control can actually lead to better, not worse, long-term decisions that benefit shareholders, not management. After all, a family controlling a company is free to make long-term decisions without worrying what others think.

Finally, Weetabix management was unusually uncommunicative with investors. There were no fancy lunches at gilded brokerage offices within the City of London. There were few corporate news releases besides mandatory half-year and full-year results. There were no opportunities to meet with management at analyst meetings. Indeed, the annual chairman's letter to shareholders in the annual report provided the bulk of the information investors would receive. Numerous efforts notwithstanding, it was years before I met the CEO, even though my clients then held nearly 16% of the shares outstanding.

While such inaccessibility discouraged many investors, I appreciated management's practice of focusing on the company's operating prospects and letting results speak for themselves. As I saw no evidence of self-dealing over the years, I was comfortable with management's success at building shareholder value. Best of all, the very difficulty that caused the stock to be undervalued when I first learned of it caused it to remain undervalued over time. I was delighted with the chance to continue to add to holdings at market prices below intrinsic value. By the time Weetabix's shares were acquired in 2003, my original investment had increased tenfold.

Summing Up

The bottom line is that Graham and Dodd's—and Buffett's—principles are equally suited to international markets as they are to the U.S. market. Indeed, because so many investors are scouring the U.S. markets for bargains, some foreign markets remain considerably less efficient, dominated by short-term trends, rumors, and overreactions to new developments. What could be better for value investors?

ABOUT THIS EDITION

This project began in late 2006 when I was approached by an editor at McGraw-Hill about putting together a new edition of *Security Analysis*. I agreed to take on this project as lead editor, and over the months that followed, we assembled a team of three additional editors: a prominent financial writer and historian, a leading value-investing academic, and an experienced financial journalist. We also had modern-day practitioners comment on the original text, thereby providing a fresh perspective based on their own approaches to value investing. We added a new essay on global value investing.

Because these contributions were submitted and edited during the second half of 2007 and early 2008, you will not see references to the deepening credit crisis and sharp financial market sell-off that very nearly bankrupted the venerable investment bank Bear Stearns in March 2008. The reason is that instead of focusing myopically on very recent developments, we took a long-term view that would be applicable in both good markets and bad, and, like Graham and Dodd, we concerned ourselves chiefly with "concepts, methods, standards, principles, and, above all, with logical reasoning."

We decided to base this sixth edition on the second edition of *Security Analysis*, published in 1940, because it was the most comprehensive edition, and we also decided not to alter the text of this classic work. By proceeding in this fashion, we hope that readers will gain both an appreciation for the magisterial accomplishment of Graham and Dodd in their exact words as well as insight into what is still relevant and important even in today's vastly changed world.

This project has brought together 11 contributors in a collaboration that is emblematic of the nature of the value-investing community. Many of us are business rivals, but we are also friends and colleagues. All of us know that no one of us possesses all the answers; we vividly remember our biggest mistakes as if they happened yesterday. Similarly, we recognize that none of us has perfected the art of value investing; there are always new challenges, and there is always room to improve. By assembling the diverse perspectives of these experienced and able contributors and editors, we hope to make this sixth edition of *Security Analysis* a rich, varied, and highly informed tapestry of investment thinking that will be a worthy and long-lived successor to the five preceding editions.

Seth A. Klarman
Lead Editor
May 2008

ACKNOWLEDGMENTS

I owe much to the coeditors and contributors who found time in their busy lives to share their insights and experiences for the readers of this edition. On behalf of all of them, I would like to acknowledge our authors, Benjamin Graham and David Dodd. Through their writings and legacy, they have touched each of us in important ways; obviously, without them, this collaboration would never have happened. I would also like to thank Warren Buffett for his very personal foreword and, more important, for serving as the living embodiment of Graham and Dodd's principles of value investing, sound reasoning, high integrity, and generosity through the avenues of teaching and philanthropy.

In addition, I must acknowledge a debt to Leah Spiro, who had the idea to bring together leading practitioners of value investing to tell us how they apply Graham and Dodd's principles today. This collaboration was difficult to orchestrate, and some doubted it could be done. Indeed, the project would have faltered if not for her persistence and leadership. My thanks also goes to the many professionals at McGraw-Hill—including Philip Ruppel, Herb Schaffner, Laura Friedman, Seth Morris, Lydia Rinaldi, Anthony Landi, Jane Palmieri, and Maureen Harper—who ensured that this would be a work of which we could all be proud.

Seth A. Klarman
Lead Editor

ABOUT THE CONTRIBUTORS

Seth A. Klarman, president of the Boston-based Baupost Group, L.L.C., manages a series of successful investment partnerships using Graham and Dodd principles. In his preface, Klarman discusses the timelessness of their philosophy, the changes in the environment with which value investors must work, and the unanswerable questions that will always require value investors to work hard. He is also the author of *Margin of Safety*, a classic investment book. Klarman is the lead editor of this sixth edition.

James Grant, founder and editor of *Grant's Interest Rate Observer,* has been writing about markets and financial figures for over 30 years. He is the author of five books, including biographies of financier Bernard Baruch and President John Adams. He is a founding general partner of Nippon Partners, a hedge fund that invests in Japan. Grant's introduction takes us back to Graham and Dodd's era to put *Security Analysis* in a historical perspective. He also served as an editor of this sixth edition.

Roger Lowenstein, one of America's top financial journalists, gives us his keen insights into contemporary value investing. Lowenstein is a frequent contributor to the *New York Times Magazine, Portfolio,* and *Smart Money.* He is also the bestselling author of the books *Buffett: The Making of an American Capitalist* and *When Genius Failed: The Rise and Fall of Long-Term Capital.* His most recent book is *While America Aged.* Lowenstein is also an outside director of the Sequoia Fund.

Howard S. Marks, **CFA**, chairman and cofounder of Oaktree Capital Management based in Los Angeles, was an early investor in high yield bonds and a devotee of Graham and Dodd. At first glance, those two ideas appear to be antithetical, but Marks says that's not the case. His introduction to Part II, which is about fixed income investments, explains how the ideas in *Security Analysis* can be applied profitably to today's corporate bond market.

J. Ezra Merkin, managing partner of Gabriel Capital Group in New York City, is one of today's leading investors in corporate bankruptcy and distressed securities. In "Blood and Judgement," which is the introduction to Part III, Merkin lays out various bankruptcy scenarios using real examples and analyzes them as investment opportunities from a value buyer's perspective.

Bruce Berkowitz is the founder of Fairholme Capital Management and the manager of the Fairholme Fund, a value mutual fund. This Miami-based investor offers his insights on corporate dividends and their modern-day equivalent, free cash flow. Using examples and anecdotes from his own experience, Berkowitz provides this key update to Graham and Dodd's wisdom.

Glenn H. Greenberg, **CFA**, cofounder and managing director of New York–based Chieftain Capital Management, admits flat out that he never read *Security Analysis* in business school and that even midway through his career, he found the text a bit fusty. Going back to the book after more than three decades on Wall Street, he finds it remarkable for its enduring sound advice. His introduction to Part V shows us how to assess companies and their income statements with a value investor's eye.

Bruce Greenwald is the Robert Heilbrunn Professor of Finance and Asset Management at Columbia Business School, and he also heads the Heilbrunn Center for Graham and Dodd Investing. In his introduction to Part VI, he tears apart the corporate balance sheet and shares his unique insights on this most important of financial statements. He is the author of *Value Investing: From Graham to Buffett and Beyond*. He also served as an editor of this sixth edition.

David Abrams heads his own investment partnership, Boston-based Abrams Capital Management. In "The Great Illusion of the Stock Market and the Future of Value Investing," which is the introduction to Part VII, Abrams offers his early experiences in and lessons from the investment business and makes the dry subject of warrants and options come alive.

Thomas A. Russo is a partner in Gardner Russo & Gardner, which is based in Lancaster, Pennsylvania, and is a general partner of Semper Vic Partners, L.P. Russo has specialized in global value investing for over 20 years. His essay introduces the part of the book that was never written—value investing in global markets. The subject was small bore in Graham and Dodd's day, but it is of great importance now.

Jeffrey M. Laderman, CFA, served as an editor of this sixth edition. He is a 25-year veteran of *BusinessWeek* and has written and edited articles on everything from stock market crises to trading scandals. He is now the editor of *On the Markets* and *The View*, publications that go to the clients of Smith Barney and Citi Private Bank respectively.

About the Authors

Benjamin Graham was a seminal figure on Wall Street and is widely acknowledged to be the father of modern security analysis. The founder of the value school of investing and founder and former president of the Graham-Newman corporation investment fund, Graham taught at Columbia University's Graduate School of Business from 1928 through 1957. He popularized the examination of price-to-earnings (P/E) ratios, debt-to-equity ratios, dividend records, book values, and earnings growth, and also wrote the popular investors' guide *The Intelligent Investor*.

David L. Dodd was a colleague of Benjamin Graham's at Columbia University, where he was an assistant professor of finance.

Index

Margin trading, price cycling and, 671–672

Marginal purchases, investing vs. speculating and, 102–103

Marion Steam Shovel, 330

Mark-downs to reduce depreciation charges, 455

Market, irrational behavior of, as barrier to security analysis, 69–70

Market analysis:
  Ayres mechanical forecasting method and, 702–703
  disadvantages as compared with security analysis, 703–704
  prophesies based on near-term prospects and, 704–706, 707
  as substitute or adjunct to security analysis, 697–702

Market efficiency, 624–625, 631–632

Market price, intrinsic value related to, 70–71

Market timing, 133

Marketable securities, profits from sale of, in income account, 416–420

Market-adjusted debt (MAD) ratios, 138

Markowitz, Harry, 125

Marland Oil Company, 466

Marlin Rockwell Corporation, 93*n*

Maryland Casualty Company, 218*n*

Mason City and Fort Dodge Railroad Company, 97

Mathieson Alkali, 93*n*

Maytag Company, 509*n*, 652

McClelland Stores Co., 224, 225

McCrory Stores Corp., 224, 225

McDonald, Jack, 713

McDonald's, 53

MCI, 545

"MCI: Is Being Good Good Enough?" (Mehta), 279*n*

MCI WorldCom, 279–280

McKeesport Tin Plate Corporation, 460*n*

McKesson and Robbins Company, 330, 412*n*–413*n*

Mead, Edward S., 326*n*, 371*n*

Means, G. C., 199*n*, 576, 577

Mehta, Stephanie N., 279*n*

The Memoirs of the Dean of Wall Street (Graham), 1

Mergers:
  depreciation and, 461
  market exaggerations due to, 680

Merrill Lynch & Company, 5, 44

Message Media, 267

Mesta Machine, 93*n*

Metropolitan Casualty Company, 218*n*

Mexico, 175

Meyer, Jack, 630

MFS Communications, 545

Microsoft, 54–56, 340, 342

Midland Steel Products Company, 457

Milken, Michael, 138

Miller, Bill, 282*n*

Milwaukee, Sparta and Northwestern, 153

Milwaukee Lake Shore and Western, 202*n*

Mining companies, ore reserve amortization by, 464–469

Minneapolis, St. Paul and Sault Sainte Marie Railroad, 210–211, 212, 226

Missouri-Kansas-Texas Railroad Company, 146, 205–207, 212, 318

Missouri Pacific Railroad Company, 152–153, 199*n*, 212, 646

Mobile and Ohio Railroad, 222*n*, 693–694

The Modern Corporation and Private Property (Berle and Means), 199*n*, 576

Mohawk Hudson Power Corporation, 306, 307

Mohawk Industries, 342–343

Mohawk Mining Company, 567, 585
Mohawk Rubber, 517, 519
Montana Power Company, 506
Monthly statements as information
source, 90
Moody's, 97
Moody's Manual, 78n
Moody's Manual of Industrials, 591n
Moody's Manual of Investments,
448n–449n
*Moran v. United States Cast Iron Pipe
and Foundry Company,* 198n
Morgan Stanley, 5, 44, 626
Mortgage(s), purchase-money, 243
Mortgage bonds, 215–218
Mortgage companies, 187–188
Mortgage guarantees, 215–218
flame-out of, in early 1930s,
10–11
Mouquin, Inc., 638n
Mullins Body Corporation, 678, 679
Mullins Manufacturing, 90, 678,
679
Munger, Charlie, 58
Murray Corporation, 328–329
Mutual savings banks, selling down
of, investing and, 50

N
Nairn Linoleum Company, 684
National Acme, 330
National Biscuit Company, 141–142,
251, 350, 351–352, 353, 462–463
National Bondholders Corporation,
682n
National Broadcasting Company,
471
National Cloak and Suit, 383n
National Department Stores, 198
National Distillers Products
Corporation, 308
National Electric Power, 240n
National Enameling and Stamping
Company, 460n
National Hotel of Cuba, 235n

National Investors Corporation, 368,
369
National Lead Company, 429
National Radiator Corporation,
243n
National Sugar Refining Company,
160n, 460
National Surety Company, 218
National Trade Journals, Inc.,
294–295, 296
National Transit Company, 416
Nature of business as qualitative
element in analysis, 83–84
Neisner Brothers, Inc., 225
Neisner Realty Corporation, 225
Nelson Act, 270n
Neporent, Mark, 280
Nestlé, 716, 719
Netherlands, 174, 175n
New Idea Company, 637n, 674
New Jersey Zinc, 92n
New York, Chicago and St. Louis
Railroad Company (Nickel
Plate), 417, 444, 447, 448, 597,
644, 645, 646
New York, New Haven and Hartford
Railroad Company, 147n,
242–243, 315n, 322
New York and Erie Railroad, 152
New York Central Railroad
Company, 226, 645, 658
New York City, 216, 249–250
New York Curb, 92n
New York Edison Company,
243–244
New York Moratorium Law, 252n
New York Savings-bank Law:
bond investment criteria imposed
by, 170–179
provisions of, 177–178
New York State, 233n
New York State Railways, 235n
New York Stock Exchange, 235n
New York Stock Exchange firms as
investment advice source, 260